The World Bank UNVEILED

Inside the Revolutionary Struggle for Transparency

"To many people engaged in the effort to mitigate the effects of poverty around the globe, the World Bank is a black box. Its development contributions and its great potential are hindered by processes and systems that obscure rather than illuminate. David Shaman undertook yeoman efforts to reform the institution, using modern communications technology to achieve more transparency. Now **in this superb book, Shaman reveals the resistance he faced and offers important recommendations for reform.** He explores the crisis of identity that has plagued the Bank since its creation: Is it a financial institution requiring appropriate confidentiality and the discretion of a bank, or is it a development agency whose mission requires openness, participation and widely-shared results metrics? Shaman leans toward the latter. This view **merits deeper reflection and debate which this book should provoke."**

—**J. BRIAN ATWOOD,** DEAN OF THE HUBERT H. HUMPHREY INSTITUTE OF PUBLIC AFFAIRS, UNIVERSITY OF MINNESOTA, AND FORMER ADMINISTRATOR OF THE U.S. AGENCY FOR INTERNATIONAL DEVELOPMENT

"David Ian Shaman's *The World Bank Unveiled* is required reading for anyone who believes public institutions should be transparent and accountable. His hard-won insights provide valuable guidance for concerned citizens and government watchdogs."

—**MELANIE SLOAN,** EXECUTIVE DIRECTOR, CITIZENS FOR RESPONSIBILITY AND ETHICS IN WASHINGTON

"In this book David Shaman takes us on a conducted tour of what many regard as one of the world's more extraordinary institutions, the World Bank. This is in the context of his efforts to promote B-SPAN, an internal World Bank service he launched to provide video coverage of important events and analyses both to the Bank itself and to its external stakeholders. He captures very well the mix in the Bank of everything from enormous ability focused on advancing the cause of the poor to bureaucracy devoted to empire-building and the denial of information, with no holds barred in naming his adversaries and identifying their defects. Given this mix, **you can rely on finding something to love or hate in the Bank, depending on one's prejudices."**

—**JOHN WILLIAMSON,** SENIOR FELLOW, THE PETERSON INSTITUTE FOR INTERNATIONAL ECONOMICS, AND AUTHOR OF THE PHRASE "WASHINGTON CONSENSUS"

"This is a knock-out of a book. It tells the inside story of how a small group of "guerrilla" staff members, initially working on environmental issues, wheeled and dealed to get the World Bank to accept unedited presentations of its activities both to its own staff and to the wider public. And of how some Bank managers out-machiavellied Machiavelli in their efforts to wrestle control from them so that they could use the technology (webcasting to stream video content over the Internet) to present a more sanitized version of the Bank in line with corporate objectives. I know of no other study which illuminates the "street-level" politics of a multilateral organization so well, or which shows culturally quite different notions of "transparency" and "accountability" being used as weapons in bureaucratic struggles over budgets and authority."

—**ROBERT H. WADE,** PROFESSOR OF POLITICAL ECONOMY AND DEVELOPMENT, LONDON SCHOOL OF ECONOMICS, NOTED EXPERT ON THE WORLD BANK AND RECIPIENT OF THE LEONTIEF PRIZE IN ECONOMICS 2008

The World Bank UNVEILED

Inside the Revolutionary Struggle for Transparency

David Ian Shaman

PARKHURST BROTHERS, INC., PUBLISHERS

Parkhurst Brothers, Inc., Publishers
Little Rock, Arkansas

PARKHURST BROTHERS, INC., PUBLISHERS

Our National Conversation
Raising the level of public discourse

www.pbros.net

Parkhurst Brothers books are distributed to the trade through the University of Chicago Press Distribution Center. Copies of this and other Parkhurst Brothers, Inc., Publishers titles are available to organizations and corporations for purchase in quantity by contacting Special Sales Department at our home office location, listed on our web site.

Printed in Canada

First Edition, 2009

12 11 10 9 8 7 6 5 4 3 2 1

Library of Congress Number: 2008909926

ISBN: Hardcover 978-1-935166-03-0 [10 digit: 1-935166-03-4]

ISBN: E-book 978-1-935166-06-1 [ten-digit: 1-935166-06-9]

This book is printed on archival-quality paper that meets requirements of the American National Standard for Information Sciences, Permanence of Paper, Printed Library Materials, ANSI Z39.48-1984.

Dustjacket/cover design:
WENDELL E. HALL

Page design:
SHELLY CULBERTSON

Acquired for Parkhurst Brothers, Inc., Publishers by:
TED PARKHURST

Editor:
ROGER ARMBRUST

To Misha and Sophia Elena

who will inherit a world that we leave them.

acknowledgements

No endeavor of merit, whether it is climbing a mountain or running a political campaign or writing a book, is the result of any one individual's toil. To be sure, credit may be directed on to a single person, but in retrospect (and retrospect is necessary) all achievements of note include the inputs of many people. This book is no exception.

I learned something long ago: the threads of simple, innocuous and often unrelated events can intertwine and evolve into something far larger and more significant. That is how our lives often unfold. That is how this book came to exist. Therefore, I am the product of a thousand influences, from people who wrote profound chapters in my life to those who were only footnotes. Each holds some place in whatever I have achieved. And, accordingly, in the context of this effort there are literally hundreds of people whom I have interacted with that have helped shape the pages that follow. It is with regret that I cannot thank them all.

Nevertheless, a few stand out and I could not go further without noting their contributions. First would be my mother, Diana Shaman, whose unyielding determination to help in any and every way warrants an appreciation that cannot be equaled. Her sound judgment and counsel permeate these pages. I am also indebted to Dr. David Wheeler, my friend and mentor from the World Bank, who in large part is the most important protagonist in what follows. With all the members of his "team," he followed a simple and astonishingly little used management theory of empowering others to fulfill their potential. To the extent that my talents allowed, I have tried to do just that and his gift I was grateful to have received.

During this journey, I have received counsel from Jim Kessler of Third Way, a political think tank in Washington. His wisdom has been clear, precise and invaluable as I moved forward. He also, coincidentally, put me in touch with Ted Parkhurst, my publisher. I am grateful to Ted for taking interest in this project and believing in me and what I was trying to achieve. The ending for this book may have been far different otherwise. Concurrently, a debt of gratitude must be directed to Roger Armbrust, my editor with Parkhurst Brothers Publishing. Roger spent months working with me to refine the text and without him it would not have been as good.

There are others to thank as well. There is Joan Baum, a wordsmith aficionado, literary critic and my friend who sustained my confidence with her enthusiasm and advice. Tessa Warburg, a British author and publisher, and my aunt, who with candor and flair readily helped me navigate the peculiarities of the book industry. Craig Meisner, a World Bank economist and colleague, was immensely helpful to me as I was conducting research for this book. Mark Davis, a former Bank economist, was also a constant source of encouragement. Don Reisman of the Resources for the Future, an environmental think tank in Washington, provided me with an invaluable service by critiquing my text at a critical point. His advice was the genesis of a profoundly important and positive change in the way the book was written.

Finally, there is my wife Irina. I had already been working on the book for nearly a year when we first met and until its publication she knew of no time when I wasn't working on it days and nights and weekends. Her endless patience was a critical component for its completion. For that alone (and other reasons), I love her.

table of contents

PART I

a path to peace

In the spring of 2007, Hugo Chavez, Venezuela's socialist-leaning president, did what he had enjoyed doing since rising to power in 1998: He stuck his finger in rich countries' eyes. Chavez announced Venezuela would cancel its membership in both the World Bank and the International Monetary Fund (IMF). Some viewed the move as symbolic. Venezuela, benefiting from huge oil reserves and rising oil prices, had just paid off its World Bank debts years ahead of schedule. Moreover, the country's IMF debts had been cleared years earlier; in fact, the Fund had already closed its Venezuelan office in 2006. Others viewed the move as political. Chavez would soon seek an end to presidential term limits. Rejecting the monetary harness of wealthy capitalists would be popular with voters. Yet something else was afoot.

Chavez also announced he would seek to launch a Bank of the South (Banco del Sur).[1] The new bank's membership would consist of South American nations that would pool resources to finance regional development projects. The Bank of the South, he hoped, would usurp the role played by the World Bank and IMF, as well as the Inter-American Development Bank. These international financial institutions, he suggested, were pawns of economic powers, most notably the United States.

Chavez was not alone in believing that the World Bank and IMF loans to poor Latin American countries saddled them with few rewards other than mounting debt. Other Latin American governments, desperate for World Bank and IMF capital, agreed. The two lenders had actively pumped money into the continent, but the funds were tied to unpalatable "conditions." Then, according to the terms set by the loans, the debtor nations were forced to cut spending for social programs, privatize their state-owned industrial sectors, devalue their currencies, and reduce trade barriers. The U.S.-based financial institutions said these loan requirements, called structural adjustment lending, would improve the infrastructure within these economies, and allow for growth and poverty reduction.

The results, however, proved far from successful. The United Nations' Economic Commission on Latin America reported that the region's per capita income grew by only 9% between 1980, when the World Bank's structural adjustment lending commenced, and the year 2000.[2] By comparison, per capita income had grown 82% from 1960 to 1980. Growth following the new Millennium to 2005 had proved even more anemic at 4%. Poverty was gripping Latin American societies, and income inequality between rich and poor within individual countries was also profound. In addition, the crippling debt that hobbled these governments since the late 1970s remained a burden.

While rejection of the World Bank's and the IMF's austere monetary conditions became publicly popular in Latin America, Washington hardly uttered a word of concern. Many there considered the Chavez maneuver the machination of a left-wing politician whose yearning for power and dislike of the U.S. grew more visible and strident by the day. With the World Bank's and the IMF's six decades of experience, who could possibly replace their development expertise and sizeable reserves, Washington argued. Yet by winter, in a stunningly short period, seven South American countries gathered in Argentina's presidential palace to announce the Bank of the South was no longer a concept, but a reality.

The consortium of Venezuela, Ecuador, Bolivia, Brazil, Argentina, Paraguay and Uruguay agreed that the Bank of the South would initially focus on development lending which would compete directly with the World Bank's portfolio. Emergency aid initiatives, as characterized by the IMF's activities, would be tabled for future consideration. Importantly, Bank of the South membership would not be weighted—

meaning that, unlike membership in the World Bank and the IMF, each country would receive an equal vote and thus an equal say in how the new lender conducted business. As of 2008, the new bank was open for business. Loans were to be made without "conditions."[3]

At the Bank of the South's inauguration, Ecuadorian President Rafael Correa said, "South American nations will be able to put an end to their political and financial dependence that they have had with the neo-liberal model."[4] Even Brazil, with its strong relationship with the World Bank and the U.S. government, joined as a founding member. Perhaps then, a comment by Brazilian President Luiz Inacio Lula da Silva seemed the most emphatic one made that day.[5] "Developing nations must create their own mechanisms of finance instead of suffering under those of the IMF and the World Bank, which are institutions of rich nations," he said. "It is time to wake up."

The World Bank's public position, however, was characteristically understated, and similar to how it has reacted to developments over the years that have run counter to its agenda: Denial. "As far as the World Bank is concerned," said Augusto de la Torre, the institution's chief economist for Latin America, "this new initiative is not perceived as a competitor."[6]

To be sure, the success of the Bank of the South is not guaranteed. Relative to the World Bank's depth of experience and financial resources, the new lender is weak. It began operations in 2008 with $7 billion in start-up capital while the World Bank's lending in any given year averages about $20 billion.[7] In addition, the World Bank lists thousands of projects in its pipeline and hundreds in operation throughout Latin America. Some critics have suggested the Bank of the South would be overly political in nature, and unable to match the World Bank's technical assistance.[8] Nor would it be able to handle future emergency financial crises that the IMF was designed to address.[9] While all legitimate, these concerns do not address perhaps the most salient point: The Bank of the South now exists, and the underlying reasons for its existence have been decades in the making.

The World Bank, an experimental brainchild of American and English economists, stands two blocks from the White House. It lends money and provides technical advice to the developing world's poor governments to enhance their economic growth and development, and to reduce poverty. Its reach is enormous. Thousands of personnel are involved in education, health, agriculture, environment, transportation, electric, water, sanitation, information technology, and financial and legal reform projects, to name a few. It hosts an array of research teams renowned throughout the academic world for their excellence. Its pedagogical training branch instructs thousands of government officials each year on the latest trends and practices in economic development. Since its inception, it has implemented tens of thousands of projects and loaned hundreds of billions of dollars. Nevertheless, questions remain as to whether the world's poor are less poor, or whether the disparities between rich and poor have decreased since the World Bank began.

The Bank of the South's emergence symbolized an ongoing dissatisfaction with the World Bank by its client members. But it has not been the only example. In fact, signs of the World Bank's deteriorating financial influence have been gathering over the last two decades. Angered by the conditionality of Bank loans, borrowing governments have increasingly sought out private-sector investment alternatives. While poorer clients were changing their borrowing strategies, the Bank's lending portfolio was evolving in tandem. The Mexican peso's collapse in 1994, an event partly attributed to the Bank's loan conditionality that forced the government to privatize its banking sector, provided the impetus for rapid change.[10] In reaction to a potential influx of legal and illegal immigrants, the U.S. government quickly put together a massive emergency lending package of $40 billion for Mexico. The U.S. package solidified the fiscal situation, but in its aftermath, it did something else. It sent the private sector a signal that a safety net existed when investing in foreign markets. Within two years, private capital flows into the developing world skyrocketed to $250 billion. Concurrently, Bank lending to the poorest countries declined sharply as its portfolio focused on a wealthier strata: middle-income client countries. Questions arose as to whether the Bank had outlived its usefulness.

In a 1999 article in *Euromoney*, Adam Lerrick, a Carnegie Mellon University economist, launched an assault on the tenets of the Bank's lending composition.[11] Recipients of Bank aid who had no international bond ratings declined from 40% in 1993 to 1% in 1999, Lerrick stated. Of the 4,100 loans made the previous seven years, his research revealed only 22% had gone to countries with low ratings. During this period, eleven key clients accounted for 70% of total flows. The remaining 30% went to the other 145 Bank clients. Structural adjustment lending had risen during the decade from 20% to 63% of the Bank's portfolio, he added. In essence, Lerrick suggested the Bank was deserting poor countries in favor of safer loans to middle-income developing countries. In a 2005 follow-up analysis for *The Wall Street Journal*, Lerrick concluded the trends had remained consistent.[12] Moreover, the Bank was lending almost exclusively to middle-income countries, yet these nations were increasingly borrowing from the private sector.

While the Bank was trying to increase its lending to powerful borrowers such as China, Indonesia, Brazil and Mexico, these countries began to reassess the institution's merits. Research in 2006 by Ngaire Woods, an Oxford University academic, revealed this: Starting in the 1980s, the Bank instituted a series of lending-fee changes that shifted the burden of financing the organization from donors to borrowers.[13] In turn, despite higher fees from private-sector investors, borrowers began more actively soliciting non-Bank sources for financing. In response, the Bank reduced its loan fees and lending limits. Still, the hemorrhaging continued. From 2001 to 2004, the Bank's income from borrowers' fees dropped by almost $4 billion. In fact, at a time when stakes for the poor were growing more desperate and international security threats more apparent, the Bank was moving in the opposite direction—taking fewer risks in its development lending, and lending almost exclusively to countries that could afford alternatives.[14]

While the Bank's portfolio has been metamorphosing, another disturbing trend has materialized, first codified by a 1991 internal Bank investigation called the Wapenhans Commission.[15] The panel reported that almost 40% of the Bank's projects had failed. Ten years earlier, the Bank claimed the level was 15%, meaning that by the institution's own measure of effectiveness, its success rates had declined by 150% during the 1980s. The commission also noted that an additional 30% of projects were in serious trouble by the fifth year of implementation. The commission further found that Bank personnel ignored local input and bullied borrowing governments to adopt loans as the Bank had written them. Project appraisals were slanted in such a way as to quickly secure loan approvals. And, there was more. The report stated that over 60% of the audits either provided insufficient information or had been conducted so soon after the final lending disbursement that it was impossible to accurately gauge effectiveness. In other words, the Bank could tell when a project failed, but it couldn't tell when a project succeeded.

In the aftermath of the Wapenhans Commission, the Bank invested more funds in project evaluation, and claimed its success ratio climbed to nearly 80% by the end of the 1990s. Critics remained skeptical. In preparation for the 2002 Monterrey Conference that codified the Millennium Development Goals, the Bank issued a report about its lending effectiveness.[16] The report cited important progress in China, India and Uganda, and suggested the Bank had recovered from the stumbles of an earlier time. William Easterly, a former Bank economist, offered a contrarian view.[17] Aid to China and India, Easterly suggested, represented a small fraction of their Gross Domestic Products, and had not been a major factor. He acknowledged Uganda was a low-income country with strong growth, but said the report neglected 54 other low-income countries where Bank lending had yielded zero per capita growth. In fact, Sub-Saharan Africa's debt tripled between 1980 and 1994 from $58 billion to $165 billion. About a third of the debt came from capitalization of interest and much of the rest from servicing the existing debt to prevent default.

The Bank's financial impact has continued dissolving since the middle of the 1990s. Belief in its lending effectiveness has been crumbling for even longer. And a third leg of this paradigm—the decline of its moral influence—has weakened the institution's ability to steer the course on the war against global poverty.

The Bank's mission statement notes, "Our dream is a world free of poverty." It is hard to imagine a nobler mission. Yet six decades of acting in secrecy has hardened a perception of the Bank. Many see it as a monolithic culture where well-connected financiers close their doors to deliberate on the fate of millions; and it is only when these insiders unlock the doors that people living in poverty learn what has been decided about their future. Like the other problems identified above, this image has existed for many years. Donors mistrust the Bank because they fear it overstates the effectiveness of its lending operations. Borrowers feel the Bank imposes lending conditions that have not significantly reduced poverty, and in some cases have increased it. Non-governmental organizations (NGOs) and community-based representatives believe the Bank shuns accountability for its actions, and manipulates information as propaganda rather than as an opportunity to honestly share knowledge.

While the image of the Bank as a monolithic society has been present since its inception, it was during the 1970s that it began drawing the attention of community activists. They watched with alarm as the Bank's lending activities were increasing environmental degradation, deforestation, and population dislocation. Infamous debacles in the Amazon and India during the late 1980s accelerated concern. Activists began suggesting these blunders occurred because the Bank seemed accountable to no one, with almost no transparency in its decision-making process.

Sensing change in the geopolitical winds, the institution implemented a Disclosure of Information policy, and launched an Inspection Panel to monitor whether lending met acceptable standards. The Bank also subsequently sought greater collaborative opportunities with NGOs, but they were at the margins rather than the core of its agenda. After a period of détente, critics suggested the institution had engaged in appeasement strategies filled with enough loopholes to avoid substantially altering the status quo.[18] Throughout the 1990s, an eclectic group of activists grew increasingly vocal and aggressive about organizing protests. The Bank, they suggested, had become a vehicle for wealthy nations to extract resources from impoverished nations. The institution's cultural instincts to make decisions behind closed doors and limit community activists' participation enhanced this image. By the middle of the decade, thousands of protestors had taken to the streets chanting that the Bank had run its course. By the end of the decade, even the protests had evolved, morphing into burgeoning violence.

Concern about the Bank's lack of transparency and accountability has never abated. Recent history offers a useful example. The absence of openness in selecting Paul Wolfowitz, a Deputy Secretary of the U.S. Department of Defense, and subsequently Robert Zoellick, a former U.S. Trade Representative and Deputy Secretary of the U.S. Department of State, as Bank presidents have drawn the ire of development think tanks, NGOs and even some of the institution's client governments.

In the spring of 2005, following the announcement that Bank President James Wolfensohn would depart at the end of his term, intense speculation began about his successor. Traditionally, the U.S. had selected new Bank presidents. But because of gnawing discomfort over the process's secrecy and the lack of participation by the Bank's full membership, a consortium of development think tanks and NGOs questioned the selection's legitimacy. They characterized the choice of Wolfowitz as secretive and to have excluded voices of developing countries that would be affected by the decision. Two years later, Wolfowitz would become embroiled over allegations of improprieties in his personal ethics, and he was forced to resign. The selection process that anointed Zoellick to succeed Wolfowitz again raised the same transparency issues and concerns Bank critics had voiced previously.[19]

Concurrently, critics also suggested that the representation of the Bank's board of directors is overly skewed in favor of rich donor nations at the expense of poor borrower members. The weighted voting of the board's representatives, a legacy institutionalized at the Bank's inception, means those countries who donate have a greater say in how loans are spent and those that borrow have less say. If in principle, this doctrine seems to have some degree of legitimacy, in practice it has become a lever that serves to bend poor countries into submission. The U.S., United Kingdom, France, Germany and Japan each have their own executive director. The 19 other executive directors represent the rest of the world. One African director represents 24 nations. In fact, Sub-Saharan Africa accounts for 27% of the Bank's membership but only 8% of its voting shares.[20] Calls to reduce these disparities were rebuffed until November 2008 when a global economic crisis compelled major donor and emerging-market countries to agree that some reform on board representation was in order.

The terrorist attacks of September 11, 2001 provided a unique opportunity for the Bank to rearrange the development paradigm. During the months preceding the attacks, the Bush Administration had begun a rigorous campaign to remake the Bank from a loan-making institution into a grant-making one. The Bank should defer to the private sector when middle-income countries sought loans for development, Administration officials suggested.[21] Indeed, the institution appeared to be the object of its scorn. U.S. Treasury Secretary Paul O'Neill suggested it had squandered billions of dollars in aid and failed to reduce poverty. Even voices from the left, such as Jeffrey Sachs, the United Nations' point person on the Millennium Development Goals, were calling upon the Bank to move toward massive debt forgiveness and grant making. On the eve of the terrorist attacks, Washington was bracing for an onslaught of 100,000 demonstrators who months before had battled with police in the streets of Seattle.[22]

Following the terrorist attacks, the U.S. development agenda underwent a quick mutation.[23] The Administration paid outstanding arrears owed by the U.S. to the United Nations.[24] Then it lifted nuclear-testing sanctions on Pakistan. Then the Bank and IMF became objects of heightened interest as the U.S. began using their lending instruments to solidify support from Pakistan in the new war. The Administration pressed the Bank to focus on developing countries specifically willing to fight Al Qaeda.[25] U.S. Treasury officials lobbied the Bank to add anti-money-laundering components to its projects. The U.S. representative to the Bank's board voted to begin lending to Pakistan for economic projects other than humanitarian aid. And, despite Pakistan's history of misuse of development aid and a checkered record on meeting lending conditions, the IMF abruptly approved a massive loan.[26] By

2008, Pakistan and Turkey, two Islamic countries critical in the war on terrorism, represented the bulk of the IMF's portfolio.[27]

Were these developments unusual? Given the overall context of the Bank's history, the answer is no. The U.S. government had simply reverted back to the same prism with which it had viewed the Bank throughout the Cold War. During the 1950s, '60s and '70s, the U.S. used the Bank's lending pipeline as a way to persuade impoverished Third World dictatorships to align with the West in the struggle against the Soviet Union. In the post-Cold War period, American efforts focused on using the Bank as an instrument for opening up emerging markets to trade and investment. The new battleground had become the war on terror.

Many might question how much progress has occurred and debate the tactics used. For example, a key resource for extremists is Pakistan's madrassas—religious seminaries that educate nearly two million poor children about the Koran. They are funded by local mullahs, which make the seminaries popular for families without other means to school their children. They are also widely seen by Western experts as factories for aspiring terrorists. However, in the middle of 2005, *The Wall Street Journal* reported Pakistan's public school curriculum for 25 million students was even more pernicious in its religious extremism.[28] The *Journal* noted only 2% of the country's Gross National Product was devoted to education, a ranking among the lowest in the world. A fraction of the resources devoted to the war on terrorism could have funded education and curriculum reform in Pakistan as a way of bleeding dry Al Qaeda's most valuable resource. But despite all the monies channeled into anti-terrorism and development aid redirected to Pakistan, the only Islamic nation with nuclear weapons, this had not materialized. In late 2007, following the first attempted assassination of former Prime Minister Benazir Bhutto, *Newsweek* magazine called Pakistan, not Iraq, the most dangerous country in the world.[29]

As his term as Bank president neared completion in 2005, Wolfensohn made a candid admission. He noted development aid from donor nations had declined to $56 billion annually, the lowest per capita level in four decades. Instead, rich countries were investing $300 billion each year on domestic agricultural subsidies and $900 billion on military expenditures.[30] The 2004 World Development Indicators, the institution's annual statistical report, suggested the percentage of the extremely poor had been halved between 1981 and 2001, but even senior Bank officials acknowledged that China and India accounted for the bulk of progress.[31] Poverty and disease remained unabated throughout much of the rest of the developing world. Current trends suggested most developing countries would not achieve the Millennium Development Goals, targets set by UN member countries on poverty reduction by 2015, unless rich countries dramatically increased aid. Instead, the outgoing Bank president acknowledged donors were focused on the war in Iraq and anti-terrorist activities. "The world is out of balance," Wolfensohn said.

Wolfensohn has cited the 2001 terrorist attacks as the event that demonstrated there were no walls between rich and poor. Many in the development community believe the lessons of September 11 are clear: The resource that fuels Islamic extremism is chronic poverty in a desperate region. Increase opportunities for economic development and education, build infrastructure and improve governance, and the ability to recruit militants would decline. Yet eight years later, it is clear the donor community has viewed the event essentially as a terrorism issue, and the development community led by the Bank has not effectively convinced them to believe otherwise.[32] Instead of being at the forefront of the war on terrorism, development institutions have been relegated to the sidelines in a supporting role.

U.S. promises made in 2002 on the Millennium Development Goals have been largely unmet. Six months after the terrorist attacks, President Bush announced the launch of the Millennium Challenge Corporation (MCC) that would increase U.S. development aid—tied to conditions—to $5 billion by 2006. Unfortunately, only a handful of countries have met the MCC's criteria for aid.[33] Moreover, the funds actually dispersed have disappointed many (about $3 billion by the middle of 2007) and subsequent Congressional actions have reduced the program's appropriations.[34] Allegations have also been raised that the Administration has used MCC funds to help its allies or as a political weapon against countries lukewarm in support of the Iraq war.[35] In 2003, the Administration announced it was financing a $15 billion aid package to combat HIV/AIDS in Africa and the Caribbean. While both actions increase American aid levels, some critics believe these efforts have not lived up to expectations. More importantly, it pales in comparison to financing of the war in Iraq, which is now measured in the trillions of dollars.[36]

In addition to the Millennium Challenge Corporation and the AIDS package, the Bush Administration doubled development aid in real terms during its time in office. Nevertheless, most observers believe it had a mixed record of success and under-performance. On September 24, 2008, *The New York Times* reported, "Aid from the world's developed countries fell by almost 13 percent between 2005 and 2007 to under $104 billion, after inflation. The aggregate aid budget of the most developed nation's amounts to 0.28 percent of their gross national income, woefully below the target of 0.7 percent agreed to by world leaders in 2002. Only Sweden, Norway, the Netherlands, Luxembourg and Denmark meet the target. Canada's overseas aid amounts to 0.28 percent of its income. Japan's is 0.17 percent. The United States, shamefully, is at the bottom of the list, spending 0.16 percent of its income on development assistance."[37] Most foreign aid expenditures during the Bush Administration went to finance some aspect of the war in Iraq. The underlying causes of terrorism such as poverty, disease, malnutrition, inadequate education, insufficient water and sanitation, lack of land tenure and property rights, corrupt governance, and human rights abuses still wait for adequate funding. Those directly involved in the fight against terrorism predict it will be a war waged for generations.

A June 2005 UN progress report on the Millennium Development Goals, released in anticipation of an upcoming G-8 summit, offered sobering data.[38] More than one billion people lived in abject poverty. Some 800 million did not have enough to eat each day, and more than one-fourth of children in the developing world were undernourished. More than a billion lacked access to safe drinking water. While international attention focused on Rwanda, the Balkans and other conflict areas that claimed twelve million lives from 1994 to 2003, eleven million children died *each year* during the same period because they did not have access to inexpensive vaccines or mosquito nets. Concurrently, aid levels amounted to one-quarter of one percent for the world's richest countries. Moreover, much of this aid was directed at natural disasters such as the 2004 tsunami. Current population and environmental trends were predicted to create an intolerable situation. "We have the means at hand to ensure that nearly every country can make good on the promises of the Goals," UN Secretary General Kofi Annan said then. "Our challenge is to deploy those means … Let us be clear about the costs of missing this opportunity: Millions of lives that could have been saved will be lost; many freedoms that could have been secured will be denied; and we shall inhabit a more dangerous and unstable world."[39]

The summer of the UN report's release offered hopeful signs. As Live Aid musicians took to the stage, the G-8 Summit convened in Scotland. G-8 leaders pledged to increase development assistance by $50 billion in 2010. They also agreed on debt forgiveness for 18 impoverished nations, mostly in Africa. Yet questions remained. The rich countries had pledged significant infusion of development funds in the past. Would they deliver this time?[40] Some critics bristled it would take a half decade to disperse funds while thousands were dying now. Some worried the key issue of agricultural subsidies had been tabled for another time. (The G-8 nations would continue to bicker over the issue throughout the year until World Trade Organization negotiations collapsed in 2006).[41] July, however, proved also to be the cruelest month. As the summit was ending, London exploded. Terrorist bombs claimed 50 lives. In a bizarre juxtaposition, politicians, financiers, rock stars and their fans, and terrorists were embroiled in a global orgy for attention. It also offered a frightening reminder that poor countries do not have the luxury of time, and rich countries and institutions such as the Bank do not have the option to fail.

Wolfensohn's acknowledgement prior to the G-8 Summit that relative aid levels were declining and the Millennium Development Goals would not be met in the poorest countries was an admission:

The Bank had not been able to position itself to make the case that fighting poverty was a priority in the post-9/11 environment.[42] In the summer of 2007, the key issue that confronted Robert Zoellick as he began his term as Bank president was convincing donors to fully replenish International Development Association funding that occurs every three years. "But continuing that aid, and perhaps increasing it, is now a major hurdle...Wealthy countries are balking because of their own budget problems and lingering questions after recent turmoil over the Bank's relevance, its priorities and its effectiveness," *The New York Times* wrote following Zoellick's appointment.[43]

With these perceptions in place about the Bank's lending conditions, its project effectiveness, and its accountability and transparency, to whom among donors, borrowers and civil society actors can the Bank make its case?[44]

In 1999, two World Bank researchers joined others in concluding the institution had reached an important crossroad. But unlike its external critics, the two men believed their positions as Bank insiders might allow them to play a unique role in helping to bring about change. They had worked within the organization for almost a decade, seeing first-hand the Bank's strengths and weaknesses. The institution's waning portfolio and hardening image as a monolithic society now motivated them to embark on a remarkable journey. They wanted to see if it was possible to increase transparency—indeed, bring real transparency—to the Bank. This could increase opportunities for those affected by its decisions to participate in the process. They also wanted to show skeptics that a significant part of the institution was listening and shared their concerns. They did not view transparency as a panacea for the Bank's ills. Nor did they believe it would guarantee better policies or better results. But they did believe that increasing such openness could lead an insular culture, with its proclivity to make deals in back rooms, toward greater accountability, and thus provide critics with a greater understanding of how its policies were made.

Beginning in the mid-1990s, a series of unlikely and unrelated events had led them down this path. During this period, new information technologies were sweeping through the world. The Internet and email communications were making it possible for groups and individuals to meet one another for the first time, and to network with each other.

There was also the work of the two researchers themselves. Their investigation of environmental conditions in the developing world had led them to a series of discoveries as to how unregulated and informal activities could induce behavioral change. Among the most important: A powerful new program in Indonesia where the government disclosed the environmental performance of industries to the public, resulting in radical pollution reductions. The two Bankers realized public disclosure of information once kept secret possessed the capacity to improve people's lives in dramatic and unexpected ways.

The researchers decided to launch a new experiment. Amid the background of a monolithic organization under siege, they began to use these new information technologies to implement the lessons they learned from their environmental research. The subject of their analysis was the Bank itself. The vehicle they employed was an Internet-based broadcasting system that aired uncensored internal Bank meetings, opening the institution's doors for the world to look inside.

Their initiative, however, faced formidable foes. The Bank's culture, hardened over a half century, viewed information as power. Hoarding and shaping information paralleled its instincts. Revealing and sharing it did not. Indeed, many within the organization considered it an anathema. The institution's bureaucracy also was an opponent. It was comprised of numerous fiefdoms. Their rulers viewed the status quo as a mechanism for advancement and greater power. They saw information disclosure and transparency as dangerous threads that could unravel their foundations. On this fractured terrain, a war flared between the proponents of cultural change and the status quo. Over five years, it twisted and turned with each side alternating in triumph.

Former U.S. Treasury Secretary Lawrence Summers once suggested that development banks in the post-Cold War world would play a similar role to that of security organizations following World War

II.[45] That has turned out to not be the case. The Bank is the leading international development institution in the world. Its relevance is essential to the future of the war on poverty. Yet the future of its relevance is not assured. In announcing the Bank of the South initiative, Hugo Chavez suggested, "Sooner or later, [the World Bank and IMF] will fall due to their own weight."[46] Many believe that may come true, but that chapter is not yet written.

The researchers had been considered mavericks by Bank standards even before they began on this new endeavor. That they wanted to increase the institution's transparency made them revolutionaries. The struggle in which they became engaged might then serve as a litmus test for the Bank's future: Will its ability to reduce global poverty dissolve over time, or will it successfully embrace change as a path to reach its potential? To understand how the Bank has arrived at this crucial juncture in its history, one first needs to cleave through the mists of time. What follows is the story of a revolution to transform the World Bank, and a case study of the Bank's power to transform people's lives.

PART II
threads

1

July 1944 proved a seminal moment in world history.[1] American and German soldiers squared off in the fields near Normandy. The Red Army launched a pincer movement in Belarus and a half million of the Third Reich's troops disappeared. Hitler survived an assassination attempt by his own officers. The U.S. 1st Armored Division gained the heights above the Orlo River north of Rome.[2] There was heavy action in New Guinea, Saipan, the Solomon Islands and Burma. Preparation for the invasion of the Philippines was underway. A wire out of Jerusalem said hundreds of thousands of Jews were being deported to SS prison camps in Poland for extermination. The report, however, could not be substantiated.

In the United States, Thomas E. Dewey secured the Republican nomination for the presidency at age 42. Rumors raged that Southern Democrats would force Roosevelt to drop Vice President Henry Wallace from the ticket in the fall. Most attention focused on Senator Alben Barkley of Kentucky as his replacement, though Harry Truman of Missouri was also mentioned. Truman, incidentally, said he was not interested. A wave of walkouts by disgruntled steel and coal mine workers disrupted large facilities in Pennsylvania. Many worried about the impact on war operations. Blacks in Georgia attempting to register for the Democratic Primary were refused ballots by local election officials. A million New Yorkers cooled off at Coney Island for the holiday weekend. Paul Robeson, Jose Ferrer and Uta Hagen closed a record run of 296 performances of "Othello" at the Shubert

Theater. The St. Louis Browns were on their way to the only pennant of their half century of existence. And, in July 1944, bankers and diplomats from 44 countries gathered at a New Hampshire resort called Bretton Woods. Their purpose was to meet the challenge of creating a post-war economy that President Roosevelt called a test of the Allies' capacity "to cooperate in peace as we have in war."

By the thousands, men lined sidewalks around induction centers across the nation as 1942 began. The temper of America is slow to move when unsettled, but quick to act when angered: And the dawn raid on Pearl Harbor had inspired a rage not seen since the Lusitania's sinking. While the military was still tabulating losses from Hawaii, U.S. Treasury Secretary Henry Morganthau was already pondering the kind of world the men on sidewalks near his office would come home to after the war.[3] He decided to commission a study devising a post-war plan to prevent the "currency disorders" responsible for the economic and political instability leading up to World War II. He turned to Harry White, a leading economist in his department, to develop a strategy. White soon envisioned a system that would create two institutions. The first would tie the global economy to the gold standard as a way to protect the exchange rate from fluctuations and inflation. To shield this system, a second institution would operate as a lender of last resort to supplement financing by private capital markets. This second institution, a "Bank for Reconstruction of the United and Associated Nations," would be financed by capital infusions from member governments, and subsequently be bolstered by growing reserves, revenues from its lending, and perhaps further capital infusions.[4] To move his concept to application, White began collaborating with John Maynard Keynes, a renowned English economist who was formulating a post-war international stabilization fund on behalf of the British government.[5]

For the next two years, White and Keynes and their teams drafted and reworked the plan. By early 1944, White decided it had crystallized enough to hold an international conference in the summer to begin implementation. The gathering's primary emphasis was to establish a system of currency stabilization. Instituting a bank for reconstruction was considered a secondary objective.

White and his contemporaries viewed an International Bank for Reconstruction and Development (IBRD)—not as an altruistic endeavor to relieve poverty and suffering—but as a way to prevent the political extremism of communism and fascism that characterized the 1920s and 1930s. "There is nothing that will serve to drive these countries into some kind of ism, communism or something else, faster than inadequate capital," White famously said at the time. Reconstruction of Europe's devastated infrastructure would be the primary focus.[6] Attendees, as an afterthought, included 'development' as part of the new bank's mandate.[7] If funds remained, lending might be considered for projects outside the war zone. Moreover, economists and policy planners at the time conceived of development differently than we do today.[8] During the 1940s, much of the world still consisted of colonies or territories of the principal nations conducting the war. Independence for many populations remained decades away. For conference planners and attendees, development translated into creating physical infrastructure to exploit natural resources and generate economic growth for their colonizers.

The conferees adopted the model proposed by White and Keynes: The Bank would raise capital by selling bonds based on member countries' financial guarantees. Financially strapped by the war, England and other representatives deferred to the United States as their chief underwriter. The preeminence of the American position proved useful for Roosevelt's emissaries in resolving contentious issues in such a way as to insure their enduring influence. Most notably, the U.S. solidified dominance with the adoption of a weighted membership system.[9] In direct contrast to the UN's adoption of a one country-one vote structure, a member's influence on Bank policy and lending would be a reflection of its economic salience. This determination virtually guaranteed that the major economic powers would control the institution in perpetuity. Negotiators also acquiesced to housing the new institution in Washington and provided its executive directors with permanent residency.[10] This gave White House officials close proximity and seamless access to the Bank's key policymakers in an era when satellites, computers, and the Internet had yet to exist.

If the World Bank was born during the deadly struggle between the Nazis and Allies in the hedgerows of France, then it's feasible to suggest the seeds of its birth were sown at Versailles in 1919. During those negotiations, the victorious Allies set peace conditions so severe, Germany was fated to decades of economic uncertainty and political instability, thereby setting the stage for a subsequent world war. The creation of the Bank and the International Monetary Fund (IMF) was an acknowledgement Versailles had failed the peace after World War I much as Europe's monarchies had abdicated the peace in the four decades leading to 1914. The Americans and the British believed these new institutions, which would include the United Nations, would be critical to staving off a third cataclysm. And, known only at the highest levels of the American government and military, something else made establishment of global economic stability urgent: A realization that the coming atomic age would make such a war apocalyptic.

In December 1945, the Bank's Articles of Agreement were ratified by 28 governments with one notable exception: The Soviet Union. In the wake of Winston Churchill's Iron Curtain speech and a series of communist uprisings in Eastern Europe in 1946, the Soviets withdrew their membership and called the Bank an instrument of American foreign policy.[11] Indeed, the sun had set on the English empire; and with Moscow's abdication, the terrain had been ceded to the U.S. For the next half century, the Bank would be seen as a pawn in the struggle between East and West.

Yet even as the original mission was unfolding, it was ending. In 1947, the Bank made its first loan of $250 million for the reconstruction of France, but it had become obvious the scale of rebuilding Europe was beyond the ability of the fledgling lender. With the unveiling of the Marshall Plan, the Truman Administration signaled the removal of the Bank as the lead agency in the European renewal.

Instinctively, the institution moved to remake itself as a development organization. At the time the conference convened at Bretton

Woods, an estimated 60% of people in the Third World lived in abject poverty.[12] Life expectancy in Mexico was 40 years. In parts of rural India, it dropped to 25 years of age. Disease and starvation routinely killed millions, almost all of it outside public view in the industrialized world. But in this dramatic and permanent shift from reconstruction to development, an awful truth was revealed. There was no clear sense of what development meant, how to promote or measure it, or whether prevailing economic theory could address the profound issues surrounding global poverty.[13]

As the Bank evolved into this new role, intellectuals from rich nations and their counterpart elites in the developing world began to engineer initiatives on behalf of impoverished communities with unique, complex, and fragile economic, political and social orders.[14] The stresses that developed between donors and borrowers from the outset permanently etched into the Bank's DNA a sense of conflict within its membership.

Throughout its early years, the Bank was a cautious lender, working meticulously to establish credit worthiness. To achieve this, it focused resources on financing large infrastructure projects because the era's prevailing notion believed that capital accumulation provided the foundation for economic growth. By the mid-1950s, pressure from critics compelled the institution to rethink its role in facilitating development. A metamorphosis began. In 1955, the Bank established the Economic Development Institute (EDI) to foster learning and training of client-country policymakers. In 1956, the International Finance Corporation (IFC) was created for investments in the private sector. The defining event of this evolution, however, was the establishment of the International Development Association (IDA) in 1960. IDA offered cheap loans to the poorest countries and repayment rates so elongated they were essentially considered grants. Recognizing an opportunity to increase its clientele by lending for agriculture, water sanitation, education and other areas, senior Bank officials realized IDA could also serve as a vehicle to force donors to markedly increase capital infusions. IDA funding, however, arrived with a caveat. Monies came, not from bonds, but from donor members' capital infusions which needed to be replenished every three years. Prior to IDA, the Bank pursued only the soundest investments. Now, the riskiest nations were prime candidates for its lending. Both factors served to exacerbate existing tensions between the Bank and its political adversaries in donor governments. These tensions have never abated.

For the first quarter century of the Bank's existence, the term "poverty" rarely appeared in its annual reports; and a sense grew by the late 1960s that its portfolio of individual projects had not fundamentally altered the development situation for many poor countries.[15] Robert S. McNamara, a former U.S. Secretary of Defense and the Bank's president from the late 1960s to early 1980s, decided to move the organization away from its prevailing emphasis on economic growth toward a more holistic philosophy. McNamara was influenced by two important economic theories that had gained credence during his time in the Kennedy Administration.[16] The first came from Theodore Schultz, an influential economist and Bank critic who believed the institution needed to shift from delivering physical capital, such as large infrastructure projects, to fostering human capital by investing in education and health care. The second theory came from an Administration colleague, National Security Advisor Walter Rostow. He urged the Bank to focus less on the economic disparity between nations and more on the income inequality within nations. McNamara's Bank began to alter its mission toward poverty reduction. Basic needs would be met through sector investments. Accordingly, new departments for rural and urban development, agriculture, health, population, education, and nutrition were formed. Income distribution and the number of people living on a dollar a day became key barometers for measuring how well the Bank was doing. Correspondingly, lending expanded rapidly.

But while the Bank president was calling for eradicating poverty by the end of the 20th century, the institution struggled with its new agenda. It lurched uncertainly toward aggressive social engineering to redistribute income and alleviate poverty. Then, suddenly, while beginning its great endeavor to remake itself and the future of millions, its chance disappeared. In 1973, the Yom Kippur War fueled the impetus for the Arab oil embargo a few months later. The embargo sent shock waves into the global economy as prices escalated. Oil-importing nations, particularly in Latin America, began borrowing more heavily to finance further imports. For the balance of the decade, commercial lenders rescheduled debt while the Bank was lending to these borrowers. Within a few years, numerous developing countries were saddled with destabilizing debt imbalances. A concurrent growth in bilateral and private-sector lending undermined the Bank's influence, and weak institutional capacity by its clients to absorb the loans curtailed McNamara's agenda.

To address the emerging debt problems, McNamara announced a new strategy to promote lending for structural adjustments to debtor nations. The new concept would veer the organization away from its emphasis on poverty reduction to concentrate on implementing macroeconomic reforms. To reduce debt and stabilize these fragile economies, the Bank would impose "conditions" as part of its lending terms. Highly indebted borrowers would be forced to reduce trade barriers by replacing quotas with tariffs, reduce inflation, reduce public spending, increase savings and balance budgets. And, since highly indebted borrowers remained in desperate need of capital, they agreed to the Bank's terms.

Structural-adjustment lending became the centerpiece of the Bank's philosophy, and it energized intense debate as to whether its policies were benefiting or hurting the poor. Throughout the 1980s and into the early 1990s, the institution came under intense scrutiny from skeptics on both the far right and far left. Conservatives supported structural adjustment as a mechanism to remold the Bank as a facilitator of private-sector lending since it pressed borrowing countries to reduce trade barriers and open their markets. Nevertheless, they sought to curtail replenishments of IDA funding, pressuring the institution to reduce its lending portfolio and move into making concessionary grants. They also attacked the Bank as an ineffective bureaucracy that had become bloated during the McNamara era.

This new school of development economics that favored

structural adjustments, however, was not well received by the Bank's borrowers. The prescription for reducing trade barriers and public spending and currency devaluation imposed serious hardships on developing countries. Austerity measures proved harsh and, indeed, counterproductive as many borrowers had problems implementing them. It also reversed policies the Bank had previously fostered, which created doubts about the lender.[17] Concurrently, the Bank did not really understand the domestic political uncertainties that endangered the policies from the start.[18] The two factors in tandem proved disastrous. Most global regions, other than East Asia, experienced a serious decline in growth during the 1980s. Economies in Africa and Latin America were particularly hard hit.

Bank capital predicated on "conditions" may have been based on sound economic principles, but the condition of debtor nations worsened. As the Cold War blazed on, many in the development community came to view adjustment lending as a cynical prop for Western powers to finance autocratic regimes willing to side against the Soviet Union. With the negative image of the Bank hardening, so did the resolve of a then-burgeoning community of non-governmental organizations (NGOs). By the late 1980s, these stakeholders became increasingly vocal. They began to question whether the institution's resources were being used to propagate poverty and sanction dictatorships. Adding fuel to the NGO fire were lending debacles by the Bank in Brazil and India that caused significant environmental damage, deforestation of rainforests, and desecration of indigenous populations.

These embarrassments led the Bank to commission two important reviews that validated concerns of critics in the donor, borrower, and civil society communities. The first, the Morse Commission, examined the fallout from a dam-lending project in India that displaced tens of thousands, leading to street clashes with local authorities. Allegations suggested that root causes had been a lack of transparency and accountability in the Bank's decision-making process.[19] The Morse panel then found systematic failures ranging from human rights violations to breaches in the institution's own environmental guidelines.

A second investigation reviewed the quality of the Bank's lending portfolio. The Wapenhans Commission, led by a former Bank vice president, revealed flaws in the quality of the Bank's work as well as its internal appraisal system. Wapenhans also called into question the institution's legitimacy. With the IDA replenishments concurrently being negotiated, senior Bank officials sensed that donors had shifted their thinking about its funding from an act of collaboration to an act of burden sharing.

By the time its annual meetings convened in Madrid in 1994, the Bank was reeling from the criticism. Madrid brought further calamities. Thousands derailed the gathering with street demonstrations and disruptions of the Bank's conferences. When then Bank President Lewis Preston stood up to address attendees, protestors on the atrium roof dropped fake dollar bills with anti-Bank slogans on the audience. "50 years is enough," they chanted. Many in international policy circles wondered if they were right. Questions of whether the Bank was capable of completing its mission intensified. Some even speculated the Bank could soon disintegrate.

The next spring, Preston resigned because of ill health. The Clinton Administration's replacement was James Wolfensohn, a charismatic investment banker with a long track record of successes. Wolfensohn, a philanthropist, Olympic fencer, part-time cellist, and at the time of his selection chairman of the Kennedy Center for Performing Arts, had been angling for the position since McNamara's term. The Bank he inherited was much like a once-handsome boxer who could no longer move with cunning—legs lethargic, torso sagged on the ropes, looking for the bell for oxygen. Bureaucratic, conservative, obsessed with the machinations of internal processes, the Bank had become an organization reacting to external events rather than driving them. Staff often joked the Bank's ultimate goal was to drive itself out of business and it sought to do so as slowly as possible. In its new president, the institution found a man determined to reorder the dynamics of how it operated.

2

In contrast to James Wolfensohn, no Oval Office interview anointed me when I joined the Bank. In fact, when the temp agency offered a two-week assignment, I refused. I had done a short stint at the Bank once before and found it boring. It wasn't immediately obvious to me what the organization did, though staff seemed to specialize in moving large amounts of paper from one desk to another. Then, I reconsidered. Two weeks seemed a long time not to worry about a paycheck.

I had come to Washington four years earlier to pursue an interest in politics. Yet, with each step I took in the halls of Capitol Hill, a black cloud loomed above me. The first Congressman I worked for would be convicted of embezzlement and sent to jail. The second Congressman fared better. His constituents preferred him as a private citizen to Senator. And, the third Representative wore large JESUS pins on her lapel, garishly colored suits, and feathers in her hat; so when she sat on the dais of committee hearings, she looked like a Christmas tree in a winter forest. She, too, was indicted as a prelude to retiring from Congress.

I was not entirely convinced I would destroy my party if I did not leave politics, but the opportunity to test the theory had not yet arisen when the door at the Bank opened. It was July 1993, and the agency placed me with a new research unit that had started just a week earlier. My job would be to run a few calculations and place the results in graphs. It was pretty straightforward and, despite little aptitude for numbers, I didn't botch it. This pleased the office manager. She struck up a conversation and learned I had once been a newspaper reporter. A couple days later, a youthful man with white hair, moustache, and convivial disposition stopped by my desk. He ran the unit. "We're a brand new research team working on environmental issues in the developing world with a particular focus on industrial pollution," he began. "We need someone with research skills. Your background could be helpful. What would you say if we extended your assignment to two months?" I had little ambition to work at the Bank, but it surpassed my ambition to work at finding work. "That sounds pretty good," I said. My new manager was David Wheeler.

Wheeler had a comedic cynicism about politics and bureaucracies, and since we had this trait in common, an immediate bond formed. Raised in Missouri and West Virginia, he was a robust concoction of rebel and hillbilly. He had also been educated at some of the country's most elite institutions. Still, despite the academic credentials, he was fond of noting the most important lessons he learned about life came from his time in the Army during the 1960s. After the military had had enough, he became an econometrician working extensively on the analytical nexus between industry and environment. Prior to joining the Bank in 1990, he taught applied econometrics and microeconomics at Boston University, MIT, and the University of Zaire. He also managed a research institute in Indonesia investigating industry and trade issues, and co-founded a second one in the U.S.

Nobel Laureate economist Robert Solow once said, "In the long run, the economics of natural resources and the environment is as important to our well being as the economics of money and banking."[20] Nevertheless, despite civil society's sustained scrutiny of the environmental impact of its work, the Bank had not learned the lesson when Wheeler arrived at its Industry Department. Its Environment Department did not yet exist. All that had evolved since the 1970s were a few "end-of-pipe" components for pollution control, occasional financing of clean technology installations, and some environmental assessments as components of larger lending activities. By anyone's measure, this activity was modest. Over the previous decade many of its client countries had launched their own environmental management agencies. But these agencies were poorly funded, poorly equipped, and without adequate data to make informed choices about regulation. Because of its own hesitancy on financing environmental activities, the Bank was not well positioned to provide meaningful technical assistance to these fledgling agencies.

Wheeler identified the core concern the Bank historically held on environment lending in a 1991 paper when he wrote, "Much of the Bank's policy advice has reflected the widespread conviction that a very large gain in discounted net welfare accompanies the transition from Path 1 (no environmental policy and unsound economic policy) to Path 2 (no environmental policy but sound economic policy), even if the short-run adjustment costs are high. Environmentalist concerns are, however, very controversial among development economists who fear unwarranted costs in the transition to Path 3 (sound economic and national environmental policies). This fear has been compounded by the recent emergence of Path 4 (sound economic, national environmental and global commons policies), which reflects global commons concerns."[21]

Policymakers in the developing world were generally reluctant to invest scarce resources on environmental problems when there were pressing poverty, illiteracy, and health care needs. Most Bank economists also assumed pollution was the inevitable price of economic development. They theorized it was necessary to get rich first and clean up afterwards. This positioned the issue as one of 'either-or' rather than examining tradeoffs between benefits and costs.

Wheeler and a smattering of allies said their research did not support such an assumption. Industries provide vital employment opportunities, they noted, but they also pollute. The researchers understood communities might find some acceptable tradeoff between environmental degradation and the economic opportunities provided by local industries. Their objective as economists was not to eliminate pollution but rather to find a level that balanced both needs. In fact, they believed common ground could exist where the industrial sector's economic growth and employment gains served as a valuable component for a sustainable environment with poverty reduction. Misguided policy choices had as much or more to do with degradation as did economic growth, they suggested.[22]

For example, sectors that assembled materials were less polluting than sectors that processed them. Therefore, where an economy invested resources impacted pollution levels. Plant-level factors also determined the amount of pollution and a facility's ability to be in regulatory compliance. Factories, even in the same sector or location, polluted differently because plant characteristics were integral to environmental performance.[23] These factors included input prices, plant technologies, operational efficiencies, the environmental orientation of the workers, owners, suppliers and/or consumers, abatement costs, existing standards, and monitoring and enforcement practices by regulators. Additionally, market characteristics, the availability of cleaner technologies, and financing mechanisms to upgrade machinery were also influential. As a result, pollution abatement costs varied widely across and even within industries.[24] A contrarian group of economists within the Bank believed that, with the right instruments, most plants could attain significant levels of abatement at modest costs.

Another prevailing theory of the period suggested that poor countries with little or no environmental regulation would become "pollution havens" if trade barriers with rich countries were lowered. This theory assumed wealthy nations would successfully seek to purchase access inside impoverished nations for their refuse. Wheeler and his colleagues believed this notion was not necessarily true.[25] Based on the data they were examining, clean and dirty plants coexisted in both rich and poor countries. It appeared more likely that dirty industries found sanctuary in protectionist economies rather than open ones which were quicker to adopt cleaner technologies. Even if poor countries could not invest in environmental protection, it did not denote a lack of interest. They saw problems their wealthier neighbors had, and indeed were often facing problems their industrialized counterparts had never confronted. Rich economies that hadn't invested in cleaner production technologies from the outset paid an enormous cost in human suffering and cleanups. The Superfund program in the U.S. was a prime example, costing taxpayers hundreds of billions of dollars. Polluted economies were poorer than their leaders believed, the researchers concluded, and under appropriate circumstances clean production was feasible in developing countries. Indeed, in the absence of capital for clean technologies, many poor countries had adopted monitoring and enforcement standards based on Western models. Such methodologies, however, were costly, and developing countries predictably devoted financial resources to other pressing needs. They needed a tool to help prioritize their environmental problems so they could address them within the limitations of their scarce resources.

The ideal level for pollution existed where the cost of control equaled its societal gain.[26] Too much pollution meant communities paid excessively in damages and remediation. Too much pollution abatement meant lost jobs and a slowed economy. But where those lines crossed was difficult to define. Certainly, theoretically models had their place, but the reality was painfully stark. Millions of people in the developing world were dying as a result of the environmental degradation that their national economies created. A Bank estimate from the mid-1990s suggested that two million Chinese died annually from pollution.[27] Millions more became incapacitated. Air pollution in major cities had forced people to use face masks as routine daily wear. Some rivers were little more than sewers, and acid rain blanketed large geographic regions. The impact on public health was so enormous that senior government officials could no longer ignore its threat to their relentless quest for massive economic growth. And, in the developing world, China was far from alone in this struggle.

Wheeler and a few colleagues began pursuing a methodology that would accurately estimate the point where costs equaled gains. They began with an analysis of the Toxic Release Inventory (TRI), a U.S. Environmental Protection Agency (U.S. EPA) database of publicly available information on chemical releases reported annually by industries.[28] The researchers then negotiated an agreement with the U.S. Census Bureau to access another database of confidential information on 20,000 industries covering all manufacturing sectors.[29] This coup allowed them to match plant-level manufacturing information with the publicly available data from the TRI, thus assembling a database of emission coefficients. These coefficients would allow regulators and economists to estimate pollution load by industrial sector for major water and air pollutants.

By 1991, the small team had designed a first-generation Industrial Pollution Projection System (IPPS).[30] IPPS used manufacturing data to estimate industrial pollution in developing countries. Most developing countries had little reliable information on environmental performance, but they usually had detailed industry information on employment or outputs. IPPS converted this information into pollution intensity profiles (pollution per unit of output, value added or employee). Unlike previous engineering estimations, IPPS used actual reported emissions and production data from industrial facilities. The database held environmental, economic, and geographical data on 200,000 firms covering 1,500 industrial sectors on all major operating technologies, and on hundreds of pollutants.

The researchers were also interested in the toxicity risk different pollutants posed, and concurrently began developing a second inventory.[31] It was critical for regulators to identify pollutant volume; but it was also necessary to understand toxic risks, since public exposure to small levels of one pollutant could be more hazardous than exposure to another's larger levels. Both assessments would be critical for regulators in priority-setting exercises.

Finally, the team focused on identifying what abatement of pollutants would cost.[32] Factory owners would refrain from cleaning up if these costs were unknown. The group began an analysis of the U.S. Commerce Department's Pollution Abatement and Control Expenditures (PACE) database. It revealed that abatement costs were relatively minimal in the beginning, and rose sharply as a factory continued to reduce pollution. This meant it could be relatively inexpensive to reduce large amounts of pollution if regulators and firms fully understood where to target their resources. For factory managers, it provided an opportunity to reduce pressure from regulators at minimal cost. Regulators would also be empowered. They could focus scarce resources on polluters with low abatement costs, thereby protecting the environment with minimal impact on the local economy. Just how powerful this dynamic was revealed itself a few years later when research in China found the pollution tax 50 times lower than what was optimal. The level of pollution control by regulators at the time had only valued an individual's life at a few hundred dollars.[33]

The rudimentary IPPS model was applied for an exercise in preparing the Bank's seminal 1992 World Development Report on the environment.[34] But some Bank counterparts openly wondered whether U.S.-based pollution intensities could be used to approximate pollution in the developing world. In the fall, the team sought to expand the system with plant-level data from other countries. Funding, however, remained elusive. In a memo to key department heads he titled "Neiman Marcus Information at Kmart Prices," Wheeler made a plea to Bank managers to "slide the money into the position formerly occupied by the mouth," noting "This potential mother lode is accessible at marginal cost. We're playing with no net here. If I can't get enough support, we'll simply have to shut down our operation within a month."[35] The plea brought $35,000, enough to keep the research sustainable.[36]

Wheeler and his allies began encouraging senior Bank officials to expand research on industrial pollution control. Since environmental protection had never been a Bank priority, their pitch focused on identifiable synergies.[37] First, polluting economies were inefficient economies, which is what the Bank was in the business to fix. They drained clients of productivity because they were wasteful, unhealthy, expensive to clean up, and reduced the ability of these countries to promote economic growth and reduce poverty. Second, such research dovetailed with the Bank's technical assistance activities to develop national environmental action plans for nascent regulatory authorities. Technical assistance needed sound econometric analysis.

The proposal cleverly identified weaknesses in the Bank's policy dialogue that it could strengthen: Offering modeling instruments at a time when the organization was about to expand lending on the environment. It also piggybacked on the Bank's environmental miscalculations from prior years that had left it with a tarnished reputation. By the early summer, the Bank's Research Department announced it would launch a new division on Environment and Infrastructure. Wheeler was named "acting" chief, a title that suggested his interim status would be one of assessment for both him and the new line of research.

Work began immediately to broaden the IPPS with emissions and abatement data from developing country sources.[38] The unit soon collected an array of talents. Mala Hettige, an economist from Sri Lanka who played a leading role in developing IPPS, would use the tool to conduct country-level surveys. Shakeb Afsah would use his engineering and public policy degrees from India to help Indonesia implement a radical new environmental management program. He would be joined by Benoit Laplante, an environmental economist from Canada studying how regulatory structures influenced plant-level behavior. Econometricians Susmita Dasgupta of India and Hua Wang of China would analyze China's manufacturing sector and regulatory efforts in order to develop abatement opportunities. Mainul Huq of Bangladesh would survey factories in South Asia to identify variations in how they behaved in the absence of formal regulation. Sheoli Pargal, an industrial economist from India, would seek to identify why plants complied with existing regulations. Muthukumara Mani, an environmental economist also from India, would conduct an extensive cross-country analysis of water pollution. David Gray, a Scottish geographer, became the unit's Geographic Information Systems (GIS) specialist conducting spatial analysis of the unit's pollution intensity calculations. Dave Witzel, an American, would work on IPPS projections as well as the team's database systems. The unit, however, was not focused exclusively on industrial pollution. There was analysis of the environment's impact on health, as well as research on HIV/AIDS and infrastructure issues. One particular infrastructure specialist who joined the unit would play a pivotal role in the great debate the Bank would one day face. A Tanzanian, her name was Frannie Humplick.

Initially, I was put to work creating spreadsheets, but as I became indoctrinated into the program, I soon began editing the team's research papers.[39] The two-month contract led to a position as a research assistant.[40] Wheeler enlisted me on a two-year pursuit to uncover and collect pollution data from Bank sources, engineering firms, embassies and environmental agencies throughout the world. The data collection work introduced me for the first time to a historic reluctance within the institution toward information sharing, even among Bank colleagues. Who had information had power, and some saw no advantage in voluntarily giving it away. The large majority of Bank counterparts willingly shared information, but a number called their data "proprietary," or cited confidentiality agreements with clients, or considered the exercise of creating a global database on pollution emissions futile. Others suggested their data might be available if we provided funds. Moreover, a subtle but obvious hostility appeared from a cadre of counterparts in the Environment Department, who suggested IPPS undermined its own in-house modeling tool. While both tools sought to achieve the same outcome, IPPS was ideal for initial prioritization assessments while the other system was useful for going in-depth with a particular sector.[41] In essence, Wheeler's model undercut theirs, and some counterparts were resentful. From our perspective, however, it was questionable as to whether the Environment Department's tool could play a fully useful role at all in pollution prioritization exercises in the developing world. Wheeler recalled one early meeting between him, Emmanuel Jimenez, a fellow research division chief and a Bank environmental colleague who questioned the value of using a system calibrated with U.S. data. Jimenez responded by noting, "The alternative is nothing." Wheeler rejoiced in what he called "Manny's Maxim," as IPPS had little competition.[42] Within a year of its launch, Bank units as well as a number of environmental agencies and research institutes had used IPPS. In time, it would be implemented in dozens of countries by Wheeler's team, other Bank personnel, and numerous researchers around the world.[43]

Just a few months earlier, Wheeler had published *The Economics of Industrial Pollution Control*, a paper that laid the foundation for the team's research over the next decade.[44] It surveyed ten countries in both the developing and industrialized world to compare their regulatory models, practices and results. The paper suggested that pollution control was influenced by many factors: Local social values, transaction costs, institutional capacity, enterprise ownership, pollutant risk, and geographic characteristics. Policy options such as volume-based limits, taxes, and fees were all important in these agencies' ongoing environmental management, but something else caught Wheeler's attention. He noted market reputation and potential consumer liability promoted significant cleanup in rich countries including the U.S. Part of this could be attributed to the establishment of the TRI. Yet even in some developing countries without strong enforcement capacity, plants and communities were negotiating pollution control. Something was occurring beyond the traditional practice of environmental management: There appeared to be a new trend toward an informal approach to pollution regulation. Wheeler's discovery proved profound. It would set the stage for an unheralded new way to protect the environment. But more than that, it would unleash forces, spinning faster and faster beyond control, to grip the very essence of the Bank itself.

3

In 1992, Mainul Huq, Wheeler's colleague in the Industry Department, boarded a plane for his native Bangladesh. His mission: To conduct surveys of the fertilizer sector's environmental performance as part of the cross-country analysis Wheeler was preparing for *The Economics of Industrial Pollution Control* paper. Bangladesh had few regulations, and with little incentive for factories to reduce the amount of their contaminants from entering rivers, the researchers expected to find their polluting behavior unrestrained. They were wrong. In fact, they found wide variation in performance.[45]

But why would clean facilities exist in a poor country that could not enforce pollution control activities? They learned that communities were not powerless. In fact, localities had negotiated compensation for damages to their fisheries and rice paddies, and in some cases forced plants to install wastewater-treatment measures. They had organized boycotts, launched court actions, applied pressure through political or religious intermediaries, and had even threatened violence. This had become clear: In the absence of effective enforcement by regulators, communities had been entering into informal negotiations with local facilities. Mounting evidence suggested informal arrangements were already playing a central role in environmental management of some developing world societies. New databases were uncovered in Thailand and the Philippines that produced similar observations.[46] These events contrasted sharply from traditional environmental management practices. An unusual phenomenon was taking place, intriguing the researchers.

The opportunity to learn more came in 1994. BAPEDAL, the Indonesian environmental agency, invited the team to analyze the impact of a new program urging industries to voluntarily disclose their water emissions.[47] The data paralleled what the researchers had found in other developing country settings. Indonesia had a highly developed regulatory regime, but the nation suffered from severe, growing pollution levels. BAPEDAL's repertoire of monitoring and enforcement tactics seemed too conventional to create much impact. The researchers wondered if the informal social arrangements impacting pollution levels elsewhere in South Asia might work here. Could orchestrating public participation in pollution control provide regulators with a new option for environmental management? They were aided by a visionary thinker inside BAPEDAL: Its deputy director, Nabiel Makarim.

Makarim was also a careful observer of environmental management efforts elsewhere, and he had made the same discovery. He saw the impact the TRI had in the U.S., as well as on public pollution inventories in other industrialized countries. These inventories were complex, but citizen advocacy groups with sufficient technical expertise had played a crucial role by analyzing the data and informing the public of the dangers it faced.[48] Manufacturers had responded accordingly by reducing their pollution levels. BAPEDAL did not have such an inventory; and even if it did, Indonesia's community-based organizations did not have the expertise to analyze it for the public. But something else about Indonesia's culture gave him an opportunity to change their behavior. Reputation matters everywhere; yet in Indonesia, saving face was an integral part of its society. Makarim envisioned a system where factory behavior could be disclosed to the public as a way to influence the industry's actions. Such an initiative would need to rely on sound information; but if the data could be repackaged in a way understandable to the general public, it might form the basis for a powerful regulatory tool. Indeed, game theorists might suggest public disclosure of non-compliance formed a credible threat, since it imposed the certainty of exposure, shame, and damage to a factory's reputation.

Pollution inventories were not new. In fact, they were not even an invention of the West. Their antecedents could be traced back to Asia, when Japanese communities started negotiating emission disclosure agreements with industries in the 1960s.[49] Japan's citizenry enthusiastically embraced industrialization following World War II. Local plants were seen as harbingers of the public's wellbeing. But as unrestricted discharges became recognized as the source of health problems, attitudes changed. The first advocates of change interestingly enough were ordinary housewives concerned about their children. Over the course of two decades, activists lobbied local governments to pressure polluters, or employed clever awareness-raising campaigns. Strong initial resistance from manufacturers and government officials began to melt. By the early 1980s, cities throughout Japan began enacting ordinances recognizing the public's right to know about pollution, and mandating public inventories be collected.

Just as the Japanese were embracing the concept with increasing momentum, a chemical release from a Union Carbide facility in Bhopal, India killed thousands. Horrified citizens in the U.S. began voicing concern about toxic risks from industrial facilities in their communities. The U.S. Congress subsequently passed The Emergency Planning and Community Right-to-Know Act of 1986. It mandated that a database of publicly available information on toxic chemical releases be reported annually by manufacturing sources.[50] The Toxic Release Inventory, however, did not come into existence without a fight. Industry lobbyists in Washington argued the public would not react rationally to the legal release of chemicals since the government would play no interpretative role. They argued confidential information would be lost to domestic and international competitors. But Bhopal had shaken the American public in much the same way as Three Mile Island and Love Canal had. The lobbyists lost.[51]

For the first time, manufacturing performance would be linked with accountability. Naturally, pressure grew on industries to change. Environmental NGOs filled the void left by government to analyze the data and lead campaigns for improvement.[52] Local communities followed suit by entering into direct negotiations about abatement with neighboring facilities. Adroitly, some manufacturers repositioned their loss in Washington as a win.[53] Large companies such as Boeing and Monsanto made substantial reductions, and proclaimed themselves as good corporate citizens. Some began issuing annual reports to shareholders, consumers, and civil society activists about their environmental management efforts. Though public disclosure had been a "powerful motivator," there were carrots among the sticks. Many manufacturers learned for the first time about their pollution levels and the hazards they created.[54] The new information also compelled more efficient production methodologies to reduce abatement costs. In the aftermath of the TRI, Canada, the United Kingdom, and other industrialized countries began to create their own public pollution release inventories.

Makarim asked Wheeler and his team for assistance to build the system he now envisioned. On one level, the concept would parallel work done with the TRI, but with a twist. The TRI analysis done by American NGOs did not provide easy comparisons of performance between industries. Makarim wanted a rating system the public could easily understand. Without sufficient capacity by NGOs in Indonesia, responsibility for managing the system would have to be BAPEDAL's.

The new program had three objectives. It sought to hold the poor performance by some manufacturers to public scrutiny in order to shame them into compliance. It also sought to provide positive incentives through public recognition of good performers. Finally, the program's transparency and public scrutiny also would create incentives for BAPEDAL to perform well.[55] Wheeler secured funding from Richard Calkins, the Bank's Country Director for Indonesia, to send Shakeb Afsah overseas to help Makarim design and implement a pilot.[56] A momentous experiment was underway.

The integrity of the data analysis was critical. A rating mistake might unduly enhance or tarnish a company's reputation. In either case, the program's image would also be imperiled; a mistake in one ranking would call into question all the rankings. Care also needed to be exercised with how information might be perceived by the public, since the program could not analyze the health impacts of emissions. Analysts needed to assimilate the data into a format that no one could misinterpret. Monitoring officials would quantify results through random on-site inspections. The new system was called the Program for Pollution Control, Evaluation and Rating (PROPER). It provided color-coded assessments of pollution performance. Gold meant a firm was excellent. Green meant a factory did well by Indonesian standards. Blue symbolized existing standards had been met. A rating of red signified minimal standards had not been met, even if some abatement work had occurred. Black meant bad in every sense of the word.[57]

By March 1995, BAPEDAL was ready to begin. Three-hundred-fifty plants were solicited for data on their water effluents. A computerized model tabulated the responses, and by June, the Ministry publicly announced the results. There were no Gold performers. Five received a Green rating, 61 a Blue, 115 Red, and six were rated as Black. Almost half the factories, however, did not bother to respond, and of the 187 plants that did, almost 60% had failed to meet national standards.[58] But integral to the program was Makarim's knowledge of Indonesia's social and cultural norms which resisted confrontation. When BAPEDAL Minister Sarwono Kusumaatmadja announced the results, he also noted: Firms who had failed to meet minimal standards would have until December to improve their performance before their names would be revealed to the public. It was a brilliant ploy. Polluters could save face through the grace period; but it also gave the agency time to strengthen its legal position should it subsequently initiate sanctions against recalcitrant polluters. The agency had put its reputation on the line as well. The failure rate suggested it was confessing its own ineffectiveness to the public. If PROPER imploded or factories simply refused to respond, the agency's image would be tarnished for years to come. The clock was ticking for both sides.

Makarim's gamble paid off. BAPEDAL's public announcement spurred extensive media coverage and public concern. The regulators began receiving queries from factory owners who had previously spurned the program. They wanted to know how they could join. By the December deadline, when the government publicly revealed the names of factories still out of compliance, the Black category had declined by 50%, the Red category by 6% and the Blue category had increased by 18%. Overall, an 8% improvement in environmental performance had occurred during the grace period between private and public disclosure.[59] By September 1996, a little more than a year after the launch and nine months after public disclosure of plant performance, there were no more plants remaining with a Black rating. The Red category declined to 87 firms, and those with Blue ratings increased to 95. Compliance increased by 50% from when the program was launched, and it had rendered a 40% decline in the target group's water pollution levels.[60] By increasing public awareness, regulators were also building new coalitions within and between communities and their representatives—coalitions they hoped would help insulate programs from opponents in industry and other government agencies. Regulators assumed that once exposed to this new flow of information, the public would react strongly against attempts to have it discontinued.

Follow-up research several years later by Afsah and Resources for the Future (RFF), an environmental think tank, suggested that a key reason for PROPER's success was that it was often the means by which factory owners first learned of their plants' environmental performance.[61] Plants' internal awareness was a powerful factor driving improvements. The program significantly impacted BAPEDAL as well. The need for accuracy compelled the agency to increase inspections, and improve the quality and reliability of its data collection and verification. Makarim had been able to better both his agency and the environment, and all within a modest budget. Prior to public information disclosure, agency expenditures on monitoring and enforcement had yielded almost no discernable pollution reductions. Previous experiences in Asia suggested information disclosure might be a low-cost opportunity to influence plant behavior. The hunch proved right. PROPER cost BAPEDAL $100,000 during the year and a half the pilot was underway. With 187 plants rated and sizeable gains achieved, the cost per plant was about a dollar a day.[62]

Regulators in other countries began watching PROPER to gauge its utility for them. In the fall of 1996, the Philippines Department of Natural Resources (DENR) asked Wheeler's team to help them launch a similar "EcoWatch" program.[63] Two years later, the results mirrored what had happened in Indonesia.[64] The concept of empowering the public through knowledge sharing continued to take hold elsewhere. In 1998, Mexico's environmental agency, Procuraduria Federal de Proteccion al Ambiente (PROFEPA), announced it would rank the environmental performance of 3,000 industries and publish the results as a way to provide incentives for pollution reduction.[65] The Centre for Science and the Environment (CSE), a New Delhi based NGO, launched a Green Rating Project to rank environmental management by Indian industries, and soon received a government grant to disseminate the results.[66] The Uttar Pradesh State Pollution Control Board in India announced it was launching a program.[67] The European Commission announced plans to create a register similar to the TRI of pollution from 20,000 major facilities.[68] Colombia's Minister of Environment traveled to Jakarta to meet with Makarim, and inquiries were coming in from Bangladesh.[69] Moreover, others were internalizing these lessons and making innovations in their own policy arenas. In England, the government began implementing public performance audits to compare spending in counties and cities on education, sanitation, police, fire and other services.[70]

All these initiatives were germinating in largely open societies. What was startling was the concept of public information disclosure began taking hold in closed societies as well. In 1998, Wheeler's colleague Hua Wang negotiated the launch of a pilot program in China of air quality ratings for 50 cities.[71] "Releasing the numbers is a revolutionary concept for the people and the government," said Lu Xinyuan, director general of SEPA's Department of Environmental Protection, Enforcement and Inspection, sometime thereafter.[72] "We were worried that people would complain that air pollution is too serious. Instead, the consciousness of people has been raised. And they feel the government trusts them with the facts, so we are gaining points from doing this."

Critics, however, questioned the quality of the data, and suggested the government was using information disclosure as a way to build momentum with the public for closing economically inefficient plants. Nevertheless, in the process, a line had been crossed. A year later, Wang convinced his counterparts to launch public information disclosure pilots in the Huhhot and Zhenjiang municipalities, and later extended the program to cover Jiangsu Province.[73] In 2002, the government of Vietnam followed suit with their own program.[74] Even in places where Wheeler's team had no dialogue, ripples were being felt. The mullahs of Iran approved the launch of a Green Industry program that provided public recognition of plants that were good environmental performers.[75] The concept of public information disclosure was a quantum leap out of character for all these authoritarian and secretive societies. The impact on them from this newly embraced notion supporting transparency might not be fully known for generations. But by 2007, China's National Environmental Protection Agency announced it would take its program nationwide.[76]

The Bank team never suggested that information disclosure was a substitute for monitoring and enforcement, or taxes, or clean technology transfers, but rather a complement to these other efforts.[77] The team concluded that perhaps a hybrid system would prove most optimal. Regulators would conduct monitoring and risk analysis, and provide what they learned to communities which then could negotiate directly with factories to implement local standards. If necessary, community agents could return to the agency for legal support and enforcement. Though the community's role in making these programs successful was paramount, the equation required balance. As exemplified in the public disclosure activities in all the Asian examples, effective leadership made action possible. Leaders such as Makarim and Victor Ramos in the Philippines emerged at the agency or community-level, spurring change. When firms, which had much to gain from the status quo, were recalcitrant about improving, these figures often engaged in personal diplomacy with plant managers, or involved NGOs to apply pressure. The lesson was clear: Change agents must be strong, and their leadership sustained for their work to be effective.

Research by the team and by others suggested pollution levels were greater in poorer communities because, in part, the poor were less aware of what pollution was taking place, and less educated about the importance of environmental quality.[78] Information disclosure provided some comparative balance. Citizens would be concerned about the potential health impact of the pollution levels that were revealed, and they would also be concerned about the comparative injustice of living with pollution levels far different than those faced by their wealthier neighbors. By the end of the 1990s, public information disclosure initiatives in Indonesia, the Philippines, and elsewhere seized the imagination of those in the environmental management field. Tom Tietenberg, a leading U.S. environmental economist, described the concept as "the forerunner of a whole new approach to pollution control."[79] "Sunlight is the best disinfectant," wrote Howie Severino, a *Manila Times* columnist.[80] "The information age has created new ways of letting it shine through." Perhaps the key role of the program, Severino suggested, was less its ability to reveal egregious polluters, but rather "to empower people."

The permutations of where empowerment could lead were endless. The research team foresaw public information disclosure's potential application well beyond the field of environmental management, for the concept of a well-informed public defined the team's activities thereafter. One simple idea had produced remarkable results in some of the world's most polluted developing countries. And, in an altered form, it would soon boomerang to change the very history of the Bank itself, and in a profound and powerful way.

4

There was an important difference between the research Wheeler's group was conducting and that of other Bank units. The Bank's classical approach to research was in response to the institution's operational units' needs. Economic theory, however, could not often account for real situations. One problem involved the lack of data because it was scarce. The opportunities to conduct experiments were sporadic. Wheeler's solution was to establish collaborative arrangements with environmental agencies that provided learning opportunities. Regulators received help building their capacity with cost-effective regulation and through a dialogue with the Bank. In return, the team got data and the opportunity to fine-tune its theories in actual settings. While colleagues were analyzing data and designing hypothetical policies, the team took the next step: Using data to build tools that changed results on the ground. The tools also enabled users to identify their own choices. Developing collaborative arrangements with policymakers in regulatory agencies was therefore considered essential. These "living laboratories" as Wheeler characterized them, allowed clients to define their objectives while the researchers analyzed their implementation.[81] The methodology also emphasized that pilot projects demonstrate feasibility and effectiveness before scaling up. At the heart of the work was the notion that the research would not address the symptoms of pollution, but identify sources, and build policy options based on sound econometrics. To do so, it was necessary the unit include not only economists, but also engineers, geographic information specialists, and communications and computer technology specialists.

Full agreement, however, was not forthcoming. Lyn Squire, the

Bank's research director, was unsure about Wheeler's methods, and by 1995 decided not to confirm him as the unit's chief. The announcement stunned the team. It had become a close-knit group and cohesive under Wheeler's tutelage. He, too, was left shaken. Suddenly, everything was uncertain. Who would become the unit's manager? What would it mean to the research program? Had the research just been graded? It could not be known, at least for a while. Disturbed by the development, I launched a campaign to advocate on Wheeler's behalf.[82] A letter signed by every member of the division went to Squire urging his reconsideration. It produced two results. Squire never responded, which provided me my first concrete example of senior management's indifference to the views of its staff. Wheeler, however, saw the effort differently. It was a watershed moment for the two of us, and formed a bond of friendship that transcended the Bank.

Skepticism about us appeared in other Bank circles. A core group of environmental officials found our interest in public information disclosure disconcerting. As environmental regulators, auditors, engineers and project financiers, they had been trained to work within the existing methodologies. Informal regulatory initiatives radically departed from long-held views on environmental management. Viewing us with suspicion, these influential critics honed in on PROPER's work.[83] Firms might report more emissions, they suggested, but they were still under-reporting pollution; and BAPEDAL was too undermanned to effectively monitor them. They also noted that some firms remained out of compliance. They wondered why attention was focused on egregious polluters when their emissions and effluents were outweighed by those who were simply out of compliance. They suggested the agency's data and collection methodology was weak since it had refrained from judicial action, perhaps in fear that a negative court ruling would endanger the entire program.

Fortunately, there was a silver lining. Informal mechanisms might not have been well understood by the Bank's engineers and auditors and by some regulators, but in the field of environmental economics, these trends were gaining resonance. A few months after downgrading Wheeler's status, Squire signaled his support for the research. In a note to Michael Bruno, the Bank's chief economist, he said the work on industrial pollution was a good candidate for a future World Development Report or Policy Research Report, the two flagship publications of the institution's research.[84]

As 1996 closed, the work had blossomed to the point that Wheeler was calling it a "new paradigm" on industrial pollution control. Squire asked the team to present its findings to Bank President Wolfensohn.[85] The old model, the president was told, established a system whereby the state through its agents—regulators and courts—managed behavior. Regulators set standards and used tax incentives, then devoted resources to monitoring and enforcement. Civil or criminal penalties for non-compliance would then be imposed by the courts. But the old model was not replicable in most developing country settings. The scarcity of human and technical resources, the lack of information and analytical capacity, bureaucratic institutions, and changing political governments made these systems ineffective. Developing country regulators needed, by necessity, to expand their toolbox and so they had. In the new model, they called upon other actors to play decisive roles, including communities and NGOs.[86] These actors were negotiating their own arrangements and modifying firm-level performance. In this mix, the team had discovered a third agent: Consumers and investors.[87] A tarnished reputation might lead to consumer boycotts. Concern over litigation or judicial penalties might affect decisions made by investors and financial markets.

With the state on one end, communities and NGOs on another, and consumers and investors on the third, the new paradigm for pollution control in the developing world formed a triangle with manufacturers in the middle. This model had multiple agents and multiple incentives, so it was necessary for institutions such as the Bank to rethink the appropriate role it could help regulators play. In their new role, regulators would no longer be confined to just monitoring and enforcing the rules. Instead, they would gain leverage through non-traditional programs that harness the power of communities and markets. Regulators remained essential, however, because information is paramount. Effective regulation would be impossible unless agencies had reliable data and integrated systems to help markets and communities make appropriate assessments of a factory's performance. To achieve maximum effectiveness, regulators would identify the most serious polluters, and target their resources toward them. Regulatory agencies would improve effectiveness by allocating fewer resources to conventional enforcement, and more to the generation of information products. In this new role of orchestration rather than dictation, regulators would influence polluters indirectly by increasing environmental awareness within communities, by promoting public disclosure of factory performance, by reaching public agreements with firms regarding abatement, and through technical training of environmental personnel in polluting factories. This new paradigm was startling and radical because it promoted a transfer of significant control from regulatory agencies to communities.

In retrospect, the team concluded that, through its collaboration with regulatory counterparts, it had changed its view of pollution regulation from the project's inception.[88] Conventional policy discussions had been too shallow and too narrow. Too shallow, because they devoted inordinate attention to instrument choices while ignoring the preconditions for applying any instrument effectively; too narrow, because they continued to focus on the interaction between state and factory as the sole determinant of environmental performance. Thus, the researchers argued, there was a need for a less heroic but broader model that included communities and markets in the dialogue.[89]

With Wolfensohn in support, momentum began to build for publication of the research via a major policy report. Collaboration, data tools, and public information were part of the Wheeler doctrine. There was another component. During the implementation of PROPER, Chief Economist Bruno issued a memorandum emphasizing the importance of "research with impact." Wheeler dutifully followed up on Bruno's mandate with a note to Squire.[90] "Our implementation strategy may be rather unusual by traditional [Research

Department] standards," he wrote, "but it does seem right for the times. We want to do work which is judged highly relevant by our colleagues in Operations and new environmental protection agencies in developing countries. We want them to use our results, and we want our interventions to make a difference for environmental policy. While continuing to stress high-quality empirical research, our program and staffing strategy also reflect the need for a mix of skills which are useful for technical assistance and outreach."

Dissemination of research had never been a strong characteristic of the Bank. The department's traditional methodology was to draft papers, vet them internally or within a select group of external academics, and then submit the final drafts to refereed journals for publication. Wheeler wanted to stretch the boundaries to encourage cross-fertilization with Bank operations, external academic counterparts, and other stakeholders. But a vehicle was needed. Unknown to all, a new phenomenon was about to unfold that would change everything: The Internet.

5

In 1962, J.C.R. Licklider, an MIT professor, became head of computer research at the U.S. Defense Department's Advance Research Projects Agency (DARPA). Licklider had been theorizing about the potential of computer networking. Inspired by the research, Lawrence Roberts, a fellow MIT researcher, soon joined him. Roberts had been reading research on packet-switch communication by Leonard Kleinrock, a UCLA academic. Unlike circuit-switch communication, packet-switch communication allowed messages to be broken into packets that could travel separately to a destination before recombining. Licklider, Roberts, and Kleinrock began to look into creating a packet-based computer network. They found researchers from the RAND Corporation interested in creating a decentralized system that could survive a nuclear attack from the Soviet Union. By late 1969, four computers were installed in different locations, ready to conduct an experiment by typing "Login". In Los Angeles, a computer technician typed "L." His counterpart in Palo Alto said it was received and responded with an "O". Then, the system crashed. "L" "O," however, was a phonetic success. It was also a technological transformation. As the joke would later go, Al Gore, then covering a war in the Vietnamese rice paddies, had just invented the Internet.[91]

The Internet was an association of computers that allowed information and data exchanges. Over the next two decades, it remained the domain of a few hundred computer programmers, engineers, and academics. Then, during George H.W. Bush's presidency, momentum began building to broaden its scope. Toward the end of 1994, Wheeler and I became aware of the Internet because an environmental consortium sent us a letter that it had posted some of its data online.[92]

A light bulb went on. We were a new unit, so much so that most of our research counterparts were only vaguely aware of us. Environmental economics was also relatively new, and academics from other disciplines viewed it with some skepticism. Perhaps this new tool could get them acquainted with our research, and help us solidify funding in upcoming budget allocations. There were other obvious benefits. Department economists traditionally disseminated research by distributing draft working papers to colleagues and a select circle of external academics. Drafts would be refereed, rewritten, and ultimately forwarded to established journals for publication. The process often took as long as two years. The Internet represented an instant way of disseminating our outputs. We could get feedback quickly from a wider audience than we had traditionally sought, and without the delays or costs of paper mailings.[93]

Wheeler enlisted Dave Witzel, our computer maven, and me to create a website for the unit. In April 1995, we posted a single page describing the framework of the IPPS research.[94] We were one of two units in the department to have done so. The IPPS summary page received 368 hits during the month.[95] This rudimentary exercise allowed us to make an immediate observation. Far more people were accessing the website page than were phoning or mailing us for paper copies of IPPS or any other research. The three of us sensed from our dim corner of cyberspace the outline of a door with blinding light on the other side. The next month, our page was accessed 747 times.[96] A new business line appeared in the making.

We caucused with Mala Hettige, our IPPS specialist, to put the entire IPPS paper and our abatement research online along with some datasets. To free the team from the potential avalanche of readers' questions, I took the lead in responding to inquiries via a new electronic mail account that we established.[97] Witzel concentrated on creating HTML files and getting them online. Bit by bit, sections, tables, and figures were loaded. We completed the project in time to encourage attendees of the Bank-Fund annual meetings that November to access our new site. We billed it as the Bank's "first full text, full data, research report on the World Wide Web."[98] Our file transfer numbers jumped to 5,700, representing an increase of more than 1,500% since our launch.[99] We had become the dominant website in the department.[100]

Though mundane by current standards, at the time we were collectively startled by what we were witnessing. The growth potential of this new medium dumbfounded us because we knew Internet access was hardly universal. Most of the Bank's stakeholders had no access. Many did not yet know the technology existed. Yet we were receiving feedback from environmental ministries, universities, and research institutes with whom we had never previously had a relationship.

When the U.S. Environmental Protection Agency created a link to our site, other research organizations followed suit. Our numbers escalated sharply. I created links back to them as well as links to major search engine sites, such as the newly formed Yahoo.[101] When I sent an email to a small group of academics—with whom we had shared previous exchanges—to learn their impressions, they indicated our data was being incorporated into their own research.[102] Indeed, the new access to IPPS had allowed some to alter their methodologies to ascertain more robust findings. Our new website was starting to impact a whole community of environmental economists. Increasing the dialogue had a reciprocal effect. We became more knowledgeable about what the larger community was investigating, and it alerted us to potential opportunities for collaboration.

As 1995 waned, we made a crucial observation: Two additional units in the department were now posting material. Teams studying economic growth and compiling the Living Standard Measurement Studies (LSMS) enjoyed widespread attention from audiences traditionally interested in Bank research. Both fields vastly surpassed the popularity of our niche area, industrial pollution; and the other teams had uploaded a sizeable number of files on their sites from the outset. Predictably, they received the bulk of traffic from the start, but they did not continue to make investments as we did.

We were consistently adding new files. This resulted in repeat visits from previous viewers, as well as from new visitors. Our market share of the department's website traffic began to increase. Perhaps, since other economists had been trained to disseminate information via traditional methodologies, they viewed contributions to the Internet as one-time projects. Wheeler, Witzel and I realized otherwise. We viewed the new medium as a process. Adding and expanding was the new methodology.[103]

The other units had exponentially larger audiences to draw from, but it was our site that was rising. To build a successful website, we instinctively understood that attracting viewers would not be the goal: Attracting repeat viewers would be. Building the site would make them come once. Updating the site regularly would compel them to return. The hypothesis proved robust. After tracking data for a couple months, we saw our traffic had doubled.[104] The number of papers delivered via the site grew by 25%.[105] Yahoo's index had picked us up as well. By the fall, my work on data acquisition and research support had become secondary. I focused on website development.[106] At our site's April launch, our page was tenth in the top ten of the Research Department's most accessed website pages.[107] By January, we owned all top ten spots.[108]

In early 1996, major investments began. We altered the home page and added new papers and modeling tools. The expansion compelled me to actively begin marketing.[109] We encouraged environmental organizations with in-house publications to mention our new Bank site's creation. Articles about us appeared in magazines and journals. Paper summaries about the site were distributed at major Bank events. Intense cross linking began between other Bank and non-Bank websites. I queried counterparts for their email addresses, if they had one, and whether they had colleagues who also might be interested in our efforts.

In the spring, Wheeler put together a proposal for "IPPS Dissemination: Promoting Research with Impact."[110] It requested a year's funding to expand the website. The IPPS paper and emission parameters had already been downloaded hundreds of times by regulatory agencies, environmental NGOs and research institutes in over 40 countries. Our website had far outpaced anything we had disseminated by paper. Our mailing costs had been virtually eliminated. Moreover, the new medium was impacting the team's sense of our role as researchers. We had already evolved from traditional creators of hypothetical models and data analysis to activists providing technical assistance. Now we were morphing again as a portal where regulators could learn about success stories elsewhere, and have assistance replicating them locally. In the span of a few months, the Internet had become critical for successfully applying the modeling systems our team had built.

Wheeler pitched the proposal as an experimental website outside the Bank's "firewall."[111] Despite noting Internet access didn't exist in many client countries, and might not in the near future, Gregory Ingram, Director of the Research Advisory Department, approved funding for $40,000. He recognized the importance of providing online access for users with the research and datasets.[112] Translation: We could play with the Bank's money, but we wouldn't be recognized by the organization as one of its official sites. To keep our flanks covered, we agreed to display a disclaimer that we were an experimental site. We characterized our results as "intermediate," and the status of our research as on-going. We began collaborating with Prosody Communications, an external vendor that Witzel was leaving the Bank to manage. The new site went into business in

October 1996. The Internet phase of our extraordinary Bank experience was in a full-growth mode.

Wheeler, Witzel, and I formed a seamless troika. Witzel handled technology. I did marketing. We worked on content and imagery jointly. Wheeler provided post-mortem reviews. Our tiny cabal became a powerful laboratory of innovation: Seeing opportunities and capitalizing upon them; broaching possibilities to one another that in turn spawned new ideas. There was no playbook. In fact, the medium was so new we really didn't have examples to guide us. Intuition, imagination, and common sense were our guides. What we achieved in this remarkable period is now considered standard practice, and has been replicated with success by thousands of others. But at the time, if others were doing what we were doing, they were like us, alone within their own cavity of creation.

We talked about a new hypothesis we called 'critical mass.'[113] We believed if we could establish ourselves as the preeminent site in our niche area, then at some point we would need to do little marketing. The site's traffic would grow under the weight of its own momentum. Long before the Bank moved to create a comprehensive website, we had understood the medium's importance: To set our development agenda, and to leverage Bank assets as well as external resources, establishing a forum for stakeholders to gather and consort as a way to create knowledge. "When we go to conferences, it is clear that many of the participants in our specialty area are familiar with our site and through it our materials," Wheeler wrote, looking back.[114] "Since the site has a unique specialty topic in public disclosure and informal regulation and the impact of these approaches, there is no comparable resource. During the lifetime of this project, these topics have been accepted as mainstream approaches both within the Bank and the broader development community. And the main component of this acceptance has been the availability of [our website's] 24x7 broadcast facility."

The collaborative spirit spawned creative ways of presenting and packaging information. The site's graphics were overhauled. We corrected papers and vetted links. PowerPoint presentations made to Bank officials, client country regulators or academic counterparts were uploaded. Country-specific sections of research went online. I envisioned electronic newsletters as a key vehicle for driving traffic to the site; they would do more than inform, they would build clientele. Correspondingly, I began cataloguing a database of email addresses—from our informal network developed over the years—to serve as the foundation for monthly distributions.

To increase awareness, we decided the site needed a new name. In the fall, the Economics of Industrial Pollution page became New Ideas in Pollution Regulation (NIPR).[115] In a fortunate twist for launching as an 'experimental' site, we were able to skirt the labyrinths of the Bank's medieval Internet infrastructure to establish our own address, http://www.nipr.org.

In a note to NIPR's new audience, Wheeler announced, "As important as it is to let the research community know about [our] results, it may be more beneficial to use the Internet technology at hand to serve for interactive and collaborative arrangements with our audience and colleagues in the field. We propose to create opportunities for economists, academics and researchers to comment on [the unit's] research, ask questions, offer their own research for review or comment and interact with others with regard to their original research ... our concept is to make the NIPR site a gateway of communication on the economics of industrial pollution control for Bank and non-Bank economists and academics. [We] believe the idea of creating a dialogue between non-Bank people on issues of mutual interest is an exciting opportunity for all of us to learn about new and innovative research happening around the world, and to provide commentary and thoughts to research that is developing."

This notion offered a subtle but powerfully important proposition.[116] It suggested the dialogue did not necessarily have to include the Bank. It might be sufficient for the organization to serve as a conduit for dialogue amongst and between clients, much in the same way our research had revealed developing country environmental agencies were acting as conduits of information for negotiations between communities and factories. With our hardly realizing it, the

Internet was transforming us as well as our research.

In late 1996, in response to media leaks of information contrary to official Bank positions, Bruno issued a departmental note on dissemination etiquette. Sensitive information, he directed, should be vetted by the institution's External Affairs Department.[117] NIPR already carried disclaimers noting research papers were personal opinions, and did not formally reflect Bank policy. As long as the disclaimers were prominently displayed, Wheeler felt we were safe.[118] The Bruno memo, however, underscored senior management's sensitivity about information dissemination. It also hinted at a growing schism of thought emerging within the organization. On the one hand, the culture of the Bank favored hoarding and hiding information. On the other hand, senior officials were beginning to recast the institution's image as a "knowledge bank." Moreover, the Internet's nature contradicted Bruno's edict, for it embraced open and transparent exchanges of information. The Bank's power brokers were trying to ride a wave over which they had no control.

NIPR's growth accelerated. "This thing is fabulous, guys," Wheeler wrote Witzel and me.[119] "If we can just keep Bankenstein at bay until NIPR is too big to stomp, we'll set a new standard here." Witzel, however, reiterated a growing concern. "Sometimes it gets a little depressing waiting for that big foot to come down," he noted.[120] "Good intentions aren't enough."

But as the year ended, our course, running counter to the Bank's culture, was firmly fixed. We sent out our first newsletter identifying three objectives for our audience. First, NIPR would serve as a vehicle to disseminate current and future research outputs from our team. Second, it would create a forum of dialogue between us and counterparts in academia, regulatory institutions, and civil society. And finally, it would serve as a platform for the research outputs of those outside to the Bank. The pledge was subtle yet profound. We were stating publicly that we would give non-Bank academics a stage for publishing their materials and communicating with one another. External stakeholders would receive a voice where no outlet had existed before. Since we were an experimental site, we had the flexibility to act in a way unavailable to us if NIPR had been an official site.

NIPR evolved into three sections to correspond with the major themes of the research: Industries' pollution and abatement behavior; the community's role through informal measures such as information disclosure; and the impact of consumers and financial markets in forcing firms to internalize pollution's costs.[121] We entered a period of innovation and vibrancy. Enthusiasm drove creativity and we played with the Internet as a child would a new toy. Most of our ideas struck us as common sense, but they were powerful drivers of traffic.

We launched an Introductions page to make good on our pledge to establish an interactive site, and economists and academics across the globe started discussing their own research, and soliciting each other for collaborations.[122] We launched a new section to house the ongoing research and media reports on PROPER and EcoWatch. We entitled it Transparency: A Regulatory Strategy. We added a What's Hot section. We added a Hosts section providing pictures and brief biographies of the team members.[123] OnTheNet, a compendium of the most innovative environmental websites we could find, went online.[124]

We added an internal search engine, and worked diligently to get the site listed on what were then first-generation search engines such as HotBot, WebCrawler, PlanetSearch, and InfoSeek.[125] We posted information on upcoming environmental conferences when alerted by our viewers.[126] We assembled regional pages to focus on where our research was concentrated. The regional pages inspired us to create a section on ministry websites. This EPA's of the World section sucked in visitors like a circus entering a small town.[127]

It didn't take long to realize the results of our work. Dozens of new readers signed up each day to receive our newsletter. Our mailings encouraged them to ask questions, provide comments, offer us their own research, and learn who else from the Introductions section might engage them in collaborative relationships. To download our datasets, we asked users to register with their email addresses, which was another driver of volume for our newsletter distribution list. Traffic doubled at the start of 1997, and was growing at a torrid pace. Three months into the year, it had climbed 300%.[128] During the first quarter, our papers were downloaded over 500 times.[129] At an average of six dollars per paper mailing, NIPR had saved the department $3,000.[130] By the mid-point of 1997, some 2,000 papers had been downloaded by readers from 57 countries.[131] Over the final six months of the year, just 10 of NIPR's 36 available research papers were downloaded 3,400 times by users in more than 90 countries.[132]

Everything was exceeding expectations, with one fundamental exception. One afternoon, Witzel and I met with a counterpart in the Asia region to discuss an extensive project to link materials from their website to ours. We asked for subsidization, but our colleague had no money. Indeed, while NIPR was already far down the road, other units in the Bank could not get funding to even launch a website. The Bank had not significantly valued the Internet, even three years into its applicability as a mass medium of communication. Most sites had been put together to cover a bureaucratic flank, but they remained hollow and barren of information.

Almost the entire Bank had reacted to the rise of the Internet by freezing in place. Individual units wondered what to do. What information would go online? How would it look? How would one site's appearance and content be coordinated with other departments? Who would vet the materials? What language and protocols would be used? In contrast, we operated on a simple edict succinctly espoused by Nathan Bedford Forrest, a Confederate cavalry officer during the American Civil War: "Get there firstest with the mostest."[133] Our methodology was to establish an overwhelming presence, capture the terrain, keep surrounding new ground, avoid the checks and balances deployed by the bureaucrats, and use the theory of "critical mass" to create an unstoppable momentum. To "get there firstest with the mostest," we employed a more modern colloquialism, Nike's "Just do it."

In fact, funding for NIPR, and for me, would terminate in June, 1997 at the close of the fiscal year. Wheeler labored constantly to float research proposals and review trust funds to find spare cash. He even raised the idea of selling advertising space on NIPR.[134] If we moved on the advertising front, he warned of the likely outcome that would follow: Colleagues would be angered at the 'prostitution' of the institution, and would suggest our research's 'commercialization' was a scandal. But as soon as the dollars started flowing our way, they would look to cash in on the concept as well. His prophesy was good for a hearty laugh, but it also had the ring of truth.

Funding for the research also remained problematic. In 1992, a last-minute plea had saved construction of IPPS. Collaboration with Bank operations for individual projects had sustained the pipeline, but to expand our existing relationships with countries mandated sustained funding. Clients valued the expertise we provided, and Wheeler noted the programs being implemented needed three to five years to mature.[135] It was critical, therefore, the Bank demonstrate its commitment so our partners not perceive the collaborative program as a passing fad. He asked for $300,000 per agency in seven countries we had concentrated upon. While expensive in comparison to counterparts' research proposals, the payoff would also be large: The Bank would be positioned at the "leading edge of international environmental policy reform." Wheeler also returned to Greg Ingram for additional website funds. Ever a master of the bureaucratic bait-and-switch, Wheeler noted Squire was pushing the team for a major policy report on its research.[136] The website would serve as an integral multi-media component to exponentially magnify the impact of the results.

The crisis soon reached the breaking point. My contract was ending, and without departmental financing for me or approval of the website proposal, my work on NIPR would terminate. Wheeler had requested funding me for two years, but it was too late. I had an offer outside the Bank, and it came with a deadline. We sat down. "I have to give them an answer today," I told him. He was not optimistic, but agreed to give Squire's office one more call. Just as I was about to make my phone call, Wheeler popped his head in my office. Squire had approved.[137] I was under contract again for two more years. But there was a glitch. The Human Resources Department, he wrote me in a note later that day, "just couldn't deal with our salary proposal; had to increase it! Man, this place is f----- up, but we might as well relax and enjoy it, right? I hope we have your understanding on this one, comrade. Yours in fiscal rectitude ..."[138]

NIPR could continue, but a new dilemma unfolded. The department had recognized our success. It wanted to move NIPR back inside the firewall so we would become an official Bank site.[139] We were leery. NIPR's experimental status had allowed us to develop it without the constraints of irrelevant bureaucratic limitations. It looked and functioned differently from all other sites in the Bank, and therefore attracted a following unlike any other. Would our formal association with the Bank and its dam-building and forest-cutting projects be harmful? We wondered if bureaucrats would seek to homogenize us to prove a point. With Wolfensohn and his senior management implementing a massive Bank reorganization via a new plan called the Strategic Compact, there were even rumors the Research Department might cease to exist in the near future. We discussed the issue intensely. Witzel noted the importance of branding. "The NIPR brand is beginning to work. We talk about it; people are starting to identify it on the Net and in newsletters, magazines. Brands based on [the] Bank … tend to disappear every few years. With that you lose name investment."[140] He had touched upon a key point: The nature of the institution's bureaucratic culture to stifle heterogeneity, even when it had proven successful. Wheeler concurred. "There's no historical record of any sponsorship of creative play by the Banco, to put it mildly," he noted.[141]

We debated what to do by reading Dilbert cartoons religiously. Funding for a site outside the Bank had an end date. If NIPR was an official site, we could probably get subsidization from Ingram as the dissemination vehicle of the team's larger research project. Finally, we opted to bring it inside.[142] The Bank as an institution was making so few inputs on the Internet that we sensed it was still far from a point of seeking to homogenize all its sub-sites. (This proved correct. It wasn't until 2004 that the Bank moved to introduce conformity for all Bank sites. Until then, site developers were free to tailor the content and graphics of their sites to what they thought would work best with their stakeholders.) Ingram asked for only a few stylistic changes, and word filtered down the reorganization would do little more than change the department's title to the Development Economics Research Group (DECRG).[143] Whatever machinations we were going through were now irrelevant to the organic growth of NIPR. We were free to continue our research and dissemination activities uninterrupted. By the summer of 1997, the number of registered readers for our monthly newsletter climbed above 1,000.[144]

We thought the biggest beneficiary of our Internet experiment would be our own department. Since its emphasis was on long-range research questions and associated policy implications, we believed more research sites would prove quickly popular with the academic and developmental communities.

Management did not share our viewpoint. Indeed, it did not begin a serious discussion about developing a departmental website until early 1998, almost three years after we began actively using the Internet to communicate. Though we openly espoused the Web's potential, senior managers acted diffidently. Finally, with Lawrence Macdonald—the department's chief communications officer—pushing hard, management invested resources and found the water warm.[145] In 18 months, the department captured a quarter of the Bank's traffic.[146] By opting in, the department was not only recognizing the strength of our position, but institutionalizing it as well.

Differences, however, remained. The most distinct one was on emphasis. Management wanted to use the website to communicate more closely with the Bank's operational side, an internal audience. NIPR was focused on creating collaborative relationships with client-country development practitioners and other external stakeholders. The goals, and the audiences, were different. Our directions were unaligned. In retrospect, it was not a surprise the Bank was reluctant to embracing the Internet as a communications tool. The Internet empowered individuals, and often the transfer of this power came from institutions and nation-states. It was not a native instinct of the Bank.

In the spring of 1997, we made a prophetic discovery. The Bank's External Affairs Department (EXT) had made a videotape of an interview we did with Nabiel Makarim during a visit to the Bank the previous summer. Wheeler, an avid reader of technology magazines, learned it was possible to convert the analog video files into digital ones that we could then load onto a website. The ability to stream video on computers had reached the mainstream. We could put the Makarim tape on NIPR![147] But the technology of converting video and audio files into a web-friendly format was so new that Bank technology specialists were unfamiliar with the application. Wheeler encouraged the department to invest in video streaming, but predictably, they declined. Wheeler moved preemptively, purchasing his own encoding package, and downloading free streaming software.[148] After processing the tape, Witzel loaded it on NIPR. It represented the first encoded file ever assembled for a Bank site.[149]

Wheeler queried counterparts in the Environment Department about streaming their videos and conferences.[150] The proposal, however, elicited little interest. One respondent wrote, "I don't know what to answer because I don't know enough to know what to say."[151] We did a tour of their site. "ENV continues its tradition of bullshit web pages," Wheeler wrote me. "I hit the button for the ESSD Conference and got their 'bye, bye' notice."[152]

By the beginning of 1998, our mailing list had reached 2,500. Hits to the site climbed to 83,000 by April, representing a 200% increase from the start of the year.[153] When the year closed, NIPR's traffic accounted for half of the entire Research Department's site.[154] It was five times larger than the highly financed survey data it sought to showcase. NIPR was one-third the size of all traffic registering with the Bank's Public Information Document centers.[155] The cost savings from reduced mailings had reached $20,000.[156] Moreover, we accounted for one percent of all web traffic coming to the Bank.[157]

We had become the preeminent sub-site within the Bank, and the external web community had taken notice. The U.S. Environmental Protection Agency applauded our "innovative use of the TRI," and encouraged the Bank to take steps in assisting client countries to establish similar systems.[158] The National Academy Press cited us for excellence.[159] NIPR had risen to the top of major search engines such as Yahoo, Alta Vista, InfoSeek, and Lycos.[160] Internet dissemination of our research was affecting activities of our counterparts in the regulatory institutions. Ministries throughout Asia and Latin America were learning about public information disclosure and informal regulatory mechanisms through NIPR, and beginning to apply the tools and lessons we described within their own settings. The cross fertilization filtered out to the academic community as readers commented on NIPR's importance in their own economic work. Even website developers inside the Bank wrote to say they considered NIPR a model of best practice. "Maybe we should propose that the website budget be allocated on use rates rather than politics," Wheeler quipped.[161]

That year, the Bank launched an Intranet (internal only) website to parallel its public site. The move reflected a priority for making information available to internal audiences, but it also hinted at a conundrum. On one level, the Bank was an organization possessing proprietary information. The Intranet provided a platform to distribute it appropriately. Yet how could it be protected from public leakages? On another level, the Bank was a highly evolved bureaucracy. Its history of fiefdoms created a natural reticence toward transparency and sharing information with stakeholders. The organization's cultural instincts compelled participants to pursue internal website dissemination during an epoch when external pressures were growing on the Bank to be more transparent. This unspoken tension would become a defining issue for our team in the years to come.

The Intranet's creation also led to a crucial epiphany. For years, the Bank published a weekly staff bulletin about project and lending developments, meetings, seminars, and other announcements. The bulletins had been distributed in mailboxes; but following the launch of the Intranet, they disappeared. The information was soon being uploaded online. It was logical, but people were accustomed to being informed by paper mailings. The efficiency of using the Intranet to disseminate information was paradoxically inconvenient for workers used to having a brochure to flip through each Monday. And not all the information from the hard copy version was making it online. I noted the change to Wheeler. He agreed and then had a revelation: "A lot of this information is being lost," he said. "These meetings would be interesting for many people. One day, we should film them, and put them on the Internet." My eyes narrowed. Somewhere in my mind a door was opening again, and behind it was another intense light. We agreed to keep the thought in our heads. For now, the environmental research was still growing, and we were driving toward a finale.

Our counterparts in the Research and Environment departments, however, continued to view us with jealousy. Their praise was muted. They questioned results. They bristled at the attention we garnered, and suggested we were seeking publicity.[162] Environmental officials even went so far as to suggest the only Bank website about pollution should be the one they maintained, though theirs was an empty shell.[163] We realized public recognition was a byproduct of our success, not the reason for it. Nevertheless, we had become too noticeable for the taste of some. "There are days when I'm worried that we're what Louis Pasteur was trying to stamp out," Wheeler wrote me.[164]

But the results could not be ignored. Following a report to our senior management about our web activities' validity, a Research Department economist, Gunnar Eskeland, made this observation: The new Bank Chief Economist Joseph Stiglitz and Director Squire's "noticeable amazement" might compel the department to move beyond its traditional print methodology of dissemination.[165] Lawrence Macdonald, when pressing the advantage with success, wrote, "This type of recognition shows the value that a well informed and dedicated content provider ... supported by his managers, can bring to our knowledge creation and knowledge sharing efforts."[166] Even the Environment Department finally accepted our offer to put the full text of its Pollution Prevention and Abatement Handbook on NIPR, then followed with a request we also offer the text of its annual report, *Environment Matters*.[167] Both departments had stood on the sidelines until NIPR had proven itself. Thereafter, they started their own website development.

We never stopped making investments into NIPR's juggernaut. Between the fall of 1998 to the close of 1999, page requests climbed more than 300%.[168] Hits reached one million annually.[169] Our newsletter list ranked second only to the Bank's own list.[170] When the industrial pollution research project finally ended in 2000, NIPR had captured a staggering 2% of the Bank's entire Internet traffic.[171] Even without further upgrades following 2001, NIPR for years remained the highest search item on Google for industrial pollution. In 2002, when we sent the last NIPR newsletter, our mailing list had reached 14,000.[172] Three years later, without further mailings, it had reached 18,000, and was still the Bank's third-largest mailing list.[173] Our hypothesis about reaching "critical mass" had come true.

Because we started early, and the institution was slow to recognize the Internet's value, there were no rules to define how NIPR would evolve. We made our own decisions, defining issues, questions, and precedents as we viewed them in the context of our research. Often we did this intuitively, but sometimes to elude the monitoring of bureaucrats. Staying out of view (hard to do with a website) was another strategy for insulation. We realized institutional power brokers did not value our methodologies or the Web's transparency. They instinctively sought conformity as a way to reaffirm their authority; and indeed, NIPR proved unique within a sea of mundane Bank websites during the Internet revolution's first decade. Prior to the Internet, a select group of academics and economists accessed Bank research. NIPR's ability to increase stakeholder participation was an accomplishment. But what senior Bank officials had not understood was that their participation had enriched us, too.

In 2000, the Internet Working Group, an informal collection of Bank website and technology specialists, hired an external vendor to review the nearly 1,000 sub-sites in the institution's Internet infrastructure.[174] They found it disorganized, dated, sparse, littered with broken links and files that didn't load. There were few opportunities for the public to ask questions. Many sites were little more than shells to cover an obligation, or were implemented as one-time projects.

Bank managers had limited their investments. We understood launching a website was only part of the equation. Making investments in building an audience was most of it. In each area where the Bank had been weak, we had been strong. Consequently, the reviewers ranked NIPR as the institution's best site.[175] It would take years before a smattering of Bank sites would rival NIPR for its depth and creativity. Most never did. But by 2000, Wheeler and I had already moved on. Like two boys who found a treasure map in the attic, NIPR had revealed the future and we were racing to meet it.

6

In the soft spring light and the hard winter air, men would rise in the morning and descend from the inclines that drifted below Mount Washington and Allentown and Duquesne Heights into a simmering cauldron. The boiling mills were the heart of the city and the universe of the men who lived on the hills. They were the very greatness of the country itself. Yet somehow, Rachel Carson felt differently. She grew up on a farm just outside the city, where she wandered the streams and groves—a stark contrast to the grey haze wafting over the town and its people. She left the farm near the mills to go to school. She studied writing and then zoology with a desire to "make animals in the woods or waters, where they live, as alive to others as they are to me."

She combined her interests with a writing position at the U.S. Bureau of Fisheries, over the years becoming a respected editor. She began to write books exploring a theme that held her since childhood. Mankind, she believed, was not separate from nature, but interrelated and dependent upon it. She gained some notoriety, but not widespread acceptance. America was moving in a different direction. The Pittsburgh steel mills, Detroit assembly lines, and Texas oil rigs were building an economic power. They were building an empire. One day, she received a letter from a friend who mentioned thousands of birds had died near where she lived. The friend thought it was from heavy spraying of pesticides. It rekindled an interest in Carson. Years earlier, she had wanted to write a magazine article on the same subject, but the editor had said no. This time, she began researching the issue, gathering evidence, and compiling what she learned into a book. "What I discovered," she said, "was that everything which meant most to me as a naturalist was being threatened, and that nothing I could do would be more important."

When *Silent Spring* was published four years later, it was the proverbial stone thrown into the water, causing waves that rippled to a broadening scope of America's society. The book documented the harmful effects of chemicals on the environment, and suggested a causal link between DDT and cancer in humans. The nation was stunned. Citizens began organizing to ban spraying in their communities. The U.S. Department of Agriculture was flooded with letters voicing concern over DDT's unfettered use on farm produce. The chemical industry reacted by suggesting Carson was a hysterical extremist, but momentum was building against it. President Kennedy ordered an investigation, and a committee of scientists found there was indeed a direct correlation. The committee also concluded something else: The government had done nothing to protect people.

Like Upton Sinclair's *The Jungle* that chronicled egregious conditions in Chicago's meat packing industry six decades earlier, *Silent Spring* compelled the government to act. In the aftermath of its publication, federal legislation was enacted to protect widespread wilderness areas, create the Environmental Protection Agency, protect drinking water, improve air quality, and eliminate DDT use throughout the country. The impact of the book, however, went even further. Concerned citizens took their own initiative. In the years that followed, environmental interest groups—such as the Environmental Defense Fund, the Wilderness Society, the National Resources Defense Council, and Greenpeace—formed to protect and inform the public about ecological abuses. Carson's cause had spawned a movement.

Gaylord Nelson grew up in a politically active family in a small, northern Wisconsin community. His great grandfather helped found the state Republican Party, and he remembered how his father took him to watch the legendary Robert LaFollette speak from the back of a train. Nelson entered politics, and reached the United States Senate, where he pursued an interest in conservation and natural-resource issues. Following the publication of *Silent Spring*, he introduced legislation to ban DDT's use.

In 1963, Nelson convinced President Kennedy to tour nationwide, promoting conservation; but the effort did not galvanize public interest. Nelson began looking for another vehicle. It came six years later. Inspired by the heated anti-war movement then pulsating through the nation, he thought he could link the protestors' "flower power" momentum with its natural affinity for the ecological commons. He announced he was organizing a nationwide grassroots demonstration on behalf of the environment. It was scheduled for the following year. The gambit worked. Wire services carried the pledge, and inquiries from across the nation came pouring in to Nelson's office. *The New York Times* reported, "Rising concern about the environmental crisis is sweeping the nation's campuses with an intensity that may be on its way to eclipsing student discontent over the war…"[176] By the time Earth Day was held on April 22, 1970, an estimated 20 million people participated in gatherings throughout the country.

Carson and Nelson were hardly alone in their environmental awareness and activism during this period, but their efforts offered seamless bookends to their cause. Carson's book brought environmental protection into the political forum, and created a cadre of citizen activists. Nelson's advocacy moved the issue into the public mainstream. Environmental activism did not grow rapidly, but shocking events such as the toxic poisoning at Love Canal and near catastrophe at Three Mile Island prompted outrage and fear, keeping the issue keenly in the public's consciousness.

Toward the end of the 1970s, a surprising twist in the evolution of environmental awareness occurred, and in a most unlikely place.[177] The industrial base of planned economies in the Soviet Union and its allies had sustained its political and military infrastructure during the Cold War. It had also wreaked enormous environmental degradation. Environmental protection was a distant concern because Socialism's priority was industrial production. To keep the economy salient, the government had subsidized heavily polluting industries. As conditions deteriorated, labor and citizen groups voiced concern. Using environmental protection as a platform, they began public protests that ultimately served as a mechanism for democratic reform. Throughout the 1980s, these burgeoning green movements in Poland, Bulgaria, Georgia, Czechoslovakia, Yugoslavia, Hungary and East Germany, with labor union counterparts, planted seeds of public discontent within their Marxist societies. Half a century of superpower posturing may not have been as significant to the downfall of the Soviet Union as the rising demand for environmental protection. If communism had been the triumph of the proletariat over the bourgeoisie, then what was to be made of the heroic counterinsurgency that led it to incite civil unrest? Leninism had sought to unite the workers of the world, yet the bitter irony was laborers undermined the autocracy of these political theorems. By the early 1990s, green movements in Eastern Europe had created ties to NGOs in the West.

When the conferees at Bretton Woods gathered to discuss the global economic order of the post-war world in the summer of 1944, civil society participation and environmental protection were not on the agenda. Just a few dozen "consultative groups" were listed with the UN following the war. By the close of the Millennium, the list had grown to 1,500.[178] Organizations such as the Sierra Club, The Wilderness Society, Friends of the Earth, and Greenpeace that formed in the aftermath of *Silent Spring*, had become powerful. Moreover, the perspective of these civil society actors had evolved. Instead of focusing exclusively on the environment, a new generation of NGOs began to address a wide range of issues including international development, population growth, and human rights. They became specialized and sophisticated. By nature and design, many were confrontational. Aided by increasingly dynamic information technologies, these disparate NGOs and civil society actors began working together across national and international boundaries, forming transnational alliances.

In the aftermath of the Soviet Union's fall, civil society attention began turning to resource questions left unattended during the Cold War. In the vacuum created by the fall of communism, NGOs and other civil society activists began to examine the inequities of international poverty and manipulation of the global economy by large multi-national corporations with the aid of donor nations such as the U.S. As seen by these activists, the balance of power was moving away from sovereign states, particularly those in the developing world, to industrialists and their proxies in the international financial arena—the non-elected international financial institutions (IFIs). Viewed within this prism, the industrialized world had relegated the impoverished of the developing world to the precipice of extermination. Western NGOs observed the impact environmental activism had made in the former Soviet Union, and logically concluded lessons learned there could provide the impetus for broader reforms.

The Bank had already established a reputation among NGOs as a monolithic society. For years, the Bank had reluctantly interacted with civil society representatives. Bank leadership assumed that, once these actors came on stage, they could not be removed. They would present difficulties by taking positions contrary to the Bank's. The Bank had, therefore, focused its relationships on a few dozen strategically chosen organizations, relegating hundreds of others to the sidelines. Civil society activists watched with increasing alarm as the Bank's lending activities throughout the 1970s and 1980s led to environmental degradation and population dislocation. Its structural adjustment policies also hampered the economies of developing countries that they had sought to grow. Infamous debacles in the Amazon and India during the late 1980s accelerated their concern. Still more enemies surfaced in 1991 when an internal memo from its Chief Economist Lawrence Summers (now President Barack Obama's chief economic advisor) was leaked to the media.[179] Summers wrote, "I think the economic logic behind dumping a load of toxic waste in the lowest-wage country is impeccable, and we should face up to that." Many were outraged, but few were surprised. "Of course he would write that," said a Greenpeace official. "The World Bank has been acting this out for decades. We just got an inside look at their thinking for a change."[180]

The environmental debacles were possible, NGOs charged, because the Bank's operations provided for no accountability or transparency. Monitoring the geopolitical winds, the institution began a strategy of appeasement. It hired personnel to increase its dialogue with civil society activists. Lending projects with environmental-abatement components climbed incrementally. In 1989, the Bank's board of directors formally endorsed a Disclosure of Information policy. But activists felt the measures had not substantially altered the status quo.

U.S.-based NGOs began an aggressive effort to influence Congress. They called for reducing America's critical funding contribution to the International Development Association (IDA) unless the Bank made a major concession by improving its accountability to stakeholders. Senior Bank officials bristled at their audacity. Client countries also worried and openly wondered if the Bank was being unduly influenced by NGOs whose agenda reflected their parochial Western values. The tactic, however, proved effective. Congress began debating substantial reductions. By 1993, the Bank appeared to capitulate when it established an inspection panel to investigate future charges of corruption or violations of the institution's lending or operational activities.

Bank officials hailed the panel as a major step forward. They noted that although the Bank funded the panel, it reported directly to the board of directors; and while the president nominated members, it was the board that approved them. Therefore, the panel was completely independent of the influence of senior management, officials suggested. Critics, however, felt a hollow victory had been achieved. The panel was prohibited from investigating complaints regarding actions by governments and their implementing agencies. Jurisdiction was limited to some branches of the Bank but not all of them. Nor could the panel investigate loans no longer active in order to see if restitution could be made for violations. Critics also noted that, while the panel could investigate alleged violations and make recommendations, it did not have the authority to review management's subsequent actions. Finally, when an investigation was requested, it could not be done on the basis a Bank project had caused harm, but only upon a charge there had been a violation of Bank policy.

The international trade battles of the early 1990s that focused on large treaties such as the North American Free Trade Agreement (NAFTA), and not the Bank, marked a key turning point in the NGOs' emergence as stakeholders of influence in the larger debate about global development.[181] Opponents to both NAFTA and the entrance of the U.S. into the World Trade Organization (WTO) a year later fought hard but lost. Heavily funded and politically connected corporations had compelled Congress to give its approval. The activists took a step back. They had neither the money nor the access their opponents enjoyed, and concluded they could not compete playing the inside game. A new strategy was needed. They resumed the tactics they employed as embryonic civic-minded organizations. They would return to the outside game. They would build large grassroots followings that emphasized the disenfranchisement of individuals in a monolithic society and the value of civic engagement.[182]

Their first success came in Madrid in September 1994. More than 100 NGOs, under the banner "Fifty Years Is Enough" to mark the half-century since the Bretton Woods conference, banded together to derail the Bank's annual meetings. But greater victories were in store. The NGOs' strategy was to develop coalitions to speak over politicians' heads directly to the public. Just as they began, they received a gift that made it much more possible. The advent of the Internet and email proved precisely the weapons capable of escalating public engagement. Through tools that made the globalization of communications possible, the age of anti-globalization had arrived.

The ascension of James Wolfensohn to the Bank's presidency in 1995 brought with it a period of détente. Wolfensohn realized the institution had been blindsided by the intensity and ingenuity of

NGOs' public relations campaign in Spain, and he began a concerted effort of personal diplomacy. "We must embrace all the players," he said.[183] After decades of ignoring NGOs, Bank literature started suggesting civil society could play a valuable role in fostering development, improving government accountability, and giving voice to the poor.

The NGOs' level of antagonistic rhetoric began to abate, but it did not disappear. Even if NGOs had received more sympathetic counsel from the Bank's titular head, in their eyes the Bank was not changing measurably. NGOs sensed the Bank's willingness to increase their participation was a tactic to mute criticism. Paul Nelson, an associate professor of international development at the University of Pittsburgh—in his 2000 paper *Whose Civil Society? Whose Governance? Decisionmaking and Practice in the New Agenda at the Inter-American Development Bank and the World Bank*—suggested the relationship had highly confrontational encounters over issues of infrastructure, structural adjustment lending, energy, and involuntary resettlement of indigenous populations.[184] The Bank subsequently sought collaborative opportunities, but they were at the margins rather than the core of its agenda. While NGOs won concessions on environmental and social projects, the Bank's major emerging trends were on structural adjustment, governance, and private-sector lending.[185] These areas remained largely untouched. Moreover, NGO input was allowed in some sector-level planning, but the more critical country-level processes remained off-limits. Their victories, Nelson concluded, were measurable, but only within the "context of institutional arrangements."[186]

The détente that marked Wolfensohn's early period dissipated. "The Bank had been targeting partnerships with NGOs for a couple of years," admitted one Bank country director, "but from an operational point of view, it had done very little." Activists realized that while the Bank could no longer overtly ignore them, their input had been minimized or came so late in the planning process as to be nebulous.[187] As the 1990s waned, the mood darkened considerably. They began to categorize the Bank, along with its Bretton Woods sister, the International Monetary Fund (IMF), and the World Trade Organization (WTO), as agents of globalization. Globalization helped rich countries grow richer by aiding the interests of multi-national corporations. It came at the expense of impoverished nations, and the Bank, they charged, was one of the primary culprits. They raised other charges: Its structural adjustment lending had buried poor countries in insurmountable debt and its myopic policies had led to increased environmental degradation, relocation of indigenous populations, and destruction of some of the world's cultural heritage.

The Bank, IMF, and WTO inadvertently aided the growing crescendo by holding annual meetings and periodic global conferences. These gatherings provided NGOs with rallying points. A smattering of street protestors showed up at the Bank-IMF annual meetings in 1998 and 1999.[188] This received nominal attention from the media. Management yawned. Protestors carried signs and casually mingled with Bank workers on the sidewalk. A few wore colorful outfits. The flashpoint, however, was just below the surface. It would ignite in November 1999, three thousand miles away at the WTO ministerial meeting in Seattle.

NAFTA laid the groundwork for activists to mobilize in mass. In Madrid, NGOs made it clear to the Bank they would no longer be ignored. Seattle represented a third critical juncture in the discord, and the most serious because it suggested for the first time things could become violent—that someone might literally try to torch buildings associated with these organizations and the people inside them. Local authorities anticipated a small gathering, but tens of thousands came, and their mood was ugly. One group blockaded key intersections and shattered storefronts. The immensity of the gathering fed the chaos. Police responded with tear gas, pepper spray, and finally rubber bullets in a scene eerily reminiscent of the Vietnam War era. Hundreds were arrested, and the meetings collapsed. Euphoric protest organizers announced a Mobilization for Global Justice would march against the Bank in the spring at its next annual meeting.

The emergence of NGOs as influential players in the development arena offered interesting dichotomies. Like the organizations they chastised, they were often dominated by academic elites.[189] Though they claimed to be governed by stakeholders who voted through their donations, these ties were fleeting at best.[190] Moreover, they were essentially unaccountable to anyone even as they were demanding accountability from international organizations such as the Bank. Indeed, more specifically, the anti-globalization movement had many contradictions. It comprised a myriad of interests that under normal circumstances, would have worked against one another—such as students seeking to improve the working conditions in developing countries and labor unions worried about losing jobs to Third World economies. At times it appeared to be a reincarnation of the old "flower power" movement for peace; but it also included anarchists for whom no form of international governance was acceptable. Many influential NGOs that railed at globalization as the "Americanization" of the world were created and based in the U.S. Moreover, the anti-globalization movement was itself transnational, and therefore the product of globalization. And, in perhaps the oddest irony, positions the movement took were often out of sync with views of the impoverished nations it claimed to represent.[191]

The protest movement made a point of linking globalization with environmental degradation; and, while research suggested possible linkages, the answers were not clear-cut. Trade opportunities led to increased road construction to improve access from rural areas to markets. This impacted forests. It also increased demand for agricultural products, which increased the burden on vulnerable flora and fauna. On the other hand, trade liberalization frequently led economies to eliminate subsidies that supported highly polluting industrial sectors.[192] Additionally, significant research suggested rich nations did not necessarily dump their wastes on poor nations, as was originally believed.[193] Still other researchers looked at the movement's economic arguments, and suggested the data didn't support anti-globalization's suppositions. For example, it was true, as the protesters charged, that globalization helped some economies more than others. However, most research suggested open economies enjoyed growth and poverty reduction far more often than closed economies.[194]

But analysis was not what mattered now. Reality was. April 2000 saw 20,000 protestors descend upon the Bank at its annual meetings in Washington, and business in the nation's capital virtually ceased. The Bretton Woods institutions turned into a walled encampment with barricades spanning several blocks, and rivers of police ringing its complex. Senior officials ordered workers home. The District of Columbia police arrested 600 people the first afternoon. By the third day, hundreds more protestors stood across the street chanting. With my ID tucked securely beneath my shirt, I waded into the crowd with a camera. In every direction I turned, people were wearing gas masks. A line of police in full riot geared swayed a few yards before us. I lifted my camera to the masked faces, and each time a hand would raise and shake. Their message to me was unmistakable: The World Bank was an institution under siege.

7

In the spring of 1998, Joseph Stiglitz, recently appointed as the Bank's Chief Economist, and Lyn Squire decided the Bank's 2000 Policy Research Report (PRR) should be a compendium of our industrial pollution activities. While it signaled their recognition of its value and what the research team had accomplished, it also suggested an official end date for our project. It was an artificial deadline, and saddled us with a troubling conundrum, for the key premise of our collaborative relationships was the pledge of our ongoing and long-term partnerships. The Bank's history was that of terminating lines of research so as to foster new endeavors. Sometimes this was appropriate. Our project had lasted six years, and some departmental counterparts believed it had run its course. While well-intentioned, this viewpoint, nevertheless, had a weakness. It made the institution vulnerable to criticism it was not willing to fully invest in partnerships or long-term analytical programs.[195]

In fact, our research was still deepening. The application of environmental taxes and charges in the developing world were essentially unknown prior to the mid-1990s. Now, new lines of research on China, the Philippines, and Colombia had been launched and were blooming. Moreover, public information disclosure was spreading rapidly across China and elsewhere.

Developing capacity inside governments to help them administer their affairs meant creating opportunities for new knowledge, as well as a stable environment within which the client country and donor institution could collaborate. If people, programs, and priorities constantly changed in one or both, sustainable development would logically become harder to achieve. Knowledge takes time to evolve, to be disseminated and accepted. Progress often occurs in bursts, first in the scientific community, and eventually in society, team researchers wrote in one paper. Then they added a post-script: Knowledge can also be lost. Then progress could evaporate as well. For example, the East Asian financial crisis in 1997 led to the eventual ouster of Indonesia's Surharto government. Makarim left BAPEDAL, and without a champion, funding for PROPER ended.[196] Subsequently, Shakeb Afsah, a key architect of the program from our team, analyzed the impact of the financial crisis on the country's production and environmental performance.[197] He found factory output declined 18%, yet pollution intensity from industrial water effluents increased by 15%. This finding contradicted assumptions that negative or even low economic growth would reduce industrial pollution. In fact, as a result of the crisis, industrial pollution had grown because plants were adjusting their abatement efforts in response to lax regulatory monitoring and enforcement and the advent of higher pollution control costs.

In early 1997, the Bank embarked on a new initiative to re-invent the institution as a "knowledge bank." The purpose of the Knowledge Management System (KMS) was to collect the institution's knowledge, case studies, and datasets in a central location for staff and clients. The initial emphasis would focus on providing Bank staff with "just in time" information, but eventually government representatives, universities, foundations, and other institutions would gain access to this evolving clearinghouse of development knowledge. The vision represented a major strategic shift and cultural adjustment for the organization, and even the KMS designers acknowledged the difficulty. "A challenging implementation issue will be achieving the necessary organizational culture shift away from an individualistic node of working and storing knowledge, towards a sharing team-based mode of work. A sustained management effort over several years will be necessary to effect the change ...," they noted.[198] A sustained program would indeed be crucial. Knowledge sharing couldn't be viewed as an organizational fad. Organizers noted serious private sector initiatives devoted as much as 10% of their budget on knowledge management. The Bank would only provide 2%.[199]

The Economic Development Institute (EDI), the Bank's pedagogical arm, was designated to lead the building of the system. But EDI's mission posed a serious challenge to effective implementation that the Bank's senior management never fully grasped. EDI conducted training and designed learning courses as a way of building capacity within client countries. The KMS report noted the conundrum. The risk, as they saw it, was that "we are approaching this as a learning organization."[200] Along with a colleague, I was asked by the division to conduct some analysis of the effort. Our report was tinged with doubt. "The KMS's task of changing the Bank's culture from hoarding information to sharing information is formidable ... given that in a recent survey approximately 50% of those interviewed indicated that managers discouraged sharing information with other divisions, we remain skeptical," our report noted.[201]

Our philosophy on knowledge sharing differed substantially from the mainstream of Bank thinking. The Policy Research Report (PRR) would prove it. In the winter of 1998, Wheeler began drafting *Greening Industry: New Roles for Communities, Markets, and Governments*. It represented a completely new approach to how PRRs were written and produced. For the first time the principle audience would be laymen rather than economists. It was produced in four-color with a complete version online at NIPR which housed links within the report to working papers and external websites.[202] The online version dismayed officials from External Affairs who worried that if people were allowed to download the report off NIPR it would cut into print sales. But as Lawrence Macdonald, our department's communications liaison, succinctly noted, "We are in the development business, not the book business!"[203]

Greening Industry's main theme: Evidence did not support the assumption that industrial pollution was unchecked and worsening in the developing world.[204] To be sure, industrial pollution was exacting a heavy toll in the Third World; but substantial documentation showed pollution intensities falling as industrial bases were expanding. Our data did not corroborate a widely held belief that environmental degradation would increase until development generated enough wealth to promote pollution control and abatement. Developing countries were enacting an extraordinary range of innovative programs as they no longer adhered to the premise that pollution was an acceptable price to pay for development. At the core of understanding these issues: Identify motivations and constraints faced by polluters while helping regulators identify where abatement costs equaled social gains. The report then documented six years of the team's research, and the innovative programs for which we had been privileged to serve as collaborators.

The report revealed a number of new insights. First, public information disclosure had become a new force in environmental management. Second, we provided detailed accounts of programs actually working in the developing world. And, finally, we documented the first systematic evidence on causes of factory-level pollution in the developing world.

Greening Industry noted keys to effective pollution control: Public information, participation, commitment by government to decent standards, cost-benefit analyses, and understanding abatement costs for plants. Studies had shown reducing emissions at the source is cheaper than cleaning degraded air, land, and water. We believed the Bank was well positioned to show and support opportunities; but once governments saw the value of a program, they would find resources to expand it.

Greening Industry also acknowledged an unfortunate fact of life: Poor people suffer from more pollution simply because they are poor. However, where poverty was the root cause of pollution exposure, taking steps to rectify environmental injustices might be unnecessary and could even backfire. More specifically, we believed promoting economic growth while ignoring pollution damage to ecosystems, public health, and industrial efficiency was not cost effective. Nevertheless, when the cost of saving lives with pollution control exceeded its cost from other means, then it made sense for societies to divert resources to other approaches.

Greening Industry issued a warning to the Bank. Investing in large lending programs that sought to address a myriad of environmental issues would overwhelm regulatory agencies. Massive programs would distract agencies with limited capacity from confronting their most critical problems, and ultimately compromise their other activities. Focused, targeted pilot projects would provide the lessons and experiences necessary to move environmental reforms and sound management policies to the next level.

Looking ahead, we suggested a scenario where population and economic growth increased while poverty declined. Global warming, deforestation, loss of biodiversity, and other problems would remain daunting; but we were optimistic. Still, our own work only focused on one basic question: Can local (not global) pollution be held within acceptable bounds while industry continues to grow? For this question, at least, the answer appeared to be yes—if regulators and their donor counterparts were clever and careful.

The dissemination of the *Greening Industry* report marked a radical departure from the traditional print methodology of previous Bank policy research reports. First, the entire paper became available on the Internet via NIPR, with links to other research papers and organizations noted in the report. Then, the report's print version included a CD-ROM that housed the entire NIPR website, with its related research. Finally, a live Internet telecast (webcast) of the conference was produced and seen by audiences worldwide. Major conferences unveiling the report were held in Washington, Colombia, and Thailand. And, on the way to Bangkok, my colleague Susmita Dasgupta and I met with Vietnamese officials about public information disclosure, prompting them to request translation of *Greening Industry* into Vietnamese.[205] At the conference, the Thai government announced its environmental agency would launch public information disclosure.[206] Then China announced it would hold a conference on public information disclosure the following year. When the report was finalized, translations had been requested for French, Spanish, Chinese, Vietnamese and Arabic versions.[207]

As news surfaced about intense interest overseas for the report, Macdonald wrote the department's management about the effectiveness of the team's operating methodology.[208] "*Greening Industry* was published in October 1999," Macdonald said. "To judge by the rather limited media coverage, one might have concluded that the study was not making much of a splash. Yet the new ideas about pollution regulation attracted a great deal of attention within relevant sectors. Starting well before the publication of *Greening Industry* and continuing long after, the [department]-sponsored New Ideas in Pollution Regulation (NIPR) website and email newsletter built a global community of people who were exploring the practical application of these ideas ... We all know there are many other instances in which Bank research findings set in motion a chain of events that ends with changes on the ground that enable poor people to improve their lives. But it's not often that we can see the links so clearly. It's a useful example to keep in mind for the next time that somebody asks about the impact of Bank research."

But a clique within the Environment Department felt we had stolen their thunder. We were entrepreneurial and innovative, which fell outside the mainstream of consensus gathering that was the norm at the Bank. Starting as early as 1997, Wheeler made a concerted effort for closer integration. He broached a plan to the department's senior officials to inventory the organization's priorities and allocations, identify gaps, and establish a framework for addressing them. For us, the payoff would be obvious. Integrating the unit's research into the Bank's operational network would insure steady funding support, and institutionalize our modeling and technical assistance exercises. But there were risks. Wheeler acknowledged, "I have no idea how this will turn out, either for our work program, the scale of our operation or the style of our work."[209]

Its reception was lukewarm. After the European Commission began to promote pollution inventory exercises within its membership, Wheeler encouraged the Environment Department to collaborate. He wrote: "Given our demonstrated support for public disclosure, we may have a rare opportunity to join forces with some NGOs that are frequently our strongest critics. An extension of our pilot public disclosure programs in several developing countries to a full international collaboration might be just right for the times."[210] There was no response. Since NIPR's inception, repeated offers to host the department's materials on NIPR were rebuffed before the benefits were starkly obvious. We were dealing with a fiefdom.

In 2000, the veneer came off. Carter Brandon, a colleague supportive of our work, was developing a mission to India to discuss best practices with their environmental officials. He wanted Susmita Dasgupta to explain some of our programs. It drew a sharp rebuke from a Bank environment official assigned to the region. Our approaches were "exotic," she suggested.[211] "If evaluation criteria have something to do with outcomes, environmental performance of industries in China and Indonesia is much worse than in many other countries which did not experiment with innovative approaches but focused on getting basic regulation and compliance in place …," she said. "I am not saying that these are not interesting examples, but their value is limited and can be understood only in the broader context of 'international good practice' in pollution management, based on lessons summarized in the Pollution Abatement Handbook and other serious analyses …Somehow we, as a unit, indeed, seem to underutilize/ignore expertise/experience we have ..."

Our team was angry, but publicly silent. Wheeler wrote Brandon a private note revealing our sentiment: "After all these years in the Bank, I'm still a little shocked by how ridiculous smart people can sound when they're working an agenda too hard. Pollution charges and public information as 'exotic'—riiiiight. I think it's particularly hilarious that we're singled out for blame in 'dubious' places like China and Indonesia. Total spending by our team on environmental management in those places: Probably $400K over seven years. Total spending by the Bank on 'non-exotica' during the same period—dunno, maybe $150 million? As my daughters would say—Hellllo??!"[212]

Fortunately, not all in the Environment Department felt disenfranchised by our methods. In fact, we had support from one key stakeholder—and a powerful one. Kristalina Georgieva, the department's director, understood what we were doing. She embraced our enthusiasm for public information disclosure and informal regulatory activities, perhaps because she was from Bulgaria and a product of the green movement a decade earlier. She had once been arrested by its Communist authorities for her activism there. And, importantly, she would make public her support for us a few months later, at a pivotal juncture in our episodic journey.

8

With the industrial pollution research and *Greening Industry* projects winding down, we had reached a crossroads.[213] The researchers on the team would move on to new projects; but NIPR's maintenance, and my association with the unit, would end unless alternatives arose. Two presented themselves. The institution's digital abyss seemed a compelling irony when the Bank's 1998 World Development Report addressed Knowledge for Development. The report suggested developing countries should institute policies that enabled them to narrow knowledge gaps with the donor nations.[214] Our Internet success, mission, and history of client collaboration inspired Wheeler to think seriously about the digital divide in the developing world. He formed a new proposal in the summer of 1998. Mainul Huq had returned to his native Bangladesh. The two researchers decided to explore the concept of setting up computers with Internet connections in rural sections of both Bangladesh and India.[215]

The project would focus on what changes new digital opportunities produced at the village-level. Conditions in the villages would be surveyed to establish benchmarks prior to Internet access, and at regular intervals thereafter. Two control groups of villages with similar characteristics, but one without Internet access would be selected. Survey data would allow the project team to measure changes in both groups. The concept offered a unique opportunity. Villages would be utilizing brand new technologies for the first time, and our observations would come from unbiased sources. Futurists such as John Naisbitt and Alvin Toffler had suggested new communications technologies would provide rural residents with substitutes for the face-to-face contact found in large cities, and would mute migration and perhaps eliminate large urban communities.[216] Some hypothesized the Internet might provide opportunities to generate economic growth. Others thought it might homogenize indigenous cultures, or empower dominant cultures to expand their influence. The digital village proposal sought to identify the veracity of such theories.

South Asia seemed an ideal laboratory for observation. India and Bangladesh had stunning poverty, and rural communities that had never even encountered technologies as modern as the analog telephone. But these countries had something else as well. Entrepreneurs operating in the 1980s, such as Dr. Muhammad Yunus of Grameen Trust and Sam Pitroda of the Indian Telecom Commission, were developing the lending and telecommunications infrastructure to make Internet and cell phone access widely available. Pitroda complained development institutions viewed telecommunications as inappropriate for unsophisticated, rural populations. He considered it as essential to the poor as any of the Bank's lending for health, sanitation, or transportation.[217] Huq and Wheeler agreed.

Initial response from Bank colleagues was favorable, so much so Wheeler asked me to consider moving to Asia to manage the project with Huq.[218] Serious discussions ensued on funding and project implementation.[219] Yet, somehow the concept could get no further. Funds moved toward other ventures. Perhaps a low-key, decentralized, and analytical approach was not sexy enough for the times. Soon thereafter, the Bank launched The Global Development Gateway (GDN), an Internet platform of development information, tools, and resources for donors and stakeholders that cost tens of millions in seed money.[220] It was quintessentially Bank-esque, with a centralized administration and governing board, and carefully administered satellite sites. The focus was on harmonization of services and homogenization of information. A coalition of NGOs suggested the GDN would amount to little more than a Bank-run editorial board.[221]

Others in the development community followed suit. The UN Development Programme (UNDP) cosponsored a massive undertaking called NetAid.[222] NetAid would become the world's biggest website, boasted the UNDP director Mark Malloch Brown. UNDP then condescendingly added it would connect the "know's and the know not's" to enhance development.[223] Spectacular concerts on two continents, modeled after the Farm Aid of a few years earlier and Live Aid of a few years hence, rolled the effort out. Within two years, the UNDP jettisoned the project. These ventures stood in stark contrast to the quieter and more decentralized pilot approach suggested by Wheeler and Huq.

By the summer of 1999, momentum for the digital village had stagnated. My mind returned to a conversation Wheeler and I had shared the previous year—filming policy events at the Bank for viewing via the Internet. I encouraged him to revisit the webcasting idea, and as the season waned, he warmed to the concept. A series of test cases had cemented our notion that such an endeavor was possible. We had made a videotape of Nabiel Makarim discussing PROPER which had been made available on NIPR the year before. This realization, that we could make video materials available on the Internet, led us to another one: We could make news as well as conduct research. We could document experiences in our client countries in a way simple to understand for audiences not versed in environmental economics. Wheeler squirreled away funds for the purchase of a camcorder. I went to Colombia in the spring of 1998 to make a film about its pollution charge program.[224]

The Bank's culture coerced staff into viewing the Internet with suspicion. Information needed to be carefully choreographed and sanitized. The Internet was hardly the medium for such a philosophy, so the material that made it online to Bank sites often amounted to propaganda. Moreover, the flow of information was moving in only one direction: From Bank sources to clients and institutional stakeholders. Little value was placed on providing a forum for reciprocal views or knowledge sharing. For example, a number of observers suggested poor information or misinformation disseminated by the Bank and IMF actually facilitated East Asia's financial crisis in the late 1990s. Bank Chief Economist Joe Stiglitz was one such critic. He was forced to resign when his observations became uncomfortably public.

David Rothkopf—a visiting scholar at the Carnegie Endowment for International Peace, and former Clinton Administration official—in the spring 1999 edition of *Foreign Policy*, suggested we had entered an age of systematic and deliberate disinformation. "Governments still regularly provide economic information that they know or might reasonably conclude is inaccurate," Rothkopf said.[225] "Often, financial institutions not only accept this information but also relay it to their clients as fact when it suits their interests. In addition, financial institutions offer themselves as independent analysts and providers of market information when, in fact, they have a variety of conflicting interests that shape their presentation of the 'facts' … the market remains confounded by old habits of secrecy and a system that has been rigged by insiders to serve their needs at the public's expense."

Rothkopf had only reiterated a commonly held view. Indeed, whatever differences the Bank's rich-country shareholders and poor-country stakeholders, along with anti-globalization and civil society activists had with one another, there seemed to be a universal agreement among them: The Bank was a monolithic society where small groups of elite officials would meet behind closed doors on policies affecting millions of people, and then would open those doors to announce what they had decided. It was therefore a stark irony when the Bank spoke about promoting transparency in the financial markets, or increasing accountability within developing countries, or forcing governments to meet stringent conditions before receiving loans. There was never discussion about increasing transparency or accountability within the Bank itself.

We saw the Internet as a place to create what academics such as Nobel Laureate economist Amartya Sen called "social capital."[226] In contrast to the "perfect" information released by colleagues, much of our content was classified as "drafts" and as evolving concepts. We freely recognized weaknesses, ambiguities, and contradictory analysis. And, we quickly embraced the concept of receiving information from counterparts. In fact, it was part of our mantra to create opportunities for them to provide new perspectives on our research, and develop independent collaborative arrangements with other counterparts completely outside our domain of influence. We actively featured research papers of outside academics on the front page of NIPR or in our newsletters. Since we did not feel constrained by the cultural fiefdoms that inhibited others in the Bank, there was no inconsistency in collegially featuring their outputs and events as well. Our objective: Create a medium where anyone interested in our niche subject area could communicate, because we believed such an approach would benefit all.

We envisioned that the theoretical underpinnings of the new webcasting system would come from the public information disclosure systems we helped design and implement. Critics suggested public information disclosure programs were destabilizing, but we believed people panicked when they were surprised by news and the potential impact on their families. Public information, however, was founded on the opposite philosophy. Giving people full information about a subject promoted long-term perspectives and practical approaches. Originally, our technical assistance on the environmental information disclosure projects was seen as a way to improve performance and accountability of firms and agencies, which would help make their conditions comparable to their richer neighbors. But as we studied PROPER and EcoWatch, our concept of the original precepts evolved. We began to view public information disclosure as a formula to promote transparency and accountability beyond environmental management. We observed how its application was a way to reduce abuses and promote equity in an increasingly diverse array of sectors in both the industrialized and developing worlds. Bank technical specialists, with our help, used the concept to assist regulators in choosing water concessionaires in the Philippines.[227] In Uganda, the government announced how it was distributing money to school districts through the newspapers and radio as a way to reduce embezzlement.[228] In Indonesia, something similar happened when a Bank project mandated competitive bids on infrastructure projects be announced to the public.[229] In the United Kingdom, the government disseminated information comparing province-level spending on various service sectors.[230]

And, our sense of urgency was never greater. Five decades of intransigence by senior officials had devolved into an angry, chanting mob of thousands at the Bank's front door. This time they had come with gas masks. Who knew what they would bring next.

For these many reasons we decided to move forward on building a webcasting station that would become the platform for an Internet-based, global public policy network. And, there was one more reason as well. For all the disdain critics expressed about the institution, its management, its bureaucracy, and its culture of fiefdoms, we understood they had not had the opportunity to see the Bank as we had seen it: As a human organization, good as well as bad. For behind the glass and steel partitions, the Bank was composed of thousands of people that cared, who worked ceaselessly and sacrificed time with families, and sometimes their health, to make the world better. They also had something to say and share beyond the sanitized rhetoric. We wanted to help them.

Bureaucracies, said a friend who worked in one, like to keep all blades of grass trimmed to the same level. The irony here is these environments can be fertile for subversion because, despite the overwhelming conformity by the masses, invariably there are those who see weaknesses inherent to blind adherence. It provides ferment for viruses. Our nonconformity didn't qualify us as revolutionaries. Yet without realizing it fully, we were morphing into the architects of an unannounced revolution to change the culture of an institution that had hardened during half a century. Two outliers in the bureaucracy were going to inject a virus into the system to see if, beyond its rhetoric, the Bank could truly become open, transparent, and accountable to the people it served. The tenets of a profound experiment were in place. The subject would be the Bank itself. What we would learn would challenge the very precepts of its commitment to its mission and stakeholders.

The threads of more than a decade had wrapped and entwined. From the environmental catastrophes that prompted new reporting systems to our voyage of discovery about public information disclosure in the developing world, from the evolution of civil society activism with its focus on the Bank to a new president also seeking to change the institution's cultural dynamics, from the creation of new information technologies to our own understanding of their potential, we had reached a unique moment. Development theory was merging with the Internet age. But could this change human nature? The chromosomes that prevented the Bank from being transparent remained deeply entrenched. Following markedly different paths in life, Wheeler and I had arrived at the same place. Where we were, we were not sure. Where we were going, we did not know. What we would become, we could only anticipate. But we were headed onto dangerous ground. Moreover, it was not just that we were traveling into foreign and hostile territory. We, ourselves, were dangerous. We had become dangerous.

PART III

build it and they will come

1

1999/2000

By early November 1999, the heavy lifting for *Greening Industry* had been done. The moment had come to move on implementation of the webcasting initiative. In a note to Witzel, Macdonald and me, Wheeler immediately identified the key question that would shape the venture: Funding.[1] Unspoken was a desire to keep the effort inside the department, but knowing management's appetite for dissemination, alternatives were mandatory. We would have to choose carefully.

Wheeler offered three preliminary scenarios. First, we might consider External Affairs (EXT). The Bank's public relations branch would likely have money, and on the surface there appeared synergies with a system designed to broadcast. But there was a key weakness. EXT would view the system within the parameters of their public relations mandate. Top Bank officials would instinctively use it as a platform for delivering sermons. Institutionally, we would be like a recently hatched chick alone in its nest. We would not be able to deny such requests if they came early in our development. We labeled this problem the "cult of personality" scenario. The Bank operated like any other large bureaucracy. Senior managers would quickly use the service to position themselves or their policies. Moreover, staff would actively facilitate this desire following a natural inclination to be seen as helping their superiors succeed. Their actions would be cyclical. The result would be predictable.

A second option was the Bank's recently launched Development Gateway. Headed by Lyn Squire, who had resigned as the department's research director, the Gateway was a web-based platform to house development information from the organization as well as non-Bank providers. Wheeler suggested the Gateway might present us with a paradox: It could become so information-intensive that it would lack the flexibility to allow a glitzy webcasting initiative. Having leeway to develop simultaneous newsy and showy qualities would be important for us. This reflection seemed sound.

The third possibility: Base the project inside the World Bank Institute (WBI). The successor to Economic Development Institute, WBI had been charged with fulfilling Wolfensohn's pledge to transform the Bank into a knowledge sharing institution. Wheeler noted WBI spearheaded the development of a Global Distance Learning Network in client countries. The benefits of using such a network to disseminate a webcasting station's content were obvious. But with intuitive foresight, he added, "This thing would probably wither if it got forced into some kind of Procrustean bed."

But first we needed a lesson on the concept's applicability. We used the launch of *Greening Industry* to unofficially begin our new effort. Promotion of previous PRRs had amounted to press releases from EXT and a Washington ceremony with the principal authors. To heighten anticipation of their unveilings, EXT planted stories in major newspapers, magazines, and journals, and embargoed text coverage in the days leading up to the release.

Wheeler and I thought the release strategy should have an aspect not considered before by the Research Department or EXT: A live webcast. Several hundred people would be in Washington for the *Greening Industry* conference, but many more would not. A webcast would allow them to participate by observing the event from where they lived. To increase their opportunity to interact, we decided to set up a real-time email chat room where viewers could post questions or comments.

Webcasting struck us as a logical development in our dissemination efforts. During the four years we managed NIPR, we had attracted tens of thousands of visitors accessing research on a relatively narrow subject. NIPR taught us important lessons, most notably that if a website could be seen as a leader in its niche, aided by then-emerging, powerful search engines, it could co-opt the market by "reaching critical mass." At that point, the momentum of the Internet itself would solidify the website's ranking in perpetuity. Webcasting was seen as another tool to aid our momentum.

There was a problem, however. Though the technology had existed for several years, it had not been tried in the Bank. In fact, the Information Solutions Group (ISG), the Bank's technology unit, had virtually no experience with it; so they could not provide assistance. ISG had the ability to stream video over an internal cable channel to Bank staff, but we needed external access. Witzel put us in touch with Netcast, a company that conducted live webcasts for corporate clients.[2] A Netcast technician and I met to connect ISG's fiber lines from the conference room to their server. Then, we contracted with the General Services Department (GSD), the Bank's audio/video unit, to film the event, and connect their cameras to Netcast's streaming server.[3] While we micromanaged every other aspect of the conference, Netcast and GSD ran the webcast.

Everything worked. Cameras and wires connected without problems. The feed was transmitted, and didn't crash. A smattering of people logged on to watch. It was more than the alternative, which was nothing and that was good. The Washington conference on *Greening Industry* on November 22, 1999 signaled the end of our six-year research project, but also the beginning of a powerful new endeavor.

Wheeler and I reflected on the venture's success and what would be necessary to scale up. We were starting at zero. We didn't understand the technology. We didn't know about our capacity. We weren't sure who would be interested or whom we would reach. We weren't sure what kind of content we could capture, and we didn't know if what we captured could be delivered consistently. Nor did we know how much the enterprise would cost or where the money would come from. And, perhaps most importantly, we didn't know if Bank personnel would give us access to their events. The time had come to find out.

Our discussions culminated in a second concept note by Wheeler to Michele de Nevers, the new director of WBI's Environment Pillar, that codified our goals.[4] He had actively recruited de Nevers, an organizational maverick with a no-nonsense personality, as a patron to help fund the project. The note suggested we would create a daily webcasting news service that would respond to breaking events with video coverage, interviews of relevant policy makers and stakeholders inside and outside the Bank, and with links to related video presentations, documents, websites, and datasets. With hat in hand, Wheeler suggested WBI could play a significant role since it served as the focal point for the Bank's knowledge-sharing activities.

It was a three-pronged pitch. With funding for *Greening Industry* ebbing, Wheeler also encouraged de Nevers to recruit me as her new communications person, citing the dominance of NIPR.[5] In a timely turn of events, an internal review of the Bank's Internet operation ranked NIPR as its top website. Then, a few weeks later the Research Department gave the team an award for *Greening Industry*'s success.[6] While a new position with de Nevers might serve as catalyst for the webcasting project, Wheeler and I also hoped her interest might compel our own department to keep me.

To move beyond vision toward reality, we needed a second pilot. We got our chance sooner than expected. Starting in the 1980s, partially in response to the developing world's greater concern about natural resource degradation, biodiversity loss and industrial pollution, and partially because of its own missteps that enraged civil society activists, the Bank began hiring technical specialists to manage environmental components of its lending. For years, these internal environmentalists toiled in ignominy as lending portfolios were driven by the institution's financial barons. The Bank was a laboratory where financiers, economists, engineers, and bureaucrats thrived. Project managers were reluctant to aggressively enforce environmental standards on their lending programs, fearing it could slow or derail projects or escalate costs. Predictably, they had their eyes on the larger picture, where ascension through the bureaucracy was facilitated by how much lending they could orchestrate. Projects moving through the pipeline were the thoroughfare to advancement. Environmental components were the slow lane.

By the late 1980s, however, activist scrutiny had increased its cadence. As things change in the world, institutions also change because they are infiltrated by people who bear the weight of causes larger than themselves. The Bank enacted new steps to mitigate the criticism. An Environment Department was established to review projects, add protection and sustainability components, and mainstream lending in the consciousness of Bank operations. Lending for environmental activities increased. A manual of environmental standards was codified, which personnel had to follow. Then, in 1993, because of the need for a related research component, our unit on environmental economics was established.

While the culture of the institution adapted, it had not changed substantially. Nevertheless, environmentalists inside the institution gained momentum. They updated the organizational guidelines first introduced a decade earlier. The unveiling coincided with our publication of *Greening Industry*. It also coincided with the violence at the World Trade Organization meetings in Seattle. The next target of the anti-globalization movement was the Bank's annual meeting in April. The window the Bank environmentalists had been seeking for more than a decade had just opened. We saw it, too.

With the hammer of the protestors poised to descend, the Environment Department decided its conference in March would become a forum to enact a comprehensive overhaul of the institution's strategy on sustainable development practices. The Environment Forum would bring staff from around the world to Washington to discuss how Bank practices could be modified.

In this precise moment, we recognized a perfect opportunity. Just seeing if we could webcast the event would be a first litmus test of the institution's tolerance for transparency.[7] This offered two challenges: Could we get the Environment Department and its related Sector Board to agree to our coverage; and could we manage the technology to deliver the content without mishaps.

Wheeler's close working relationship with Kristalina Georgieva, the Environment Department's director, proved pivotal. With credentials as a reformer from her days in Bulgaria, she joined the Bank in the early 1990s ready to shake up an establishment apathetic about environmental sustainability. She arrived during a period when like-minded thinkers wanted to reposition the institution on a range of social development issues including gender, cultural heritage, and indigenous rights. Wheeler succeeded in creating a three-way alliance with her and de Nevers. Both agreed to fund the pilot if the Sector Board would allow it. The proposal: A live webcast covering two full days, as well as an archive of the sessions along with post-production work on interviews with important stakeholders whom Forum organizers invited. An important hurdle was cleared when the Sector Board accepted.[8] A subsequent note from Wheeler to the Research Department's management noting the Sector Board's approval closed the bureaucratic loop.[9]

To help with orchestration, we rehired Netcast to set up a fiber connection to their streaming server, and a separate computer to receive feedback from viewers.[10] ISG would make the feed accessible to Bank staff in Washington and its global offices, and would house the material we developed afterwards on their server.[11] We hired Mind & Media, a video production company, to digitize materials and help with post-production.[12] We then contracted with Forum One, Dave Witzel's new firm, to create web pages, and arranged to have GSD send a camera crew.[13] EXT agreed to help us conduct interviews and disseminate documents to the media.[14] Finally, NIPR and the Environment Department's website would jointly link to ISG's server to allow public viewing of the webcast and post-production materials.[15]

Before the first chair was placed and the first person seated, a remarkable thing had already unfolded at the Bank. The Forum, an internal strategy-making session for a Bank department, was being transformed into a highly inclusive event. Policymakers from around the world, including leading actors in our research, were invited to participate. More surprisingly, some of the Bank's harshest critics—such as Friends of the Earth (FOE) and World Resources Institute (WRI)—were being given a seat on the dais to discuss the institution's strengths and weaknesses.[16] And the circle was being reinforced with our live webcast and online discussion forum.[17]

Sensing the opportunity to push the agenda boldly to the forefront of Bank thinking, Georgieva fired an immediate salvo to open the Forum. "The Bank is changing," she declared in her opening remarks.[18] "Our mission is to fight poverty. It is obvious to us that to deal with poverty, you must take the environmental challenges into account, but this is not obvious to many people." Georgieva made it clear: If the Bank was to adopt a more environmentally conscious attitude, then its agenda would still be too narrow. Its modality of operation needed to become more transparent, accountable, and supportive of stakeholder participation. Ian Johnson, her superior and Vice President of the Environmentally and Socially Sustainable Development network (ESSD), reiterated the sentiment.[19] "While we go about preaching openness, consultation, participation, we have to live up to it in the institution," he said. "We can't do what we used to do in this institution, which was to close ranks, close doors, have internal discussions, be very pleased with ourselves, then bring in our external affairs. We've got to be more open, more inclusive, more debate-oriented."

The message reverberated with the invited audience. "I can see a lot of dynamic changes at the Bank," said Victor Ramos, the former environment minister who enacted EcoWatch in the Philippines.[20] "Ten years ago, there was a lot of suspicion from developing countries for the Bank on how sincere it was on the environment … (Now) our presence here, for you to invite us, the open debate, the webcast around the world."

WRI's Frances Seymour, traditionally a tough Bank critic, said, "With very few exceptions the Bank is increasingly open about environmental issues. We had little problem getting access to information, access to people's time. We were amazed with the candor, especially in places where staff thought the Bank got it wrong." But she added a cautionary note. "The Bank's negative image lingers in many borrower countries. So I think it is unfortunate a flap at [a recent] forestry policy review caused some senior Bank managers and the Board to conclude the openness is a bad thing, because I think it helps the Bank in the long run."[21]

The Environment Department had moved proactively in a new direction, but it was not overall Bank policy. Adrian Fernandez, an environmental official from Mexico, clarified why transition for the whole institution was necessary.[22] "We have to promote accountability," he urged. "When you are in a country where every four to six years, 90% of the people in office are pushed out and replaced by other people, you had better strengthen other stakeholders in society. They are going to be there forever pushing and fighting on the same issues. We must strengthen other actors in society. That will guarantee continuity in long-term policies ... By providing information, by leaking information to the public, by making public statements, by getting together with NGOs, with the private sector, academia, with everybody, we become stronger, and we can sit at the table with the Finance Minister and Trade Minister."

While the Bank's environmentalists were trying to create a new way to do business, we were trying to create a new business. We were researchers who analyzed data and wrote reports. Development of a website had been, by industry standards, an unusual deviation. Webcasting was an even more radical departure. This new medium also presented special challenges. Building a full-fledged system would be a process of trial and error, but the immediacy of the Forum's needs kept the learning curve short. Even after four years of immersion in the Internet age, I jokingly told Wheeler I was still a "paper guy." ISDN lines, fiber connectivity, chat rooms, kilobits, kilobytes, video conferencing, phone jacks, streams, downloads, multi-boxes were, as far as I could tell, among the great mysteries of mankind. In orchestrating the setup, I was reduced to asking inane questions and using "duh" repeatedly.

The Forum's webcast, nevertheless, went flawlessly. It received 443 viewers from 28 countries, who watched on average for about 30 minutes.[23] The online discussion elicited comments and queries from five continents. Afterwards, we ate and drank ourselves to sleep.

Wheeler and I analyzed the two webcasts. Both had been highly successful pilots; but the question was how easily and affordably could webcasting be expanded into a full-time service. With a late go-ahead to perform the Forum webcast, we had had little time to build audience awareness. Our only marketing had been a last minute newsletter to the NIPR email list, and despite limited advance notice, more than 400 people watched.[24] About half the audience tried to download video files via a modem, rather than accessing through a network. We speculated this group was mostly from the Bank's client countries, and therefore exactly the type of participants we wanted. In the weeks following the live event, more than 50 people from 16 countries accessed the archives.[25] These numbers represented viewers who had volunteered to register, but didn't include other users, who for their own reasons, did not want to register. It was obvious we were on to something.

Wheeler sent a note to Georgieva and de Nevers stating the project had set "a new standard for transparency and outreach in the Bank … and just at the moment when folks outside are attempting to paint the Bank as a closed, arrogant, undemocratic institution. After all, it's precisely these issues that seem to get our friends in the street most wrought up. Some may be beyond dialogue, but the larger world out there will undoubtedly be interested."[26] To Witzel and me, he sent a second note. It was "nice to be moving along in cyberspace while they're 'dancing in the street' across town," he noted.[27] He cited Gil Scott Heron's 1960s poem "The Revolution Will Not Be Televised," and closed by suggesting, "Thanks to the Net, I get this funny feeling that the next Revolution will be live!"

Behavioral tendencies are difficult to change quickly, however. They generally evolve over time. Not long after the Forum website was finished, a senior environmental official ordered a number of background documents removed.[28] Wheeler and I thought it was a curious juxtaposition to have a public strategy consultation when the background documents were private. Wheeler noted the obvious.

"These reflexes are deeply ingrained within the Bank," he said, and then working behind the scenes he had the request reversed.

Other unwelcome events unfurled. WBI put a freeze on hiring new staff; and de Nevers had to rescind an offer she wanted to make to me.[29] On the heels of giving me its annual performance award, the Research Department said my services no longer warranted funding, and encouraged me to take WBI's offer.[30] Later in the year, WBI relaxed its freeze, and de Nevers was again set to hire me; but Human Resources decided my degree in journalism was insufficient to qualify me for a communications position.[31] Chuckling over the paradox of the Bank's wisdom, Wheeler said he would piece together small pools of budget to keep building the webcasting venture.[32] De Nevers then quickly agreed to provide a small appropriation with the understanding we would focus on environment-related events.[33]

The promise of the Forum suggested our moral compass might be coming into vogue. It would, however, not be enough to create a technology-based mechanism for delivering information. In his original concept note to de Nevers, Wheeler defined a model we hoped to develop.[34] Using a recent flood in Venezuela to illustrate, he said the webcasting service would react by showing footage of the disaster, interviewing Bank and non-Bank experts on the country or issue, streaming related seminars, and linking to websites, video, and print materials, as well as to the Bank's publications store for instant online ordering. The Forum project allowed us to assess all the issues associated with a webcast and its post-production and to compare the result with the model initially suggested.

Wheeler and I entered a period of intense discussions. The issues we debated framed the challenges that would unfold in the years to come. Would our initiative mimic C-SPAN by having cameras simply turn on and record what transpired? Would we include only Bank events or also events from elsewhere? Would we have a passive service, recording events that were requested, or would we actively seek to create content by soliciting organizers and conducting interviews and journalistic investigations? Would we try to record just a few key meetings, or seek as many as possible? Would we include the institution's social and ceremonial functions, or stick strictly to its policy dialogues? Would we create a post-production component to edit materials? Would we seek audience participation via online forums? Would we archive content for short periods, or permanently? Should the website serve as a repository for all sorts of video files from NIPR, EXT, and other Bank units? Would we charge for coverage? Would we host advertisements if funding became a problem? And, most importantly, could we motivate individuals, inhibited by the Bank's culture and often restricted by their operational mandates, to embrace a new activity emphasizing transparency?

We realized some of these questions would resolve themselves through time, and trial and error. The question was whether a conservative institution—where geopolitics and macroeconomics merged, which took pride in being a bastion of international powerbrokers, that employed a culture of withholding and using information selectively and awarded bureaucrats for loyalty and discretion—would be the same institution that created, maintained and tolerated a transparent window on its own activities. To our knowledge—aside from C-SPAN's coverage of U.S. Congressional floor activities, and occasional scandal-related hearings—this would be the world's first backdoor channel into the meetings and activities of any government, international, private-sector or civil-society organization. Only through enlightenment offered by time would the answers be revealed.

2

To pursue something this unlikely, we decided to implement Wheeler's guiding mantra: Better to ask forgiveness than permission. We would build the system quietly. We would reveal little beyond what was necessary with senior officials. We would go slowly, testing technologies and applications. We would selectively build a coalition of support. We would seek to establish a model we thought appropriate, and then set precedents which would make it difficult for adversaries to decouple. We would fly as far under the radar screen as we could before the establishment would notice. By then, if we had manipulated the terrain well enough, the webcasting station would be too much a part of people's consciousness to reign in or disassemble.

With all the hard work behind us, the real labor had just begun. Now, we had an immediate and overwhelming priority, one essential to the entire endeavor's success. We needed a name.

Sometime while preparing for the Forum, Wheeler and I began leaning toward the moniker of B-SPAN.[35] There had been vigorous debate over various suggestions: World Bank TV, World Bank Webcast, World Bank Netcast News, B-CAST, Bank Cast, Bank-SPAN, and a number of other names were floated. Which one of us came up with the name remains lost to history; but the moment B-SPAN was mentioned, we both liked it. We didn't know what SPAN meant (it stands for Satellite Public Affairs Network), but we knew it was what we needed. It had the tone and feel we thought would epitomize the project. It positioned the viewer's mind to intuitively realize what we wanted them to understand.

The name B-SPAN was a take-off on C-SPAN, the American cable industry's television and radio station that broadcasts sessions of the U.S. Congress, and some public meetings of the White House, federal agencies, and Washington policy institutions. The C-SPAN model was to simply turn the cameras on, and record what took place. A highly transparent approach, it provided viewers with an objective format for judging the session and its participants without subjective editing. It achieved what we were pursuing. In addition, C-SPAN's transparent format was well known in the public policy community. We theorized that people would instinctively understand the principles surrounding something called B-SPAN. We briefly considered calling C-SPAN to ask if there were legal issues which would preclude using the name, then speculated it was a Pandora's Box better left unopened. We decided to let them sue the Bank if they ever wanted to follow up.

Two other issues also needed to be resolved quickly. First, we needed money, and no one would underwrite the project until we learned more about its costs. Yet we couldn't evaluate the costs until we better understood the technology. We needed to conduct our own webcast. Even though we had managed two productions, our knowledge remained limited since we had hired an outside vendor to run both. We needed to know precisely the cost of delivering one event, thus defining the project's scale and scope.

The costs associated with using external vendors had been significant, and we knew they were not sustainable. Still, it might be possible to have an external vendor manage parts of the system while we focused on content delivery. We began looking at potential vendors, getting references from Witzel and skimming the Internet. The scales of economy provided by a large organization, however, made a service administered completely inside the Bank likely the most affordable option. There was only one place to start.

ISG was the one Bank unit with some knowledge of webcasting. It had established a cable TV channel to transmit occasional Bank events which staff could watch on their office computers. No one had ever considered using the transmissions for external purposes. But at $500 an hour, it was expensive. Moreover, ISG did not view it as an important part of their business model. Their mandate was to manage the institution's telecommunications system, install and fix computers, facilitate video conferences, build websites, and maintain servers. Webcasting was seen as a burden. Without a mandate to provide it, and without an expectation of generating revenues, no infrastructure for webcasting had been put in place. ISG also did not have the capacity to generate website content, so it couldn't create the interest necessary to build a clientele. Without a regular clientele, the price of any individual webcast would remain prohibitive. Therein lay a conundrum. Without an audience, infrastructure could not be built; but without the infrastructure, there could be no audience.

During our period of post-Forum fermentation, we adopted a core objective: B-SPAN would become a virtual library of videos on development discussions.[36] As the number of events we covered grew, it would create a stockpile of videotapes for viewers to select. To achieve the library concept, we would need to permanently archive video files on a server. The time had come to develop our first crucial relationship.

I called Chongman Kim, who managed ISG's internal webcasting activities, and he agreed to meet.[37] He quoted me a storage fee of $500 per gig for seven days; but he also suggested that archiving a stream represented the least expensive part of the process. Wheeler, whose nose was regularly buried in technology magazines, realized Kim's pricing structure was unrealistic in comparison with the prevailing market.[38] It was apparent no one had asked ISG this question before. Since seven days was not what we had in mind, I queried Kim about the costs of a dedicated server.[39] He estimated we would need $10,000 to acquire the hardware, $100,000 for the software and operating licenses, and $15,000 for annual maintenance.[40] Wheeler and I knew these costs would break us before we could begin. The response raised another problem. How were we going to maintain a server? We were developing a content-based system using a particular technology. We didn't have the training, aptitude, or interest to run servers. We needed another option, and we needed ISG to give it to us.

Casually, I suggested to Kim that we would start exploring how to build and maintain our own server.[41] Server maintenance was ISG's core business. Nothing creates a sense of crisis like the possibility one might inadvertently create a competitor for oneself. Kim responded accordingly.[42] "ISG is not comfortable allowing individual units in the Bank to purchase and maintain their own servers," he said. "This would create a highly complex network structure." I agreed, but what could we do, I asked. He offered me the arrangement I was hoping for. He would set up a server where we could dump video files, and we would pay him a monthly maintenance fee of $2,000. It wouldn't sustain large volumes, but it gave us breathing room. "I think that works," I said, and suddenly we had something we could afford.

Our initial inclination was to develop a live service.[43] To do so, ISDN lines—fibers that transmitted a camera feed to a laptop connected to a video server—would have to be available where an event took place.[44] A website would then provide the link to the video server that viewers would use to "stream" the video file over their computers. ISDN lines were not cheap to install, and only a few large conference rooms at the Bank had them. Bank seminars, however, were held in rooms throughout six office buildings along its Pennsylvania Avenue corridor. The vast majority of rooms had no ISDN cables. Having GSD transport cameras to six buildings might create havoc. We wondered if establishing a connection in one place within the main headquarters might make everything more efficient.[45] It might also serve as an incentive for event organizers to schedule events there. Kim said it would cost $700 to establish a line in a room we had permission to use, and another $100 a month for maintenance.[46] This sounded expensive as well, but I began exploring locations with an eye on lighting conditions and proximity to the Environment Department. When ISG subsequently revised its installation and maintenance costs downward, I alerted de Nevers, who then got the acquiescence of Ian Johnson, the Environment Department's Vice President, to hook up a room nearby.[47]

Filming events was another piece of the equation. Like the server side of the venture, we did not have the equipment, staff or ability to do it ourselves. We had established a cordial relationship with Sefik Cardak, who ran the GSD camera teams that covered the *Greening Industry* and Forum events for us. Their costs, however, were also too high for the amount of volume we wanted to generate. GSD charged Bank units $350 to cover two-hour events. Hiring external vendors to film events was not an option. They were more expensive. We needed a better rate. I sat down with Cardak.[48] "Paying $350 per event is fine for Bank units who occasionally use the service," I said, "but we want a discount because we are going to generate immense volume for you." It is the rare manager who cannot see the advantage of telling superiors he found a customer to substantially increase his business. Cardak suggested $250 was as far as he could go. I said okay, grabbed his hand for a quick shake, and ran out of his office.[49]

When we conceived of B-SPAN, we did not believe coverage should be limited to only Washington events.[50] We wanted the system to have the flexibility to webcast from overseas as well. If this was going to be a piece of the business, it would be too expensive to send camera teams and server technicians on the road. We would probably need local vendors to film and stream it back to headquarters. We also considered purchasing a camera capable of streaming (the first commercial ones had just come on the market), going on the road and doing it ourselves.[51] Cardak, however, delivered the notion a body blow.[52] Suitable cameras would cost $20,000, he said. Then there are expenses for wireless microphones, power cords, tripods, travel and per diem for you to leave Washington, he added. For the moment, we would have to table this part of the agenda.

Our webcasts would be unedited and uncensored.[53] Post-production of video remained under consideration, but the Forum had demonstrated its difficulty.[54] It was time-consuming and expensive. To be part of the model, it would have to prove quick and inexpensive. We turned to WBI's Global Development Learning Network (GDLN) to find out more.[55] GDLN had television studios capable of editing video. Wheeler, de Nevers, and I met with John Middleton, its manager, and his deputy Phil Karp to discuss using their facilities to film events, and hiring them to post-produce our unedited materials to create new products. Wheeler and I quickly became leery. Sensing wolves near the lair, we worried GDLN would wield its considerable influence to co-opt B-SPAN, and merge it into their business model.[56] We decided to let them conveniently forget us.

By the end of May, I presented Wheeler with preliminary cost projections.[57] Server hosting would cost about $24,000 annually. Installation of an ISDN line in a dedicated conference room was a one-time charge of $2,000. Production costs, derived from discussions with GDLN, would run $25,000 yearly. Editing videos were estimated at $45,000 in the first year; but with technology improvements and practice, we thought we could halve these costs in the second year. Forum One maintained NIPR for $15,000 annually, so we assumed the rate would hold for B-SPAN. However, if we hired someone internally, website maintenance might decline. If we achieved our goal to cover 100 events during the first year, it would cost $25,000 for camera services. Depending upon how scenarios unfolded, we estimated the first year would cost $165,000, and drop to $116,000 in the second year.

Our initial analysis revealed depressingly high hurdles. Eliminating post-production and refraining from using GDLN's studios would certainly reduce the figures; but the projections did not include my salary as producer or compensation for Wheeler's technical assistance.[58] In addition, identifying the cost of a single event remained a floating target. We would need to create one to make an accurate evaluation. Given the costs, B-SPAN would be expensive, perhaps prohibitively so. It would be difficult to convince anyone in the Bank to underwrite a startup of this magnitude. We needed different options, or we needed to change the model of a live webcasting system.

We were building our ship plank by plank. Next, we needed a website. Wheeler's love of gadgetry was a driver. His constant search for new inventions, innovations, and software programs translated into a bombardment of possibilities for us.[59] With notes from Charlie Parker or John Coltrane emanating from Wheeler's computer, I'd come into his office to listen to him riff about something he just downloaded. A typical salvo to my email might note, "A new version of PlayStation has just launched, 100,000 hits in the first minute, check it out."[60] Another time he wanted to know if it was possible to program an algorithm to speed up audio so busy "listeners" could participate.[61]

Wheeler was a zealot for technology, but I had a theory: He was simply trying to keep up with three teenage daughters. There were times, however, when I had to lower expectations. When he heard about Flash technology that made images magically appear and move around the website, he expressed great enthusiasm. I hated to disappoint "The Professor," but we were on a tight budget.[62] Witzel was also excited. He sent similar emails suggesting things he had come across.[63] One that stood out was EXBTV, a recently launched daily webcasting station streaming government news conferences. High-profile journalists such as Hugh Downs and Jed Duval had joined, but the venture soon shut down. The moral I drew from the quick fizzle: Have enough patience to build a solid hull.

Wheeler felt it imperative to have a formal website running to show de Nevers the project was moving forward. I was well-versed in managing content, but I didn't have the experience or time to build pages. I began looking for someone who would fit seamlessly into our operation, and found Polly Means.[64] Means worked on a variety of Research Department websites, including for a brief period NIPR. She was quick and competent, essential characteristics for what we needed. Her manager agreed to let us purchase some of her time. Early in June, I placed a request with ISG to establish an address; Wheeler mocked up a couple simple prototypes, and Means built a crude home page.[65] It was a dummy site and not pretty, but we existed in cyberspace. That was the marker necessary to keep in the good graces of our benefactor, de Nevers. Afterwards, I asked Witzel to draft a contract for Forum One to develop a full-fledged website.[66]

The time had come to make decisions about our operational model.[67] Our goal was to have a daily news-oriented broadcasting system. Internet audiences, however, have notoriously short attention spans. It would be difficult keeping someone watching a two-hour webcast. On the other hand, our experience from the Forum suggested editing footage into an abbreviated package for viewers was so time-consuming and expensive, it was unsustainable. We mulled over the merits of eliminating small chunks of dead air and breaks between speakers, but even this task would soon be overwhelming. Moreover, it raised a serious question. Would audiences suspect our edits doctored the content or modified its tone? Would the removal of dead air and momentary flubs call into question the integrity of the entire webcast? It would be too high a price to pay.

The themes that emerged from the Forum established a framework for B-SPAN's principles on transparency and accountability. We realized that by turning on the cameras and filming what took place without any editing, we could fulfill these objectives. Keeping someone watching for the full-length of an event might not be possible, but we accepted this as a sound compromise for getting the transparency model launched. We could revisit the question of segmenting events into smaller pieces when time and resources allowed, but editing was not an option.

We also decided it would not be feasible to allow Internet audiences to actively participate in live events via chat rooms or other discussion forums.[68] We were concerned that presenters and hosts would resent the additional work necessary for producing online chats, and might not agree to our participation at all. We were at the beginning, and not along the way. What we needed now, more than anything, was access. Our thinking was solidified during a meeting I had with Ron Kim, manager of the Bank's Discussion Forums, a real-time online chat room designed to supplement WBI courses or major Bank initiatives.[69] Kim thought moderating live discussions did not work well, since viewers from other global regions would need to watch during hours they normally would be sleeping. Though we were moving rapidly away from a live model because of the costs, Kim's reflections, coupled with our reluctance to pressure seminar presenters, ended this part of the project's development.

We also had to decide what kind of content B-SPAN would webcast. Intuition told us B-SPAN would define itself through a natural selection process, partly of our making, and partly by others. Some events would be interesting and valuable, and others not. Some event organizers would reject external dissemination out of hand. Others would embrace it. It would start as a moving target. We knew that we did not know, so inevitably institutional players would perform a central role in defining content. To some extent, pragmatism would also be our guide.

Wheeler had gotten de Nevers to fund us with seed money to begin the project. Since she was paying the freight, we decided not to grow our initial coverage beyond her environmental mandate. This also meshed with her conception of the service: She wanted coverage of events she couldn't attend that day, but might wish to see later. We did know, however, we did not want management molding B-SPAN into a forum for sermonizing or proselytizing. The Bank already had

External Affairs. We would steer away from speechmaking from senior officials, unless given in a forum where audience participation and dissent were possible. We would also refrain from covering ceremonial functions devoid of policy dialogue.

The second content-related decision involved whether we would produce events only viewable by Bank staff. In April, de Nevers forwarded a note from a unit wanting to webcast a discussion on poverty reduction strategies, but only for internal consumption.[70] We had no content to offer. Now we were being offered something. It was also clear to us some events would only be suitable for staff. But B-SPAN was invented to open to the public Bank meetings that previously had been unseen. Using it to webcast to internal-only audiences would undermine this goal, as well as encourage the less courageous instincts of our colleagues. For the moment, we were the only option available, and therefore in the enviable position of outmaneuvering potential critics. We tactfully informed de Nevers it was our way or no way. We also believed it would not take long for our way to look appealing. In fact, we suspected we would need only a few users at the outset to build our momentum quickly. Natural instincts would begin to act out. As staff saw others webcasting events, they would not want to be left behind, and would seek us out.

There was also another source for content we thought was needed to complete our agenda.[71] Institutions outside the Bank held their own events on issues related to development. These would include other multilateral lending institutions, such as the IMF and Inter-American Development Bank (IDB), as well as numerous policy groups, think tanks, and special interest organizations headquartered in Washington and elsewhere. Without them, the goal of making B-SPAN a truly inclusive platform for communications would never be fully complete.

I decided to employ two strategies to determine coverage. The first would be an open invitation. If staff wanted their event covered, they needed only to contact us, and we would help. The second was to use my intuition, drawn from my background in journalism and years inside the Bank. If an event captured my interest, if it had "sex appeal," I thought it might do the same for others. I would pro-actively reach out to its sponsors.

Aiding the effort would be our electronic mailing list. In the four years of building NIPR, we had created the second largest list in the Bank, with more than 12,000 subscribers.[72] It was an extremely powerful tool for disseminating information, and would serve as the baseline for creating a second list for B-SPAN. Into this database we had also added 1,500 new electronic subscribers from the Forum, an extraordinary coup.[73]

To succeed in our highly conservative environment, we would have to move quietly, keeping the institution's bureaucratic tendencies muted. Like the river that flows past rocks embedded in its basin, we would have to maneuver on shifting terrain. We would coerce when practical, and bend when necessary. And we knew from the start, ambivalence would be an important ally. Bank staff tended to think their work highly important (we were no exception), and paid little attention to things unrelated. In organizations like the Bank, the myopia was magnified a bit more. Having senior people not notice us—because they were busy saving the world—was a very useful behavior for us to leverage. While we weren't trying to hide what we were doing, we didn't want to draw unnecessary attention to ourselves, particularly from EXT. Since they were the official voice of the Bank, they might object vehemently to anyone outside their department seeking to systematically disseminate external content. Most staff would think we naturally overlapped, because the objectives of B-SPAN were not fully clear to anyone but us. To communicate the differences would be detrimental. Wheeler was inclined to pro-actively establish a cordial relationship. I, however, was concerned EXT might object to us, or take B-SPAN over if they thought it worthwhile. I pushed hard for anonymity until we were too well-established for EXT to undermine. Wheeler finally agreed.[74]

Throughout the spring, I tracked event information by any means available.[75] The Bank had no systematic mechanism for informing staff of events at its facilities. Personnel working at one of the world's most information-laden institutions—a global leader that three years before had announced it was transforming itself into a "knowledge bank"—was reduced to plastering elevator walls with leaflets of upcoming events. I read them daily. Some information came via email, but it was sporadic. So I dutifully compiled a list of every unit in each department, and contacted them asking to be placed on their distribution lists.[76] By June, I had developed a network that alerted me to almost everything taking place. Perhaps in this one respect, it made me the most informed man inside the institution. I put together an event sheet, updated it daily, and sent it to Polly Means at the close of each week to post on the website.[77] B-SPAN's schedule turned out to be more comprehensive than EXT's, the department responsible for keeping Bank staff informed via the Intranet. Naturally, I reviewed their daily updates to add anything we might have missed, an act I called "innovation." Wheeler also forwarded notices he came across.[78] "Yo Spanable," read one note.[79] "Today's catch … sushi, fried or Spanable, could be delightful," read another.[80] I wrote back that events would be categorized as "eminently BEESpanable, possibly Spanable or definitely Bexpendable."[81] We began looking for an event suitable for launching our maiden attempt.[82]

De Nevers' purse was limited.[83] Wheeler had finagled funds within our department to cover some of my salary. Long-term sustainability, however, would depend upon resources neither possessed. De Nevers continued to gauge GDLN's interest.[84] Middleton told her he had met with Bank President Wolfensohn, mentioning B-SPAN could fill GDLN studio time with content.[85] But Wheeler and I remained uneasy.[86] Something about GDLN's operation was making us hesitate.

At the end of June, Wheeler, de Nevers, and I met to assess progress and next steps. She wanted to increase B-SPAN's involvement with her department.[87] Ever clever, she wondered, if she was going to share the wealth, how she would share the pain. Her interest raised a red flag with us. If our financing became too WBI-centric, then there was a distinct possibility a service intended for the entire institution would become absorbed in one specific department's agenda. Conversely, if we did not find a reliable funding source soon, B-SPAN was doomed. De Nevers felt it was time for a public announcement.[88] We wrote a note for Ian Johnson to send to his department a few days later, encouraging them to use the service.[89]

In preparation for Johnson's note, I wrote a lengthy mission statement on B-SPAN for our new website. "For many years, the World Bank has hosted regular luncheon seminars, workshops and conferences in its Washington, D.C. headquarters where the world's leading experts came to discuss the latest developments in their sectors. Unfortunately, these live events were only attended by a small fraction of the potential audience interested in participating. B-SPAN seeks to fill this gap by allowing anyone with Internet access an opportunity to watch an event live or afterwards through the archived files on its website. B-SPAN capitalizes on World Bank President James Wolfensohn's efforts to transform the institution into a 'knowledge bank.' In 1999, President Wolfensohn said, 'We have got a knowledge bank that we are building, so that wherever you are, you don't have to come to Washington for information, you can get it locally.' B-SPAN delivers on that pledge. The webcasts will be a free service to any Internet user, who will need only to download a free version of RealPlayer, a software that allows the playing of live webcasts and archived videos on a personal computer … The power of B-SPAN is that it seeks to inform and empower others to think, debate and act. 'This knowledge issue is not just a cosmetic issue,' said President Wolfensohn. 'In the next five years it is central to the issue of development.' B-SPAN forms a foundation upon which to build a bank of knowledge."

Shortly thereafter, a colleague called me to say his team in the Bank's Middle East region "hungered" for such an initiative. He characterized B-SPAN as a "brave" effort. As we would learn, he could not have been more right.

3

We now had our basic institutional arrangements in place. ISG would manage our server and GSD would film our events. A website had been built, prepped with information, and someone had been found to maintain it. There was a bit of capital to finance initial operations. B-SPAN's operational model was solidified. We were open for business.

The conversation with de Nevers hardened our focus to seek a diversified revenue stream. While environmental issues would dominate our service in the early stages, sustainability depended upon Bank-wide usage. Wheeler recognized de Nevers' seed money would not last indefinitely, and the search for additional partners began.[90] Logically, we solicited the Research Department first.[91] It would be a good match. Our chief interest was the policy dialogues the institution offered, and its research seminars were ideal. They were informal, low-key, and rich sources of information; and if a recording flubbed in any way, it would not cause great outcry. We assiduously wanted to avoid high-profile events in the early stages. Our paranoia that senior officials might use B-SPAN to fulfill personal agendas remained high.

In late July, responding to Johnson's email, an official with the Bank's Europe and Central Asia (ECA) region contacted me.[92] With the Bank's annual meetings coming up in September in Prague, he wanted interviews of authors for various environmental strategy papers. He hoped webcasts would initiate widespread discussions among Bank staff prior to Prague. It looked promising for us.

With a sense of urgency, upgrading the dummy website became our next priority. We contracted with Forum One to build a quick prototype.[93] Witzel understood our objectives, and the shareholders and audiences we sought. We were confident he would build a site viewers found dynamic and easy to navigate. Forum One encouraged us to consider a far-ranging package containing technological bells and whistles, and audience analysis; but the moment was not right.[94] Our near-term objective was simple, fast, and cheap.

Witzel cautioned us that C-SPAN might object to our B-SPAN moniker and move pro-actively against us.[95] Wheeler found an interesting parallel in the 2000 U.S. presidential campaign when candidate Ralph Nader's ads parodied the MasterCard "Priceless" commercials. The company sued to pull the ads. He, too, was concerned. Since our website was going to be housed within WBI's Internet infrastructure, he suggested a middle ground.[96] "Why not have an address like 'worldbank.org/wbi/wbtv' that didn't mention B-SPAN and kept recognition muted in the early phase?" he offered. I remained opposed to the compromise. "It would create too much confusion," I countered.[97] Debate continued until we agreed our concern reflected more paranoia than the situation warranted. We went with http://www.worldbank.org/wbi/B-SPAN.[98]

As August started, Wheeler wanted a second cost analysis to assimilate new information gathered since the first projection. These costs included his oversight and my production expenses, Forum One's web-design contract, website administration by Means, and ISG's server maintenance and camera costs. Determining camera expenses was bedeviling since there was no way to estimate how much filming would be requested. Our guess was we would need cameras once for each day the Bank was open during a year, approximately 260 days. That would come to over $90,000 annually, an enormous expense. First-year cost estimates now floated between $254,000 and $211,000. Some of the expenses involved one-time acquisitions, but second-year estimates only dropped a bit. On the surface, it sounded expensive; yet in reality, we were attempting to launch a global communications network on the cheap. For the moment, without an underwriter, we would need to charge users. The calculations suggested a single event would cost between $812 and $977 in the inaugural year. It would drop to $700 in the second season. It was a gloomy scenario. We wouldn't see much usage at these prices.

Wheeler suggested offering a live-service event for $250, and charging $150 for events shown as archived video-on-demand files.[99] I ran new calculations.[100] We would have to film five events a day to meet our expenses. Any way we ran the numbers, we were going to have trouble convincing Bank colleagues the service's value was worth the expense. It compelled us to make an important strategic decision. We decided to forego charging customers initially. We would first interest them in using the service, and then make sure we could deliver content efficiently.[101] The point at which cost and willingness intersected would remain momentarily open-ended. My analysis suggested the final answer would hinge on whether we could "successfully market B-SPAN as a service quickly enough to increase the volume to cover the initial outlays before WBI pulls the plug."[102]

The challenge was obvious; and it included another glaring weakness. We had no capacity to encode videotapes before they could be loaded on to ISG's server. We would have to rely on ISG for this as well, but they charged $100 for every tape processed, and were reputedly slow and unresponsive.[103] Witzel suggested we outsource this part of our service, but we were inclined to keep everything in-house.[104] Doing so enabled us to maintain greater control. Nevertheless, B-SPAN would live or die based on how quickly we could encode videos and load them on servers. We decided talking with external vendors would be prudent.[105]

Throughout August, preparations intensified for the environment strategy interviews. Forum One and I created a B-SPAN logo, a home page with a news bureau design, and a newsletter registration page.[106] We also put together visitor instructions for downloading RealPlayer streaming software, a necessary component for watching our video files.[107]

Cost-projection research continued, too.[108] We confirmed video archiving was not nearly as expensive as ISG had suggested. Moreover, Witzel found their streaming charges unrealistic compared to external vendors.[109] ISG wired the conference room we designated with an ISDN connection; and we tested it with a camera team to ensure a live stream functioned seamlessly.[110] It did not. We still operated on the assumption we would try to convince event hosts to schedule their seminars in our specially wired room.[111] If they resisted, our back-up plan was to get them into GDLN's studios.[112]

By the end of the year, however, we had scrapped both options. Then Chongman Kim, ISG's webcasting liaison, handed us a gift.[113] He agreed to waive server charges for three months while we sought to establish the system.

B-SPAN made its debut on September 7, 2000 with three events.[114] The inaugural seminar featured Richard Klein of the Potsdam Institute for Climate Impact Research. I decided to record Klein's discussion for subsequent viewing rather than live, because the ISDN test had not proven faultless.[115] Without a reliable stream, I had hesitated on pre-event marketing, a prerequisite for a live webcast. Later in the day, a regional official sat down with Alexandre Marc and Marjory-Anne Bromhead, social development and natural resource specialists for the Bank, to talk about the draft strategies they had prepared for Prague.[116] I stood in the back of the room, double-checking camera angles, and jotting notes for the summaries to be featured with the videos. For a moment, my eyes went blank. I had an overwhelming sense the first waves of a memorable voyage were sweeping below my bow.

4

Storm clouds were immediately in the offing. Wheeler informed me Real Networks might phase out its free RealPlayer streaming software.[117] They were actively pushing for a monthly subscription service. This would be injurious but was obviously out of our control. If external viewers were forced to make purchases, most would opt out, possibly curtailing dissemination to developing countries. There was only one thing to do: Keep working with the free version while it lasted, and monitor Real Network's success with its subscription model. Adding to the difficulty, Bank staff had an older version of the software installed on their hard drives.[118] It was not compatible with videos we were streaming. As word about B-SPAN had filtered out, we started receiving inquiries from staff unable to stream files. The short-term solution was easy: Get staff to download the right version. The reality, however, was that users often did not have the time or aptitude to load the correct RealPlayer. ISG planned to correct the problem by installing an upgrade on people's computers, but implementing a new system was months away.[119] Until then, we would be forced to do a lot of handholding. To head off the trickle before it became a downpour, I wrote detailed instructions and had Means link it to every page.[120] We were now in the curious position of being able to webcast B-SPAN outside the Bank, but not easily inside it. However, there was a silver lining. We had the ability to stream content to the world without senior officials knowing precisely what we were doing.[121]

Other obstacles rose before us. EXT launched World Bank TV to webcast daily reports from the Prague meetings.[122] Fortunately, these were no more than five-minute vignettes with little substance. The reports terminated when the meetings ended. Then Polly Means's manager suggested too much of her time was being co-opted by B-SPAN.[123] Luckily, our department's management began to encourage its managers to get staff time subsidized through other Bank units. The directive allowed us to cover a sizeable chunk of her expenses with WBI's cash, and the manager's concerns faded into the background. During the weeks ahead, we would run into an assortment of technical glitches. Files were encoded, streamed, or loaded on servers incorrectly.[124] There were hardware and software crashes. The problems, however, were predictable. All of us were learning how to webcast for the first time. By Christmas, we were crawling faster and faster.

I focused my energy into selling the service. To create the event, it was first necessary to create the desire. I talked to prospective clients about the Internet's power, the medium's immediacy, the enormous constituencies that could be harnessed, the importance of sharing knowledge with their networks and receiving feedback, and the cost effectiveness of disseminating via webcasts versus traditional print outlets. Some voiced concern regarding our presence.[125] They suggested the informality of the discussions would make them largely irrelevant. Others worried proprietary information might escape.

This was no surprise. Staff remained wedded to the concept that information released into the public domain needed to be highly structured and vetted.

Where I found uncertainty, I moved aggressively to modify viewpoints by changing my pitch. "Transparency can mollify the growing chorus of Bank critics about your work," I suggested. Even the newness of webcasting itself prompted discomfort. Presenters and hosts jokingly asked if they needed makeup. To reduce the underlying anxieties entwined with making a "public" presentation, I joked back that we would provide makeup artists.[126] As the fall unfolded, we began to attract a growing interest.

The issue of outsourcing our encoding, streaming, and storage components remained an open question.[127] Chongman Kim seemed supportive, but he was an elusive figure disappearing for weeks at a time to handle Bank activities overseas. His absences became a running joke between Wheeler and me.[128] For the moment, however, our complaints were muted. ISG had temporarily waived its storage costs and encoded a smattering of tapes, but this wouldn't sustain us long.[129] Witzel began introducing us to vendors, but two hurdles remained in our minds: Cost and control. Outsourcing archives for storage on a vendor's server would be a significant expense, though ISG's quote was even higher. Nevertheless, having archives housed on a server external to the Bank might create proprietary concerns in the future. Would putting Bank information on external servers create a backlash against us? We also wondered that if our relationship with the vendor ended for any reason, how much would it cost, and how long would it take to move archives back to a Bank server? We didn't have the answers, but we could speculate.[130] We decided to redouble our efforts to convince ISG to incorporate high-volume server storage and maintenance services, combined with lower charges, into their business model. To accomplish that, we needed to first convince them B-SPAN would be a permanent fixture.

Practicality was also dictating the model. Event organizers were increasingly inviting B-SPAN to participate because they recognized its value. They were less willing, however, to move to the room we had specially wired for live feeds.[131] We had to come to them, which meant we were moving inexorably away from a live webcasting model to a recording and archiving system.[132] Our principles were also evolving when our vision of the path we wanted to take was not clear. Once we covered a water sector event that was nothing more than a promotion of services that water technology companies were offering to staff.[133] Private companies and consulting firms often came to the Bank to inform staff about their products and services. This was appropriate, but it was outside the parameters we had defined as permissible for the service. We adapted by adding a disclaimer: B-SPAN did not endorse products discussed during our webcasts. We also made it a point to more carefully scrutinize the context of the events before sending cameras.[134] We were in our infancy and learning. We moved on.

In October, the Bank's Rural Development network organized a seminar series on its new strategy, scheduling several leading scholars to speak. They invited us in.[135] Lynn Brown, the series' organizer, noted, "It would represent the first time that a strategy process has used this technology to really involve the field teams. For us that is exciting, because at the end of the day much of the work for getting our strategies implemented comes down to work at the front line in the mission offices, and yet generally these staff are the least involved in actually drawing up strategy."[136]

Shortly, thereafter, the Urban Water and Sanitation team asked us to cover their lecture series for the next two years.[137] These requests signaled growing recognition by institutional players that B-SPAN was a vehicle that could help achieve their communication objectives. New words started appearing in emails. People began referring to events as "Spanable" or having them "B-Spanned".[138] We had entered the Bank's lexicon! And, we had stopped crawling.

Customer needs changed our model from a live system to one that produced archived materials on demand. This changed the production process as well. Instead of streaming live events, the emphasis had switched to encoding tapes; but ISG was taking too much time to turn them around.[139] A pile flowered on my desk. And, at $100 a tape, in bulk it represented a crushing expense. If we could not post content rapidly, we could not aggressively publicize our service. If we could not expand quickly, we would be vulnerable to an equally quick demise. Clients would expect a quick turnaround, and if we couldn't deliver, our credibility would be called into question. We were also concerned delays might cause de Nevers' support to waiver, and with it the paychecks that subsidized the project.

Wheeler suggested exploring whether other Bank teams were encoding. I found a team in the Latin America (LAC) network that was putting short documentaries on the Internet. They acknowledged they had the know-how, but couldn't make B-SPAN their priority.

Then I thought of asking Means if she would be interested in learning the encoding process. She responded positively, and a door opened for us.[140] Overnight, we went from ISG's mercy to bringing this component of the system in-house. Her acceptance offered distinct advantages to our evolving model. We immediately began thinking about purchasing equipment, installing it in her office, getting her trained, and internalizing the encoding process into our system.[141] This development offered distinct advantages. Means would not be as expensive as ISG. She was also interested in B-SPAN, which translated into the quick responsiveness we needed to keep content moving. Then, by chance, we learned our department had purchased encoding equipment the previous year.[142] We received permission to use it. Means started researching hardware and software upgrades to optimize the process.[143] Even Kim saw the advantage of removing this burden from his plate. He agreed to provide her training.[144]

As we prepared a public announcement about B-SPAN's launch using NIPR's email distribution list, a revelation dawned on us. The more our dialogue with ISG continued, the more territory and responsibility they ceded to us. Aside from server hosting, we had forgone live webcasting, taken over encoding and streaming activities on equipment we possessed, and were purchasing disks for our storage needs. Kim even found a 100-gigabyte hard disk he would donate to our cause. We now had enough capacity to keep us floating into the next fiscal year.[145]

Our popularity was growing inside the Bank, as was our relevance outside it.[146] We scheduled nine events in one week in November, and ten more in early December including our first major presentation. The Sixth Conference of the UN Framework Convention on Climate Change had just concluded in The Hague. Robert Watson, a senior environmental official at the Bank, came back to Washington to report on the negotiations.[147] With a packed gallery listening, Watson discussed climate changes from the time of the Spanish conquistadors to the present, followed by a variety of projection scenarios for the 21st century. He concluded that, without a doubt, human behavior was affecting the global climate. The pronouncement was perhaps the first time the scientific community had so emphatically stated its views in public on the link between humans and global warming. And, B-SPAN had captured it for the world to see.

In fact, as 2000 drew to a close, B-SPAN had become a cornucopia of fascinating exchanges on policies and issues across the spectrum of human development. The events themselves were wondrous. Wheeler and I hardly had to do more than email each other with "Yo, Spannable" for some were irresistibly "Spannable." The significance of the debates we witnessed the first few months confirmed our highest aspirations for the venture. The topics included:

- Saving the Rainforest through Poison Dart Frog Ranching
- Immunization: The Uganda Experience
- Reaching the Poorest in Thailand: Bringing Culture and Art to Children in Bangkok's Slums
- Tracking the Global Pandemic of Road Traffic Accidents
- Economic Valuation of Improvements in Air Quality in the Mexico City Metropolitan Area
- Stock Market Responses to Bank Restructuring Policies During the East Asian Crisis
- Politics, Growth, and Inequality in Rural China: Does it Pay to Join The Party?
- Establishing the Rule of Law: Creation of Constitutional Courts in Eastern Europe

- How to Avoid HIV, Smoking, Under-Five and Maternal Mortality, and Thus Live Forever
- Using Information and Communication Technologies to Empower Women in the Middle East
- Restructuring Small and Medium Enterprises under Russian Conditions

The speakers were equally impressive. The Bank received regular visits from presidents and ministers, as well as economists, academics, and researchers from leading international universities and think tanks. There was also room at the table for smaller research outlets doing field-level work in the Bank's client countries. B-SPAN offered everyone's voice an opportunity to be heard. In the first three months of existence, B-SPAN hosted a quarter of the 100 events held at the Bank.[148] We found ourselves scheduling more and more events outside our environmental mandate, as staff from other parts of the Bank heard about B-SPAN and sought us out. It was just as we had hoped.[149]

We understood B-SPAN would not be sustainable if it only covered environmental issues. We needed to expand B-SPAN's scope almost immediately. As noted, we began looking inward to see if our dissemination prowess would interest the Research Department.

Wheeler's investigation of moss hidden by rocks unearthed a deal with Lawrence Macdonald.[150] Macdonald, an early enthusiast of NIPR, understood—in a way his supervisors did not—that our website empowered the department by increasing its reputation as a resource of substantive research. In B-SPAN, he saw the power to leverage even more value. He agreed to appropriate $5,000 for partial coverage of weekly events the department hosted on a variety of research themes.

Our work, however, would not be without its challenges. While many of our colleagues were leaders in their fields, they were markedly less knowledgeable about the future of the web. One day, not long after we began covering research events, an economist asked me for a tape of her seminar. I explained the event was online and could be accessed anytime. Moreover, it was our policy to keep it archived permanently. But she needed a videotape, she explained, because she didn't know how long the Internet would last.

Fortunately, a few did. Quick to recognize the value of Macdonald's deal was Bill Easterly, an economist whose instincts ran counter to Bank orthodoxy.[151] He managed the Macroeconomics seminar series for the department, and was perfectly comfortable in leading discussions with odd but intriguing headlines such as "Growth Implosions, Debt Explosions", and "My Aunt Marilyn or Nonzero: The Logic of Human Destiny." Martin Rama soon followed his lead.[152] Rama organized the department's seminar series on Poverty and Applied Microeconomics. Since he was stationed in Paris, he quickly understood the benefit of a service that let him view events he could not personally witness.

It had been a successful debut. We were producing tangible products. Washington, however, is a town about processes not products. It has no manufacturing base. Cars, books, or clothing are not produced in Washington. Ideas are its commodity and trade. At the Bank, the products of its culture are also processes. Process is the nexus around which people coalesce and fight. It is often the first and final result, and something to which Bank staff is often beholden. But process had little to do with B-SPAN. B-SPAN was built with an entrepreneurial acknowledgement that the power of producing products that generated ideas was the most valuable process of all. We now had a product by which an organization, driven by process, was indebted: The product of ideas. That our system could still fail, we had no doubt. Territorial claims, underlying jealousies, hidden collusions, funding shortfalls were all weapons that cabals within a bureaucracy could use. For the moment, we still remained under the radar, and as 2000 waned, our reach was expanding rapidly.

5

2001

Our roles had solidified. Wheeler kept institutional players content or oblivious, sought funding, and provided strategic advice. Day-to-day implementation and making calls on the ground were my responsibility.[153] The delineation was sound. Wheeler remained deeply involved in his research, and still managed a team of economists with no relationship to B-SPAN. B-SPAN was an interesting and entrepreneurial venture, and surely one with significant ramifications; but he could only be as deeply involved as his other work allowed. He recognized and anticipated the project would be only as successful as I had the ability to make it. B-SPAN would therefore begin and end as a product of my ambition.

Having a smooth operation was the essential challenge for the moment. The technology was relatively new and we were new to it, so we learned as we went; and there was much to learn. The learning curve on encoding took longer than expected, and Kim was often on mission overseas, unable to troubleshoot our problems. Even more serious, once we did encode a tape, he was unavailable to load it on ISG's server. Adding to the difficulties, ISG had no backup for him. The percentage of our materials that was unavailable was building at an alarming rate. Clients would forgive our hiccups for the moment, but how long would they indulge us? Our job was not to find out. At one point, in frustration, de Nevers suggested drawing up a performance contract for ISG. We figured out a way to use the problem to our advantage. One day, Kim returned to headquarters. "Life would be easier for you if we were authorized to have direct access to the server," I suggested.[154] He saw the utility of the notion, and suddenly our logjam was broken.

With new events now going online, I focused attention on our ability to increase the volume of content. Our first-generation technology only allowed encoding of 26 minutes of video at a time. This forced us to segment events into several awkward sections, and multiplied the amount of testing of streams we needed to do. Means had to constantly monitor the process, clear her hard drive when it was full of data, and start encoding the next segment. To mitigate this problem, we decided to section the streams with each new speaker or topic. Means encouraged us to upgrade our antiquated system, so she could compress more volume for longer periods of time.[155] It was sound advice. I asked her to research a suitable solution for us. A few months later, when she offered her recommendations, we empowered her with our Nike spiel to "just do it."[156]

Instead of outsourcing key activities, necessity compelled us to handle important components ourselves. We had negotiated a reduction in server costs from $24,000 to zero, and had motivated ISG to purchase additional server capacity. Additionally, we were now able to post materials to ISG's server ourselves, something no one else in the Bank could do.[157] With Means in the fold, we could encode at minimal cost. She had even received free training from ISG. Our filming was being done at discount. With bargaining, improvisation, and perhaps some witchcraft, we had winnowed away a significant amount of our projected expenses.[158]

Wheeler ran new expense numbers for de Nevers.[159] Variable costs depended on the amount of volume we produced. Wheeler estimated we had the ability to generate 40 videos a month. This translated into an annual budget of $250,000, but our strategy was to get Bank-wide financing. If we could get four other networks to help, we could offer a full-time service for which the yearly bill for individual departments would not exceed $50,000, a small sum by Bank standards. As other departments saw the benefits the original investors enjoyed, we believed they would opt in as well, driving costs down rapidly.

Fixed costs for our salaries were, in fact, the variable in the equation. The Research Department was showing reluctance to finance the project or cover my salary which had been our Achilles heel from the beginning.[160] Wheeler appealed to de Nevers to budget a two-month extension for me while we sought alternative arrangements.[161] A few days later, de Nevers approved his request. March was the deadline to figure something out. We were, in an institutional sense, on life-support.

To adapt to the shifting tide, we changed the emphasis toward marketing.[162] Though public notice about B-SPAN had been made previously via one NIPR mailing and Ian Johnson's announcement, it was time to leverage what momentum we had generated with our maiden newsletter.[163] The database of subscribers for B-SPAN mailings originally had been derived from NIPR. But from now on they would diverge. New additions to B-SPAN's list would not be included to NIPR's and vice versa. However, since NIPR's mailing list of 12,000 subscribers was second only in size to the Bank's own newsletter dissemination list, B-SPAN was an offspring with pedigree.

Interest in B-SPAN, however, would rise or fall on its own merits.[164] We featured Watson's presentation on climate change; an Ian Johnson discussion about The Hague negotiations; the original environmental strategy interviews, and an event on illegal forestry activities in Cambodia. We were immediately flooded with congratulations from enthusiastic recipients. *The Scout Report*, a weekly compendium of newly discovered web resources for researchers and educators, featured B-SPAN prominently.[165] *The Lancet*, an Internet journal, showcased our launch as well.[166] The days that followed were spent walking users through the intricacies of streaming files, and fixing bugs that cropped up.[167]

Following the newsletter, de Nevers set up a presentation for her WBI colleagues.[168] We showed them the website, demonstrated how videos streamed, and documented initial traffic analysis and anecdotal feedback from enthusiastic viewers. De Nevers thought things had progressed well.[169] She wanted to lobby GDLN for $100,000 to help with cameras, studio time, and web maintenance. The underlying sentiment suggested she wanted WBI to maintain a dominant position. Wheeler, however, wanted to press vice presidencies and thematic groups around the Bank for appropriations. She asked him to recalculate our cost projections based on the assumption that the project was going to full scale (i.e., as a full-time Bank-wide service). De Nevers also planned to update Bruno Laporte, WBI's new Knowledge Management chief, on our activities. Laporte was to become a pivotal figure in the months ahead.

To solidify our institutional support, I launched a host page with de Nevers' picture and title featured prominently.[170] With Means able to post new events on ISG's server seamlessly, and create links to them, our site began to blossom with content covering a range of subjects and global regions. I was now able to spend less time fixing bugs and invest more time on reviewing tapes, writing summaries, and marketing.

B-SPAN started to enjoy the same creative epoch NIPR had during its early development. A plethora of datasets, and documents associated with events went online. An "On Air" banner was placed above available videos to give viewers a sense they were accessing a dynamic and changing site. We routinely changed pictures on the front page to highlight interesting events that came online. Substantial cross linking from event pages to Bank sub-sites generated cross pollination, and promoted the service with customers. We installed a rudimentary search engine, and added a "Did You Know" section to provide visitors with useful tips on implementing the RealPlayer streaming software.

It had been our hope B-SPAN could be free to anyone inside the Bank who wished access. Nevertheless, we remained a barebones operation desperate for revenue. We continually reappraised event pricing. The fluctuations were a matter of striking a balance between getting them to ante up and what Wheeler called "keeping the ceiling repaired."[171] He was obsessed with keeping our fee minimal. It was a smart tact. Whenever we could lower costs (our biggest expense by far was hiring camera crews), we passed along the savings. We were always a step away from disintegration. But we were convinced minimizing charges maximized opportunities to cover events while keeping potential rivals away. In time, building volume would make our system solvent. The logic was hard to refute but, as we would learn, not universally accepted.

There were certain trip wires we would not touch. David Gray, our former colleague from NIPR days, had become GDLN's coordinator for Latin America. He caught wind of what we were doing, and became interested in linking his video materials with our site.[172] He was sitting on a pile of cash. I toyed with the idea of having him create content, and pay us a fee to feature it on B-SPAN, but much of Gray's material turned out to be short documentaries and back-to-office (BTO) reports of Bank staff on oversea missions.[173] Despite the need for funds, we decided violating our operating principle of unedited public offerings was too great a sacrifice. I politely declined.

Still, we continued to make some sales. A short conference on exchange rates generated $450.[174] A second conference on intellectual property rights featuring senior research officials netted another $1,300.[175] We put the day-long event up so quickly, Wheeler bragged to Nicholas Stern, the Bank's new chief economist, about B-SPAN's efficiency.[176] With the rent not assured, we were looking for every edge we could get, and hoped the Research Department would reassess helping us. Macdonald lent a hand by putting us in touch with organizers of a conference on International Development Goals.[177] They voiced concern, however, about having it in the public domain. Wheeler and I conferred. We recognized some discussions might raise confidential information, and for legitimate reasons needed to remain private. We agreed the organizers could select which sessions would be public and which private, but stuck to our guiding principle that what B-SPAN covered would be uncensored. We viewed partial coverage not as selective editing, but good policy. The organizers accepted our proposal.[178]

Then a large cache fell into our laps. Dani Kaufmann, manager of WBI's network on governance, asked de Nevers if we would provide a platform for his video materials.[179] The offer meant a new line of content, and opportunity to broaden our reach as well as, importantly, access to $15,000 in his wallet.

Though I worked relentlessly at selling the service, B-SPAN's operational mantra of "flying under the radar screen" remained fully in place. One day, an EXT liaison sent us a note asking what we were up to.[180] Alarms bells went off for Wheeler and me. Fortunately, paranoia is usually more hype than reality. After providing information on pricing and logistics, we disappeared into the woodwork again.

Kaufmann's funds, along with the deal Wheeler negotiated with Macdonald, and seed money still available from de Nevers, were keeping the lights on. It also kept us away from more daring financing ideas. We had deliberated about finding external advertisers for the website—*Bank World*, an internal publication, had established this precedent already—or seeking subscribers from Washington's think tanks and NGOs.[181] Our concept was that external content providers would be part of B-SPAN's evolution, but it was a risky play this early in our development. For the moment, it was better to develop the internal terrain, institutionalizing the service before allowing the rest of the world to opt in.

Kaufmann's infusion came with an important caveat. Aside from a couple of small buckets, almost all our financing now came from one department. It moved us away from a Bank-wide financing model, and increased our vulnerability to be molded by WBI's agenda. But for the moment, existing today would allow us to define tomorrow.

Surviving allowed us to think of other adventurous ideas. Each Bank network had regular staff-only, sector board meetings on recent developments and initiatives within their policy niche. What if we could webcast these meetings?[182] And why stop there? The Bank's executive board of directors met regularly to discuss institution-wide issues and approve lending initiatives.[183] We dreamt of the day we could open these discussions to the public. But to even hint at such interest was akin to suggesting we had become marauding pirates. We kept silent, scoping the coastline for potential breaches.

Loading files on ISG's server, however, had not turned out to be flawless.[184] We were experiencing significant problems transferring files, and Kim was unavailable to help. Additionally, security breaches of Bank servers shut down our streaming capacity for extended periods. The deck kept shuffling. Our attention skipped from technology to marketing to financing, then back to technology. If B-SPAN was going to get where we wanted it to go, we would have to continually smooth the institution's rough edges.

Despite warnings, our volume had caught ISG by surprise.[185] They suggested building a new server, mostly for B-SPAN's use.[186] If so, it would keep us solvent well into the next year. But prudence suggested we adopt a wait-and-see attitude, and explore our options.[187] It was the era of the dot.com boom, and we were being wooed from all sides.[188] There were inquiries from SiteBurst, Escene, Mind & Media, Vodium, Virage, Streampipe, Digital Island, Akami, and others offering attractive interfaces, streaming capacity, and hosting platforms. But what if a vendor went out of business? This was a hurdle we did not know how to overcome so we continued to reject the idea of an outside vendor.

In the months ahead, I sensed ISG becoming more responsive to our needs. The appeal for outsourcing, though not terminated, waned. However, one service floated by vendors, that ISG could not yet provide, resonated. Our website used a traditional HTML format where Means manually updated pages. A San Francisco-based company touted a database that would automatically push content loaded on our website to other Bank websites. The idea of creating a new presentation, and having its link automatically generated on hundreds of other websites, was compelling. But using a California company to house it seemed impractical. We wondered if someone closer to home, and who knew us well, could provide it when the time was right. Forum One came to mind.[189]

Filming posed its own set of problems. Many of our "stars" had not yet adapted to having a camera in the room, nor understood the importance of speaking directly into a microphone. We fitted main presenters with wireless mikes. A second wireless was available for people who had questions. Unfortunately, since discussions were informal and spontaneous, participants often found it inconvenient to wait for a mike to be passed to them. Others simply forgot to wait. A couple of economists who managed the research seminars pressed us to have stand-alone microphones on the table, but this would force the camera teams to provide a soundman.[190] It was a cost we could not afford, and stationary mikes would also pick up unwanted sounds. These explanations were shrugged off. Nor were camera teams always reliable.[191] At times they went to the wrong room. Sometimes they didn't show at all. Moreover, a percentage of tapes were unusable because of poor lighting or inadequate sound. Cameras also remained our biggest expense; and while we sought further reductions based on growing volume, GSD would not budge.

Our effort had not gone unnoticed. On April 1, B-SPAN achieved cult status within the Bank. We were lampooned in the annual *Bank Swirled*, a tongue-in-cheek publication written by staff that poked fun at the organization.[192] *Bank Swirled* spoofed a Bank mission, characterizing it as Survivor 3 (after the reality TV show). Naturally, coverage was brought to viewers by B-SPAN. Wheeler and I were giddy, doing proverbial high fives by email. In Bank terms, we had arrived … as a comedy act.

In the spring, Wheeler scored a major coup when he convinced senior Research Department officials to have us cover the Annual Bank Conference on Development Economics (ABCDE) with residual funds left from its travel budget.[193] The ABCDE Conference was the department's largest event. It convened economists from around the world to discuss the year's key research. Days later, we achieved a second big success when the InfoShop, the Bank's publication outlet, invited us to cover the unveiling of Maurice Strong's new book, *Where on Earth are We Going?*[194] Strong, a senior advisor to then-UN Secretary-General Kofi Annan, was one of the world's most influential environmental activists. Wheeler called him a "real macher." And, over the summer, we would record our first (but not last) Nobel Prize economist, Amartya Sen, lecturing on the importance of preserving cultural heritage. The "machers" were starting to come aboard.[195]

B-SPAN was beginning to look like the daily webcasting service we had envisioned. By the end of April, we were averaging an event a day. I had become the master of a three-ring circus: Planning events; scheduling camera crews; collecting tapes; watching and summarizing videos; tracking down papers and links; feeding content to my web administrator; vetting web pages; and letting clients know their information was available.

But not everyone was on board. Early into our participation with Bill Easterly and his Macroeconomic seminars, he organized an event with IMF counterparts.[196] When our film crew showed up, however, they were barred from the room. Confusion followed. The IMF officials insisted their events were off-limits. Some in the Bank may have been willing to experiment with transparency, but its sister organization was not yet ready. Easterly suggested the IMF had a "secrecy habit," but I already had them on my radar screen.[197] I would revisit them when the time was right.[198]

At the conclusion of the fiscal year, we received a major break. Zmarak Shalizi, the division manager who had replaced Wheeler, was given a one-year assignment to lead a team of researchers working on the prestigious World Development Report. Wheeler returned to his former role as acting division chief.[199] It provided him complete authority over the division's budget. Since NIPR had not yet officially concluded as a product line, much of my salary could suddenly be subsidized with division funds. Reality also set in. We were a three-person team handling an unfathomable amount of work. For me, B-SPAN had become a very personal endeavor. I babysat every nuance and attended every detail. No decision, large or small, was made without my fingerprints. The enormity of what we sought to accomplish, however, could not be done by one person, no matter how competent or faithful to the task. I decided to volunteer an idea. "We should consider adding someone," I told Wheeler. He found Nick Bowden, a young consultant doing administrative tasks in the Bank's Social Development network. Wheeler wanted to split Bowden's time between webcasting and another project he managed. Having his feet in both allowed Wheeler to pay Bowden's salary with the Research Department's money. A meeting was arranged. Bowden was congenial and interested in what we were doing. I said okay. Our little team had grown to four.

At the beginning of June 2001, I sent de Nevers a progress report.[200] There were 26 events online with 70 hours of viewing materials. Twenty-four additional events were in production. Since our launch the previous September, we were averaging one-and-a-half events a week, and the rate was growing steadily. Discussions primarily covered the Environment and Research Departments, but had also branched out. The tone was optimistic. The huge Environment in June conference was about to unfold. It would focus on how to implement the strategy determined at the 2000 Forum by showcasing regional efforts, highlighting linkages between biodiversity and sustainable development with poverty reduction, identifying ties between climate change and Bank lending, and exploring closer partnerships with other multilateral organizations. We were again getting unprecedented access with coverage of eight events over two weeks.[201]

Identifying linkages between the environment and poverty was ambitious. It was also critical to the Environment Department's effort to become relevant with the lending side of the institution. To achieve their objective, conference organizers looked to B-SPAN to enact a key component of its communications strategy. Concurrently, we got a second feeler from EXT. Nicole Frost, who managed the Bank's most valuable Internet real estate, its home page, wrote to say she thought we were doing interesting things and she might like to feature some of our events.[202] Though we reacted with our normal trepidation, it was a pleasant note. Wheeler and I saw an opportunity.[203] The Environment Department's earlier call for transparency was unprecedented in the Bank. As part of our dissemination campaign, Frost agreed to feature B-SPAN in two places.[204] Though we would one day come to dominate the Bank's home page, this was our first taste. A B-SPAN link was then included in the Bank's online journal, *World Bank Today*, for the first time.[205] Witzel, who monitored traffic on Bank sites, sent a note shortly thereafter: B-SPAN had vaulted into the top ten of WBI's most active websites.[206]

Earlier in the year, Chinese officials had asked us to organize a conference in Nanjing on public information disclosure.[207] The Research Department responded with a grant for us.[208] Wheeler asked me to participate. As the mission drew near, ISG finally began an upgrade of streaming software on Bank computers.[209] Our handholding would not be necessary much longer. In one final session, we covered Vinod Thomas, WBI's Vice President. Some of his staff had trouble accessing his speech, and it elicited a flurry of worried emails.[210] A deeply ingrained "blame-avoidance" instinct within WBI quickly emerged. Someone questioned why the Bank needed this technology. A colleague immediately concurred. I weighed in to note ISG's upgrade was imminent, but a senior GDLN official criticized me for not consulting more closely with his technology people.[211] It was an unnecessary slap in the face, but provided Wheeler and me important intelligence as the alliance between B-SPAN and WBI began to tighten.[212] GDLN suggested we re-encode all our videos using a previous version of RealPlayer software.[213] De Nevers asked if I had a response.[214] I did: Silence. I left for China.

The objective of the mission to China was to preach the gospel of public information disclosure. It was exciting to consider the enormous potential transparency might one day have within this Communist regime. Yet, in a sense, the venture had already become part of my past.[215] The question going forward: Could I make transparency a way of life for my own organization? Just prior to the conference, my colleague Hua Wang had convinced the Chinese to pilot public information disclosure systems in a couple of provinces.[216] B-SPAN was also opening the Bank to the public in an unprecedented way. It seemed for a few short weeks that the sun was shining all over the world.

During my absence, Wheeler kept opening windows in the Bank. Consistent lobbying finally convinced the Research Department to ante $25,000 for blanket coverage of any of its seminars. Wheeler immediately offered free service to all.[217] Easterly and Rama, who had been enjoying partial coverage, quickly requested full-time service.[218] Soon, Beata Smarzynska, manager of the International Trade series, opted in as well.[219] The team administering the Finance series followed on her heels.[220] Wheeler's best pitch was saved for my return. He had secured funding for me, with a raise, for most of the new fiscal year—partly from de Nevers, and partly from reserve funds left in his budget.[221]

In August, Witzel ran a traffic report for us.[222] A year earlier, we had recorded 204 requests for web pages on our embryonic site. By June 2001, we were close to 16,000 page requests. It was a jump, but by any analysis still quite modest. Perhaps the stars were aligned, but only time would tell if B-SPAN would become truly valued.

Even if B-SPAN remained a modest service in mid-2001, we were still the leader of the pack. Wheeler forwarded an article of a new system being launched by the Massachusetts Institute of Technology. Called MIT-World, it would be a 24-hour, seven-day-a-week, video-on-demand system covering school seminars. The article said, "Before this idea becomes a reality, the project must overcome the technical difficulty of storing and then serving a massive video archive to a potentially large audience." Sound familiar? Wheeler asked me. Their price tag was a mere $2,500 per event. Wheeler suggested it was "nice to have MIT on our 'trailing edge,' eh?"[223]

The new encoding system Means purchased was installed over the summer. Tapes could now be encoded in their entirety, but ISG's server continued to be plagued with streaming problems. Nevertheless, signs of our progress were undeniable. Wheeler did a Google search and found B-SPAN had 700 links cited.[224] At the end of August, President Wolfensohn asked WBI to prepare notable examples of the Bank's knowledge sharing activities for his speech at the upcoming annual meetings. The GDLN official who had just rebuked me sent a note asking for a couple of paragraphs on B-SPAN.[225] I found the irony delightful and had a memo back to him the next day.[226]

A year before, mass demonstrations against the Bank during its annual meetings had paralyzed Washington and descended into violence. Expectations for September were that 100,000 protestors, five times the number of the 2000 protest, would gather. With anti-globalization activists hot on their trail, Bank and IMF officials agreed to a public debate during the meetings. An "informed public discourse of the global economy is clearly needed," said an IMF spokesman.[227] A debate forum was set up with a coalition of activists which included such groups as 50 Years is Enough and Jobs for Justice. De Nevers caught wind of it, and suggested to EXT Vice President Mats Karlsson that it be carried by B-SPAN.[228] Wheeler forwarded the exchange to me, saying with characteristic understatement, "Dis could be interestin' … remember joking around about the 'roving camera' from B-SPAN out there during the demo? Hey, we could be closer than we think!"[229]

Polishing continued. To prevent earlier snafus like the Easterly-IMF event, we decided to implement a new policy: Verbal and written permission from presenters would be necessary before we scheduled cameras.[230]

As volume accelerated, a proliferation of new topics went online. Our burgeoning success, however, revealed a weakness. All content posted was permanently archived, yet our backup system was dangerously antiquated. A server crash, a distinct possibility given the environment, might translate into a catastrophic loss for us. Means suggested purchasing a CD burner, allowing us to jettison the original tapes we stored.[231] Wheeler signed a check immediately. This also alleviated a tangential problem. With our growing popularity came numerous requests by event organizers and speakers for copies of videotapes. They felt they needed something tangible to hold on to even though our files were permanently archived. Requests quickly grew beyond the point where we could fulfill them. We decided to ask the camera teams to provide us with only digital tapes.[232] It would improve our efficiency by streamlining the encoding process; and since we no longer used analog files, we could shift client requests to GSD, which could copy videotapes for a nominal fee.

When our third newsletter was released in September, it highlighted the major environment conference held in the summer, but the breadth of offerings now included finance, governance, macro-economics, micro-economics, and trade events.[233] The size of the newsletter mailing list was also growing exponentially. Like NIPR, B-SPAN was accelerating under the weight of its own momentum.

The next day, four planes fell out of the sky.

6

September 11, 2001 was a world-wide revelation. Many of the Bank's staff came from the world's poorest societies, and they, too, were stunned by what had happened. But the development community had a fundamental problem of its own making if its leaders believed the poor were "know-nots" rather than "have-nots". As I read obituaries in the daily papers, a bitter anger grew. It returned me to a fundamental question. What was B-SPAN all about? The answer brought me to an understanding: Our mission—and the Bank's—was more important now than ever. B-SPAN had to do more than survive. If we failed, we would not fail ourselves only.

To provide comparison with Witzel's analysis, I asked ISG for its traffic data. In July, we had 700 visitors who recorded 21,000 hits.[234] In August, it climbed to 1,200 visitors and 43,000 hits.[235] The next month 2,700 visitors made 57,000 hits.[236] By November, we had reached 66,000 hits. ISG's data indicated B-SPAN's growth was outpacing NIPR's, the standard bearer of Bank websites, at a similar point in its history.

The numbers motivated another round of marketing. I went through the Bank's Internet infrastructure, lobbying dozens of website administrators to include links of videos we had about their subject areas. I also targeted the event hosts and speakers with mailing when their sessions went "live".[237] There was some novelty in being the star of a World Bank webcast, and I wanted to maximize the appeal that generated. Undoubtedly, presenters would forward my notices to their colleagues and students for further review, thereby enhancing the impact of any single event.

The tactic started paying dividends. Gobind Nankani, the new vice president of the Bank's Poverty Reduction and Economic Management (PREM) network, asked us to webcast his department's weeklong conference the next spring.[238] PREM Week 2002 was a signature Bank event, and a promising sign of our acceptance within the organization. With PREM in the fold, Wheeler noted Human

Development (HD) would be the only major policy network that had not yet contracted with B-SPAN.[239] By the end of the year, consistent and diplomatic inquiries had them nibbling as well.[240] We had a growing sense the lights would be staying on for a while.

Awareness of B-SPAN brought solicitations that we host video content already created by others.[241] It was a tricky line to walk. We could use the money and content, but this moved us in an uncomfortable direction. It was someone else's production, perhaps choreographed, and would co-opt valuable server space at a time when our own access seemed uncertain. Moreover, if we accepted one solicitation, what would prevent others from seeking wholesale dumping of their video files on our server? We backed away to pursue a venture squarely of our own agenda.

Our parameters had evolved. The time seemed right to try a quiet pilot. I started a dialogue with the US-Asian Environmental Partnership (US-AEP), a consortium promoting environmental technology exchanges between the U.S. private sector and Asian businesses.[242] They hosted seminars, and had an interest in our *Greening Industry* research. Hua Wang was invited to discuss the NIPR team's pollution levy work in China. A second event would feature George Frampton, the former chairman of the White House's Council on Environmental Quality during the Clinton Administration, discussing the World Summit on Sustainable Development that was to be held shortly in Johannesburg. I negotiated an agreement with US-AEP to pay our camera costs while we would subsidize everything else. Both events went smoothly, but the burden of arranging logistics for external events proved unsustainable for the moment. The precedent, however, had been set. B-SPAN's future direction, if there was to be one, was now very clear.

On the heels of Halloween, a sinister development arose. A WBI official requested we webcast one of their events, but to keep it private by making it password protected.[243] The request obviously violated the sanctity of our transparency pledge. We declined. But it launched a dialogue between Wheeler and me: Should we create a website for internal-only events. It was a conundrum. We were only interested in pushing B-SPAN to the limits of our capacity. An internal-only venue, separate and unattached in any way to B-SPAN, would not violate its transparency principle, but would steal time and energy from our agenda. On the other hand, to cede the terrain to someone else inside the institution might inadvertently create a dangerous competitor. I advocated we let the issue rest until forced to act. If cornered, we would then move to capture the territory, give the platform an androgynous name, provide minimal resources to maintain it, and do no marketing. We had Means create a mock website, which she code-named "Peekaboo."[244] We were now enabled to react on a moment's notice.

The year 2001 ended with reflections. The September 11 terrorist attacks reaffirmed a belief: No matter what sand bars might be erected inside the Bank, we would seek to endure. We had learned much about diplomacy. Wheeler and I applied the lessons liberally within the sphere of B-SPAN's influence. They began with our most important client, Michele de Nevers. Her satisfaction stood at the top of our agenda. We worked hard to make her feel we were completely responsive. She reciprocated by giving us the latitude to run the program with minimum oversight. She also protected our flanks from the bureaucracy's conservative instincts. In the wake of 9/11, she received an angry missive from a managing director, one of the most powerful officials in the Bank.[245] This knowledge sharing activity called B-SPAN was unknown to his staff. It seemed to answer to no one, he said. All was well, de Nevers calmly wrote back. A potentially dangerous encounter was averted.[246]

I worked hard to develop a second key ally: Polly Means. Her blunt manner concealed a warm personality, and our friendship grew. Her expeditious assistance was essential. I made sure she felt a sense of ownership in how B-SPAN ran and looked. She was encouraged to provide advice on Internet and technological issues, and often her views became our policy. While her official duty was to serve the Research Department, she was quick to handle our issues because of the loyalty we collectively developed for the endeavor. Means was integral to our success, and I never neglected to emphasize that point in my conversations with her or my correspondence with others. As a result, her devotion to B-SPAN from the beginning remained unquestioned.

I meticulously worked to develop three other instrumental relationships. I began by adopting an important principle: No matter the misstep, the most valuable outcome was not to assign blame or sidestep it myself, but to learn its lessons for tomorrow's show. It started with Sefik Cardak who managed the Bank's camera teams. We developed a cordial friendship, and would often humor each other on the trials of working in a large bureaucracy. Budget restrictions forced his department to rely on inexperienced contractors, so Cardak often worried about incurring a client's wrath over a camera mistake. When the occasional catastrophe occurred, I invoked my principle, focusing on what came next, thereby eliciting a loyalty he shared with few others.

Chongman Kim, who managed the Bank's video servers, frustrated us with his periodic absences as one glitch after another plagued our embryonic venture. Yet it was hard to be upset for long. He agreed to almost everything we asked; and when available, he was as helpful as could be. Whenever I spoke with him, I always started my salutations with a heartfelt, "Chongman, my man!" and he would reciprocate in kind.

Finally, there was the newest member of our team, Nick Bowden. The two of us were different in personality and disposition. Alabama born and bred, he was a cautious soul, and the underlying principle driving B-SPAN remained unknown to him. But he worked hard, and as the year waned, I began to rely on him to shoulder more of the burden of summarizing events and filling in on other miscellaneous responsibilities. I envisioned Bowden would soon become the main correspondent and writer for the system as I moved on to a new role, expanding B-SPAN's reach.

New achievements were scored daily. But money, remained in short supply. When 2001 ended, B-SPAN had been in business for nearly two years, and we were still walking a fiscal tightrope. Our accomplishments, however, had been possible because we were small.

Key decision makers at the Bank were mired in the importance of their work, so we were free to carefully define our parameters, and empowered to set precedents we believed critical to the future. De Nevers had insulated us from WBI's natural inertia. Wheeler, the Zen master, knew how to manipulate the institution at its margins, and had built informal coalitions to give momentum to our ideas. But in 2002, everything would change. B-SPAN's transparency model would face a series of pivotal challenges, bringing it to the brink of destruction.

7

2002

As dawn broke over our third season, we featured a rich and diverse selection of tapes. There was Mary Robinson, a former President of Ireland, discussing human rights; Nabiel Makarim on environmental governance in Indonesia; former White House aide George Frampton on the Earth Summit; social development in Afghanistan; the internationalization of Jerusalem, and more.[247] We created a series of new features on the site, among them a B-SPAN Personalities page to display prominent individuals we had online, and a History section with snapshots of previous home pages we had developed as the site evolved.[248] We added another feature highlighting several minutes from notable events, extracted as a promo to encourage viewing of the full event.[249] A page of links to organizations that appeared on B-SPAN was started.[250] In a sense, we were sailing before a stiffening breeze. But serious weaknesses remained. Piecemeal funding measures could not sustain us, and the mechanics of our operation—camera and streaming services—though improving, remained undependable.

As the year began we realized we had to rethink the technological side of the revolution. The server deal we had negotiated with ISG in 2001 was an interim arrangement. While ISG was not charging us, the server was not exclusively ours either. Though forewarned, ISG had not anticipated the volume of material we were loading on to their video server. Their model was designed for occasional efforts that needed hosting for short periods of time. We were sending them tapes daily, and telling them the archiving was permanent. The problem, however, was ours. By December, the original server was out of space. We were forced to stop adding files until a new arrangement could be negotiated.[251] Kim suggested it would be expensive.[252]

Our old colleague David Gray came to the rescue with an offer.[253] He was putting together a consortium within the Bank for exclusive use of a dedicated video server. The cost for any single investor would only be $5,000. We had material waiting to load immediately, and much more anticipated for the pipeline. The offer was an affordable lifeline. Moreover, we guessed we would end up using the lion's share of space. This assessment proved correct. When ISG had the server ready for use two months later, we started loading files in bulk.

To be sure, so many problems remained that we began to give them nicknames. The flood of requests for free service was labeled the "deadbeat" problem.[254] We worked on the "glazed eyeball" problem by jazzing up the website.[255] The "free advertising" problem of external vendors selling their services was addressed with disclaimers that we were not endorsing any product.[256] The "dollars for dumping" problem was characterized by delicate negotiations to dissuade others from using our valuable server space.[257] Then there was the "Magda" problem, named after a Bank official.[258] This was a serious one indeed, for it symbolized the dichotomy of the Bank. As many others have noted, the Bank's conservative culture evolves like a glacier, and B-SPAN sought radical change.

The "Magda" problem evolved when at a colleague's request, we scheduled coverage of an event; but when our camera team arrived, the hostess balked, refusing to let them film. B-SPAN had a two-year history of collegiality with her department's management, but she suddenly used the incident to encourage her colleagues to participate only in internal webcasting. We began toying again with resurrecting "Peekaboo." The solution to the "Magda problem," Wheeler told de Nevers, was to push fearful colleagues to stay with the public channel. In an aside to me, he noted the weight of bureaucratic momentum can stifle many good initiatives. Fortunately, it could work in our favor as well. Magda, motivated by the timeliness of her important work, was soon conquering new challenges. She forgot us like yesterday's lunch, and "Peekaboo" never saw the light of day.

Many Bank staff, however, empathized with her. Shortly after the incident, it became clear to us that many in the Bank felt uncomfortable with B-SPAN. I became aware of a conference sponsored by the Bank's Middle East and North Africa (MENA) region that I thought was particularly important for us to cover.[259] The organizers, however, were decidedly less enthusiastic. They were not comfortable having the sessions made viewable to the public, they said. I prodded. They parried. Our discussions went on for weeks. Finally, they declined. I was dumbfounded. The conference was about the growth of transparency in the Middle East.[260]

Contrast this with the way B-SPAN was viewed outside the Bank. Oxford University, for example, inquired as to how they could start their own webcasting station.[261] Could the notion of a B-SPAN spinoff be far behind, I wondered. I also started receiving resumes from job seekers, including someone working at C-SPAN![262]

Suddenly, our storm-tossed voyage took a new turn. When B-SPAN was launched at the beginning of the Millennium, it owed its start to a combination of Research Department brain power and WBI underwriting. During our two years of operations, however, WBI's leadership expressed no interest in us, and in fact, seemed unaware of our existence. All that changed in a day.

In December 2001, Frannie Leautier was named WBI's new vice president. She immediately wanted to know more about us. Leautier was a remarkable figure at the Bank. She had joined the institution ten years earlier, and had risen through the hierarchy with meteoric speed. Aided by a stint as President Wolfensohn's chief of staff, her ascendancy in such a short period was astounding. And, in a fortunate stroke of luck, one of her first Bank assignments had been as an infrastructure economist under Wheeler's management. She was our old colleague, Frannie Humplick, which had been her maiden name. Having her at the top of WBI's bureaucracy would prove essential in the months ahead.

De Nevers and Wheeler set up a meeting with her in January to demonstrate the service.[263] It produced a stunning result. Leautier enthusiastically bought into the transparency concept. She told de Nevers she had the leeway to spend funds to enlarge the system. De Nevers immediately suggested we cover any worthwhile event and forgo charging anyone for the balance of the fiscal year.[264] We could even hire additional staff if necessary. In bureaucratic parlance, we had scored a coup. After months of high seas regarding finances, there was a break in the skies. Wheeler extended my consulting contract through the rest of the year.[265]

Wheeler understood our window would not remain open indefinitely. He believed by ramping up quickly, momentum would work in our favor. If we could capture all departments and sectors in one swoop, they wouldn't have the courage thereafter to turn off the spigot to stakeholders watching their events. He began contacting senior officials throughout the Bank, offering free service.[266]

He considered the time it took to summarize each event as the biggest obstacle to rapid expansion.[267] I estimated each took about six hours on average, but the summaries were vital. Many visitors did not have the time to watch events in their entirety. Others had problems with connectivity that prevented them from accessing the streams. The choice, as Wheeler saw it, was either to shorten summaries or hire new writers. There was logic in what he said, but I counseled a different approach.[268] Perhaps, rather than increasing staff, we could assess how the current team might absorb added volume, and instead invest resources in new technology.

We increased Bowden's writing responsibilities, and I began looking at ways to improve our encoding system a second time.[269] We only had one line, and the encoding card we had purchased the previous summer contained unanticipated bugs. Camera teams also continued to film in analog and digital formats. A second line capable of processing both was necessary. We considered purchasing a portable system, but $25,000 was beyond our budget. My focus returned to improving our hardware and software components. Since volume was a looming issue, Means wanted to increase our ability to compress data, thereby reducing the encoding time.[270] Following discussions with RealNetwork, we settled on a state-of-the-art system that captured and compressed data in one step, and pushed out tapes at twice the speed of before.[271] We could also stream at different rates simultaneously. At $6,000, the new line cost the same as the system from the year before, but allowed us to corner the market against any internal competitors. Moreover, we also could reduce competition outside the Bank since the institution's scales of economy made us far less expensive. Once both lines were operational, we would be able to encode as many as five events a day.[272]

Another bottleneck we needed to address was the transfer format for video tapes. We were encoding the camera team's analog and digital tapes with an analog VCR system. Even when a digital tape was provided, we had to transfer it to an analog format, and then back to a digital file. To bypass the process, we needed a digital VCR. I logged on to my computer and found something compatible with the digital format GSD used. We purchased two to service both encoding lines.[273]

I returned to Forum One to develop a proposal for building a content management database—the kind described by the dot.com vendor a few months earlier.[274] It would replace our static HTML website. Witzel had developed one for Macdonald, who encouraged us to make a deal with Forum One so our websites could automatically integrate our videos with his research outputs.[275] Search and retrieval would be vitally important as we increased production. What caught our attention was the ability to automatically distribute our content on somebody else's website. The concept involved managing a generic host page where we would add new videos, placing them in categories we could automatically load as a link on to other websites. Theoretically, such a database could allow us, with one click, to change hundreds of websites. Today it would be the Research Department's site. Tomorrow we could capture the rest of the world. The synergies were clear.

There was one sticking point. Macdonald's template was housed on Forum One's servers. Our relationship with Witzel, however, was long and close. We moved to make a deal. The terms of reference (TOR) I wrote up for the contract noted B-SPAN now had over 100 videos in its permanent archive.[276]

The new environment with the sudden increase of cash flows elicited more interesting intelligence about WBI's bureaucracy. De Nevers had kept an open channel of communication to GDLN regarding use of their video services should gaps occur with GSD's camera teams.[277] One day a request came in to cover an event, but GSD was not available. De Nevers sent GDLN a note asking for help.[278] The response, received a month after the event concluded, suggested we consider hiring an external vendor.[279]

Leautier's checkbook allowed us to reassess the balance of our pricing structure. Wheeler and I ran new numbers.[280] Two-hour seminars would be free, half-day events $300, one-day events $800, and two-day events $2,200. The new pricing structure encouraged use of shorter, more cutting-edge seminars and research discussions rather than conference-length events. Conferences co-opted our time and resources, and these more formalized gatherings kept us from pursuing informal and spontaneous seminar-style discussions.[281]

This also led to an editorial decision. We fully summarized all events, but that could not continue if we hoped to increase volume. We decided to stop summarizing conferences, and only provide basic information on who spoke and on the general lines of discussion. We invited sponsors, however, to provide fuller synopses, if they wanted to invest their time. The philosophy behind the shift in pricing was subtle, but important. Pricing was, for the moment, no longer critical to keep the project going. Now, we could use it as an incentive to encourage staff to use our system as often as possible.

By the end of February, manipulating prices for longer events seemed more abstract thinking than strategic development. Just a month after Leautier's directive, our volume was exploding. In fact, we were turning events down because there weren't enough camera teams to field our requests. Traffic climbed explosively. From December to January, web hits jumped 25% to 79,000. Visitors rose 50% to 3,500.[282] We were closing in on a rate of one million hits a year.

The two months ISG took to set up the server for Gray's consortium forced us into the equivalent of a black hole in cyberspace. Without server space to load files, tapes were encoded, summarized, and stockpiled. It had become a dangerous threat to our credibility. I met with Research Department specialists knowledgeable about servers. They suggested we bring the activity in-house, but the learning curve would be vast. The consortium server arrangement was an interim solution. Something permanent was needed, and if ISG couldn't or wouldn't deliver, we were going to have to adapt accordingly. I corralled Kim for a face-to-face meeting.

"We now have a vice presidential mandate to go Bank-wide," I began. "We are no longer just streaming research, environment and WBI events. We are no longer small and we are here to stay. Server breakdowns and shortages are happening too frequently. We've been deflecting angry clients. But can we do this indefinitely?"

Kim suggested B-SPAN was now competing with services offered by ISG, but I corrected him.[283] "It's true", I said, "ISG streams and stores video files for Bank clients, but B-SPAN is a one-stop shop for scheduling, encoding, streaming, archiving, summarizing, content management, and content dissemination. There is no way ISG could duplicate what we are doing. Additionally, our event costs are being fully subsidized by WBI. We don't need to charge Bank users. You can't compete with a zero charge."

Then I produced a stick followed by a carrot. ISG could compete with us and pay the price when it failed to duplicate our service, I suggested. It could continue not taking us seriously, and risk the ire of senior officials who wouldn't understand why their department's content was not viewable. Or they could take us seriously, be reliable in the service they now provided, and get paid appropriately. Kim's eyes widened. He understood. Whatever unspoken battle his department had been waging with us was over. He agreed to build a server arrangement similar to one established with Gray. I agreed to pay his price as long as it was competitive with external vendors. I had left no room for doubt with our colleagues in ISG.[284] Yet, as it turned out, the greatest danger to B-SPAN was much closer to home.

8

Finally, the consortium's server became operational.[285] With the leak repaired, our dam immediately burst. Dozens of new events—from land use in Africa to education and employment for women in post-war Afghanistan, to development in Muslim societies, to natural disaster management—flooded online.[286] Our environmental roots had been left far behind.

The explosion of new videos elicited an interesting response. From viewers outside the Bank came the usual plaudits.[287] The view inside the Bank was decidedly less enthusiastic. We started fielding criticism. Some wondered why we would stream files when not everyone in the world had access. They questioned whether B-SPAN had relevance when many people in developing countries could not log on to the Internet at all.

The inability of potential users in developing countries to access streaming files was a problem we acknowledged. In many countries, the infrastructure to support high-speed communication lines was not yet available. Even at relatively slow speeds there could be problems. We, however, had adopted a philosophy taken from an icon of American pop culture, the movie "Field of Dreams": "Build it and they will come."[288] Regular checks of our traffic data showed viewers were coming, and in growing numbers each day we existed. This divergence of views highlighted an interesting schism between the Bank and its stakeholders. Bank insiders, uncomfortable with non-choreographed events, were obsessed with releasing perfect outputs. We believed people living in poverty didn't have the time to wait.

As we predicted, the advent of B-SPAN was creating internal debates and revelations for Bank staff. One environmental specialist asked if we could film events that included non-Bank presenters. A water sector administrator said her team was debating the merits of allowing external audiences to access their events.

Following a highly publicized split with its management, Research Department economist Bill Easterly left the Bank. His successor showed considerably less appetite for dissemination of the Macroeconomic series.[289] For the first time in the history of the institution, individuals were being forced to choose whether transparency was a core operating principle or a necessary rhetorical tool to pacify external stakeholders. It was a period of push and pull. B-SPAN had exploited a handful of opportunities to promote openness, and the longer we were in business, the more opportunities there would be to exploit. We hoped the cumulative sum of our success would bend the Bank's culture of secrecy irrevocably in favor of our direction. It was slow going, but wave by wave we were advancing.

Word about Leautier's support seeped through WBI's bureaucracy. Staffers managing a video conference on food security issues asked to have coverage online in time for a briefing with the vice president.[290] Their meeting elicited a statement from Leautier. She said she found B-SPAN valuable for the Bank's country-based staff which could not attend events in Washington. Then she added something else: President Wolfensohn's wife Elaine was also a frequent viewer of B-SPAN.[291]

The comments got us thinking. If the president's wife watched, the likelihood the plug would be pulled on us had declined markedly. Leautier's statements also noted the system's value to staff, not outsiders. It suggested the audiences we and the vice president valued might be different, but not exclusive of each other. For the moment, it was irrelevant. B-SPAN's security was not likely to be threatened by management at the top of the Bank's structure. At this level, occupied with the geopolitical forces pressing the institution, senior officials would either embrace us conceptually or ignore us completely. Rather, the danger, as we perceived it, came from within the ranks: Those seeking to co-opt resources to fulfill personal ambitions.

The temporary resolution of server difficulties allowed enough respite to daydream. In a note to Wheeler, I laid out an ambitious agenda. Upon installing the two encoding lines, we would place renewed emphasis on marketing the service internally. I would soon begin a campaign to get B-SPAN's logo on Bank sub-sites carrying links of our video streams. If possible, we would quietly begin soliciting external partners in the international development and Washington policy communities.[292]

I also wanted to purchase a streaming camera so we could leave the Bank headquarters to record events.[293] Newly developed cameras were now on the market that could encode and stream content directly to video servers, a technology that would allow us to stream content directly from camera to website without having to return to headquarters to encode tapes first. I began looking into specifications, and dreamed of exotic vacation opportunities. The terms of a permanent server arrangement still needed to be negotiated with ISG, but it was possible to use the momentum we now enjoyed to stream Bank events within 24-hours. We were on the verge of a startling breakthrough.

By April, B-SPAN had arrived at an important buoy. Means and I finalized specifications for a second encoding line, and started on procurement.[294] We moved the balance of a remarkable array of stored events into the public domain. In less than two months, we published seven newsletters.[295] A plethora of new offerings became available, such as malnutrition in South Asia, industry and country collaborations on HIV/AIDS programs, the cost of migration restrictions in China, economic progress ten years after the Soviet Union, and immunization efforts in Sub-Saharan Africa, to name just a few.

B-SPAN's home page now listed almost every Bank network and region. Those that were out, wanted in. Freed for the first time from funding shortfalls and technological restrictions, content volume continued rocketing. The Bank, formerly staid and insular, had been transformed into a flourishing garden on which B-SPAN was the window.

The progress was noticed elsewhere as well. An editor with the U.S.-based Voice of America wanted to disseminate our information to their network of reporters covering Asia.[296] The University of Iowa was running a technical assistance program for African universities, and wanted CDs of B-SPAN events.[297] "Yo, DS," Wheeler wrote, "just did my periodic visit, and the front page is looking good. Our only problem is that we make most of the Bank's web stuff look boring by comparison!"[298]

New traffic highs were recorded. Hits increased 70% from March to April.[299] We were closing in on an annual rate of two million hits. Visitors doubled. "This is what people in the development field have been waiting for," said one viewer.[300] Another called our archives "an amazing collection of resources."[301] A third said, "I'm quite impressed of your work in making webcasts available to us who wish we were in many places at once."[302] Another wrote, "We will be pleased to inform others in the Africa Virtual University network who would certainly benefit from this virtual library of information on development and poverty reduction."[303] A fifth viewer stated, "I would like to say how amazed I am by your website and the amount of information that is readily accessible."[304]

Viewers logged on from 88 countries.[305] They came from Harvard, Stanford, Yale, the European Union, the World Health Organization, the Organisation for Economic Co-operation and Development, the United States Senate, the U.S. Energy Department, NASA, IBM, Boeing, Daimler-Benz, Bloomberg Financial, and John Deere. They were all watching us. De Nevers was watching, too. She informed Wheeler she was going to ask WBI to create a permanent position for me to manage B-SPAN.[306]

Even when some hesitated, the new Bank transparency initiative provided powerful incentives to convert. One day, I learned an expert in Islamic affairs was scheduled to discuss the role of madrassas in fostering development in Muslim societies. Madrassas, schools that use the Koran as the foundation for their teachings, play a central educational role in some Muslim countries, especially Pakistan. In the aftermath of September 11, these schools had been vilified by many for spreading hatred about Western culture and fostering a climate that encouraged terrorism. I asked the speaker if he would like to appear on B-SPAN. But with the emotions surrounding the issue in the months following the Al Qaeda attacks on the U.S., he declined.[307] I wrote him again.[308] Because of recent events, much of the world had only one viewpoint of madrassas, I suggested. B-SPAN would provide him a unique opportunity to share another viewpoint. He reconsidered and granted permission for us to attend.[309]

Outputs were being matched by inputs. B-SPAN's four-person team was working at a frenzied pace. More than 30 events were covered in April, and May was just as torrid. The Bank's Environment Department contracted with us to cover their massive Sustainable Development Month.[310] There, President Wolfensohn spoke about the Bank's environmental strategy leading up to the Johannesburg Earth Summit.[311] Martin Indyk, a former U.S. Ambassador to Israel, addressed security and development in the Middle East.[312] Jane Goodall, the anthropologist, discussed biodiversity in Africa.[313] Maurice Strong, one of the world's leading environmentalists, suggested that changing government incentives and subsidies was the way to achieve sustainable development.[314] Herman Daly, also a renowned environmentalist and a professor at the University of Maryland, talked about redefining the sustainability concept.[315] The climactic event, however, was Jeffrey Sachs's address on the economics of sustainability.[316] Sachs, a macroeconomist, had become widely known for his shock therapy approach to stabilizing economies in Latin America, and aiding Eastern European countries following the collapse of the Soviet Union. Sachs called upon rich countries to provide large cash transfers to the developing world and debt forgiveness for the poorest countries.

"Poverty in the developing world will never disappear without sizeable transfers," he said in his address at the Bank. It was a powerful moment. I made a frenzied push to have his speech online by the close of the day. By the next morning, when we sent out a newsletter announcing its availability, we had proven it was possible to make B-SPAN a 24-hour service.

Wheeler was ecstatic. He characterized our coverage as the "second window on the Bank in full flower," and described what we had done as the realization of our dream.[317] Per his marketing strategy, he passed along the good vibes.[318] Leautier wrote that everyone who crossed her path said we were a big hit.[319] When our most prolific month concluded, Wheeler wrote me a private note. "Have we really done this? What an amazing resource," he said.[320]

Kim contacted me with ISG's server proposal.[321] They wanted $20,000 to license and install a system exclusively for us, plus a monthly maintenance charge of $1,000. It would allow 500 viewers to access our streams simultaneously, and would provide 100 gigabytes of space with the capacity to add an additional 100 gigs. 200 gigs of space would last a year, perhaps a bit more. That was acceptable, but the ceiling on simultaneous usage made us ponder. Knowledgeable colleagues suggested the proposal was expensive, and probably negotiable. I laid out the options for Wheeler.[322] External vendors offered smaller installation fees, but sizeable maintenance fees. Then there was the issue of storing files outside the Bank firewall, and bringing them back inside should a vendor go out of business. Still, we had finally brought Kim to the table. Now the bargaining could begin. Enough space was available on the server already set up for Gray's consortium to keep adding files for a couple of months. We had time to ponder.

Kim made the decision for us. A few weeks later, he made a second offer.[323] He would add 50% more space, lower ISG's monthly maintenance fee, and install the server within two weeks. The fiscal year was dwindling. We had money now. Once the calendar reached July 1, signaling a new fiscal year, it was not likely WBI would allow us to enjoy the same wealth. The offer provided all our storage needs for at least a year, and our files would remain inside the Bank's firewall. We took the deal.[324] As it turned out, ISG was working on so many other things they never did get around to charging us anything. It ended up being a very good arrangement for B-SPAN.

Forum One worked energetically to develop a plan for our content management system's integration with Macdonald's. Wheeler and I had been part of the Research Department for almost a decade, and understood the potential power of combining resources. As Forum One's plan became more detailed, however, we faced a strange irony: B-SPAN could become too closely entwined with the Research site. The implications were that we might evolve into a system valued by the academics but by relatively few others. Our goal was to make B-SPAN an institution-wide system that anyone would be interested in using. We began to fear implementing Forum One's plan would drive us in too narrow a direction.[325] I called David Hobbs, Forum One's developer, and broke the news: The contract remained in place, but we would need time to deliberate how the database would reflect our long-term objectives.[326]

Over the next few months, Hobbs and I continued to talk, meet and exchange notes.[327] The key challenge: How to create topic and sub-topic headings within the database that reflected our understanding of how the Bank defined itself, rather than how it had been defined by the Research Department. Forum One also suggested we survey visitors as to their country of origin, their work, how often they visited, and what they liked about B-SPAN.[328] Certainly, there was value to the information, but I questioned the importance of this data so soon in our development. We were still forming, and our audience was still growing. Organic growth might eventually lead to mistakes, but prejudging our audience might lead to larger problems. I tabled the idea.[329]

In anticipation of the traffic we would drive to his site following implementation, Macdonald asked about the size of B-SPAN's newsletter list.[330] My review found that at 12,000 subscribers it was 3,000 readers larger than our own department's list. The only two bigger lists were NIPR's and the World Bank's.[331]

Our experiences had taught us the culture of the Bank was reactive. I wanted to use our broadcasting system to push the boundaries. If the objective was to broaden B-SPAN from a reactive service covering events to a proactive service creating events, then we also would have to be transformed. I began looking for opportunities, and found one in Professor Samuel Paul.[332] Paul, the chairman of the Public Affairs Centre in Bangalore, India, was coming to the Bank to talk about public services in his country. He agreed to be interviewed. Unfortunately, with the whirl of activities on both our parts, we couldn't coordinate schedules.[333] I shelved the initiative, but with the understanding I would revisit it one day.

Just then a new opportunity, one vastly different but equally exciting, offered itself. Viet Burger of GDLN sent a congratulatory note.[334] GDLN's resources, he said, extended far beyond headquarters to included learning centers in dozens of client countries. These Distance Learning Centers (DLC's) were often owned by the client country rather than the Bank, and were created to facilitate distance learning between the institution and stakeholders. He wanted to know if we would like to advertise our offerings through the DLCs. The invitation suddenly suggested we might be able to bypass the bureaucratic quagmire represented by GDLN's central management that had had us hesitating. Our antennas started quivering.

I sat down with Burger and his colleagues Claude Salem and Mwangi Wachira. The DLCs were equipped with high-speed connections to facilitate video conferences between local stakeholders and Washington. Using B-SPAN's content as a way to entice them to visit DLC facilities was a win-win scenario. The DLCs would see an increase in the number of people using their network. We would increase viewers who had limited Internet access. Enthusiasm at the table began to build. We discussed piggybacking on the existing activities of local DLCs by advertising presentations at specific times, or offering a series of moderated discussions around a specific B-SPAN video. Burger and Salem wanted to charge to recover costs for the moderated discussions, but this raised a red flag with me. It might be appropriate for tailored products, I acknowledged; but B-SPAN was a free Internet service, and should remain so to people who wanted to visit the DLC to watch one of its files. They conceded the point, but we agreed to keep the concept of charging open for later discussion. We also discussed modes of delivery, such as the possibility of downloading files to servers in the field, live webcasting from the Bank, and making CDs for distribution. Questions remained, but our discussion was off to a nice start. Burger sent a note to GDLN's management, and Salem wrote DLC site administrators.[335]

Only a few minor adjustments remained with GDLN. Combined with the pending implementation of Forum One's database, B-SPAN was on the verge of a historic breakthrough: Wholesale dissemination of content using the Bank's existing infrastructure. Then, suddenly, three events unfolded in rapid succession that irrevocably changed the landscape for B-SPAN.

9

In the middle of June, Macdonald approached me with an offer.[336] The Bank's former Chief Economist, Joseph Stiglitz, had recently won the Nobel Prize for Economics for his research on markets with asymmetric information. Now he was returning to the Bank to discuss his new book, *Globalization and Its Discontents*. Macdonald wanted our coverage, but there was a condition.

Stiglitz had left the Bank under a cloud. He had been highly critical of the Bretton Woods institutions for their handling of the East Asian financial crises of 1997-98. He was then pushed out of the Bank for the public stridency of his views. The new book harshly questioned the logic of policies implemented by the IMF during financial implosions in Indonesia, Thailand, and other economies. Stiglitz would not be alone at his book launch. The IMF had caught wind of the event. It had pressured the Bank to schedule a panel discussion between Stiglitz and IMF Research Director Kenneth Rogoff, who would defend the Fund from Stiglitz's allegations.

The controversial nature of the event compelled Macdonald to impose conditions for allowing B-SPAN to attend. First, we could not advertise on our website that we would be covering the book launch.[337] Nor could we characterize the meeting as a "debate", but rather a "discussion." We agreed to his conditions, though soon after Macdonald allowed us to do some advance promotion. While B-SPAN could film and put the archive online afterwards, we soon learned the IMF had contracted with ISG to internally stream the event live to its own staff. Though hundreds would be in attendance, the Bank had not consented to a similar live stream to Bank staff. Moreover, while the meeting was open to journalists, the nervousness felt by both institutions over the explosive nature of Stiglitz's criticism—and potential fallout from the discussion—compelled them to characterize the event as "private." Its contents were to be considered off-the-record.

The Stiglitz-Rogoff "discussion" of June 29, 2002 proved to be a seminal event in B-SPAN's history.[338] It started in an ivory tower of the intelligentsia and descended into chaos. B-SPAN served as the fulcrum. The dialogue began modestly enough. Dirk Koehler, the publisher of the Bank's book division, said the institution was not afraid of providing Stiglitz with a forum for a book critical of the Bretton Woods institutions. To considerable laughter, Koehler reminded the journalists in the room the entire event was off-the-record. Our camera in the back continued to roll. Nicholas Stern, Stiglitz's successor as chief economist and host of the discussion, offered his hope the "debate" would be about issues and not personalities. It seemed a curious comment at the moment, since civility was the standard by which all discussions at the Bank took place.

Using a professorial tone, Stiglitz began by noting globalization had benefited some, but not all countries. Those that had benefited most had done so by using their leverage as strong exporters, while keeping their markets closed in return. He suggested special interests in the industrialized world were manipulating trading rules in the current wave of globalization. Stiglitz then characterized rapid capital-market liberalization as dangerous. The IMF's support of that approach, for example, had caused financial pain in Malaysia, and international trade agreements had reduced Sub-Saharan Africa's gross domestic product by as much as 2%. The IMF bailouts had not been effective, and had, in fact, benefited foreign creditors, he suggested. By raising interest rates during the East Asia crisis, the IMF had exacerbated the region's problems. The Fund, he believed, needed to be more transparent and accountable. Stiglitz then concluded that reforms in the IMF were needed.

Rogoff stood up. His tone was caustic.[339] He immediately suggested Stiglitz was so eager to take credit when things turned out well, he respected no one but himself. The book, therefore, was long on innuendo but short on footnotes. His ideas were controversial, Rogoff said, and the rhetoric was more suitable for a snake oil salesman. In fact, it was Stiglitz's criticism of the IMF during the financial crisis that had truly undermined the Fund's efforts. Naturally, the IMF sharply disagreed with Stiglitz on inflation policy and raising debt, he said, and noted President George Herbert Walker Bush once called such policies "voodoo economics". Rogoff asserted it was Stiglitz who failed to engage the Fund in a policy dialogue during his tenure as chief economist at the Bank, not the other way around. *Globalization and Its Discontents* was riddled with inaccuracies and slander, he said. Rogoff then went on to suggest that until the mistakes were deleted, the book be removed from stores.

For a moment there was a stunned silence. Then an uncomfortable rumble began to rise from the audience over the personal nature of the attack. In my almost decade of watching and participating in Bank meetings, nothing like this had happened before. I had the tape rewound immediately and raced up to Means's office. I buried myself in writing the summary, and had Means juxtaposition photos of Stiglitz and Rogoff side by side on our home page. By the end of the day, a Friday afternoon, the tape was encoded and summarized. We were ready to go.

Just as we were about push it over the firewall, Macdonald called. Nicholas Stern, the chief economist, wanted us to shelve our broadcast. A diplomat by nature, he had been shaken by the dialogue. Even though Rogoff had read a prepared statement signed off on by the Fund's top management, Stern called the event an embarrassment for the IMF. He was fearful fallout from B-SPAN's airing would exacerbate existing tensions between the Bank and IMF.

Suddenly, we faced a problem that extended far beyond the current situation. We were being censored. I protested vehemently to Wheeler.[340] "Stern is calling the book launch a private event," I noted, "but how private can it be with media and several hundred staff from both institutions in attendance?" People throughout the Bank were already asking to view the stream. If we couldn't show the video, it would affect B-SPAN's integrity as an honest broker of information. Failure to disseminate the Stiglitz controversy now might mean we could be viewed as another tool of the Bank's public relations strategy. Censoring B-SPAN also made a mockery of the Bank's claims of embracing transparency, which of course only validated Stiglitz's argument that the Bank did not. Finally, pulling this event would set a terrible precedent. Would the Bank start asking us to pull other events because of controversial content? We already had dozens of those online.

Wheeler agreed. I began looking for options that might be palatable to Stern.[341] Perhaps we could keep it off the home page, or not announce it was online, or announce it only to Bank staff, or make it available at a future date. But we were shoved into the untenable position of trying to define the terrain as a way of manipulating choices made by others. Wheeler was in a difficult spot. I was pushing hard, but confrontation with management was a no-win game. He said we should wait, and let emotions cool over the weekend. This debate would go higher than the Chief Economist's office, he thought. We agreed, however, there was one line in the sand we would not cross. We would not accept a request to edit the tape and present a muted version on B-SPAN.

On Monday, chess pieces began moving. Rogoff's statement appeared on the IMF's internal website. Macdonald called me. Caroline Anstey, Wolfensohn's chief spokesperson, wanted to have the unedited video stream put online for internal viewing only. We had it accessible moments later. For the first and only time in its history, B-SPAN produced a webcast for Bank staff exclusively.[342] Macdonald carefully edited the corresponding text to make it read as blandly as possible.[343] We were now halfway to where we wanted to be. Like the Zen Buddha seeing all players and potential moves, Wheeler predicted more would unfold. We just needed patience.

On Tuesday, the IMF took another step. They went public by contacting the media with a statement.[344] Macdonald called me again. The Bank now wanted the video on B-SPAN to be available externally, so the public would have the Bank's side of the story.[345] It was on our home page within moments. The next day the *Washington*

Post and *Financial Times* and a number of international media outlets ran stories on the sparring match.[346] In its article, the *Financial Times* noted that the Bank had a video of the debate available on its website, and FT.com had a link to B-SPAN.[347]

When the smoke cleared, we had gotten everything we wanted.[348] The Stiglitz-Rogoff confrontation, as controversial and contentious as it was, was publicly available on B-SPAN. It was a huge win for us, and we had even captured international notoriety in the process. Wheeler and I recognized, however, the incident raised serious questions. B-SPAN had been the Bank's pawn in a public relations battle with the Fund. We had been used, not as an honest broker of information, but rather to suit management's purposes when positioning itself before the public. Wheeler thought there was also a silver lining. We had been useful, too, he suggested; and by performing a valuable task, the Bank's ruling class would see us as an ally. Since we had helped the institution during a difficult moment, some chits had been collected. Perhaps now, Wheeler speculated, the notion of B-SPAN as a "back door channel" for disseminating information would gain acceptance among the institution's powerbrokers.

Just when we came up for air, a new crisis unfolded, and we were submerged again in turmoil. Two days after the Stiglitz-Rogoff event, the Research Department held a conference on Culture and Public Action.[349] It featured Stern, Nobel Prize winning economist Amartya Sen, and many of the department's economists and researchers. Vijayendra "Biju" Rao, a department economist, organized the event and requested our presence.[350] Everything seemed normal. With the drama of the Stiglitz-Rogoff affair successfully behind us, we had no premonition that this conference would turn into a litmus test for B-SPAN's survivability as a medium for transparency.

The second day of the conference—the day Wolfensohn's office asked us to make the Stiglitz tape available to Bank staff—Jeffrey Hammer, a Research Department economist, made an off-the-cuff remark about President George W. Bush.[351] A few days later, Rao called me. "Hammer's comments are offensive," he said. "They will embarrass the Bank if they become public on B-SPAN."[352] I hadn't heard what Hammer said, but I reminded Rao about our policy of not editing content. Rao said that the policy was fine, but we still needed to edit the comments out. I understood he was concerned about fallout, and wanted to give him an option he could live with. We would be willing to pull that section of the conference, I offered, provide it to him to edit as he saw fit, so it could be released on his website. As noted earlier, it was our policy to webcast only parts of conferences organizers agreed to make public. The rest of the conference could appear on B-SPAN unedited, and we would provide a link from our site to the edited file on the Research Department site. "That is unacceptable," Rao said in a matter-of-fact tone. He was going to have Chief Economist Stern order us to edit the tape for viewing on B-SPAN. Somewhere over my head a bomb exploded. In a moment, a request had escalated into a declaration of war.

The implications were immediately obvious. I phoned Wheeler. We understood if this situation did not resolve itself exactly as we needed it to, it would destroy all we were attempting to achieve. Lose this one battle, and the concept of a transparent service was over, and forever. Stern knew little about B-SPAN, and had shown no previous interest. His primary experience with us was the just-concluded tightrope act of airing Stigltiz-Rogoff. He had already expressed considerable discomfort with the notion of a transparent webcasting station operating within his domain. Nor would he understand the significance of forcing us to edit Hammer's comment. We had to resolve the crisis before this powerful authority had the opportunity to act.

We debated what to do. We didn't know if the Chief Economist was in Washington, but the moment he would weigh in, our situation would become untenable. If we were cornered into a yes-no argument, we were sure to lose the battle and possibly B-SPAN. Wheeler asked if there was anything on our website that referred to our policy of maintaining transparency by not editing content. There was. I sent Rao the text, along with a note restating our commitment to resolving the situation to his satisfaction, and in a manner consistent with the principles decreed since B-SPAN's inception.[353] There was just a small problem. The principles were laid out in an informal declaration of intent by Wheeler and me, with de Nevers' support. Now we needed a formal declaration.

Rao did not respond. Instead, his manager, Martin Ravallion, did.[354] He wrote Wheeler suggesting I was being obstinate. He was sure Hammer would agree to have his comments taken out. Wheeler provided me institutional cover.[355] Shaman was just doing his job, he parried. He runs the site according to the principles established by WBI. B-SPAN is their show, he suggested. We were just around to develop the system on a cross-support basis. It was a half-truth, but Wheeler was hoping to diffuse Ravallion's ire.

To me, Wheeler noted the significance of Rao having Ravallion pressure us, not Stern. The politics of asking the Chief Economist to participate might be weighing on Rao's mind, he thought. Wheeler had bought some time, but we needed something else. As a senior manager, Ravallion was better positioned than Rao to call Stern if we continued resisting his demands.

We began discussing the politics of involving Leautier. We wanted her to believe B-SPAN was developing in fairy-tale fashion. We loathed telling her—and de Nevers, too—about any difficulties or breakdowns. So, we didn't. When problems arose, we addressed them ourselves, going out of our way to keep bad news quiet. "Managers don't want to hear about problems," Wheeler was fond of saying. "They want you to solve them." This problem, however, could not be solved through diplomacy, hard work, or chicanery. We had never sought Leautier's involvement before. We wrestled with the pros and cons of doing so now.

Ravallion wrote back promptly.[356] "I don't think B-SPAN can survive without a little flexibility to deal with embarrassing mistakes," he said. "If this got out, the backlash could be very damaging. Nor do I think that the compromise to B-SPAN's objectives for removing one indiscreet comment is so great. It seems to be one thing to not require editing and quite another to insist that there is no editing when it is asked by the source."

After mulling it over the next morning, Wheeler decided to move preemptively. He sent a lengthy note to Leautier asking her guidance on the no-edit transparency policy.[357] The note acknowledged presenters and organizers had the right to pull an event off B-SPAN, but that we would not edit events we presented. The no-edit policy had been respected by all the principals during the just concluded Stiglitz-Rogoff controversy, he added. "By preserving this principle, we hope to maintain our credibility with our audience," Wheeler said. "But now the evolving issue with the Culture and Public Action Conference compels us to seek reiteration of the vice president's support to these operating principles." Leautier responded immediately, stating she was in full support of B-SPAN's transparency principle.[358] We were euphoric. "Viva B-SPAN," the Professor wrote me.[359] Shortly thereafter, he let Ravallion know of Leautier's reaffirmation of support.[360]

Ever the sage of diplomacy, Wheeler's note to the vice president named names. Though not vituperative by instinct, he wanted Leautier to know who the culprits were. A couple of days later, Rao called to say they would be glad to accept our compromise.[361] He asked for the tape so he could have it edited and posted on another website. I dutifully handed it over. Without B-SPAN's encoding equipment, however, he soon learned finding an alternative was neither quick nor easy. We had cornered the market. Two weeks later, Rao returned the tape. "After a further look, Hammer's comments were not so offensive after all," he said.[362] When commenting on a colleague's paper on HIV/AIDS, Hammer had said "perhaps the author sees the Mother Theresas' and Martin Luther Kings' of the world making policy, but I sometimes see the Mugabis' and Bushes', and the other Bush and Reagan and Nixon. Anyway, it's not obvious the right people are making these decisions."

Rao asked me to put the tape online in its entirety. Despite Rao's and Ravallion's insistence that he felt as they did about the comments, Hammer never did mention his opinion on whether the offending remark should have been edited out.

The funding given NIPR for its subsidiary maintenance of the *Greening Industry* report was ending in June. Wheeler had led a persistent campaign to keep B-SPAN wholly within the Research Department, but word filtered down management would move in the opposite direction. They would no longer provide any budget to support B-SPAN. This was a disappointment, but not a shock. The only prominent official who had voiced any interest for B-SPAN over the past two years was Macdonald.

But we were already too successful to die. De Nevers convinced Leautier to subsidize the system's full cost, but the arrangement came with a shift in management. Wheeler would remain in the Research Department, leading the Bank's work on environment economics. His formal involvement would end. We had enjoyed an unusually close working relationship for over a decade, an unheard of length of time within the Bank. It was a profoundly sad moment. De Nevers was also moving up WBI's chain of command. Instead, management of B-SPAN would fall to Bruno Laporte, recently appointed as WBI's knowledge and learning director.[363] June closed with Wheeler meeting de Nevers and Laporte to discuss the formal transition. Laporte wanted to come over to the office to meet Bowden and me.[364] Wheeler set a date at the start of July, and asked me if that was okay. I took a deep breath, and said yes.

PART IV
red sky in morning, sailor's warning

1

In the two and a half years Wheeler and I built and nurtured B-SPAN, we had made the simple idea of broadcasting Bank events to the world a reality. Our system had flaws because the institution was psychologically and technologically unprepared for it. Therefore, a gestation period was inevitable. Nevertheless, B-SPAN worked. It was applauded from every region on the globe because it brought the Bank closer to its stakeholders. It repositioned a monolithic society into one that was more transparent and accessible to the people it served.

We also knew this was not enough. The system had been built by flying under the radar, carefully picking battles we could win, and avoiding ones that might unsettle senior officials with the authority to terminate B-SPAN outright. Given unknown currents, we had charted our course carefully, and moved it from shoals to sea. Yet, the journey had only begun. We needed to go much further to create a global system where news and events were webcast both from the Bank and back to it.

And, we were startlingly close as well. The explosion of content, the spectacular rise in traffic and newsletter subscriptions, the new content management system that could spread our videos to hundreds of interested websites, the recent negotiations to disseminate content via the Distance Learning Centers (DLCs), the international attention from the Stiglitz book launch, and the reaffirmation of our transparency principle from Frannie Leautier, the World Bank Institute's (WBI) vice president, all suggested we could reach the horizon via a few more tacks into the wind. But the attention had come at a price. We were no longer invisible.

B-SPAN was much like a virus. We had entered the institution's body, and while many supported us, the notion of transparency was still new to others. The concept of openness made those bureaucrats entrenched in old ways of thinking uncomfortable. They saw us as more than just an oddity. We had become a threat to the way they conducted business and built fiefdoms. Transparency thrives by throwing back the curtains and letting the light shine in. Autocrats, bureaucrats, and technocrats like to operate in the shadows, leery of exposure that might reveal their operational methodologies. The question of whether we could function effectively was now known. The question of whether we would survive was not. The answer to whether the virus we represented would become accepted or expunged would come in the months ahead.

2

The day B-SPAN webcast Stiglitz-Rogoff around the world, we met with the new WBI managers to begin the formal transition.[1] Laporte arrived in Wheeler's office with Andrei Tolstopiatenko, the manager of the Knowledge Learning Pillar's Internet Strategy Team (I Team) and Hector Montenegro, an IT specialist. Wheeler started discussing B-SPAN's concept in-depth, and naturally mentioned the coup we were just then enjoying.

Laporte expressed enthusiasm for our project. He thought it was wonderful. Tolstopiatenko stood in the corner, behind Laporte, and said little except with his eyes, which opened and narrowed with the dialogue. Tolstopiatenko would replace Wheeler in the formal day-to-day oversight of the project and of Bowden, and me. Montenegro also spoke little, but did note archiving files permanently didn't seem realistic.

The comment was irksome. Why would he say that so quickly? The creation of a virtual library was one of our core objectives. "For the moment, nothing will change," Laporte said. There was no space into which to move Bowden, me, or the encoding equipment, he added; so we would stay in our current offices until the end of the calendar year. The meeting ended. Wheeler thought it went well. I agreed it was cordial, but the thought of leaving Wheeler for these strangers made me uneasy. We went back to administering B-SPAN.

Signs of change, however, became immediately obvious. I encouraged Wheeler to follow up on the purchase of the streaming camera we wanted.[2] We had missed the procurement deadline for the recently concluded fiscal year, but it would be invaluable for our development. Wheeler was supportive, but thought it best if he opted out of any involvement. "It might cause resentment with the new managers," he said.[3] We also learned permanent positions would not be created for B-SPAN as de Nevers had intended.[4] Laporte had decided Bowden and I would remain as short-term consultants on six-month contracts that would then be extended for the balance of the fiscal year, if the new managers approved of our performance.

Two weeks later, Tolstopiatenko called me. He wanted to meet for lunch. He was very interested in our traffic statistics, especially what was being recorded on Kim's video server.[5] We set a time. I felt apprehensive. I couldn't say why.

Andrei Tolstopiatenko grew up in the Soviet Union, a society where guidance flowed in one direction.[6] He had completed dual PhDs in mathematics and physics, and had spent the better part of a decade as an academic in Moscow. There, he acquired a specialization in educational technologies. He came to work for the Economic Development Institute, the predecessor to WBI, in the early 1990s. Colleagues thought he was extremely bright, especially with technologies. They also characterized him as ruthless. Peers often found Tolstopiatenko maneuvering on terrain outside his authority, and doing so effectively. He had been groomed in the Stalinist approach to management, and now that B-SPAN was under his authority, he was going to be the boss.

He started our meeting by asking about traffic B-SPAN generated. I discussed statistics compiled by ISG, but he stopped me. "This is HTML information," he noted. He wanted information on the video files: How often were they streamed and how long were they watched. Traffic data was generated for all WBI sites, and this information was needed to complete his monthly reports, he said. Instead of pulling data off ISG's server, he wanted Kim to automatically push the information to him.

"Just a glance at our trends shows things are going well," I offered. "We're just starting. Big numbers will come soon." But he was only interested in the video data. The rest of what we were doing seemed a distraction. He also wanted to see the terms of reference we had developed for the Forum One database. "It is unrealistic to keep archives indefinitely," he continued. "B-SPAN needs to be incorporated into WBI's business model. I need to know how much server space is available since WBI events will now become B-SPAN's priority." Then, he added, B-SPAN would no longer subsidize the costs of seminar events. In one fell swoop, he was shifting B-SPAN's direction on a number of fronts.[7]

I took a deep breath. I told him I would try to get Kim to set up an automatic push of video data to his computer. He also asked me to set up a meeting between Montenegro and Means to review our encoding operation.[8] The meeting was over, but Tolstopiatenko's questions kept reverberating in my head. He had this habit of narrowing his eyes into a squint whenever I spoke, as if listening especially hard for weaknesses. My apprehension grew.

I mentioned my uneasiness to Wheeler, who suggested I send good news anytime it arrived. Operation Feel Good, as we dubbed it, was launched immediately.[9] For the opening salvo, I forwarded Tolstopiatenko a collection of comments from viewers who expressed their appreciation of B-SPAN.[10]

Administration of B-SPAN continued for the moment without change. I learned Hernando de Soto, an economist of substantial influence, was giving a presentation at the Bank. We made arrangements to cover him.[11] With our plans already in place, we received a request by Caroline Anstey, Wolfensohn's spokesperson, to cover de Soto.[12] This raised a concern. Had the Stiglitz affair put us so squarely on EXT's radar they now felt comfortable telling us what to cover? We had always had the latitude to move in any direction we believed appropriate. It was possible a dangerous battlefront was opening. Our approach all along had been to adopt the great Chinese militarist Sun Tzu's philosophy of possessing terrain before the enemy understood its value. We were already covering de Soto, so there was no need to respond to Anstey. But on the deeper question we would have to wait for further evidence. EXT, however, operated the way the rest of the Bank did, running from one crisis to the next. In the months ahead, we were fortunate. No other high-profile events took place, and as with others, we disappeared like the setting sun from EXT's view.

The de Soto event was a good one.[13] He had written several influential books, including *The Mystery of Capital: Why Capitalism Triumphs in the West and Fails Everywhere Else*. He began by noting entrepreneurs flourish in the West rather than the developing world because Western societies established methods by which people could trust one another. The basis of such trust was legal documents which identified wealth and ownership. These tools allowed capital markets to grow.

"Instead of measuring poverty by how many people live on $2 a day or less," de Soto said, "the Bank should measure how much of the world is covered by acceptable standards of law." Much of the developing world, he suggested, owns and operates "dead capital," i.e. capital generated outside the law. De Soto believed dead capital far exceeded foreign investments and developmental lending. He encouraged the Bank to reassess the way it measured poverty.

We had the event online the next day. EXT's internal web-based news service, *World Bank Today*, ran a story with a link to our video. It was the second time we had partnered with them. A couple days later, I sent out our second newsletter of the month with de Soto as the main feature. Shortly thereafter, the de Soto webcast appeared on the Bank's home page. My hope of having B-SPAN's icon permanently on the home page was growing. Though we had no way of knowing it then, in the months ahead the relationship with key EXT counterparts would prove to be a lifeline for B-SPAN in thunderous seas.

Kim agreed to automatically push data from his video server.[14] Tolstopiatenko wrote back minutes later. He wanted the data immediately, going back to January.[15] I noticed my new supervisor had a habit of characterizing all his requests as "urgent." The next day, at the weekly staff meeting of the I Team, Tolstopiatenko presented more interesting dictums.[16] He repeated the assertion B-SPAN would align its business model to meet WBI's needs. "B-SPAN's primary audience should be Bank staff, not viewers in the developing world," he suggested. B-SPAN's budget would be very tight. Therefore, short-term concerns would take precedence over long-term considerations. Revenues we generated from conferences would not be enough, so we must begin charging the full costs of our services for seminar events, he said. "The video traffic data," he added, "would be useful in analyzing which files are being watched and how to target B-SPAN's coverage." Montenegro added that files not streamed enough warranted removal from the video server.

Here, I decided to probe, testing a modest defense. "One of the key operating principles B-SPAN offers the public is a virtual library of development discussions," I noted. "When a visitor comes to B-SPAN to access a tape, they will also find numerous other videos available on the same issue. Just because I'm not interested in reading Tolstoy today, doesn't mean I should take it off the shelf since I may wish to read it tomorrow."

Tolstopiatenko remained unconvinced by the analogy. Perhaps he did not like Tolstoy. "We will prepare surveys to study our audiences so as to target demand," he said.

"The filming quality of events is unsatisfactory," Tolstopiatenko continued. "B-SPAN's informality is a weakness. Productions should take on a stage appearance." He wanted us to identify locations with optimal lighting, and then push event organizers to use those rooms. "Portable lights should be brought in if necessary," he added.

I knew the Bank's penchant for making public information "perfect" had just appeared on stage as well. Bank staff was just becoming familiar with having a camera standing unobtrusively in the back of the room. A "lights, camera, action" atmosphere would quash the spontaneity of the discussions, and people would be frightened into sanitizing everything they had to say.

The I Team's manager was not finished. "The website is not acceptable either. It needs to be identical with the WBI template." He wanted Forum One's database development halted immediately.[17] Tolstopiatenko closed the meeting with a final reiteration. "B-SPAN will begin to focus on WBI's needs rather than the Bank's," he said.

By the end of the day, Tolstopiatenko and Montenegro had disseminated a draft work program for B-SPAN.[18] The meeting had left me stunned. The memo codified my alarm. We may have been born a knowledge sharing venture, but the note said B-SPAN would become integral to WBI's Learning Portal. This suggested a radical alteration. The share of WBI events would increase, the new manager wrote, and more events would be done in GDLN studios, and significant charges would be imposed. The website would be revamped to conform to WBI's template. ISG's video server data would determine if an event was archived or deleted. Moreover, videos would be edited and converted into new products for WBI's pedagogical activities. Tolstopiatenko's draft strategy represented a shocking reversal of all Wheeler and I had built.

Though Wheeler was no longer a part of the project, I was determined to keep him involved as an informal presence. It was a role he was willing to play. Tolstopiatenko's determination to change the fee structure and archiving policy would have a terrible impact on B-SPAN, I told him.[19] Billing task managers would cause many to opt out at a time when they were first becoming familiar with the service. Raising revenue at this point in our development was not nearly as important as generating content, growing a client base within the Bank, and an audience outside it. Tolstopiatenko was unmoved by the revenues raised by conferences, but there were options. We could renegotiate our rate with GSD, raise our conference charges, limit the volume of events we covered (though I considered this highly undesirable), encourage event organizers to use GDLN studios (though I considered this impractical), and purchase the streaming camera which would pay for itself quickly from the savings of not using GSD.

Evaluating video traffic so as to make judgments about archiving, I believed, was another mistake. We were still developing, and essentially unknown to the outside world. Many Bank staff was also not aware of us yet. We needed prolonged exposure before we could start analyzing our audience intelligently. Also, how could we know what our audience would find interesting? How many people would have found an event on madrassas worth their time before September 11? What was not consequential today might be critical for people to watch tomorrow. We had also promised clients and audiences our files would be permanently archived. If this promise evaporated, then perhaps our credibility would as well.

Tolstopiatenko's position on server archives suggested something more than a concern about budget constraints. Savings that would result from removing files from our archives would be marginal at best. The cost of storage space was also declining rapidly as the technology advanced. If viewers couldn't find an event on our server, then we would need to provide them a CD. The time and labor needed for providing CDs was far more expensive than housing a video file on a server. Additionally, what sort of explanation were we going to provide our Bank colleagues whose events no longer existed? Before Tolstopiatenko became supervisor, we had finally secured a server arrangement with Kim for almost 300 gigs of storage space. This amount of space was enormous. We didn't have a storage problem, unless of course, the new manager had ideas on how to use the space that didn't involve B-SPAN. I didn't have the answer to that, but I was listening to him carefully. Tolstopiatenko was emphasizing the need to incorporate B-SPAN into WBI's business model. He was saying B-SPAN needed to be reassembled to package and promote WBI programs.

This was going in the wrong direction. I needed to do something to stop it before it went too far. I sent viewer commentaries on

B-SPAN again to Tolstopiatenko but also copied Laporte.[20] Then, I ran into Jonathan Maack, a Bank staffer in the Social Development unit. Maack had high praise for our coverage of Stiglitz-Rogoff. I asked him to send me an email with his thoughts. He agreed. "It was courageous and smart of the Bank to go forward with this strategy. The organization showed its commitment to transparency and allowed outside viewers to form their own opinions rather than relying on the media's spin of the events. All of the people to whom I sent the link were impressed that it was available," he said.[21] I forwarded the note to both managers.[22] Operation Feel Good was well under way.

When the de Soto discussion became available, Tolstopiatenko wrote me it had "great learning potential for use in corresponding WBI courses."[23] But, I felt I could confront him only so far. The key, I believed, was to maintain an alliance with Wheeler and de Nevers that would provide me access to an informal power structure of key B-SPAN stakeholders. They were more influential with Leautier than either Tolstopiatenko or Laporte, and could mitigate efforts to change B-SPAN's direction. Wheeler forwarded Maack's note to de Nevers and alerted her to the growing friction.[24]

The Knowledge and Learning Services division was a newly formed unit in the Global Knowledge Department of WBI.[25] Laporte, as its head, called for a retreat where new members could learn about each other's work.[26] He asked me to make a presentation. I sensed an opportunity.[27] If I could lay out a strategic vision with a grounded perspective, then perhaps I could alleviate growing misconceptions on Tolstopiatenko's part, as well as help others understand what we were doing.

Laporte asked me to sit next to him. Then, I began.[28] "A couple of years ago, tens of thousands of people, angry about enduring poverty in the developing world, angry about macroeconomic policies of institutions such as the World Bank, coalesced into what we now call the anti-globalization movement. And at the core of their frustration was the notion that these institutions were places where PhDs gathered in a room, closed the door, discussed issues affecting the fate of millions, came to a decision, opened up the door, and announced to the world what had been decided.

"We realized the time was right to open those doors, and let the world see what was actually discussed and debated at the World Bank. So we created B-SPAN. At its core, B-SPAN was started with a few simple, but fundamentally important principles. First, it would be a transparent, open window on Bank activities and discussions, which would be uncensored and unedited. That meant if something controversial was said or someone was critical of the Bank, we would not edit it out of the broadcast. This would assure B-SPAN's audience of thc authenticity of what they were viewing, and allow them to trust what they watched was not being molded for spin control or to disseminate a 'message'. Second, B-SPAN would be a free service, because its medium for broadcasting was the Internet. We knew the heart of our audience would not be World Bank staff, but rather the millions of people in our client countries, many of them quite poor, desperate for the latest information and thinking on development issues. Toward that end, we use free software that allows viewing of video/audio files on the Internet. Our third principle was that B-SPAN would serve as a virtual library, a permanent archive of videos on development. This would allow visitors to come to B-SPAN for a particular selection, and see a range of videos on similar issues, to provide them an impetus to generate new ideas. We also knew development issues which were not high-profile today, might well be some time in the future; so a quick and easily accessible archive would be essential for that knowledge dissemination.

"In the past two years, many people have come to us and asked 'Is B-SPAN a technology?' and we have said, 'No.' They have come to us and asked, 'Is B-SPAN a website?' and we have said, 'No.' We tell them B-SPAN is a broadcasting system that broadcasts information, ideas, and news—just as a television station broadcasts information, ideas, and news; just as a newspaper broadcasts information, ideas, and news, or a radio station, or a news magazine. Only B-SPAN uses this new medium of the Internet to broadcast."

I also noted B-SPAN wanted to be a full partner in the department's activities, packaging events in their course materials and training modules, attracting stakeholders into GDLN facilities by disseminating content through their network, and allowing staff in global offices to create content and send it back to B-SPAN.

When I was done, Laporte praised the service as a "wonderful initiative." Throughout the day, people called the concept inspirational.[29] Tolstopiatenko seemed to have a slightly different take. He glared at me when I had finished talking, and left the retreat moments later.[30]

Things were moving quickly. Wheeler and I discussed finding a mechanism to insulate me from Tolstopiatenko. We decided to create an advisory committee for B-SPAN. It would consist of senior officials who would report to Leautier.[31] Our objective was to eliminate unwise policy decisions Tolstopiatenko might seek to deploy. Wheeler raised it with de Nevers, and she broached it to Karin Millet. Millet, the new manager of the Global Knowledge Pillar and Laporte's direct supervisor, was supportive. She sent Laporte a note, and he responded that it was a terrific idea.[32] For tactical reasons, we never suggested my inclusion. That allowed us to eliminate Tolstopiatenko from consideration as well.[33] The committee agreed to meet in September, following the summer break.[34]

My counterpart was also maneuvering. He sent Laporte his draft work strategy, and stated I had been one of its drafters.[35] This was designed to give Laporte the impression I fully supported the profound changes Tolstopiatenko called for.

He upped the ante immediately. At the next I Team meeting, he announced B-SPAN would begin a new product line showcasing WBI's training materials and learning courses.[36] The pilot for the new line would be an edited tape of a WBI workshop.[37] Wheeler responded adroitly. He suggested we create a box on the website that identified these tapes as edited products offered by WBI.[38] The goal was to make the distinction so obvious that our audience would know the additional products were not part of B-SPAN's core service. We decided to call the concept WBI Presents. I suggested allowing Tolstopiatenko to move ahead with his pilot. When it came to fruition, we could then inform him it violated the vice president's edict. It would squeeze our new adversary into a corner. It also had the further benefit of allowing him to define the outcome rather than us forcing the issue.

Traffic information remained a contentious issue as well. The I Team wanted us to chart data from archives we had been collecting from WBI's Finance Pillar.[39] This request was misguided. Our audience was generic. We weren't making any particular effort to market finance issues; and if the traffic wasn't strong in this area, I didn't want it used as a precedent for taking down files.[40]

Tolstopiatenko sensed the opposition to his proposals, and my speech at the retreat had had minimal effect on him. As far as he was concerned, he was the owner of the system. His strategy to align B-SPAN to meet WBI's needs would go forward. He began pushing harder on the pilot to have B-SPAN webcast edited materials. But he also understood he did not know enough about what we did, and how we worked, to undertake drafting a formal strategy by himself. He asked me to write a new draft work program for the current fiscal year.[41] I realized he would view anything I wrote as a yardstick for whether I would bend to his will. As of yet, no one had expressed interest in helping develop the program, but a clear determination to use our resources to market pedagogical activities and products had become obvious. I now envisioned that my draft strategy version could serve as a second and more valuable opportunity to define the program and set the parameters for our formal integration.

I decided to draw some lines in the sand. An excuse was needed to delay Tolstopiatenko from forcing edited products online. For the moment, Means controlled access to our video server. I told him no new products could go online until a formal strategy had been drafted, negotiated, and agreed upon. I assumed Laporte had informed Tolstopiatenko of the proposal for an advisory committee. I also sensed Tolstopiatenko wanted to implement his initiatives before the committee convened in September. He wanted the draft immediately.[42] My deadline was a few days hence. I closed my door and, without answering the phone for two days, began to write.

The document I created was comprehensive, describing all our activities, and addressing the proposals Tolstopiatenko had put forth within the context of our original mandate.[43] It allowed me, for the first time, to define the battleground.

I positioned traps throughout the draft. The opening line announced B-SPAN was invented to provide public viewing of Bank policy dialogues in a transparent and unedited format. Moreover, the primary audience was not Bank staff, but external stakeholders. Bank personnel who could not attend events were important, but secondary. I added B-SPAN would be a resource for WBI's knowledge and learning activities where appropriate, meaning as long as it was within our mandate.

I divided the draft strategy into several subjects: Website refinement; technology; content; traffic and marketing; WBI knowledge and learning portal issues; and budget. Knowing Tolstopiatenko's desire to have our site look like every other WBI site, I wanted to retain our unique character. I emphasized the importance of our branding efforts to make B-SPAN identifiable as a transparent window on the Bank. Audience recognition of our product line would be critical, especially in light of Tolstopiatenko's agenda to add learning products. Here was a marker for my adversary. If he blurred the product lines and diluted the public's understanding of what we did, he would be responsible for undermining our mandate.

This was followed by a logical conclusion: Refinement of B-SPAN's website could include WBI's pedagogical products, but it would need to be clear they were different, additional, and separate offerings. Once both sides agreed to this premise, then WBI's products could be added immediately. There was just one hitch. There were no new products yet available for Tolstopiatenko to add. They would have to be created; and it would be time consuming, and probably expensive. So, I added a twist. The burden of creating new products would rest with Tolstopiatenko and his shop. We would be willing to provide oversight, but only for purposes of quality control. Since the I Team already had a host of other burdens, I knew creating these products was problematic. I also added a point about halting implementation of Forum One's database. It was complete and ready for

B-SPAN's use. The database would also help identify user interests, something Tolstopiatenko desired. He had mentioned substituting another database he planned to create. If he wanted to kill the Forum One system, then his would have to be operational immediately. It would be another burden for the I Team.

Keeping technological considerations in mind, my goal was to keep our system moving forward, and pushing out content to our audiences. Improvements and refinements were fine, as long as the headaches fell on the I Team. For example, if Tolstopiatenko wanted B-SPAN's videos synchronized with the presenter's PowerPoints as he had stated, his team should be responsible for building a program that functioned quickly and effectively. I knew from an exercise we did for Dani Kaufmann, WBI's governance expert, the previous year, it would be no small feat.[44]

I made what appeared to be a concession to Tolstopiatenko; but it was something Wheeler and I recognized would benefit our service, and reinforce our no-edit mandate. We would adopt indexing of content, breaking videos at logical points so viewers did not have to stream everything if they were only interested in a particular section.[45] Tolstopiatenko had talked repeatedly about the poor quality of B-SPAN's recordings. This seemed a useful place to offer an olive branch that we were willing to work together, especially since the problems were fixable. We would draft shooting, audio, and lighting guidelines (not mandates) for GSD to follow. We would also try to identify ideal locations for events to be held, and encourage organizers to conduct their seminars in those rooms. We had already tried and failed with this, but there was no need to argue its likelihood, for it was another place where I could say I said "yes."

With regards to our encoding operation, I kept filling the bucket with sand. We had a system that worked well. If there was material the I Team wished to add for WBI Presents, B-SPAN didn't have the capacity. The I Team, which also had encoding capabilities, would have to do it themselves. Finally, on the subject of servers, I made two points. I reiterated B-SPAN's core principle: Video archives were permanent, and I noted our space was for future B-SPAN events. Tolstopiatenko would need to negotiate his own server arrangement with ISG to house his materials. A trap was set here. To house his files on B-SPAN's server would again violate our no-edit policy. I sought to soften the sting as well. The cost for server space was dropping continually, I said. Finding another affordable arrangement should be no big deal.

While Tolstopiatenko had made no overt suggestion he wanted to orchestrate content on B-SPAN, I decided to co-opt the terrain nevertheless.[46] We would manage it. His repeated forays about our traffic strongly hinted he wanted to use weaknesses as an excuse to remove our archives from B-SPAN's server and replace them with his pedagogical content. It was mandatory to undermine this effort with a reasonable argument.

I attempted this by acknowledging the need for a better understanding of traffic data to identify our audience and their tendencies, but I also pointed out our traffic was growing steadily. We were only just tapping our potential. WBI's audience of officials and academics in developing countries numbered in the thousands. B-SPAN's potential audience was six billion, the vast majority of whom had never accessed the Internet. I also noted the audience for WBI's course and learning materials differed dramatically from B-SPAN's. Though these audiences weren't mutually exclusive, they were not the same. To re-engineer B-SPAN to serve WBI's audience would negate B-SPAN's usefulness. Given these parameters, traffic analysis and viewer surveys should be seen as useful in identifying audience interest and marketing opportunities rather than limiting content.

The document closed with a discussion of budget issues. I stressed the importance of keeping seminar-length events free to event hosts. Conference charges could be increased, charges for supplemental video services could be added, and new revenue generation strategies could be considered. It was critical to head off any effort by Tolstopiatenko or Laporte to impose charges for seminars.

It was a tough document, but fair to B-SPAN. We had invented the system to achieve specific objectives. While willing to give ground to assist our new colleagues, their objectives had to fall within our parameters. To do otherwise would have been an abrogation of our responsibilities, destruction of our vision, and to have two years of toil subrogated to another's parochial agenda. With the lines drawn in the sand, it was now up to Tolstopiatenko to decide whether to wage war.

I had something valuable on my side. Space was not yet available for Bowden and me in WBI's suite of offices. We remained in our current location until the end of the calendar year. The value was less "out of sight, out of mind," though that was helpful, but rather quick and invisible access to Wheeler for thoughts. I realized Tolstopiatenko and Laporte would know we remained in close contact. We agreed it best to keep Wheeler removed from any involvement in my day-to-day interaction with either. It would undermine my position, and his, to do otherwise. Since he was no longer the manager of B-SPAN, he could not be seen as orchestrating events from behind the scenes. To do so would destroy his credibility, not so much with Tolstopiatenko or Laporte, but with Leautier and Millet. Ultimately, survival of B-SPAN would depend upon them. Public involvement with me would also not allow Wheeler to play the one role he formally could: Principal stakeholder and member of the advisory committee. Wheeler would be a silent partner, but silent or not, we knew Tolstopiatenko and Laporte would know he was there, somewhere, operating in the shadows, working informal alliances they would not know about, or be able to control even if they did.

Bowden and I were gathering intelligence everyday about Tolstopiatenko. What we had learned was not good.[47] He is ruthless and punitive, people in WBI said. You are only short-term consultants. Cross him at your peril. Trying desperately to keep our sense of humor in the gathering storm, Wheeler and I coined a new nickname for Tolstopiatenko: Comrade A. At first, we wondered if what was evolving was simply a clash of personalities or a misunderstanding of B-SPAN's intentions. Yet it was increasingly clear we had competing visions. In thinking more reflectively about his motivations, I found it obvious Tolstopiatenko was uncomfortable with the medium's transparency. But he was also a practical individual. He wouldn't mold an agenda around philosophical issues. I came to the conclusion Tolstopiatenko wanted to use B-SPAN's resources—as well as capitalize on its successful branding—to promote his own product line. There remained a still unanswered question. Was Laporte aware of the developing chasm? Did he support Tolstopiatenko's vision for B-SPAN?

Tolstopiatenko responded quickly to my draft.[48] He acknowledged the prudence of distinguishing between edited and non-edited events, informal seminars, and formal learning products; but he considered the WBI Presents concept a non-starter. "I don't want a distinction between the product lines as B-SPAN is now a part of WBI," he said. "There are target audiences WBI wants to reach and B-SPAN needs to account for them." He was upping the ante again, but Wheeler and I had Leautier's dictum in mind when we created the WBI Presents concept. We may have been revolutionaries, but we were also realists. We knew things couldn't be black and white. Integration into a new unit meant it would be necessary to *appear* to cede terrain. The goal was to offer compromise without giving ground that was of value. If Tolstopiatenko wanted to cross this line, he would then have to square off against the vice president. He could ask Leautier to change the mandate or accept a differentiated product line, but he couldn't move preemptively because he knew it would be leaked. Bureaucrats may mercilessly punish those beneath them, but they rarely confront their seniors. That is their edict. We were creating a situation Wheeler fondly characterized as using institutional momentum to work for us. Sun Tzu would have instinctively recognized the terrain.

Tolstopiatenko had additional questions about the draft strategy. He asked for a meeting. We sat down in his office. He conceded B-SPAN should not be revamped into a training tool for WBI, but it needed to go beyond its "informing" function, he said. He wanted to have WBI products housed on B-SPAN's servers. I stayed mute and forced my expression to remain impassive. He remained steadfast in his desire to have an undifferentiated product line. He probed further on my definition of the "no editing" mandate. "Should videos not have some technical editing to improve consistency and clarity?" he asked. I held fast and wondered if he knew B-SPAN's principle was supported by Leautier. He paused and seemed to collect himself. He suggested a few minor changes, but offered little further resistance for the moment. He asked me to draft an addendum further clarifying B-SPAN's principles, editing parameters, and what type of events would be eligible for our service. I readily accepted. It was another opportunity to define the terrain. Perhaps he viewed it as a last chance to mute tensions with me. The addendum I planned would reinforce the walls already fencing him in.

To get a better sense of how B-SPAN's integration into WBI was actually unfolding, I put together a list of requests we had already accepted or resisted.[49] I tabulated 26 areas where we had acquiesced to Tolstopiatenko's requests. These included having WBI learning courses and training materials on B-SPAN via WBI Presents. I had also conceded using our server space to house his materials, halting Forum One's database development, indexing content, synchronizing PowerPoints, improving video quality, gathering video traffic data, surveying audiences, and more. There were only six areas where my refusal had been steadfast: Allowing the editing of B-SPAN products, having B-SPAN's videos merged seamlessly with edited WBI materials, removing archived files from our server, charging Bank task managers for coverage of their two-hour seminars, prioritizing WBI events over other Bank events, and conforming our website to WBI's template. These were areas where I would resist hard or not budge at all; but on some I had not informed Tolstopiatenko of where I stood. The longer I could move camouflaged on these battlefronts, the more time I had to build an impregnable position.

In writing the addendum, I created a linguistic version of a shell game.[50] New WBI products that were policy discussions and unedited could go online. WBI course or learning materials would not be eligible outside a clearly defined and separate window. On the issue of using B-SPAN's server to house WBI materials, I consolidated Tolstopiatenko's gains with a nuance. This could happen, but B-SPAN's video content had priority. The addendum noted the motivations of content providers to have minor "technical" editing to correct misspeaks, delete inaccuracies, confidential admissions, or controversial statements were understandable. Nevertheless, it was a violation of B-SPAN's operating principle. I also noted that, when informed of our operating mandate and the reasons behind it, no one had decided to withdraw their event. Our archives had climbed above 300 events. I added a final point. The operating principle was B-SPAN's trademark, and a mandate WBI Vice President Leautier stated could not be violated.

I scheduled a break for myself in mid-August. The morning of my departure brought further revelations. Millet convened a division-wide meeting to discuss WBI's Internet site. Millet was new to WBI, so no one knew her opinion on anything. We found out quickly. She liked B-SPAN.

"I've seen several events and am excited to have this addition to WBI's website," she said.[51] "B-SPAN is demonstrating to the Bank the importance of transparency with the outside world. By contrast, WBI's website is too WBI-centric. It makes finding information about the Bank difficult. With regards to its Internet strategy, WBI needs to change its mindset; and to do so, the department's website needs to be revamped to move it beyond WBI's parochial needs." Her unsolicited words could not have been more welcome. Tolstopiatenko seemed shaken. He followed Millet into the elevator talking intently to her as the doors closed. I went on holiday. It would be the last one I took for two years.

3

During my leave, Millet convened a meeting with the I Team. Bowden reported she reiterated her enthusiasm for B-SPAN. "B-SPAN is a leading example of the kind of service WBI should be moving toward," she said.[52] She joked with Bowden. Could she switch jobs and work for us? Tolstopiatenko stepped in. Had she seen our draft work program? She had, Millet said, and she liked what we had accomplished and planned for the coming year. It must have been another difficult moment for him. And, many more would lie ahead, for both of us.

Upon my return, I was greeted by more good news. Tolstopiatenko's website analysis for WBI revealed B-SPAN was among its most powerful attractions.[53] Wheeler was pushing the margins from his end. He sent me a note that a meeting of the advisory committee would convene soon.[54] He had been updating de Nevers on the transition, noting Tolstopiatenko's efforts to reconfigure B-SPAN's model and slow down the operation with meetings, forms, and requests. It amounted to behavior Wheeler considered bizarre.[55] It's obvious, he said to her, the new supervisor didn't care about B-SPAN, but did care about how our resources could be used to pursue his own agenda. Since the managers above him had only good words for us, perhaps there was a simple solution: We report directly to Laporte or Millet.

The advisory committee meeting, however, proved less than whelming. The group agreed to the transparency model of providing unedited content. This meant introduction of edited WBI content would have to be a differentiated product line. The I Team could have responsibility for the new product line, but we were in charge of the day-to-day management of ours. Disputes within the team could be referred to the committee. These agreements solidified territory we already held. They did not help us gain new ground. When Wheeler suggested oversight responsibility be removed from Tolstopiatenko and given to the committee, Laporte balked immediately. He refused to consider any change in the succession of authority. He was not going to allow an outcome that raised questions about his management. Wheeler demurred and then finally deferred to him.

Afterwards, Wheeler thought the meeting went well. I was less impressed. "Of course, Laporte would accept transparency in the face of three powerful advocates," I noted. "But we need autonomy from Tolstopiatenko, and now the results of the meeting place him even more firmly in control as its operating authority." The obvious had been accomplished, but not the objective. Wheeler encouraged me to meet with Laporte. "It will give you a chance to get to know each other as well as give Laporte a sense of where you want to take B-SPAN," he suggested. I called Laporte and he agreed to meet.[56] He was looking forward to finally sitting down with me, he said. Wheeler encouraged me to take the high road, and avoid talking about the struggles I was having.

Tolstopiatenko's demands escalated. He wanted an agreement on results we would accomplish during the fiscal year.[57] We would also have to submit a performance assessment of actions taken and completed each month.[58] He wanted protocols drafted for materials appearing on B-SPAN.[59] There were revisions necessary for the strategy paper.[60] Then, there were revisions for the revisions. Answers to questions were followed up with more questions. And, there were endless rounds of meetings. We were slipping into a malaise as our time was being invested in paperwork and away from moving content.

On a wide range of fronts, Tolstopiatenko was employing tactics to slow B-SPAN down. He announced that with the halt of Forum One's database, his chief programmer, Patrick Tse, would develop a video-on-demand database for B-SPAN that mirrored Witzel's system.[61] Means was still encoding videos and making our website updates. Tolstopiatenko wanted her terminated and the encoding equipment moved to a space near him so Bowden would take over the activity.[62] Wheeler and I had once considered this, but found the trade-off unacceptable.[63] It would reduce the amount of events Bowden could summarize and we could make available to the public. However, I could not overtly refuse. Tolstopiatenko had suggested on several occasions he could find no justification for keeping Bowden otherwise. Means was my loyal bulldog at the gate. She refused anyone's request for changes or updates unless I gave approval. I now began to speculate whether physically moving the machines also meant losing final authority over access. I needed an argument that would meld our competing objectives. I noted her fees were nominal. Such a move would not provide cost savings since she was working many more hours than she actually billed. It worked. Tolstopiatenko wanted to know her expenses to compare them with those of external consultants.[64] I then turned my focus to the Bank's Director of Knowledge and Learning.

Bruno Laporte was a French national who had been with the Bank for nearly two decades.[65] He had worked on education during much of this time. Before, he had been a loan officer in the private sector and an economist in the Ivory Coast. He had mastered the Bank's code of conduct, knew what it took to advance within its hierarchy, what superiors would accept, and what they would frown upon. He was a consummate bureaucrat. His new position gave him responsibility for making knowledge sharing activities a part of the unit-level activities across the institution. Unfortunately, given his new status as the Bank's guru on knowledge sharing and learning, he was saddled with a peculiar irony: He was somewhat visionless.

Our meeting took place on the first anniversary of the terrorist attacks on the U.S., and we took a moment to reflect with sadness on the occasion. Following Wheeler's advice, I offered Laporte a perspective of sunshine and roses. In the aftermath of Stiglitz-Rogoff, we enjoyed a 70% increase in visitors and 40% increase in website hits, I told him.[66] August statistics were also strong.[67] We were on pace to reach two million hits annually.

He thought things were going well, too, but inquired whether our transition under Tolstopiatenko was difficult. Sensing a trap, I relied on Wheeler's instincts. It would be better to see how Laporte acted in the aftermath of our meeting to gauge his true intentions. I suggested we were doing our best to make the transition a smooth process, and then identified areas where B-SPAN was accommodating WBI's needs. This seemed to satisfy him. He wanted me to develop a PowerPoint presentation that I could present to the Learning Boards throughout the Bank.[68] "B-SPAN is a resource they should know about," he said. I began discussing the vision we had for B-SPAN: Developing content from resident missions to include on the site; disseminating content via the GDLN's Distance Learning Centers; conducting interviews of Bank staff and guests on development issues; and offering the

Washington policy community an opportunity to provide content to our system. "These are good ideas," he said.

With him moving in my direction, I sought to solidify support on key struggles I was having. "Keeping B-SPAN's archives permanent is central to our vision of creating a virtual library of development discussions as well as an historical record of the Bank's work," I said. I offered Laporte an analogy: "A farmer had many kinds of vegetables he wished to sell in the city. As he passed the first town, he sold one type of produce, and in another town he sold another vegetable. He still had not reached the city, and he had many more types of vegetables yet to sell. If the farmer suddenly returned home knowing only what the two towns purchased, he would never fully understand how many of his vegetables were in demand." Laporte smiled and said he understood. "The solution," I said "is to purchase server space as necessary. Since costs are dropping, this will be less of an issue in the future than at the moment." Another way of reducing costs, I suggested, would be to purchase our own camcorder with streaming and encoding capacity. The investment would pay for itself if we filmed 15 or 20 of our own events. I closed by making a pitch to maintain the distinctive characteristic of our website. "The branding of B-SPAN has been important to its strong growth over the last two years," I noted.[69]

"My door is always open to you if there are any problems," Laporte said to finish the meeting. Then, he added, "We are meeting without Tolstopiatenko. Discussions on B-SPAN need his involvement." The open-door policy apparently closed at the first hint of trouble. He suggested convening a B-SPAN meeting involving everyone soon.[70]

Upon learning of Laporte's intention to have a meeting, Tolstopiatenko took decisive action. He requested an immediate discussion with ISG on video server issues.[71] When he had first been given responsibility of B-SPAN two and a half months earlier, he wanted ISG to feed video traffic data to him. I sent this along, but ISG had followed its normally laconic method of facilitating requests. Now, the I Team manager implored them on the urgency of accessing their log files.[72] Why did he want it so badly? He had just released his monthly traffic report which showed us growing dramatically. Everything seemed fine for B-SPAN. But I hadn't realized I had a blind spot.

The joust of thrust and parry seemed to be going in my favor. It seemed while all was not well, we were well. Strategies deployed to change the transparency model and eliminate B-SPAN's archives had been countered by actions to hamstring Tolstopiatenko. Tactics designed to muddle our operation had been muted. B-SPAN continued to function without significant delays.[73] Even Tolstopiatenko's desire to jump start WBI Presents remained mired in his own swampland of paperwork. In actuality, I had no intention of implementing WBI Presents. Wheeler saw my acquiescence as a gesture of good will, and while I made the gesture freely when necessary, I never did anything to foster action. I knew once an alternative product line appeared on B-SPAN, I would never be able to eliminate it. And, just as bad, if it became inactive due to the I Team's neglect—a distinct possibility—it would be a festering sore of dead space on our website. Then, at this sensitive period, when we seemed in Laporte's good graces, we glanced against the shoals, and disaster struck.

Noted economist Daniel Yergin was coming to the Bank to discuss a PBS documentary on his book, *Commanding Heights: The Battle for the World Economy*.[74] The book and film addressed the evolution of the global economy during the 1990s, a critical decade when the communist powers dissolved and globalization accelerated. Laporte asked me for coverage.[75] Unknown to us, a request had also been made to ISG to stream the event live to Bank staff.

This was the first time GSD taped a recording during a live webcast. They decided to use the same camera for both purposes. With GSD technicians in a control booth, ISG called intermittently during the event to adjust lighting levels for their live stream. Our videotape ended up underexposed. I called Cardak to find out what happened.[76] Knowing the keen interest by EXT and Laporte to have it online immediately, I made a tactical blunder.[77] I made the video public. The final product was dark enough to produce an immediate reaction. Feeling his prestige was at stake, Laporte called me.[78]

He was terribly concerned about the quality of webcast, he said. We needed to fix it immediately. Tolstopiatenko followed suit. It was an outrage that a video of such poor quality was online, he said. I had erred grievously by making it available, he suggested.[79]

The bulk of the day was spent working with GSD to improve the tape.[80] I also tried a preemptive measure, suggesting to Laporte that, to eliminate similar occurrences, I would draft filming guidelines specific to Internet recordings.[81] By coincidence, several days earlier I had met Peter Midgeley, a Bank consultant who was knowledgeable about filming webcasts.[82] I called him and he agreed to help draft the guidelines.[83] I also made it a point to insulate GSD from Laporte's wrath by stating they were helpful in fixing the problem and we had enjoyed a long history of collegial relations. Late in the evening, an improved version went online.[84] The next day, I handwrote a carefully worded explanation of GSD's actions, and asked Cardak to send it back to me by email.[85] It mitigated much of the blame on GSD by explaining that the problem resulted from technical reasons brought on by the concurrent live feed. And, it absolved B-SPAN of any blame.

The damage, however, had been done. Laporte, while relieved about our fixes, responded with a refrain picked up from Tolstopiatenko about the inadequate quality of B-SPAN's filming.[86] Video quality was a serious issue he wanted addressed at our meeting, he said. After three months under his management—but only after the *Commanding Heights* event and Tolstopiatenko's meeting with ISG on video traffic—Laporte confirmed a date on his calendar for his first detailed examination of B-SPAN.[87]

In the struggle between Tolstopiatenko and me, the key question Wheeler and I could not answer was where Laporte stood. At first glance, he seemed to support B-SPAN. This meeting would offer tangible evidence as to which way he was really leaning.

Not knowing the agenda of the meeting, I prepared for what I knew would come: The untimely video quality of *Commanding Heights*. I offered an explanation about the unique circumstances under which GSD had filmed the event. I noted my discussion with

GSD about filming guidelines, their support, and the drafting of the protocols with Midgeley's input. The guidelines, I added, would not have prevented the problems with the Yergin event. Trying to head off any potential discussion about eliminating GSD in our operational model, I noted they had been highly responsive to us for two years; and because of our unique discount, they lost money when they filmed an event for B-SPAN. "Despite problems encountered with *Commanding Heights*," I closed, "it is important to remember B-SPAN's value is not in any particular event, but in the culmination of many."

The pitch fell on deaf ears. Tolstopiatenko produced a list of twenty videos in our stock of 300 that "proved" B-SPAN had systematic problems. He believed B-SPAN was so littered with poor quality that the entire service was compromised. Videos were choppy, full of delays, and hard to see. If he was having these problems using a high-speed connection, it would be impossible for Bank clients with low-speed connections to "download" files, he said.

Laporte said he was very concerned about the fallout *Commanding Heights* would have on the division's reputation. Other than the people in the room, no one had complained about the quality of the event. I knew no one ever would. I also realized that was irrelevant. "All these videos will need to be fixed," Tolstopiatenko said. Laporte concurred. Tolstopiatenko thought we would have to reduce our volume to ensure each offering was of the highest quality. Laporte concurred again. Given the gravity of the situation, Laporte said he could no longer support any effort to market B-SPAN to the Learning Boards or other potential clients.

Tolstopiatenko went further. "Quality is not the only problem," he began. "Every video from 2002 had been digitized incorrectly since you had encoded them at a rate too high to be viewed by low-speed users. Therefore, all files from 2002 will need to be encoded again, and perhaps until this is done, all these files should be removed from B-SPAN servers." This had come out of left field. I didn't know what he was talking about. Ever cautious, Laporte moderated this suggestion. "We should only re-digitize files generating the most traffic from July and August," he said. By now, they were piggy backing on each other's comments with increasing zeal in their voices. I had lost control over the meeting, and now thought only in terms of damage control.

Then Tolstopiatenko dropped a well-concealed bombshell. He had taken a look at ISG's video traffic data, and it revealed important information.[88] "What is that?" Laporte asked expectantly. "The fact is very few people watch B-SPAN's videos," Tolstopiatenko said, "and the few that do stay online only for a minute or two and then leave. Most viewers watch a few moments of a high-profile event like Stiglitz-Rogoff. That one event accounted for more than 75% of B-SPAN's video traffic the previous month. The vast majority of traffic Shaman touted is visitors accessing HTML website pages. Essentially, B-SPAN's video content is unused."

"This is very disturbing," Laporte noted. "Can you dispute these numbers?" he asked me. I had no answer. "One has to wonder if B-SPAN is worth continuing," Tolstopiatenko suggested.

I was mute, listening in stunned silence. We were hemorrhaging. Laporte and Tolstopiatenko continued their discussion as if I were no longer in the room. My participation, indeed my presence, had become largely irrelevant. We will need to analyze audience interest and use further, they said. B-SPAN must conduct a user survey to determine more clearly how it is used, and whether webcasting is a viable service for WBI, they concluded.

The meeting ended. Laporte got up abruptly, turned without looking at me, and left as if he had witnessed an execution. Tolstopiatenko was smiling. "That was a tough meeting, yes?" he said in his thick accent. He suggested further recalcitrance might end in my termination. My hands twitched. On the commanding heights, the winds had shifted. Comrade A was boss and master of B-SPAN.

4

The night gave me time to absorb the shock of the day, to understand the battlefield's terrain as defined by Tolstopiatenko, and the tactics he had employed. The blows had to be softened. The wounds had to be healed. I began carefully maneuvering in the underbelly of the trenches. The next morning, as promised during the meeting, I delivered a draft of survey questions.[89] The draft camera guidelines were submitted to the I Team for comments, to which Tolstopiatenko appended text about portable lights.[90]

I turned to Means for analysis of allegations that we had incorrectly encoded events. She suggested Tolstopiatenko was clueless.[91] She had not encoded anything at a single high-speed rate. Everything we streamed was at multiple rates.[92] The RealProducer software we used insured viewers would receive the most appropriate stream, so long as they had the correct settings on their computers. Moreover, viewers did not download B-SPAN's files, but streamed them. File size, therefore, was irrelevant. If Tolstopiatenko was having problems, Means surmised, it was because he was using an incorrect version of RealPlayer, or the connectivity setting on his computer was wrong. It had nothing to do with the encoding process. I forwarded Means's analysis along with a note suggesting we would work on the problematic tapes if Tolstopiatenko insisted, but within the context of this clarification, he might wish to reconsider.[93]

He called for a meeting.[94] "B-SPAN should encode video streams at only one rate," he began. Means countered.[95] Tolstopiatenko was now playing on her turf. "If your objective is to improve viewer quality, then offering only one rate would mean high-end users would receive a lower quality stream," she noted. It was the opposite of what Tolstopiatenko was advocating. He was boxed in on this front, and broke off his attack. He also conceded his computer's configurations for the RealPlayer connectivity settings might be off. "Re-encoding all B-SPAN's archives," he acknowledged, "no longer seems necessary."

He tried a new tactic. Staff that used laptops while traveling had trouble receiving our streams. B-SPAN was webcasting globally, but Tolstopiatenko was suddenly worried about a few dozen personnel. His aggression had reached inane proportions. Means noted again it was an issue of adjusting connectivity settings and that was up to the viewer and not the province of B-SPAN. Faced by a technical expert, Tolstopiatenko had been vanquished. Nevertheless, the next day at a meeting chaired by Millet and Laporte, he criticized us on the issue of connectivity. For the moment, it was not necessary to win debating points. More importantly, we had won on the substance by sidestepping a roadblock that would have crashed our system.

Tolstopiatenko's mind was working hard with new schemes. He suggested not paying GSD for tapes he believed of questionable quality. I chose to ignore the comment. He suggested getting the Bank's legal department to grant us permission before making our events public. This was a death threat, and we both knew it. Here, I needed to respond. "If you do something so obvious to destroy the service then you will become the focus of attention," I offered. This hit the mark. He dropped the idea on the spot.

He tried a new maneuver.[96] To improve the quality of B-SPAN's offerings, we would need to synchronize them with PowerPoints. Means noted many web browsers could not support such a template.[97] In fact, ISG had also urged Bank staff to avoid using them, since it would create problems for low-speed connections, which was, of course, the situation in most of the developing world. Implementation would grind B-SPAN to a standstill since an inordinate amount of time would be necessary to synchronize PowerPoints with each event. Given our fragile status, to confront Tolstopiatenko with a refusal was out of the question. Instead, we agreed it was an excellent idea, but unfortunately we didn't have the knowledge or resources to implement it. Knowing he had his people running in a thousand directions that had nothing to do with B-SPAN, the idea was stillborn.

I was performing two jobs simultaneously: (1) The rear guard action to prevent my managers from destroying B-SPAN, and (2) B-SPAN's work. Events continued to be covered and put online. Newsletters continued to be written and disseminated.

As our reputation grew, we were increasingly being asked to webcast the institution's most important events. In October, we covered Jared Diamond, a distinguished author discussing the historical antecedents of globalization; the Bank's Poverty Reduction and Economic Management (PREM) network's Poverty Day 2002; the UN Population Fund's Executive Director Thoraya Ahmed Obaid on problems presented by overpopulation, and China's Vice Minister of Finance, Jin Liqun, on China's entrance into the World Trade Organization.[98]

Tolstopiatenko demanded a list of every event we covered during the year.[99] This order actually worked to our advantage, for it provided an effective marketing tool to demonstrate our reach. B-SPAN had produced 217 events during the preceding year, amounting to more than 600 hours of programming time.[100] Generating content was at the heart of B-SPAN's power. Wheeler and I understood processing a few carefully orchestrated events to ensure perfection before release was a typically bureaucratic reflex. Tolstopiatenko was impressed by our production level, but said the new emphasis on improving quality would mean our volume would need to drop.[101] Laporte seconded the notion.[102] Wheeler thought if we could keep driving traffic, it would undermine tactics Tolstopiatenko might employ. Laporte would never agree to move decisively against B-SPAN if our numbers kept growing. So I pushed hard to keep the flow of service uninterrupted by the larger strategic struggle. And, our traffic was growing.

Operation Feel Good resumed in full throttle. I asked Macdonald, the Research Department's communications chief, to write me a note on how he found the service.[103] He "continued to be impressed by B-SPAN," he said. "This is a great Bank-wide service, an example of scaling up the power of knowledge by capturing and sharing with the world events that would otherwise be available only to a limited audience of Bank staff and their invited guests. It not only makes an important contribution to our dissemination of knowledge and development, it also helps de-mystify the Bank. The display of transparency helps to dispel the belief that we are a closed institution that enforces some sort of orthodoxy. The integration of content from across the Bank is especially valuable since it means that event organizers can benefit from your economies of scale, and that users searching for online video of Bank events can find it all in a single place." His comments were forwarded to key players in the struggle.[104]

The screws kept turning. Laporte and Tolstopiatenko wanted a meeting to assess progress.[105] The tension Bowden and I were working under was palpable. He confided to me he was losing sleep.

I began the meeting by discussing activities to address the video and audio quality. I had met with GSD, GDLN's Studio Team, and other webcasting experts to develop camera guidelines. I now visited each event to conduct sound and lighting checks with the camera teams, and inform audiences about why cameras were in the room and the importance of using microphones. I also reviewed each tape afterwards. Bowden and I had worked on the files Tolstopiatenko identified as problematic to improve audio or lighting quality where possible.[106]

Tolstopiatenko responded he remained deeply concerned. He then suggested it was time to change B-SPAN's model from supply- to demand-driven. This inferred we should move away from accommodating requests from colleagues, use his traffic data to determine usage, and then cover only those events. It was another recipe for destruction. "Video traffic is disappointing enough to warrant terminating B-SPAN altogether!" he suddenly exclaimed.

With the consensus of the advisory committee's edict still fresh in his mind, Laporte was more cautious. "You should halt marketing of B-SPAN until the quality of problematic videos is corrected," he ordered. He wanted B-SPAN to index events by speaker and session and synchronize PowerPoints. I quickly acknowledged full support. Laporte also wanted us to work with the Instructional Design (ID) team within WBI to improve presentations made during our events. The instructional designers helped speakers with the structural presentation of WBI's training materials.

Laporte was providing a clear signal he supported Tolstopiatenko's notion of choreographed productions for B-SPAN. Instinctively, both men were introducing Hollywood-type ways to perfect content for a system moving in the opposite direction. I said we would be delighted to work with the ID Team. The exhaustive work Bowden and I had done between the two meetings paid off. Laporte was somewhat mollified. We had bought some time to reestablish our footing.

The next day Laporte issued a quarterly assessment of accomplishments and goals for his new division.[107] He was rosy about the future. The "interaction of the learning, knowledge and Internet application teams is showing great promise," he said. One of his priorities, of course, was to create an encouraging environment. Laporte said he was ready to "recognize accomplishments and value each member of WBI Knowledge Learning such that innovation, synergy and risk taking are encouraged." B-SPAN was in WBI Knowledge Learning and we were family. It was now official. We were happy.

Tolstopiatenko, however, was still on a war footing. The Learning Support Group within the division asked me to discuss B-SPAN at a seminar they were organizing. The event would convene webcasting practitioners from outside the Bank to educate staff on the opportunities the technology could provide them.[108] The day before the seminar, I learned Tolstopiatenko had caught wind of my appearance.[109] He had demanded to speak ahead of me. Just before we went into a packed room, he pulled me aside. "Don't misconstrue my comments as being negative," he assured me.

It was then I realized after traveling the peaks and valleys of life, I had finally met Darth Vader. After the initial presenters finished, he began. "WBI is running B-SPAN, but there is little interest by audiences for watching unedited videos," he said. "At most, a motivated viewer will watch only for a few minutes. For example, the average viewing time for B-SPAN's most popular video, Stiglitz-Rogoff, was only five seconds. WBI is debating the legitimacy of webcasting as a sustainable service."

A Bank manager had just informed a public audience the project he administered was worthless. I was livid. I barely began my remarks before curtailing them altogether to address Tolstopiatenko's comments. "Full analysis of B-SPAN's service is premature," I said. "We are a new venture tapping into a global audience that for the most part has no Internet access. Those who are online and streaming video are only now getting familiar with the technology." Tolstopiatenko's comments and mine must have puzzled the audience. He did not stay for further discussions. When my comments concluded, he stood up, offered a smile, and stepped out of the room.

The event organizers were also angered. Like murky water turned clear, Comrade A's strategy had been clarified: Look for imperfections in the system; magnify them in the most negative light; divert resources needed elsewhere to address shortcomings; invest time on paperwork and administrative requests; slow production as much as possible; highlight weaknesses in traffic; terminate the service; co-opt the physical infrastructure; and fold budget savings into activities where credit would go directly to him. Since the summer, I had been on the defensive, reacting and ameliorating his assaults. The Learning Support Group event signaled his resolve to keep punching until there was a knockout. I decided the time had come to launch a counteroffensive.

5

Four months earlier, I had extended my hand to greet Tolstopiatenko, and in return received a blow to the face. From there, the two of us were staking claims to territory. Tolstopiatenko was used to terrorizing subordinates, but not their resisting. His agenda didn't include B-SPAN. We had resources that could be used for his projects. We must have looked like an antelope in the presence of a lion. And, who did we think we were—two short-term consultants who meant nothing to WBI? Our contracts were counted in months. With Laporte's acquiescence, he had the power to terminate us at will. As documented by his history with us and others in WBI, Tolstopiatenko's nature was to plot in silence, then to pounce quickly and decisively. Now, with Laporte giving public signals of his dismay with B-SPAN, he was openly attacking on many fronts. Master Sun would have recognized we had reached "dying ground." I had to fight for B-SPAN hard, or it would die. I was working deep into the nights, maneuvering on dozens of issues, searching for ways to destabilize his assaults.

That we had not been destroyed, I attributed to three reasons. First, we received public recognition from Leautier. She thought B-SPAN was wonderful, and said so often.[110] It was hard to terminate something your vice president makes a point of praising. Second, my informal alliance with Wheeler and de Nevers provided a check on Laporte and Tolstopiatenko. It was the fear of what they did not know that kept both from moving boldly, the same fear that also made both quintessential bureaucrats. Finally, there was the power of B-SPAN itself. It was supported by the majority of Bank staff. A steady flow of emails from them reached my inbox, and per Operation Feel Good were quickly forwarded to my supervisors.[111]

Wheeler and I discussed going directly to Leautier, since her public support for B-SPAN was being contradicted by its administration. I was optimistic if we presented our evidence, she would support a change in management; but Wheeler was more cautious. "The realities of administrating a sizeable bureaucracy," he suggested, "may compel or restrict her from meddling with the directives of her management team." He thought she could go either way, and put the odds at 50-50. We understood if we went to Leautier and she was not disposed to become involved, I would soon be terminated. Within a few months, B-SPAN would continue in name only, and become something very different. Once the cord was pulled, there would be no turning back: It was for all the chips. We termed reaching out to Leautier as the "nuclear option."

I was increasingly inclined to go nuclear, and with Tolstopiatenko's public condemnation of his own project, felt it was time for Wheeler to pull the trigger. He had remained reluctant, but thought Tolstopiatenko's action warranted his dismissal from the Bank. Now he was on the verge of making a move. I suggested he wait while I prepared documentation of actions Tolstopiatenko and Laporte had taken since July.[112] If he walked into the vice president's office with everything at stake, I wanted him armed with every bit of weaponry I could find. He reverted to his Zen methodology. It wouldn't be needed. He would just make the case there was no blame to assess, just competing visions of the service. Still, we agreed to monitor developments a bit longer.

I decided to lay further groundwork with Leautier that B-SPAN was highly valued by senior Bank stakeholders. Chief Economist Stern had hosted Jin Liqun, China's Vice Minister of Finance, when he came to the Bank a few weeks earlier to discuss his country's entrance into the World Trade Organization. I asked Macdonald if I could draft language for a dissemination note Stern would send. He agreed, and Stern said he was "grateful to our colleagues at WBI for B-SPAN's coverage." Macdonald forwarded the note to the Research Department, to Bank staff in the East Asia region, and at my request, to Leautier.[113]

Tolstopiatenko's blitzkrieg needed to be checked. With the next meeting on B-SPAN scheduled for the first week of November, I began preparations. For me, B-SPAN had always been an intuitive creation. It grew organically, and followed the pattern of my mind and instincts. Statistics were useful barometers, but I relied more on the feel of the invention with feedback from constituents to chart our course between wave and wind. The I Team manager lived in a world of numbers. The force of Tolstopiatenko's authority resided in his ability to convince superiors his assertions carried the ring of truth. It would be his turf, but it was there I needed to wound him, crippling his credibility.

During the first Laporte meeting in September, Tolstopiatenko revealed a covert strategy for undermining B-SPAN by using ISG's video server data to suggest interest in our streams was nominal. He began producing monthly reports on video traffic that quantified the data in a number of different ways.[114] I started culling through the reports to find information that might offer a different perspective. I called Witzel to ask his thoughts as an expert on Internet traffic statistics. He believed ISG's data upon which Tolstopiatenko had built his case was suspect.[115]

First, I reviewed trends and time lines from HTML and video data to provide the baseline on the direction B-SPAN was moving. The HTML traffic, from Witzel who tracked B-SPAN since its inception in 2000, and from ISG as of the next summer, revealed strong and steady growth.[116] I already knew this, but wanted charts for Laporte to visualize our growth, and leave no room for doubt. In fact, B-SPAN's climb was quite powerful. During July 2001, we had received 21,000 hits and about 700 visitors. By October 2002, we had risen to 177,000 hits and 9,400 visitors. I Team members had recently suggested web hits were a poor barometer for measuring usage, so I ran trends for a variety of indicators: Page views; visitor sessions; international visitors; multiple visits; number of countries where visitors resided; and more. By every indicator, the trends made the same statement. We were experiencing rapid growth.

Tolstopiatenko had insisted ISG's HTML traffic data was not as accurate as statistics he compiled each month. He used algorithms from a subset of their information, so I gleaned through his reports from when he first began documenting B-SPAN. Each indicator he assessed—successful page requests, unique visitors and data transferred—also revealed B-SPAN was growing more powerful with each passing month. I massaged the data further to create a ranking for B-SPAN against all the other WBI websites charted. Since formally joining WBI, B-SPAN ranked as one of the top five websites in the department for page requests and visitors.[117] If Tolstopiatenko wanted to derail us, he would be destroying one of WBI's best performers.

Next, I analyzed the video data from ISG's server files.[118] If all I had was an argument on the HTML side, but nothing of equal weight on the video side, B-SPAN would remain vulnerable to Tolstopiatenko's charge the value of the service was nebulous. Here I had a problem. In July, the Stiglitz-Rogoff event had generated a spectacular spike of interest. It skewed the data, both for that month and subsequent months. Without the aberration, data from August and September showed small progress for hits, visitors, visits, and page views, but I needed to make a better case before Laporte.

The initial review offered interesting information, but all grim. Data from June through most of September indicated almost all our video traffic had been generated by Stiglitz-Rogoff or the Hernando de Soto lecture. Everything else barely made it on the report. Data for October said something different. Usage was much more evenly spaced. Stiglitz-Rogoff and de Soto still generated the strongest usage, but other events were sparking interest. This was good, but I needed more.

During the September meeting, Tolstopiatenko—in his analysis of the video traffic—said the *median* length of time a visitor watched a B-SPAN file was only five seconds. Five seconds meant they really weren't bothering to watch. But the *average* length of viewing time for the month was more than ten minutes. Something was afoot. I queried Wheeler for a perspective. He noted the average and median offered two different ways of analyzing a data point. He suggested reassessing the median as well as charting quartile data points. Stiglitz-Rogoff profoundly dominated the video data. It warranted further inspection. The day we offered the public access to the event, Stiglitz-Rogoff received international attention in the media. A surge in traffic to our site was created. It was a spike of dramatic proportions, far stronger than anything we had seen, or ISG's video server had ever experienced. ISG could only provide access to 500 simultaneous streams. With so many visitors trying to procure the stream at the same time, the traffic had congested a pipe with limited space. Congestion caused constant buffering, or stopped people's access altogether. The day's congestion had skewed our statistics, and given Tolstopiatenko the hook he was looking for. The statistic he used to question B-SPAN's value was an outlier all along, only now I knew it too. I crunched the numbers for August and September, and found the median average time for visitors was eight minutes, then 35 minutes. Tolstopiatenko's assertion had been simply a highly selective truth.[119]

I now had something to question the legitimacy of his best argument about our video usage. I wanted to say something positive as well. He had compiled data from July through October on an indicator called the Activity Level by Length of Visit. This indicator measured activity levels by each minute, such as how many people visited B-SPAN from 0 minutes to 1 minute, or from 1 minute to 2 minutes, and so on up to 19 minutes and over. This analysis had several sub-variables, and Tolstopiatenko had chosen to highlight the percentage of total visits. The duration of visits of one minute or less accounted for more than 75% of total visits. This meant three out of four people accessed a video file for a minute or less, and then logged off. Extrapolated for the first five minutes, the percentage of people logging off rose to 85%. This suggested we were irrelevant. However, I identified a different sub-variable Tolstopiatenko had chosen to ignore. It was the percentage of total views. It said one out of four streams was curtailed before one minute, and a little more than 40% during the first five minutes. That put us in a better light, even if moderately. This variable also revealed something else. More than 40% of the views continued to stream for 19 minutes or more. This statistic meant that the people who viewed the streams really valued the content. Tracked over four months, the trend for these variables was unmistakable. The number of views streamed for less than five minutes dropped from 62% to 40%. The number of views streamed for 19 minutes or longer rose from 20% to 42%. The longer we were in business, the more our video files were considered valuable and were being watched.[120]

I had a hypothesis about Tolstopiatenko's data I wanted to test. I again reviewed the HTML data ISG generated on B-SPAN. This data, which recorded strong growth, replicated the video data. The vast majority of visitors, 83%, logged on to the website for one minute or less. One quarter of the total views was for one minute or less. I began looking at other Bank websites, including the most powerful sub-sites the institution offered. The HTML traffic data for all the Bank sub-sites said the same thing. My hypothesis was correct. The traffic patterns for HTML and video files were similar. Now, I had a story to tell.

To set the stage, I wanted to prevent Tolstopiatenko from

knowing what I had learned. I documented all the requests made from the previous meeting that had been completed.[121] They included working with WBI's instructional designers to improve seminar choreography, completing the filming guidelines, creating a frequently-asked-questions page on connectivity issues, offering an audio-only file to compliment the video files, and working on synchronized PowerPoints. Tolstopiatenko had no reaction other than I had addressed the memo from the B-SPAN team to the I Team when in fact B-SPAN was part of the I Team.[122] The venom was seeping through.

The meeting began with a positive development. Laporte asked me to take the minutes.[123] I realized I could now write the history of what was said. Tolstopiatenko made his opening move. Our coverage of one of Wolfensohn's Presidential Lecture Series preempted a previous website built by WBI to house these events. I wasn't familiar with the existing WBI website, and had only responded to a request for coverage, I said. The suggestion we were trying to steal WBI's thunder was easily batted away. We would be happy to provide links to the WBI site from any future presidential lecture we covered, I offered.[124]

Then Tolstopiatenko launched into a new assault on video quality. We had been forewarned. The day before, Tolstopiatenko told Bowden he planned to shut B-SPAN down at the end of the fiscal year. A sympathetic I Team member then alerted Bowden to Tolstopiatenko's next point of attack. "B-SPAN's video quality for the last twenty events was unacceptable," he continued. "They were much too dark."

I didn't want to let him run too far with this gambit in front of Laporte, who was highly impressionable, allergic to negative news, and reluctant to immerse himself in the substance of programs he supervised. I cut him off. "Andrei's opinion on video quality is not shared," I said. "The medium of webcasting does not lend itself to high-quality video in the same way television or movies do. Quality is lower for webcasting because the video signal is compressed during the encoding process, and data is lost when it is streamed. Frame rates between television and webcasting are also different. When B-SPAN's streams are viewed from our computers, Bowden and I have not found any problems with quality. Perhaps there is a problem with his monitor, and it is affecting his perception of lighting and brightness." Bowden immediately said he would look at Tolstopiatenko's computer to see if the monitor needed adjusting. The onus of proof had turned.

Bowden discussed work he had been doing with I Team colleagues Patrick Tse and Hector Montenegro on synchronizing PowerPoints with video. He had learned about new software from RealProducer that could do synchronizing more effectively. Tolstopiatenko interjected. As soon as he learned of the software, he had received purchase approval from Laporte, he said. I drove home our point, however. B-SPAN was working on the issue, had done the research, and found a solution. We were responsive.

Tolstopiatenko finally turned to the issue of traffic. I remained silent to let him use his ammunition before I counter-attacked. "In October, WBI's overall website traffic rose 10%, but B-SPAN's only rose 5%," he began. "In fact, traffic on B-SPAN's video server declined by 5%."

Bowden objected: "People come to B-SPAN to see new offerings. With the current emphasis on video quality, all our time is being spent monitoring and improving old tapes. We have not been able to make many new events available." It was a good point. Laporte reiterated his belief a loss of volume was acceptable as long as quality improved.

In the September meeting, Tolstopiatenko had suggested we include an audio-only component with our video streams. Now he wanted to highlight its success. "The audio stream of Jin Liqun discussing China's entrance into the WTO is one of B-SPAN's top ten files," he announced proudly. "That is excellent," I said. "Where did it rank?" Seventh, he noted. "And, out of curiosity, where did the video file of the Vice Minister rank?" Second was the muted response. His thunder stolen, I asked him if he had any further thoughts to add on B-SPAN's traffic. No, that was it. Then, I said I had a few things I wanted to share.

I disseminated several documents. One itemized all the reasons beyond our control that might prevent a viewer from viewing one of our streams, including the lack of marketing. This was an attempt to change Laporte's current stance. This document also revealed the Bank's Online Media Briefing Center was routinely accessed by 20% of the registered journalists for any single event advertised, but it was a different 20% with each event. The example sought to suggest that only 20% may have responded to any particular event, but a much higher percentage was monitoring. The same could be said of B-SPAN's events.

Two graphs offered on HTML traffic plotted a variety of indicators showing accelerated growth. A third chart documented video traffic Tolstopiatenko had compiled from July through September on the percentage of total views. I described how Stiglitz-Rogoff had created an aberration in the data. The graph showed most B-SPAN visitors were staying five minutes or less, but those numbers were declining significantly. Concurrently, the trend for visitors staying 19 minutes or longer was growing markedly. "These trends make a clear statement," I said. "They show more people are viewing our content for longer periods as our service grows. That means our audiences increasingly value our service. Andrei's own numbers are revealing something irrefutable. Additionally, these trends follow a similar pattern for HTML websites. There is really no difference between how our video files are being used as opposed to any HTML website in the Bank."

The pitch to Laporte was registering. He was nodding. In the September meeting, he had asked whether Tolstopiatenko's data could be refuted. Now, I had called into question the legitimacy of his entire argument, not just a particular statistic. Tolstopiatenko's eyes were narrowing. They began twitching. He tore off his glasses and brought the graph closely to his face.

Laporte was in full retreat as well. "B-SPAN should work on anticipating client needs. This will require marketing. We should have some focus groups," he suggested. He would be happy to help. He called for another meeting at the beginning of December to chart developments, and then got up to leave. Before he could, both Bowden and I emphasized traffic numbers may rise or fall from month to month, but our trends were positive and exciting. In surrender, Tolstopiatenko also acknowledge B-SPAN's traffic was strong. Laporte walked out the door.

I turned to Comrade A. "For future meetings on B-SPAN, I think it would be appropriate for you to share any video traffic you find before the meeting rather than during the meeting. Don't you think this would be appropriate?" I asked. "Yes, it would be appropriate," he admitted. His face was in disarray. Then I walked out.

6

Laporte's philosophy was to concentrate on the big picture and hear no evil. He delegated day-to-day management to subordinates while he espoused the virtues of the Bank's Knowledge Sharing Program in high-profile conferences throughout Europe and North America. Tolstopiatenko was applying time-tested autocratic tactics while relying on his technical reputation with Laporte. Their approaches worked in equilibrium with each other. I knew the key to B-SPAN's survival would be to continue building traffic and good will among clients by moving content through the system.

Seasoned bureaucrats, however, make excellent weathervanes. Sensing the current moving against them, they started tacking. For months, good news forwarded to Laporte had been met by silence. Now he began responding, and featured B-SPAN in the department's newsletter.[125] Leautier continued to praise B-SPAN and his public rhetoric had to match hers even if his private actions differed significantly. The longer he stayed on this course, the more difficult it would ultimately become for him to change direction.

Tolstopiatenko was also moving backwards like a man reeling from a blow. His monthly survey of traffic noted B-SPAN for the first time.[126] A few weeks earlier, someone from the Bank wanted to feature several WBI videos on his unit's website. Now, surprisingly, Tolstopiatenko wanted to know why B-SPAN's videos weren't being highlighted.[127] I knew the winds may have shifted, but Tolstopiatenko's nature had not changed.[128] He would see our meeting as a temporary setback. It would be imperative to keep his activities under close scrutiny, and wait for when he would strike again.

Tolstopiatenko forwarded the latest video data. They confirmed the trends I had highlighted. The requests generated during the meeting were quickly completed. While it was necessary to let B-SPAN's supervisors know I could hit back, it was equally important to remain responsive to their concerns. I sat down with Cardak to discuss the lighting issue raised by Tolstopiatenko. Cardak said bringing portable lights to each event would require adding an additional person to the camera crew. It would escalate our costs by an additional $350 to $600. Since we were receiving a discount for GSD's services, those savings would be wiped out. I knew this point would resonate with Laporte, since he increasingly asserted budget restrictions were beginning to impact B-SPAN's funding. Adding lights would also neutralize the existing lighting contrast in the rooms, so PowerPoint presentations would be difficult for attendees to read. I drafted a note for Cardak to send back to me on the consequences of additional lighting, and then forwarded it to our managers. The timing was perfect. Cardak's "email" reached me in the evening.[129] The next morning, Tolstopiatenko wanted an update, and I forwarded the email that had arrived the night before.[130] He responded by suggesting the lighting issue be dropped altogether.[131]

I also looked at the specific events he said had problems. It was obfuscation. Only two out of twenty events had questionable lighting issues. I forwarded my analysis to Laporte.[132] I also began pulling tapes I normally would have left online if they skirted too close to what I thought B-SPAN's supervisors might deem problematic. These tapes were brought to GSD for further processing in the hope they could be saved. To cover my flank, whenever staff complained about delays, I noted we were a small team backlogged with overwhelming volume.

New shafts of light began to find us. Jeff McCoy from EXT said they would start featuring more of B-SPAN's coverage on the Bank's home page.[133] He wanted to coordinate with us on future coverage. Wheeler forwarded my analysis of the video data and Forum One's HTML information to de Nevers, to keep her firmly in our camp.[134] Coincidentally, Laporte ran into de Nevers and suggested B-SPAN's traffic was faltering badly. But she already had our information in hand. Perhaps it was time to talk, de Nevers suggested.[135]

Wheeler wanted to frame the discussion. Striving for diplomacy, he suggested to de Nevers no one was to blame for Laporte's and Tolstopiatenko's criticisms of B-SPAN.[136] It was simply a case of competing visions. The managers wanted high-quality productions of glamorous Bank events. B-SPAN was designed to just be there covering as many events as possible, and making them available quickly. Wheeler noted, "By their round-hole criteria, B-SPAN may always be a 'failure,' even if, by square-peg criteria, it is a brilliant success." Wheeler and I carefully discussed the punch line. His recommendation was B-SPAN should continue to develop according to its original mandate. If Laporte and Tolstopiatenko found this option incompatible with their philosophy and wanted a plausible exit strategy, Wheeler would be happy to reclaim management.

In retrospect, to hope the offer would be taken seriously was myopic. The first priority of a bureaucrat is to take credit for successes. The second is to find scapegoats for failures. If a scapegoat cannot be found, the final priority is to find an explanation where no blame could be linked back to them. For Laporte to accept such an offer would be to admit his management had been a failure. He would not relinquish control of B-SPAN.

As the calendar moved into December, the clock was ticking for Bowden and me. Our contracts expired at the end of the month. No renewal for us meant B-SPAN was finished. It was the key tactical weapon Laporte and Tolstopiatenko could use to bend us into submission. It was possible they might say they inherited a flawed project that needed to be terminated. On the other hand, as Wheeler pointed out, if they renewed our contracts, more senior officials would assume any failing of B-SPAN would be their responsibility. It was delicate for all involved.

Evidence of capitulation, however, was already in the air. In helping Laporte prepare a presentation for Millet, Tolstopiatenko listed B-SPAN as the first service the I Team provided.[137] Individual I Team members began opting out of the next scheduled B-SPAN staff meeting. As a result, Tolstopiatenko decided to drop it altogether.[138] When EXT ran our coverage of a conference on disability and development attended by Queen Noor of Jordan and U.S. Senator Ted Kennedy on the Bank's home page, Tolstopiatenko sent us a congratulatory note copied to Laporte.[139] To Bowden and Means, I wrote, "I couldn't run this thing without you, though I suspect more likely you could run it without me."[140] "We will always need you to be the strong arm," Bowden wrote back.[141]

Since momentum was finally moving in our direction, I decided to speed it along. Laporte had said his door was always open to me. Now, I thought to test how wide. I asked for a meeting and he agreed.[142] Good news came shortly before we sat down. We were setting traffic records on all major indicators.[143] Hits climbed above 190,000. Visitors rose over 10,000. Page views went past 80,000. We had jumped to third place for page requests among 72 WBI sub-sites. Well over half the page views for our video traffic were now five minutes or longer, and 43% of visitors were online for ten minutes or longer. Half our traffic came online during non-working hours, suggesting B-SPAN was being accessed in other time zones, or used in this one as a supplemental tool. During the calendar year, web hits increased 259%.[144] Page views grew by 205%.[145] Visits rose 193% and visitors escalated by 330%.[146] The numbers were solid. We were winning. I documented a range of other positive developments and suggested solutions to points of friction in recent weeks. Then, with the bases covered, I tried to corner Laporte on our contracts. "The terms of reference we should write for January should include a strategy for marketing the service," I suggested. He did not respond to my suggestion, but otherwise the meeting did seem to go well.[147]

Knowing Laporte would communicate the results of the meeting to Tolstopiatenko, there were two messages I sought to convey: First was to let Laporte know how well things were really going. His understanding of B-SPAN had been colored by the filter of Tolstopiatenko's lens. Second was to remind Tolstopiatenko it was possible for us to skip over him up the chain of command. The I Team manager said he heard we had had a good meeting, and would I share my traffic analysis.[148] Both messages had registered. The next day, I sent a note formally requesting renewal of our contracts.[149] There was no reply.

The final days of the year wilted. B-SPAN continued to pump out content. I sent the two managers a note that December's traffic was about to shatter all previous records.[150] Laporte only wanted to know about video data that would not be available until January.[151] As Christmas loomed, I sent a final note about our contracts.[152] Again, there was no response. Bowden and I made preparations to leave for Christmas and perhaps for good. Then, we got the news. It did not come in a formal note or call from either manager, but by chance. Bowden ran into one of the administrative assistants for the division. "Yes, your contracts have been renewed for six months through the balance of the fiscal year," he noted.[153]

There was no other feedback with the exception of B-SPAN's constituents, Bank staff, and external viewers who marveled at the offerings made available each day for more than two years. Thus 2002 ended. It had been a tumultuous experience. But there would be no holiday. Another tough year was about to begin.

7

2003

2002 did not end in a draw. B-SPAN still existed. On every battlefield our adversaries chose, they had been outmaneuvered and defeated by short-term consultants working on part-time remuneration with no formal authority. The only arsenal in our repertoire was an unwavering belief in B-SPAN, and the integrity to defend it. These men had the power to end our association with B-SPAN and the desire to use the power, but we continuously made them too impotent to act. But it was illogical that they could not see the advantages of embracing B-SPAN. It was generating high praise from staff and stakeholders alike. Yet neither manager wanted to reverse course and reap the benefits of B-SPAN's success. In 2003, both chose to continue waging war.

B-SPAN had allies, of course. Bowden and Means fought in the trenches, helping me respond adroitly to attacks. Wheeler stayed unobtrusively in the background, offering counsel and taking the temperature of senior officials as events evolved. Further in the distance was de Nevers, and even further afield was Leautier, whose public pronouncements of praise had proven stifling to those who plotted to destroy this unique and transparent internal broadcasting station. The vice president, however, was not aware of the war being waged by her subordinates. Her public compliments were coincidental. The timing for us was fortuitous.

Never did I believe the ground I was defending was for me, though the stakes were personally high. Nor was it even for those supporters inside the Bank who used B-SPAN to communicate. Rather, B-SPAN was for the stakeholders the Bank served. They needed to know the Bank could be an honest and engaged partner in their struggle. They now knew there was a transparent means of communicating with the institution. That would vanish if B-SPAN ceased to exist. If B-SPAN survived under its original mandate, the Bank would move in a profoundly new direction. To lose the battle would mean the institution would drift irreversibly backwards, and recede into the mists of monolithic secrecy. Our battle was being fought on behalf of millions who had never heard of B-SPAN or the World Bank, and perhaps never would.

Certainly perspectives on B-SPAN varied widely in WBI. This was possible because, in bureaucracies, information filters from top to bottom quickly, but the flow in reverse happens slowly, if at all. I was reminded of this when one day I ran into the vice president. She was hearing great things about us and was quite happy about our progress. The compliment was gratifying, but it was what she wasn't hearing that was troublesome.

Revelations about our mantra of "dissemination with impact" floated back to me. A friend in Moldova congratulated me on our coverage of Jared Diamond's speech.[154] Our former nemesis Biju Rao requested traffic analysis of the research seminars he hosted.[155] Twenty or thirty people attended his events. My investigation revealed the archived files were being streamed to three or four times that many viewers each month for months at a time.[156] January's statistics reported B-SPAN had become WBI's number one website for page requests.[157] Moreover, WBI's share of page requests within the Bank's overall Internet infrastructure had grown from 11% to 16% during 2002. B-SPAN, more than any other single WBI site, had been responsible for driving this increase. Wheeler wrote me to say B-SPAN now accounted for 2% of all Bank traffic.[158] It was a stunning revelation. Yet, Tolstopiatenko continued to remind us we remained a pilot project that could be shut down any time. Still, the bite was already gone from the I Team manager's attack. He and Laporte no longer mentioned B-SPAN's traffic as a concern.

Positive developments continued. Our archives were getting richer each day. I began marketing again. I pressed for inclusion on Bank newsletters with distribution lists of five hundred or more, and sent tailored emails to their editors informing them of content specific to them.[159] It paid an immediate dividend. Nick Harrison, the editor of the Bank's *Week in Review* newsletter, said he was looking for new and innovative content.[160] He would begin highlighting our events each week. B-SPAN had moved past NIPR to become the second largest newsletter distribution list in the Bank, but Harrison had the largest. It was a nice payoff on both ends. By the fall, Harrison wrote me a note he had become reliant on B-SPAN to provide material for his newsletter.[161] Other newsletter editors began following suit. I started a new tactic. Now, when an event on water issues in Ghana became available, for example, the Bank's director for Ghana and the sector manager for African water issues would receive a tailored note from me.[162]

One day, EXT's liaison for Europe and Central Asia wrote to ask if B-SPAN would host a videotaped briefing by the European Bank for Reconstruction and Development (EBRD) on the economic progress of the transition countries in the former Soviet Union.[163] I immediately accepted.[164] It was valuable content, and importantly, the event had been held inside the IMF. My previous attempts to entice the IMF to disseminate events on B-SPAN had been rebuffed. It was an unusual opportunity, and a precedent I hoped to exploit when the current struggle within WBI settled down. It went online without further discussion. By degrees, the Bretton Woods financial institutions were becoming acclimated to us. Then, abruptly, the weather changed again.

Tolstopiatenko reemerged from the reeds. We had video files on three different ISG servers. He wanted them moved to one server, and reiterated interest in deactivating those B-SPAN files generating low demand.[165] This request coincided with the formal introduction of the database Tse designed as the substitute for our Forum One system. It was called Video on Demand (VoD), generated a vanilla look and feel, and was gratingly boring.[166] More importantly, it did not duplicate the most essential reason we had Forum One's system developed. It was not capable of pushing our content to other websites. The chaos of transferring files to the new database would also be considerable. I wondered how much of our content might not make it. Then Laporte sent a note criticizing old text on the website that described what the B-SPAN station did.[167] He wanted the copy vetted by all I Team members. Laporte had little time for substantive involvement, but he had time for this. I wet my finger and stuck it in the air.

With space finally available, Bowden and I moved our computers, files, and encoding equipment out of the Research Department and into offices near Tolstopiatenko and Laporte.[168] Wheeler thought it might be helpful, because we would officially be part of the tribe. I was less sanguine. The die had been cast and the course charted. Wherever we sat, we would be considered insurgents. The next week a large group of our Research friends took us to lunch for a touching farewell.[169] The comparison with where we were headed could not have been starker.

The timing of Laporte's note was important, because it was a period during which I hoped to marginalize Tolstopiatenko. To head off further agonizing B-SPAN meetings, which had become forums for I Team adversaries to take shots at us, I asked again to meet Laporte alone.[170] He granted the request.

B-SPAN had experienced a nice run. I thought the timing advantageous to push my agenda. I asked him to give B-SPAN autonomy from the I Team and to allow us to report directly to him. I knew Laporte would need a rationale to consider such a drastic move. I elaborated. "When B-SPAN was originally aligned within WBI Knowledge Learning," I said, "it was perceived as a website and linked up with the division's web-design unit, the I Team. There are, however, 80 websites within WBI, and none are part of the I Team. More importantly, we are a news-broadcasting system. The I Team has no experience operating such a system. It is true we have technological needs fulfilled by I Team members, but those service requirements are no different for the 80 other WBI sub-sites. From our perspective, autonomy to report directly to you would lift a huge burden from the I Team."

Laporte listened intently without interrupting. When I finished, he said he was already thinking about separating us from the I Team, but no formal move could be made until the fiscal year closed. It wasn't a promise, but the response generated hope. In the meantime, he asked me to work more collegially with the I Team. I said I would do all I could. I decided my first peace overture would be to start attending Tolstopiatenko's weekly I Team meetings again, after having abandoned them in the fall.

Per Operation Feel Good, I emptied the spigot. December's hits had jumped to 223,000, and page views to 112,000, both all-time highs.[171] Hits had grown 81% since August. Page views had grown by 75%. Bank servers had crashed several times during the holiday recess, but there seemed no stopping the B-SPAN tsunami.[172] Testimonials from supporters were coming in waves.[173] "If we were a stock, our stakeholders might consider retiring," I joked.

Yet even here, with the wind filling all sails, a thread of discontent was being sown. Laporte and Tolstopiatenko had pressed aggressively for months to synchronize video files with a speaker's PowerPoint presentation. A pilot Bowden and Montenegro, Tolstopiatenko's I Team colleague, created had proven too cumbersome. Bowden continued his research, and found new software that could do the synchronization quickly and efficiently. He also found someone with the experience to implement it. Dany Jones was a consultant who worked closely with Peter Midgeley, editing video files for the Bank's Transport unit. With his contract expiring, he was looking for a new assignment.[174] It would be a good fit, and would help me move Bowden off encoding and into writing exclusively. I could devote less time to summarizing events with him and more time to preaching the gospel. It might also translate into an increase in our operating budget. I decided to raise a trial balloon.

"Jones would be a great addition for us, even in a part-time status," I suggested. Laporte was supportive, but wanted to run it by Tolstopiatenko first. The seeds for the next important struggle had just been planted. We moved on. Laporte wanted to understand more clearly how staff felt about B-SPAN. He asked me to meet with someone in the unit who had experience in developing focus groups. Regarding the perspectives of B-SPAN's most important clients, the Bank's stakeholders, Laporte did not express an interest.[175]

For a brief period, a lull ensued. Like two boxers gasping for air and assessing rope burns, both sides paused to await the next round. Bowden sounded out I Team colleagues to decipher Tolstopiatenko's intentions. They had become less enamored by his management style. Before our arrival, his authority was unquestioned. The destabilization created by the furor between Tolstopiatenko and B-SPAN, however, now empowered some members to openly criticize him.

A new opportunity unfolded. It had been a year since my discussion with Burger, Salem, and Wachira about pushing B-SPAN's content through the GDLN Distance Learning Centers throughout the world. Two administrators from the Tanzanian DLC were visiting Washington, and the troika wanted them to meet with me.[176] After debriefing the Tanzanians about B-SPAN, we discussed how content could be provided and used, and how the DLC could market the material to attract customers. I asked the officials what topics were of relevance to their stakeholders, and said when new events in these targeted subjects came online I would alert them as part of my outreach activities. I also suggested having subjects identified might allow us to target events more strategically. As had been the case once before, we all left the meeting sensing the enormous opportunities before us. If the Tanzanian DLC could be used as a prototype to push out B-SPAN's content, the enormous GDLN infrastructure might be activated to achieve spectacular results.[177]

Afterwards, I put together a memorandum for the Tanzanians that outlined collaborative opportunities.[178] Based on subjects they cited, our archives held 34 events they could offer clients immediately. Marketing opportunities I suggested for their consideration included advertising events shown at specific times, offering ongoing viewings of events related to a specific topic, and combining our videos with their related course and training activities. Finally, I floated a long-held strategic goal of having Tanzanian DLC stakeholders who were experts in their fields, conduct their own seminars to be filmed on-site in Dar es Salaam, and sent back to B-SPAN for airing. I copied Laporte and Monika Weber-Fahr, the new GDLN manager.[179] Neither, however, reacted.

As mentioned before, the GDLN network was vast, but had many weaknesses. With a mandate to fill the studio time of its DLC satellites, it nevertheless offered little self-generated content. Salem had been telling Weber-Fahr routinely about B-SPAN's free content.[180] She expressed no interest. Salem tried a new tactic. He asked me to put together a proposal to apply for trust funds.[181] These funds represented targeted sources of donor funding administered by the Bank. The proposal was to visit DLC facilities in several regions to educate them about B-SPAN resources, and to develop location-specific marketing opportunities with stakeholders. The application went nowhere. As much as was possible within the limits of my time and energy, I sought to kick the ball down the field. But it could only go some of the way. To cross the goal line would require Weber-Fahr's approval. With Tolstopiatenko and Laporte at my heels, clear signals were needed. Salem and I were getting none. Weber-Fahr's inertia—or was there more to it?—prevented us from capitalizing on this unique window. In the months that followed, the Tanzanians routinely thanked me for the updates they used to attract customers.[182] No word ever came from GDLN's management.

Burger continued enthusiastic communications with liaisons in the field.[183] Soon thereafter, David Mikosz, who administered DLC facilities in the Kyrgyz Republic, Uzbekistan, and Tajikistan, responded.[184] He wanted to offer B-SPAN products. In fact, Mikosz went a step further. He liked my idea of stakeholders generating content, and suggested an event he had in mind. I suddenly vacillated.[185] "While B-SPAN remains open to the possibility of receiving information such as the conference you cited, it would seem appropriate to build a solid system outwardly before adding a component that redirects information to us. There is room for both, and in time there will be both, but it's probably best for us to walk before we can run," I wrote back. The fact remained that I was waging a two-front war: Running a webcasting station and institutionalizing the concept of transparency. I had no moments to spare, and opening a potential third battlefront with Tolstopiatenko and Laporte posed much risk. Yet Mikosz was presenting an opportunity to bypass GDLN's central management to begin germination of my goal for decentralizing content generation. Circumstances would lead me to believe I had made a serious mistake.

Like a shark, agitated but unable to act, Tolstopiatenko thrashed in the background. He tried a new tactic. He hinted Tse's VoD system would become an internal webcasting service.[186] Conceivably, such a service would rival B-SPAN, and compete for the same clientele. Tse had finished a new prototype. It was strikingly similar to B-SPAN, right down to the language used to describe itself.[187] I forwarded the link to Wheeler. Obvious plagiarism, he called it.[188] "Typical Bank behavior," he added. "Lurk until something looks proven, then copycat."

We resumed our old debate on establishing Peekaboo or ceding the terrain to Tolstopiatenko. It was a delicate question. The instincts of bureaucracies run deep and last long. We had spent three difficult years trying to change the culture. It was happening, but with the establishment of an internal-only system, Bank staff might begin to revert to its instinctive antecedents. To allow Tolstopiatenko to launch such a service would be to voluntarily accept an ambitious and dangerous competitor—one with a vendetta, and the ability to destabilize our delicate progress. I reverted to my original position. I told Wheeler, as before, if an internal service was created, we were best served by controlling it ourselves. We could have it, not promote it or provide it with the bells or whistles clients received from B-SPAN, and perhaps even use substantial charges as a way of creating a disincentive for turning away from B-SPAN. He agreed. There was no easy answer, but my instinct was to delay until necessary. When Comrade A moved, Peekaboo would emerge above the waves like a fog.

I also sensed the advent of VoD was a ploy by Tolstopiatenko to co-opt daily management of B-SPAN. He was pressing to have our website deactivated so the VoD database would become the formal vehicle for public access. He ordered me to identify the cost of employing Means as our website administrator.[189] Her encoding role had been assumed by Bowden. Tolstopiatenko wanted to encourage Laporte to eliminate her involvement entirely. Tse, as developer of VoD, would manage functions Means performed. Since Tse worked closely with Tolstopiatenko, our adversary suddenly would control any material that went on B-SPAN. It was a clever maneuver, and while I could identify the dangers, identifying opportunities to sidestep them were more problematic. I made the unavoidable inquiries, and forwarded Means's expense sheets.

We already had had reminders about the fragility of transparency within multilateral financial institutions. Given the context of the Peekaboo versus VoD debate, the next example was timely. Various UN agencies were coming to a Bank-hosted gathering on preserving cultural heritage and protecting the rights of indigenous peoples. It was an excellent opportunity to highlight activities underway. Everyone agreed except one agency representative. Informal discussions shouldn't be made public, she said. Informal discussions were what B-SPAN was about, I argued. I tried persuasion. All the other agencies had agreed to the webcast, but none would have the opportunity to communicate their achievements unless all participants agreed. They might wish to know why you are refusing to join in, I told her. Nice try, she suggested, but refused to budge. Our offer of coverage had to be cancelled.[190]

Our core business continued to be successful as ever. The volume of material remained intense. By March, our archives streaked past 350 events.[191] As a team, we were getting sharper with each passing day. When Irish Prime Minister Bertie Ahern spoke at Wolfensohn's Presidential Lecture about Ireland's economic growth during the 1990s, and the lessons it had learned about development, we provided a stream within a few hours.[192] To minimize our turnaround time, I convinced EXT to give me Ahern's embargoed speech.[193] When they agreed, it signaled to me in EXT's eyes, B-SPAN was a growing presence. With Ahern featured on B-SPAN's home page so quickly, we had even scooped EXT, which did not report on Ahern until several days later.[194] Despite all obstacles put in our way, we were leaving our opponents behind.

Tolstopiatenko called for another meeting, but it was scheduled in the midst of our coverage of Bertie Ahern and a series of related Environment Department events.[195] I politely declined and suggested we reschedule in April.[196] Such a response would have been unfathomable a couple months earlier. Now, Tolstopiatenko meekly accepted.[197] Instead, he spent his time extolling to Leautier and Millet the virtues of a new effort by the I Team. This project "proved the value of the 'extended' Internet Team," he wrote them.[198] Laporte was quick to add he was also "very impressed and proud."[199] The new product line was cartoons-on-demand. The target audiences for our WBI managers and for B-SPAN were very different. Laporte and Tolstopiatenko had the I Team use resources to showcase its services to an internal audience, namely WBI colleagues and senior management. We were pushing out knowledge about development issues to the entire world. Their focus was straight up. Ours was straight out. I sensed the steam had gone out of B-SPAN's opponents.

But I was wrong. Clouds were forming again on the horizon.

I sent a request to Laporte and Tolstopiatenko to hire Jones to install the software we purchased to synchronize PowerPoints with videos.[200] I was offering them a low-cost, short-term solution with an experienced consultant, and hoped the results would compel them to keep Jones on-board indefinitely. Neither manager responded. Bowden followed up with Tolstopiatenko a few weeks later.[201] "It's frozen for now," he responded. "Please tell David that next time he should talk to me before he submits anything to Bruno."[202] He believed I had encroached on his territory. The temperature moved from simmer to boil.

Tolstopiatenko wasted little time in firing a second salvo. For WBI's annual Knowledge Forum, Bowden developed a draft brochure on B-SPAN.[203] When it was forwarded to the I Team for comment, its manager reacted. "B-SPAN is not an Internet broadcasting station," he charged.[204] Rather it was a simple encoding service. He also criticized traffic data Bowden had chosen to highlight. To a non-partisan outsider, whether B-SPAN was a station or a service might seem a nuance. Inside the trenches, it symbolized the crux of our internal conflicts. Comrade A had reemerged from the sidelines, and signaled he was ready to lock horns again.

I was ready, too, and responded immediately.[205] His position was nothing short of astounding, I suggested. I provided a lengthy quote from my speech given at Laporte's retreat the previous summer, refuting the perspective he embraced. B-SPAN was not a technology or a website, it read. It was a broadcasting system that used the Internet as its medium to communicate news, information and ideas. The stage had been set for the next important confrontation.

April exploded onto the scene. My habit, as each month began, was to check traffic data for the previous month. March heralded more excellent news.[206] Web hits had climbed to a quarter million, putting us on pace to generate three million annually. Visitors climbed to 12,000 and visits to 22,000. Growth remained unquestionably strong.

In light of the cancelled B-SPAN meeting a few weeks earlier, Laporte asked me to stop by to give him an update.[207] The March numbers were timely. He reacted with indifference. Here I was handing him great news, something he could cite to superiors as a success story under his command, yet he acted as if I was wasting his time.

I tried a new tactic, one Wheeler had suggested. "As B-SPAN's popularity has grown, demand for our services has increased," I told Laporte. "We need a budget increase, and perhaps you might make a request to the vice president early in the deliberation process for the next fiscal year." The rationale behind the increase request for B-SPAN was that it would mean an increase in Laporte's overall budget, a prospect almost all bureaucrats relish. Without the slightest hesitation, he said, "Absolutely not. The vice president indicated there would be no budget increases in July." In fact, Laporte wanted us to start implementing a user fee, and ordered a proposal drafted.

I was hearing nothing good. I tried an end run. "We are facing a growing backlog of events. Now that the RealPresenter has been purchased, if we could hire Dany Jones temporarily to do the encoding and simultaneous PowerPoint synchronization, it would free Bowden to tackle our surplus." Laporte asked whether I had discussed the matter with Tolstopiatenko, and I noted he had stopped the request. "Well, that's whom you need to talk to," he countered. Like a rat in a maze, I kept running into walls.

I had always followed Wheeler's advice not to criticize Tolstopiatenko in front of Laporte. But now I had had enough. "Frankly, I don't trust Tolstopiatenko," I said. "He's done nothing but undermine me. He keeps me from doing my work by shackling me with paperwork or complaints about miniscule problems. He keeps me from growing B-SPAN. He takes steps to injure the system."

In a normal environment, I would have been writing my termination notice. But B-SPAN was not a normal situation. It was a high-profile venture achieving spectacular results with plaudits from its vice president and from peers throughout the Bank. Laporte was pinned down and could not move. I repeated my desire for autonomy to report directly to him.

"That is not going happen," he snapped. "Tolstopiatenko's your boss and you're going to make that relationship work!" For a moment, we both paused. I reached into a folder and broke the silence by reading Tolstopiatenko's email to Bowden about freezing our request to hire Jones. Laporte's expression changed. "Well, that's an inappropriate response for a manager," he agreed. He asked me to forward the email to him. He would query Tolstopiatenko as to where the request stood.[208] It was a concession, but the meeting ended with both us still steaming.[209]

The next morning, Tolstopiatenko called me into his office. I closed the door. "I'm trying to decide whether to replace you as manager of B-SPAN," he began. The temper I had kept in check for months finally exploded. "Fine! You've just threatened me," I roared. I got up and began to leave. He asked me to stay, and said something conciliatory. He wanted to have a productive relationship, he added. "I'm sick and tired of you stabbing me in the back," I countered. I was in a full rage. "If you want a productive relationship, you will need to build trust," I added. "That means stop criticizing B-SPAN in public and start saying good things. That means stop undermining our work." I spewed for a while. The volume of my voice carried into the hallway, likely ending old rumors and beginning new ones. Tolstopiatenko suggested there were misperceptions on both sides. He asked if we could make a fresh beginning. I calmed down. We agreed to start again.[210]

We addressed some of the current sticking points between us. The I Team was developing a team brochure.[211] The information Bowden had provided on B-SPAN cited ISG's traffic numbers rather than his. I agreed to use Tolstopiatenko's data. He said he wanted I Team members to install the RealPresenter rather than hiring Jones. For a pledge to change his tune toward B-SPAN, it seemed like a worthwhile trade. I said ok. We parted. Later in the day, I met Laporte outside the building. It was common for me to not see him for weeks at a time. Our bumping into each other was coincidental. He said he heard I had met with Tolstopiatenko. "After he threatened to fire me, I think our meeting went well," I responded. Laporte was smiling. "If

B-SPAN was a sunset activity, it would be different," he said.[212] But it was not.

8

These exchanges represented the earthquake beneath the waves of a sun-filled ocean. The enormous stresses that had been building for months were somewhat relieved. Though the underlying differences in our philosophies remained in place, there was now an unspoken understanding that covert and overt activities to undermine B-SPAN would stop. Though I had no evidence, I suspected in the days following these discussions, Laporte chastised Tolstopiatenko for his management style. The email exchanges between the I Team manager and me even gained a note of civility.[213] For the moment, the bureaucrats appeared to have accepted, if not embraced, B-SPAN's existence. With the marketing and dissemination strategy I had recently developed, I hoped I could finally start to build something extraordinarily powerful. Though B-SPAN seemed to have found a safer port, it was less clear whether Bowden and I had as well. Our contracts expired in less than two months. The clock was ticking again for us.

One day I received a call from Carter Brandon, an environmental economist in the Bank's South Asia region, and an old ally from our NIPR days. Jeffrey Sachs, recently appointed as Special Advisor to UN General Secretary Kofi Annan on the Millennium Development Goals (MDGs), had asked his assistance in setting up a video conference. He would be in Washington, and wanted to dialogue with a group called the World Affairs Council of Oregon. Brandon asked me to help.[214] I smelled a scoop.

Sachs began the video conference with a speech that mirrored the one he gave at the Bank a year earlier. He implored the donor community to increase aid to alleviate Third World suffering, but the emphasis now was different. He strongly criticized the Bush Administration's decision to begin a military conflict in Iraq. The war, he estimated, would cost $200 billion over the next three years. Citing a World Health Organization (WHO) study, he said just $25 billion invested for drug and nutritional assistance would save 20,000 lives worldwide every day. That would translate into eight million lives saved each year. He went on to cite a CIA report asserting economic hardships and mass deaths from preventable diseases were underlying causes of why numerous governments failed. Failed states were breeding grounds for terrorists and their networks, he said. As the UN's chief advocate for achieving the Millennium Development Goals, Sachs called on the United States to redirect its scientific, technological, and financial resources into development.[215]

Afterwards, I discussed what we were trying to achieve with B-SPAN, and how we would be streaming his discussion to tens of thousands of viewers in our global community. Sachs was immediately excited. We began talking about synergies between us and his work with the UN and Columbia University's Earth Institute.[216] The conversation put my WBI experience in focus. Here, a stakeholder, in this case a prominent personality, instantly recognized B-SPAN's potential whereas B-SPAN's senior management, after a year in control, still did not.

Internal politics aside, client pressures continued unabated. We marched double time to get Sachs's speech online immediately. B-SPAN was a juggernaut, but the volume of material dropped upon our tiny team was becoming unimaginable. Plaudits were coming in just as quickly. One came from Michael Carnahan, director of the World Affairs Council of Oregon, the recipient of Sachs's video conference feed.[217] "That a record of the event is publicly available at all is the first huge gift," Carnahan said. "That someone took the time to summarize the presentation, identify its parts, and even suggest a highlight, all available on audio or video, is just plain amazing. What a service!"

Plaudits aside, there remained enough challenges internally to keep us from enjoying the fruits of our labor. It was too early to tell if I had achieved some sort of détente, or whether the other side was catching its breath, and lubricating its firearms again. To the rest of the world, we were popular, and it translated into a sizeable backlog of inventory. To remain popular, we needed to winnow it down, but we were imploding from our own success and our management continued to deprive us of resources. Then a new problem emerged from an unlikely source.

B-SPAN's participation had been requested again for the Environment Department's annual series of month-long events.[218] One of them featured Wheeler leading a discussion on where the Bank was financing environmental activities. Following *Greening Industry*, my old unit launched a new project to quantify where the Bank was spending money on the environment, and using GIS to juxtapose the analysis with actual conditions in the Bank-designated priority countries. The results suggested the Bank needed to rethink where it was investing resources. In a sense, we had traveled full circle because this was Wheeler's first appearance on B-SPAN. The event was notable for another reason: It would result in a rift between B-SPAN and its original ally.

The Environment Department had been our first client, and their relationship was central to the genesis of B-SPAN. Yet a new group of people had taken over their outreach activities from the team that had worked with us during the 2000 Forum. Word began filtering back there were problems with our coverage. We had been asked to cover Environment Department Director Kristalina Georgieva's presentation on the internal administration of her department.[219] Though I was attending fewer of the events we filmed, I was in the audience for this one, because the next session was Wheeler's presentation. It struck me as odd Georgieva's discussion was being made available; but if the Environment Department wanted it online, then perhaps transparency was reaching a new level. It was not. Galina Arkusinski, their communications liaison, wrote she wanted the presentation taken off-line.[220] Realizing from my attendance that the discussion addressed internal departmental matters, I quickly complied.[221]

During the Stiglitz-Rogoff discussion, Wheeler and I had settled on a policy regarding clients' rights. Ultimately, we decided the client should be able to request material be withdrawn. The final responsibility for whether B-SPAN hosted a video would be theirs. What remained less clear was exactly how "client" was defined. As we saw it, the client was the department or division director or project task manager. Administrative staff would not have authority to make this decision on behalf of their managers. We thought it best to cleave the line this way to prevent a scenario where staff, rather than managers, were making decisions on public dissemination. We understood something about the institutional mindset. Staff would instinctively fear that their superiors might make controversial comments on B-SPAN that they felt might be best kept private. Flushing out bad moments was good staff work. Of course, it was a double-edged sword. Who was to say where the best interests of B-SPAN lay.

I received a follow-up note from Jo Albert, the department's learning coordinator.[222] She didn't realize B-SPAN was a public website, and now wanted all proceedings taken off until reviewed, she said. The request troubled me in several ways. First, we had had a long and fruitful history with the Environment Department. That someone there didn't know what B-SPAN did was odd. Moreover, they had solicited us to make these events public. We had only complied. Did Albert now want them to be for internal viewing only? What was less clear was whether Albert had the authority to make such a decision. Did we need to hear from the presenters of each session, or Georgieva, or perhaps from Ian Johnson, the department's vice president? In addition, these events had already been public for several days, and were featured with top billing in our newsletter.[223] This probably prompted Albert and Arkusinki, two people unknown to me, to act. But how would our audience react to the sudden disappearance of material? There were no simple answers. With my next B-SPAN meeting imminent, I needed to keep things quiet, and stall for time.

The day before the meeting, Tolstopiatenko asked for a pre-meeting update.[224] He wanted to draw up funding scenarios, echoing Laporte at our recent talk. Because of an internal department policy, no WBI service, including B-SPAN, could receive a direct transfer of funds from Bank clients for services rendered. I anticipated their interest in what they called "cost recovery," and developed some options I would present the next day. I discussed them briefly.[225] Then Tolstopiatenko offered some ideas as well. One was to take down B-SPAN's archives, and sell the space to other Bank units. "What would be the point of B-SPAN if we didn't have anything online?" I asked. He awkwardly acknowledged the point, and then mentioned the synchronizing software we purchased for B-SPAN had been installed by Montenegro for the VoD database. We would need to order a second package for us.[226] The software wasn't expensive, but had been ours and he was telling me it had been confiscated. In the spirit of détente, I said nothing. Still, I left his office wondering if he was just being malevolent or had no understanding of the impact of his actions.

By the time the meeting began, Sachs, Irish Prime Minister Ahern, and Kumi Naidoo, a leading South African anti-apartheid activist, already graced B-SPAN's front page.[227] New traffic numbers revealed the percentage of total views for five minutes or less had dropped to 36% while those above 19 minutes had climbed to 53%.[228] Mimicking what American presidents say before Congress each year, I began "The State of B-SPAN is strong."[229] This elicited laughter but it was hard for anyone to suggest otherwise.

I tackled the revenue issue head on. "It is true," I said, "WBI has financed B-SPAN, but we are an institution-wide service. We should reach out to vice presidents and sector and regional networks for co-sponsorships with annual funding requests. The funding requests might begin modestly, yet revenues raised would supplement WBI's investment and would insure coverage of events throughout the institution. It is also time for WBI to change its policy of charging for its services with other Bank units. B-SPAN charges for conference-length events to subsidize free coverage of seminar-length events. This policy gives seminars that lack funding a forum through the resources of well-subsidized conferences. Charging more for conferences is appropriate, for these events have ample budgets for dissemination; and the volume of material they generate co-opts the time and resources of our small team."

Without realizing it, I had made a tactical misstep. Laporte was incredulous. "We are not getting paid for work rendered?" he asked. This shouldn't have been news to him. One of his primary responsibilities was managing the budget for teams under his supervision. Then he asked a ludicrous question. "How much do we charge for covering seminars?" One of our core practices since Leautier's assumption of the department had been to provide free coverage. After a year of administrating B-SPAN, Laporte still did not know how we operated. The question revealed in an instant how disengaged he actually was, and how much he had relied on Tolstopiatenko for information about the program.

"We subsidize all costs of covering seminar-length events," I said. "Well, that must end," he responded. "We need to start charging task managers every time they use B-SPAN." I was appalled. It was exactly the wrong approach. Line managers often didn't have funds to cover the costs of making their events available on B-SPAN. If such a policy was in place, only those with sufficient money could use B-SPAN. We would be creating a "have and have-not" society within the Bank.

I began an appeal. "Vice presidents and networks have sizeable funds available. I want to create partnerships at the start of each fiscal year. For a few thousand dollars, an amount networks would hardly notice, packages of events could be purchased, and individual task managers could receive coverage without giving it a second thought. We could even ask Leautier to make such an appeal on our behalf."

Laporte frowned. He could never ask the vice president to do such a thing, he said. But he wouldn't say why. He wanted to know how much it cost WBI to subsidize one B-SPAN event. Tolstopiatenko leaped up. He estimated $1,000. I knew the guess was inflated conjecture, and said I would research the question. The discussion on cost recovery ended. The meeting moved on.

"It would be a good time for a survey to better understand client demand for the service," Tolstopiatenko suggested. Laporte picked up the banner. "In fact, earlier in the day, Karin Millet said the division should be looking at just this question," he noted. "If demand exceeds supply, then a survey could measure Bank clients' willingness to pay." I smelled a setup, and was struck again by a sense that, before our meetings, the two men carefully scripted what cards they would play, and how they would put them on the table. Bowden and I agreed to begin developing a survey.[230] Laporte wanted a follow-up meeting in two weeks.[231]

Then, as the gathering drew to a close, Laporte threw another haymaker. "B-SPAN should only cover events reflecting the Bank's corporate strategy priorities," he stated. Tolstopiatenko quickly agreed.

What those priorities were, I had no idea. I had never heard the phrase before. Did it mean some events were acceptable, while others had to be turned away? Did it mean B-SPAN would no longer be an open service for staff to communicate with their constituencies? I sensed new problems at hand that could impact B-SPAN gravely. Imposing a charge for B-SPAN's seminars could alone destabilize our client base at a time when it was growing but still vulnerable to pricing shocks. I dialogued with Wheeler. He suggested caucusing with de Nevers when the situation ripened to a critical point.

Laporte and Tolstopiatenko walked off the stage. Albert and Arkusinski walked back on. I convinced Albert to temper her desire to remove everything.[232] She focused on two events, including Wheeler's presentation. To maintain the policy, avoid an undesirable precedent, and keep the squabble from Laporte and Tolstopiatenko, I decided on a two-pronged strategy. I explained our policy of acceding to requests from event managers, and Albert agreed to let the event's co-sponsors, Kristalina Georgieva and Kevin Cleaver, the Bank's rural development director, decide.[233] I agreed to temporarily remove the two events she had pinpointed, pending further clarification from those officials. Cleaver, a featured guest in one of B-SPAN's first webcasts and an old fan, responded shortly he had no problems with the content.[234] Wheeler then wrote Georgieva to say he noticed his event had been removed from B-SPAN.[235] As the presenter, he hoped it would be reinstated. Arkusinski wrote Wheeler back to say she would be happy to ask B-SPAN to make the link public again.[236]

April closed on a promising note. Traffic records continued to be broken.[237] I decided to conduct a more comprehensive review of ISG's statistics. It was revealing. Our video website, in comparison to more than 250 Bank HTML websites, was in the top 22% for web hits, top 14% for page views, top 25% for visits, and top 20% for visitors. B-SPAN also accounted for 13% of WBI's top 1,000 documents and 17% of its top 1,000 single access pages. B-SPAN's team had jelled into a fast-acting, collegial unit motivated by a "bunker" mentality because of the constant fire. We were generating huge amounts of content, and since B-SPAN had something to sell, the public was buying.

As a result, we had become a dominant site within WBI. Now, we were beginning to achieve the same within the Bank's entire Internet infrastructure.[238] Then, EXT's Nicole Frost said she would create a B-SPAN link on the Bank's home page.[239] It appeared overnight. Concurrently, B-SPAN covered an event on grassroots radio stations in Africa. EXT's *World Bank Today* wrote a story on the session, and asked for our video to help with background information. The reporter, Craig Mauro, skimmed the website and called me. He wanted to write another article, this one about B-SPAN.[240]

With issues of traffic and video quality ameliorated, B-SPAN's battle lines now formed around cost recovery. The intermediate step for determining the new policy would be the survey Bowden and I drafted, with inputs from I Team members.[241] Basic questions asked how often staff requested help, whether targeted audiences were internal or external stakeholders, whether their expectations had been met, and suggestions for improvement. The final question asked clients if they would pay for the service. Clients had three choices: They could pay by the event; through an annual allocation; or they could indicate an inability to pay for the webcasting at all. I sent the survey to 61 people who had been our event liaisons. Ultimately, 15 responded.[242] Seven said they were willing to pay by the event.

May was ebbing. The time was marked with quiet as both sides prepared for the next anticipated confrontation. Then, the other side made its move. In asking for the survey results, Tolstopiatenko announced they had decided to start implementing charges shortly.[243] He wanted a breakdown of costs for producing a single event, as well as proposals from me to justify the policy.

This irked me sharply. An important decision was being made without waiting for survey feedback, and I was being asked to provide the "spin" to cover their tracks. The best option, I wrote back, was to keep the service free.[244] Maintaining B-SPAN's volume allowed it to retain its value to WBI. Other options included charging more for conferences, renegotiating GSD's fees, and if absolutely necessary imposing a nominal per event fee ranging from $50 or $100. I forwarded a second note about our cost structure.[245] Salaries, camera costs, website maintenance and equipment acquisition costs (there were no server costs since ISG had yet to charge us) came to $163,000. Given that our volume continued to escalate, per event costs would continue to decline. As it stood, without summarizations, since summaries were not necessary for making a video available, a single B-SPAN event cost WBI less than $400 to produce. I realized Tolstopiatenko would not like the memo. I learned subsequently he did not even forward it to Laporte.

The uneven and unpredictable quilt of positive and negative signs continued to be woven. The quality of our content remained extraordinary. Mamphele Ramphele, a Bank managing director, spoke about growing up as a black in South Africa.[246] Author John Clark discussed the role of civil society in the globalization process. Afterwards, he joked that my summary was so accurate I had no future in journalism.[247]

Roberto Zagha, a senior economist in the Bank's Poverty Reduction (PREM) network, was organizing a new lecture series entitled *Practitioners in Development*. The lectures would feature influential economists and development practitioners throughout the world discussing their experiences. He had been asked by de Nevers and Leautier to have the lectures featured on B-SPAN.[248]

It was another major coup, but unlike previous milestones, the *Practitioners in Development* series would prove pivotal for us in the months ahead. As a prelude to the series, John Williamson, a former Bank economist who was famous for originating the phrase "Washington Consensus," was invited to discuss his perspectives over the past twenty years.[249] Williamson said he coined the phrase to describe key economic reforms he believed were necessary for Latin America during the late 1980s. The region had been plagued then with large deficits, inflation, and devaluation problems. "In the intervening years, however, the Washington Consensus has come to mean something very different," Williamson suggested. "It has evolved into a euphemism for all unpopular macroeconomic reforms imposed upon developing countries by the international financial institutions."

The lecture series officially started several weeks later when former Chilean Minister of Finance Alejandro Foxley spoke about improving income distribution while maintaining fiscal discipline during Chile's economic difficulties of the 1990s.[250] Over the next year and a half, B-SPAN covered every series speaker. They represented a long list of distinguished development giants.

As May concluded, Wheeler had an impromptu meeting with de Nevers and Millet.[251] It was an opportune moment to get their assessment of our transparency effort. Both remained enthusiastic. Privately, de Nevers reiterated her pledge to push for permanent positions for Bowden and me. Communication between levels of the department suggested something was endemically wrong with WBI.

I opened our June meeting with an overview on charging options, event costs, and survey results.[252] Laporte said the time had come for B-SPAN to align itself with the strategic objectives of WBI by implementing a new pricing policy. Then, in a curious moment of bureaucratic double-speak, he added, "B-SPAN's pricing policy would be a reflection of WBI's corporate priorities rather than a concern for cost recovery. B-SPAN should cover events where it could have the most impact on WBI's priorities." Tolstopiatenko followed his lead. "There should be flexibility in the model for WBI to subsidize B-SPAN's costs for events it felt worth covering," he said.

The two were suggesting B-SPAN should outright exclude events or use charges as a disincentive, thereby diminishing the ability of some parts of the Bank to use the system. By their measure, it was all very reasonable. They were WBI managers administering a service that should achieve departmental objectives. There was only one problem. B-SPAN had been invented to serve the whole Bank, not any one part of it. That we were housed in WBI was a quirk of fate. It was the same clash of philosophies that had marked our relationship from the beginning.

When the results of the survey were reported, both managers expressed enthusiasm. Wasn't it marvelous that seven respondents accepted the idea of being charged by the event, they said. I suppressed a laugh, and then tried a counter maneuver. "Only one of the seven responses came from someone who is in a budget-deciding position," I noted. The respondents had been mostly support people. This surprised both men. Laporte was visibly upset. He had wanted to go forward immediately with a pricing model. Now he had no justification to do so. "WBI pays for everything it does. I don't see why B-SPAN should be fully subsidized by the department," he said. I parried. "B-SPAN's success stemmed from the volume of content it produced. If we implement seminar charges, volume would drop. Then B-SPAN's value to the Bank, and concurrently to WBI, would decline." I tried a feint. "We cover numerous conferences, events that have significant budget support. Why don't we raise our conference charges?" Laporte asked what percentage of our events were conferences. About 10%, I answered. "Not good enough," he responded. My mind was racing. I needed something better. "Opinions are needed from senior sector leaders and task managers to determine their willingness to pay for seminar coverage," I noted. "We should hold focus groups." The suggestion sought to play on Laporte's cautious bureaucratic instincts. It worked. He said yes.[253]

Laporte then asked about the nature of our clientele outside the Bank. I noted it was mostly academics. On the surface, an objective observer might infer this was positive, since WBI was the pedagogical arm of the Bank. Not so. "Academia is not who B-SPAN should serve," Laporte said. "WBI's mission is to build client capacity and B-SPAN should be helping WBI's clients." It was an illogical statement. Tolstopiatenko began firing rounds. "Perhaps from now on Shaman should stop being involved in event selections, and the decision should be done through a committee process."

Laporte thought only high-profile events like Stiglitz-Rogoff (which curiously was the most controversial of all our events) warranted B-SPAN's coverage. "The true value of the service is the smaller, cutting-edge discussions," I countered. Bowden added B-SPAN's strength was its transparency. "Transparency was yesterday's problem," Laporte retorted. "B-SPAN should not continue to be an open window on Bank activities. It should serve WBI's corporate strategy. If the only issue is about B-SPAN's transparency, then it might as well be housed in EXT." I was dumbfounded. Laporte had just said a remarkable thing. He closed the meeting by stating he was sure Leautier would not support a service used primarily by academics.[254]

As always, these meetings revealed Laporte's frame of mind, and just how far apart we were on how B-SPAN should be used. I had felt from the beginning his opposition to B-SPAN was not preordained, though his enthusiasm for our transparency edict was rather lukewarm. Instead, Laporte seemed like an overwhelmed manager overmatched by events. He administered a sizeable group, and was being squeezed by funding limitations. Certainly, I had to weigh all the oddities that came from a volatile environment, so it was possible to feel a trace of sympathy. This meeting put things in clearer perspective. My conclusion, therefore, was inevitable. Laporte was more than just inept. He had become a dangerous antagonist.

Afterwards, Tolstopiatenko stopped by and I was able to learn more about Laporte's thinking. "B-SPAN didn't actually have a specific budget allotment in the division during the current and upcoming fiscal year," he said. This meant, since it wasn't a specific line item, it was up to Laporte to determine how much was spent. Additionally, all funds were fungible. Money not spent on B-SPAN could be spent on activities where Laporte had a personal association. Moreover, every dollar B-SPAN raised in charges was revenue he could direct into his pet projects. The notion of B-SPAN selecting specific events and charging Bank clients to support WBI corporate priorities was just a ruse. Tolstopiatenko leaked another nugget of valuable intelligence. Over the next six months, Laporte would seek to make half of B-SPAN's content learning courses and training activities. If he succeeded, it would mean the death knell for B-SPAN.[255]

Laporte wanted a focus group convened before the end of the fiscal year, then just two weeks off.[256] I recalculated event costs, and drafted an invitation to sector managers. My note on cost analysis prompted a sharp rebuke from him.[257] Why had I not described how B-SPAN would align itself with WBI's corporate priorities?

But what were WBI's corporate priorities? They had not been defined by WBI's senior management. They were not written anywhere. In short, no one really knew. With all that was swirling around us, I had put together another comprehensive document on B-SPAN's vision and objectives.[258] With inputs from Bowden, the document included client and traffic analysis, product analysis, revised cost estimates, competitor analysis, pricing strategies, and operational and strategic initiatives, including suggestions on closer alignments with WBI's pedagogical agenda.

The juggernaut of incoming content remained unabated, and I refused to turn away requests. The volume was driving traffic that in turn undermined Laporte and Tolstopiatenko's ability to destroy B-SPAN.

Bowden, however, was frustrated. He was encoding and summarizing an overwhelming amount of content, and worried that delays in making events public would hurt our reputation. He was sick of the dysfunctional environment our managers had created. The strain was enormous. Our contracts expired in days, and we were battling for our institutional lives.[259] Our nerves were fraying. We began bickering.

I continued to rely on Wheeler to play the inside game. He sent an appeal to de Nevers for dedicated funding.[260] If Laporte didn't believe in the program, perhaps it could be arranged that Shaman report directly to Millet, he suggested. To test the buoyancy of Wheeler's note, I had an impromptu caucus with de Nevers. She suggested maybe the best thing would be to move B-SPAN into EXT. The notion of moving B-SPAN out of WBI had long been on our minds, but we needed autonomy. Though autonomy might leave us unfunded, we needed independence from the political agendas of any branch of the institution. Moving to EXT also had the distinct potential of leading to irreconcilable differences, since our agendas were diametrically opposite. As the public relations branch of the institution, EXT was focused on enhancing the Bank's image. By contrast, B-SPAN was an open forum that allowed the world to see the Bank as it was. Moving B-SPAN to the president's office would place us in an artificially high political environment. We couldn't go back to the Research Department. Where else could we go? Until a haven revealed itself, I reluctantly concluded we would have to remain where we were. The message we kept hearing was Leautier and Millet believed in our transparency model. If Laporte and Tolstopiatenko didn't believe in B-SPAN, then we should report to a new manager. I wrote Wheeler to suggest he ask de Nevers float his own name to Millet.[261] The fiscal year was ending. It seemed like a useful moment to again make such an appeal.

On our flank, Albert and Arkusinski fired another salvo. They decided Wheeler was not the event host but simply a presenter and that Las Vidaeus, the department's deputy director was the host. They said Vidaeus wanted Wheeler's presentation taken off B-SPAN.[262] I remembered a Civil War anecdote of how the North captured two English officials aboard a rebel ship, and held them prisoners. When Queen Victoria hinted she might declare war, Lincoln freed the pair. "One war at a time," he said. I capitulated, and had Wheeler's presentation taken down.[263]

In preparation for the pivotal focus group, Bowden and I decided to stack the deck with allies. I asked de Nevers to attend, but she had a scheduling conflict.[264] Tia Duer, Bowden's former manager and WBI's new business development leader, however, responded positively. She was staunchly opposed to the charging scheme. We needed more help. I appealed to Macdonald who agreed to attend. Nine managers attended the session, including two who would have important roles in B-SPAN's future: Erik Johnson and Kathy Sheram.[265]

Laporte opened the session by asking the Bank managers where they thought B-SPAN could be improved. One by one they stood up and applauded the system. B-SPAN was helping them reach their constituents, they said. Some added personal praise of the work Bowden and I were doing, and for our responsiveness to their requests. I stood in the corner, expressionless and silent.

One noted the importance of our free coverage. Laporte took the cue to suggest B-SPAN might have to begin charging. Macdonald interrupted. "Any charges would have to be miniscule since B-SPAN is a public good for the Bank. A substantive charge would force me to seek budget approval with each event, and would essentially curtail my use of the service." Beata Smarzynski of the Research Department's trade team followed suit. She used B-SPAN often, but charges would end her ability to rely on it any longer. Duer went further. "Charges will kill B-SPAN," she said. "There is too much concern inside the Bank over issues of cost recovery." Reiterating the appeal I had made all along, if there were to be charges, she said, "They should be institutionalized on an annual basis rather than at the event-level. Task managers will not have the funds at their disposal to cover individual events."

"Everything has a cost," Laporte countered. "For example, providing coffee to the focus group is a cost to WBI."

"Information is different than coffee," Duer shot back. "It is hard to capture the private benefits of the knowledge sharing B-SPAN provides. B-SPAN's information is a public good. The ability of internal clients to access B-SPAN's services freely is essential, because it is for the good of the entire institution." For a moment, the room was silent. Macdonald re-entered the fray. "Having charges to create a revenue stream should only be a secondary consideration," he said. "More important is to monitor B-SPAN's value as a public good." The comments left Laporte visibly shaken. He changed the subject, and asked for suggestions on how B-SPAN could be more effective.

Macdonald noted the importance of B-SPAN archives. "Different people will value different events at different intervals," he said.

Laporte referred a question to me about the makeup of our audience. "It is mostly academics in the OECD (Organisation for Economic Co-operation and Development)," I said. However, I added, anecdotal evidence suggested many of these academics were residents from developing countries attending OECD universities. Laporte, whose role was supposed to be facilitator, switched hats in midstream to offer an opinion. "If that's the case, B-SPAN is not reaching the right clients." Macdonald stopped him in his tracks. "Those are important users," he countered. "Those are the users who return to their countries to become policymakers."

Laporte switched gears again. While he supported the notion of transparent, unedited events, he wanted to know if anyone supported edited content. The query made the support he espoused suddenly seem shallow. No one replied. The conversation drifted off to other subjects. As it ended, Macdonald said the Research Department was very happy with B-SPAN's services. Laporte agreed. "It has been a very successful program," he said. He then left the room with a stunned look on his face.

The next day, I forwarded the minutes to Laporte's attention.[266] Bowden added a compendium of innovative suggestions the group had offered.[267] Our emails, however, were too late. Laporte had already left on a brief vacation, but not before he had sent WBI's senior management his vision for the upcoming year: B-SPAN would begin featuring learning events.[268] There was one more piece of information forthcoming. Our reward for the year's accomplishments had been determined. One of the division's staff assistants said Bowden and I would not receive a new contract.[269] We would be given a 40-day extension to catch up on our backlog of events. When the summer ended, senior WBI officials would meet to reorganize the unit for the year. Then management would decide what to do with us. Laporte and Tolstopiatenko had gone to the edge of the cliff and punted to another day.

9

The business model I wrote for B-SPAN charted a course for growth beyond the current fiscal year and into the future.[270] Its foundation was an analysis of our achievements for the past year. There was deployment of new features, such as indexed streams by speaker or subject, modified streaming rates and audio-only files, as well as improvements in video quality. During the year, we had worked with 44 different Bank units and covered 199 seminar-length events and 12 conferences. Our traffic growth was an unparalleled documentation of success. The cost to put the average event online, including GSD's charge of $250 per event as well as our summaries, came to $450. I also compared our charges with ISG and external vendors. Both were prohibitively more expensive than ours. I included revenue generating options for further consideration.

Also addressed was B-SPAN's strategic alignment with WBI. We had provided extensive coverage of core areas of the department's mandate: Environment, poverty reduction, human development, and private-sector development. I also noted, "To more fully understand the needs and concerns of internal clients, B-SPAN is convening focus groups in FY'04. This will help B-SPAN align its work program to more adequately meet those needs, as they can be met within the context of strategies and objectives being determined by [the division]." I had learned something from my WBI managers. It was classic "bureauspeak." The final section addressed operational plans to improve our service. Improving search functionality, linkages with other Bank sites, pushing content through the Distance Learning Centers, and covering events outside the Bank to create two-way knowledge sharing opportunities were enhancements I envisioned.

With the business-model document, I added a cover note to Laporte. I asked for his guidance and counsel in implementing the proposals. Based on my knowledge of his understanding of B-SPAN, I included something else. It was the operating principles by which we existed. They were simple and spelled out: Unedited videos to guarantee authenticity to the public; permanent archiving to create a virtual library; and free service for Bank clients so they might easily communicate with their constituencies. The document was a comprehensive review of where we had been and where we planned to go.

It also unveiled a serious break in my relationship with Bowden. Our alliance had frayed during the months of relentless work and tension. We shared the same philosophy on B-SPAN's mission, but over time our perspectives on what this vision was worth began to diverge. My view was that B-SPAN's mission was more important than anything else. My colleague had tired of constantly having his employment in jeopardy. He could hardly be blamed. The strain had taken its toll on both of us. Laporte's rebuke for not providing a strategy for aligning with WBI's "corporate" priorities incensed Bowden. He suggested it was a deliberate act of defiance on my part.[271] In reality, Laporte's scolding had caught me by surprise, since his request for such a document had been made casually in one of our staff meeting months before. Instead, I viewed his reaction as a contrived excuse to act punitively, rather than genuine interest in our work. My assessment in the fullness of time proved accurate. After I forwarded a revised document to Laporte and Tolstopiatenko, neither man ever acknowledged its receipt or mentioned it in any way ever again.

Upon his return, Laporte had effusive praise for Tolstopiatenko's introduction of VoD.[272] The deployment, however, had me rankled. A number of the videos were from B-SPAN, but there was no attribution they came from our system. I called him on it, and he agreed to cite us as the source of our own content. He also made a request. He wanted to justify implementing seminar charges, and he wanted me to figure out what those arguments would be. I had to give him credit. He had chutzpah. Still, I refused.

The truly important indicators remained positive. Kemal Dervis, the former Minister of the Treasury and Economic Affairs for Turkey, appeared on the next edition of the *Practitioners in Development* series.[273] Dervis was the Bank's Poverty Reduction and Economic Management (PREM) network's vice president in 2001 when Turkey's prime minister asked him to stabilize rampant inflation and implement structural reforms. Our coverage was seamlessly coordinated with a *World Bank Today* article and placement on the Bank's home page.[274] B-SPAN's home page was arguably stronger: U.S. Health and Human Services Secretary Tommy Thompson speaking on AIDS funding for the Caribbean, Chilean Finance Minister Alejandro Foxley discussing growth strategies, macroeconomist Jeffrey Sachs advocating for increases in water projects to achieve the Millennium Development Goals (MDG), and Bank Chief Economist Nicholas Stern analyzing key drivers of development, were just some of the selections then available to viewers.[275]

Following our publication of the Dervis event, Laporte asked if it was possible to synchronize PowerPoints with the video.[276] I shook my head in wonder. It was clear: Laporte only cared about harmony. Anything regarding substance was not of interest. Yet what he missed was that the battle for B-SPAN's soul had been driving the friction all along. My understanding of his methodology crystallized. He would respond with alacrity to superiors or complaints from institutional counterparts. Since his focus was on pleasing those ranked above him, it left him less time to learn the mechanics of what he administered. As a result, he never appreciated the impact his actions might have on programs he oversaw, other than how the decisions would be perceived by more senior officials. Laporte was most skillful where he spent the bulk of his time: Ingratiating himself with more powerful officials.

In mid-July, Wheeler sent me a note. Laporte wanted to meet him.[277] He did not say why. We began to speculate. Perhaps Laporte was considering Wheeler's proposal to be reinstated as manager of B-SPAN. We agreed he would say little, and if Laporte made an important decision to the contrary it would have to be vetted by the advisory committee. When Wheeler and Laporte met, Laporte admitted Tolstopiatenko had been a disaster, so much so he was going to be sent to a training course to improve his managerial skills. However, it was out of the question to have Wheeler resume control of B-SPAN. Laporte simply had called the meeting to tell him B-SPAN must have a long-term strategy. It must evolve to adopt WBI's objectives rather than its current institution-wide mandate. Frankly, he wasn't sure Shaman was up to the job, he said. As a courtesy to one of B-SPAN's key stakeholders, he was reaching out to Wheeler to hear his views. Perhaps Laporte was hoping for enough understanding to allow him to terminate me. Wheeler's response was succinct and firm. Shaman is exactly the man you need. He left Laporte with much to think about.

Millet held a meeting for her entire unit to review the year's accomplishments. She called B-SPAN one of WBI's shining lights. It was, she said, "phenomenal."[278] Laporte was running out of options.

Summer is a time of relaxation for most Bank staff, many taking their allotments of vacation time. Tolstopiatenko made his annual trek to the Black Sea. Laporte retreated to his native France. For Bowden and me, there was no time off. We worked furiously without any breaks, to winnow the immense backlog we had not processed due to months of turmoil. If we were going to be terminated, we wanted at least to leave the slate clean for our clients.

Laporte had left open the possibility of further focus groups upon his return.[279] In anticipation of this, I began a quiet campaign to solicit the views of the sector managers who had been invited but were unable to attend the first meeting. Their opinions ranged across the board. Some expressed willingness to pay for B-SPAN by the event. Others said it would end their relationship. Any way I looked at implementing the cost recovery approach, it meant the same thing. Some could pay and the rest would watch. WBI would have created a "have and have not" society inside the Bank, which would present a significant irony, considering the institution's mission.

With our managers away, B-SPAN functioned smoothly. As our backlog diminished each day, I mulled over new schemes. I checked Millet's schedule, and thought about requesting a meeting with her. She had praised B-SPAN repeatedly in public and voiced enthusiasm to Wheeler just a few weeks before about what we had accomplished with our initiative. She was Laporte's boss. She worked just down the hall from us, but one irony remained regarding her. We had never met.[280] She did not even know what I looked like.

Leautier did know what I looked like; and in the end, her constituency was the one that counted most. I was keen to find opportunities where we could make her shine. When she participated in a summer video conference with several African trade ministers, we had the event online immediately.[281] There was a quick payoff. *World Bank Today* picked up our stream. As long as we could make the vice president look good in front of Wolfensohn and the Bank's board of directors, we would look good, too. She sent me a complimentary note a few days afterwards.[282]

In fact, we were now featuring so many of the Bank's important events, EXT's Nicole Frost said our billing on the Bank's home page would become permanent. In turn, I convinced Loli Arribas-Banos, who administered the Bank's Intranet page, to also provide a permanent B-SPAN link. We were covered, both inside and out.[283] Not all events, however, were open to us. Former President Jimmy Carter was invited to speak to the Bank's board, and the event was being filmed for internal viewing. Sensing an opportunity to crack into the board's forbidden world, I made a query.[284] The foray generated serious mulling, but the reaction I received was not the one I hoped for. They declined.[285] Allowing B-SPAN's coverage of President Carter would set a precedent for opening a board proceeding to the public, they said. That thought never occurred to me, I responded. The Hail Mary had fallen short, but had been worth throwing nevertheless.

My growing relationship with Craig Mauro and the *World Bank Today* team had helped me maintain their interest in writing a story about B-SPAN. It would make Bowden and me publicly synonymous with B-SPAN, and I hoped would cement job security for us. It would be quite a leap for Laporte to pull the plug after such a public plaudit. I mulled over the article's timing to maximize its impact. The WBIGK Pillar was meeting at the end of August to discuss organizational realignments. Delaying until September, however, would increase the number of Bank staff returning from vacations who would read it. In the end, Mauro determined its timing. He was too busy at the moment, and couldn't get to it until the fall.

As the summer waned, Bowden and I had whittled our backlog to a manageable level. I came across a Dilbert cartoon that seemed apropos for our situation. Dilbert's manager was commending him for performing well doing two jobs during the year. He had no budget to offer a raise. All he could offer was an "Attaboy" award. Unfortunately, he didn't want to cheapen the "Attaboy" system, so that was not forthcoming either.

Upon Laporte's return, I maintained pressure by submitting an update on our progress during his absence.[286] July's HTML traffic had reached an all-time high in hits and page views.[287] We were now generating over three million hits annually. During the summer, we had launched more than 40 new events, and more were coming online. In recent weeks, we had coordinated with *World Bank Today* to feature four of our videos with their articles. They had used our links 15 times since the previous July. EXT had agreed to feature a permanent B-SPAN link on the Bank's external and internal home pages, and a number of prominent Bank sub-sites had followed suit. Most major Bank newsletters were disseminating B-SPAN's content, and we were now regularly providing content to the Development Gateway.[288] The note was copied to Millet. We were pouring a constant and continuous stream of water on Laporte's fire. There was no response, but there could be no doubt he was smoldering.[289]

I was starting to feel confident enough about survival to offer some tongue-in-cheek exchanges with the team. To Bowden and Means, on the prospect of finally catching up on our backlog, we had done "the unthinkable, the unfathomable, the unforgettable and the unimaginable …" It was still possible we would have our contracts terminated shortly, "but, of course, we could use a little time off anyway."[290] To Wheeler, I was even more audacious. When one of the Bank networks sent out a mailing to its subscribers about one of their events on B-SPAN, I noted we were on the verge of becoming institutionalized.[291] Anecdotal evidence suggested my confidence was well founded, but I was still far from the truth.

Tolstopiatenko's house of cards finally collapsed at the end of August. He called us into his office upon his return from vacation.

Also in the room were Erik Johnson and Ron Kim, co-managers of the Knowledge Sharing (KS) team under Laporte. He was brief. Management had decided as part of the Pillar's reorganization, B-SPAN would formally leave the I Team and move to the KS Team. Tolstopiatenko said we were being moved because management recognized we were content providers. It was a face-saving story management invented to cover its original gaffe of merging us with I Team. His fourteen-month rule had dissolved like a passing front of rain and fog. After sailing without a compass for a very long time, I could finally look up and see stars. Tolstopiatenko's traffic data for July closed the loop on his tenure over B-SPAN.[292] Our page requests had climbed to 160,000, jumping over 30,000 from the month before. Under his reign, B-SPAN had become the second-most active website within WBI. Comrade A had presided over our triple-digit growth from the previous year.

PART V
by dawn's early light

1

It had been a miraculous feat. Powerless and temporary gnomes had ousted a heralded and cunning manager. Though Tolstopiatenko began the relationship capable of destroying anyone in his path, he had become persona non grata, even within his own I Team unit. Interestingly, I had mixed feelings about the announcement of his departure. I was ecstatic that I was rid of a disruptive influence over B-SPAN. Our power struggle seemed to have ended, and to the extent the department could say it publicly, management's decision about Tolstopiatenko's incompatibility with B-SPAN was a vindication of all our efforts. However, he was the devil I knew. My counter maneuvers had left him largely ineffectual, and his influence had been waning for months.

On the other hand, I knew Ron Kim, one of my two new managers, only slightly, and Erik Johnson, the other, I did not know at all. Obviously, Millet and Laporte had given me a pass this time. If friction developed between the KS Team and me, no matter the cause, management would view me as the problem. I needed to establish a working relationship with the new managers. It would mean accepting compromises and implementing items on their agenda. I had drawn a line in the sand that I had not allowed Tolstopiatenko or Laporte to cross. The question was whether Johnson and Kim believed in what we were doing to make B-SPAN grow.

Johnson and Kim split the management of activities within the KS Team, and jointly decided Johnson would take the lead on

B-SPAN. He made an immediate overture. It marked a radical departure from Tolstopiatenko's style of dictation. He wanted to listen. He wanted to learn about B-SPAN and Bowden and me. Concurrently, he wanted us to get acquainted with his team's work. He and Kim, both Americans, shared a low-key manner and a willingness to consider new information, and alternative viewpoints, while making decisions. They had a sense of humor. They mocked the Bank's stifling bureaucracy.[1] It was a refreshing departure from the squalls and frothing seas of the previous administration.

Shortly after Johnson took control, he and I sat down to discuss Laporte's extension of our contracts for the calendar year's balance.[2] That gave Bowden and me a five-month window to sway both supervisors. Johnson noted the Bank might revamp its hiring of temporary workers with a new category called Extended Term Consultant (ETC). Over the previous two decades, the institution had increasingly relied on temporary consultants [they had received various titles such as Non-Regular Staff (NRS), Long-Term Consultants (LTC) and Short-Term Consultants (STC)] to help line managers fill interim gaps in their program activities. This growing group of consultants often had the same responsibilities as regular staff, but few benefits and little job security. But it had been a comfortable arrangement for the Bank.

As an international organization, it was not subject to the same labor laws imposed on businesses under U.S. law or that of any other country. By the mid-1990s, the Bank was running an enormous sweatshop where many core activities were designed and implemented by a workforce with no voice and no rights. The inevitable abuses that arose created intense resentment from a growing percentage of the Bank's workforce. To ease the pressure, the institution was considering a proposal to reduce the number of STCs by creating ETCs. An ETC would have all the benefits of normal staff for two years. Then an ETC could be hired as a regular staff member, be returned to STC status, or forced to leave the Bank.

Two years of job security seemed an unfathomable luxury. I was sure I could get B-SPAN to where it needed to be by then. I told

Johnson I was willing to take the gamble, but he was aware of our history of recalcitrance with Tolstopiatenko. "We are new to each other," he said. "I want to see how things will work out before recommending an ETC appointment." I had heard this before from Laporte when B-SPAN joined WBI. Johnson and I made an agreement. If things went well over the next few months, he would push getting Bowden and me converted to ETCs in the next fiscal year.

Johnson made another gesture.[3] He wanted to collaborate in growing B-SPAN's influence. He had had ongoing discussions with the Bank's Transport Department about knowledge sharing activities. They had a database of video events. I was familiar with them because Dany Jones had been encoding their videos. Johnson encouraged me to reach out to see if there were opportunities to utilize their content.

Tolstopiatenko had exited, but a problem remained. Laporte still wanted cost recovery for B-SPAN. He was pressing Johnson hard to get something in place. My new manager made it clear: My future was contingent on implementation of an acceptable plan. But he was also building a bridge. He had listened closely during the focus group discussion in the spring. Johnson said he recognized B-SPAN was a public good. "For the moment, seminars will remain free," he said. "Work on raising conference charges and creating other financing alternatives."

Laporte wanted to know if we could implement a subscription-based service.[4] I met with EXT's publications unit to learn about their experiences charging for online products. Sources from poor countries would need to be excluded, and the technical ingenuity necessary to charge only sources from rich countries was complex. The hurdles were so considerable EXT had abandoned its effort. Laporte remained momentarily aloof, so I dropped this approach to explore a more palatable option.

Shortly after our migration to the KS Team, Ron Kim suggested, "Much of B-SPAN's difficulties are because Laporte senses he is not getting enough credit for its success."[5] Kim had regular access to Laporte. Their relationship was cordial, and to some extent he had a pulse on what Laporte was thinking. Behind an expressionless mask, I was befuddled. If we had only had the foresight to name the endeavor Bruno-SPAN, we could have been living in harmony. Then eliminating our transparency principle, deleting our archives, diluting our product line, derailing our production rate, alienating our institutional partners, and passing costs off to other Bank units would not have become issues. Obviously, Laporte couldn't be blamed for distancing himself from a site breaking WBI's traffic records and receiving global plaudits when none of the credit was going to him.

"Laporte should stop worrying about whether I cite him," I responded. "If he was smart, he would stand up and just take credit." Kim smiled and nodded. His remarks, however, were enlightening. Wheeler suggested I could mollify the Knowledge and Learning Director by taking Wheeler and de Nevers off the Host page, and putting up a photo of Laporte.[6] It might have been good politics, but I was in a cockfighting mood. I said no.[7]

When Leautier raised the issue of cost recovery for B-SPAN during a meeting of WBI's leadership, Laporte's anxiety intensified.[8] He became adamant about deleting any expenses other than the salaries paid to Bowden and me. Then, before Johnson could begin his assessment, he moved preemptively. Laporte ordered us to halt underwriting further filming charges.[9] From now on, clients wishing to use our service would be responsible for all filming expenses. Johnson protested and I followed suit, but Laporte refused to discuss the issue. I knew our ability to serve the Bank would be seriously compromised. Afterwards, Laporte confided to Kim that frankly he did not care about what impact the decision had on B-SPAN. The clouds darkened further when word leaked out from the I Team that Tolstopiatenko was suggesting our salaries should be based on commissions.

Laporte ordered me to provide further options he could present to the vice president.[10] I again put the onus on well-subsidized conferences. I was covering old ground, but conferences co-opted our time and resources. I suggested doubling our charges. For months, I had tried pushing Laporte in this direction, but he did not believe the idea worth considering. Then he heard it again from Wheeler during their summer meeting. Suddenly, the notion had validity because Laporte was motivated by sources.[11] He heard subordinates, but he listened to superiors and peers. I also suggested marketing to external content providers such as policy institutes, NGOs, think tanks, and community-based organizations, and charging them to put content on our system. Finally, I added a cautionary note. Defray costs to clients without resources, I appealed. Implementing charges will have important implications, and should only be done on a trial basis.

I began to ask myself a question. If the department was no longer willing to subsidize B-SPAN as a public good, then what was holding us to WBI? We could run the service anywhere.[12] I ran into de Nevers one day. She had also been thinking about the problem, and thought Wheeler should contact EXT's Vice President Ian Goldin. I wrote Wheeler to nix this suggestion, but the issue was still relevant.[13] We had circled a maze of waves only to return to the same longitude and latitude. We needed autonomy to run the system effectively. WBI certainly wasn't the answer. EXT was not likely to be either. I floated the notion of the Operations Evaluation Department (OED) because of their ombudsman role within the institution, but Wheeler was unconvinced. "This will require further thinking," he decided. Until then, I needed to traverse a fractured terrain of ice floes.

After Laporte announced the new policy, Wheeler and I began to co-conspire. One of the Research teams had immediately canceled further coverage of their series.[14] I forwarded their note to Wheeler.[15] Under the guise it was a Research Department event, he wrote Leautier to ask her to consider moderating WBI's approach toward imposing charges.[16] She signaled interest, but not a commitment, in making some accommodation.[17] I began tracking how clients responded to the new charges. In the opening weeks of implementation, 25 events were cancelled or refused.[18]

Still, our first month under Johnson ended with promise. Exciting events such as India's progress in achieving the U.N.'s Millennium Development Goals, U.S. Congressman Michael Oxley's assessment of investor confidence in the aftermath of the Enron and WorldCom collapses, and perspectives of women in the post-conflict Tajikistan and Iraq, went online.[19] September's traffic charted spectacular highs.[20] We were now on a pace to accumulate four million hits annually. I probed the numbers more extensively. B-SPAN had 11 pages in the Bank's directory of top 1,000 documents, and 16 pages were in the top 1,000 single access pages.[21] We had also become the most heavily trafficked website in WBI.[22]

Tolstopiatenko remained active, pushing for migration of our website into VoD.[23] Defeated on his initiative to merge product lines, he had rejected WBI Presents as an alternative to focus on populating VoD with content for internal viewing. Under his plan, B-SPAN would serve as the portal for external viewing. Johnson also saw the merger as a chance to make his imprint on B-SPAN.[24] Our traffic was surging under the current format, but I observed the importance my new manager placed on migration. Supporting him offered me an opportunity to cement a relationship that had begun on a promising note.

Converting our website also offered technical advantages. We could reduce the time it took loading files on the site and indexing streams by speaker or topic. But the migration came at considerable sacrifice.[25] Casey Stengel, the legendary manager of the New York Yankees, was once asked by reporters which player was most important to his championship teams. He said he never played without his "man." They assumed he was talking about Joe DiMaggio or Mickey Mantle or Whitey Ford, the obvious superstars, but he wasn't. He meant Yogi Berra, his durable catcher who was a clever and clutch performer.

Polly Means was B-SPAN's Yogi Berra. She was always there for us, and always delivered. With the migration of our HTML website into VoD, Bowden, Tse, and Montenegro assumed her responsibilities for uploading materials on the new database. Means's costs were minimal, but her impact had been significant. With her gone, I fretted over how quickly our events would get online.

The challenge of the merger was two-fold. First, we wanted our site to convey features that gave it a news-oriented feel. Tse was a skilled programmer, but was less concerned about aesthetic issues. His database vision was to portray a bland, corporate image. Tse was also an important member of the I Team. Its previous dysfunctional relationship with B-SPAN meant initiatives he spearheaded had been underutilized. He harbored enough resentment that even Johnson found him prickly. Johnson rejected Tse's initial draft, and further collaboration from the programmer was suddenly not forthcoming.[26]

Secondly, B-SPAN's streams resided on an HTML website. To get them in the VoD database would mean inputting them manually. I feared some archives might be lost in the transition.[27] Johnson was sympathetic. He collegially shared thoughts and suggestions. The grueling summer had hardly ended, but I already gained a sense the new manager recognized what we were trying to achieve.

In fact, some of Johnson's ideas were very creative.[28] Building on our own notion of a "webzine" style, he suggested we advertise events in our pipeline the way commercial video stores did. Soon, we had "Upcoming Events" with release dates listed on the home page. He also suggested having "Special Focus" sections on the home page so visitors could view thematic collections.[29] These sections would then change regularly to accommodate new Bank initiatives or topical subjects. We settled on four for the initial launch: Wolfensohn's Presidential Lectures series; the Practitioners in Development lecture series; the Building State Capacity in Africa series; and the Pro-Poor Growth and Inequality series.[30]

A new friction unfolded with Tolstopiatenko. With the migration of the Host Section into VoD, I added Johnson's photo and title.[31] The I Team manager, still reeling from the debacle of having B-SPAN wrested from his control, caught wind of the update, and wanted to be included.[32] I was apoplectic. Johnson played diplomat. He realized Tolstopiatenko managed WBI's Internet applications, and therefore could still create problems if he so chose. Johnson brokered a compromise. A line at the bottom of the Host Section page would read VoD had been developed by the I Team under the "leadership" of Tolstopiatenko. I grimaced and moved on.

With the migration in full swing, Johnson and I turned our attention back to the thorny issue of cost recovery. The challenge was to build a model that mollified Laporte and still provided a system clients found affordable. If they left B-SPAN, their content would go with them, and the station would lose value.

Over the summer, WBI had been given responsibility for a Wolfensohn initiative to organize a massive conference in Shanghai on scaling up successful poverty reduction projects. The two-day conference would gather political leaders, development practitioners, economists, and civil society activists from across the globe. As a prelude to Shanghai, GDLN facilities would host a series of video conferences addressing country-specific cases of poverty reduction activities. Johnson and I used a request from one of the WBI organizers as a starting point for building a revised scheme.[33]

The model recognized Laporte's order to pass along filming costs to clients, but it also placed emphasis on providing discounts for volume bookings. Concurrently, we increased charges by 50% for conferences.[34] Since GDLN filmed video conferences in their studios, we agreed to provide them free access to B-SPAN. The Shanghai part of the equation would be given a price based on volume. In this one case, at least, we had found a way to sidestep the impact of imposing charges; but then again, it was already WBI's show. Also promising, Johnson was receptive to opening B-SPAN to external content providers. The carrot was my suggestion that we could charge them for gaining access to our audiences.

Laporte played his cards close to the vest. He had not revealed his thinking about options I had already suggested, or his discussions with Leautier. In fact, Johnson was miffed that Laporte had move preemptively to pass along filming charges.[35] He decided to take Laporte's temperature and came back disillusioned. "Laporte," he said, "remains uncommitted to B-SPAN's long-term prospects." He was worried Laporte continued to be attracted to the notion that B-SPAN's termination would translate into a savings for his unit. I had an additional concern. Johnson and I agreed revenues generated by our charges would be reinvested into B-SPAN, either to subsidize events Bank clients couldn't afford, or to enhance the system's technological capacity. Laporte assured Johnson he wouldn't touch these funds for other uses, but I worried the pledge had not been unequivocal.[36]

Two problems complicated our effort. First, the department did not have a formal mechanism to allow the transfer of funds from other Bank units for services WBI rendered.[37] That meant there was no way to administer charges. For months, B-SPAN had charged Bank clients for coverage of conferences; but for reasons beyond our control, we had not been able to collect. Marshall Schreier, the department's senior budget official, suggested a solution for the Gordian knot: Bowden and I could be hired as short-term consultants for several days by Bank units to cover their conferences.[38] With Bowden disillusioned about the situation inside WBI, I decided to remove him from the equation. I talked it over with Johnson. It would be a personal sacrifice on my part. I would have to track down my own paychecks, which would have to come from a myriad of budget sources throughout the Bank, but this approach would save WBI money because other units would be picking up some of my costs. "I will do it if the money saved goes back into B-SPAN," I said. Johnson assured me of his support, but it was a risk. Laporte could arbitrarily squirrel away money we saved for his own activities.

The second complication: Bank guidelines suggested budget transfers between departments should not be for less than $5,000.[39] It would therefore not be possible to charge another unit for individual seminars. Even under a worst-case scenario, our charge would fall far below that level. I fell back to the original notion offered to Laporte in the spring: Creating annual partnerships with Bank departments. Johnson and I began discussing possibilities.

I continued seeking a channel to Leautier through Wheeler, suggesting he try to get a commitment from her to reinvest revenues back into B-SPAN, and allow us to solicit external revenue sources.[40] With assurances on either point, Laporte would be outmaneuvered from making further assaults on us. To pressure Laporte's flank, Johnson forwarded him a long list of cancellations due to the new charging policy.[41]

As the website migration neared completion, we began a series of quality control checks to make sure links worked and streams played.[42] I had stayed in contact with Craig Mauro of *World Bank Today*.[43] We agreed the launch of VoD would provide the impetus to tell our story Bank-wide for the first time.[44]

My original objective remained in place. Laporte had given no indication he would continue to employ Bowden and me beyond December. Instead, the grapevine suggested he wanted to shelve B-SPAN entirely. Having the larger Bank community learn the story of how we built B-SPAN would make Laporte think twice about firing us. I had gotten to know Johnson well enough to feel comfortable confiding in him. I suggested the pending article would also help the KS Team receive an unusual publicity scoop. He cautioned me to cover my bases by keeping Sunetra Puri, WBI's communications director, informed. Puri had never acted collegially towards us. I sensed she saw B-SPAN as an unwelcome competitor. She might try to redirect the focus to a more WBI-wide perspective. Johnson, however, was right about the politics. Shortly before meeting Mauro for the interview, I stopped by her office. It placed Puri in the loop, but because of the timing, it closed before she could enlarge it.[45]

With our quality control completed, the new site officially launched at the end of October.[46] Since a number of video files had yet to migrate, we decided to keep the original HTML version operational until then. The new home page rotated current highlights, which then included a discussion on post-invasion Iraq, growth strategies for the South African country of Lesotho, and a conference on the impact of infrastructure on the poor. Every time a viewer clicked the home page, they would find a new event had rotated to the top as the lead item. The sidebar had other recent releases. Below were the four Special Focus sections, and at the bottom of the page was a space for Upcoming Releases. Johnson had successfully coordinated a disparate group to build an improved and dynamic website.

Mauro finished a story draft a few days later, and forwarded it to me for review.[47] It included several of my key quotes which sent messages I needed to make public. First, B-SPAN was not just about featuring high-profile events, I said. "The value is in covering the small, cutting-edge research seminars where new ideas are discussed and debated." Secondly, I noted, "We don't edit so no one can accuse us of spin control. Authenticity is necessary and debate is healthy." Next, I called B-SPAN a "backdoor window into the Bank where outsiders can get an unfiltered view of dialogues taking place. To my knowledge, no other developmental, governmental or private sector institution has implemented an internal communication mechanism where complete transparency forms the basis of the model." Finally, I said the model worked. We had more than 500 events online, and over the previous year our traffic had tripled.

Still, the article needed something that officially sanctioned the endeavor. Mauro suggested a quote from a supervisor. I queried Johnson about Leautier. He agreed.[48] We drafted a statement and forwarded it to Puri for review.[49]

At the new website debut, Tolstopiatenko unveiled a new strategy for the struggle he refused to abandon. The advent of the VoD system, with its internal platform for edited products and learning materials, meant terrain Peekaboo was designed to protect had been ceded to Tolstopiatenko. The VoD system still mirrored B-SPAN's look and graphics in substantive ways; but more importantly, Tolstopiatenko announced plans to launch an external VoD site with edited content.[50] Johnson and I immediately objected.[51] A competitive database with edited content that looked like B-SPAN would confuse visitors, we argued. We worried about the ominous possibilities a competing service might present.

This issue would engage us in long discussions in the months ahead. For the moment, Johnson was able to pressure Tolstopiatenko to change VoD's look enough so it no longer plagiarized B-SPAN. He warned the I Team manager against bringing his new concept over the firewall to the public.[52]

November's traffic data revealed a spectacular 33% increase over September.[53] I relayed the news.[54] Johnson responded with his thumb in the air.[55] Millet sent a congratulatory note to WBI's senior management.[56] No such positive feedback was rendered from Laporte. He only wanted to know how many visitors were coming from countries WBI had designated as its priorities.[57]

I was now pounding the Knowledge and Learning director relentlessly with good news. Events, newsletters, and complimentary responses were being circulated in, out, and around.[58]

Then, I unloaded the barrel I had been priming for months. *World Bank Today* ran its story on B-SPAN.[59] When I sent a note out, people from all over the Bank started emailing back.[60] They were doing the cyberspace equivalent of standing up and applauding. Leautier led the way.[61] She wrote, "Excellent article, David. Keep up the good work on B-SPAN. It is truly a remarkable product." The rest of WBI was somewhat less impressed. Laporte was silent. Millet and Puri complained they should have been the ones to send out notices from the department.[62] Tolstopiatenko called Johnson to complain the article had no reference to the I Team for leading the new website development.[63] Millet's ire had been a miscalculation on my part for not informing her about the upcoming article. She had not previously expressed interest in disseminating news about B-SPAN, but her support was critical. I began thinking of ways to re-establish us in her good graces.

Two other developments unfolded the day the article appeared. After consistent lobbying, Nicole Frost, the EXT manager of the Bank's Internet home page, made a subtle, but important change to our link.[64] For the past few months, she had run "B-SPAN" on the sidebar. Now, she added "Webcasting" to the title. Since our earliest encounters, I had been trying to convince her of the merits of branding B-SPAN as the "Bank's webcasting station." The impact, I suggested, would be positive for us and EXT. She finally seemed to have agreed.

The second event would have a profound impact on B-SPAN. The Bank's board formally approved a new proposal regarding the status of STCs and the adoption of the new ETC category. The amount of days STCs were allowed to work would be significantly reduced.[65] ETCs would fill the gap. For Bowden and me, squarely on the front lines of an intense philosophical struggle for the institution's identity, our employment was now measured in days, not years. We didn't have the luxury for the moment to worry about what the ETC development meant for us.

I realized Laporte, Tolstopiatenko, Puri, and perhaps now Millet, viewed me as an indulgent self-promoter. I was the one announcing exciting new developments regarding B-SPAN. I wrote the newsletters, communicated with clients, and answered viewers' questions. When people spoke about B-SPAN, they routinely interchanged its name with mine. WBI's managers instinctively viewed the issue from their parochial perspective, worrying about who was receiving credit.

I did not, however, view the matter as a luxury, and would have gladly traded credit for a healthy environment. Moreover, I recognized this was an appropriate tactic in moving my agenda forward, but only if the terrain was not hostile. We had been under attack the moment we entered WBI. So, there was another perspective. I was fighting for the life of the project as well as my life in it. I viewed public relations as a tactical strategy geared to insulate me, not just from attacks, but from attempts to remove me from B-SPAN. And, by and large, the strategy had been successful. Every time Laporte or Tolstopiatenko wanted me out, they couldn't drop the guillotine because my name was so closely linked to B-SPAN.

Zagha's Practitioners in Development series suddenly entered into this equation. Wheeler saw that one upcoming guest was former Brazilian President Fernando Henrique Cardoso. The Professor suggested I interview Cardoso. I knew a good idea when it was handed to me. I ran it by Zagha, who also liked it, and suggested we could interview other guests as well.[66] John Williamson, the noted former Bank economist, was returning soon, and Lawrence Summers, the former U.S. Secretary of the Treasury, would also be visiting.

The interview concept, however, presented a danger for me. I sensed sitting alone with a former President of Brazil or U.S. Treasury Secretary would not be tolerated by WBI. However, such interviews represented another layer of protection for B-SPAN and me, so I suggested that Wheeler, Zagha and I form a panel to interview these visiting lecturers.[67] They agreed, and I was insulated nicely.[68]

Meanwhile, we rotated new offerings on our home page. Joe Stiglitz discussed his latest book, *The Roaring Nineties*, about the rise and fall of the U.S. economic juggernaut.[69] Cambodian Minister of Commerce H.E. Sok Siphana talked about his country's entrance into the World Trade Organization.[70] Mario Blejer, director of Argentina's Central Bank, discussed his work managing the country's financial crisis in 2002.[71]

We were now coordinating almost daily with *World Bank Today* to have our streams linked with their articles. Johnson thought we should take advantage of the burgeoning relationship by creating B-SPAN Alerts directed to WBI staff.[72] It was a clever publicity stunt. And, in it, I saw the opportunity I was looking for to repair my relationship with Millet. I suggested she release them to the department.[73]

The B-SPAN Alert strategy hit the mark. A few weeks later, Millet stood before several hundred WBI staff, reiterating her enthusiasm for us. "B-SPAN has become one of the department's leading products and the key tool for promoting the Bank's transparency to its stakeholders," she said.[74] Leautier followed suit and applauded its success.[75] People nodded and glanced in my direction.

My face never changed expression. It was nice to be singled out, but I had bought tickets to this play before. My stoicism was well founded. Shortly thereafter, Laporte told Johnson he did not know exactly what Bowden and I did. He wanted to merge our jobs into one position. Johnson talked him out of it.[76]

By November, three months had passed since Laporte changed B-SPAN's pricing policy, enough time to get a sense of its impact. Initially, there had been a strong backlash. Now clients were returning.[77] They compared the fee's impact on their budgets with B-SPAN's influence on their communication strategies. For the moment, their choice was clear. B-SPAN was winning. The recovery of volume, however, hadn't happened in a vacuum. Other managers had come to accept the new fee structure, and perhaps even acknowledged its logic from their institutional perspectives. Many, like Laporte, were bureaucrats used to manipulating internal budgets to maximize gains for their agendas. The recovery of volume was a result of B-SPAN's success. We had become ubiquitous. We had moved beyond just a fashionable way of communicating to become the mainstream model.

I was relieved, but I also didn't think I had been mistaken. I remained convinced our market was highly vulnerable to pricing shocks. It was a slippery slope. Further ones would destabilize our system. And, in two respects, my prediction still rang true: Clients were returning, but overall volume had declined; and the number of presentations with less-prominent personalities was disappearing at a prodigious rate.[78]

The decline in cutting-edge events was predictably augmented by glitzy ones flowing through the pipeline. Lectures by Blejer, Stiglitz, and Siphana were followed by Peter Piot, the UN under secretary-general and executive director on UNAIDS.[79] Dr. Piot said the pandemic's infection rate had not leveled off, and was now threatening new global regions such as Eastern Europe, China, and India. Prevention initiatives and falling drug prices offered hope, but Piot stressed the development community needed a more synchronized and coordinated effort to avert a global disaster.

Leszek Balcerowicz, the former deputy prime minister and finance minister for Poland, spoke about the uneven progress of Eastern Europe and the former Soviet Union in transitioning from communism to free-market economies.[80]

Freed from the poisonous yoke of Tolstopiatenko's constant checks, B-SPAN was flowering. Even Laporte faded from view for a time. With the harmony provided by Johnson's oversight, he was no longer calling for draft strategies, work programs, or monthly meetings. The B-SPAN Alerts also provided us with a mechanism to jump a level of the bureaucracy. By interacting directly with Millet, we had eliminated almost all contact with Laporte.[81]

But Laporte reappeared. Johnson called me into his office one day. His face was downcast. "Laporte has spent what was budgeted for your salaries," he said.[82] As he explained it, Johnson had asked Laporte to authorize routine spending requests for the first half of the fiscal year. Laporte apparently mistook that to mean the entire fiscal year. For a moment, the two of us sat in dumfounded silence. "B-SPAN is too far down the track," Johnson assured me. "Laporte will find some discretionary funds or use money saved from our new cost recovery policy." I agreed. If B-SPAN folded because of a funding miscalculation on Laporte's part, it would backfire on him.

Wheeler had a different take.[83] He speculated it was a deliberate ploy by Laporte. "Pry more money out of the vice president so as not to divert existing funds from his own priorities," Wheeler suggested. "It's an old trick." Either way, whether it was a detestable tactic or administrative blunder, the result was the same.

VoD needed significant fine-tuning. Our original HTML template divided selections by region, topic, or sub-topic. As our archives grew and diversified, new categories were created. Tse's template followed the Bank's standard taxonomy. Unfortunately, this protocol was too broad to allow for effective searching. Visitors, trying to find selections in specific categories, ended up with so many offerings as to make the search engine useless. Recognizing the problem, I gathered with relevant KS Team members, including Tse, Bowden, and taxonomy experts from ISG, to develop something appropriate for B-SPAN.[84] But we were all moving on too many fronts to fix the problem quickly. B-SPAN was now stuck with an unwieldy search engine.

Equally intractable was Tse himself. As an ardent ally of Tolstopiatenko, collapse of the transparency model would elevate the marketability of his programming skills. He proved to be the antithesis of Means and procrastinated habitually with requests to update the site. My fear that valuable archives wouldn't make the transition from the old website prompted him to accuse me of trying to undermine VoD.[85] Johnson, too, had become frustrated by his recalcitrance.

Following the launch, I suggested we add a Related B-SPAN Videos selection on the database. This would allow us to generate traffic to salient materials on our archives. Tse refused. Instead, he was going to create a platform on the database that would offer two selections: B-SPAN and B-SPAN2 for edited products. Johnson and I caucused. Tolstopiatenko was attempting an end-run.[86] Though the terrain on an internal platform had been ceded, its value was reduced because staff realized B-SPAN's could reach external audiences. Moreover, Tolstopiatenko didn't have access to our newsletter list and couldn't match our marketing prowess. The internal VoD was listless, but Tolstopiatenko's renewed drive to make it external crossed a dangerous threshold.

"Tolstopiatenko is seeking to capture territory by degrees, but we cannot allow it," I told Johnson. "Bureaucratic instincts die hard. If he offers Bank staff the opportunity to have their video products carefully edited for external consumption, they might begin to turn away from the transparency model. We must claim this area for ourselves." I raised an old idea: WBI Presents. Johnson thought it worthwhile, and floated a compromise scenario: The I Team could build it and I would manage it. For the moment, we would let things unfold to see how Tolstopiatenko would react to the suggestion.

I prepared a concept note on WBI Presents.[87] Potential uses for the VoD database included internal dissemination, external dissemination with unedited content, and external dissemination with edited content formats. While I Team technicians could create the system and its content, they were poorly positioned to manage content. They simply didn't have the communication skills necessary for keeping these sites viable. I didn't overtly push for assuming these responsibilities myself, but suggested instead they should fall under the auspices of KS Team managers, Johnson and Kim.

If Tolstopiatenko was trying to create a competing service, having its marketing under our control would stymie him. Initially, we would direct clients to B-SPAN. If they insisted on editing content, only then would we provide them with WBI Presents. I also noted blurring of product lines was prohibited, as it would confuse viewers and violate B-SPAN's mandate. Naturally, we wanted to provide disincentives for the competing service. By using B-SPAN, we would disseminate to our global audience. If Bank staff wanted to use WBI Presents, they would have to do their own marketing. In addition, WBI Presents should have a higher fee structure, I suggested, since editing consumed more time and resources. Clients looking for editing help could use I Team resources.

Providing Tolstopiatenko and his team an opportunity to be buried in editing videos seemed adroit. It would leave them less time for causing mischief. I suggested revenues raised by WBI Presents should be split between KS and the I Team. The proposal boxed him in nicely, but there were some weaknesses. The line of authority would have to be cleared with Laporte. How he would see the issue was still an unknown. Secondly, ISG and GSD performed the same activities. If WBI got into the business of competing with them, I wondered if B-SPAN would suffer retribution.

Johnson favored creating a box on B-SPAN for an edited line rather than an entirely new look. There were pros and cons for both approaches; but we agreed any new product must look distinctly different from B-SPAN. I suggested calling a line housing WBI course and training materials "Classroom," and Johnson thought the name would sell well with management. We also agreed, as long as the unedited content was on B-SPAN, edited materials from the same videos could go on WBI Presents. We did diverge on one point. I was reluctant to rush forward. WBI Presents represented a product line moving in a radically different direction to the transparency model. However, Johnson wanted to pre-empt further maneuvering by Tolstopiatenko. He immediately sought Laporte's endorsement.[88]

My relationship with Bowden was rapidly deteriorating. We had weathered a difficult environment under Tolstopiatenko, and fought the struggle arm in arm. But it had taken its toll. Bowden wanted less stress, which meant capitulating every time Laporte pushed to take B-SPAN the wrong way. I also had traveled a long distance, and had no plans to turn around. We began to clash repeatedly. He no longer agreed with strategies and tactics I suggested. Feeling our divergence, I stopped soliciting his advice, and began to work on activities without his counsel.

This further alienated him. He was increasingly critical of the most mundane details. The slightest omissions were blown out of proportion. He was frustrated by the quality of GSD's work and wanted me to crack the whip. What he failed to understand was video quality—though always important—had been essentially a tactical weapon for Tolstopiatenko and Laporte. Its relevance as a fault line in our struggle had been traversed long ago.[89] Bowden also chaffed for the opportunity to do something more than encode videos and write summaries. We both knew instinctively that WBI's management was never going to allow him to grow beyond what he was doing. As our alliance was disintegrating, my bond with Johnson was deepening.[90] He understood where I was going and wanted to go there too. He also sensed the fissure with Bowden, and stepped into the void.

Claude Salem had abruptly abandoned GDLN a couple months earlier to move into Leautier's office as a senior advisor.[91] He told me privately his relationship with its manager, Monika Weber-Fahr, had dissolved. From his new position, he continued trying to generate interest in merging B-SPAN's content with the Distance Learning Center facilities.[92] He heard about a special Bank fund for dissemination activities as part of the institution's 60th anniversary. Nicole Frost was seeking proposals, so he suggested I reach out to her. She agreed to make a case on our behalf.[93]

Our concept was to put together several B-SPAN programs related to a specific theme, work with a sector-specific specialist who would serve as facilitator, and create courses that could be conducted in the various DLCs. The cost would be modest, perhaps $25,000. If successful, the pilot could be replicated in other DLCs. Salem, Frost, and Johnson, who volunteered to join the effort, thought the pitch was tailor-made for the trust fund. The proposal committee, however, thought differently. They dismissed the idea immediately. B-SPAN's dissemination via the DLCs was an obvious EXT initiative, they explained.[94] It should be financed there.

The proposal to disseminate B-SPAN's content via the DLCs had prophetic symbolism for our transparency crusade. Not long after this effort died, de Nevers forwarded a note to me.[95] Leautier had been visiting the Philippines when the Bank's Country Director Robert Van Pulley expressed interest in having B-SPAN's videos disseminated through local Public Information Centers (PICs), which are offices where Bank documents are made available to the public. The Philippines had a number of satellite locations. I forwarded the concept note, which Salem and I had developed, to de Nevers, who sent it along to WBI's senior management.[96] Again, we heard nothing. We had the desire to get moving. We had interest from the field. We had products that would cost the department little to repackage. But, we couldn't get anyone with authority to take the idea seriously.

Bad news and good news sprinkled intermittently. I pursued the interview concept for the Practitioner in Development Series. It came to fruition in December, when Wheeler and I together with Roberto Zagha and his colleague Indermit Gill talked with former Brazilian President, Fernando Henrique Cardoso.[97] The four of us beamed as we gathered with the President before he spoke to a large Bank audience.[98] Cardoso said that prior to his term in office, Brazil experienced strong economic growth, but significant poverty remained. During his presidency, he focused on reducing infant mortality and raising education levels. Twelve million Brazilians were lifted out of poverty during his tenure, but he acknowledged it could have been more. The international financial crises of the 1990s had retarded Brazil's economic growth; and he believed part of the blame resided with the Bretton Woods institutions. President Cardoso thought the time had come for reforms to be implemented at the Bank.[99]

As the Bank was being dressed down, good news was arriving for B-SPAN. Following our publication of the European Bank for Reconstruction and Development's transition report on Eastern Europe's economic progress, I began communicating with one of the IMF's public affairs liaisons, John Starrels.[100] I suggested, with the precedent set, B-SPAN should be webcasting more IMF events. "Our traffic is strong and growing stronger," I said. "If you look on the Bank's home page, you will notice our latest links to the Development Marketplace and Stiglitz's book launch on *The Roaring Nineties*." Starrels was intrigued. He said he would discuss the possibility of our streaming their ongoing Economic Forum Series with his colleagues.

However, there was one small problem. We were now charging our Bank clients for the service, albeit in the form of passing along filming costs. I needed to find a financing mechanism palatable to potential non-Bank clients. The fee also had to be higher than what we charged Bank customers, who would be in an uproar if they found out it was otherwise. Access to the IMF was far from assured. I knew Starrels would walk if I asked for too much. I decided to take a calculated risk. I believed once hooked, the IMF would become amenable to negotiating a fee. I suggested a free trial to see how things went. The day Wheeler and I interviewed President Cardoso, Starrells called to confirm B-SPAN could have access to the IMF.[101]

The developments with Cardoso and the IMF represented the realization of a vision Wheeler and I had shared long before. B-SPAN had become a transparent medium for policy presentations of Bank events, development discussions from outside the Bank, and interviews with important policy makers. It was a highly transparent and journalistic endeavor. Under Tolstopiatenko, this dream had no chance. With Johnson, we were moving forward dramatically. It was an exciting moment. I began to think the time had come to contact policy groups around Washington en masse, to make them aware of our service and offer them the opportunity to participate.

A new blip appeared on the radar. EXT was redesigning the Bank's home page. Based on surveys, they wanted to highlight ongoing themes of the Bank's work program. Frost sought comments from key Bank participants.[102] It was a laudable goal, but the redesign deleted B-SPAN's name from the sidebar, and replaced it with a generic "Video" category. After two years of lobbying EXT that B-SPAN could be a brand to drive traffic to the Bank's website, we had abruptly taken a step backwards.

I made an immediate appeal to Frost.[103] "The branding of B-SPAN makes an imprint on the consciousness of Bank stakeholders at a time when the institution is competing with a phalanx of competing voices in the development field," I argued. I noted since

B-SPAN's name first appeared on the home page in July, our traffic had almost doubled; and I listed how B-SPAN helped deliver on each of the objectives EXT sought with the redesign. Johnson and Ron Kim followed with their own appeals.[104] Frost was sympathetic, but non-committal.[105] Several days later, the new Bank website was unveiled. The listing for B-SPAN had changed to "Videos".

Johnson, Kim, and I continued to plead that EXT reinstate our name on the home page. We tried a middle ground and suggested "Video" remain and a "More on B-SPAN" logo be added.[106] This was rebuffed.[107] Frost said there were a variety of sources for video content within the Bank. She didn't want to divert visitors to a single source. It was a reasonable response, but upon review I found the other sources were mostly obscure. None compared to what we were doing. I requested a meeting.[108]

Johnson and I sat down with Frost and McCoy.[109] I noted there had been a spike in our traffic after the B-SPAN title was added to the Bank home page. "Losing the branding will impact us negatively," I said. "We would be willing to create a box on B-SPAN's home page with the listing of all the other video sources EXT wants to publicize." Frost remained reluctant. "EXT surveys indicate stakeholders are confused by the multitude of Bank products," she said. I realized then the public relations branch of the institution was philosophically uncomfortable with branding product lines. The great irony, I believed, was effective branding would serve to decrease the public's confusion. She offered a concession and agreed to change "Video" to "Webcasting."[110]

After eighteen months, I finally found a way to please Laporte. My willingness to hire myself out on three and four-day STC contracts to other Bank units for conference coverage had saved Laporte $7,500.[111] He happily reported the results to Leautier, and the vice president was equally enthusiastic in her response. The exchange closed the year for B-SPAN. It had been twelve months of riding roller-coaster swells.[112]

Under Tolstopiatenko, B-SPAN had weathered a dangerous hurricane. But we had stayed the course, keeping both our principles and wits. And it was B-SPAN's adversaries who had gone under. Johnson offered us a fresh sea. Even with problems caused by Laporte, the layer of cover Johnson provided allowed us to break free of many bureaucratic shackles. As importantly, the new manager also felt a sense of involvement in helping B-SPAN expand in new and dramatic directions. As with other entrepreneurial endeavors, whether we were doing well or were on the verge of collapse depended on which day, and which moment of the day the question was asked. But the year had been spectacular in substantive ways. I crossed my fingers. With just a little luck, 2004 held forth even greater promise: Achievement of the dream Wheeler and I had envisioned years before—a webcasting station that would catapult the Bank into the 21st Century by changing the way people around the world who were involved in poverty reduction communicated with one another.

2

2004

A new year did not alleviate ongoing flashpoints. Though our contracts were extended for the balance of the fiscal year, long-term job security for Bowden and me remained in limbo. Bowden was complaining with greater frequency on a variety of issues.[113] Significant flaws remained with VoD. Many archived events had not transferred over. The HTML version was still accessible, negatively impacting traffic data to the new site; but I opposed deleting the former until the migration was complete.[114] The structure of the new site's search engine was ineffectual, but no one had time to address it. On the WBI Presents/Classroom proposal, I was fighting a rear-guard action, voicing acquiescence while hoping Laporte's ineffectual leadership would delay creating a prototype. And, perhaps most importantly, B-SPAN, unlike almost all other Bank sites, had breaking news with deadlines. Yet Tse's procrastination when updating the website posed a serious obstacle.

We needed to do three things: (1) Insulate ourselves from the parochial whims of Laporte; (2) avoid mission creep by making training videos available, and (3) capitalize on the interview with Cardoso and our new relationship with the IMF to create access for other external content providers. I decided to seek a meeting with Leautier.[115] She quickly agreed, but her schedule was filled until mid-February.

I realized meeting the vice president would represent a watershed moment for the transparency movement. I had been preparing the stage for months, copying her with a steady stream of good news on event coverage, traffic trends, and responses from clients and consumers. We were old associates. Our relationship went back a decade to our days under Wheeler. But since she had become vice president, I had never met with her privately. She seemed highly insulated in her new responsibilities. Our only contact had been chance encounters where pleasantries were exchanged or through an occasional email. I kept my pending meeting secret from everyone except Wheeler. I knew, however, I would risk injuring my relationship with Johnson if he was not informed prior to my walking into Leautier's office. Nevertheless, once Johnson knew, Laporte was sure to find out as well. I decided to play it close to the vest by informing Johnson of the meeting only a few days before it took place.

Wheeler thought that continuing under our STC contracts was no longer viable. The time had come to push Leautier directly to give us ETC status, he said. The pitch would be based on this supposition: Stability was necessary for ensuring the long-term viability of the system. "Asking for resources to expand B-SPAN is not enough," Wheeler said. "The vice president will ask you what you would want. Think carefully about how to answer the question."[116]

As predicted, Laporte found funds to cover B-SPAN's salaries for the balance of the fiscal year.[117] Now I hoped the conference charges I generated could be used for new hardware and software acquisitions or other project initiatives. Johnson and I convened to discuss potential ideas. Though B-SPAN was the only part of his unit making money, Johnson raised the possibility he might also want to use some of the revenues for other KS activities. Collegiality in the current environment was an important parameter. I raised no objection.[118]

On the eve of our second Practitioners in Development interview with macroeconomist John Williamson, I received our first official feedback from the mountaintop. Frost had given Wolfensohn a presentation on the new Bank external home page.[119] He complimented her on B-SPAN's coverage of Cardoso, which seemed to suggest he thought we were an EXT product. Wheeler wrote me, "Hey HeDMan, so UDMan".[120]

Williamson reiterated many of the themes he raised in his initial appearance on B-SPAN.[121] The Washington Consensus was originally formulated not as a prescription for development, but rather policies the donor community supported for Latin America during its fiscal difficulties of the late 1980s, Williamson said. He added that it had then evolved to mean a generic economic framework that the Bank, IMF, and the U.S. Treasury Department supported for developing countries. Williamson analyzed the original policy reforms of the Consensus, and concluded by suggesting the Consensus was now dead. A profound gulf had developed between the Bretton Woods institutions and the Bush Administration.

By the middle of January, Tolstopiatenko was on the move again with VoD.[122] To have it compete directly with B-SPAN for the same events would catapult the department into open warfare. Johnson and I met to cement our strategy.[123] Johnson thought Laporte would support the idea of having him and the KS Team managing both external sites. We also agreed VoD would need to look different from B-SPAN, and its users would have to do their own marketing. To create further disincentives, this service would have to cost significantly more than having the event shown on B-SPAN. Johnson reiterated interest in a "Classroom" box, for he believed a clearly defined new product line housed within the transparency model would depressurize the situation. How revenues from the new site would be divided remained an open question. Our plan was solidified: We would manage marketing and client relations, and would channel Tolstopiatenko and his people into technical activities.[124] As the meeting broke up, I told Johnson, "If Tolstopiatenko wants a new line of business then he is welcome to take over our encoding tasks." He smiled.

Comrade A tried a new tactic.[125] He surreptitiously sought a managers-only meeting regarding another proposal. Tolstopiatenko wanted to establish a generic website entitled WBI's Video Library.[126] It would serve as a gateway for all the video product lines housed by the department, including those of B-SPAN, the external VoD with edited content, the internal-only VoD site, and perhaps other video products. Visitors would be forced to access this initial page before finding B-SPAN. Additionally, Tolstopiatenko wanted all visitors to fill out a request form that would, in effect, encourage them to consider alternatives to B-SPAN. Finally, he suggested allowing clients to request B-SPAN's services, but then host the stream on their own website instead.

"B-SPAN is a corporate and public relations tool for the Bank," he said. And, in an interesting reversal, he now claimed the I Team was in the knowledge sharing business rather than an encoding and streaming service. Johnson asked for my perspective. "DOA," I said. "It is another flanking maneuver to reclaim ground he already lost." Johnson concurred. "Our first line of attack," I suggested, "should be to query whether WBI is suited for this line of work at all. It will put Laporte in a position of making departmental decisions for the vice president. It might also jeopardize B-SPAN's existing relationship with ISG and GSD, since the proposal has the potential to impact their business models as well." But Tolstopiatenko had one customer interested in his ideas: Laporte.[127]

I ran into Laporte as he was headed to and from the meeting. I decided to give him an opportunity to come clean, since he did not know I knew what was taking place. "What's new," I asked. "Business as usual," he said, twice. In recent weeks, when seeing me, he had taken to asking what new offerings I was putting up on B-SPAN. This was camouflage to feign interest, but I had grown tired of the game. When he asked this time, I told him I was trying to pump traffic. From now on, could he go to the site to see for himself? The managers-only meeting also included Tolstopiatenko's staff. Johnson said he had felt ambushed.[128]

Johnson and Tolstopiatenko began exchanging notes to seek a middle ground.[129] Tolstopiatenko remained steadfast on having a central portal to access B-SPAN and VoD. Finally, Johnson tired of the struggle. I believed Tolstopiatenko didn't have the capacity or ability to run a service on his own. "What if we just let him take it on," I said. "If he fails to deliver, he would cut his own throat. If he tries to undercut our pricing constraints, we could call him on it. If he deliberately tries to steer clients away from us to create market share, we could call him on that." Johnson thought it over and said okay.

Tolstopiatenko was a badly damaged, but still dangerous, opponent. He needed to be dealt a decisive blow. I began quietly toying with an idea. When Tolstopiatenko disabled the Forum One database for B-SPAN, he had deliberately created an opening to develop his own system. What emerged was VoD.[130] But WBI had spent $40,000 on the Forum One system, and its designer, David Hobbs, now worked in ISG. I asked Hobbs if he would give me a detailed account of the similarities and differences between the two databases.[131] I knew a major one was that the Forum One system could push our content on to other websites, but VoD could not. I hoped there would be other differences, and a complete comparison would be highly unsettling for Tolstopiatenko if it became public. I decided to keep it in my pocket until pushed into a corner by suggestions of a competing system.

In late January, I checked the Bank's home page to see how much of our content was being featured. B-SPAN's moniker was gone, but B-SPAN was not. We comprised eight of the 39 total links, more than one-fifth of the Bank's home page. When informed, Leautier was ecstatic, Millet was complimentary, and Laporte was silent.[132]

Cardoso's interview was featured on the Bank home page and in the Bank's *Week in Review* newsletter. It marked a subtle but important shift in thinking by these outlets.[133] Perhaps without realizing it consciously, they had come to acknowledge B-SPAN's journalistic antecedents. They were providing a secondary dissemination vehicle for our news-making content. Our successes inside the Bank were translating into victories where it counted most. Traffic skyrocketed in December.[134] Our page requests hit 330,000, a jump of 80,000 from the previous month. B-SPAN, the most powerful website WBI hosted almost from the moment of Tolstopiatenko's departure, had markedly outdistanced departmental competitors. Viewers were tuning in from Azerbaijan. They were tuning in from Cambodia. They were tuning in from Oman. They were tuning in from Iran.[135]

Our third Practitioners in Development interview featured Yegor Gaidar, the former prime minister and minister of finance and economy under Russian President Boris Yeltsin.[136] Gaidar had been pivotal in helping Russia transition from a command-and-control to a market-based economy following the Soviet Union's disintegration. He would gain additional world attention in late 2006 for a sudden illness associates suggested was linked to the Alexander Litvinenko spy-poisoning case.

Zagha and I sat down with Gaidar for an enlightening discussion prior to his lecture. Following the August 1991 bloodless coup in which Yeltsin rose to power, Gaidar said his immediate concern was developing sound institutions. He noted Russia did not have the luxury of a gradual transition to a market-based economy as China did, because the Soviet Union's collapse was sudden and unexpected. Russians had lived with 75 years of socialism, so changing the culture would take time. For years the Russian economy contracted. The privatization process was chaotic, and oligarchs vulcanized national assets. It wasn't until 1999 that the country experienced sustained growth through the enduring strength of the industrial infrastructure originally established under communism, Gaidar said. But such growth was not sustainable, he warned; and Russia's financial future would be tied to how successfully its economy transitioned again into investment-based growth.[137]

Our internal successes remained hard won. Johnson said Laporte was unwilling to offer ETC status to Bowden or me when the new fiscal year began.[138] Then, my deteriorating relationship with Bowden finally collapsed. He had changed content I prepared for Frost without my knowledge.[139] I was upset he made the decision without my input, but he thought he should now be making content decisions. He called me a glorified scheduler. I exploded. A bloodletting on both sides settled into an uneasy truce. I would make decisions on communication strategy, but would seek his input if he had an interest in something particular. He would focus on technology. We had come to an unspoken understanding. Bowden had crossed a line he should not have, and wouldn't again.

I turned to a more strategic matter: Generating a revenue stream from outside the Bank. Johnson suggested I get my ducks in place before making an attempt.[140] I turned to WBI's budget staff, who said it would be legal by Bank rules. All an external provider needed to do was write a check. Then I queried Cardak, who said GSD would welcome the extra business. But then Johnson had reservations. He wanted to ask permission.

"That will only put Laporte in a position to nix the concept entirely," I told him. "It would be better to find a provider who is willing to pay us. We might start with the IMF. Once we have a check in hand, we could give it to Laporte, and request that it be spent on KS activities. Whether he uses the money for KS or not, once he deposits the check he will by proxy have sanctioned the precedent for our seeking external clients. Perhaps on further reflection, we might just tell Leautier what we have accomplished, and bypass Laporte altogether. First, though, I need a check."[141]

Two years after joining the department, Laporte held a meeting to formally introduce B-SPAN to his unit.[142] To assuage his claim to ownership, I suggested Bowden give the presentation. I would weigh in on Q&A if needed. It was uneventful except for one sensitive moment. In discussing activities we hoped to achieve in the future, Bowden noted possible dissemination via the DLCs and acceptance of content from external content providers. Tolstopiatenko leaped up and expressed concern over infringement of presenters' copyrights. Kathy Sheram, a senior learning officer in another part of the unit, immediately concurred. I noted B-SPAN was a public website and, like any news service, lifting sound bites is a common practice. The objections were temporarily overcome, but I sensed Tolstopiatenko was contemplating yet another line of attack. And, regarding Sheram, it was obvious the bureaucratic instincts within WBI were firmly entrenched, and pulsated at the mention of B-SPAN. Copyrights were a Pandora's Box. I worried that if lawyers got involved in vetting B-SPAN's movements, we would be finished in a matter of months.[143]

Sheram asked us to meet with the instructional designers of her learning unit.[144] They were interested in using our content to help them build training courses for WBI. Johnson and I thought a pilot would be useful, but Sheram wanted us to take the lead. This made no sense, since her people designed courses. Then, Sheram again raised her concern about copyright issues. She worried that using our content in their courses would violate the intellectual property rights of presenters. I reiterated B-SPAN was a public website, and our policy was to refer copyright matters to secondary users. If Sheram or someone else wanted to use our materials and thought permission was necessary, she or they would be responsible for tracking down the original source. She suggested she would seek counsel with the Bank's legal department.[145] A couple weeks earlier, Bowden had attended a legal department seminar on copyright issues, and one of the lawyers had told him B-SPAN represented a complex dilemma.[146] I now told Johnson that Sheram's meddling could lead to a very dangerous situation.[147] He agreed.

But before the lawyers could get to us, in early February we brought three more important events into the fold in quick succession. The importance of these presentations was yet further evidence of the vital role B-SPAN was playing in disseminating critical information on development to global audiences. Lawrence Summers, then Harvard University's president and former Bank chief economist, and former U.S. Treasury secretary, gave the next Practitioners in Development lecture.[148] Summers said he drew several key lessons about development from his experiences in the 1990s as Treasury secretary. The most important lesson was that the quality of institutions and the efficacy of political administrations were central to development. He believed the global financial crises during this period revealed that resources devoted to averting future problems would do more good than those mitigating collapses once they began. Summers also suggested a financial system that allowed the richest country in the world to borrow at a less than one percent rate from the poorest countries in the world was seriously flawed. He expressed concern over the fungability of development assistance, and closed his speech with a jab at the Bush Administration by lamenting its apathy toward aiding the world's impoverished.

Perhaps by coincidence, Laporte sat down next to me to watch the speech. He said he was fascinated that we were trying to disseminate B-SPAN content through the DLCs, a tidbit picked up from Bowden's presentation. What the devil was he talking about? Salem and I had been sending him memos about the idea for well over a year.[149] Why the sudden interest, I wondered. I would find out shortly.

At the second event, IMF officials discussed Russia's growth since its fiscal crisis in 1998.[150] They suggested positive trends resulted from the government leveraging its vast oil reserves. They cautioned that wavering structural reforms, ongoing corruption, and President Vladimir Putin's arrest of oil mogul Mikhail Khodorkovsky, threatened the fledgling business environment. The seminar was a seamless compliment to our coverage of Gaidar a couple of weeks earlier.

The third event suggested that our foray to become pro-active and create news had gained acceptance. Chris Neal, who had replaced Macdonald as communications liaison for the Bank's chief economist, asked if we would interview Francois Bourguignon, the newly appointed chief economist about his visit to India.[151] I accepted on the condition the interview wouldn't be a puffy feel-good session for Bourguignon.[152] Neal agreed to the terms, and I suggested we conduct the interview jointly.

Bourguignon said, despite the strong growth in India in recent years, he and other academics had not been able to quantify corresponding reductions in poverty.[153] The new chief economist discussed a theory he called the "poverty-growth-inequality triangle." He believed there was a relationship between growth rates and inequality. Bourguignon suggested that "if there was growth but no change in inequality, one should expect to see a reduction in poverty. If inequality increased when there was growth, then the impact of growth would be diminished." Bourguignon went on to say that by international standards, inequality in India was relatively low. If this changed, however, the impact of growth on poverty would be reduced. He then suggested this had been the case in China where, despite rapid growth, increases in inequality muted poverty reduction.

Neal began to steer Bourguignon on a tangent, but I forced the interview back to inequality in India. I noted that in a previous speech, Bourguignon had suggested redistribution policies for India were not currently necessary. He seemed momentarily unsettled, but said he still supported the position, with some caveats. India had started to implement more social development policies, and he would encourage them to do more. "A prospering middle class has increased inequality in rural areas, which would require redistribution activities," he noted. "This would necessitate more investments in education and training."

I asked if there were parallels with China. Bourguignon sidestepped the question by suggesting increased trade between the countries had created new opportunities for India. The interview closed with my asking if research on equity and social inclusion would be the pillars of his tenure as chief economist. Bourguignon said if this could be accomplished, it would be a major achievement.

When he saw the tape, Wheeler was pleased.[154] "Ten years ago, the thought of a Bank official giving personal opinions about development policy would have been inconceivable," he said. The transformation of the institution's culture could in large part be attributed to B-SPAN, he suggested.

The Environment Department's series of conferences and seminars was around the corner. I touched base to get a sense of what level of participation by B-SPAN they wanted.[155] I was in for a surprise. They had decided to keep everything private except for two innocuous seminars.[156] I was stunned. Just four years earlier, we had piloted B-SPAN with a live webcast of the department's two-day strategy session that brought participation from stakeholders from around the world. Now, their dialogues were practically off-limits. It was a complete reversal, and another signal B-SPAN's crusade to institutionalize transparency could easily fail. Transparency was not the way the Bank did business. Rather it was the fashion of the day, depending upon who was managing policy at any given moment.

I went to Krysten Ebro, the EXT liaison who had worked with me on the 2000 Forum, to protest.[157] "The signal the department is sending to the public is wrong and could damage its credibility," I suggested. I sought common ground based on an earlier conversation with Johnson. Two opportunities were missed with the Lawrence Summers lecture. The first was his cancellation of our interview, but EXT had also cancelled its request to conduct a live webcast.[158]

Johnson and I were interested in picking up the flag. In the past, I was concerned about ISG's ability to deliver, but this ebbed over time. I realized ISG was much more comfortable with the technology, and if a client was willing to subsidize the increase in cost, it would be a valuable service we could facilitate.

Jeffrey Sachs was scheduled to be the keynote speaker for the lead event of the Environment Department's month of activities.[159] In a bit of a surprise, Johnson said Laporte was willing to let us pay for the session with money I had raised for selling my time to other Bank units for webcasting their conference events.[160] I told Ebro it would be a bonanza for her colleagues, then began navigating my own channels through Wheeler to prod de Nevers and Georgieva.[161]

Georgieva, however, was no longer at the helm. Without her leadership, the Environment Department's instinctive reflex was to withdraw from its previous openness. This shift provided a graphic demonstration of how easy it was for the institution to regress any time pressure for transparency eased.[162]

There were other examples. A few days later, former Bank President Robert McNamara visited the Bank to discuss *The Fog of War*, a film about his time as U.S. defense secretary managing policy in Vietnam. Though the event was open to hundreds of Bank staff and invited guests, EXT had the session filmed for internal viewing only. I requested EXT put it on B-SPAN.[163] They refused.[164]

Still another unit was hosting a discussion on social services in Cuba. The Bank had no formal program or lending initiatives with the Cuban government, so when I queried the event manager, it came as no surprise she espoused reluctance.[165] "Of course, I love B-SPAN and fully support transparency," she stated, "but a webcast will curtail the openness and informality of the discussion."

I pointed out capturing such events was the reason B-SPAN had been created. For example, there was Jeffrey Sachs's speech chastising the donor community on the Bank's home page. There was Stiglitz-Rogoff and other spirited discussions. "Cuba is a politically sensitive subject," she countered. "We wouldn't feel comfortable talking about this in public."

I parried, "Cuba is politically sensitive, and I would understand completely if you and your colleagues walked away from my offer. But did you know that the Bank's Managing Director Mamphele Ramphele and WBI Vice President Frannie Leautier had a video conference on Cuba's social services aired on B-SPAN a couple weeks back? If two of the Bank's most senior officials can talk about social services in Cuba in public, perhaps you could as well."[166] The task manager was chagrined, but she did not change her mind.

Shortly after airing the IMF's Economic Forums, I learned their chief economist, Raghuran Rajan, would be hosting a session on "Sixty Years Later: Why the IMF is Embraced Yet Misunderstood." An old Research Department acquaintance, Shanta Devarajan, was participating, so I asked him if B-SPAN could cover the event.[167] He said yes, then wrote back to say Rajan said no.[168] I let it go, but wrote Devarajan to say, "It seems that if the point of the discussion on the IMF's part is to be better understood, it sends a curious signal that they wouldn't want to share it with more people."[169]

Transparency was a pretty dress to own for some, but inconvenient to wear. Individuals in the Bretton Woods institutions were learning that B-SPAN was not an abstraction anymore. There were no more test cases to follow. There was no more waiting for precedents. There was only the willingness to stand up and embrace transparency, or revert back to instinctive monolithic behavior. That was not to suggest there was no progress. Biju Rao, who challenged us on our editing principle that led to Leautier's edict fully supporting our transparency model of no editing, hoped I could make the McNamara event public.[170] It was interesting for me to note: Once the concept of openness was accepted and people understood its merits, perhaps they might actively embrace it. Still, I had to be pragmatic. There were supporters and there were converts, but there remained an entrenched resistance to the cultural change we sought, as if it was a plague.

In this environment of successful coups and potential trapdoors, a major earthquake hit WBI. The jet stream for B-SPAN would be transformed instantly and irrevocably.

3

I was meeting with Salem to see how we could generate enthusiasm for our pet project to push B-SPAN's content through the DLCs when he gave me an odd look. "Something large is afoot in the department," he said.[171] He did not know what it was. Leautier's office subsequently called to postpone my meeting for a few weeks. Then, the announcement came. Millet was leaving the Bank, and Leautier had decided to dissolve the entire Global Knowledge Pillar.[172] The implications, though not fully known then, would be enormous. Laporte and a few personnel including Johnson and Ron Kim would move to the vice president's office in July. Many other pieces of the Pillar, such as the I Team, were being absorbed by GDLN. In a hastily convened meeting, Laporte said it was an open question as to what would happen to B-SPAN. He had talked to Monika Weber-Fahr about having it join GDLN. He was also talking to EXT. I was appalled. Either outcome would bring disastrous consequences.[173]

I sought Johnson out. He said Laporte had gotten the idea of having GDLN take B-SPAN based on our Knowledge and Learning meeting days before. Johnson thought the concept wasn't yet solidified, but the window for changing it was extremely tight.[174]

I needed to think fast. Suddenly, the meeting with Leautier had taken on a significance of profoundly greater importance than I first anticipated. I still hadn't informed Johnson I was going to sit down with the vice president. I knew instinctively what I needed to do. Now I had to have enough time to make it into Leautier's office before a public announcement relegated B-SPAN to a fate I could no longer influence. I asked Johnson to stall Laporte until I could come up with something. He subsequently sent Leautier a note asking her not to decide prematurely about a permanent move.[175] He did not copy Laporte. Leautier wrote back to say B-SPAN's placement remained an open question.[176]

I caucused with Wheeler to vet my strategy.[177] "I'm going to ask the vice president for autonomy by moving us into her office," I told him. "Such a shift would give me a chance to finally operate B-SPAN without the parochial constraints of departmental bureaucrats."

I also knew it was an all-or-nothing proposal. Rejection could doom B-SPAN. Acceptance would embolden it. It would give me a chance to grow the system to its full potential. I also knew the notion of reporting directly to the vice president was a non-starter, so I would advocate for the re-establishment of the advisory committee composed of Wheeler, de Nevers, and Johnson. I would answer to them, and they would report to the vice president. Wheeler was supportive but doubtful she would accept the idea. I sought out de Nevers.[178] She was agreeable as well, but also registered skepticism Leautier would buy in.

The vice president held a meeting for the department to discuss the dissolution and its impact on WBI's work program.[179] She noted many of the Pillar units would be placed within GDLN and hinted B-SPAN would be included. I realized Laporte and Weber-Fahr had sought her out already, but hoped a decision had not been finalized.

I was also gathering information on Weber-Fahr, and the news was not good. The intelligence coming in called her autocratic, dictatorial, and highly bureaucratic. "Do you know what a micromanager is," one senior GDLN official asked me rhetorically. "Well, she is a nano-manager."[180] With GDLN's pedagogical mandate, B-SPAN would be pushed to produce complementary and highly stylized product lines. I sensed the stakes were growing more critical by the moment. Weber-Fahr symbolized a return to the terrible storms B-SPAN had just weathered. Salem said he had abandoned his work with GDLN because of her. Now, I sought his help to dissuade Leautier on a merger.[181] He agreed.

It was then I revealed to Johnson my proposed meeting with Leautier. My chances of reversing the policy were dimming and I knew it. Johnson encouraged me to paint the differences between GDLN and B-SPAN as starkly as possible. "Show the vice president B-SPAN's potential revenue generating power if it is not married to GDLN's agenda," he suggested.[182] I began working deep into the nights at a furious pace to synthesize and refine my arguments.

I developed a three-pronged agenda.[183] The first item for the vice president's consideration would be a strategic vision for B-SPAN. It would lay forth the fulfillment of our original concept, as well as an evolution in my thinking about what B-SPAN should become. Throughout its first four years, B-SPAN had been reactive, recording events requested by Bank staff. Now, it had started to evolve into a pro-active system with its interviews of policymakers. There had also been an expansion from covering only Bank events to including external content providers such as the original US-Asia Environmental Partnership events and more recent IMF seminars. It was possible to move beyond these test cases to webcast a variety of external partners.

I called the concept "multi-directional knowledge sharing." B-SPAN would serve as a hub of videotaped policy dialogues on development. External content providers would be research and policy institutes, universities, think tanks, NGOs, or community-based organizations that could provide video content on discussions about international development issues. Additionally, there was another group I called "reverse content providers." These were staff in the Bank's country-based offices and the DLCs' stakeholders. They could produce their own events, and send the video materials to B-SPAN for dissemination on our website.

This would create win-win scenarios. First, we could gather valuable content. Second, we could create a revenue stream from non-Bank sources to subsidize the system in the absence of adequate funding from WBI. By providing an outlet to hundreds of thousands of viewers globally, we would be presenting knowledge sharing opportunities for these external partners that they could not duplicate for themselves or find elsewhere.

The concept would have profound implications. A modest investment by the Bank could result in its becoming the focal point for a vast reservoir of development dialogues. Essentially, the system I was seeking to build would make the Bank the epicenter for an untapped market.

A typical scenario might unfold as follows: A research institute in East Asia, studying agriculture issues in the region, would film a gathering of experts and stakeholders for a discussion. The tape would be sent to B-SPAN for encoding, streaming, dissemination and marketing, which then would be watched by agricultural researchers, policymakers, and stakeholders globally. It could potentially influence their work or spur reciprocal dialogues. The first target would be the wealth of materials available in our own backyard—the Washington policy community—but this could quickly be expanded. Numerous policy discussions were being held outside the Bank every day, but like pre-B-SPAN days, almost none of it was being captured for posterity. The market was B-SPAN's to own.

The model could include new products tailored for redistribution. B-SPAN could edit or craft video products for inclusion in other product lines, such as WBI course or training materials, so long as the original unedited source was in our archives. This could be extended to external clients such as research, academic, or media outlets. For instance, an event featuring a major personality would be shown in its entirety on B-SPAN, while a news organization such as CNN or the BBC might feature a snippet on its evening broadcast. And, B-SPAN could apply a charge for reuse as well.

Like with the DLCs, the proposal could also foster dissemination in other global networks such as the Development Gateway and Global Development Network. Additionally, the strategy would establish a live webcasting component of premiere Bank events, and would seek to increase the percentage of non-English webcasts. None of these activities, however, would be possible if B-SPAN were immersed within GDLN's agenda.

The second prong addressed financing. I wanted to move the vice president's mind away from viewing B-SPAN as just recovering its costs, and toward the understanding that there were great opportunities for revenue generation as well.[184] Instead of creating lose-lose scenarios by charging Bank task managers each time they used the service, B-SPAN would seek partnerships at the departmental level. While departments were preparing their annual budgets, we would negotiate packages of service each year, allowing them to webcast as many events as they envisioned necessary. This would provide B-SPAN and WBI a guaranteed revenue stream. Partnerships could also be created with our external clients. The creation of tailored products would provide an additional revenue source.

The final prong would be to create ETC positions for Bowden and me. Without security for its staff, B-SPAN was doomed. I put together figures on revenue generation goals and cost parameters for salaries and hardware/software acquisitions through the next three fiscal years. The lynchpin of all of these goals would be our autonomy. Without it, B-SPAN would inevitably grind to a halt.

Armed with facts and figures, I met with Leautier. I had just fifteen minutes on her calendar to make my case. I began by documenting some of what we accomplished over the last two years, including the recent pro-active format of interviewing policymakers. Then I laid out the cornerstone of my vision: B-SPAN as a hub for multi-directional knowledge sharing. What I was offering was an opportunity to transform not just WBI but the entire Bank in a profound way. The mechanism I proposed would bring the institution closer to its stakeholders and its stakeholders closer to the Bank and one another. The Bank would evolve from an organization dispensing development advice to a repository for harboring development knowledge and dialogue.

The opportunity was now in Leautier's hands. "I can make it possible as I have made B-SPAN itself possible," I said. All she had to do was accept. I then discussed other complementary pieces of this vision: Accessing content from external sources, live webcasting of important events, and creating tailored products for redistribution. She said she was receptive to all of it, and asked that I set up a live webcast of the massive Shanghai conference coming that summer.

Then, the vice president's secretary opened the door. Her next appointment was waiting. But many important issues remained. I asked for a few more minutes and began racing through the rest of my agenda. Touching upon the impact of the cost recovery policy on B-SPAN, I encouraged Leautier to create departmental partnerships. She promised to revisit the issue. I turned to the matter of ETC status by noting Bowden and I had been living on two and three-month contracts for two years. "We need security," I said. She scribbled some notes and said she would personally look into this for us.

Finally, I turned to the issue of autonomy. "For two years, B-SPAN has been asked to implement agendas other than its own," I said. "Now there is strong consideration to place B-SPAN within GDLN. To achieve the vision I just now defined, we need autonomy. Bring us into the front office, and create an advisory committee to serve as a management mechanism."

The moment of truth had come. Without the slightest hesitation, Leautier refused. "If I left, the next vice president would wonder why B-SPAN was located in the front office," she said. "This would make you vulnerable. Who would protect you should I leave? There has been some misunderstanding about your merging with GDLN. B-SPAN will not be part of GDLN."

Leautier became emphatic. "It will simply be under the management of Weber-Fahr. No, far better to be under her. She will protect you. She will fight to get you resources. This is in your best interests," the vice president declared. The look on my face must have registered skepticism, for Leautier added a caveat. She suggested I meet with Weber-Fahr and tell her my strategic vision for B-SPAN. "If you still felt uncomfortable, you can revisit the alignment with me."

I was boxed in. It was, as Don Corleone said in The Godfather, an offer I could not refuse. But I was shaken and badly. Instinctively, I understood B-SPAN was on the precipice of catastrophe.[185]

In an exchange of notes the next day, I expressed my appreciation to the vice president for her time.[186] She wrote back, "B-SPAN is a highly strategic tool and I take a very personal interest in it."[187] No time had been wasted communicating the results. That morning I received another email. It was from Monika Weber-Fahr to request a meeting.[188] A highly nuanced game of three-level chess was already underway between us.

PART VI
the crucible

1

B-SPAN had become a tale of two cities.

In February 2004, evidence of the transparency juggernaut was quantifiable.[1] This had happened despite its immersion into a culture that found it distasteful to its palate. In less than a year and a half, B-SPAN had become the most heavily trafficked of WBI's 70 websites. We now routinely received 300,000 page requests or more each month, and were even leaving this marker behind. And, while these numbers were rapidly growing, so was the distance with other WBI sites. But traffic data was only one yardstick to measure the webcasting station's impact. A sense was hardening within the institution that B-SPAN, despite or because of its transparency principle, was a key venue Bank staff needed to communicate with stakeholders. Sprouting like wildflowers, our logo and links were mushrooming on dozens of sub-sites in the Bank's sprawling Internet infrastructure.[2] And, perhaps most importantly, B-SPAN had become the fulcrum where major debates about the Bank and its development role were taking place.

The pivotal conversation with Leautier was followed shortly by Sachs's keynote speech launching the Environment network's month of events. After significant debate, Bank officials finally decided to allow him to give the address.[3] Their vacillation had caused cancellation of our live webcast, but not our participation. It became quickly obvious why they had hesitated. Sachs, in his role as special advisor to UN General Secretary Kofi Annan and director of the Millennium

Project, minced no words.[4] The challenge for the donor community was to help the developing world reach the Millennium Development Goals (MDGs), he said. "Halving poverty by 2015 is achievable. In fact, the scientific, technological and financial infrastructure already exists to eliminate global poverty by 2025 if it is implemented conscientiously and passionately. The only ingredient missing is the will." With war raging in Iraq, Sachs noted the U.S. was spending $450 billion annually on military expenditures, but just $13 billion in development assistance. "There is a woeful lack of support by the U.S. on its agreed commitments to achieve the MDGs," he added. "And, the international community's structural adjustment policies exacerbate poverty in the developing world."

His voice resounded with disgust. "Things must change," he emphasized. "The donor community must stop telling the poor to live with poverty, and do more to get the poor what they need, such as medicines and soil nutrients." The U.S. was clearly the focus of Sachs's ire, but not all of it. He went on to note, "The Bretton Woods institutions deserve much of the blame for forcing poor countries to make do with the limited resources provided by donor countries. Instead of berating poor countries, the Bank and the rest of the development community should start representing them more forcefully before the powerful."

It was a stunning moment. Sachs, possibly the most famous development practitioner of our era, had accused the Bank before hundreds of its staff with reckless malfeasance. More fundamentally, the UN was telling the U.S., the Bank, and the IMF that their failure of leadership resulted in unnecessary hunger and disease in the developing world. It was a bombshell.

I began to set the timer. I contacted Ravi Rankur, the administrator for Sachs's Earth Institute website, to suggest he make our stream available on his home page.[5] "You may want to do this quickly as there is no telling how the Bank's management might react," I said. I also encouraged him to have the stream available through Sachs's affiliated UN Millennium Project website.[6] Rankur was excited.

Then, I turned to displaying the speech on our home page.

Normally, banners for featured events offered mundane titles. This one originally stated, "Jeffrey Sachs on ESSD and MDGs". The Sachs speech, however, offered a unique opportunity to highlight an event of important news value. I crafted a new title and asked Bowden to paste it online. He reacted violently. He was adamantly opposed to creating a precedent suggesting we had a news story. "It is exactly the precedent we should be setting," I countered.[7]

The headline now read, "Bank Must Change to Reach MDGs, says Jeff Sachs."[8] It was a watershed moment. Here was an *internal* communication medium publicly suggesting the possibility its own institution was not in compliance with stated objectives. It was akin to a corporation confessing on its website that it knew its products were defective but sold them anyway. Nothing like this had happened within the Bank before. Afterwards, Wheeler said, "B-SPAN's brilliance is it provides plausible deniability for the Bank's management.[9] Messages emanating from B-SPAN are unofficial, so Wolfensohn never needs to respond to external queries. He can support Sachs's position without being tied to it." Still, the message had been sent. After the Sachs speech went online, I half-jokingly told Wheeler I would file for unemployment, and then stopped taking calls in the event a senior official might phone demanding the video go off-line.[10] None did.

But the Bank did respond. About a week after our Sachs coverage, Shengman Zhang, the Bank's managing director and second most powerful official, offered a rebuttal.[11] To assist low-income countries, he said, the Bank's main vehicle was implementation of Poverty Reduction Strategy Papers (PRSPs). This process helped countries set targets, develop and monitor indicators, articulate policies, and arrange financing requirements to achieve the MDGs. Zhang added that Bank research, data collection, financing modalities, monitoring reports, human development activities, lending programs, and partnerships with other donor agencies formed the foundation of its advocacy role. The managing director, however, neglected the key point. He never addressed Sachs's central assertion: The Bank should stand up to the Bush Administration for reneging on U.S. aid commitments. Zhang's response also appeared on the *World Bank Today*, an internal organ. His speech was available to Bank personnel but inaccessible to the general public. He was simply shoring up staff morale.

The Bank's two main public outlets presented curiously different spins on B-SPAN's stream. The massive newsletter, the *World Bank Week in Review*, sought to moderate its punch. Its title was a muted, "Donor Country Responsibilities," and the text made no allusion to Sachs's charge of negligence.[12] Two days later, Frost placed the stream on the Bank's home page with a headline almost identical to B-SPAN's: "The World Bank and Donors Must Change to Reach MDGs Says Jeff Sachs."[13] It was a remarkably courageous step. The Frost headline would remain online for an astounding six weeks. The juxtaposition of these acts—trepidation and acknowledgement—was implausible. The constant in the equation driving these actions: B-SPAN.[14]

The debate over the Bank's development role continued through the transparency medium. Kwesi Botchwey, the then executive director of the African Development Policy Ownership Initiative and former minister of finance for Ghana, lectured at the next Practitioners in Development Series.[15] Botchwey said a decline in donor aid was linked to sub-par performance in Sub-Saharan African economies during the last quarter century. He pointed to structural adjustment lending by the Bank as a key factor. "These policies skewed decision-making within African governments and eroded national ownership of reform agendas," he said. "There is evidence trade liberalization has increased unemployment while rapid industrialization has led to wage inequalities." He added, "Development for the region must include more than income growth. While the donor community focuses on improving governance, it has placed too much emphasis on eliminating corruption, but not enough on the root causes of market failures such as institutional inefficiencies and vested interests of informal power brokers in the private sector."

The Bank's own analysis of poverty reduction in Sub-Saharan Africa supported Botchwey's premise. Annual per capita income for the region was just $650; and this figure dropped by half if South

Africa was excluded from the equation.[16] The high incidence of AIDS, malaria, and deforestation rates was accelerating poverty. Even Bank officials admitted that reaching the MDGs in the region was unlikely.[17] During our interview, I asked Botchwey if he agreed with Sachs's assertion the donor community needed to do more to fulfill its commitments on achieving the MDGs. He thought the Bank had made strides in recent years, but concurred.[18] "The institution needs to advocate more on behalf of the poor," he acknowledged.

Botchwey and Sachs were in the same camp on the key development debate of the post 9/11 era. There were others, however, who suggested institutional reforms and capacity building were necessary before large aid inflows could effectively reduce poverty. The Bank, concerned with how shareholders and stakeholders judged its performance, justifiably sought to place its poverty reduction accomplishments in an appealing light. China and India were often cited as examples of effective Bank lending. B-SPAN provided an equal forum for these voices as well. For example, Zhou Xiaochuan, the governor of the People's Bank of China, followed Botchwey. Zhou said that since the 1970s, market reforms had lifted 400 million people out of poverty.[19]

More powerful events came online. Jagdish Bhagwati, a renowned economist from Columbia University and author of a new book, *In Defense of Globalization*, spoke at the IMF's Economic Forum.[20] Bhagwati characterized the anti-globalization movement as one with two camps. The first he labeled "rejectionists," and thought it had no interest in negotiating. The second group he identified as those who worried about the negative economic impact of globalization.

Bhagwati thought their concerns were fundamentally over social inequities existing in a globalized world. His research sought to better understand whether globalization was helping or handicapping the world's social agenda. He used an example of child labor in Vietnam to illustrate his conclusion. "Increasing Vietnam's access to foreign markets allowed rice exports to rise and created more wealth for farmers," he said. "This allowed them to use fewer child laborers and increasingly children returned to school. As income levels rose, so did national education rates, especially for girls." The downside of such economic progress was that domestic concerns compelled U.S. politicians to promote international labor standards that, if not met, could lead to trade sanctions. In other words, donor nations forced structural adjustments on developing countries that lacked the capacity to assimilate these reforms.

When the Sachs stream appeared on the Bank's home page, I had written Leautier: "Your leadership within WBI has led to the Bank's growing embrace of greater institutional transparency." [21] She wrote back, "You have been the heart and soul of B-SPAN's principles. Great news and good job!"[22] It was a promising response, but I was struggling to fit its meaning within the context of our organizational realignment. After the Botchwey interview, I asked Wheeler for an assessment: Did he think we had finally institutionalized B-SPAN? He was candid. "No," he said, "but the multi-directional initiative you proffered to Leautier was a clever ploy for sustainability."[23]

The conflicting currents that embodied institutional thinking about transparency warranted a logical explanation. My hypothesis was the Bank had evolved significantly during the Wolfensohn era and to some degree even before then. Policy dictation was decidedly less from the top down. Opinions, in contrast to past Bank doctrine, were coming increasingly from varying sources within the organization. B-SPAN itself had likely played a role in facilitating this trend.[24] Senior management was bending to competing demands from shareholders and stakeholders, and was becoming more responsive to the scrutiny of external critics.

The stolidly hierarchical structure had weakened, but only to some extent: The ancient concept of fiefdoms remained. Now, middle-management individuals controlling turf had greater leverage to use their resources in support or in subtle opposition to the institution's prevailing platform of the moment. Some opted to test the limits. Others stayed far from the line. Since fiefdoms populated the Bank, there was room for B-SPAN to develop informal alliances. Where support or opposition resided depended upon the individual warlord. The theory had credence from our experiences with de Nevers, Tolstopiatenko, Laporte, and Johnson. But they were B-SPAN's history. Despite all our accomplishments, the voyage was precarious again. A new fiefdom had to be traversed: Weber-Fahr's.

2

B-SPAN would remain part of the KS Team through the balance of the fiscal year, another four months. Nevertheless, Salem and Johnson encouraged me to prepare a detailed work program. A choreographed game plan, they believed, would lessen Weber-Fahr's instincts to manipulate.[25] I began the endeavor immediately.

Much grief was endured with Tolstopiatenko and Laporte, because they never formally acknowledged or agreed with B-SPAN's transparency and archiving principles. Upon our entrance into WBI, we had mistakenly assumed Leautier's staff would implement her policies. I would not make the same mistake twice. The draft work program now sought to steer Weber-Fahr toward the notion that homogeneity of B-SPAN's product line had led to its success.[26]

I wanted to start the dialogue with the suggestion that she would accept separate websites to accommodate alternative product lines, and reasoned it was always possible to fall back to creating a Classroom/WBI Presents section on our home page. I also hoped to denude habitually parochial thinking within WBI that B-SPAN was a house organ; I would emphasize the benefits it offered to the entire Bank organization.

Tolstopiatenko was also on the move under Weber-Fahr's supervision. He would likely encourage her to create a competitive service, so his alternative vision remained viable and dangerous. Included in the note was the strategic vision on multi-directional knowledge sharing and new product lines. Codified targets for revenue generation, however, were not identified. Setting specific targets, I concluded, would leave us vulnerable if they were not met. Dialoguing about budget issues also raised related questions about ETC status for Bowden and me, an issue I wanted the vice president to decide directly.

To help guide the discussion, I decided to send the draft work program to Weber-Fahr in advance of our meeting.[27] I asked Wheeler and Johnson to comment.[28] Wheeler thought it sounded good, but Johnson lobbied me to make important changes.[29] He encouraged me to delete references to B-SPAN as a homogenous product line, to acknowledge acceptance of a "Classroom" product line, and to push Weber-Fahr directly on the ETC issue.

Weber-Fahr was also preparing for our meeting. She sent a series of messages through conduits. In our weekly KS Team meeting, one attendee said the GDLN manager had called B-SPAN a simple digitization service.[30] Weber-Fahr met with Bowden and characterized B-SPAN as a cog in her machine. Cost recovery would remain a priority, but what sort of plan she supported was not revealed. She also repeated the prevailing department refrain that B-SPAN would become a venue for WBI's learning events.[31] Weber-Fahr had made it clear: The Tolstopiatenko-Laporte doctrine would remain in effect.

She also had an important message for Bowden.[32] His role as B-SPAN's primary encoder would not change. It eliminated his hope, and mine, that he could evolve beyond his technological responsibilities.[33] Unsurprisingly, on the eve of my meeting with Weber-Fahr, Bowden announced he had accepted a position elsewhere in the Bank.[34] His involvement with B-SPAN would end at the close of the fiscal year along with the KS Team. Johnson thought Bowden's departure would provide me with leverage to lobby Weber-Fahr to create two staff positions: One to replace him on encoding, and another to assume the writing responsibilities that would increase under the strategic vision for which Leautier had voiced support.[35] With the upcoming budget contractions that WBI had announced, I thought Johnson's proposal had little chance of succeeding. Moreover, through the grapevine, I was hearing there were many people on Weber-Fahr's hit list.

We finally sat down at the end of March. Weber-Fahr was short and bland. She wore her blonde hair curtly cropped, and her face owned few wrinkles from a lifetime of playing poker. She had a curious habit of inserting American clichés in her speech, though they usually came out awkwardly. However, she was highly educated, and had joined the Bank under its vaunted Young Professionals (YP) Program.[36] Young Professionals were the Bank's equivalent of first-round draft picks, and were often groomed for senior management positions. Differences between Weber-Fahr and her B-SPAN predecessors quickly became apparent. She spoke carefully seeking to create impressions rather than to reveal information. And, the impression the diminutive German created dwarfed even Laporte and Tolstopiatenko in one surprising respect: She was a super-bureaucrat.

I asked her if she supported B-SPAN's principles.[37] "I do," she said. Did she support the vision outlined in the work program? She said yes again. To reassure her we were moving in the same direction, I noted two-way knowledge sharing would mean costless new product lines for GDLN's infrastructure. Weber-Fahr said she would be under significant budget constraints in the coming months, so I described my revenue generation strategy. She responded positively. "The notion of establishing departmental partnerships rather than charging task managers for individual events is a useful approach. Why don't you draft a letter I can have Leautier send to other vice presidents?"

But the promising start faded. I had habitually come to use the generic "we" when describing what B-SPAN did. Now, Weber-Fahr pressed me to describe what I specifically did to manage the system. I discussed my responsibilities and then did a tour of the website.

She paused when she saw the Sachs event. Her eyes focused on me dully. "Are you proud of that?" she asked. "I am. I am proud of that," I responded. The exchange was revealing. In a moment, we instinctively understood each other. Regarding B-SPAN's dissemination of the Sachs speech, Wheeler predicted I would hear nothing from the most powerful players in the Bank. From our experience, it had always been mid-level managers building fiefdoms on the road to greater authority who had been concerned with the transparency model.

"You are very entrepreneurial," Weber-Fahr noted, "but now is a time for pragmatism. With the budget constraints I now face, I'm compelled to keep you as an STC for the balance of the calendar year. After that, funds will be in place to make you an ETC." Something about the statement didn't sound right. "Why will funds suddenly be available in the middle of a fiscal year that aren't available now?" I asked. Boxed in a corner, she admitted she wanted to see if she was comfortable with me before deciding on giving me ETC status. It was the same sentiment expressed by Tolstopiatenko and Laporte, and even Johnson. The meeting ended. I had a bad taste in my mouth.[38]

Every time I answered the riddle, someone arrived to say the rules of the game had changed. After eleven years as a consultant, what did I have to do to make the team? Johnson was also disturbed by Weber-Fahr's rejection.[39] He encouraged me to press my case. On the spur of the moment, I knocked on her door. "Past accomplishments and plaudits of previous managers are all fine," she said in a halting monotone. "I will even give them consideration, but if I can't offer you ETC status in July, we can discuss an exit strategy." I told her that would be fine and left.[40]

Johnson was incredulous about Weber-Fahr's response. Wheeler was livid.[41] I decided to press Leautier.[42] "I empathize with managers facing budget constraints, but they always have these restrictions," I noted. "That will never change. Based on B-SPAN's reputation, Bowden has been hired sight unseen as an ETC in another part of the Bank. I don't believe I am asking for more than I deserve, only what I deserve." The vice president said she would talk to the GDLN manager and follow up with me.[43]

Weber-Fahr had given mixed signals. On the one hand, she said she supported the transparency model, but on the other she would not commit herself to its architect. I thought hard about our conversation, and realized she had told me only what I wanted to hear, but not what she was really thinking. She wanted to buy enough time to bring B-SPAN into her shop.

Why this was happening remained unclear. Perhaps Leautier had concluded for budget or realignment reasons she needed me to move into GDLN with B-SPAN. Should I bolt and B-SPAN subsequently collapse, the fallout for WBI would be substantial. It was Weber-Fahr's job to keep me for the moment. If the GDLN manager didn't believe in the model, perhaps I could use her verbal pledge of support to tie her into a public commitment.

She asked me to give a presentation at her next staff meeting.[44] The parallels with the retreat Laporte hosted two years earlier, when B-SPAN first joined his unit, could not be missed. At that time, a bitter battle was already forming with Tolstopiatenko over the notion of transparency and permanent archiving. As baseball legend Yogi Berra once said, it was "déjà vu all over again." Before GDLN's staff, I provided an overview stressing the importance of the transparency principles as the foundation for past growth and future success.[45] Weber-Fahr offered no reaction.

Bank Swirled, the annual April 1st publication spoofing the Bank, devoted a half page to parodying B-SPAN.[46] We were featuring a diverse range of programming. The 8 a.m. show *Morning Inspiration* aired live coverage of Wolfensohn's prayer breakfast with the Republican Party faithful. There was *Africa in the Morning* at 8:30 featuring Gobind Nankani, vice president of the Poverty Reduction network, practicing his Esperanto with closed-captioning for hearing-impaired viewers. The topic of discussion: "How Joe Stiglitz was fired for our sins." *Lunchtime with Jim* at 1:00 p.m. featured an announcement from the White House Rose Garden with Wolfensohn stating he would not oppose amending the Bank's Articles of Agreement to ban gay marriage. At 9 p.m., the Bank's version of reality TV with *Lost in Translation* was shown. This edition featured a jetlagged economist dreaming of a world free of poverty meeting a lonely newlywed in the Grand Hyatt Shanghai bar. Parody was *Bank Swirled*'s forte, but even its editors would have been hard-pressed to assimilate the April Fool's joke the Bank was playing on the real B-SPAN.

3

Weber-Fahr seemed alarmed B-SPAN would feature Sachs questioning Bank wisdom. President Wolfensohn, however, confirmed Wheeler's theory. In fact, he moved beyond Shengman Zhang's reaction to embrace what the UN's special advisor to the MDGs had said.

"People in developing countries have the same hopes and aspirations as those living in industrialized countries," Wolfensohn noted in a speech before Washington religious leaders that B-SPAN covered.[47] "The challenge of helping three billion people who live on less than two dollars a day is enormous. Reaching the MDGs is less about money and growth and more about equity and justice. Rich countries have promised to build capacity in poor countries, increase aid and open their trading markets. Yet the $50 billion in annual development aid represents just 0.2% of GDP in rich nations. In comparison, these same countries spend $350 billion annually on agricultural subsidies to supplement their domestic markets and $900 billion in military expenditures." Wolfensohn paused and declared, "If the rich thought there was a wall between them and the poor, then it tumbled down on September 11, 2001. The U.S. must provide greater leadership. They must lead governments of the industrialized world, all of whom have an obligation that transcends economics and addresses issues of humanity."

Since its inception, we had scrupulously avoided having B-SPAN become a venue for what Wheeler and I called the "cult of personality." We didn't want the system to become primarily a platform for senior Bank officials to voice objectives at the expense of giving space to lesser-known academics addressing cutting-edge issues. This objective had been weakened by Laporte's decision to transfer GSD's bills to internal clients.

As predicted, high-profile events had become the lion's share of our offerings. However, without adoption of the proposed revenue generation strategy, this trend would continue, and our hands were tied. Accordingly, I had never featured a newsletter to our 16,000 subscribers where Wolfensohn had been the central figure.[48] His speech, however, had been a remarkable public rebuke of the donor community's commitment to the global poor. It far surpassed traditionally muted Bank rhetoric about its contributing members. I decided the time had come to give the Bank president his due.[49]

For the moment, revenue generation still had legs. A couple of weeks earlier, Millet had convened a final meeting of her division.[50] There Leautier noted WBI, along with most other departments, would experience budget reductions over the next three fiscal years. Accordingly she had brought my revenue generation plan before the Bank's board of directors. "The approach merits consideration for other product lines within WBI," she said.

Weber-Fahr dutifully stepped in line. The basis of the note I was drafting for Leautier would be an analysis Weber-Fahr requested from me on each department's involvement with B-SPAN during the year.[51] In creating the original revenue generation model, Johnson and I developed a sliding scale of services.[52] For example, if a network wanted ten events per year, it would cost so much. If they wanted twenty events, a lower rate per event might be offered. Weber-Fahr said she liked the approach.[53] She wanted to share my research on usage with Leautier, Millet, and Laporte for a final review before implementing the strategy. The concept of creating partnerships was moving forward.

Revenue generation, however, posed a conundrum. The partnership proposal seemed ideal for building a client base and institutional support for cost sharing. It was, however, difficult to implement because of WBI's own limitations on receiving budget transfers from other Bank units, and because of Bank-wide guidelines that frowned on transfers under $5,000. Johnson suggested creating partnerships with vice presidencies starting at $5,000. This would guarantee a minimum level of coverage during a fiscal year, and the sliding scale would determine how much. Unless WBI's management implemented a mechanism to circumvent the charge-back restriction, it was the only feasible proposal we could come up with.

We both agreed, however, to some extent B-SPAN should remain a public benefit. Under this philosophy, our proposal provided non-partnering networks with the opportunity to use B-SPAN a couple of times a year for free.[54] Budget might not be available for these clients to disseminate content via webcasting, but we didn't want to eliminate them altogether. They may have a critical event or two each year where they needed B-SPAN's help. Even if WBI wanted to say "no," I wanted B-SPAN to say "yes."

With Johnson still formally managing B-SPAN until the end of the fiscal year, I turned my attention to setting a precedent for an external pricing model. Establishing something now, I believed, would be critical, given the developing environment. I called John Starrels, the communications official at the IMF who had granted us access to its Economic Forums.[55] The week before, Starrels wrote someone on the KS Team.[56] "Most large institutions, including the IMF, are grappling with the heightened information demands being placed on them in the wake of the Internet revolution … in an effort to respond to never ending inquiries, the search for new ways of thinking about and supplying knowledge to a diverse public, I was lucky enough to come into contact with [B-SPAN]," he said.

He agreed to meet me and brought one of his colleagues. I described B-SPAN's development, and how its transparency had allowed the system to evolve into a communication juggernaut. "I can make your events available to tens of thousands of viewers each month," I offered. "These are audiences to which you currently have no access." Their eyes widened, and they expressed amazement for what had been accomplished. "It's important you recognize the inevitability of modifying our collaboration from a free trial into a fee-based service," I noted. "I can't avoid that from my end." They nodded. They wanted to participate. They would talk with their management.[57]

Several weeks later, I followed up with Starrels. Bank clients were paying $350. Offering something comparable would make us vulnerable if leaked to our enemies. But gauging his pricing sensitivity would also be difficult. "John, we can do this for you at $500 per event," I suggested. "Too expensive," he replied. "$500 is too expensive for the IMF," I asked. I let this sink in for a moment. "OK, why don't you make me a counteroffer?"

Starrels said he would discuss it with his manager. But I had been around the Bretton Woods institutions long enough. I knew I would need another source to establish my precedent.[58]

Johnson was also exploring opportunities to attract external content providers through his network. He found Omer Karasapan, a communications official for the Bank's Middle East and North Africa region. Karasapan recommended a partnership with the Bank's Moroccan office to have events filmed at Hassan University and aired on B-SPAN. He even had a name for the new spin-off: A-SPAN, short for Arabic-SPAN. We enjoyed the laugh, and the next day Karasapan sent a note to Rabat to broach the idea.[59]

With money accrued from my conference charges, Johnson and I discussed equipment we could purchase with the savings.[60] I suggested acquiring a camera with encoding capacity. Originally, such an acquisition would have been designed to reduce B-SPAN's costs and dependency on GSD. Now, it offered different advantages. Clients without capital for GSD's charges could be covered; and we would be able to record events outside headquarters. It would also eliminate the necessity to encode tapes. This offered additional advantages. By encoding instantaneously, we could stream events immediately instead of days or weeks later. Reducing the processing rate would simultaneously allow us to increase the volume and value of the service, as well as our ability to generate revenue. Johnson suggested we might want to consider purchasing a couple of cameras and loaning them to GSD. It was a great idea, and might even allow us to negotiate another discount on their charges, since they would be using our equipment.[61]

Johnson had wanted to remain involved in shaping B-SPAN's future. Knowing the dangers Weber-Fahr posed, I wanted him involved as well. But a dysfunctional thread was enveloping his effort. In the spring, based on the negative reaction from Laporte's forum on charging fees to Bank clients, we thought it best to conduct a survey before presenting a formal proposal on revenue generation to WBI's senior management. However, when Johnson sought to raise the issue with Weber-Fahr, she refused to respond.[62] In fact, her silence toward him was unsettling. It seemed she no longer considered Johnson involved with the system, and was signaling that further inputs were unwelcome. Her behavior suggested she was preemptively co-opting terrain.

My time became increasingly fragmented. We had been ostracized by Laporte, forced into an organizational realignment by Leautier, left without adequate resources by WBI's management to address the institution's expanding requirements, and refused guidance by Weber-Fahr.[63] A system with high internal and external demand being administered by a pair of temporary consultants without sufficient budget did not make sense. At this point, Bowden was splitting his time between B-SPAN and his new position.

Leautier and Weber-Fahr had been unequivocal in their original statements of support for B-SPAN's strategic vision, but their actions suggested otherwise. I sensed that, whatever plans they had, they were not divulging. Weakened by his lame duck status, Johnson felt less and less empowered to make strategic decisions without input from Weber-Fahr. He would have put himself at risk to do otherwise. However, on all issues other than revenue generation, she remained aloof. Even when pressed for comments during chance encounters, she couched her language in double entendres.

Weber-Fahr's veiled messages convinced me fire lines were needed to protect B-SPAN's transparency. Increasingly, I began to view expanding B-SPAN's reach as a strategy for protecting it from the most dangerous bureaucrat we had yet faced.

With demand outpacing capacity, Bowden became adamant about declining requests for coverage.[64] When one of our encoding lines froze, Johnson concurred with Bowden.[65] But I loathed turning clients away. I offered a compromise: I would not solicit business until we whittled down the backlog, but I would not refuse unsolicited requests.[66]

Johnson was also eager to find a replacement for Bowden. He

hired Ann Vroom, an agency temporary with web development and computer skills.[67] Vroom quickly leapt into the gap. Her aptitude for encoding and workaholic personality proved invaluable. The logjam of unprocessed events began to dissipate. There was, however, something quirky about Vroom's character. She was highly focused and humorless. I couldn't put my finger on it, but it did not seem to matter. B-SPAN was moving again.

Meanwhile, B-SPAN's growth continued unabated.[68] In March, we registered 350,000 page views—100,000 page views more than WBI's second strongest website, and 200,000 more than its third. The numbers had jumped 25% since the beginning of 2004. Even by hopeful standards, it was startling. To gain a sense of the ground, I looked at GDLN's data.[69] GDLN was a multi-million-dollar venture with 70 satellite facilities around the world. Our budget was measured in the thousands. Their page views had not reached 100,000.

To assimilate the pieces of Millet's unit that she had absorbed, Weber-Fahr convened a series of strategy sessions on GDLN's reorganization.[70] "Frannie wants our new unit to more effectively reach mass audiences," she said.[71] "But new ways of scaling up outreach activities will have to be done within increasing resource constraints. GDLN also has to help WBI fulfill its mission of operational relevancy with other Bank units." In other words, GDLN was in business to support WBI's pedagogical mission.

B-SPAN's objectives were quite different, and any reasonable interpretation of her message suggested the transparency model would be disassembled or molded to fit this need. Still, I sensed GDLN's reorganization had not yet crystallized. Leautier continued voicing support, and Weber-Fahr was being careful to not stray too far behind, at least in public. Perhaps resource constraints meant existing staff could be assigned to B-SPAN to implement the vision Leautier and Weber-Fahr said they supported. I toyed with a peculiar notion: I might end up managing some of Tolstopiatenko's old staff.[72] But true intentions remained unclear, and the signals were mixed. It could go either way.

Weber-Fahr followed the introductory discussion with a full

day "big think" retreat of senior staff and key clients.[73] As the only B-SPAN person left standing, I was invited.[74] The retreat was meant to give people input on where Weber-Fahr might put pieces of the puzzle. How units and personnel were organized was important, but of equal interest to me was reading the tea leaves.

It brought me a surprise. Throughout the day, members of the new unit kept praising B-SPAN. People I had never met said B-SPAN was essential to their work. They enthusiastically embraced the concept of B-SPAN as a multi-directional hub. Leautier stopped by to share thoughts. "I'm a big fan of B-SPAN," she stated. In fact, the vice president was so effusive with praise, one of my new colleagues asked if I was sending her kickbacks. We laughed, but I was watching something else. Weber-Fahr was characteristically expressionless and silent.

Leautier continued: "The Bank has not done well in the area of capacity building with its client countries. WBI is good in this area, but is not well immersed in the Bank's operational work. With donors increasingly linking aid to results, budgets are being reduced. WBI needs to match its product lines more closely to its clients' needs. For example, I'm impressed by how academics are using B-SPAN products in their classrooms. B-SPAN is an outstanding example of 'massification.' 'Massification,' however, remains a challenge for WBI generally."[75]

I was trying to read between the lines. Leautier was sending a message that she wanted the reach of GDLN's activities to expand beyond the limits of its resources. But was that message meant for me or Weber-Fahr? I had been emphatic with the GDLN manager on a couple of occasions.[76] "B-SPAN is at a critical juncture in trying to satisfy internal demand with inadequate staff," I had pleaded. "Bowden is phasing out. Vroom is a temporary fix. Two full-time people are needed in addition to me if we are to keep the service responsive to our clients." Weber-Fahr had remained coy with her responses.[77] For several weeks, I had been toying with the idea of taking my case to Leautier directly. The vice president's remarks suggested she understood my predicament and was encouraging

Weber-Fahr to make resources available.

Leautier's remarks also suggested other things that moved against B-SPAN's well-being. Budgets were being cut. If B-SPAN wasn't important to Weber-Fahr—and increasingly it was becoming obvious it was not—then the road ahead would be treacherous. The life could be squeezed out of us.

The vice president also said WBI needed to match its product lines more closely to client needs. WBI products were course materials, training modules, and classroom sessions. The department's success was measured in how many stakeholder participants it trained. That suggested B-SPAN might become a venue for these materials. Was Leautier saying B-SPAN worked so well, WBI needed to change it? Was its ultimate value as a marquee brand and potential for massive dissemination? If that was the case, then the transparency model would die.

The dialogue was moving in opposite directions simultaneously. Leautier's obsequious praise had left me cautiously optimistic, with the emphasis on *cautiously*. It wasn't adding up. I needed more information.

I got a bit the next day. In a note summarizing her perspective on the retreat, Weber-Fahr said, "Customization and massification are not necessarily contradictory, nor mutually exclusive. We need to think intelligently, together with WBI course teams, on where and how customization and massification can be combined."[78] In the days that followed, she pressed me for written details of my daily work routine down to the percentage of time spent on any particular task or activity.[79] I had the palpable sense she was methodically and deliberately extracting from me a manual of how to run B-SPAN should one day I disappear. Clouds were thickening on the horizon.

The retreat examined several different operational structures the revamped GDLN might adopt. Weber-Fahr convened another meeting to hone in on a selection.[80] The first model was a status quo approach that left its small and disparate teams intact. The second model merged B-SPAN with GDLN's Studio Team. The third model embraced the same merger, but also put us under a newly conceived

Business Development Unit. This unit would seek to create new types of product lines from pooled resources within the unit.

When asked about the competing proposals, I spoke about the power of having entrepreneurial relationships between teams. “Having flexibility to seek and capitalize on opportunities within and between teams offers considerable advantages,” I suggested. “B-SPAN could work with the Studio Team to create new video products, identify content applicable to new products developed by the Learning Team, and coordinate with GDLN staff to push materials to content-starved DLC studios.”

Han Fraeters, a distance learning specialist who was also joining GDLN, suddenly stopped me. “Perhaps you have too much a sense of ownership for B-SPAN now that it is going to become a GDLN product,” he offered. I reacted sharply. “I do have a strong sense of ownership as I am the only champion B-SPAN has.” Heads were nodding. The majority of attendees were inclined to adopt the status quo model, but by the end of the day it was clear how they felt was irrelevant. Weber-Fahr had decided to go with the third option to place B-SPAN under a newly created Business Development Unit.[81] I had a growing sense of her management approach. She would ask for opinions, but it was done for the sake of political expediency. The only opinion she valued was her own.

The immersion into GDLN was going to be problematic. I believed to the extent it was possible, it would be necessary to broaden B-SPAN’s repertoire as a strategy to protect it. I decided to revisit an old theme. Because of hesitation elsewhere, we had missed opportunities to conduct live webcasts of Sachs and Summers. I kept trying. Shirin Ebadi, the 2003 Nobel Peace Prize winner for her work on human rights in her native Iran, was coming to the Bank to speak at Wolfensohn’s Presidential Lecture series. The series organizer in EXT was interested in my offer to webcast the event live.[82] We convened a meeting with her team, ISG, and GSD.[83]

Since live webcasting had almost no precedent at the Bank, it became clear many others visualized the final objective but not the route necessary to achieve it. The EXT event team’s concept of outreach to develop an audience was to contact their media sources. This made a live webcast irrelevant; the only ones accessing the stream would be a couple dozen journalists. Outreach to the public, therefore, would have to be done by B-SPAN. That meant sending newsletters days before to build audience interest. But before alerting B-SPAN's community, I wanted to make sure ISG and GSD conducted a successful test.[84] The Ebadi event had a complication. She would be speaking in Farsi. ISG believed it could stream the Farsi and the English translation simultaneously, but did not know definitively. They agreed to move up their test to accommodate my newsletter, and reported back both languages could be streamed live.[85] But they weren't sure enough bandwidth existed for our anticipated audience.[86] They decided to run a separate internal stream for Bank staff. The Ebadi webcast would serve as a test case for all of us.

Problems predictably ensued. Final checks were concluded only moments before Ebadi spoke, and only the Farsi version went to the public. When queried as to why the English stream was missing, the explanation was that only one stream could go out. That contradicted their earlier information. By the time it was switched to the English translation, much of the audience had abandoned hope and moved on. B-SPAN's post-event response was no smoother. Bowden had largely moved on to his new assignment. Vroom was unavailable. Tse said B-SPAN was not his responsibility. The system was stranded by its own constraints. The encoded streams did not go online until long after EXT's website stories went public.[87]

Shirin Ebadi's speech mirrored the appeals voiced by Sachs, Botchwey, and Wolfensohn. She made a passionate plea to donor nations to do more to help the world's poor.[88] But there was an important difference between her and the three others. They were leaders in economics and development. Ebadi rose to prominence by speaking on behalf of the disenfranchised and risking imprisonment for doing so in her repressive society.

"Poverty in the developing world," Ebadi said, "adversely impacts the economies of the industrialized world. Who can accept the disparities of a world where life expectancy in Japan is 82 years but just

35 years in Sierra Leone?" She issued a stark warning to the Bank. "Business conducted by the donor community with dictatorships and undemocratic governments emboldens them to neglect human rights. At some point those regimes will collapse and the oppressed will condemn the institutions providing funding that sustained their oppressors."

A few days later, I read on *World Bank Today* that B-SPAN was covering the Research Department's Annual Bank Conference on Development Economics, the main event the chief economist hosted each year. I had asked the communications liaison if they wanted to move forward, but he never followed up.[89] Now, I queried again, and was told that since it was mentioned in a *Today* article, we should make the arrangements.[90] It was another data point for a growing body of evidence: Many Bank staff focused so intently on their superiors that they were not thinking hard enough about the institution's stakeholders. WBI, GDLN, EXT, ISG, GSD, and the Research Department were all working to facilitate the inside game. It seemed only B-SPAN was consistently thinking about the outside game.

With eddies swirling around me, a new threat appeared in the currents. Demand remained constant, but Bowden and Vroom were only working part-time.[91] With Weber-Fahr's refusal to reveal how she would staff us, Johnson felt compelled to seek a stop-gap solution. He decided to hire someone to help with the summarization.[92] Bowden complained. "We should turn down requests," he argued; but Johnson decided to move ahead. Vroom suddenly balked and said she wouldn't tolerate having another person working around her. She announced she was quitting immediately.[93] Johnson and I were stunned. Only urgent promises that we would not take on additional help convinced her to stay.[94] Monitoring the email exchange between Vroom and Johnson, I noticed she sent him lengthy descriptions of all her activities down to the most mundane details every day. Johnson noticed it, too, and had become annoyed. We were desperately shorthanded, and those with authority to make resource decisions had abstained. For the moment, a crisis had been averted; but it dawned on us Bowden had become a malcontent, and Vroom was a highly volatile and unpredictable personality who had come into our midst.

Weber-Fahr held meetings with GDLN's new members about their assessment of the new model.[95] In preparation for my meeting, I asked Drew Stewart of the Studio Team to review strengths and weaknesses of our potential realignment together. A formal merger would provide B-SPAN access to state-of-the art studios to interview policymakers. It would also, in some cases, improve video quality and ease reproduction of CDs and tapes. But there were more minuses than plusses. GDLN's studio environment would give a choreographed feel that contrasted to the informality of events we produced. The interaction between presenters and audiences would be altered noticeably. The schedule for studio time was also rigid, making the prospect of moving previously planned events problematic. Getting things in synch would be virtually impossible. We would end up doing nothing but logistics. Stewart and I agreed we were better off remaining apart.[96]

When Weber-Fahr and I sat down for our second face-to-face meeting, the agenda was to discuss viewpoints on the realignment.[97] I also hoped it would be an opportunity to appeal to her again about the urgency Johnson and I felt about B-SPAN's inadequate manpower. But she had something else on her mind. I informed her about my discussion with Stewart. This surprised her. She asked where else I saw B-SPAN being merged. I said I didn't know there were other possibilities. "That is a problem," she retorted. "In fact, you in particular are a problem. I've been canvassing people in WBI and am hearing you are efficient, creative and successful, but it was best to leave you alone. My challenge is to mold B-SPAN into the framework of my overall operation. You have come to view B-SPAN and yourself as synonymous."

I realized my exchange with Fraeters several days earlier helped to cement this impression. It was also clear she did not think I was a team player, which was a dangerous perception within the instinctively rigid, hierarchical, and authoritarian structure she administered.

She continued: "GDLN needs a greater sense of ownership over

B-SPAN to help it grow." This comment struck me as odd. I had spent two years describing how B-SPAN could help GDLN. I realized Weber-Fahr was now hinting at how B-SPAN would be assimilated into her fiefdom. I had already realized that her vocal acceptance of my strategic vision was a tactic to merge B-SPAN into GDLN with minimal friction. Now I wondered to what degree our visions were in competition. She went on. "You have a big vision for B-SPAN, but it can go farther by implementing newer, smaller projects I have in mind."[98] She didn't elaborate.

Weber-Fahr was using the meeting as a referendum about me, and I was gauging each sentence, splaying them fully to elicit their true meaning. Her speech moved to a new subject. I was a skillful operator, she suggested, but I maneuvered on the organization's fringes and amongst its shadows. This assertion, given the context of the players and the situation we found ourselves, spoke volumes. Quite literally, my methodology was foreign to her. She found it frightening. She was a career woman at the Bank; and anyone she could not dominate and manipulate automatically was a threat needing to be eliminated. I let her attack soak in for a few moments. It was now clear Weber-Fahr would move forward with the idea of merging B-SPAN somewhere, most likely with the Studio Team. Also unspoken but clear, I would begin the new fiscal year under a contract with a few more months of guaranteed employment. And, I could be assured the clock was ticking.

I finally responded. "Suggestions I am not a team player have been taken out of context. When B-SPAN formally moved into WBI, Andrei Tolstopiatenko took steps to disband the project. I stopped him until Karin Millet saw fit to remove him completely. I did this because B-SPAN was an institution-wide service, and not a trophy for his showcase. If anyone has come to see me otherwise, then the viewpoint is groundless. I have only sought to protect B-SPAN principles. Let's examine the current manager. Erik Johnson and I didn't know each other when he took B-SPAN over. However, under his guidance, it has become a team effort, and he views me as a team player. I encourage you to solicit his thoughts directly."

Weber-Fahr's reaction struck me as peculiar, not so much for what it said about me, but what she was suggesting about herself. "You operate at a very high standard of conduct," she began. "You expect the same from others. This means you work with a high level of honesty. My challenge is to find someone within the unit who could work with your strengths and overcome your weaknesses in championing B-SPAN throughout the GDLN." She did not specify whether my standards were a strength or a weakness.

I returned the conversation from theoretical to practical matters. "I believe it's time for WBI to stop thinking about B-SPAN as a project and treat it as an institutional service," I suggested. "It needs to be staffed adequately to insure growing demand does not overwhelm existing resources. This would damage WBI's reputation. Come the new fiscal year, Bowden and Vroom will be gone. Johnson has been reaching out to you to find and train replacements before the current team leaves."

Weber-Fahr's response was enlightening. "The Bank does not always put money into things it says it supports," she said. "B-SPAN will operate as a low-cost initiative. College students will be hired part-time to fill the writing gap created by Bowden's departure." My mind went blank. B-SPAN was on the cusp of becoming the most powerful communications medium in the history of the Bank. Did she say she was going to run the service with college students who had time between classes?[99] She continued. "The greater challenge as far as I'm concerned will be integrating you into GDLN rather than appropriately staffing B-SPAN. I will be carefully thinking about who will be your new supervisor."

I soon learned Weber-Fahr's selection to oversee B-SPAN, Kathy Sheram, was the most bureaucratic person available. In fact, her absolute adherence to all Weber-Fahr's dictums was the key tactical reason for the choice.

The battleground in which I engaged Tolstopiatenko and Laporte was being revisited. Our engagements had been mostly head on. Overt fighting inside bureaucracies is unusual, but waging war against my adversaries had freed B-SPAN to become successful. Nevertheless, it was meaningless to the department's senior officials. Within WBI, the victory of transparency over propaganda had not been institutionalized. Leautier had allowed old terrain to be retraced with a new adversary. Instinctively, however, I sensed the tactics would be different. Overt confrontation would not be employed. This engagement between the micromanager and the lone crusader would be subtle and silent.

Understood immediately was that Weber-Fahr would seek to use her authority to compartmentalize and marginalize my inputs into B-SPAN. Alternatively, I would seek to use the good will we had developed throughout the institution to protect B-SPAN's sacred principles. However, my dream of building a system to change how the institution communicated in the new Millennium had been—in the course of one conversation—eliminated.

Regarding the coming storm, I knew I was at a distinct disadvantage. I had none of the formal levers of control. Any influence I had was informal and based on reputation. There was one further disadvantage for me that hadn't existed when I first engaged Tolstopiatenko and Laporte. I had been given an unofficial label among department officials as a malcontent. It was why I had worked hard to earn Johnson's support, and was grateful for his collegiality. The label wasn't warranted, but in politics the perception of reality *is* reality. It was another quiver Weber-Fahr had in her arsenal.

The perception of a particular relationship is also based, in part, on relationships one has with others. At the time I met Leautier to ask for autonomy, I was burdened with an unfortunate history with two of her key managers. To have an openly frictional relationship with Weber-Fahr would reinforce the image Laporte and Tolstopiatenko had painted for the vice president.

I needed a quieter, more subdued approach to protect B-SPAN. I would have to give ground and give it openly. My strategy therefore would be to yield on everything regarding style, and say nothing in response to openly hostile rhetoric. The strategy would focus on protecting only what was of substance to the principles and the content. Nothing else mattered. And, I hoped the more ground I yielded on style issues the more it would appear I was indeed the good soldier. I wasn't sure the strategy would work, but it was all I had.

Weber-Fahr would also work quietly. Aloof and unemotional by nature, she had gained a reputation as blunt and straight-talking. Her style intimidated staff into obsequiousness. Since they were quickly forced into subservience, GDLN personnel rarely questioned or challenged her. In meetings, she made it a point to ask for opinions, but close examination revealed choices made were ones she originally supported. Staff, interested in surviving, picked this up immediately. Dissenters had a way of disappearing. Since dialogue moved in only one direction, subordinates often suggested their relationship with Weber-Fahr was open. At least we know where we stand with her, they said.

But what would happen with someone on the other side of a philosophical divide that could not be bridged? Weber-Fahr inherited the Bank's lightning rod for transparency. I inherited a completely institutionalized bureaucrat. She knew I would take stands based on principles. I knew she would move with ruthless cunning to find points of weakness before launching a kill.

Assimilation into GDLN was now moving in a precarious direction. At a time when B-SPAN was on the verge of an historic breakthrough as a global communications system, the seeds for its destruction were also being planted. Aside from the occasional rhetorical flourish from the vice president, there was little to keep the ship I built afloat. If Leautier wasn't going to fund B-SPAN, then Weber-Fahr certainly wasn't going to either. The dance between us was a prelude to choreographed execution. With me gone, the GDLN manager, as the I Team manager had wanted to do before her, would mold B-SPAN into a propaganda tool to please the department's most senior officials. Alternatively, funds might also be eased out of the system until it was deemed extraneous to WBI's mandate, and pawned off on another vice president, or it was muted into a benign entity, or it collapsed. All were distinct possibilities.

The signposts were now clearly pointing in a particular direction. Johnson saw it, too. Weber-Fahr continued to ignore attempts he made to talk to her about opportunities B-SPAN afforded GDLN. Rumors continued to circulate it would become a venue for learning products.[100]

Johnson was candid with me. "You've burned some bridges in WBI," he said. "Your relentless defense of B-SPAN's transparency has made enemies of Laporte, Tolstopiatenko, and Tse. Even Bowden feels alienated. They are all talking to Weber-Fahr and coloring her vision. And, she is not bothering to get alternative viewpoints."

He paused to let the gravity of what he said sink in. Then, he continued. "You have a small business owner's approach to building B-SPAN.[101] It is a rare strength in the Bank. Paradoxically, it is also perceived as a threat when practiced inside a bureaucracy. That makes you personally vulnerable. I'm hearing from management initiatives that will spell the end of B-SPAN as a transparent service. They will seek to transform it into a medium of propaganda through pedagogy. You will have to make a decision."

He was right and I knew it. B-SPAN, which so recently had sailed in the sun, was being forced to tack back into a storm.

Now it was time for me to decide who to become.

4

The formal power structure of WBI was coagulating into a unified front against B-SPAN's transparency model. All that stood in the way: One temporary consultant's personal conviction and a highly enthusiastic audience.

None of the turmoil enveloping B-SPAN was visible to the public. Perhaps more importantly, it was invisible to Bank personnel and to almost everyone in WBI as well. For two years, a vigorous war raged behind the doors of half a dozen people over what kind of institution the Bank would become. No one else knew. People only knew what B-SPAN did. And, they clamored for more. The April traffic results revealed a painful truth to B-SPAN's antagonists.[102] It had shattered its record high set in March for page views by 50,000. With 400,000 page views, it was on pace to record about five million page views annually. Since the start of the year, we were reaching between 20,000 and 25,000 visitors each month.[103]

I had a palpable sense things had accelerated to an uncontrollable speed. Demand continued escalating; yet with each new achievement, the situation was spinning more inexorably out of control.[104] I was moving on two fronts, each designed to keep B-SPAN solvent: Grow it where possible; and create moats for its protection. By the late spring, I was still hiring myself to other Bank units for their conferences.[105] With the savings accrued, Johnson, our new IT specialist Bryan Waller, and I investigated hardware acquisitions to make B-SPAN more dynamic.[106]

Concurrently, we were encouraging Karasapan to get the Moroccans interested in launching A-SPAN, though only silence was forthcoming from Rabat.[107] With the end of the fiscal year just weeks ahead, we were getting desperate. If new hardware was not identified and purchased and a precedent with A-SPAN established, Johnson's formal control over B-SPAN would terminate and the possibility that Weber-Fahr would champion either initiative was nil. In the next few months, I realized the B-SPAN experiment could move one way or the other, and the change would be irrevocable. Only one question remained. Could I create an environment that made the transparency model's demise so personally injurious to Weber-Fahr she would refrain from destroying it?

In mid-May, Weber-Fahr convened a final retreat to discuss implementation of the model she had chosen for GDLN.[108] B-SPAN, she had decided, would not be aligned with the Studio Team after all. Instead, she had created a tier of development operatives who would work with various sub-units within the new division. B-SPAN was identified in Weber-Fahr's matrix as a "special project." Kathy Sheram was assigned to supervise B-SPAN. Weber-Fahr had chosen carefully.

Sheram, an American with flowing clothes and long, graying hair, had the appearance of an aging flower child. A former Peace Corps worker, she would hint with pride how she had come of age during the anti-Vietnam War generation. Yet the suggestion was draped in irony, for Sheram had made a career of fitting snugly into dolorous bureaucracies. Following Weber-Fahr's lead, Sheram was an enthusiastic disciple of "nano-managerism." She had led Laporte's instructional designers with a pleasant demeanor and cheery attitude. Nevertheless, her team disliked her.[109] By inserting herself into every aspect of their work, the designers complained she buried them in endlessly mundane and duplicative activities. The practice made her look as if she were actively managing, but subordinates found her a dead weight that moored their work into lethargy. Weber-Fahr, a careful observer of character, understood this. She had thought hard about who could slow B-SPAN down. Sheram was a logical choice. She could have ground General Patton to a halt.

The problem was recognizable immediately. The retreat sought to simulate day-to-day activities of the new work routines. In a hypothetical exercise Weber-Fahr created for us, someone wishing to disseminate a learning event to private audiences came to B-SPAN for help encoding the video.[110] I couldn't have been more overjoyed. Sheram was pleased, too. "B-SPAN should not simply encode the video," she squealed. ""It should also be the medium to disseminate it to 'select' audiences."[111]

Waller, who was spearheading our effort to acquire an encoding camera, organized a demonstration from its vendor.[112] The camera worked flawlessly, but with one important glitch. It used a different format than the Bank. It appeared we had run into a wall. Montenegro, who had joined our effort, came up with a clever solution.[113] "Instead of cameras, why not purchase encoders and lend them to GSD," he suggested. "Whatever they film for you can be encoded simultaneously." Johnson and I were suddenly excited. It eliminated the need to manually encode while offering clients immediate dissemination. Montenegro had identified a potential breakthrough for the volume and staffing problems we suffered. I called David Leonard, Cardak's manager in GSD, and asked if we could meet with him about the idea.[114]

The next day, we gathered to gauge Leonard's interest. I pitched it as a win for both sides. "You can gain a new service to offer your clients," I suggested. "When B-SPAN isn't involved in the event, GSD is free to use the encoder to help other Bank clients." Leonard liked the idea, but was cautious. "There will be a learning curve for our people, and they will need training," he noted. I said we understood and would accommodate for it. The group agreed to move ahead.[115] A few days earlier, Johnson had calculated my efforts had saved the department $30,000.[116] Johnson wanted to acquire a Niagra Max, a one-piece system ISG was using.[117] We had enough cash for two.

Weber-Fahr caught wind of our activities. She demanded an immediate meeting.[118] I described our efforts to delete encoding from our production activities, Montenegro's solution, and the deal we had negotiated with GSD. She instantly objected. "We should have these encoders for GDLN's use," she said. My eyes widened, but I said nothing. "We shouldn't be lending encoders we purchase to another unit. And, GSD shouldn't be allowed to use them with other clients. Rather, the encoders should be used by our studios, and carried to and from there if GSD uses them on a B-SPAN event."

"Where's the incentive for GSD?" I asked. "Without it, the deal will die."

"The incentive," she responded, "will be GSD can charge WBI a higher rate which GDLN could then pass along to B-SPAN's clients." She was suggesting we turn an incentive into a disincentive for our customers.

It occurred to me a revenue generation proposal Johnson and I had submitted to her days earlier was probably dead on arrival.[119] Moreover, it suggested previous pronouncements on her part about supporting our partnership approach had been another tactic to quell dissension for merging B-SPAN and GDLN.

"Perhaps the service should take a new name under GDLN," she continued. "We might call it G-SPAN." "You mean like God-SPAN," I offered hopefully. The room roared but beneath the surface the point she was making was serious. Weber-Fahr, still six weeks removed from B-SPAN's formal management, was already cannibalizing the system by destroying the deal with GSD, and stealing the encoder while driving our charges upwards.

G-SPAN suggested something quite different than B-SPAN. Created to serve the Bank's 10,000 workers and millions of its stakeholders, B-SPAN was now being treated as the personal property of one highly ambitious manager. That wasn't new, but in the past, B-SPAN had informal shareholders powerful enough to protect it. I sensed, however, this was no longer the case. I also felt something else. Weber-Fahr had used the meeting to test how pliant, resistant, or resourceful I would be. Neither of us came away happy.

The Niagra Max story had a post-script. Waller picked up interesting intelligence following our meeting.[120] Weber-Fahr authorized its purchase for GDLN's studio.[121] The Studio Team, however, didn't have use for the equipment, so she cancelled the purchase.[122] She would be taking over B-SPAN shortly, and the encoder would have reduced the costs B-SPAN incurred that had so troubled department officials. Johnson was incredulous.[123] I, however, was not. It simply confirmed what I suspected all along about Weber-Fahr's intentions for B-SPAN's future.

5

Karasapan's dialogue with Morocco had yielded nothing. But, as one door closed, another opened.[124] Moira Enerva of the Philippines Public Information Center (PIC) was in Washington, and asked to see me.[125] "The Philippines has twelve PICs," she said "and its visitors are eager to access B-SPAN's video streams." Sensing an opportunity, I shared my vision of creating two-way knowledge sharing with B-SPAN serving as a hub for content generated by PICs. "Perhaps a prototype event could be held," I offered. "Should it be successful, the Philippines could become the leading PIC in the Bank's global network." I suggested meeting PIC staff in Manila, and some regional satellites to discuss ways to merge B-SPAN's content with their knowledge sharing activities. From there, I would oversee a pilot event. Johnson and I hoped a quick success before the end of his tenure would provide an example replicable throughout the Philippines and at other global PICs.[126] Enerva became excited. She would talk to the Bank's Country Director, Robert Van Pulley, when she returned to Manila. But time was running out. Johnson and I had control over our funds for only a few more weeks before the fiscal year ended.

The PIC pilot, however, died at birth. Johnson reported Laporte had "mistaken" the money I had saved the department for new revenue.[127] Then, he had spent the bulk of it on his own projects. Johnson was livid. I was dumbfounded by the explanation, but not the result. It was just as I had predicted. With a little money left, we could only finance part of a trip to the Philippines. With the fiscal year finished, Manila did not have enough left in its till to get me the rest of the way. Laporte's style could be encapsulated in one final exchange near the end of his tenure running the division. A WBI member wrote him asking the difference between knowledge sharing and learning. The Director of Knowledge and Learning for the Bank wasn't sure. He sent a note to his staff asking if someone knew.[128]

I turned my attention to the massive Scaling Up Poverty Reduction Conference in Shanghai, just days away.[129] During our February meeting, Leautier had asked me to arrange a live webcast of the two-day event.[130] It was an important objective for her, but also a complex puzzle. In the early spring, I had caucused with Yan Wang and Han Fraeters, WBI's point people, arranging logistics. They asked me to identify technological needs and funding parameters.[131] From my experiences during the *Greening Industry* launch in China in 2001, I knew mistakes could be made. Not having direct oversight of Chinese personnel might easily lead to problems. I couldn't offer guarantees unless I was in Shanghai to manage things, I cautioned.[132] But the prospect was not likely, as WBI was already experiencing cost overruns.

I learned no plans were in place for filming.[133] To set up a webcast, it would be necessary to find capable vendors in China. Language would also be a factor, and then there was the Chinese government itself. They had not signed off on a live event; and their instincts about transparency were remarkably similar to that of many of WBI's managers. Moreover, word leaked back that the Bank's China office was reluctant to consider live webcasting because they anticipated a negative reaction from the government.[134] Johnson was in a humorous mood. He forwarded me a note about the Chinese style of transparency.[135] They had allowed then U.S. Vice President Richard Cheney to conduct a live broadcast, but it was aired without advance notice, and subsequent transcripts on Chinese websites had been censored. "Finally, they're moving in the right direction," I quipped.[136]

ISG technicians would be managing technological needs for Shanghai. Fraeters and I met with them to discuss how they could help.[137] "How much of an audience do you anticipate?" they asked. "Given Shanghai is a global event, we should be prepared to host several thousand simultaneous requests," I suggested. But ISG had doubts about WBI's commitment. Their concern was well founded. De Nevers confided to me she thought WBI's effort had been haphazard and chaotic.[138]

Late intervention by ISG secured a streaming vendor, but the conference posed sizeable logistical challenges.[139] Presidents from five countries would be joined by Wolfensohn and forty other ministerial heads. Five live video streams in high- and low-speeds would webcast the language spoken on the floor and the English translation.[140] And the streaming capacity had to accommodate potentially thousands of viewers. In addition to the proceedings in the main convention hall, twenty plenary meetings would take place, involving a thousand participants. Convention hall events would be live, but the smaller meetings would be taped and encoded by us. There was a lot that could go wrong, and "Mr. Murphy" was not disappointed.

Problems began immediately. Several hours before the start, ISG forwarded links to Tse and Montenegro to load on B-SPAN's home page.[141] Montenegro's computer, with the latest software, tested the stream successfully. Mine, with the Bank's standard, received nothing. That meant few staff would be able to watch from headquarters. I alerted ISG, which responded it would work when the event went live.[142] That turned out to be incorrect, because the vendor was using a different codex altogether.[143] Viewers tuning in at the start of the conference watched a pre-recorded feed, but not the actual proceedings. ISG wasn't able to post the correct links until half the first day had concluded.[144] Moreover, archives of the live stream were accessible only to the fastest connections, and did not include English translations.[145] The live webcast had stumbled badly. Problems would persist through the second day, but ISG played it coyly.[146] Leautier was told things went smoothly. Everyone else fell in line. No questions were asked. Nothing more was said.

The saga, however, did not fully end there. Plenary sessions were filmed for subsequent encoding by B-SPAN. GSD's Leonard had been sent to Shanghai to oversee the vendor's camera teams. With a multitude of simultaneous sessions, he was by himself and overwhelmed. Sessions were not filmed according to the guidelines WBI required B-SPAN to maintain. They were also taped in the incorrect format.[147] It would take months before the formatting could be fixed and videos made available. Millions had been spent on Shanghai. For a few thousand dollars more, WBI could have gotten a suitable webcast as well.

The final month of Johnson's administration began with my meeting Wheeler.[148] He marveled at how Weber-Fahr tacked in one direction and then another on B-SPAN. "At least the tenor of the discussion is different than a year ago when Tolstopiatenko was openly trying to terminate the system," he suggested. I acknowledged the point, but noted the warning signs for the transparency model were ominous. What we knew was that we didn't know. Weber-Fahr's administration was a month away. Only time would reveal her precise plans.

In the wake of the IMF's rejection, a new opportunity finally arose to offer the service externally. I learned Resources for the Future (RFF), an environmental research organization in Washington, was filming an event on Chilean water regulations.[149] I inquired if they had interest in B-SPAN hosting their video.[150] Since they were doing their own filming, I offered to make it available for $300. Meg Keller, one of their communications liaisons, responded positively.[151] Afterwards, I discussed the venture with Michael Hensler-McGinnis, her supervisor. He was apprehensive. "Why should RFF share its content with B-SPAN?" he asked. I explained B-SPAN would introduce RFF's research to tens of thousands of development stakeholders who had never heard of his organization before. He nodded, but we did not yet have a deal.

By the middle of June, Vroom's enormous emails had frayed Johnson's nerves to the breaking point. He asked me to see if I could dissuade her, but she waved me off. They continued uninterrupted. She complained bitterly to Waller about occasional shortcomings in the system. Little could be done to mollify her. Waller, too, was losing his patience. Then, without warning, she announced her agency was having problems processing a payment, and abruptly quit B-SPAN for the second time.[152] Weber-Fahr had yet to assume control, but Johnson no longer had funds to hire a replacement. B-SPAN had come to a standstill.[153]

Sheram stopped by my office. As Weber-Fahr's surrogate, she wanted to speak with Vroom and couldn't find her.[154] "What are you going to do about the problem?" she asked. I was perplexed. It was an illogical question. "The problem is not new," I said. "Johnson and I have been seeking guidance from Monika for months to stabilize B-SPAN's ad hoc arrangement since Bowden left. We've been recommending options, but heard only silence. People are complaining about delays. WBI's reputation is at stake." Sheram's reaction was curious. "This project is simply an unfunded mandate," she stated and walked out the door. It was an interesting phrase. I began to think about what she meant. I would hear it often in the months ahead.

On a whim, I stopped by de Nevers office to update her and gauge reaction.[155] "After two years of withholding resources, B-SPAN is barely sustainable," I said. "Without adequate staff, it can no longer function. Soon there will be no one aside from me." She was surprised. She didn't know things had deteriorated so badly. She didn't think the vice president knew either.

The next day, I saw an opportunity to drive the point home. EXT was hosting another President Lecture with Juan Somavia, the director-general of the International Labour Organization. Frost and event organizer Maya Brahmam asked for a live webcast.[156] During previous weeks, Wheeler, Johnson, and Ron Kim had quietly suggested I consider letting a crisis occur.[157] I did the calculations. EXT would howl if we pulled out. With the Shanghai tapes of the external plenary sessions now back in Washington, WBI's senior officials would be anxious to get everything online. For both, a sense of urgency existed.

I called Johnson. "Now would be good," I said. He agreed. I wrote Brahmam back. "We no longer have staff or resources at this time to cover events. I sincerely regret this. Best wish with your event."[158] WBI's senior management was copied on the email.

Brahmam called immediately. Frost followed suit. "What's going on?" they asked. "I couldn't say, but if you have a problem, you should write the vice president," I suggested.

De Nevers sent a note.[159] She had spoken to Leautier, who wanted the Shanghai tapes online as soon as possible. They would find budget, and if I needed to find an external vendor to encode the tapes, she would allocate funds for this as well. As for B-SPAN, de Nevers reported the vice president wished to say she remained a "committed supporter" and it would be fully staffed. De Nevers said Weber-Fahr had everything worked out for the new fiscal year.

I sensed the ploy had accomplished little. The vice president cared that the Shanghai tapes might be delayed, but the point was missed.[160] Finding budget to encode tapes was not the issue. Having adequate personnel to work on B-SPAN was.

As Johnson neared the end of his tenure, he continued trying to splice things together. In a note to Sheram, he said hiring an agency temporary to replace Vroom would leave B-SPAN just as vulnerable.[161] He suggested hiring a consultant to be trained by Bowden.

Finally, after months of silence toward him, Weber-Fahr responded in the aftermath of our cancellation of the Somavia event.[162] She liked Vroom's long daily summations. She was enamored by Vroom's ability to create pictures of computer blips, encoding shortcomings, and tape mislabeling in her emails. Weber-Fahr couldn't do that. She wanted someone to teach her how. She told Johnson she would rehire Vroom. There was some logic to the move, for Vroom was experienced, efficient, and inexpensive. There was, I sensed, an ulterior motive as well. Weber-Fahr and Johnson shared the same view about Vroom, but formed opposite opinions on the value of her explosive personality. Johnson realized Vroom could cripple B-SPAN. Weber-Fahr realized keeping Vroom allowed her to turn the system on and off at will.

The irony of the situation was never clearer. Internally B-SPAN was chaotic. Without adequate manpower, we were drowning in our own success. Between the lines, careful observation suggested plans were being assembled to disassemble the transparency model.

Paradoxically, outwardly, all appeared well.[163] The momentum of the B-SPAN juggernaut was accelerating faster each day. The level of coverage was intense, and new traffic highs were consistently recorded. During the previous few months, we had migrated to a new website, interviewed leading global policy makers, conducted live webcasts of major events, and were now extending our reach beyond the confines of the Bank. None of it would have been possible without Johnson's support. But now, like a U.S. presidential transition where the government moves from the control of one party to the other, his authority had evaporated, and a very different philosophy was forming in its place.

The KS Team convened one last meeting to say goodbye.[164] The staff gave me a card with well wishes. There was a pervasive sense of concern in their notes: The road I was about to walk would be difficult, and perhaps not navigable. I was quite touched, and now, alone. A fan closed the Johnson era with a prophetic email to me.[165] "I appreciate the excellent program. The World Bank is truly becoming what Wolfensohn has pursued—a knowledge bank," he said.

It was the best of times. It was the worst of times.

6

Wheeler was gone. So were Means, Bowden, and Johnson. Now, I had Weber-Fahr and Sheram. They called an immediate meeting.[166]

"There had been a debate as to whether B-SPAN would be given to EXT or remain within WBI," Weber-Fahr began. "The EILT (The Extended Institute Leadership Team was the senior management body for WBI of which Weber-Fahr was a member.) decided B-SPAN should stay within WBI, and they want it to start offering edited products and learning activities. A new model will be implemented. Your job for the next six months is to keep B-SPAN running, put together a cost recovery model to generate income for the department, and develop learning products to put online. I want you to draft letters to Bank vice presidents on new charges for B-SPAN's services. Your contract will end in December, and you can apply for your position in competition with other candidates. In the meantime, I will finance B-SPAN as a low-cost initiative using part-time college students to fill staffing needs."[167]

I suspected she had made a persuasive case before her EILT colleagues, but perhaps Weber-Fahr was simply being the good soldier. Either way, the transparency model was dying before my eyes.

The first checkpoint was codification of a results agreement.[168] In the world of our fathers, workers would punch a clock when they entered and left the factory each day. The Bank's version of that was results agreements. Since these agreements documented what happened in real life, they were redundant before even being created. In the hands of benevolent managers, it rubber-stamped what both parties already understood. In the hands of autocratic managers, they were used to punish personnel who failed to live up to each and every letter. How results agreements were written and interpreted was important. And, in this sanctuary of bean counters, Sheram was a cleric. I realized mine would leave no room for carrots.

Weber-Fahr and Sheram focused on three areas: How B-SPAN was administered; how a yet-to-be selected cost recovery model would be implemented; and what new learning products would be produced.[169] I was confident the first two items would be easily handled, but the last one was a concern. There was nothing in my experience to suggest I knew how to produce training and course materials. Sheram became intensely interested in this activity. Weber-Fahr, who began our relationship emphatically stating her support for B-SPAN's principles, had taken off her mask. I wondered if WBI Presents or Classroom could be created as a separate entity. Perhaps if I volunteered the name G-SPAN, we might live happily ever after. Perhaps.

We met repeatedly to hammer out language. I entered the meetings good-naturedly, but for Sheram it was a passionate experience. Never had so many pencils been used to tweak so little; but these were the margins where she wrote her biography. She obsessively included as many sticks as she could find. I casually attached neutral phrases like "as resources allowed."[170]

One area remained where Weber-Fahr's agenda and mine might be in sync. Verbally, she continued to suggest support for my revenue generation plan.[171] This carefully fell in step with Leautier's current public stance. In actuality, she had hinted otherwise with the Niagra Max escapade. How B-SPAN created its own revenue was an enormous issue. Success in this area might provide me with enough maneuverability to protect or expand B-SPAN in other ways. A fumble would cripple everything.

In the waning weeks of Johnson's administration, Weber-Fahr had asked me to draft letters for vice presidents throughout the Bank.[172] Now the time had come for her to make a decision on the revenue generation proposal. Each letter was individually tailored to note how many times B-SPAN had been used by each department during the previous fiscal year.[173] The proposal Johnson and I suggested offered several scenarios: Coverage of 10 to 19 events annually at $150 per event; 20 to 29 events at $125; and 30 or more events at $100 apiece. If a vice president chose to forgo a partnership with us, individual events could be contracted at $200. To retain B-SPAN as a public service, we suggested each vice president without a partnership could receive up to three events each year for free.[174]

Instead of charging clients admission every time they came to the door, I wanted to create long-term relationships based on mutual interest. In the end, whatever price structure B-SPAN charged for its service would be new revenue for GDLN and WBI. If this was the road WBI was forcing B-SPAN to take, I believed the wisest course would be to initially impose smaller charges so clients could become acclimated, and factor our fees into future budget calculations. Then over time, as the clients came to rely on the service and saw its value, prices could escalate. Large fee increases imposed immediately would alienate clients. Prudence, rather than greed, was, in my judgment, the order of the day.

There were some variables involved with the draft. It was difficult to reconcile pricing options. Raise them too high and clients would cry foul. Keep them too low and WBI's managers might suggest I was trying to sabotage the effort. But where those lines crossed was impossible to say. Weber-Fahr had not pursued our suggestion that clients be surveyed before solicitations were made.

The draft also made some assumptions. One was that these partnerships would not include GSD's costs of $350 per event. So, when B-SPAN charged $150 for our services, the actual cost to the client would be $500. Second, WBI would have to revise its charge-back policy with other Bank units. Implementation of a new policy with other units would ease, but not prevent, B-SPAN from moving forward with its revenue generation proposal. The third assumption, and weakest, was WBI was interested in the impact on B-SPAN's clients.

My concern about pricing entailed more than its impact on volume. It was critical to the issue of transparency itself. For a time, B-SPAN had offered free service for Bank content providers. When fees were imposed, volume declined. Another fee hike had a potentially destabilizing impact. Without sufficient resources, a vast section of the Bank would be effectively cut off from B-SPAN. If the intent was nefarious, eliminating clients could become the first form of censorship. This moved beyond the motivation shown by Laporte, for he had merely been genuflecting to the budget whims of upper management.

Weber-Fahr was different. She had an instinctive dislike for the transparency model. She understood manipulating pricing meant over time much of B-SPAN's clientele could be eliminated, thereby rendering the service impotent. It could then easily be re-engineered into a platform that gave voice to senior players and official views.

But reducing the eligible pool of content was only the first step in destroying B-SPAN's transparency. Another stated strategy was to create events for selected audiences. It was a second form of censorship. Under this scenario, instead of editing content, external audiences would be kept from receiving content. From there, it was only a short leap to providing choreographed products, such as learning courses or training materials that preached particular outcomes or viewpoints. The final and fatal blow to the model would be editing of content so nothing deviating from the company line could escape to the public. There was already evidence of movement in this direction. One of Sheram's first official acts was to have the two of us attend a demonstration ISG organized: A vendor had developed software to edit videos that were already online.[175]

Weber-Fahr responded to the draft letters with a request to conduct cost analyses.[176] "The relationship between price and cost does not have to be one-to-one," she said, "but we should know what we are doing." I responded with analyses similar to the estimates provided Laporte months before.[177] It took the cost of salaries and divided it by the number of units covered. A unit was defined as one two-hour event. A day-long conference was considered four units. We had concluded FY'04 with an astounding 363 units processed.[178] My time had been divided into scheduling, quality control, event summarizing, newsletter dissemination, and marketing. Bowden's time had been divided into encoding, technical enhancements, quality control, and event summarizing. A percentage of time devoted was given to each activity. The final estimate of cost came to $289 per unit.[179] Sheram thought I should include indirect costs such as time Johnson spent on us the previous year, and overhead expenses for computers, office space, lights, and anything else I could find.[180]

While I waited for B-SPAN's managers to decide, I turned my attention back to developing external content. The Washington policy community had dozens of organizations holding events. Very few had possessed the foresight or budget to film and archive them. Those that did had produced piecemeal archives. It was a sizeable body of content waiting for a host; and B-SPAN was uniquely suited to capture a market no one else knew existed.

But the timing was wrong. Six months earlier, I didn't have the resources, and Johnson was just warming to the idea. Then, the IMF pilots dried up, and the RFF was still embryonic. Now, it was painfully obvious there was no way to trust Weber-Fahr or Sheram. The results agreement could not leak what was a cornerstone of B-SPAN's strategic vision. If either Weber-Fahr or Sheram declared opposition, it would eliminate my ability to explore future opportunities. Johnson concurred with the view.[181] I altered course, and decided to suggest B-SPAN disseminate content via the Bank's Public Information Centers. We had received inquiries from them, and if the PICs staged seminars inside DLC facilities, it would be difficult for Weber-Fahr to suggest the initiative ran counter to GDLN's strategic objectives.

But the RFF effort had taken root inside me. I was reluctant to let go; yet if I moved forward, it would have to be done covertly. I had verbal support from Leautier on the initiative, but this was meaningless as soon as Weber-Fahr objected.

I hatched a new plan. I asked Hensler-McGinnis, RFF's Internet manager, to meet about establishing a partnership.[182] If a deal could be put in place with him, it could be replicated elsewhere. The plan was to hold his checks in abeyance until a substantial amount accrued.[183] Once deposited, I hoped to produce two results. The infusion of revenue would be high enough to force Weber-Fahr to accept this new source of funds. Of course, it was possible she would reject the money; but since she was complaining about budget cutbacks, it would put her in an odd position. Acceptance of the money, by caveat, also meant Weber-Fahr had been maneuvered into acknowledging B-SPAN as a forum for external content sources. Two birds.

One stone. If.

Hensler-McGinnis and Keller were thrilled their event was featured on B-SPAN.[184] To further their enthusiasm, I had placed it at the top of our home page, so the outcome of our burgeoning partnership was as highlighted as possible. Hensler-McGinnis, however, remained reluctant about paying a fee. "If we're providing the content, perhaps B-SPAN should pay us," he suggested. "Keep your content," I said. "We want it, but don't need it." His involvement needed some reinforcement, so I revisited my earlier pitch about the return RFF would get for its investment: Its research would be exposed to thousands of development stakeholders in over 150 countries who have never heard of the organization.

That resonated. "My internal politics dictates I come up with revenue for providing access to our audience," I noted. "If I don't get this part of the equation right, the bureaucrats will kill the idea, and both B-SPAN and RFF will end up with nothing." He okayed the deal, but asked for a price reduction. Since RFF filmed and encoded their events, I agreed. I sensed I couldn't go below the price proposed to Weber-Fahr for single events done in the absence of partnerships. That meant $200. In the interim, we committed to collecting the fee as a bulk sum before cashing in. I walked out of the room with a partnership in one hand. The other hand held civil war.[185]

It was the summer season. There would be few events to cover, and time to winnow the backlog. Now, Weber-Fahr would be accountable for delays; but she had a plan, and revealed it in stages. First, she hired a college intern to help with event summaries, and unleashed the reconstituted Vroom on encoding. Vroom's extraordinarily detailed daily reports also reemerged, and they took on the quality of a compulsive obsession.[186] Much more importantly, if anything was out of place, she wailed with dismay. I had made it a point to keep my distance, so barbs were directed elsewhere. But it didn't take long to conclude she would be a highly valuable pawn to Weber-Fahr and Sheram. Vroom's meticulousness intensified the cookie-cutter operation B-SPAN's new managers sought to employ. A third dangerous foil had entered my world.

The results agreement helped Weber-Fahr develop a strategy to become immersed in the mechanics of B-SPAN's operation. She demanded weekly face-to-face reports from me, with an itemized breakdown of who used B-SPAN down to the staff assistant, name and date of events, as well as a step-by-step handbook on how B-SPAN performed its work.[187] It was unusual for any Bank manager to seek such detailed information from a subordinate, but the rationale behind the tactic was clear. Having her fingers in B-SPAN's nooks and crannies would make it easier to mold it into what she desired. My exact hours of arrival and departure were to be strictly recorded.[188] It was mandatory to have a chalkboard posted outside my office to note any moments I was away.[189] One-half hour was allowed for lunch. My key to B-SPAN's encoding equipment room was confiscated.[190] But if each directive of this authoritarian-style management was meant to demean me, I did not feel unduly slighted. Weber-Fahr dehumanized all her staff in the same way.

July moved quickly. Sheram said there had been an evolution in thinking about B-SPAN's organizational realignment.[191] Weber-Fahr wanted to merge B-SPAN into a unit that would house all of GDLN's multimedia services. Han Fraeters would be running the Multi-Media (MM) Unit. A Belgian national who had researched the educational applicability of video conferences and learning models of virtual universities, Fraeters had joined WBI the year before as an instructional designer.[192]

I knew he had Weber-Fahr's ear. I wondered if he would protect B-SPAN's transparency model from being flooded with learning and choreographed training products. I sought him out.[193] He seemed sympathetic. "It is a simple solution to protect B-SPAN's integrity," he noted. "All that is needed is to create a second web interface for learning products, even if the background encoding and database technologies are shared with B-SPAN."

This was good. On this point, we were on the same page. The Multi-Media Unit was to serve as a one-stop shop for a range of learning, design, and technology services GDLN would offer. Its mission would be to assist all WBI staff with their course and graphic design, encoding, and video editing needs.

"Bank staff outside WBI will be charged, and B-SPAN's cost recovery model will be the prototype for how the rest of the unit will apply their own charges," Fraeters said. I noted, "B-SPAN clients might request subsidiary services such as production of CDs, duplication of videos, or editing of video files for their secondary use." Then I made what I thought was a reasoned and reasonable offer. "B-SPAN will forward these clients to the rest of MM, and we can share the new revenues generated."

We had come to a chasm. "Weber-Fahr will refuse such an arrangement out of hand," Fraeters stated. "She wants absolute custody over all revenue to dispose of as she sees fit." That raised an obvious question from me. "If revenue B-SPAN generates is spent on some other part of GDLN, where is the incentive for B-SPAN?"

He was blunt. "The incentive is not to risk being labeled by Weber-Fahr as a problem." From our work together on Shanghai, I felt Fraeters knew the pulse of departmental politics. I sensed he was not wrong. His summarization of Weber-Fahr's stance on how B-SPAN should approach revenue sharing, however, was missing just one thing: Logic.

With the documents requested from me in hand, Weber-Fahr moved quickly to take control over B-SPAN's mechanics. She scheduled a meeting to identify indicators for every step of B-SPAN's production process from an event's scheduling to its availability online.[194] In preparation, she had Vroom develop a PowerPoint detailing the production process from her perspective as the encoder.[195] Then, Weber-Fahr launched a blitzkrieg.

"This information will help me allocate future resources," she said. This statement was received by me with extreme skepticism. "It is important to create a tracking system for B-SPAN's production process to insure its transparency," she continued. I was fascinated by how Weber-Fahr used the word "transparency." She never missed a beat. "B-SPAN's new model will house events exclusively for internal audiences or other special audiences.[196] Learning products will also go online on B-SPAN. In addition, it is costing GDLN money to keep

B-SPAN's files on a server. If clients do not subsidize them, B-SPAN's archives will have to come down. Perhaps files can be warehoused for up to a year, but afterwards it will be the client's responsibility," she declared.[197]

Weber-Fahr's sweeping destruction of B-SPAN was not yet done. The marketing routine I had perfected the previous fall came under attack. When a video went online, I would routinely send the client a note to say they could now access their event. This note would be copied to anyone the client originally invited to the event. It seemed common sense to surmise if those invited guests could not attend the actual function, they would appreciate knowing it was archived on B-SPAN.

Not so. Weber-Fahr characterized this as an infringement on people's privacy.[198] "It is wrong to notify anyone other than the original host of the event," she said. "No one has ever complained to me," I responded. But she was not going to tolerate differences of opinion. "As far as I'm concerned, I only care about the client and not the audience," she retorted.

I paused for a moment. It was an amazing comment, and reminded me of Laporte's statement a year earlier that transparency was yesterday's problem. I asked if she actually meant that. She did. She repeated the phrase verbatim. "The audience is the client's problem," Weber-Fahr concluded.

Smelling blood, Vroom leapt in. "Do we realize Bank people are saying very open and honest things on the videos we are streaming to the world!" she exclaimed. "People might not realize how public their statements are when they reach the Internet. We need to start thinking about that a lot more seriously." Weber-Fahr was nodding vigorously. She asked Vroom to develop a matrix of indicators to monitor a tape's evolution through the production period.[199] The meeting concluded with a demand for weekly meetings so Weber-Fahr would be updated on everything B-SPAN did.[200]

Everything about her, it seemed to me, was duplicitous. I felt she had bastardized the concept of transparency to fit a narrow view of the world. Instead of referring to B-SPAN's principles or content, it had become a mechanism to make staff accountable for her every twist of the screw.[201]

Moreover, transparency now meant providing content to selected audiences.[202] B-SPAN's principles, embraced by hundreds of Bank colleagues and tens of thousands of external stakeholders, were now being casually discarded. I believed only the vice president had the authority to change them; and if they were going to be altered, I was determined to hear it from Leautier personally.

There could be little doubt the production log was a tactic to mitigate my inputs rather than a method to improve efficiency. It would lose importance the moment I disappeared from the scene. And, the GDLN manager's rhetoric about saving money by deleting B-SPAN's archives simply had no supporting evidence. GDLN had never spent a dime on the archives, or for that matter, on B-SPAN itself. Nor would it be expected to do so in the future if my revenue generation plan went into action.

I sought Wheeler's counsel.[203] "Codification of the production process does not worry me," I noted. "I can give GDLN as many widgets as it wishes. I see this as only about style and simply the price these bureaucrats need paid to be fed. The dangers posed to the substance of B-SPAN, however, have my attention."

I believed Weber-Fahr's diatribe about needing a detailed tracking system to help future resource planning was a ruse. If the operation slowed down, our monthly scorecard of indicators to WBI's senior management would show a decline. A decline in productivity would provide GDLN's manager justification for diverting further resources away from B-SPAN.

Wheeler agreed the process of creating and counting widgets was nothing more than a ploy to strangle me. "We should have thought of driving B-SPAN's growth by creating infinite file tabs and worksheets first," he joked.

But I was not in a humorous mood. "The problem," I said, "is victories won over Tolstopiatenko and Laporte have not been institutionalized." Wheeler had instinctively surmised this during our conversation months earlier, after the Botchwey interview, when he suggested the model remained in treacherous waters. "I specifically asked the vice president for autonomy so B-SPAN would not have to travel this path," I said. He agreed. "If I'm going to go to war with Weber-Fahr, I need to know where Leautier and de Nevers stand. If they support her effort to make B-SPAN a parochial platform for learning products, then there is nothing more for me to do than strike my sails," I concluded.

"Would WBI let B-SPAN move to EXT?" Wheeler mused. "EXT has allowed some highly controversial B-SPAN events to go on the Bank's home page." I suddenly found the option palatable.

The question became how to reach the vice president. I could seek her out directly, but that would expose me as a dissident. If Wheeler approached her, I would have no plausible deniability that I had asked him to intercede. I could approach de Nevers, but she had never expressed anything more than mild tolerance for my desire to shape the course of B-SPAN's direction. Wheeler said he would ask de Nevers for a meeting to pick up information.[204]

The next day, I refined my thinking. "Ultimately Leautier will have to be confronted," I told Wheeler.[205] "Timing is critical. If I move too early, I will be seen as a troublemaker. If I move at precisely the right time, I will only be seen as championing B-SPAN's principles." I surmised I needed to move when Weber-Fahr did. More likely, however, if I moved at all, I would be hung out to dry. Wheeler would have to get the commitment by meeting her directly.

"Emails," I told him, "are open for misinterpretation. This will have to be done face-to-face, where body language and voice intonation are on display. If she wavers, then you can press her to allow B-SPAN to migrate to EXT, or at least have a second skin to accommodate [learning products]." But already my skepticism about Leautier was growing. I added that if Wheeler could persuade Leautier to agree, it was best to get it in writing.

I decided to dig a trench to protect a flank. I visited Chongman Kim in ISG.[206] I wanted to build a case regarding Weber-Fahr's effort to destroy B-SPAN's archives.[207] The server deal I negotiated with him when B-SPAN was housed in the Research Department had cost

WBI nothing. ISG had never charged WBI for purchasing, building, or maintaining B-SPAN's server during the three years since.

I asked Kim how much space we had used. He calculated barely half. Enough space resided on the existing server to keep B-SPAN uploading video files at its current rate for another two and a half years. I asked how much it cost to load new events or keep them archived. He said virtually nothing. Then, I confided GDLN was thinking about deleting B-SPAN's archives. He was dumbfounded. "Taking files down makes no strategic sense," he said. "In fact, it would be politically damaging to WBI. I don't think Weber-Fahr would be foolish enough to try." I asked for a favor. "Would you hold off on any bills for the foreseeable future?" Kim said he would be happy to help me.

Nano-managing went into full effect. I was peppered each day with dozens of emails and phone calls on obtuse details. A complete review of camera guidelines was conducted.[208] All events required posted signs and leaflets distributed to inform participants their comments would be made public on the Internet.[209] Weber-Fahr rewrote all correspondence to clients. When I announced I would take time off, the paragraph I drafted to let clients know what to do in my absence was redrafted by Sheram three times and then redrafted again.[210] The new managers acted as if they were fixing a failed service, but these tactics masked an obvious motivation. The absence of resources and guidance during the spring precipitated a backlog of unprocessed materials. If subsequently Weber-Fahr dissolved the backlog, it would enable her to suggest she improved a delinquent service. Creating a monitoring process that slowed the service to a crawl would not get her such accolades, unless it was combined with a supplemental strategy. She had one.

As was her nature, she revealed her plans in stages. Now, she announced Leautier would not send Bank vice presidents the letter on pricing options until the fall, when staff returned from their vacations. A rationale was not provided; but the decision pushed the matter a full quarter past the start of the fiscal year.

Weber-Fahr wanted an explanation of my pricing rationale.[211] I said B-SPAN's value to WBI and the Bank was relative to the amount of new content it offered.[212] The goal was two-fold: Acclimate clients to paying a fee; and implement a benchmark for earning money. If initial fees were overly high, WBI would be criticized for escalating costs too quickly, and volume would decline. Whatever fee was implemented would represent new revenue to the department, as well as a reduction in its commitments to finance the service.

In her response, she suggested charging more: Departments contracting with B-SPAN for 20 events should pay \$250 each; for 30 events, \$200; and 50 events, \$150.[213] Weber-Fahr also proposed eliminating the option of viewing B-SPAN as a free public service. I provided an evaluation of how the two proposals would have fared with actual usage during the preceding year. Under Weber-Fahr's scenario, B-SPAN would have created one partnership for 50 or more events, two at 30 events, and two at 20 events for a total of five partnerships.[214] My proposal would have generated nine partnerships. By charging less, we would actually make more. I made it clear I was ready to implement whatever management decided.

Outwardly, I appeared tranquil. There was no hint of the defiance that marked my time with Tolstopiatenko or Laporte. No task was denied. No objection was voiced. Nevertheless, through an intuitive understanding of what I represented, Weber-Fahr was making it clear I was a mortal enemy. Her aggression began to evolve into desperation. She cordoned off other parts of her work to focus on B-SPAN. I had the distinct perception she seemed obsessed, probing for opportunities to injure me. Then, inadvertently, I handed her one.

Fraeters, Sheram, Vroom, and I met to discuss Weber-Fahr's goal of merging B-SPAN with the MM Unit.[215] Fraeters began with an explanation of the production process under development by MM. Sheram recapped how B-SPAN was "finally transparent" because it could chronicle its own process through a detailed tracking system. Fraeters said updates to Weber-Fahr for the MM Unit weren't necessary. Sheram said B-SPAN was a special case. I remained silent. The dialogue continued for a while. Sheram talked dreamily about how B-SPAN would soon stream WBI's learning events and training courses.[216]

Then, something inside Vroom exploded. Nothing was good enough with the equipment, she roared. "Everything revolving with B-SPAN is subpar," she railed. She started criticizing GSD as dysfunctional. Suddenly, there was a spark. My powder had dried. Fearful Vroom would provide Weber-Fahr another lever to destabilize B-SPAN, I broke my silence.

"Actually, I've been working with GSD for four years, and the quality of their work has improved markedly. The perception their work is inadequate is mistaken."

Nobody ever said no to Ann Vroom. She bristled. First, it had been Johnson and then a string of others. Inevitably, it was going to be my turn. The meeting ended. Sometime toward the end of the day, Vroom finished encoding a tape. She burst into my office and hurled it at me. I followed her and demanded an explanation for her behavior. She refused to respond and slammed her door. I should have let it go at that. Instead, I blundered and visited Weber-Fahr under the guise of seeking advice on how to communicate with Vroom.[217] Weber-Fahr laughed and called her "an old warhorse." She would consider a replacement in the fall. "Until then, I suggest you make peace with her," she offered.

The next morning, Sheram walked into my office and gleefully announced Weber-Fahr had contacted the Bank's Mediation Office to officially intervene in the unfolding crisis.[218] In Bank parlance, handing a relationship to the Mediation Office is an action taken when open warfare cannot be settled by other means. Because of its serious nature, it is a step of last resort, not a first.

"Monika is worried it might impact B-SPAN's productivity," she proclaimed. It was nothing more than a cynical ploy to paint me as a malcontent. Vroom and I worked separately and hardly ever interacted under normal circumstances. Moreover, the "old warhorse" was as prodigious as ever. It was also a dereliction of duty by Weber-Fahr. Instead of managing, she was resorting to manipulation to achieve a more strategic outcome. Instead of defusing tensions, she sought to escalate the confrontation under the guise of seeking mediation. The move made public one of her strategies in framing the debate over B-SPAN with Leautier and her senior aides.

"I do not see a need to seek mediation," I said. "You could refuse," Sheram responded with a smile. "As you know, Vroom has a history," I noted. Sheram said she didn't know what I was talking about. When I mentioned Waller had visited her a few days earlier to complain about Vroom's behavior, she knew she had been exposed. "This whole thing is hurting production," she stammered. Sheram was groping for an exit strategy. "How?" I asked. "This conversation," she said, "is taking away valuable time."

I was inclined to refuse, but still wanted a second opinion. I asked Johnson for thoughts. He was flabbergasted. "I'm a marked man," I said. He agreed.[219] He believed Vroom was unstable, but counseled me not to ignore the mediator. The issue resolved itself quickly. I called to say mediation was unnecessary. Vroom did the same. Without two willing parties, the mediator was forced to close the file. I sensed I had dodged a bullet, but for how long?

Thereafter, Vroom's production log became Sheram's bible. The log provided her an opportunity to focus on what she did best: Delve into process for its own sake. Daily meetings were convened to identify where individual tapes had progressed in the production line. No stone was left unturned to insure the matrix was filled out correctly.[220] Though eyes would roll and glaze, even forgetting to initial something was a key issue for discussion. Her adulation for the insignificant was uncompromising. She cheerfully noted backlog was shrinking, as if to suggest the matrix was responsible but the eventless summer was not.

As my summer leave drew near, Sheram became more frantic.[221] Meetings were often scheduled twice a day. At one point, she rooted through months of files to list every task she or Weber-Fahr had requested.[222] She implored me to respond. It was a meticulous note that would have filled a law professor with pride. But it did reveal a *small* weakness. Sheram had trouble remembering things. In meetings, she would repeat questions answered moments earlier. Just minutes after her email, I wrote back that almost all these requests had already been met.[223]

I prepared for my first extended leave in more than two years. There was a great deal to think about. The paradigm Weber-Fahr created between us had three main fault lines: Transparency, budget, and control. After her initial subterfuge, she wanted to eliminate B-SPAN's transparency. On a tactical front, she had tried baiting me for a reaction by announcing B-SPAN would edit content, distribute to selected audiences, and blend product lines with learning and training content.[224] To her chagrin, I was not responding.

Moreover, reality was sobering. The Studio Team did not have the capacity to absorb this additional task. The MM Unit would provide video editing services, but it only pooled existing, not additional, resources. And, segmenting Internet audiences between public and private events was a technological hurdle requiring significant development.

I had decided upon entrance into her fiefdom that I would wait for Weber-Fahr to move first.[225] Then, I would seek clarification from Leautier and other stakeholders to determine if these activities were appropriate from their perspective. If it turned out Weber-Fahr had made policy in a vacuum, it would be a quick checkmate. I considered this terrain a draw until there were new developments.

The second fault line was budgeting. I had no formal authority, and only the power of a logical argument as persuasion. Weber-Fahr and WBI seemed determined B-SPAN should be run as a "low-cost" venture. It was possible she might opt for a strategy to penalize clients. Already known was that revenues B-SPAN raised would be used on her own priorities. I believed cost recovery would lead to a rapid decline in B-SPAN's ability to function, and a subsequent reduction in revenue. Conversely, I was convinced my strategy of revenue generation would make money. Then it would be a matter of who would be able to present the more convincing case: That (1) less revenue was an indicator of reduced client interest, and therefore a good reason to deactivate the system, or (2) a bad policy had led to a bad result. This, of course, pre-supposed one other thing: Senior WBI decision makers actually cared how B-SPAN was being managed. Since a final decision had yet to be made, it was difficult to assess future moves.

Each fault line was a tactical battleground for the real issue of importance to Weber-Fahr: Control. I cared about B-SPAN's transparency. Her obsession to dominate anything in her orbit of influence overrode all other considerations. Not being in control was the same as being out of control. It was an anathema to her.

Weber-Fahr's formal authority provided obvious advantages. She had regular access to Leautier and senior WBI officials, whereas I had none. Should I seek an audience with Leautier, Weber-Fahr would charge me with disloyalty, and Leautier seemed malleable enough to agree. Even if I did contact Leautier, it could be just once. Weber-Fahr could easily create new situations to put B-SPAN's credibility or my employment into question.

All of these considerations had weighed on my mind, and Wheeler's, during the difficult period under Tolstopiatenko and Laporte. We had refrained from "going nuclear" before, and it turned out well. Since this option hadn't been used, it was still available, but it was like going to Vegas and putting everything down on one color. On this part of the paradigm, I was on fragile ground.

Sun Tzu would have suggested the battleground was clear. With Weber-Fahr, Sheram, and Vroom circling, I was surrounded. The storm was before me. I wanted Weber-Fahr to believe I could be molded in whatever pattern she chose. The more she would press, the more I would acquiesce. I would become absorbed in the folds of the storm until I was at rhythm with its turning. If the storm would allow it, I would become invisible and silent within its groaning wind. And, I would wait for the clouds to break. If that break ever came, then I would strike back.

7

At the invitation of a friend, I boarded a plane and slipped into the silence of the former Soviet Union. Sheram kept busy testing my out-of-office message repeatedly, and designating Vroom as B-SPAN's chief spokesperson during my absence.[226]

During the lull, Wheeler caucused with de Nevers.[227] "B-SPAN is on solid ground," she told him. "There is no desire in the department to jettison it to EXT." She believed B-SPAN had been institutionalized to the point where it would not be eliminated. Wheeler seemed reassured, but I was concerned. The point was not where B-SPAN would be, but what it would become. I realized de Nevers had disengaged. She was no longer in the loop. By the Black Sea, I dreamt of the enormous burden that would greet me upon my return.

In August, Salem, the former GDLN official who had tried to get B-SPAN disseminated through the Distance Learning Centers, quit the Bank. His farewell note to department officials made a veiled reference to his former supervisor.[228] "I leave feeling that I can point to where my contribution has brought us incrementally forward, but that this could have been delineated and wider ranging were it not for the risk adverse, bureaucratic reflexes of career-obsessed, desk-bound managers," he said. Concurrently, Bruno Donat, GDLN's chief communications official, sent an email on the principles of behavior for Bank managers to the entire unit.[229] It emphasized constructive behavior and positive feedback. Donat suggested both were missing in GDLN, and left the unit a few months later. A third senior official, Mwangi Wachira, also disembarked in frustration.[230] As the summer unfolded, more began to flee.

Montenegro was equally displeased with the new environment.[231] He noted there was a formal procedure to oust dysfunctional managers. Internal regulatory controls, however, essentially eliminated palace coups. It meant building a small following of courageous individuals willing to raise a complaint to senior management. Obviously, it would be no small feat with livelihoods on the line, and given the types of personalities that deliberately sought careers in large bureaucracies.

A tightened fist greeted my re-emergence from the former Iron Curtain. A meeting was convened upon my arrival.[232] Several new events had been scheduled, and the very survival of WBI seemed to depend on their outcome.[233] Based on Vroom's ongoing dissatisfaction with GSD's work, Sheram believed it was necessary to double-check the camera team's "professionalism."[234] Creation of a routing slip for each new video was added to the production log.[235] A checklist of questions to ask clients requesting service was developed.[236] Summaries needed to be written in a standardized format.[237] Daily meetings scheduled to monitor new developments amounted to little more than discussions about typing mistakes.[238] I was yawning my way into a coma.

"Charging for archives will begin in the near future," Sheram announced one afternoon.[239] I woke up. She seemed pleased to add the Bank normally deleted its archives after five years.[240] In the eight business days following my return, Sheram wrote me 69 emails.[241]

An interesting dynamic had emerged. Under the guise of creating order, Weber-Fahr and Sheram created a climate of fear and disorder. Everything was treated as a crisis. It was not an unintended byproduct, for the objective was choreographed terror. To enhance this environment, all requests were categorized as urgent or vital. Creating imbalance was a mechanism to satisfy their instinct to dominate and control. Without control, they felt dysfunctional, but by creating chaos they were dysfunctional. The new rules were designed to channel most of my time into managing the process of production instead of producing new content. But I had seen that act before. This behavior had been a favorite tactic of Tolstopiatenko.

Johnson had been right about the unbiased nature of Vroom's venom. With Sheram's myopic nature, the pendulum predictably swung her way. One day, she tallied the scorecard numbers for B-SPAN events during the summer.[242] Vroom criticized her for not including some videos she had encoded.[243] The snippet was oddly satisfying, for Sheram and Vroom complemented each other nicely. Sheram was a niggling micromanager and Vroom was a combative technocrat with a virulent distaste of authority. The combination was lethal. I wondered when Vroom would self-destruct.

It took one more day. Montenegro showed me a bizarre email from Vroom, beginning with her coming down with food poisoning and ending with an abrupt decision to leave.[244] When Sheram decided to hire a newly arrived college student, Annie Spencer, instead of Vroom, she abruptly quit B-SPAN for the third time.[245] Montenegro was pleased. So were Stewart and Waller. Our encoding activities would be significantly impacted, but with so few events coming online the larger significance seemed to be that Weber-Fahr had lost a valuable pawn. Vroom's note also provided additional intelligence. Weber-Fahr had asked her to encode a training course. The GDLN manager was moving forward with her agenda.[246]

Sheram informed Weber-Fahr B-SPAN's backlog had been eliminated.[247] They congratulated each other. Unmentioned, however, with all the time devoted to making widgets, B-SPAN had done only a few events during Weber-Fahr's three-month reign.

Sheram continued. "Permission will be requested of clients to notify B-SPAN's public when their event goes online."[248] That was curious. "Since B-SPAN is public, why would we need their permission?" I asked. Weber-Fahr responded. "Serious consideration is being given to restricting the public's access to B-SPAN," she said.

Sheram noted WBI's Human Development pillar "loved" the idea of having B-SPAN house their learning products. I did not respond. Weber-Fahr went on to praise her own decision about informing B-SPAN speakers and attendees that the Chatham House Rule was not in effect.[249] "This is being done," she said "so secret information will not be revealed." Weber-Fahr's decision about the Chatham House Rule presented a bit of a conundrum. The rule essentially provides anonymity for speakers and their organizations, even if their comments are made public. It was difficult for me to oppose since B-SPAN was a public service.

Still, there was little doubt about her motive. Aggressively informing people their comments would be made public would logically dampen the dialogue. Instead of encouraging participants to speak freely, Weber-Fahr was using the Chatham House Rule as a ploy to stifle discussion, debate, and the open exchange of ideas. Again, I said nothing. I realized she lived in a world that revolved around tactics. It was, however, a world with little semblance to reality. Once Weber-Fahr's attention turned away from our struggle, whether B-SPAN participants knew the Chatham House Rule was in effect or not would no longer be relevant.

Sheram announced Vroom had left. Spencer would take over encoding duties with interim help from Montenegro until a replacement was found.[250] I feigned surprise.

Weber-Fahr again turned to the issue of charging clients. She had made a final decision on cost recovery. Clients would now be charged a flat rate of $350 for B-SPAN's services, to be contracted on a per-event basis. Over the summer, GSD had raised its fees to $400 so the cost of getting an event on B-SPAN would become $750.[251] Less than a year earlier, it had been free.

She did not think it would impact volume or affect scorecard indicators. It seemed like another ruse to mollify me. Weber-Fahr had said repeatedly the cost recovery policy would be made by Leautier. My results agreement stated it would be determined by the EILT, WBI's senior management body. Yet Weber-Fahr's nature was to act unilaterally. I asked for further clarification on how the decision had been made. She did not answer the question directly. Instead, she said my note "had been taken into consideration but the decision to price B-SPAN at $350 was selected to parallel our actual costs."

This was wrong. My analysis estimated the cost to be $289. B-SPAN had evolved from a free good to a service where Weber-Fahr said the price-to-cost ratio did not have to be equal. Now, it had changed again. She was literally planning to make a profit on her Bank colleagues, which was against departmental rules. Her response also suggested she made the decision herself, but for the moment that was an assumption on my part. I would need further information.

"Demand will be assessed to determine whether to continue the service since WBI's management will not fund B-SPAN," she continued. My expression offered no reaction. Sheram now carried the banner. "In fact, GDLN is seriously thinking about including additional costs in B-SPAN's fee to account for office overhead and Montenegro's time. Charges may climb to $900," she suggested. Sheram added another thought. She believed it was "entirely consistent with B-SPAN's principles that it offered edited products as well."[252] I remained mute.

The decision on what fees to charge meant many things immediately. Customers would be charged a high fee without surveys or focus groups to provide input, which Johnson and I had repeatedly warned against. Weber-Fahr's opinion, it seemed, mattered more than customers. There also would be no warning to clients, so there would be no time to adjust their internal finances to meet the escalation. And, there would be no letters to vice presidents around the Bank, or sliding scale for services purchased in bulk, or plans to create partnerships. Once a client stepped in the door, they would be handed a bill.

Clients reacted predictably.[253] They began protesting and cancelling. I soon decided to begin covert lobbying against the scheme. It was a calculated risk. If my encouragement to clients to make their objections known leaked, I would be in a fatal position. Yet, if the new fee structure remained in place, B-SPAN would be strangled to death.

With two bad choices, I went forward.[254] Mojgan Sami, who managed events for the Social Development network, expressed dismay at the new pricing structure. However, she did not cancel.[255] I called her to suggest she reconsider. "If enough clients opt out," I explained, "WBI's management will be forced to reassess the new policy." She agreed and sent me a note criticizing B-SPAN for suddenly escalating its fee structure without seeking input from clients.[256] "The sudden increase will not allow units to allocate funds in their budget cycles to address its knowledge sharing activities," she wrote.

Then, I asked Hafed Al-Ghwell, who managed the Bank's InfoShop, if he might help. He had contracted with B-SPAN regularly, and agreed the new pricing mechanism might be a serious burden. He wanted to assess its impact first, and promised to keep our conversation confidential.

I knew Sami's email would elicit an immediate response from Weber-Fahr. It would provide an interesting juxtaposition to how she responded to Johnson's months of inquiries about a range of important policy issues. It took a half-hour.[257]

"I fully sympathize with your concerns regarding an unexpected price increase," she said. "In reviewing the various services provided by WBI's GDLN and Multimedia Division, we were forced to take a hard look at what we provide to the Institute and to the rest of the Bank. B-SPAN is one of the services for which we were forced to begin instituting a charge back process."

It was an important admission. Weber-Fahr was stating publicly B-SPAN was incidental to the department and not a priority. Moreover, since WBI wasn't going to pay for it, it would transfer the costs to the rest of the institution. If that was the policy, then there was no longer a legitimate rationale to continue housing B-SPAN, other than the fact it made the department look good and had been placed under Weber-Fahr's control.

According to the GDLN manager, the $350 didn't include indirect charges such as equipment costs, server costs, and web maintenance costs. This suggestion was consistent with Weber-Fahr's habitual pattern of misdirection. How could anyone other than those intimate with the details know that B-SPAN's equipment had been bought years before, and GDLN had not paid for any of it; or that server costs were zero, or web maintenance costs were already factored into the cost analysis I had provided her? Lastly, Weber-Fahr said, "Without some support from B-SPAN's clients we will be forced to discontinue the services." Now, finally on public record, she had gone one step farther than Tolstopiatenko ever did.

A few weeks later, Sami asked me if discounts were possible.[258] Weber-Fahr's thinking about cost recovery continued to evolve. She did, after all, want partnerships. She would now grant clients who contracted with B-SPAN for ten events the eleventh event free.[259] I told Sami of GDLN's offer.[260] She walked away and was not heard from again.

Under the guise of efficiency, chaos was now the rule. When we produced our next Practitioners in Development lecture with Rima Khalaf Hunaidi, assistant secretary-general and regional director of Arab States for the UN Development Programme, it took on a circus atmosphere. With Vroom gone, Montenegro on leave, and Spencer not yet trained, Sheram scrambled desperately looking for someone to encode the tape. The Studio Team was requisitioned.[261] A new tactic was introduced into our equation: The blame game.[262] A client with an event online wrote to request the text be edited, but no one was available to access the database. When the client complained, Sheram called me into her office to admonish me. B-SPAN's new management was immersed in the search for weaknesses. Successes were irrelevant. The situation was deteriorating by the day.

Observing Weber-Fahr's modalities had been useful to me in helping choose my own. Her opinion was the only one she valued. Since other voices were extraneous, I stopped responding. It was a reversal of the tactics I used against Tolstopiatenko and Laporte. With them, I had engaged in vociferous debates, and offered responses based on the merits or weaknesses of opposing arguments. With Weber-Fahr, I had grown quiet by design. The longer we were chained together, the less I spoke. Soon I became silent. I also took it as a given she would conduct much of what she did in secret. So, there would be some things I wouldn't know. I knew, however, if I listened carefully she would often reveal clues as to her intentions. And, I had a secondary source of information for what happened behind closed doors: Sheram.

Sheram was an ardent advocate of a widely popular doctrine of business management best characterized as "Talk first, think." She continually revealed tidbits in her daily meetings that alone suggested little, but when woven together spoke volumes.

Sheram followed an August holiday with a September vacation.[263] While meeting to temporarily pass the baton to Stewart, I raised the subject of cost recovery.[264] "How was the price set at $350?" I asked. She fell into the trap.[265] "Weber-Fahr made the decision."

I hypothesized Weber-Fahr had possibly pulled an interesting switch. She unilaterally decided to charge Bank clients $350 to use B-SPAN without input from the EILT. Then, in asking the senior management body of WBI to approve charging $350 to WBI staff, they would have thought they were permitting Weber-Fahr to expand an ongoing policy. Instead, Weber-Fahr had made the decision for them, and she was covered on both ends.

There was another reason for my silence, one we both understood well. It was the calendar. The moment Weber-Fahr walked into my office the previous March, I sensed I was on borrowed time. Now, there was a deadline. My contract ended at the conclusion of the year, less than 90 days away. She had alluded to a process of soliciting for other candidates for my position and the issue was a Damocles sword over my every word and deed.

We were like two basketball coaches trying to manage a clock unwinding to the last possession. Weber-Fahr used production logs, regulations, forms, and meetings to attack B-SPAN and provoke a response. I remained mute, offering no resistance, yielding to everything she sought, since it mostly impacted the system's style. She had not yet moved to change the substance of the model, so I was content to hold my fire.

I reasoned she might wait until I was gone. Certainly, the contract would expire, but it could not be allowed to simply expire. The service was recognized throughout the Bank for its unprecedented success. Leautier had gone on record numerous times as a fan and supporter. Traffic, until recently, had been soaring. Not renewing my contract would raise too many questions. Since I was giving her no cause for dismissal, she would need to manufacture one. Time was running out for both of us.

One quiet afternoon, I sat down with Wheeler for a long discussion.[266] I catalogued for him the chain of events.[267] At the beginning there had been Weber-Fahr's statement of unequivocal support for B-SPAN's principles, the strategic concept of multi-directional knowledge sharing, and a revenue generation plan based on partnerships. This had been followed by decisions to house edited content and training and course materials; to remove our archives or charge clients for their maintenance; to restrict audience access by offering content through permission-only passwords; and to refrain from asking clients for their inputs on fees.

From there it went on to abandoning the revenue generation

model based on partnerships; adopting a cost recovery model based on per-event charges; using revenues raised by B-SPAN on other GDLN activities; remaining silent on resource needs during Johnson's tenure that created sizeable backlogs; and creating a production log that redirected staff time into its maintenance rather than the production of content.

Furthermore, she destroyed an encoding arrangement with GSD that would have simultaneously increased efficiency and reduced costs; she terminated marketing activities on the premise B-SPAN audiences were inconsequential; and used the Chatham House Rule to mute dialogue. She rejected content distribution to the DLCs; used part-time college students to run the system; sought to eliminate my contact with clients through a variety of tactics; and used an incident with Vroom to manufacture a record of insubordination.

It was a grim picture. Wheeler suggested it was time to fold my cards on WBI Presents. If Johnson still managed B-SPAN this would have moved forward. I had not raised it because I had been too busy running in place to complete Weber-Fahr's process-related objectives. But on this angle of the terrain, Johnson appeared to have been right to encourage action, and I had miscalculated by having hesitated.

"It would take the impetus from her," Wheeler thought. "If she rejects WBI Presents and moves to violate the mandate, you can seek restitution with Leautier. Weber-Fahr does not have the right to unilaterally change B-SPAN's principles. That is the vice president's decision. The strategy will corner Weber-Fahr."

"There is a price to be paid in the aftermath of such a maneuver," I noted. "Nothing is more important to Weber-Fahr than her unyielding ambition to control anything she touches. I am coming to the end of my contract, and will pay dearly for denying her goal to merge product lines." Wheeler acknowledged the dilemma.

I wanted to re-examine ways to move B-SPAN outside WBI. "Maybe, after all, a better residence would be EXT," I suggested. It was a tacit admission that I had failed to institutionalize the transparency model in WBI. I also understood the enormity of the suggestion, but

I was holding bad cards. I was trying to play my way into the next game.

Wheeler frowned. His thinking on the subject had undergone a revision. "I have no faith in EXT. It is too politicized an environment." Then, he came up with a fascinating suggestion. "It occurred to me in the context of your analysis of the cost recovery struggle. Why not seek out GSD to see if they have interest in assuming B-SPAN?"

A light bulb went on in my head. "B-SPAN is GSD's biggest client," he continued. "They would lose a huge amount of revenue if B-SPAN folded." Like two threads entwined, I fleshed his idea out. "GSD is a service-oriented department," I noted. "In terms of the politics, they are light years away from either WBI or EXT. They simply provide services, regardless of who the client is or what they have to say. All that is necessary is a workable pricing mechanism."

It was still a difficult question. To keep fees modest to entice clients, a GSD model would need significant volume. In a remarkably clairvoyant moment, Wheeler estimated 600 events annually. We agreed any contact with GSD would have to be kept absolutely secret. I said I would move on it immediately.[268]

A symbolic illustration of how dysfunctional our situation had become would envelop me the same day.[269] A communication official from the Latin America region sent me a cryptic email. He said an important change was needed on the website, but didn't elaborate further. I called him.

"B-SPAN's logo is on all your website pages," he began. "Everyone pictured in the logo is anonymous except for one person. Your banner has Elaine Karp de Toledo, an Argentine politician who has recently been accused of misusing Bank funds." I blinked. "What?" "Could you redesign your logo?" he asked.

Somewhere in my head I could hear an explosion. If this leaked, the calamities it would create were boundless. Changing a logo, however, does not usually go unnoticed. I said I would call back, and found myself sitting moments later in Montenegro's office. Our relationship had evolved remarkably since we first met during Tolstopiatenko's tenure. He had come to recognize the adverse conditions under which B-SPAN operated. Now, it had gone from bad to worse.

I explained the logo situation. He said he would help. Montenegro found an alternative photo which he quietly inserted into the banner. I called my Latin American colleague to inform him of the change. I also told him I needed to orchestrate some subterfuge via email, since his original request had come that way. Sheram carefully scrutinized every correspondence sent to B-SPAN's account. She would want to know what was going on unless convinced it was innocuous. My counterpart was stupefied B-SPAN operated under such conditions. He immediately wrote he wanted to change a photo on the event summary page of a seminar he helped organize.[270] Our misdirection was sewn up neatly.

Nothing was simple or straightforward in the current atmosphere. Each new development required careful evaluation. When the sponsor of another event called to request I remove a comment she did not like, I did not overtly refuse. Editing was now the official policy of GDLN.[271] Instead, I reminded her of B-SPAN's transparency principle, and suggested she reconsider. The sponsor called back to decline putting the event on B-SPAN, and I sighed with relief. When RFF called to say they had a second event for B-SPAN, I demurred for weeks and eventually declined.[272] It was simple to have Montenegro post it online, but with the production log in place and meticulously scrutinized, the risk of having an external event spotted was too great.[273] B-SPAN was moving backwards. A newsletter had not been sent since July. Though there was finally enough material, even this routine act needed scrutiny. The newsletter was the cornerstone to driving traffic, and B-SPAN's numbers were dimming. I rationalized it was part of my results agreement and went forward.[274]

One day, I had lunch with a friend outside the Bank. He offered an interesting suggestion. "You should interview Wolfensohn," he said. "The idea works on several levels. It is good for B-SPAN, and it will make it hard for Weber-Fahr to push you out. It will scare her." I agreed my sudden departure on the heels of such an interview would raise questions about her. "What autocrats hate most is sunlight shone on their manipulations to collect power," I responded. A few weeks later, EXT interviewed the president on the Intranet.[275] The kernel planted in my mind began to grow.

I asked Stewart if it was possible Weber-Fahr could be placated. He suggested I embrace the merger with the MM Unit enthusiastically.[276] I was skeptical that would be a solution, but decided to test its resonance. I reached out to Fraeters again about what the merger might mean to B-SPAN.[277] He thought Sheram would move on to other activities. I did some quick math. Once the merger was formalized by the end of the year, either Fraeters or Stewart would become B-SPAN's new supervisor, and I might be rid of an albatross. That, however, made one enormous assumption: That I survived.

With survival squarely on the agenda, I began implementing Wheeler's suggestions. First, I had a WBI graphic designer draft a box on the B-SPAN home page for WBI Presents.[278] The mock-up divided materials into "edited videos" and "classroom for learning materials." All that was needed was the correct moment to unveil it. Whether that might be when Weber-Fahr moved on merging product lines or earlier had to be assessed on a daily basis. I also stopped by to see Leonard and Cardak in GSD.

"I have something important to discuss with you," I confided, but wouldn't reveal its nature. We set a date to meet.[279]

B-SPAN still enjoyed a few successes. Hunaidi's lecture made the Bank's home page.[280] The Bank's Week in Review newsletter covered the RFF Chilean water event, not an insignificant development by my calculations.[281] But the endless laboring on extraneous tasks and the punitive atmosphere within GDLN began to erode my smooth coordination with EXT. The Bank home page was routinely changing, but B-SPAN was no longer able to synchronize its partnership.

Hafed Al-Ghwell of the Bank's InfoShop had gathered enough data on Weber-Fahr's cost recovery policy to make an assessment. He had come to rely on us as a cornerstone in his dissemination strategy, and he was one of our few customers left. He told me the new charge had caused him serious damage. He was passing B-SPAN's costs to his clients, who in turn were refusing service. A second front had been opened for me. He sent me a note strongly condemning the new policy.[282] His note, however, was not copied to Weber-Fahr. I knew she would bury the plea, once it was forwarded, with her choreographed response.

More importantly, I wanted to know where Leautier stood on the issue. I ran some scenarios around with Wheeler. To force the vice president to take a public position, I sent Al-Ghwell the canned response Weber-Fahr had written for Sami.[283] Covered on this flank, I caucused with Al-Ghwell again, and asked him to use my letter to write a follow-up response to Leautier with a copy to Weber-Fahr. If the vice president wavered, Weber-Fahr would be boxed in. If she did not, we were no farther behind than before, but with better intelligence. Where Leautier rested on the issue would be the bellwether for B-SPAN's future, and mine.

Al-Ghwell noted in his correspondence to Leautier that B-SPAN's sudden price increase represented a surge of 215%.[284] "The policy is hurting everyone including B-SPAN," he said. The vice president responded quickly, and her note mirrored Weber-Fahr's initial response verbatim.[285] Leautier did offer one additional thought. Al-Ghwell should solicit funds from his vice president in EXT to subsidize his use of B-SPAN. The suggestion placed the onus on individual project managers to negotiate deals with their superiors. Building and nurturing partnerships did not appear to be an activity of interest to WBI.

The obvious similarity of Leautier's response to Weber-Fahr's note was the result of meticulous coordination. It was almost as if Weber-Fahr had used the vice president's proxy to respond. Weber-Fahr was immersed in palace politics. It was possible she orchestrated responses through other key officials and Leautier's involvement was tangential, but I considered the likelihood slim. Nor did it matter where the truth resided. Cost recovery was the official position of the vice president. I also did not doubt Weber-Fahr surmised I had encouraged Al-Ghwell. His note to the vice president was not copied to me, but Leautier's response was. Leautier's response also reiterated a phrase Weber-Fahr and Sheram were using with increasing frequency: She called B-SPAN a "mandate without funding." That didn't seem logical. B-SPAN was Leautier's mandate. It was a perilous sign. Wheeler and I now had our data. I was gambling against long odds, and I wasn't using the house's money.

An amazing rumor began to circulate the halls of GDLN. Ann Vroom was coming back.[286] Spencer was still going through a learning curve on encoding, and backlog was growing again. Weber-Fahr decided to rehire Vroom for a fourth time, to pick up the slack and produce a manual on encoding.[287] Everyone was stunned.

Weber-Fahr's move, however, paid immediate dividends. Her first day back, Vroom fired off a salvo of angry emails.[288] She complained about the cleanliness of the encoding room. When Sheram asked her to focus on the manual, she responded with a scathing rebuke.[289] I've been mistreated, she said, and GDLN's management of B-SPAN is a fiasco. Vroom remained incensed Spencer had been hired while she continued as a temporary. I sat back and enjoyed the fireworks. Within a few days, the manual was finished. Her purpose served, Vroom was fired.[290] Weber-Fahr sheepishly admitted to me, "The old warhorse has not worked out after all."

I continued to feel vulnerable. I knew Weber-Fahr would eventually make a case for removing me. One justification: I was a troublesome individual. The mediation attempt with Vroom would serve as a useful example. I decided to maneuver pro-actively.

I visited Johnson and explained my dilemma. "Would you write me a note to say you heard Vroom had left B-SPAN, and thought it was for the best?" I asked. "I don't have to," he said. "I wrote Sheram long ago to say I found Vroom abrasive and difficult and would no longer work with her." He forwarded it to me.[291] It was ammunition to build a defense. Waller had had similar exchanges. He forwarded his correspondence as well.[292]

Within the prism of my own ordeal, I viewed the final results with Vroom as potential neutralization of at least one threat by Weber-Fahr. She could no longer suggest, at least with validity, I was causing disruptions to staff morale. Vroom's fourth departure undermined the legitimacy of such a claim. Still, I knew Weber-Fahr would say or do anything to achieve her objectives.

With the hour glass dwindling, Weber-Fahr made her move at the end of September. She knocked on my door one afternoon and sat down. "Because of the excellent work you've done running B-SPAN, I've decided to convert your position into an ETC," she said.

Something in my brain misfired. I didn't understand. Had I been operating in such a vacuum that I had misunderstood her all this time? Had all these years of warfare with WBI bureaucrats scarred me so significantly I had become little more than a delusional paranoiac? I didn't know what to say. So I said thanks. She would follow up with a note later in the day to confirm our conversation.

The note, however, dispelled the self-doubts I had suddenly roused, and revealed the true nature of her intentions.[293] My stellar performance had indeed made my position permanent, but it was the *position* she was making permanent. She was circulating an announcement to EXT, Human Resources, and throughout all available Bank channels soliciting anyone interested in becoming the new B-SPAN coordinator. The hiring process would be made "transparent" as all candidates would be reviewed by a panel. The note added she would be "very happy" if I would consider applying for the position as well. If I was interested (in seeking the position I created to administer the system I built), I was welcome to forward my resume to Sheram, who was already collecting them from qualified candidates.

Weber-Fahr, for the second time, had mocked the concept of transparency. She embraced the notion of having a transparent production process so she could identify missteps and assign blame. Now, she said it was necessary to have a transparent hiring process; everyone was encouraged to apply and would be vetted by a hiring panel of subordinates she selected. But even here, she provided an interesting twist. She was moving surreptitiously to reposition B-SPAN: The parameters of the position would be redefined by adding new requirements.[294] (1) The next B-SPAN coordinator should have a background in education. (2) The new hire should have an assortment of technology skills. Stacking the deck with the panel of which she was the final arbitrator would not be enough. She needed loopholes to provide any justification to terminate me. It would be the only way to move me out.

Though not a surprising move, nevertheless it was sobering. Weber-Fahr was using a time-honored tactic within the Bank: Redefine position responsibilities to erase wayward minions.

It must have also been a frustrating period for her as well. Early on, I had adopted a Buddha-like mantra, methodically submerging myself in the folds of her aggression to control B-SPAN. Neither the results agreement debate, invention of the production log, Sheram's micromanaging, Vroom's repeated hiring and the mediation debacle, the cost recovery fiasco, or numerous personal slights precipitated a reaction on my part. Sheram's daily meetings, designed to keep me closely in check by highlighting aberrations in performance, had dissolved so significantly that Sheram even sent me a note complimenting me on my comprehensive maintenance of her log.[295]

Sun Tzu had called my position "surrounded ground," and I had sought to disappear. The ETC conversion represented Weber-Fahr's most desperate maneuver. It suggested all previous efforts to orchestrate my ouster had failed. Ironically, it also represented her best opportunity. I had now entered "killing ground," and Master Sun said on this terrain I must fight.

It would be important to approach this challenge rationally, cold-bloodedly. I began to solicit information from people who might be familiar with the ETC process. It was a new category, and there seemed little consensus on its implementation. Some said converting an STC to an ETC could be done immediately. Others thought it mandated a formal interview and vetting process. I could seek out Leautier, but concluded while Weber-Fahr's behavior was morally indefensible, the vice president would logically think she had a bureaucratic "right" to make personnel decisions. If I sought to subvert that "right" by going to Leautier, I would be vulnerable to claims by Weber-Fahr of insubordination.

Incredible as it seemed, I concluded I would have to take my chances through a formal process in the slim hope it would be honest.[296] Still, it would be important to have a trump card. If I could not reach out to the vice president before the process, perhaps I could do it afterwards. If Weber-Fahr ruled against me, a near certainty by my calculation, I wanted Wheeler, de Nevers, and Johnson to appeal to Leautier directly. Until then, I would have to wait.

Wheeler's take was characteristically more optimistic. He noted Weber-Fahr's own email encouraged me to apply. "That will make it difficult for her to suggest to Leautier she can't work with you," he offered. "By all rational standards, Weber-Fahr has to offer you the position."

I pointed out, "Reason isn't the barometer. Power is. Functionally, Weber-Fahr cannot assimilate a situation she cannot dominate. If I were to remain, I would remain in the way. She will have trouble sleeping unless she can find a way to strangle B-SPAN in her grip. She has already done everything she can think of to strip the flower of its petals. And, even now, some aspects of B-SPAN remain beyond her control. Nevertheless, she will keep B-SPAN on as short a leash as she can. She has designated the ETC position as a developmental assignment lasting one year. It will give her the time to fold it, dump it on another branch of the institution, or as a last resort hold it meekly under her thumb. Weber-Fahr has set a deadline of mid-October to receive resumes. She is pressing for a quick conclusion."

Wheeler began to speculate: "Perhaps she already has someone in mind. Maybe the vice president is pushing her to get this over."

Clients continued to cancel at an alarming rate, but Weber-Fahr remained firm.[297] When clients offered to use their resources to market B-SPAN to help it grow in return for a discount, she declined. "There will be no exceptions on cost recovery," she stated, and no amount of fallout could dissuade her.[298]

The posture produced a noticeable contradiction. If a client complained an event took too long to put online or suffered from quality control, her dismay bordered on hysteria. Yet if the same client pleaded that B-SPAN's cost recovery was destroying their ability to communicate with stakeholders, she was indifferent. Reaction to the new pricing policy, however, was beginning to create a groundswell. Some, who based their dissemination strategy on B-SPAN's help, or had launched it because of our creation, were telling me they felt blackmailed. I began to wonder if their resentment would be enough, or come in time, to make a difference.

Something of substance finally arose between Sheram and me.[299] A client expressed interest in having us cover their conference. Under Tolstopiatenko and Johnson, the charge for a day of service had been $1,000. Under the new fee structure, Sheram said the charge should rise to $1,400. If my revenue generation proposal had gone forward, I would have been supportive. Cost recovery, however, provided only sticks and no carrots. This additional spike would hurt people. I tried to salvage something.

"Perhaps, we should consider a discount for clients who make bulk purchases," I suggested. Sheram asked if there was a reason to justify a discount. "Well, we don't summarize conferences," I offered. "This translates into a huge savings in time." Sheram nodded her head. She said she had additional reasons. "You won't have to put up notices outside the event doorway four times or check the camera team four times or attend four different rooms either," she cheerfully suggested. I listened without expression. Was it possible people could think this way? Immediately, thereafter, Weber-Fahr rendered her verdict.[300] The charge rose to $1,400.

Further signs of deterioration ensued. A notice appeared unannounced on B-SPAN's home page about an upcoming release identified only as a WBI training event.[301] Its scheduled dissemination would take place shortly after a new B-SPAN coordinator was selected.

In the spring, Johnson convinced a colleague to help purchase a substitute encoding system in lieu of the Niagra Max catastrophe. Now, Bryan Waller informed me Weber-Fahr had told him to mothball everything.[302] In June, Johnson's last month managing the system, B-SPAN remained on pace for record traffic growth. In July, Weber-Fahr's initial month in control, the system experienced a rapid reduction in page views.[303] The trend continued through August and September.[304] With the time spent marking check-in boxes, fighting fires and battling for the survival of the transparency model, no time was left to produce content or build an audience. B-SPAN had entered its first period of decline.

I continued gathering information on the ETC process. Bruno Donat, the GDLN communication officer, had gone through a similar ETC conversion with Weber-Fahr.[305] He had been shaken by a process that he said felt like an interrogation. "Behind the curtain," he noted, "Weber-Fahr orchestrated each twist and turn." He looked at me the way a soldier looks at a dying companion while thinking how grateful he is to have been spared.

Another colleague said his ETC conversion was nothing more than his supervisor clearing the name through the HR Department. This confirmed there was no requirement to convene a panel. Supervisors had full discretion to choose a process they wanted. Then, Sheram absent-mindedly revealed Weber-Fahr was advertising the position widely outside the Bank to have as many choices as possible.[306]

Since restitution with the vice president was not possible before meeting the panel, I began building a strategy. First, I channeled my energy into a resume. I wanted to create a case so powerful the panelists would be compelled to wonder about Weber-Fahr's motives. What emerged was a document that said more about staff and stakeholder desire for a transparent communication medium than it did about any personal accomplishment.[307] In five years of running a forum of unedited webcasts, B-SPAN produced 700 events that reached audiences in more than 150 countries.[308] During each of the last two years, B-SPAN's traffic tripled.[309] By FY'04, B-SPAN was the Bank's prime provider of video content. It also became one of its most trafficked websites. It generated more than three million page requests, one-half million more than WBI's second most visited website.[310] It entertained and informed more than 200,000 visitors. Its newsletter had 18,000 subscribers, the second-most in the Bank.[311] For a 'pilot project' that received ample accolades from its vice president but little access to her purse strings, the success was astounding. The resume shamed WBI. It would embarrass Weber-Fahr's inquisitors.

Next, I reviewed archives from *World Bank Today* to identify articles where B-SPAN had produced a related webcast that had not been linked. It would enrich their archives and bolster my case that B-SPAN had closely integrated itself with a key Bank communication outlet. Counterparts there were pleased.[312] The *World Bank Today* might mention a unit once in a great while (or not at all), yet B-SPAN had linked with them more than 30 times since the summer of 2002. Implementation of this additional research would raise it above 50.

Then, I moved to shore up support from key stakeholders.[313] Johnson and de Nevers agreed to be my references. That gave me three former B-SPAN supervisors. Interestingly, de Nevers asked what job I was applying for. When told, she said she was pleased WBI had decided to keep B-SPAN. This revelation was a blow. Within the boundaries of Weber-Fahr's tightly controlled fiefdom, de Nevers' claim as a key stakeholder had dissolved. I realized, in a close battle, a powerful ally had been lost.

The bolts of my infrastructure had loosened and frayed. Those empowered to protect B-SPAN were no longer interested or positioned to confront the bureaucracy's counter-insurgency to the transparency model. Institutionally, I was alone. Instinctively, I understood this had been the case for quite some time, but now I felt the burden acutely.

Into this desperate moment a kernel of hope arrived. It came in the form of a billboard posted in the hallway. The poster said famed economist Hernando de Soto would speak at the Bank.[314] The Bank's Archive Department, housed within ISG, was implementing a new public information disclosure policy. They had invited de Soto to speak at the official launch in late October. I glanced at the poster and stopped. I looked again and a dream began. The scheme I envisioned I knew would be a last stand. What was not yet known was whether it would unfold like Chamberlain at Gettysburg or Gordon at Khartoum. B-SPAN's future hinged upon its success. If the plan failed, then all else would fail, and I would disappear like the seasons.

8

While the de Soto plan developed in my mind, I moved on a second critical front. The Bank had recently convened an Organizational Effectiveness Task Force (OETF) to examine ways to restructure the institution to serve clients more strategically. Rumors swirled about a potential breakup of WBI. Discussions about GDLN's decentralization were at the leading edge of potential changes. I wanted to use these developments to my advantage. I sat down with Leonard and Cardak to unveil the idea that they might consider assuming command of B-SPAN.

"B-SPAN is GSD's most important client," I noted. "If it folds, the impact on GSD will be enormous." Both listened in stunned silence. Finally, Cardak spoke. "Those old B-SPAN clients will continue to use GSD," he suggested.

I disagreed. "We provide them a powerful way of disseminating their content," I said. "Without us, their content will be substantially less valuable." Leonard agreed. He was intrigued.[315]

I moved to immediately institutionalize the model in their minds. "B-SPAN's success," I continued, "derives from its transparency. WBI does not fully support transparency."

Leonard acknowledged, "WBI instinctively embraces a propaganda model. There are other parts of the Bank involved in video services. EXT films documentaries and related media projects. ISG has recently launched video editing services under the direction of Michael Kingsberry. I think the time has come to consolidate these disparate video activities in the Bank."

I was hearing something positive and wanted to encourage him. "If B-SPAN moves to GSD, then you will be uniquely positioned to move on consolidation," I said.

Leonard asked for traffic data to document B-SPAN's reach. I asked them to deliberate on my proposal without further discussion with their management. It would give all of us time to reflect and think through some of the intricacies of the idea. For the moment,

I was silent about the ETC panel process. When Weber-Fahr cut me loose, perhaps I could reposition myself with GSD. With their cameras as infrastructure, I could build a new system, and drive WBI out of the webcasting business entirely.

In mid-October, Weber-Fahr called a meeting.[316] The deadline for submitting resumes had almost arrived. I was still fine-tuning mine. Weber-Fahr said she assumed I would apply and would use an old resume on file. It occurred to me it would pose an enormous embarrassment for her if I opted out of the process. Of course, the outcome would be worse for me.

"I am planning to offer you the ETC position, but for transparency reasons need to look at other resumes," she stated. Obviously, she had mistaken me for the village idiot. "The process will conclude in mid-November," she added. She also announced Sundeep Kalidindi, a young IT professional, had been hired to assume Vroom's encoding duties.[317]

Wheeler thought Weber-Fahr could be held legally accountable for her comment about offering me the job.[318] I brushed off the suggestion. "If someone in WBI tells me the sun is shining, you can damn well be sure I will go to the window to check first," I replied. "She will deny the comment outright."

He prodded me to raise WBI Presents proactively, but my thinking had evolved. "It may prove inevitable, but it will be a mistake for me to raise it while the ETC process is underway," I said. "One of the ways Weber-Fahr wants to change the model is to merge product lines. If I float WBI Presents now, and she feels it doesn't go far enough, she will hold it over my head like a club while arbitrating my fate." He cocked his head and concluded I was right.

My de Soto plan suffered a stumble at the start. I needed sponsor acquiescence to have B-SPAN cover his speech. I called Elisa Liberatori Prati, the Bank's chief archivist and host of the event. "Will you want B-SPAN's services?" I asked. She wasn't sure. "It may be a little controversial," she said, "and the department might not want to allow coverage to go externally." I was startled. Failure was not an option.

"Hernando de Soto is a very famous figure," I replied. "You must be very happy to have him at your event." Prati said she was. Her department had been trying for a very long time to get him to attend. "Well, it would seem an odd thing that one of the world's most important economists is coming to the Bank to talk about public information disclosure, and his discussion is withheld from the public," I noted. "Someone might get criticized for that." Prati paused. "Could I get back to you?"

The next week, two officials from the Archivist's office called me.[319] What was B-SPAN? they asked. I dropped by their office to give them my routine overview. I still sensed hesitation. I called up the website on their computer. I flipped through our archives to de Soto's 2002 presentation on *The Mystery of Capital.* They were impressed.

"The event, however, is controversial," one of them said. "It marks the launch of a new Public Information Disclosure policy for the Bank's archives. Some information being made public was once proprietary. Some governments who made it available to the Bank on the understanding it would not become public are uncomfortable with the new policy."

I nodded. "That's understandable, but if de Soto comes to the Bank to talk about transparency and public information disclosure and his speech is not covered by B-SPAN, then you are going to have a big problem, and it won't come from me." They looked at each other. "Okay, we're in."[320] I had the event. Now, I needed de Soto.

Some months before, I had met Hernando de Soto while he was visiting the IMF. I told him B-SPAN had already covered him once. He seemed fascinated. He gave me his card. I pulled it out and began to compose a note.[321]

"As far as we know," I began, "B-SPAN is the only entity among development, government, academic or private sector institutions that provides a completely transparent and unedited window on internal policy discussions. In this sense, B-SPAN is unique in all the world. Not everyone supports transparency, but B-SPAN believes the Bank as an institution is healthier and stronger when we are increasingly open and accountable to our stakeholders. In this spirit, B-SPAN has webcast numerous events where people have been critical of the Bank, as well as supportive and none of these video discussions have been altered in any way."

I cited the Stiglitz-Rogoff debate and Sachs's critique of the Bank as examples. Then, sensing the fate of the transparency model after five years in stormy seas was hanging in the balance, I made my pitch. "We would be very grateful if you might consider mentioning that B-SPAN is webcasting your speech … and that B-SPAN's transparency model of unedited webcasts is exactly the type of activity the Bank should be embracing."

De Soto was a long shot, but I was running out of ammunition, and long shots were increasingly all that was left to me. Implicit in my reaching out to him was a candid acknowledgement that new informal stakeholders were needed to protect B-SPAN. I could not do so much longer myself. Nor was anyone inside the institution empowered or willing to help. I needed an external stakeholder powerful enough to frighten Weber-Fahr. It was a desperate and implausible scheme, but it might provide me the flanking maneuver I needed. I sent the note immediately. In life, one can do much, but some things are not within one's power to control. Now, I would wait.

I got a quick response.[322] Peter Schaeffer, de Soto's representative in Washington, called. "It is a very interesting request," he said. "I will try to get de Soto to mention B-SPAN in his speech." My ears pricked up. "Would it be all right if we got C-SPAN to cover the event as well?" he added. "I think it would be fine," I said. We agreed to talk again closer to the event, and he hung up. The hairs on the back of my neck were quivering.[323]

I caught another break later in the day. Sheram announced she would be taking her third vacation since August—the same week de Soto was speaking.[324] I needed to move with anonymity. By a quirk of fate, she was giving it to me.

The erosion of B-SPAN's client base finally backfired on WBI. The InfoShop featured an event on indigenous knowledge with Leautier as the featured speaker.[325] The Africa Region, sponsors of the event, however, declined B-SPAN's service because of the fee.

Leautier now was negatively impacted by the very policy she had allowed Weber-Fahr to enact. In a moment of theatrical folly, the vice president announced those who could not attend the event would be able to watch later on B-SPAN.

I moved to exploit the blunder by returning to Al-Ghwell. "Have the Africa Region write Leautier to apologize for not webcasting because of B-SPAN's punitive pricing policy," I suggested. It would convey the message without overtly implicating him. Instead, he sought her out directly. She shrugged off the mishap, but did offer a concession. For InfoShop events at which she would be the featured speaker, she would underwrite the cost.[326]

It was a win for Al Ghwell, but a hollow victory for me. The InfoShop was still using us on occasion, but the rest of B-SPAN's customers had largely disappeared. Since the fee's implementation less than a month earlier, 17 event organizers had declined our services. Incredibly, we had only covered 18 events since Weber-Fahr's administration began four months earlier. B-SPAN had hemorrhaged badly. Weber-Fahr's pricing model, designed ostensibly to generate revenue, was in fact reducing it. I suggested to Wheeler the outcome of reducing revenues had been deliberate, in part to minimize the scorecard numbers WBI's senior management received each month. Though I had selectively encouraged other clients to make a case to Leautier, I concluded the strategy now was no longer useful. Complaints would not dissuade the vice president, but might endanger me at a precarious time.

There was a glaring weakness for me regarding the ETC process. I had no background in education or training activities. I moved to shore up this vulnerability by caucusing with learning specialists within WBI.[327] Don Macdonald and Debra Beattie were knowledgeable and sympathetic about the hurdles I faced. They had experienced their own difficulties with Weber-Fahr and Sheram, and agreed to brainstorm an agenda with me that I could present to the panel. One evening, over beers, we vetted ideas.

My old colleague David Gray, GDLN's regional coordinator for Latin America, dropped in. He had been with Weber-Fahr at a retreat. He was also hearing rumors WBI might be disassembled. "WBI is going to suffer heavily at the hands of the reorganization," he suggested. "Since her budget is going to be cleaved, Leautier is looking for fat."

What Gray was hearing about GDLN, I found especially interesting. Until recently, Weber-Fahr had tried to micromanage the activities of regional coordinators like him. Those coordinators, however, had their own budgets and agendas, and answered only to their regional vice presidents. In their eyes, she was not their supervisor, and didn't control them the way she did GDLN's central anchor. Together with Leautier, she met Managing Director Shengman Zhang and other senior officials to say GDLN had achieved all its major objectives. Therefore, the regions should assume more responsibility for outcomes, and GDLN staff should be decentralized. She was advocating the breakup of GDLN with a small team retained within the anchor for administrative reasons. Gray thought she was looking to get out herself.

I asked him what he thought it meant for B-SPAN. "A consensus seems to be forming in WBI that technology services should be housed in ISG," he said.

Something unexplainable was happening. Weber-Fahr had advocated jettisoning millions of dollars in staff and programs while charging B-SPAN's clients heavily. Gray had no answer. He said, "For B-SPAN to survive, it will have to accept edited content."

Rumors were also rampant Leautier might be leaving the Bank as well. If she left and Weber-Fahr remained, it might spell more than the end of the voyage for me. Organizational realignment and budget contractions had placed B-SPAN in the crosshairs of a gun aimed by WBI officials.[328]

The Archivist's office called back to say they were having second thoughts about streaming de Soto. It was normal hand wringing that would soon pass, but an interesting scenario arose in my mind: De Soto promotes transparency and B-SPAN; the Bank censors B-SPAN but C-SPAN covers. "This could get very cool very fast," I wrote Wheeler.[329] "Love to watch them bureaucrats lose weight going backwards on the treadmill."

The question was no longer what Archive officials would do, but what de Soto would. I had tried without success to reach Schaeffer in the days before the speech. Then, I ran out of time.

Hernando de Soto, a burly man whose beard supported the great crown of his head, rose to greet his audience.[330] Several hundred elite economists, academics, and international policymakers had assembled to hear him. They accorded him the honor because de Soto was no ordinary economist. Like his namesake, a Spanish explorer and conquistador who marauded through 16th century Florida and neighboring territories in search of wealth, the modern-day de Soto had embarked on his own unique voyage of discovery.

While still a young man, de Soto left a successful business career in Europe to solve a riddle that troubled him: What conditions made it possible for some societies to accrue wealth while others remained mired in poverty? He returned to his childhood home of Peru in 1979 to find the answer. Peru was a laboratory ripe for economic analysis. Its population consisted almost entirely of Indians—descended from the land's ancient Incan origins or mestizos—people who were a mixture of Native American and European ancestry. The remaining peoples were of purely European roots dating from the time of the Spanish conquistadors. Demarcation of wealth and power was clearly delineated along blood lines. The Spanish-speaking Europeans were entrenched atop the social structure of the society, while the mass of Indians were under-employed and impoverished.

The military juntas, dictatorships, and feckless constitutionally-elected governments that infested Peru for generations had resulted in an economy tottering from ineptitude and corruption. By the 1960s, things began faltering badly as successive governments vacillated between increasing trade and protecting key industrial sectors. Conditions were soon exacerbated by hyper-inflation and a debt crisis affecting much of Latin America. The decline of Peru's economy led to a rise of informal, black-market activities where the entrepreneurial instincts of the poor could thrive and survive.

A century earlier, most Peruvians lived in the valleys that capture the great Andes. But, fed by grinding poverty and an absence of basic services enjoyed in the cities, a significant migration began. By the time de Soto returned to the Americas, the country's demographics had reversed. The majority now lived in urban areas along the coast. Lima, the capitol, bulged with eight million inhabitants. Yet most people remained extremely poor, and something else was afoot. The economic turbulence and rigid strata of its social culture had given rise to growing violence in the countryside. In 1980, a new movement blossomed in Peru: The Sendero Luminoso, also known as the Shining Path.

The Shining Path was a Maoist guerilla movement that enveloped Peru in turmoil. Its agenda was to replace the bourgeois government with a peasant-led communist regime. Along the way, according to the government, Shining Path was accountable for the deaths and disappearances of tens of thousands. Still, it enjoyed some support from the rural peasantry that belied logic. In part, this was derived from the guerillas' execution of wealthy merchants and landowners who were seen by rural villagers as exploiting the poor. It was supplemented by the government's initial indifference to the movement, which was interpreted by this population as apathy towards them as well. Moreover, when government retribution finally came, the massacres its military inflicted were also heinous.

De Soto, however, believed this did not reveal everything. Why would a political movement that used violence enjoy support? "I began to conduct surveys," he told his audience at the Bank. "I learned Peruvians wanted a clear sense of property ownership, and they wanted to improve their entrepreneurial opportunities. From my research, I learned the Shining Path had come to a similar conclusion. They were extending informal, non-legalized property rights in rural settings, just as Mao and Ho Chi Minh and Napoleon had done before them. In the cities, the Shining Path was helping micro-entrepreneurial activities."

But something was missing, and de Soto was not sure what. The recording of assets and land titling was not new in Peru. The Spaniards had recorded property of indigenous Indians hundreds of years earlier. To piece together the riddle, de Soto turned to the Bank for information.

"The Bank has more knowledge about failure than any other source of development information," he said to some laughter. "Knowledge must also include the knowledge of failure. The success of market economies is the knowledge of failure. I thought the Bank could provide the right sort of information to understand what was not working in Peru. I believed the Bank's archives contained the roots of success."

What he had not anticipated, he said, was that when he contacted project managers at the Bank, they were reluctant to talk to him. When he tried to access the Bank's archives for information and project reports, he was denied. De Soto believed the Bank had information that could help him understand the mystery of the Peruvian experience, but the institution had refused to share it with him. The monolithic culture that had permeated the Bank since its inception was both secretive and impenetrable. Since it was unaccountable to stakeholders like de Soto, its lack of transparency had sealed off information that could help Peru break free from an endless cycle of violence and corruption.

Initially, de Soto said, he was at a standstill, but he endured. He began contacting "friends" in governments that received Bank information. He reached out to former Bank staff and consultants to learn what they knew. He began to find out about numerous failures the Bank had experienced. The information produced invaluable knowledge about what worked in development and what did not. And, then his research began to focus on one particular project in Brazil. There, he learned that Brazilians wanted more than land titling that codified property rights. They wanted the rule of law. He subsequently learned land ownership must be tied to credit. Small business owners often get loans from lenders using their property rights as credit. Much employment in the developing world is generated by small businesses, and nowhere was that better represented than by the entrepreneurial culture of Peruvians.

De Soto's advocacy for the establishment of formal property

rights as a way to increase wealth and improve life for the impoverished was not well received by the Shining Path. It contradicted their Maoist underpinnings. They targeted him for assassination. They bombed the Institute for Liberty and Democracy, an economic think tank he had founded. But as his writings were assimilated into the consciousness of Peruvian society, things started to change. Support for the Shining Path began to weaken. Then it dissolved.

Providing property rights, land titling, the rule of law, and access to credit are the staples of a stable society, he said. "There is no excuse for holding back information when you have a wealth of it," de Soto asserted. "Learning these lessons could not have been possible without access to the knowledge the Bank had created."

De Soto offered praise for the Bank for making more information accessible through its archives. But he also noted this: He had found much of the information only because he had gone "the extra mile." He urged the Bank to go further in its disclosure initiative by making the bulk of its archives accessible. "To understand the lessons that have been learned by the Bank in development and to identify opportunities for the future, the archives must be available," he stated. "It is not only a matter of human rights, free speech, and democracy. It was the way the Shining Path was defeated."

When he finished speaking, a generous applause began.

As Hernando de Soto had learned, access to Bank information was not just a way to enhance development and reduce poverty. Increasing the institution's transparency had been a path to peace.

He had encapsulated a fundamental truth about the Bank, its impact on the world, and people living in desperate circumstances. Nevertheless, the United Nations shortly thereafter issued a progress report on global development.[331] It stated frankly mankind was losing ground. More than one billion lived in abject poverty. Most had dirty drinking water. 800 million did not have enough to eat each day. From 1994 to 2003, one hundred and eleven million children died because they lacked such fundamentals as inexpensive vaccines and bed nets. De Soto understood how important transparency within the Bank was to mitigating these conditions and bringing peace to troubled places; but he was still not aware of the full story. As the applause rose, my heart sank. He had made no mention of B-SPAN. I moved to implement the rest of my scheme.

Perhaps it was too much to hope that de Soto would come to the rescue. After all, he did not owe B-SPAN anything. Why should he have exposed himself to criticism by entering a fight of which he had no knowledge? Could he know the struggle over B-SPAN encapsulated the fundamental theme of his speech? It had focused on internal matters, but the answer from B-SPAN's perspective was, perhaps not. The next day, the event was loaded on to the website with a headline that read "Bank Transparency Can Lead to Peace Said Hernando de Soto".[332] I had the file linked to the Bank's external and internal home pages, a *World Bank Today*'s news story, as well as Wolfensohn's personal website page.[333]

Finally, I composed a newsletter. I knew in all likelihood it would be my last one. I wanted to make a statement, one final appeal to the Bank on the need for it to truly embrace transparency, not just release a few documents and say all was well.

I understood the message would fall on deaf ears at WBI, but perhaps I could reach the soul of the institution. I believed there were two World Banks. One embraced propaganda and one embraced transparency, and they were moving in opposite directions. One rejected its own fallibility, promoted its superiority, and sheltered itself within the confines of its authority. The other recognized the Bank's mistakes and limitations, and sought to be guided by the community of man. By a quirk of history, I had become the fault line between both worlds. I sat in the silence of my office, and began to write.[334]

"'Become the change you wish to seek.' "Mahatma Gandhi expressed that sentiment during India's great struggle to free itself from the harness of imperialism. Imperialism collapsed. The mantra lives on. Change is the defining constant in our world today. Globalization, war, the environment are just some examples of a world struggling to adapt to continually evolving forces. Arun Gandhi came to the Bank recently to share lessons his grandfather taught him a half century ago. Then, as now, the world was undergoing remarkable changes.

Nazism had fallen. Communists were solidifying control of Eastern Europe and China. British colonialism in South Asia was disintegrating and the region was stumbling into chaos. And through all this turmoil, Mahatma Gandhi was looking within to find answers on the meaning of leadership. Arun Gandhi said his grandfather taught him small, everyday acts can be significant. There are parallels today. In the aftermath of September 11th, Gandhi said many societies in the new millennium breed a culture of selfishness and violence. In such a world, the elimination of poverty will remain out of reach. To achieve the change we wish to seek, charity is not the answer, Gandhi said. Empathy and compassion are.

"People must change. Societies must change. And organizations must change, too. Internationally renowned economist Hernando de Soto visited the Bank on October 25th to discuss how increasing transparency can lead to peace. De Soto was on hand for the Bank's implementation of a revised Disclosure of Information Policy to make its archives more accessible to the public. Recounting his own research of war-torn Peru in the 1980s, de Soto learned that the poor wanted to benefit from the rule of law. The rule of law allowed them to establish property rights, open lines of credit and create business opportunities. He learned much of this by examining information the Bank held in its own archives. But the Bank was not making this information readily available to the public in the 1980s. Only by a concerted effort to extract the Bank's information through informal sources was de Soto able to understand the underlying currents that empowered the Shining Path, the anti-government revolutionary force. Times changed and so did the Bank. The work by de Soto and other stakeholders, as well as internal initiatives launched by Bank President James Wolfensohn, have encouraged the institution to become more open. Knowledge about what succeeds in development comes from knowledge about what does not succeed, de Soto asserted. Increasing the Bank's transparency is more than a way to increase development, he said. As he learned, it is a path to peace.

"The legendary football coach Vince Lombardi said leaders are not born. Arun Gandhi and Hernando de Soto have made themselves leaders in a changing world. Sharing knowledge, sharing information, sharing understanding to reduce global poverty is B-SPAN's mandate. As always, B-SPAN is a transparent, unedited medium that offers everyone an opportunity to see policy seminars and presentations held regularly at the World Bank. Leading experts from around the world discuss a variety of sustainable development and poverty reduction issues, and anyone with access to the Internet may view these presentations at no cost. Videos on B-SPAN are permanently archived, and can be seen at any time from its website. B-SPAN is a virtual library of information on sustainable development and poverty reduction issues.

"We are pleased to make this service available to you."

I signed it:

David Shaman

B-SPAN's Producer

9

As soon as it was finished, I pushed the send button and waited to see if there was a reaction. I did not wait long. Recipients began applauding in waves.[335] All in WBI were silent. I called Schaeffer to get an assessment of how de Soto had reacted to my request. He said de Soto used the event to test a new theory. Nothing further was offered. I asked Schaeffer if de Soto could send Wolfensohn a note thanking him for B-SPAN's coverage. He agreed and used my newsletter as a pretext.[336]

Reality returned promptly. Weber-Fahr's secretary sent a note congratulating me for being one of four finalists for the B-SPAN coordinator position.[337] The email was copied to Sheram, Fraeters, Stewart and Tolstopiatenko. With the composition of the panel now known, the GDLN manager scheduled my interview for November 11, Armistice Day. Shortly thereafter, I learned Tolstopiatenko was going on a mission and would miss the panel.[338] But it was only a small break.

As word seeped out, colleagues stopped me in the hallways to express astonishment.[339] Some assumed the panel would simply come to an obvious conclusion. They suggested I needn't worry, but it was impossible for me to explain why I did. To those closest to me, I confided I had a lynch mob on my hands. In a macabre moment of jesting, I told a friend my job was to walk the plank each day; if successful, my reward was to be allowed to walk the plank the next day as well. For three long years, my opponents had the luxury of losing time after time after time. I had never had such a luxury. By losing once, all would be lost. I had become the loneliest man in the Bank.

The hourglass dissolved to November. Fallout from the de Soto event began. Sheram returned and read the newsletter. It was remarkable Weber-Fahr or Sheram had not moved forcefully to control the newsletter earlier. Yet, there appeared reasons. They would go through somersaults to rewrite one ordinary sentence into another equally mundane. Sheram would labor for days over a paragraph, and announce refinements no one else noticed.[340] They were so focused on process that substance seemed irrelevant.

Additionally, Weber-Fahr had reduced B-SPAN's business from tide to ebb, so there was little new content to build newsletters. For all these reasons it was logical for neither to engage me on language of complex synopses, assuming the subject and text were benign.

The de Soto newsletter was hardly that. It struck at the heart of what they advocated. The concept of a transparent broadcasting medium promoting a leading figure's plea for greater Bank transparency needed to be rectified. Sheram wasted no time in making secrecy and propaganda safe within the Bank again.[341]

"Please delete the words 'transparency,' 'unedited' and 'permanently archived' from future newsletters," she wrote. "Since these policies are undergoing change, we need to start reflecting this change in our language." Sheram's reaction to transparency—to open, honest and unfettered transmissions of information to a world full of poverty—was to censor it.

Her second directive codified her understanding and Weber-Fahr's of the meaning of transparency. "The whole team now has admin access to the B-SPAN Lotus Notes account, so all comments and questions should be available to all of us ... transparency : -) !," she said.

Transparency as a means to reveal truths, to help development and to reduce poverty was simply a game for her and Weber-Fahr. Power was all that mattered to them.

Sheram's response also signaled she had become marginalized. Unleashed, with the production log as armor to furl B-SPAN's sails and steer it into dead air, she had become muddled in her own obfuscation. I had adhered to a philosophy of receding until her actions lost momentum as if mired in quicksand; and it had worked. Sheram's daily diatribes evaporated to the point where all she could fault was an occasional misspelling in the log.[342] With nothing constructive to offer, she also had little to criticize. Even Spencer had noticed the disengagement. She suggested to me she thought Sheram was incompetent. The response to the de Soto newsletter spoke less to the issue of transparency and more to an individual's intolerance of others.

Mohamed Muhsin, vice president of ISG, had a different perspective.[343] Originally, Muhsin was to have hosted the event, but a leg injury prevented him from participating. He watched it from home. Afterwards, he sent Leautier a note to personally thank me for making the webcast possible. It was a stunning surprise. After several hours of silence, Weber-Fahr recognized the futility of not responding. She sent me a congratulatory email, her only response to the de Soto coup.[344]

Leautier responded to Muhsin.[345] Her congratulations for me were perfunctory, but her note added something else. She called transparency and public information disclosure "an important topic that many people in the Bank do not pay attention to."

Bank vice presidents exchanging complimentary notes about a part-time consultant bordered on something extraordinary. The timing seemed exquisite, for it vastly raised the stakes for Weber-Fahr. People might wonder how I was being lauded by vice presidents one day and fired the next. There appeared in Leautier's response a subtle undertone of support for me regarding the ETC issue. But it also left me wondering if she was aware of what was happening at all.

I debated the question with my allies. One suggested I send Leautier a note, thanking her for the timeliness of her support especially with the panel convening shortly. Others thought it would overplay my hand. Wheeler counseled that, should things fall apart without escalation on my part, quiet intervention by the vice president might still be possible. Still, he thought I was safe. "You've just received plaudits from two vice presidents," he said. "The de Soto affair was a home run." But I felt joyless. I had needed a grand slam. I thought over how to respond to the vice president. Organizational politics differ from pure politics. They require a degree of subtlety that campaigns can ignore. I sent Leautier a simple thank you note.[346]

I ran into Bruno Laporte one day.[347] He offered another example of just how steeped in cynicism WBI's bureaucrats were. He had seen the de Soto coverage, and lavished praise on how well B-SPAN performed. "I've sent a congratulatory note to Sunetra Puri (WBI's communications chief)," he said, though he knew she had never been involved in B-SPAN. For two years Laporte never lifted a finger to help the system. Now that he was no longer involved, he thought B-SPAN was great.

To keep fires burning on the front I had created with Leonard and GSD, I generated traffic data dating back to 2001.[348] They told the story of a remarkable run. I also learned something new. When EXT asked about the impact of live webcasts with Shirin Ebadi and Juan Somavia, the initial streams reached several thousand viewers.[349] Yet archives usage was greater in the months that followed. It led to a realization. We remained a powerful driver of content long after it had originally been made available. B-SPAN's customers received interest in their aging content. Even national news affiliates couldn't do that. B-SPAN was a marketer's dream.

Days dripped into the past. I entered a period of intense preparation for the inquisition. The business of B-SPAN stopped. Survival was now the only item on my agenda. I reviewed strategic documents from the past, crafted a learning strategy from my discussions with

Macdonald and Beattie, charted traffic information, gathered testimonials from Bank clients, organized documents to defend myself from potential attacks regarding Vroom, and cleared sensitive files from my computer and office.

I was under no illusions. In the days following the panel interview, Sheram or another Weber-Fahr lackey could enter my office with security guards to escort me out of the building. I wanted to be prepared for any eventuality.

November 11th, the day Weber-Fahr and I had spent months preparing for, arrived.[350] The panel consisted of Sheram, Fraeters, Stewart, and Kiron Bhandari, a human resources (HR) representative. Hiring managers were formally excluded from ETC panel interviews, so as not to *unduly* influence the participants or process. Weber-Fahr waited quietly in her office next door.

My tension dissolved as the session started. Stewart began by asking what B-SPAN meant to me. Fraeters wanted to know about my strategy for the future. Sheram queried me on what my agenda in the first few months would look like. Fraeters wanted to know if I thought I had the ability to lead a team. He and Sheram wanted to know if I had ever made a mistake in running B-SPAN. Bhandari wanted to know if I was comfortable with webcasting technologies. They wanted specifics, and questions were designed to elicit information as well as highlight weaknesses.

To each I offered a reasoned response. To Stewart, I noted, "B-SPAN was created to humanize the Bank before its critics, as well as provide stakeholders with information to empower them to improve their lives."

For Fraeters, I diagrammed a vision of B-SPAN similar to the one I had described to Leautier and Weber-Fahr months before, and to this added a range of learning activities I planned for B-SPAN. The learning agenda I offered for their consideration was comprehensive. "We will work with WBI's course designers to extract content from B-SPAN events for repackaging in their training materials," I suggested. "We will provide the Distance Learning Centers with free off-the-shelf content tailored to attract local stakeholders to their facilities. We will partner with Bank units to launch pilot projects using B-SPAN content for their moderated discussion forums. We will market our archived content to educational publishers in the private sector. We will create specialized product lines such as tailored CDs, or videos for internal or external clients."

What I left unspoken was that all these proposals would capitalize on the existing unaltered archives. With the original archives in place, none of the proposals compromised B-SPAN's transparency.

When asked about my concept of leadership, I said, "It is simple. I will show I care about the people I work with by being attentive to their concerns and receptive to their ideas for how to improve the service. Should I continue my responsibilities, the first months will be spent implementing the learning agenda I described, assimilating B-SPAN's ongoing merger with the Multi-Media Unit, and continuation of the current webcasting operation. B-SPAN would not have been able to film, encode, and archive 700 events if I had not been able to create and maintain a host of relationships."

This prompted a response from Fraeters. He pressed hard to know if I had ever had difficulties with others. "Over five years, it was inevitable occasional misunderstandings would occur," I acknowledged. "It is a highly pressurized environment and I am not infallible; but I've served literally thousands of Bank staff, and have been thanked hundreds of times." Fraeters averted his eyes and looked down. Then, he nodded. I added, "The fact WBI has seen fit to change my STC position into an ETC position is already testament to what I have accomplished."

The panel was finished. So was I. Outwardly I had displayed only humility and good humor. When I returned to my office, however, an overwhelming feeling of anger welled inside. This collection of people—who could never have accomplished what we had, who knew nothing of our sacrifices, or had the courage to believe in something bigger than themselves—had been empowered to sit in judgment of us. Nevertheless, I had acquitted myself well. I was feeling optimistic. Based primarily on the exchange between Muhsin and Leautier, I calculated my chances of survival at about 10%.

10

Weber-Fahr immediately scheduled a meeting with Leautier.[351] It was logical she would preemptively make her case about changing B-SPAN's personnel and seek acquiescence. However, I would not wait for an execution. Like a fighter pilot, I began moving across the terrain searching for targets and strafing vigorously. I learned Al-Ghwell was lunching with Leautier. Instinctively, I trusted him. I decided to confide about the ETC process and the guillotine Weber-Fahr had built. He said he would make it a point to praise me to Leautier and elicit what information he could.

The MM Unit held an open house to display their services to department colleagues.[352] Fraeters introduced me to two visitors. Kabir Ahmed was WBI's chief administrative officer. Ziad Aladad was the department's director of operations After Leautier; they were WBI's most powerful officials. Each arrived separately, but both uttered the same thing upon meeting me: "I've heard about you." The underlying tone seemed ominous.

Then, Kalidindi was moved off encoding to administer the MM Unit's production log.[353] B-SPAN was virtually incapacitated. This caused a quick backlash. The inactivity was killing Sheram. She went on vacation again.[354]

One day, near my office, I ran into Sona Panajyan, a content editor for the Development Gateway. The Gateway hosted an enormous database of web-based development content. Originally, it had been a Bank-funded project; but it spun off several years earlier, and was now only tangentially related to the institution. Panajyan and I had crossed paths a year before when I was searching for new outlets for B-SPAN's content. For several months, I fed video links to her, but the process had proven too cumbersome to faithfully continue. She asked to meet me to revisit the issue.[355] Although GSD offered a uniquely fertile environment for moving B-SPAN away from WBI, to preclude other possibilities was a high-risk strategy. Taking B-SPAN outside the Bank would present sizeable hurdles, but this was worth preliminary exploration.

We talked about the synergies of our two systems. After a while, Panajyan finally admitted that the difficulty in absorbing content for the Gateway hadn't changed. That was odd. I wondered why she had wanted to see me, then. Our conversation reached a natural conclusion. I hesitated, feeling her out. Finally, I decided to broach my idea.

"WBI has not been an ideal incubator for B-SPAN," I stated. "In fact, GDLN is woefully overstaffed and underfunded. A process has already begun within the Bank that may result in its significant downsizing. If a breakup scenario gains momentum, B-SPAN could be orphaned. Would the Gateway have interest in hosting the service?"

Panajyan's eyes rolled in amazement. "That is highly interesting," she said. "In the right hands, B-SPAN could generate significant revenues," I suggested. She said the Gateway's new director was emphasizing the need to generate revenues. She would bring the idea to his attention and get back to me shortly.[356] We parted. Everyone exudes enthusiasm, I noted to myself. How soon she followed up would be the barometer by which her rhetoric was measured.[357] Until then, I would look for new targets.

I returned to Leonard.[358] He remained interested in acquiring B-SPAN. Our traffic data reinforced his desire. "I want to move GSD to the forefront of the Bank's mission to reduce poverty, and B-SPAN is an ideal vehicle to help me." Then, Leonard paused. His gaze focused in a locked position. "But I am not naïve. Everyone in Washington has an agenda. What's yours?"

I kept to my previous line which recycled what was publicly known. "The OETF is planning to reorganize the Bank," I said. "The impact on WBI could be substantial, and GDLN would be at the leading edge of its downsizing. Rumors are circulating B-SPAN is being shopped to EXT and ISG. I thought GSD should also be considered."

Leonard said his department was being taken over by a new director, Robert Van Pulley. I remembered Van Pulley. He had been the Philippines country director who suggested to Leautier that

B-SPAN should be integrated with his country's Public Information Centers. This meant he was aware of us, and saw in us some strategic value. Leonard thought it was time to raise my proposal with his superiors. I was supportive, but said for the moment I wanted to remain invisible. "I have not discussed this with anyone in GDLN," I explained. Leonard said no. He wanted to be transparent. I made a quick calculation. If I wanted the idea to move forward, I would have to trust him. I accepted.

Al-Ghwell reported his meeting went well.[359] He praised B-SPAN and cited my accomplishments on the InfoShop's behalf. Leautier responded positively. "She is thoroughly pleased with how you are running the service," he said. He thought the vice president was not fully cognizant of the impact of her cost recovery policy. "She told me the policy was implemented because she has come to believe the Bank views B-SPAN as a free good that WBI is saddled to underwrite," he noted. That gave the impression the vice president viewed B-SPAN as a burden with minimal ability to bolster WBI's sagging reputation within the Bank. The perception had also discounted the fact that B-SPAN's juggernaut growth had been purchased for a pittance. When Al-Ghwell informed her she had mistakenly announced a second Africa event would be on B-SPAN, the vice president shrugged it off again, and reiterated a willingness to subsidize B-SPAN's coverage of those InfoShop events in which she participated.[360]

Al-Ghwell had negotiated a private agreement with the vice president. It suggested that unlike Weber-Fahr, she might be swayed by a client's direct appeal for a reduced fee. It also seemed Leautier, unlike Weber-Fahr, didn't understand the impact of the pricing policy. We had suffered a loss ratio of 50%.[361] The vice president told Al-Ghwell her vision for B-SPAN was as a content provider of WBI's learning activities, providing targeted video clips to academic sources for training and course activities.

The nuances were important. I was advocating protecting B-SPAN in its entirety, and in addition offering materials the vice president and Weber-Fahr wanted as subsidiary product lines via WBI Presents or Classrooms to secondary markets. Weber-Fahr with Leautier's support was suggesting the learning activities should become B-SPAN's core product line. This marked the clearest signal in four years that Leautier's concept of B-SPAN was moving in the opposite direction of the original model and her initial mandate and toward Weber-Fahr's position. B-SPAN could still be preserved if it retained its transparency by offering a separate window for WBI Presents, but I wondered if I would ever have the chance to make my case to Leautier. Her remarks also did not clarify whether she was aware or supported Weber-Fahr's intention to merge B-SPAN's transparent content with edited materials, and to produce events accessible only to private audiences.

Al Ghwell said Leautier's face betrayed nothing about my situation. I concluded this aspect of Al-Ghwell's meeting elicited little. It remained unknown what the vice president knew. My strategy would be to continue providing her with positive results, so fallout from Weber-Fahr's firing me would be felt as deeply as I could make possible. Of course, if there was a pre-ordained decision, such a strategy would be wasted. There was no way to tell for the moment.

On organizational matters, Leautier confirmed to Al-Ghwell that GDLN would decentralize to the regions. With Wolfensohn's term coming to an end, she did not expect President George W. Bush to reappoint him. She thought he would depart sometime in the middle of 2005, and she would stay at least until then.

Al Ghwell raised a trial balloon of EXT assuming responsibility for B-SPAN, but Leautier had not warmed to the idea. B-SPAN was a coveted jewel to create publicity for her. Perhaps she had something else in mind. I had heard from several sources there were ongoing discussions with ISG to take B-SPAN over. I decided to follow the trail.

My strafing continued. The next day we covered an event on civic engagement that Leautier chaired.[362] I stopped by to make sure everything went smoothly. She mentioned her lunch with Al-Ghwell. She said he had introduced her to a Middle Eastern journalist recently, and another idea sprang into my head.

Then as she began the proceeding, she noted she had to leave early, but would watch the balance of the event that evening on B-SPAN from her home in Montreal.[363] The comment startled me. Getting an event online the same day was no small feat. I called Kalidindi and said the vice president had an urgent request. We had the video online and summarized hours later. Kalidindi had been uncomfortable about putting the vice president's event before others in the production queue without Sheram's approval. Though new to GDLN, he instinctively recognized the environment was so stifling that it was dangerous to do even simple things without specific guidance. I promised to allay his fears by sending Sheram a note.[364] Sheram would not object since the vice president was the event host, and more to the point, because she was away on a fourth vacation.[365]

Then, I visited Al Ghwell to flesh out my idea. "What do you think of convening one journalist from each global region to interview Leautier on her vision of development, and feature the interviews on B-SPAN?" I asked. He liked the concept, and I wrote Leautier to broach the proposal.[366]

The campaign to bolster my reputation in the eyes of the vice president intensified. The Bank's Disability Unit was holding a major conference with Nobel Laureate Dr. Amartya Sen and U.S. Senator Tom Harkin at the end of November. The unit contracted with ISG to do a live webcast. I had already negotiated to have the archives on B-SPAN.[367] I called Marco Nicoli, the conference organizer. "Who is doing your outreach?" I asked. When he told me EXT, I let him know they were not set up to reach the public. I made him an offer.

"If you agree to let B-SPAN host the live stream at no cost, we will send out notices to our newsletter community of 18,000." He enthusiastically agreed.[368] Nicoli went one step further. He would have Judy Heumann, the manager of his unit send Leautier an email praising B-SPAN.[369] I sent the vice president a message about the coup, and Heumann's note followed soon after.[370] Subsequently, Roberto Zagha and I crossed paths again. He was putting together a final report of the Practitioners in Development lecture series and wanted to create a CD with B-SPAN's files. He also agreed to send the vice president a note of appreciation.[371]

With the GSD initiative moving favorably and a new possibility with the Development Gateway, I placed my ear to the ground with ISG.[372] I was hearing that Weber-Fahr had launched negotiations with them, but Chongman Kim said he had heard nothing. That seemed feasible. Weber-Fahr normally met with his boss, Le Anh Vu. Such a move would be sensitive, so Vu would be naturally tight-lipped. If overtures with GSD and the Gateway collapsed, I still wanted an option. But raising the issue with Vu would risk exposure. For the moment, Kim's intelligence would suffice.

The clock struck December. I was immersed in the Disability Conference live webcast with its enormous phalanx of speakers.[373] Wolfensohn sent a Bank-wide note about the conference and mentioned B-SPAN's coverage.[374] It marked the first time B-SPAN had been noted in one of the president's correspondences. For one of the few times during the Weber-Fahr era, I had links prominently featured on the Bank's external and internal home pages. Heumann forwarded a second and even more generous thank you note to Leautier.[375] In fact, other colleagues were offering to write in my support, but I decided to pull the plug. It had started to become overkill. Already I felt Heumann's note was tipping the scales. I put together a comprehensive list of B-SPAN files for Al-Ghwell's InfoShop website.[376] I sensed time was tight, and I was punching hard with both hands.

No word had come about Weber-Fahr's decision. I had absorbed myself since the interview in polishing my image, but I felt the tide changing. By chance, I learned the identity of one of the candidates competing against me. It was a Bank communication's assistant with few qualifications for the position. I was not impressed. No one else would be, either. But there were two other candidates whose identity remained unknown to me.

Weber-Fahr and I ran into each other in the hallway. I offered a friendly greeting, "What's going on?" "What do you mean?" she retorted.[377] She was tense and seemed to be struggling to reconcile her decision. Even with the position redefined, no one brought to the table what I brought. She had believed the key to controlling B-SPAN was to master me, but the truth was B-SPAN was beyond anyone's total control. Its success, particularly during the last few weeks, had been a great burden for her. She was now weighing the fallout to her reputation if she fired me. Might some powerful or unknown stakeholder care about a shift in B-SPAN's management? No one could know. However, Weber-Fahr did know large organizations tend to devalue individuals. In bureaucracies, few people take stands on principle. It is rare for someone to take on a fight that is not their own. I knew that, too. My time in the Bank had been based on the premise.

I queried Wheeler as to whether I should switch direction and preemptively reach out to Leautier.[378] Before he could answer, there was a development. One Friday, a technology liaison for GDLN secretly copied me on a note she sent to ISG.[379] She asked them to extend my email account. Attached was an email from Weber-Fahr saying my contract had been "prolonged" until the end of January.

I began to internalize all the information available to understanding the meaning of Weber-Fahr's note. There were a variety of scenarios. Perhaps no legitimate alternative had been found, and Weber-Fahr was stalling for time. Certainly, I already had some evidence of the caliber of my competition. By buying extra time, she might hope I would stumble somehow, giving her an excuse to move me out. She knew me well enough, however, to know this was unlikely. This scenario had the least credence. Perhaps she was unable to resolve the growing schism between her need to control everything and the fallout to her reputation. The likelihood of this also seemed minimal. Johnson believed Weber-Fahr was the type of person who made up her mind quickly and developed a strategy to meet an objective. I agreed with this analysis. Her game plan had been clear since the spring. Clever promotional activities of B-SPAN would not influence someone with such a narrow vision of the world.

I also ruled out that her behavior was punitive. Weber-Fahr was a cold-blooded personality. Emotion never entered her thinking. Johnson suggested WBI recently converted a number of STCs to ETCs and might be having a quota problem. This didn't seem plausible either, as the position was funded, people had been interviewed, and B-SPAN was too critical to run on a part-time ad hoc basis. If Weber-Fahr was intent on immediately forcing edited content and learning materials on B-SPAN, a delay would give her the time to see how I might react. If I was pliant, then she might conclude I could continue. It would spare her any negative impact for making a personnel move. If that was the case, then I could shortly expect to see explicit guidance from her or Sheram. But I expected none. Moreover, putting edited content and training materials online were time-consuming activities. They were also expensive. Weber-Fahr had run out of time, and GDLN had no money. All the discussion about editing and training materials was not rhetoric, but since she didn't have resources, rhetoric is what it would remain. I concluded in any event she would postpone her agenda until this affair ended.

Then, there was the final possibility, of course. She had chosen another candidate who could not begin until February. For eight months, Weber-Fahr had alienated me, and knew keeping me would be keeping an enemy in her midst. She also knew I was creative enough to wreak havoc on her intentions with B-SPAN.

Wheeler agreed the extension was ominous.[380] He suggested I find out whether a final decision rested in Weber-Fahr's hands or those of a Bank sector board. Further investigation revealed the decision was hers alone.[381] That lent further credence to this last scenario. Wheeler's thinking about the process had evolved. He now felt once a decision had been reached, the likelihood of Leautier intervening on my behalf was remote.[382] "Bureaucrats loathe open conflicts," he said. "If the vice president steps in, it would mean breaking B-SPAN out of GDLN." With all that had come before, I found this the most remote possibility of all.

I secluded myself for the weekend, went through all the permutations, and then revisited them again and again. I was searching to know the unknowable. I felt like a detective looking at strands of hair from a crime scene. I needed to sift through months of evidence. Then there were the recent comments from Ahmed and Aladad, the senior WBI officials, and Weber-Fahr's own terminology to "prolong" my contract. I considered the data with sober objectivity. I reached a conclusion. On February 1st, someone new would be running B-SPAN.

The question now was could I stop the inevitable, and if not, could I move the transparency model off-shore. Wheeler was pleased about the progress with other suitors. They posed their own problems, however. The Development Gateway was outside the institution, and had access neither to Bank cameras or servers. It presented too many hurdles to consider seriously.

Instead, it was better to focus on GSD or a partnership between GSD and ISG. The GSD model had weaknesses. They had no experience encoding videos. They would have to allocate resources into maintaining B-SPAN's website. They had no video servers. Yet they enjoyed a pivotal strength. They had the cameras. On the other hand, ISG could encode and could maintain websites and video servers. Each unit could do it alone, but both would need some degree of collaboration. There was also something else to consider: The internal politics of each. This could not be gamed. It was also tangential to the question of the moment.

Wheeler's counsel had been to continue scoring public relations coups, generate supportive letters from allies to Leautier, and keep GSD interested in my offer. I realized now this held little sway with Leautier and no longer intimidated Weber-Fahr. I considered a "beyond the grave" strategy. I could reach out to HR or the Bank's Staff Association to see if I had an administrative recourse, but this seemed unlikely. Weber-Fahr's forte was to hide behind institutional procedures to achieve her aims. She would have assessed this possibility long ago.

I could threaten her with some sort of legal action, but as an international organization the Bank was effectively insulated from such external pressures. Moreover, though action of this nature might cause Weber-Fahr grief, it was also a double-edged sword. My reputation would also suffer. Friends and associates within the institution would instinctively shrink from me.

I could encourage loyal clients to refrain from using B-SPAN following my ouster, but that would ask them to take actions against their own best interests. They wouldn't do it, and I would end up losing face instead of Weber-Fahr. If they were to leave B-SPAN, it had to be clear it had come by her hand. I could return to Chongman Kim, suggesting he should now terminate our gentlemen's agreement of free service, and charge WBI for hosting B-SPAN archives. Such a shift, however, would be radical, and would catch the attention of vice presidents who had just praised me publicly. I could ask Scott Johnson, the administrator of the Bank's newsletter database, to delete B-SPAN's list. But it would mean destroying what I had spent nearly a decade building. I could send a final newsletter exposing WBI's actions, but this would be seen as spiteful without providing any structural solutions. And, I still had an option.

The delay by Weber-Fahr hardened in my mind as a signal she was formally about to move against me. I kept returning to a comment from Wheeler about the timidity of bureaucrats. He had said once a decision was made, Leautier would not have the courage to reverse it. There were too many political implications. Weber-Fahr, however, had not made her decision public. I needed to do something dramatic and do it quickly.

It was time to use the nuclear option. I could appeal to Leautier directly, but thought it would have little impact. I needed a more influential envoy. Wheeler would have to walk into the vice president's office with de Nevers and Johnson at his side to make an impassioned plea on my behalf. Anything less was checkmate. All weekend long, I felt my mind and Weber-Fahr's revolving within each other. It wasn't until late Monday I finally reached Wheeler to reveal my conclusions. We methodically examined all the evidence, and reviewed each scenario. He agreed with my analysis, but what to do next would be my call. I said I wanted to embark on a two-pronged strategy.

The first would involve contacting Roger Morrier of EXT's internal communications unit to broach the idea of B-SPAN interviewing President Wolfensohn. To sell Morrier, I would suggest scripting a set of questions vetted by the president's office. The two of us would then take turns asking them. Knowing tough questions to senior officials frightened Bank communications liaisons, it would be sold as a 'feel good' affair. We would ask soft questions such as his vision of the Bank's future, and what he considered his greatest achievements.

But I had a vision of the Bank's future, too. I would begin the interview by thanking Wolfensohn for his leadership in making the institution a "knowledge bank," and for creating an environment that made B-SPAN and its transparency policy a reality. Then, I would ask the first question. Wolfensohn would not fully understand the point I was seeking to make, but he would understand a compliment when he heard one, and would smile and nod his thanks. The acknowledgement would associate the president of the Bank with B-SPAN's transparency principle in a public forum, and put WBI on notice.

An interview with Wolfensohn would also serve another purpose. Weber-Fahr would never compromise her ego. It was more important to her than her reputation. She only respected power, and feared only those with greater power. Like my friend who had originally made the suggestion, I believed an interview with Wolfensohn would frighten her. And, if put in place, in time, she would be unable to move against B-SPAN or me.

The second strategy was to be conducted by Wheeler. I wanted the decision about the B-SPAN coordinator position forced out of Weber-Fahr's hands and into the vice president's. Three former B-SPAN supervisors presented a powerful front. I told Wheeler if he could talk de Nevers into going with him, then I could get Johnson to join them. I knew Johnson, as much as he supported me, wouldn't walk into the vice president's office with someone from outside WBI whom he did not know. For me to get Johnson, Wheeler needed to get de Nevers. She was the key. Without her, he would be alone, and though his personal ties to Leautier counted for something, Wheeler was outside WBI's internal political structure. Ultimately, despite his reputation with her, his word on departmental matters counted for little. With regard to WBI business, the vice president would give most weight to her internal politics. That was the reality, and we had to recognize the parameters unemotionally. Wheeler agreed.

Subsequently, I hoped he could deliver three messages to the vice president. First, B-SPAN's principles were her principles. She had codified those years before. I simply defended them. If she wanted to change B-SPAN into a forum for learning and training events, she never delivered the message to me. The time had come for her to formally tell us what she wanted: A transparency communication medium for the Bank or a platform of blended product lines that promoted WBI propaganda. Second, the department's image had faded within the Bank, but sometimes vice presidents are insulated from the truth. If I were to be relieved after driving B-SPAN to success, then WBI's reputation might be impacted further. Finally, a decision of this importance—to the most visible service WBI offered—was not a line manager's to make. It needed to be made by the vice president. Deciding not to act, I suggested Wheeler might say, would itself be a decision.

A small window existed. If we moved with alacrity, then we could still strike a deal with Leautier before Weber-Fahr went public. Any decision could be reversed so long as it was still private. Wheeler floated the possibility Weber-Fahr had already made it public. "It's possible de Nevers might know," he said. I disagreed. "Weber-Fahr never shares information," I replied. "She makes decisions in secret so she can move on information known only to her. That is her history. The panel will not know. Her GDLN team leaders will not know. Perhaps Leautier might be informed first, but only after Weber-Fahr is ready to reveal it to others."

Wheeler said he would call de Nevers immediately. I got on the phone to Morrier.[383] "B-SPAN reaches more than 20,000 viewers each month," I said. "The president has never had formal access to these stakeholders, and we've never had a chance to speak with him. Now he can reach them directly." Morrier was intrigued by the offer, but there was a glitch. It was an open secret Wolfensohn was negotiating with the Bush Administration about serving another term as president. The current one expired in the middle of 2005. No one knew how those discussions would conclude. Until then, Wolfensohn had sequestered himself from the media. An announcement was expected in the next few weeks. Morrier said we would have to table the idea until January. It was a setback. I didn't have a few weeks. I only had days and perhaps just hours.

Weber-Fahr struck the sail before Wheeler and I could unfurl it further.[384] She walked into my office the next afternoon. I grimaced in anticipation. She said matter-of-factly she had "not good news. Based on the panel's report, a candidate was found who will be more useful in how I plan to reorient B-SPAN. Your contract will end at the conclusion of January so you can help the new person transition into the new post." There was a pause. "During the past years, you have helped build B-SPAN to become what it is now," she resumed. It wasn't clear if she was pleased by that, but I had the impression she considered me as an interchangeable technician administering her project.

She invited me to contact Bhandari, the HR liaison from the panel, to pursue other opportunities in the Bank. Then, she added, "The change is not a reflection on your excellent work but because of B-SPAN's new direction." I sat stone-faced while she made her speech.

Weber-Fahr realized I would have figured out what the extension meant, and I might attempt a pre-emptive foray with Leautier. There was little I wanted to say. After three years of dealing with WBI's officials, I had learned to reveal little by speaking extemporaneously, and by keeping a blank expression. Both tactics had proven useful. And, even now I refused to yield to any outward emotion.

Nevertheless, I wanted to cleave through Weber-Fahr's carefully orchestrated rhetoric to reveal a truth. "Did the panel recommend someone else?" I asked. "The panel provided a report," she acknowledged, "but did not make recommendations." That confirmed she alone had made the decision.

I asked who the new person was. She said someone from the Development Gateway. She did not want to reveal a name. She closed by stating, "It would be understandable if you wished to leave B-SPAN immediately. You are free to do so, but if you want to serve the balance of your contract, I ask you confirm by email."[385] Without any hint of remorse, she got up and left. The date was December 7th, the day that lives in infamy.

11

It was a moment of profound reflection and regret for what was undone and would not be done. The next morning, Stewart knocked on my door.[386] He was visibly shaken. Weber-Fahr had just given him the news. He began groping for words.

"This reminds me of what happened to Steven Jobs at Apple Computer," he said. I was not familiar with the story. "Jobs," Stewart began, "created the personal computer that launched Apple. As the company succeeded and grew, it became filled with bureaucrats who thought Jobs was too visionary a leader. They forced him out, and subsequently Apple went into a downward spiral and collapsed. A decade later, Jobs was asked to return. He promptly cleaned house and restored the company to good health."

I thanked him for the story, and told him this event would not impact our friendship. He seemed relieved.

I remained curious about the panel process. I gently prodded him for information. He squirmed with discomfort. He was "afraid to say too much. Monika did not want me to talk to you at all, but I insisted."

"Tell me about the candidates," I asked.

"All had the same weaknesses," he said. "None had an educational or learning background." Those were the reasons Weber-Fahr had given for a change. If no one had those skill sets, it confirmed suspicions of the previous eight months.

"Who was the winning candidate?"

Stewart flinched. "Someone named Sona," he said. He didn't want to talk anymore. We parted.

Weber-Fahr said she was hiring someone from the Development Gateway. Stewart said her name was Sona. That meant it was Sona Panajyan. Apparently, Panajyan had been playing a game at my expense. When we ran into each other near my office, it was because she was leaving the interview with the panel or Weber-Fahr. She invited me to meet with her not because she wanted B-SPAN and the

Development Gateway to collaborate. Rather, she was surreptitiously extracting information useful to her in assuming control of B-SPAN. Panajyan and Weber-Fahr were well-suited for each other, I thought. They were both duplicitous.

When I finally broke the news to Wheeler, I still wanted to go forward with having a troika of representatives meet with Leautier.[387] "If there is some sort of final stand, perhaps the sinking ship is salvageable," I suggested. "Leautier is accountable for what happened, and I want the meeting to elicit some sort of acknowledgement of that."

Wheeler described the affair as a "deep institutional scandal." He was willing to go forward with my request, but wanted to offer an additional perspective. "You have some capital of good will built up with the vice president," he began. "It can be used in one of two ways. You can force her to admit complicity in the debacle, or enlist her support in establishing a transparency model elsewhere in the Bank. If WBI can't afford B-SPAN, she is closely aligned with Wolfensohn. Perhaps she can persuade the president to take the initiative. By helping you move B-SPAN or establishing a new service, the vice president would be acknowledging some degree of fault. This approach would be institutionally palatable by her count. She owes you something. It is up to you to decide how the debt is repaid."

Wheeler, the Zen Master, was often one step ahead of everyone else, myself included. His logic made sense, though experience suggested reason or loyalty held little relevance to decision-making within WBI's management. I wanted Leautier to acknowledge her responsibility. I believed it was deserved. I also wanted to continue the crusade. Wheeler was saying I couldn't have both.

There was something else to consider. If the vice president reversed Weber-Fahr's decision, what had I won? I would be wedded to an autocrat focused on using B-SPAN to suit her personal ambitions. A meeting with GSD's Leonard was scheduled a few days hence. Wheeler wanted to know its results before reaching out to de Nevers. Then Wheeler provided an afterthought. "Together we have had five years of collecting data about the Bank. B-SPAN failed inside the Research Department. It failed with WBI. Would it be any different elsewhere? Perhaps this should be a period of introspection about whether you should remain in the Bank. It may be possible to recreate what you've done outside the institution." It was a tough conversation, but we had to face reality.

Instinctively, I believed it was critical to try again inside the Bank. Everything Wheeler had said was true, but the transparency model worked. It just had not found the right home. It was certainly possible there was no right home for B-SPAN. I could accept that, but I could not walk away without one more attempt. The institution's infrastructure was uniquely suited by its economy of scales to house such a system. If I identified a place in the bureaucracy that saw an advantage in housing the model, I could still create a communication medium of unprecedented power.

B-SPAN had long been caught between two competing visions. Just how far apart those were was revealed in a meeting the day after Weber-Fahr's announcement. Each year, EXT hired Dave Witzel and Forum One to review how well the Bank's websites performed.[388] Witzel told his audience that 13 million visitors had logged on to Bank websites during the fiscal year. Each month, the Bank's Internet infrastructure recorded 70 million hits. Traffic had grown 47%.

Witzel's analysis startled me. The Bank had an estimated 1,000 sub-sites. B-SPAN was just one. In fact, it was a website that required more from its visitors than other websites, for they were HTML-based. B-SPAN was a webcasting site. It required users to download software to stream video. Moreover, Internet users by nature get on and off sites quickly. B-SPAN required visitors to invest the time necessary to watch the tapes. Yet despite these hurdles, B-SPAN's growth had tripled in each of the previous two fiscal years. I did some back-of-the-envelope calculations. B-SPAN received more than 200,000 visitors in FY04, accounting for nearly 2% of all Bank website visitors.[389] There had been only nominal funding to pay salaries for two short-term consultants, no funding to expand or adapt to growing demand, and years of staff time devoted to internal battles for survival, yet the Bank's stakeholders had made a profound statement.

B-SPAN, as a medium of communication between the Bank and the world, was valued far more outside than inside the institution.

Larisa Fastovsky, who managed ISG's server maintenance activities, called me after Forum One's presentation. She wanted to learn about B-SPAN's cost structure because ISG was reviewing its pricing strategy.[390] ISG was charging Bank clients $500 an hour to do live encoding and $100 an hour to encode videos for archiving.[391] She thought it might be possible to offer discounts for bulk service. My analysis of B-SPAN's costs came to $289 per two-hour event. If all other activities were excluded, however, B-SPAN's encoding, including indexing, was estimated to be $50 per event. Without indexing, the cost diminished to about one-fourth of what ISG was charging.

"You can reduce encoding charges dramatically, which in turn, will attract more clients and increase the volume of ISG's service," I suggested. Fastovsky also thought there was flexibility in ISG's model.[392] That's what I was hoping to hear. If I was able to convince GSD to take B-SPAN over or launch a competitive service, I needed to minimize ISG's encoding charges as much as possible. The time had come for me to begin a serious dialogue with ISG.

I continued working on GSD's Leonard.[393] His enthusiasm for a venture was paramount, but it was time to be frank about my situation in WBI.

"B-SPAN is attracting almost 2% of the institution's web traffic," I started. "The reality, however, is WBI does not support the model. As a result, I am leaving WBI. The department will start making B-SPAN a medium for presenting its pedagogical materials. It will no longer fund the transparency model. Its cost recovery policy has alienated clients and eroded B-SPAN's base. In turn, this will affect GSD's business. A proven market exists. WBI is ceding the field, but it doesn't mean the market no longer exists. The question for you is: Will those customers become yours or someone else's?"

He shifted in his seat. I continued. "My vision is to implement a model to increase demand for GSD's services. To do so, it will be necessary to create a pricing mechanism that is not about cost recovery but about revenue generation."

Leonard stopped me to query about my situation. "There will be opportunities inside and outside the Bank," I replied, "but creating a webcasting system in GSD is my chief objective. I know it works, and of all places in the Bank, GSD is best suited to launch a service. The economics makes sense. It has the cameras. The politics makes sense. GSD are service providers. You aren't in the business of making or orchestrating content, but providing technologies for disseminating it."

It was time for a reality check. "There are red flags, however. GSD should not make the same mistake WBI made in thinking of B-SPAN as a technology. It is an organic system that takes constant feeding, creative thinking, and marketing to secure accomplishments. The vision, human relationships, and institutional knowledge provided are integral inputs into the system. There is nothing to prevent GSD from moving ahead without me, but in six months you may find the system faltering, and perhaps unsustainable. Can GSD fail so prominently so quickly before a new vice president?"

Leonard shifted in his seat again. "There is another concern," I went on. "This process is dynamic. Someone else might move before GSD. The window of opportunity is now. If someone in GSD's hierarchy plays Hamlet, or says it's necessary to wait until Van Pulley officially assumes his duties, the window might close." I added a final touch. "If GSD doesn't capitalize, Van Pulley might want to know a year from now why his department had this opportunity on the goal line and decided to punt."

I didn't want to leave Leonard without a carrot. He had spoken about his interest to revamp GSD into a service provider that would move the institution into a new century. In addition to more filming and audio recording, he wanted to expand his service to provide creative editing. I wanted to complement his vision.

"You need the transparency model," I told him. "It will provide you an unlimited supply of content for your editing initiatives. It will also provide GSD with protection. If anyone suggests the Bank is spinning propaganda with edited content, GSD can always refer critics back to the original transparent source to maintain its integrity."

Leonard's face was responding positively. He said he remained enthusiastic. His supervisor wanted a report on our meeting. Leonard was leaving in a week for the Christmas holidays. I said I wanted to hear back before he left one way or the other. He agreed.

Fraeters sought me out to express his condolences over Weber-Fahr's decision.[394] He was the second panel member to voluntarily reach out to me. "She forced me to participate," he said. He confirmed the panel did not make a recommendation to Weber-Fahr. It had only provided a matrix on candidate strengths and weaknesses. "Panajyan scored higher in small-team management," he said. "You scored higher in business development."

I was not surprised by this analysis since I had been conducting a revolution inside WBI for three years. What he said next was a surprise.

"The panel was instructed by Human Resources to issue a matrix based solely on the results of questions and answers from the interview," Fraeters noted. "HR specifically instructed us to disregard any previous experience of candidates."

What he had just said was hard to believe. Candidates with unequal experience were at no advantage or disadvantage so long as they were interviewed for the position. Accordingly, five years of building B-SPAN was meaningless. The interview was given 100% weighting. That was absurd. I wondered if Weber-Fahr's hand had played an invisible role in HR's instructions. Fraeters said he had "found the whole experience thoroughly unpleasant."

And, still one more panelist found her way to me.[395] Sheram walked into my office. She wanted to know if I had any questions. I didn't. She wanted to know what I planned in the way of administrating B-SPAN until my departure. I asked her what she had in mind. She didn't know. She did, however, have one request. "I want you to figure out a palatable way to spin to the public an announcement of your leaving," she said. I found the encounter entirely consistent with Sheram's approach to everything else.

Leonard had a response from his supervisors.[396] They were not only interested, in fact, he thought they were enthusiastic. He discussed the proposal with Carl Weissmann, his manager, and together they floated it to Van Pulley.

"There are, nevertheless, a couple of caveats," Leonard noted. "Van Pulley is hiring an external vendor to conduct an overall assessment of the department. He won't move on anything until the analysis is done." I asked how long that might be, but Leonard didn't know. "It could linger for months," he suggested. I frowned.

Van Pulley had added something else. "He said launching a new service was a political decision." Leonard didn't have to explain. Van Pulley was saying he needed permission from Leautier.

This was a bad sign. Visionaries make decisions. Bureaucrats ask for permission. It was a harsh assessment to make on the spot, but it boiled down to an essential truth. Van Pulley could have been playing it close to the vest to test whether the water was warm, or he could simply be afraid. In the end, it meant the same thing.

If Van Pulley needed Leautier's permission, she could kill the venture before birth. Would she allow a competitive service? That seemed like a non-starter. The potential fallout to her reputation would be obvious.

Still, Wheeler continued to believe she supported the concept of a transparent webcasting system. "There is the rhetoric and there is the reality," he said. "Bubba," I responded "rhetoric is the reality." For me to remain in the Bank would constitute a threat to Leautier and Weber-Fahr neither would tolerate. Wheeler believed the assessment correct.

Our information, however, remained incomplete. We didn't know what the vice president knew regarding Weber-Fahr's efforts to destroy the transparency model. Wheeler believed I had built what he called "moral capital" with her. He wanted to test the theory, and suggested I ask for a meeting to help secure a new future in the Bank. Testing the hypothesis wouldn't hurt, but revealing the negotiations with GSD might. I wanted to use the meeting to assess the vice president's mind before revealing my plans or even a subtext of them.

A note I sent the next morning elicited an immediate response.[397] The vice president agreed to meet.[398] Her secretary scheduled me for

15 minutes in early January. The tone of her response also suggested awareness and acquiescence regarding Weber-Fahr's decision.[399]

Apparently some moral capital had accrued. Wheeler and I focused on the pitch. I offered an initial game plan. I would start with a review of the transparency model's success, followed by an acknowledgement of WBI's pedagogical mission, and difficulty funding a model that didn't serve its mandate. Then, I would suggest finding another part of the Bank to assume the service. I would close by suggesting a transparent B-SPAN would be Leautier's legacy.

Wheeler didn't like it. "If this is about transparency, Leautier might want to keep the principle for B-SPAN," he said. "Argue about economic issues. There are programming opportunities available to GSD that WBI cannot provide. The two departments should coordinate activities so B-SPAN continues to cover the high-profile events while GSD covers what WBI does not want." Wheeler believed over time, the market would turn to me because of my entrepreneurial nature and pricing differences.

Wheeler's proposal meant I had to make another decision. The pitch could seek to move B-SPAN to GSD, or allow GSD to implement a "complementary" service. I wondered whether I should raise GSD as a suitor at all. Wheeler thought suggesting Leautier reach out preemptively to Van Pulley might antagonize him and overplay my hand with GSD. Concurrently, he was pessimistic about Leautier.

"Vision is a function of context," he suggested. "In three years, she was happy to make rhetorical commitments and bask in the glow B-SPAN shone on her, but not once has she protected you from her subordinates." Rarely angered, Wheeler's face was flushed.

We moved to the economics of a pricing model. The proposal needed to impress upon GSD that the venture was profitable while concurrently convince Leautier it was unaffordable. Where the margins intersected remained unclear; there were many variables to calculate. "If we offered just filming, encoding and posting, we could provide a very modest price," I suggested. "Summaries and quality control of the filming would become the purview of the client." Wheeler liked it. "A barebones, Wal-Mart approach, might work," he thought.

A minimalist model, we believed, should focus on building a client base in the first year. By then, we reasoned, clients would recognize B-SPAN had become polluted with propaganda, compare costs, and switch. Wheeler then tore a page out of Leautier's and Weber-Fahr's playbook. He suggested taking "a Mafia-style approach to your meeting: Say what you need to say to get a deal, and then do what you want to do." I went one better. I said, "If I broker a deal, I can do whatever I want immediately." He nodded.

The next checkpoint was a meeting between Wheeler and de Nevers.[400] He was disappointed with her. "She could have protected you," he said. But she had not which suggested to him that she had discarded B-SPAN to focus on her own personal ambitions. I had come to the same conclusion much earlier during our initial immersion into GDLN. "She did have a career to grow," I speculated. Wheeler said he would espouse an "ain't it awful what's happened" requiem to see what intelligence he could elicit. I wanted to keep the GSD venture secret. "De Nevers is a schmoozer," I noted. "Schmoozing now is too dangerous."

The Development Gateway had been a ruse. GSD could fall apart at any moment. If I wanted to put the plural in suitors, I needed another one. I turned to Michael Kingsberry in ISG.[401] When I called him, he responded that he had been planning to call me. He asked me to visit.

I settled into his office and listened without comment as he spoke at length about a new operation he was putting together to coordinate video production services for the Bank. He acknowledged they weren't filming in volume as B-SPAN did, but their concept was to provide edited content for any video source within the institution. He asked me for thoughts.

"Our transparency model works," I noted. "The market exists and is available to whoever is willing to take it off WBI's hands. Your model is not B-SPAN's model, but you can have both. Mine will feed you with endless secondary content, but only mine can protect you and the institution from charges of creating and packaging propaganda."

Kingsberry was stunned. He did an intellectual somersault. "What you have proposed is highly interesting," he said. "I plan to raise this with Muhsin (his vice president), but no promises." I smiled. "Michael, we're only having a conversation," I replied.

Sheram said GDLN would soon inform clients they would be charged to keep their archives on B-SPAN.[402] It was not clear why I should remain in the loop on information other than for Sheram's enjoyment. Nevertheless, I now viewed these punitive acts as positive developments. Whatever Weber-Fahr did to injure the service and alienate clients could only be to my advantage.

I also learned, without surprise, Weber-Fahr had covertly sought to sully my reputation. In meeting with de Nevers, Wheeler had learned Weber-Fahr had tested her pliancy about replacing me before officially moving.[403] The GDLN manager had characterized me as a malcontent to gauge de Nevers' reaction. Weber-Fahr knew de Nevers was aware of my history with Laporte and Tolstopiatenko. Shaman, she had said, was causing problems with other staff.

In slandering my name, Weber-Fahr sought two distinct objectives. The first supported the theory she was trying to drive me out of the Bank. Second, it was useful to focus attention on me to take the spotlight off policy initiatives she implemented for B-SPAN.

When Wheeler informed de Nevers what policies Weber-Fahr was instituting, she was surprised. It was too late to matter anymore. De Nevers was disengaged and had made no effort to protect her legacy. Wheeler seemed bitterly disappointed. "De Nevers had taken Weber-Fahr's word at face value and not come to your defense," he said ruefully. Ironically, Weber-Fahr had done de Nevers no favor either. When I built the Host Section two years earlier, it gave de Nevers the lead credit for founding B-SPAN. The GDLN manager deleted it.[404] If anyone wanted to know who in the Bank to thank for making B-SPAN possible, the only person on record was Weber-Fahr.

But De Nevers had become part of B-SPAN's past. It was the present that mattered; and there were practical considerations arising from her meeting with Wheeler. Weber-Fahr had sullied my name. She most certainly would have done so with Leautier as well.

"You need to protect yourself by finding allies in WBI who will vouch for your reputation," Wheeler said. "Weber-Fahr is duplicitous. On one hand, she has told some a personnel change was to help B-SPAN achieve the new learning agenda she envisioned. To others, she said you are a troublesome subordinate she can no longer tolerate. If Leautier realizes Weber-Fahr is selling two stories, her credibility will be damaged."

It was good advice. I had many friends in WBI, but selectivity seemed to be in order. I turned to Johnson, who immediately agreed to speak on my behalf if necessary.[405] I felt Johnson, along with Wheeler, were all the character references I needed in front of the vice president. If Leautier raised the issue, I could say truthfully Weber-Fahr told me one story and peddled a second one to her. Then I would get angry, suggest something unseemly was unfolding, and demand the vice president investigate.

After a period of reflection, I settled on Wheeler's approach with Leautier. It was sound. It gave us the best opportunity to get where we wanted to go. Her Christmas message to WBI's staff listed the accomplishments for the year.[406] Many had been emboldened by B-SPAN, but there was no mention of our work at all.

Still, B-SPAN was too valuable for her to jettison. She would be instinctively reluctant. Yet within her reluctance was a paradox. She had not understood that B-SPAN was only a name. Without its soul and energy, it would wither. A colleague once told Wheeler the Bank was less than the sum of its parts. That's what B-SPAN would become.

Already, the evidence was irrefutable. In April, Leautier had spoken glowingly about her concept of "massification" and how B-SPAN was a shining example. Its tiny team with limited resources was reaching large audiences, and having an impact far beyond the value of investments WBI was making. Weber-Fahr immediately followed the vice president and said despite resource constraints, GDLN was going to successfully scale up its outreach activities.

In the spring, B-SPAN was reaching 400,000 page requests. It had taken me four years of building and holding off pirates to get there. Yet two months after their speeches, when Leautier officially handed B-SPAN off to Weber-Fahr, it slumped. In July, Weber-Fahr's first month, B-SPAN's numbers dropped.[407] Then, they kept dropping and never reversed course. Into October and through November, B-SPAN withered.[408] By December, it barely reached 200,000 page requests, mostly on the momentum of its old reputation, but just half the rate of five months earlier.[409]

The year closed. Stunning successes intermingled with horrific defeats. What Wheeler and I were attempting had no precedent. If we could move B-SPAN or launch a new service in the Bank, it would represent a monumental achievement. More fundamentally, the effort had the capacity to change the Bank forever. The stakes for the meeting with Leautier were enormous, but parenthetically only Wheeler and I knew what they were. The rest of the institution, and most notably WBI, were oblivious. We had three vice presidencies thinking and talking about B-SPAN, what it should be, and where it should go. That alone was remarkable.

In a few days, I would meet with the vice president. The outcome, I believed, would turn the history of the organization in one direction or the other. And, I could feel the tectonic plates of the Bank vibrating.

PART VII
our dream

1

2005

The new year rolled in like a storm that could break in two directions. I spent the holiday season preparing for the vice president. News of my departure began to leak, and Bank colleagues reacted with disbelief.[1] They were incredulous as to what had happened. Months earlier, my former KS Team colleague Ron Kim told me he had repeatedly seen successful programs in WBI destroyed by managers' intent on building fiefdoms of personal power. He believed this unscrupulous trait was endemic to the department's culture.[2] I now sensed the same disillusioned acceptance from dozens of friends who came to offer words of encouragement.

There were, however, still cards in the deck and important decisions to make regarding Leautier. I had made one critical decision already: Seeking Leautier's acquiescence on launching a "complementary" service rather than trying to pry B-SPAN loose from WBI. But I had yet to make a related decision: Whether to characterize the concept as still embryonic or near fruition. I would not know how to decide until perhaps the meeting itself while taking the vice president's pulse.

Preparing for Leautier was only one task. Another was to construct a business model saleable to GSD or ISG or both. It would be a tricky affair. It would have to balance knowledge privy only to the vice president while guiding her delicately in my direction. It would also have to create an economic framework to maintain the courtship of GSD and ISG.

The year's beginning brought an immediate surprise. Sheram and Stewart appeared as emissaries at my door. "Weber-Fahr wants to offer you a part-time consulting position with B-SPAN," Sheram began. "It would be for five days a month through the end of the fiscal year."[3] She laid out the terms. "You can keep your email account active to job hunt in the Bank. In return, you will be available to Panajyan so she can suck your brain to help her make a smooth transition." Chagrined, Stewart stood mute in the corner. Dumbfounded as I had been over any number of actions taken by Weber-Fahr, Laporte and Tolstopiatenko over three years, her proposal revealed a new level of callousness. I kept my face expressionless. "I'll think it over," I said.

I considered the development carefully, for it suggested a number of things. Weber-Fahr, I surmised, realized she was now alone with B-SPAN. It had been a high-flyer in the Bank. Leautier had given her the authority to fire me, but it also came with a condition: Keep the service solvent. If it sank, only one person could be held accountable, and all would know who it was. It appeared Weber-Fahr, whose persona was predicated on a lack of emotion, was having a bout of nerves. It also suggested she was concerned about fallout within GDLN. Despite her assertion to de Nevers, I was on good terms with almost everyone. What had occurred between Weber-Fahr, Sheram and me was largely secret and behind closed doors. One month after Weber-Fahr had informed me of her decision, few in GDLN other than the panel knew I was leaving. An abrupt ouster might impact morale. Keeping me on board would serve as some sort of face-saving measure.

The offer unveiled Weber-Fahr's devious nature. She had told de Nevers I was a malcontent disrupting GDLN's morale. Certainly, WBI couldn't employ such a person. De Nevers would realize she had been duped if she heard about the proposition, but since her ability to influence the ETC process had concluded, I considered the point moot.

Weber-Fahr had no shortage of ways to amuse me. The day she sent her emissaries, she also sent GDLN staff a note on the importance of positive behavior.[4] “Be positive,” it said. “Teach others to have fun and celebrate some success every day. Be constructive. Seek to make and solicit positive, constructive suggestions, every day. Help others benefit more than you do.” I was very moved by her metamorphosis.

When he heard of the offer, Wheeler thought Weber-Fahr might have learned of my meeting with Leautier. “She is taking pre-emptive action to keep you in the fold,” he suggested.[5] I disagreed with the hypothesis. “If she knew, she would wait to hear from Leautier first about the outcome,” I said. “She would want to know what was said before asking me to stay.” Of course, both theories were valid for the moment. For the time being, I decided to remain non-committal about the offer. I would make Weber-Fahr return again and again; and when she demanded a decision, I would ask for a terms of reference (documents the Bank uses to define job responsibilities). It might be useful to have something in writing.

I perfected my pitch to Leautier. In part, it codified an exacting and comprehensive defense of my reputation. I would note Weber-Fahr spent six months talking about a philosophical realignment of B-SPAN to meet WBI’s pedagogical mandate, but at no time had she suggested concern about my relationship with staff. Additionally, Weber-Fahr had asked me on several occasions to apply for the ETC position. She even told me she was going to offer me the position but needed to go through a formal process for organizational reasons. Once the panel learned of the decision, two of its members came to me to apologize and express regret. Hundreds of Bank staff viewed me as a friend, and many were trying to help me find new opportunities.[6] And finally, Weber-Fahr had offered me a consulting position despite my termination.

Wheeler cautioned me. “Don’t employ this tack unless Leautier suggests your leaving was the result of your own doing. Even then, leave out references to Weber-Fahr’s character. The vice president will view it as sour grapes.”

He also encouraged me to forgo mentioning that Weber-Fahr was changing the model. “Leautier may not be aware of what she is doing," he said. "We wouldn't want her to prevent it. If Weber-Fahr's goal is to destroy B-SPAN, we want to let her. If you attack Weber-Fahr preemptively, Leautier will likely solicit comments from her." I agreed. On the hope Leautier had not already alerted Weber-Fahr; we needed to keep this meeting secret at all costs. It might seem like a contradiction to allow, perhaps even encourage, B-SPAN's destruction. B-SPAN, however, was doomed to a servile existence in WBI. Leautier had been responsible for a colossal blunder. What Wheeler and I now sought was its demise and then reemergence in a new form elsewhere in the Bank.

In this strange nexus of exacting nuances and exponential uncertainties, I arrived at the vice president's office. I had been in her office only once before, almost a year to the day. This time I knew what to expect. Fifteen minutes. Wheeler had taken a dim view of that.[7] "Ten years of friendship and three years of service to her hadn't counted for much," he noted.

Leautier and I spent a moment on pleasantries. Then I began.[8] "WBI is in the business of producing high-quality products and services. B-SPAN is an example, and something you can be proud of." She nodded. I had gotten my first positive acknowledgement.

"That is why it can attract the high-profile events in the Bank. Those clients are willing to pay B-SPAN's fee structure. Not everyone, however, can afford B-SPAN's costs, nor does everyone need all the bells and whistles it provides." To illustrate the point, I suggested B-SPAN was like a luxury car, but that many in the Bank would be content to drive mid-size or compact vehicles. "That is why it would be useful for the Bank to have a low-cost, bargain-basement service," I said. "Such a service would be available to Bank clients who can't afford B-SPAN but still want to provide simple streams of low-profile events to their stakeholders. For obvious reasons, such a service could not compete with B-SPAN, but rather would complement it by providing a service to Bank clients for products that don't meet WBI's standards. It's not known whether such a market exists, but it is worth exploring."

Leautier was surprised. This was not what she had anticipated.

And she was nodding vigorously. "This is a good idea," she said. "I've told de Nevers about our meeting and now suggest you talk with her. Have you discussed the idea with Weber-Fahr and Sheram?" I said no. I was suddenly confused. What was she talking about? I realized she had not fully understood what I was suggesting. "Would you like me to talk to Monika?" she asked. Again, I said no. "Frannie, I want to start the service outside of WBI." There was a pause, and then her face registered her understanding.

She noted EXT or ISG might be appropriate homes for such a venture, but then encouraged me to consider launching the service outside the Bank. This suggestion lent credence to one of my post-panel theories that Leautier and Weber-Fahr wanted to get me out of the organization. "Have you thought about that?" "Not much." "What would you call it?" "I will call it Shaman-SPAN" and we both laughed.

Then I went back on message. "This needs to be inside the institution," I said. "There are political issues that would have to be overcome by allowing an external vendor to cover internal events. The technology services already exist inside the Bank. If I am going to get a low-cost service running, I need economies of scale." Leautier started nodding again.

The conversation entered a new phase. She wanted to know if I had already spoken to others. Wheeler and I agreed it was imperative to answer this question in a way that suggested I had been reactive rather than proactive. "After learning I was leaving B-SPAN, I sought out technology people inside the Bank," I said. She again raised the concept of becoming an external vendor. "You need to think about your future and what you will do in two or three years," she said.

That repackaged the exact language she used a year earlier as the rationale for merging B-SPAN into GDLN. I decided to end her maneuver. "If this works," I said, "I will not need to worry about what happens two years from now. I am worried about today."

Her face registered a concession. Then she returned to the key issue. She wanted to know whom I had spoken with. Coming to the meeting, I had wanted to keep that information generic. If her intentions were not honorable, she could easily close any door available to me. If pressed, I would reveal ISG and keep my most promising door with GSD hidden. If ISG's interest vanished, Leautier's thinking would be revealed to us. "Kingsberry," I said.

But there was something else to the conversation. The tone was light. The rapport was friendly. My mind was racing through the permutations of options and percentages for success or failure. I knew Van Pulley and Leautier knew each other. If Van Pulley contacted her and she learned I had already spoken with his team, our flanking maneuver would be dead in the water. There was much riding on a calculated omission.

I decided to take a calculated risk. "I've also spoken to GSD," I said. Her face changed expression. "Why GSD?" "Because they have the equipment and they are apolitical," I responded. "The rest of the institution simply sees GSD as a content provider."

She brightened. She knew Van Pulley, she said, and she liked him. "He is innovative and creative and has done interesting work with the Public Information Centers. Would you be able to put together a project proposal to test the market?" she asked. "Send it to me so I can present it to Van Pulley."

It was as if I had put my finger into an electrical socket. I suddenly had a potential coup on my hands. Leautier rose to signal the meeting had ended. "When is your contract up," she asked as I moved to the door. "End of the month," I said. She rolled her eyes.

The vice president was offering to serve as our emissary to GSD. Wheeler was ecstatic. So was I. If I could complete the sale between Leautier and Van Pulley, I could finish building the system Wheeler and I had long dreamed about. He pushed me to meet with Leonard immediately to come up with a document with GSD's input.[9] I stopped by Leonard's office. He was excited, too. "Van Pulley is very interested in B-SPAN," he said. "He has already scheduled a meeting with Leautier." Wheeler had a new nickname for me. He started calling me Talleyrand.

2

The current was murky and constantly changing. Minefields were abundant. There was no deal until I could make a deal. It would mean delicate tacking. The path to the objective dictated an institutional version of three-card Monte, or in language bureaucrats understand more clearly: The shell game. I had to open with a plan, and it began with numbers. Wheeler suggested a starting point of $150,000. An ETC would cost $100,000 and that was low-balling the figure since indirect costs such as office space and computers would ultimately have to be included. From there I had to work backwards to build figures for cameras, encoders, servers and a website.

The final variable was the cost of an event. We set a target price of $250 that included the camera costs for a two-hour show. WBI could not come close to such a fee. But to break even with a charge of $250, the venture would have to produce 600 shows. B-SPAN had peaked at about 363 events in FY04.[10] It was a lot to make up; and, while the Bank had an enormous amount of content, it still would not be enough. The rest would have to come from external sources; but for the moment, it was prudent to gloss over this fact.

There was no telling how strong Leonard's constitution would be, or Van Pulley's. The art of the deal mandated a model to make the new service complementary in Leautier's view and competitive in Leonard's. I had defined a no-frills model to Leautier. To sell Leonard, it would be necessary to augment the $250 fee with an *a la carte* menu of services. The *à la carte* menu would appeal to him because of his desire to build service components beyond filming and toward post-production editing. If a client wanted summarizing, there would be an additional expense. If they wanted indexed videos, they would pay another cost, and so on. To keep Leautier sold, the *a la carte* menu would have to remain silent.

By the end of the next day, I had crafted a mission statement, client analysis, cost analysis, financing strategies, first-year and second-year targets for clients, and pricing parameters. I emphasized that only a small percentage of the potential internal content had been tapped, and remained deliberately vague about how prevalent external content would become. It was important to keep morale strong. To do this, I stressed the existence of an internal market had been proven. Nearsightedness by WBI's management had caused it to adopt a pricing strategy that had B-SPAN losing market share. I even had a new name for the GSD venture: WorldCast.

The next buoy was a visit to Leonard's office.[11] I needed to shift his thinking, convincing him to embrace what I had proposed to Leautier. I was no longer advocating the redeployment of B-SPAN to his unit. I was now selling WorldCast, the low-cost alternative. The new model, I told him, was based on high volume with an *à la carte* menu and an external component. Leonard was surprised by the shift and that I had sold Leautier on the concept. "The purpose of our meeting," I told him "is to define the parameters of a service that will allow Leautier and Van Pully to reach an agreement. My proposal is going to Leautier tonight. You have an opportunity to make inputs you think you can sell to your boss."

We began crunching back-of-the-envelope numbers. Leonard felt constrained by his fixed camera and consultant costs. He wanted a specific per-event fee. I countered that volume and client needs were variables that could not be predictably calculated. We went back and forth. I kept to my position. "I need a flexible framework to take us to the next level of negotiations," I said. Finally he relented. I noted we could purchase two multi-component camera encoders for $5,000 a piece. With this initial investment, we would have instant archiving, the capacity to go live anytime, and no additional staffing needs. For another $10,000, we could purchase someone's time to maintain a website. He agreed to give me cameras for $30,000. Along with the $100,000 to cover the staff position, we had our $150,000.

"ISG will want to have input on building a new service," Leonard then suggested. I realized he had launched his own negotiations with Kingsberry. I needed to think fast. "ISG will likely provide us free server service if we cut them in on a percentage of the post-production opportunities," I offered. "I'm perfectly comfortable with a joint

GSD-ISG arrangement if that's a deal Van Pully wants to negotiate. GSD can handle the cameras. ISG can handle the encoding, server and website. Post-production of video can be shared. The webcasting service will remain the engine to feed your strategic one-stop shop concept for GSD." He smiled. We had an agreement.

With the numbers solidified with Leonard, the proposal was now ready for Leautier. Wheeler cautioned me to provide nothing to make her hesitate, and the document was stripped of anything with calories. Van Pulley got a colorful proposition called WorldCast.[12] It was multi-flavor, high-octane ice cream with cherries and sprinkles. Leautier got a document called Low-Cost Webcasting Station.[13] It was low-fat cottage cheese.

All became a deep whiteness. As I progressed deeper into its folds, less and less was visible until only darkness remained. All sound vanished as well. No response came from Leautier.[14] Nothing further was heard from GSD or ISG. It was as if they all had disappeared within the vapor enveloping me. B-SPAN had ground to a halt, too. There was only enough wind in its sails for me to steer one final episode: A Wolfensohn press conference on the Christmas 2004 tsunami disaster in Southeast Asia.[15]

Out of the silence, finally, came a voice. It was Weber-Fahr's. Her emissaries pressed me for a decision on her offer. Sheram wrote up a terms of reference and gave me a deadline.[16] "You must comply to preserve your email account," she warned. I continued to demur. Weber-Fahr appeared to find my delay incomprehensible. She leaned on Stewart to get a signature.[17] Stewart, however, had deep misgivings over the situation and his role with the panel. He had become the de facto official supervisor over B-SPAN. With B-SPAN crippled, Sheram's duty was done. Her usefulness to the GDLN manager had also concluded and she was to be reassigned somewhere else in WBI.[18] Stewart agreed to give me whatever cover I needed to pursue new employers. "B-SPAN was an 'unfunded mandate,'" he said to me. "If asked by others, I'll tell them Shaman kept it floating for five years until WBI decided to change."

Rumors continued to gain momentum that the task force was

devising an overhaul of the Bank's operations that would translate into serious carnage for WBI and GDLN. Stewart speculated that there would be plenty of blood in the water, perhaps even Weber-Fahr's. His guess was she would leave within a year. "If you had survived Weber-Fahr," Wheeler speculated, "B-SPAN still might have drowned in the developing environment.[19] WBI has no interest in B-SPAN. In the end, GSD or ISG might have been the only options to keep the service alive anyway." With the announcement of President Wolfensohn's departure in May, a game of musical chairs was already well under way throughout the Bank.

Like me, Wolfensohn was now on a short-term assignment with the Bank. My time, however, was desperately short. As it waned, ironies of the situation lengthened. Annie Spencer sent a note that her graduate studies at George Washington University cited B-SPAN's coverage of de Soto as an important source of information.[20] She expressed pride. Sheram went on record to say she thought it was exciting, too.[21] The same day, EXT featured an article on Sachs's new report on the Millennium Development Goals (MDGs).[22] The story linked to additional information about the Bank's work on the MDGs. There was no link, however, to his watershed speech covered on B-SPAN a few months earlier discussing Bank missteps. EXT's institutional memory had become conveniently absent.

Evidence of B-SPAN's unraveling also gathered. For the first time in two years, the World Bank's *Week in Review* newsletter did not feature one of our events.[23] For the first time ever, a WBI training workshop appeared on B-SPAN.[24] The barrier between truth and message that engendered three years of vicious political in-fighting had now been breached. Almost from its inception, evidence suggested B-SPAN was more valued outside the Bank than inside. Now evidence was building that external stakeholders were withdrawing as well. At a mid-January production meeting, Stewart seemed perplexed.[25] "Volume is down," he said. Tolstopiatenko's statistics for December revealed for the first time since August 2003, B-SPAN had dropped below 200,000 page requests.[26] Just a few months earlier, it had reached 400,000 and was growing rapidly. Before our eyes, B-SPAN was fading from view. Stewart asked me if I had any theories.

Two weeks after our meeting, I ran into Leautier as we were leaving the building. She hadn't read my proposal yet, but assured me I would hear from her before the week was out. GSD hadn't responded either. I considered a new tactic. Carl Hanlon ran EXT's video operations. He fed the news media with clips of materials from Bank sources. I invited him to lunch to see what he knew about B-SPAN.[27] If he sounded enthusiastic, I considered floating the notion that EXT get involved. He professed to know little about us. I dropped the idea without a mention.

I pursued leads outside the Bank. In trying to extend the reach of B-SPAN to non-Bank content providers, I had met a number of event organizers and people in video production services.

I began framing a concept for a webcasting station to serve the entire Washington development community, including the Bank. C-SPAN covered the federal government, but for the international policy community there was a vacuum. Now I wanted to see if I could bridge the channel between them and vendors I knew.[28] I began to explore whether it was possible to launch a consortium with business and technological inputs. All expressed interest, even excitement over the concept, but each declined. The content was there, they said, but the economics were not.

As one described it, "The Internet and webcasting are not well understood even by sophisticated communicators and policy makers. They focus on traditional tools for getting information disseminated and view webcasting with suspicion." My own experiences promoting NIPR to the Research Department's hierarchy and more recent negotiations with RFF suggested this viewpoint had validity. Think tanks and NGOs couldn't rationalize spending $800 or $1,000 to have a private vendor webcast their content. A vendor couldn't afford to provide a service for less.

I had been preaching a concept of a low-cost webcasting service that could meet expenses by building volume. But I was talking with business people who kept the bottom line firmly rooted at the top of their thinking. The Bank had a plethora of content. But it had something else equally of value: Economies of scale. Because of its sheer size and in-house capacity, the Bank could afford to launch a low-cost service in a way a private vendor could not. The message was clear. The Bank had the content. It had the capacity. But did it have the will?

I returned to Leonard to find the answer.[29] What I learned was equally sobering. He had met with Hanlon to discuss a consolidation of video services. EXT, however, was feeling inhibited by budget restrictions. Leonard sensed there would be no further movement with them. He also didn't know if Van Pully and Leautier had met, confirming an assumption I made when WBI's vice president had not responded to me earlier.

"Some issues have to be sorted out in ISG before B-SPAN can be assimilated outside of WBI," Leonard added. "What sort of issues exactly?" I asked. "Muhsin needs to first retire," Leonard said. "He will leave in October." That suggested Van Pulley and Muhsin had talked, and Muhsin had declined to get involved. Leonard finally noted, "There is a debate between all four vice presidencies about whether such a service should be considered a content-based or technology-based system."

I cringed. "The biggest expense," he said frankly, "is you." "Without the right person," I responded, "the system will not work." He agreed but quickly added he was only speaking for himself.

I had arrived at an institutional roadblock. The concept of a transparent communications medium, born in the bowels of an institution, and hidden from the tentacles of its bureaucracy long enough to flower, had now been mired down by the hierarchy. Four vice presidencies were debating what sort of system was sanitary enough for each to approve. It would inevitably mean some muddled bastardization of the original concept.

I studied the waves, watching them break. B-SPAN, WorldCast, or whatever name was attached to it, would be some mundane service offering known names and big events with choreographed speeches and edited for PG-rated videos. It would be expensive and unaffordable for most Bank units. A lack of resources would mean a consolidation of resources. Someone already in-house would be used to maintain a technology-based cut-and-paste operation. The concept of a news-style operation—opening a window on the latest research and debates inside the Bank, offering external organizations, researchers and practitioners a common platform to communicate with the Bank and between themselves on development and the Bank's role—would be safely buried beneath the foundation of 1818 H Street.

Leautier's end-of-year assessment of WBI was published to the entire Bank.[30] She wrote at great length about the expansion of GDLN facilities. She spoke glowingly of learning events held and participant attendance. Various publications were cited. She devoted ample space for Shanghai. She noted WBI's Governance website was one of the most visited websites in the entire Bank. She did not note the Governance site had finished a distant second to B-SPAN. In fact, she did not mention B-SPAN at all.

I had no offers, other than Weber-Fahr's, to remain in the Bank. Sheram continued threatening me with deadlines for a decision. I continued to vacillate.[31] Friends and colleagues alerted me to leads. I interviewed with one manager; she was confident I could handle the position, but worried that offering a low salary would give me an opportunity to criticize her before Human Resources. It was a very Bank sort of perspective. The exchange, however, compelled me to find out more about the limitations of STCs.[32]

I learned once I signed a contract, that unit did not have to release me if I received another offer. The information revealed a hidden agenda behind Weber-Fahr's offer. If I had agreed to her proposition, she could effectively keep me from working with any other Bank unit through the balance of the fiscal year.

There was, of course, the reality of not working at all. Weber-Fahr called me into her office.

"Will you sign?"

"I haven't decided."

Like leafless trees living in winter ground, the waning days of

January ended without promise. The final day of my contract began with yet another appeal from Weber-Fahr to come to her office.[33] In the afternoon, she appeared at my door. "Is there anything you can share with me to help us continue to run B-SPAN?" "I can't think of anything at the moment," I said. She wanted to invite me to a staff party she was holding the next day so she could tell GDLN's staff what an excellent job I had done.[34] I said I wouldn't miss it for the world.

There was still one thing left that had to be done. "Hey, hey, Bubba," I wrote to Wheeler.[35] "For more than eleven years, the Bank has been my home. As of this note, it appears, it will be my history. If I've done anything to move the institution's mission forward, then I'll have done all I could have hoped to do. The principal thanks, however, goes to you. Without your support, none of it would have been possible. I'm tipping my hat to you, my friend."

It was the end. For five years, B-SPAN and I were synonymous. We were the same. It was an extension of me. It was a breathing thing. And now it was something else or would be, and we were both orphaned and all at the same time. Two days later, my old colleagues in the Research Department invited me out to raise a glass in friendship.[36] The crucible was over.

3

The great wave of the institution's ancient culture flooded over me. With my hand outstretched, I was swept below its water line and sank to the very eddies of its bowels. I vanished. Panajyan assumed control and, like an android, B-SPAN tentatively lurched onward. The stifling price fee remained firm.[37] Organizers of ceremonial and non-policy events were invited to use the service.[38] Learning events and training modules began to appear.[39] Potential clients of policy dialogues continued to turn down the new coordinator's solicitations.[40] B-SPAN had once covered five seminars in a day. Strangled and stifled, it now covered six events in February. Traffic sagged below

180,000 page requests.[41] Ever vigilant to ward off a collapse, Weber-Far reinserted Sheram temporarily to oversee Panajyan's immersion. "This is the way the world ends," T.S. Eliot once wrote. "Not with a bang, but a whimper."

On one important point, I had been wrong. It was not the end for me at the Bank. A few weeks after my ouster and somewhere beyond the surface, a lifeline was extended. An old friend from the Research Department, Richard Fix, offered to employ me as a consultant for the balance of days in the fiscal year that had not been used under Weber-Fahr. He needed help for his Data Unit to migrate their website to a new format ISG had created to standardize Bank websites.[42] The new position would keep me on a resuscitator for a couple of months; but almost as importantly it would also provide me with a base from which to access Bank intelligence.

Leautier and Van Pulley and Kingsberry had not said yes to me. They had also not said no. The overt battle to make the Bank transparent was finished. The covert battle would now begin.

Master Sun preached formlessness. When strong, appear weak. When surrounded, recede. Prepare attacks in places the enemy knows not to defend. I dissolved into the shadows. I made few inquiries. I made little noise. I was content to monitor developments from afar so GDLN could move beyond the recent struggle to guide B-SPAN as it saw fit. My task was to fade from view and let Weber-Fahr forget I existed. If she was determined to chart a course that allowed B-SPAN to take on all the ills prophesized, then free rein would be given to let her do so.

The Bank, however, is not so large a community that secrets are kept for long. Word seeped back to GDLN that I had returned to the Bank. I continued to keep my distance, content to gather intelligence indirectly. The camera teams from GSD confirmed what I already knew.[43] Volume from B-SPAN had dropped dramatically. They estimated by as much as 80%. They also noted Panajyan had a very different style. She was impersonal and antagonistic. There was no camaraderie with the camera crews. She did not attend events. She did not do pre-event quality control of the videotaping. Instead, she only conducted post-event criticisms. She won no hearts.

With discussions ongoing over potential disassembling of the department, WBI marked its 50th anniversary with an elaborate party.[44] Celebration notices proudly listed the department's successes including B-SPAN as part of its knowledge sharing contribution to the developing world.

Under its new management, however, B-SPAN made another critical adjustment. Jeff Sachs again served as catalyst. In the wake of the UN's official report on the Millennium Development Goals, he published a new book, *The End of Poverty: Economic Possibilities for Our Time*. He returned to the Bank in late March for the first time since his watershed address the previous spring, and threw down the gauntlet again.[45] Before a standing-room-only audience, he began with a diplomatic acknowledgement of the Bank's importance in the development community, and a nod of recognition to the outgoing President Wolfensohn. Then he lambasted the institution and along the way attacked its powerful benefactors.

"Good intentions or not, the Bank needs to improve to prevent millions from dying needlessly each year," he said. "Heroism is not needed, only modest sums of promised funds from the U.S. and other wealthy nations. The MDGs are not making a difference, because the system has not changed. Rich countries are not partnering with poor countries. Millions continue to die of AIDS and malaria when treatment could be provided for pennies a day. Billions continue to live on a dollar a day." The director of the UN Millennium Project then asked his audience, "Poverty that kills can be ended, but how fast are we moving?"

The gloves were off. With niceties discarded, Sachs tore into the Bretton Woods institutions. "The Bank and IMF put budget ceilings on programs, and donors aren't stepping up to fill the funding gaps. We call this civilization," he exclaimed. "The Bank, at the bidding of the U.S, has backed privatization efforts, proposes domestic credit expansions and user fees, and urges civil service reforms. This is farcical. What is needed is investment in health, education, nutrition, family planning, soil nutrients, water and sanitation, road, power and communications.

"In reality, the cart is before the horse," he suggested. "Markets do not come to the rescue of the poor, because they attend to people who have something. Millions of farmers cannot produce food because their lands are depleted yet donors are cutting subsidies for fertilizers." Sachs railed about a U.S. Agency for International Development (USAID) project that sold a few hundred bed nets for malaria protection to African villages with thousands of inhabitants. "The bed nets, inexpensive by Western standards, are still unaffordable to the poor. Millions remain vulnerable. The situation is absurd."

The Bank lambasted, Sachs turned his rage on the Bush Administration. "The U.S.," he said, "is outside the global consensus on development. To my recollection, the president has never spoken about the MDGs."

Department of Defense Deputy Secretary Paul Wolfowitz, a key architect of the war in Iraq, had just been designated to succeed Wolfensohn as Bank President. Sachs bluntly questioned the appointment. "At a time when the decisions made by the Bank will impact poverty and development for decades, why has the Bush Administration nominated someone with no experience with development?"

A serious charge then followed. "The U.S. is a signatory to the Monterrey Consensus in March, 2002 where donor countries pledged to commit 0.7% of their Gross National Income to development assistance. In the aftermath of September 11th, the U.S. commitment remains 0.15%. UN General Secretary Kofi Annan has said global security cannot be achieved without development; and development cannot be achieved without the donor community living up to commitments made at Monterrey. I urge the Executive Board of the Bank to press Wolfowitz on whether the U.S. will increase its commitments to 0.7% before confirming his nomination."

Then he closed his speech. "We cannot let this opportunity pass," he began. "We are not here speaking for ourselves. We are here speaking for the voiceless in the world, the world's most powerless people. It is not a matter of convenience, but of life and death. Together, we can end poverty, but we have to decide to do it."

A year after his first remarkable speech, Sachs had returned to say there had been no improvement in the international community's development agenda. In the process, he had added a few electrifying twists. On the stage of the World Bank, the UN's point person on development had charged the Bush Administration with abrogating its promised commitment to save tens of millions dying in poverty. Moreover, Sachs suggested America's development policy in the aftermath of the 2001 attacks undermined its fight against terrorism. He lambasted the U.S. government for what he characterized as myopic adherence to macroeconomic policies that refused to recognize the realities of poverty. He then questioned the wisdom of the Wolfowitz appointment at a moment when Bank policy would determine the fate of generations. Finally, Sachs charged the Bank with complicity by serving as the U.S.'s proxy to the Third World. The message was none too subtle. Before hundreds of policymakers, the United Nations had told the Bush Administration, the Bank and the IMF for the second year in a row that they were collectively failing.

That was not the only powerful aspect of the event. Sachs, in a sense, was webcast and silenced simultaneously. The juggernaut Wheeler and I created could not be derailed. It would have been too obvious an attempt at censorship if Sachs's speech was not on B-SPAN.

Indeed, some aspects of B-SPAN's informal model were beyond anyone's control. Low-profile events could be excluded through internal economics but high-profile ones could not. B-SPAN's antagonists could only hope such events were not overtly controversial; but to their chagrin, angered development practitioners like Sachs and de Soto had not played along.

Nevertheless, full coverage was stifled. Panajyan's newsletter simply listed the speech as an event to promote Sachs's new book.[46] *World Bank Today* adopted a similar tone.[47] "Sachs," it said, "paid tribute to the Bank's professionalism and called 2005 a 'pivotal year' for development." The EXT article had no link to B-SPAN's stream. A casual reader might have thought Sachs had stopped by to praise the Bank and sell a few books. The webcast never made it on the Bank's home page. There was no noticeable coverage of the speech in the media. Further discussion of his remarks within the institution's walls and Washington policy circles seemed inaudible, as if nothing important had been said.

Yet, an incredibly powerful issue was at stake. Just one week earlier, at the London Conference of the Extractive Industries Transparency Initiative, outgoing President Wolfensohn had said transparency was fundamental to good governance and development.[48] But was transparency fundamental to the good governance of the Bank? Perhaps the most famous economist of our time, speaking on behalf of the United Nations, had implored Washington to change its ways. Weber-Fahr, and by proxy WBI and the entire Bank, had effectively muted his presentation so that the outside world remained oblivious.

4

As *Bank Swirled* rolled off the presses to mark its annual April Fools Day spoof of the institution, my eyes were on the horizon. Leonard said he was meeting with Van Pulley. He also said Panajyan and Stewart asked to meet with him. I cautioned him to keep silent about our discussions, and use the meeting to learn about Weber-Fahr's plans. He reported back Panajyan had no strategy for the future, other than to reiterate edited product lines would soon be introduced. WBI remained without a charge-back mechanism. Panajyan, who called the meeting and promptly showed up late, only wanted Leonard to agree to charge clients the entire $750 fee and forward B-SPAN's fee back to GDLN. He said he would think it over. He mused to me, "If GSD is expected to administer all transaction costs, what prevents us from taking over entirely? I wonder why WBI continues the service."

In one of those beautiful ironies that I found routinely taking place, Jo Ritzen, a former vice president for the Human Development

Department, returned to the institution to discuss his new book, *A Chance for the World Bank.*[49] It described his view of where the institution stood, and where he thought it needed to move to address the MDG challenges.

He suggested the private sector took a radically different approach to disseminating information about its work. "Corporations like Coca Cola and McDonald's are known in remote villages in impoverished countries across the world," he noted. "Why do they continue to spend 30% of their budget on marketing? Because that's what it takes to maintain their market share. The Bank still does not understand the importance of investing resources on communications to dialogue with stakeholders." Ritzen paused. "If the Bank doesn't make these investments, it will not be as effective in getting its policies implemented." Wheeler and I had been saying the same thing for over a decade. Ritzen's address was covered by B-SPAN, but its summary again offered no substance of what the speech was really about.[50]

More intelligence filtered in. I ran into Spencer who said, "Written coverage has virtually ended beyond the original announcement notices sent by the sponsors.[51] Panajyan is also not attending events or watching the videos." Shortly thereafter, Frost told me she and McCoy met with Panajyan. Frost thought she had little understanding of how to run B-SPAN. "Panajyan is only interested in a charge-back mechanism," she noted. "I think WBI is babysitting the service until they can find a way to get rid of it."

Another chance encounter with Stewart revealed Weber-Fahr still wanted to move forward on editing, streaming to select audiences, and webcasting training videos, but was waiting for Panajyan to learn her duties. Al-Ghwell, B-SPAN's chief client, said his usage had dropped dramatically. When B-SPAN was administered by Johnson, it covered 75% of the InfoShop events. Now coverage had fallen to 20%. He thought Weber-Fahr was destroying the service while trying to pawn it off on ISG. He called GDLN a "catastrophe."

Sensing the dynamics were evolving, I decided to throw a rock in the water. I asked Leonard for another meeting, and then applied another full-court press.[52] "You need to move immediately," I said.

"Either embrace the concept of a new service to compete with B-SPAN or co-opt it. Moving on the former will hand you the latter. Having an in-house system will drive clients to use your video services. With the content, you can create the secondary markets you want with edited products and duplication activities. And while WBI has shackled B-SPAN with a pricing mechanism alienating customers, GSD can implement one generating revenues."

Leonard expressed concern with the original proposal of $250 per event. "Don't worry," I said. "We can adjust fees to meet changing realities. Additional revenues can be generated through a menu of *à la carte* services. You can use a service to turn your unit from reactively administering client requests to proactively providing content."

He had not stopped nodding since I began. I discussed timing. "WBI is bloated, inefficient, and will be punished in the new fiscal year," I said. "GDLN no longer functions effectively at all. It will suffer staff departures and budget contractions in the near future. WBI refuses to fund B-SPAN, so it's questionable how long they will continue to operate it as well. Leautier wants to invest her limited video resources on training and pedagogy, but WBI cannot simply stop running B-SPAN. There would be too much political fallout, so they need a face-saving out. GSD can be an opportunity for them. The timing is right for GSD to step in and assume control."

It was time to twist his arm. "The window, however, will not stay open indefinitely. Weber-Fahr is actively shopping for a buyer, and that buyer may be ISG. If she cuts a deal with Kingsberry, then GSD is out, and your agenda will become a theory."

He seemed shaken for a moment. I moved to close. "Weber-Fahr is pregnant," I said, a tidbit gleaned from Stewart. "By the summer, she will be on leave, and when she returns it may well be to a new position in the Bank. WBI's interest in B-SPAN has never been lower, but if they refuse an offer from GSD, play your cards accordingly. Announce GSD will launch a new low-cost webcasting service to provide Bank clients with an alternative. It won't be long before WBI understands the implications. They will recognize the reality of who owns the cameras, and will offer B-SPAN to you.

"In two years, when this has been long resolved, there will be two ways of communicating at the Bank," I continued. "The first will be through EXT as they talk about the Bank to the world. The second will be through GSD as the world talks about the world to the Bank. It won't take long to figure out which one is more valuable. You have spoken about your vision for putting this operation at the forefront of the organization's mission. This is your opportunity." Then, I emphasized, "You can take all the credit for putting the system together as well."

Leonard felt my urgency. I wanted him to be worried about ISG because I was. There was no way of knowing what conversations were happening between WBI and ISG. He said he would seek a meeting with Van Pulley the next week. I had considered seeking more information through Stewart, Montenegro or Kingsberry, but now decided to wait. It would be prudent to learn the outcome of Leonard's meeting before soliciting others. But what if it went unsatisfactorily? There was already some evidence of skittishness among GSD's officials. Who did Wheeler or I know that could influence Van Pulley?[53]

I caucused with Wheeler on the question.[54] He sensed Leautier's silence signaled indifference rather than opposition. He believed her attention was focused on WBI's deep infrastructural weaknesses. The key, Wheeler concluded, was getting Leautier to give Van Pulley permission. Only then would it be feasible to deploy a covert emissary to compel GSD's vice president to react quickly to the offer.

Leonard contacted me shortly. Van Pulley had cancelled their meeting.[55] According to Leonard, Van Pulley was moving aggressively to reorganize his department, but Managing Director Shengman Zhang curtailed his momentum. It was a bad development. Suddenly, the wind in my sails disappeared.

A crowd of several hundred protestors convened in front of the Bank that weekend to rail against the Wolfowitz appointment. "We are not a fad. We are a movement," one organizer announced.[56] Yet the long cascading spiral was undeniable. Five years earlier, 20,000 protestors had closed off the U.S. capital to charge the Bank with dereliction of its mandate. The groundswell against the Bank had been a key driver for the creation of B-SPAN. As B-SPAN became more successful, external critics became more enlightened and less hostile to the Bank. Now the transparency model and the anti-globalization movement were drying up from the inside out.

As the window for GSD was evaporating, impromptu meetings with Fraeters, Gray and Johnson provided a periscope on how Weber-Fahr was administering B-SPAN. "The agenda for using B-SPAN as a medium for training videos and edited content remains firmly in place," Fraeters said, "but things are moving slowly. Without adequate budget, she is finding it difficult to finance these activities."

That came as no surprise to me. "The focus at the moment is to get a charge-back mechanism in place," he added.

Gray thought GDLN would suffer a 30% budget reduction in the upcoming fiscal year. "It will force Weber-Fahr to shed more staff and resources," he suggested.

Johnson met with Panajyan and didn't think she knew what she was doing. I asked him not to help, but he didn't understand. "Why do you want to see your creation fail?" I had to play along to cover my schemes. "Of course, I do not want to see B-SPAN fail," I said.

Johnson didn't think Leautier would leave until she had had a chance to assess Wolfowitz. In the meantime, he had come to a conclusion different from Gray's. "She has protected WBI well in the current budget wars," he said. Still, he thought his own future in the department was negligible. He was looking elsewhere.

March disappeared and revealed new numbers. B-SPAN was markedly more active, with 11 events. Another 13 events were covered in April. On the surface, all seemed well. Just below the waterline, another story was emerging. The arrogance of power was on full display. Panajyan's churlish behavior with colleagues continued. Weber-Fahr's punitive pricing mechanism remained unyielding. The April newsletter noted how "exceptionally busy" B-SPAN was; yet the character of its coverage had changed remarkably.[57] The webcasting service once devoted to serving the community of have-nots instead had created one. All cutting-edge discussions and research seminars had disappeared. Only prestigious personalities and high-profile conferences were covered.

Peter Bell, the CEO of USA-CARE, was a guest of the Presidential Lecture Series. The respected *New York Times* columnist Thomas Friedman, one of the world's most influential journalists, spoke at another event. Queen Noor of Jordan appeared as well. Poverty Reduction Week, Environment Week, and Water Week also came online. But like widgets on an assembly line, they were videos without context. Nothing to make them interesting or salient could be extracted from the newsletters following these events.[58] De Nevers, sounding surprised, commented on the metamorphosis one afternoon to me. "B-SPAN seems to have changed a lot," she suggested.

EXT's collegiality disappeared as well. The World Bank's *Week in Review* newsletter stopped mentioning B-SPAN by name.[59] *World Bank Today* articles now provided links without the branding I had worked endlessly to foster.[60] The Bank's home page dropped "Webcast" and replaced it with "Video." The important distinctions I had engineered were lost. And, it had been noticed. Despite the big names, viewers dropped to 15,000 a month.[61] Page requests declined to 150,000 in March and remained at that level in April.[62] In eight months, traffic on B-SPAN had declined by more than 60%.[63]

In mid-May, two conferences took place at the Bank that provided the context for an evolution in my thinking about B-SPAN's future. The first was the Global Communications Forum, an annual meeting of Bank media specialists from across the institution's country offices.

Wolfensohn, his time in the Bank waning, addressed the gathering. He minced no words. "This is not cosmetics," he said. "This is not spin and it's not a popularity contest. Your job, in addition to developing and getting out our message, is to come back to the organization with the substantive issues that our public wants us to pay attention to. You are the bridge between rich countries and developing countries. You are explaining that the role of the Bank is to intermediate and to help achieve the MDGs."[64] EXT heard Wolfensohn's plea, but were they listening?

The second event was the annual Web4Dev Conference.[65] It was a forum for international organizations to discuss website practices, trends and technologies that could impact their poverty reduction activities. With the Internet gatekeepers of the development community meeting together, an array of speakers began to reveal startling observations.

Among the speakers was Nicole Frost. She said, "The Bank is a great producer of content, but remains slow to respond to external forces."[66] My ears pricked up. "The Bank is more transparent than it had once been, but less transparent than it should be," she admitted.

Christopher Strebel of UNESCO said, "International organizations are lethargic with regards to the Internet. They need to be more entrepreneurial and less afraid of failure."[67] A third speaker discussed a new website that was not affiliated with the Bank, and had monitored the institution's recent presidential selection-process. He characterized its "democratization of the Internet as original."[68] He might have tailored his speech slightly had he been aware that B-SPAN had been empowering audiences for five years by allowing them to participate in internal Bank discussions and events.

As the session broke for lunch, I observed something else. Guests were encouraged to join "table talks" conference organizers had set up on a variety of subjects. Tables devoted to technological applications were packed. The table for Strategic Collaboration with Media Outlets was conspicuously empty.

The conference reconvened for its keynote speaker, Internet expert Gerry McGovern.[69] "Whenever you change the way you communicate, you change the way people interact," he began. It was the concept Wheeler and I had tried for a decade to get the Bank to embrace.

"The Bank," he noted, "uses the Internet reactively to state what it has accomplished. Content, however, should affect change rather than react to it. The problem is international organizations view their websites as projects when they should be thought of as processes. Long-term thinking and planning is what is needed. Like other international organizations, the Bank has viewed the Internet as a technology."

McGovern then went on to discuss how technology had driven the computer revolution for the previous thirty years. "In the next phase of the computer revolution, information and how it is used will navigate the future," he suggested.

Prior to the conference, McGovern had asked attendees to fill out a survey on what they saw as priorities for administering their websites. Now he revealed the results. Their top concern was addressing managerial interest on quality control or in the parlance of laymen: Perfect information. The survey further suggested international organizations did not feel compelled to educate audiences about their work. He summarized how this viewpoint played out: "We are important organizations responsible for doing worthwhile things, and we are the only source of this service; so we don't need to educate our constituencies." This was the standard thinking, he said.

He noted only 12% of survey respondents thought engaging audiences was important. "The Internet," McGovern reminded the audience, "is vast. Millions of websites compete for attention. Marketing therefore is critical to getting Internet surfers to focus on a provider's website. Only 4% of the survey participants think marketing is an important component of their work. There is a gap in your strategy."

There was another speaker of particular interest to me. Gerry Rice, EXT's communications director, would address the conferees during the final afternoon session.[70] I waited with great anticipation.

"The Bank's website," Rice began, "has become its main communications tool for sending messages and receiving feedback. As the Bank's chief communicator, I believe the Internet has allowed the organization to reach audiences it had neglected in the past. In my opinion, it provides the Bank with an opportunity to build relationships beyond the selling of messages."

Rice then made a startling comment: "The Bank's senior management does not understand the Internet. Nor do they understand how important a tool it is for communication with our stakeholders."

I had observed these tendencies for the last decade and had little doubt about the veracity of Rice's assertion. Still, I was shocked he had said so in public. To illustrate his point, he noted page requests and email newsletter subscriptions were rising markedly. He called them "growth industries," but added traffic data had not been enough to make the case. Management said its support needed to be tied to specific impacts in the field. To demonstrate this notion further, Rice discussed examples of how information on the Bank's website led to favorable media coverage on several projects. Clearly unspoken was another understanding: The Internet was seen by key Bank officials as a propaganda tool rather than an opportunity to create real change to impact poverty.

"If the Bank wants to be seen as a 'knowledge bank,' then the Internet will be the key," Rice continued. "Senior management says the right things about communications, but doesn't provide necessary funding because of competing priorities."

He thought this would continue and believed the Bank's muted interest for communications was due to its monopoly on development in many countries. "As a result," Rice acknowledged, "a culture of arrogance has evolved. We believe, 'We do good things, so why do we need to explain ourselves.'" It mirrored McGovern's contention.

Rice continued: "The penalty for failing to take communications seriously is critics will define the Bank rather than vice versa. But the Internet provides an opportunity to rebalance things. The environment in the Bank is less hierarchical than it was a decade ago, but timidity and fear to embrace change remain." Rice shifted his discussion to address proposals he had made to the Bank's board to improve its website. "If it fails, then I am fearful for the future," he concluded.

Within a few months, Rice announced his retirement from the Bank.

5

Intelligence continued to filter back to me. Al-Ghwell thought Weber-Fahr was still pursuing ISG. Sources in WBI said the Quality Assurance Group (QAG), an internal Bank unit that assessed the quality and effectiveness of institutional activities, had produced a scathing report about WBI. Departmental staff thought it was perhaps the toughest one QAG had ever issued.

Montenegro said WBI had finally approved a new charge-back mechanism. Weber-Fahr now had Panajyan focused almost exclusively on soliciting payments of outstanding arrears. He added something else. "Weber-Fahr still intends to move forward on editing videos, but the scarcity of funds has stunted her ambitions. And, this is interesting. WBI is reevaluating whether B-SPAN is an appropriate platform for its learning and training videos." Montenegro sounded disillusioned and seemed perplexed. "WBI talks about knowledge sharing," he finally said, "but knowledge sharing is not its priority."

Repeated forays by Leonard to see Van Pulley had failed.[71] Leonard was now counseling patience. A reevaluation was needed. Patience was not a virtue if the Bank's managing director had pressured Van Pulley to refrain from reorganizing his department and Van Pulley had stymied Leonard's initiative. The fiscal year was steadily marching to a conclusion. If July began without something in place, a whole year would transpire before the puzzle could be reconfigured. By then, all the key players would have accepted the comfort of the status quo. I feared GSD's indecisiveness would leave B-SPAN permanently frozen in WBI's glacier.

I needed an alternative to GSD. Resuming negotiations with ISG was risky. If the rumors about them and Weber-Fahr were true, my covert operation would quickly be exposed.

The two May conferences, however, offered a new perspective. Nicole Frost had long been an ally. She had put pivotal events with Sachs and de Soto on the Bank's home page and her boss, Gerry Rice, had just spoken about the importance of the Internet for the Bank's future. It would reverse our previous stance on EXT, but if the right people were positioned to protect the transparency model, I could live with the inconsistency of housing B-SPAN within the Bank's public relations arm. I decided to float the notion to Wheeler.

"Weber-Fahr has no assets to expand her agenda, but I think you're right that Kingsberry might be too close to the play," he began. "The perils of tying B-SPAN to EXT are relative. Frost's been in sync with our work in the past, and having the service in her shop would be a natural extension of her work program. There's also an additional benefit to seeing if she's interested. It would flush out GSD's intentions. Bureaucrats move slowly, but are compelled to be quick if a competitor comes into view. Your instincts are sound. Make the case."

The next week, the Bank hosted a farewell party for Wolfensohn.[72] In a video produced by EXT, a range of speakers from Bill Clinton and Al Gore to Kofi Annan and rock star Bono offered congratulations and best wishes. Various Bank dignitaries also offered their perspectives. Leautier said, "Wolfensohn taught me how my decisions have an immense impact on the world's poor." I couldn't have agreed more. She also talked about the meaning of leadership, but neglected to mention an integral component was loyalty.

The gathering gave me another opportunity to glean morsels of information from relevant players in B-SPAN's episodic journey. Paulette Wilmott, a former supervisor in GSD, provided perspective on Van Pulley.[73] "He is interested in reforming the department and making it less hierarchical," she said. "But he is also constrained by budget reductions and is looking closely at outsourcing some services. There has been ongoing talk about consolidations between ISG and GSD when Muhsin departs in October. I think Van Pulley is ambitious enough to try to acquire ISG's webcasting activities."

I found Leonard a short time later.[74] He said his supervisor Carl Wessmann wanted to move quickly on B-SPAN. They were going to try once more to meet with Van Pulley. Suddenly GSD seemed promising again.

I pursued a meeting with Frost and in late May we sat down.[75]

I already had doubts the proposal would interest her, for she had spoken pessimistically about the Bank's board approving funding for Rice's core objective to build alternative language sites.[76] Frankly, how would I be able to negotiate approval of an entirely new funding initiative? Nevertheless, there were only a few bullets left in my chamber, and little time to make a deal. I aimed point blank and fired.

I began with an overlay of the environment. There was Rice's address at the Web4Dev conference on the need for the Bank to invest in communications. There was Jo Ritzen's speech the month before providing a parallel perspective.

"If the Bank does not invest in selling its initiatives, then it risks not being able to influence those stakeholders who will be implementing them," I said. "I believe the Web4Dev conference also missed something. Participants focused exclusively on written content and neglected rich media. I think in five years the role of video and audio will be a much larger component of how websites communicate. The Bank does not want to be behind the curve again."

Frost queried me. "What makes you think this way?" I provided her with Forum One's analysis. "B-SPAN received almost two percent of all the Bank's website visitors last year. It did so without adequate staff and funding. It required viewers to download special software. It required them to invest time watching streaming video via a medium that consumers typically accessed for only moments. Think what B-SPAN could achieve with appropriate support."

I moved right to the sale. "WBI is running B-SPAN into the ground. Traffic has plunged to 60% of what it was a year ago. Eighty percent of its clients have abandoned the service. It has become a sanctuary for the Bank's rich and elite, which by the way is an irony for an institution invented to serve the disenfranchised. Hundreds have been left out, but they want back in. The market for them still exists."

Frost stopped me. "What do you want?" she asked.

"I want you to take it over," I replied. "It can produce volumes of alternative language content for Rice and generate revenue for EXT." The conversation paused as she absorbed what I had said.

Finally, she spoke. "If I make the case to Rice and Ian Golden (EXT's vice president), then I need a proposal with a 50%, and preferably a 70%, cost recovery. I need data on costs, clients, traffic, countries accessed, EXT's usage, how EXT's video team managed by Carl Hanlon would benefit, as well as examples of what the world would look like if B-SPAN didn't exist."

"Consider it done," I said. As our conversation closed, she said there was one other thing. Sunetra Puri of WBI had asked her to meet. Frost thought she wanted to talk about moving B-SPAN.

The strange juxtaposition of the Bank speaking with two tongues grew in volume. On the eve of Wolfensohn's departure from the institution, he was interviewed by PBS journalist Charlie Rose.[77] Rose asked for his opinion on the greatest challenge the development community faced as it pursued the MDGs.

Wolfensohn noted, "Rich nations have yet to fulfill their signed commitments in Monterrey. Poor nations have pledged to improve their governance and in my opinion the developing nations have made substantial progress. I have made fighting corruption a core activity of the Bank's agenda during my tenure. The key to fighting corruption is promoting transparency in developing countries. Transparency reduces opportunities for corruption. The reduction of corruption leads to good governance. Good governance leads to development. Transparency is the key."

The interview ended. I turned off the TV. If transparency was the key to good governance outside the institution, I wondered why it wasn't being practiced inside the Bank.

With music from Wolfensohn's farewell dinner wafting upwards from the floor below me, I drafted another proposal to lead the Bank towards the transparency it asked of others. Most of what Frost wanted was easily assembled. The key element would be whether I could fulfill her requirement that B-SPAN recover most of EXT's costs.

I ran the numbers. I didn't see it. Then I ran them again and then again. And, then I saw the way. When I managed B-SPAN, we had developed relationships with 59 Bank teams from 16 major networks and regions.[78] I re-engineered the sliding scale of packages. Each vice presidency could evaluate its own needs and choose a package of events suitable for its yearly dissemination strategies. Each package would provide $8,000 or $9,000 in revenue, a miniscule amount in their department's multi-million-dollar budgets.

If I could recreate these annual partnerships, I could approach full cost recovery in the first year. If I could finesse it with the inclusion of external content providers, I could exceed full cost recovery, and potentially even reduce internal fees. For the moment, I would remain silent about external content. The objective now was to make a sale to Frost.[79]

In early June, I had another chance encounter with Montenegro. With Sheram gone, Stewart back at the Studio Unit and Weber-Fahr about to go on maternity leave, B-SPAN was solely under Panajyan's command. Panajyan continued to spend the bulk of her time collecting old debts.

GDLN's new interest, Montenegro said, was getting viewers to download rather than stream files. I presumed this would allow GDLN to delete B-SPAN's archives since clients and viewers would be able to store them as they wished. Nothing had changed within GDLN. Their obsession remained on the process of production. With the decentralization of GDLN's business teams to the Bank regions soon completed, Weber-Fahr's anchor would be mostly logistical and administrative. I wondered what would happen to her.

Montenegro thought she was far too ambitious to be satisfied running a skeleton crew. "She's hoping the regions fare poorly under the new arrangement so she can swoop down to regain control," he said.

For two weeks I waited for Frost.[80] The fiscal year was ending and with it my hopes to engineer a deal. Instead of letting the clock run out, I contacted her. She had not read my proposal. Her priority was getting funding for alternative language websites.

"Taking B-SPAN in is not something I am going to fight for now," she said. "Perhaps (Carl) Hanlon might. I suggest he be brought into the discussion." I felt a lock turning. We set a date and it was promptly cancelled as Hanlon left town on family business. I heard the click.

I continued digging for clues about WBI's intentions. Johnson revealed QAG's condemnation of WBI would have little impact, as budgets had been set for the new fiscal year, and major strategic decisions would be deferred until Paul Wolfowitz, the Bank's new president, settled in. Johnson noted Panajyan had stopped working on B-SPAN because she had run out of days to bill her time.

His comment made me pause. Perhaps, after all, Weber-Fahr had not given her an ETC when she arrived, but employed her as an STC for the balance of the fiscal year. In any event, I surmised, Panajyan's ETC would begin with the new fiscal year. Therefore, WBI's plan was to hold B-SPAN through FY06. "Frannie just likes it," Johnson said. In May, however, only 10 events were covered and less than 15,000 visitors logged on.[81]

My conversations with Johnson and Montenegro led to a further revision in my thinking. Even if it was financed meagerly, Leautier enjoyed having the B-SPAN feather in her cap. Importantly, GDLN's decentralization of its business units into the regions meant its anchor was rapidly becoming marginalized. It was taking on the functions of an administrative processing center. Weber-Fahr's fiefdom was evaporating.

It also meant the MM Unit would gain importance within her organization. She would need to keep it intact and running smoothly. In a strange twist of irony, with less power for her to wield, B-SPAN might become increasingly valuable to a manager who had previously disdained it. If she actually took an interest in managing it, it could become her personal propaganda tool until she abandoned GDLN for a higher calling. It also suggested she would fight attempts by others to assume its administration.

Still, volume was down and the service remained a financial drain on the department. In theory, it was a losing proposition the way it was being administrated, but that could change. Despite fighting long and hard against a revenue generation model, Leautier or Weber-Fahr could switch gears at any time. Adopting my proposal would be no admission of failure. Such things do not exist in bureaucracies. It would be simply announced as a new strategy the vice president and senior management had designed. I hoped WBI would seek to muddle through with a minimum of effort. My slim chance of moving B-SPAN somewhere or creating a second system depended on how poorly WBI administered the service.

My proposals were not going anywhere. Though Leonard remained enthusiastic, he had not gained an audience with Van Pulley, nor expected to until the new fiscal year. Frost, despite receiving a proposal that mapped almost full cost recovery, remained focused on spending her capital elsewhere for the time being.

The enormous amount of turns the B-SPAN story had already taken took yet another twist. One day I saw Kingsberry. He was advertising for staff to help him implement his newly designed Data Asset Management (DAM) system. I used it as an excuse to meet. There are things you know and there are things you don't know, I decided. Often, one finds speculation is the basis for decision-making. It was time for my speculation regarding ISG to end. I needed to find out if rumors about a relationship between him and WBI were true. If not, Kingsberry might be able to present me with a final opportunity to rescue the transparency experiment.

The next day I stopped by his office. He said our conversation in December remained vivid, and he was serious about exploring how to bring B-SPAN into his domain. I asked him what had resulted from our first conversation. Kingsberry said he discussed the transparency model with his boss, Le Anh Vu. Vu was also interested, but pressing issues had waylaid further discussions throughout the spring. His sense was B-SPAN wasn't doing much anymore; and if it was an institution-wide service, then an institution-wide department should be running it.

Was ISG talking to WBI? Kingsberry said, "No. But, I'm leery of politics and I know that in negotiating with WBI there will be some. Before the politics can be addressed, however, I need to see if there is a business model that will work. I do not think ISG would take B-SPAN if it could not pay its way." I said it could, and I had a plan. We discussed the outlines of my concept. He wanted a proposal before meeting again.

I caucused with Wheeler to game scenarios and identify flash points.[82] The proposal had to remain hidden from WBI, but it couldn't be kept from GSD. They were the lynchpin for a deal. Somehow, they must be convinced or pressured to renegotiate their camera rates for the new service.

I was also worried about "the politics" which frightened Kingsberry. B-SPAN was a flower in Leautier's lapel. She wasn't putting much money into it, but it wasn't costing her much either. WBI, I concluded, despite its abysmal management and rumors to the contrary, would not jettison the service. Wheeler thought I was right. We decided to flip our approach back to launching an entirely independent service.[83]

I met Kingsberry again in late June. We talked in circles for a while until I said the politics might be too difficult to overcome. He agreed. "It might be best to launch an entirely new service based on establishing partnerships," I suggested. He agreed again. "It would be a natural evolution of the DAM system," he said. His team already did encoding, streaming, archiving, website maintenance and video editing. He suggested building a prototype, but he wanted to do it covertly to show his supervisors it would work before scaling up.

I began, yet again, drafting a proposal. I broke down the components of the DAM system to find an entry point for a new webcasting service.

Kingsberry's system provided everything B-SPAN did except one thing: They provided editing services along with encoding and streaming. Therefore, by caveat, they already processed unedited videos. It was an important distinction, since as a consequence no one in WBI could accuse them of launching a new service. All ISG needed to do differently was offer Bank clients a website to house their unedited products. Since it was already in the business of creating and maintaining Bank websites, it could hardly be accused of deviating from its mandate if it now maintained its own website.

The note to Kingsberry painted a clear picture of the opportunity before him.[84] It built upon lessons generated from WBI's experience with B-SPAN. The first: Given an appropriate pricing mechanism, there was an enormous market inside the Bank for a transparent webcasting service. The second lesson: Clients were highly sensitive to pricing elasticity. WBI's pricing policy for B-SPAN failed to provide clients with incentives for strategic planning. The result was the number of clients diminished and audiences declined. ISG, I proposed, had an opportunity to capture the market WBI alienated, if it shied away from a fee-based service and offered a subscription-based model.

The focal point remained finding a pricing mechanism that would attract buyers. In theory, B-SPAN's pricing reflected real costs. A new service had to do better, and substantially so if it was going to win converts.

How could GSD be persuaded? There were a couple of arguments to be made. One, ISG, unlike WBI, was a unit with an institution-wide mandate. If GSD shunned an ISG proposal that was seen as moving the Bank's mission forward, it would put GSD in an uncomfortable position. Second, and more pertinent, an appropriately run service by ISG would increase GSD's business. The proposal put forth a sliding range of subscription prices from $250 to $500. Even in a worst-case scenario, this pricing would undercut B-SPAN's by a sizeable margin. My job would be to convince buyers they would receive the same quality service for considerably less money. If ISG accepted, WBI would be out of the webcasting business in a few months.

The proposal went forward to Kingsberry at the end of June. But there was no response.

I was offered full-time employment outside the Bank, and began a new job in July.

I decided to reach out to Kingsberry again, and he agreed to meet; but on the appointed day, he could not be found. I persisted and tracked him down again. He agreed to meet but again on the appointed day, he was nowhere to be found. He did not return calls. Like Leonard and Frost before him, he walked away from the table despite having a map to institutional riches placed in his hand. My voyage had ended.

One day I saw Al-Ghwell. "Weber-Fahr," he said, "wants to dump B-SPAN but won't because the outcry will be too dangerous for her." He was the biggest loser, he suggested. Of 72 events the InfoShop hosted the previous year, he had only been able to webcast 21.

As my service in the Bank officially ended, I took one last look at B-SPAN. It was featuring an awards ceremony with the new Bank president, Paul Wolfowitz.[85] B-SPAN had become a venue for ceremonies and training courses just as Tolstopiatenko, Laporte, Weber-Fahr and Sheram had always wanted it to be. Whatever unedited content it presented was cover for the propaganda its bureaucracy needed to disseminate. In B-SPAN,. they recognized a valuable medium of dissemination. That was all.

In June 2005, my last month of Bank employment, B-SPAN's page requests declined to 126,000.[86] It was less than one-third of the level to which I had lifted the service just twelve months earlier. It plummeted to a level of activity it had not seen in years. In fact, I had said to Wheeler months before, I did not think it possible B-SPAN could ever dip below 150,000. Yet it had.

PART VIII

become the change you wish to seek: an overview and analysis of the bank's culture

1

As one walks into the World Bank's headquarters, one's eye climbs naturally up the soaring columns of glass, steel and shafts of light that house its atrium. A blue day will bathe the onlooker in a heavenly glow. This lofty view is grounded with a visionary message at the foot of the entrance. It is the Bank's mission statement: "Our dream is a world free of poverty." Dreams put into action, however, take many small steps and twists on the road to reality.

For some Bank staff, poverty is a reality. They started life impoverished and struggled through considerable odds to overcome it, if indeed one ever really overcomes it. They often have families in distant lands that remain poor, and their Bank incomes sometimes serve as a lifeline for relatives left behind.

For other Bank staff, poverty is an abstraction. They come from lives of privilege and have never been hungry. They have gone to the best universities. They have enjoyed the best medical care. They have never lived in a village with people who live on less than a dollar a day. They shuttle between first-class airplane seats and five-star hotels.

Mahatma Gandhi said, "Poverty is the worst form of violence." The age of abstraction ended on September 11, 2001 when planes and buildings and people began falling from the sky. Each day fresh obituaries appeared of people disintegrating in the carnage. Before they were murdered, they had been our neighbors, co-workers, fellow worshipers and parents raising their children with ours.

It became apparent to many at the Bank that the institution had a moral obligation to mitigate the causes leading to September 11. I, too, had a moral obligation. It was to build a medium where those who needed access to information about development could interact openly and transparently with those who had access to information. Lives were on the line. If I failed, I would not fail for myself only.

Former U.S. Treasury Secretary Lawrence Summers once suggested development banks in the post-Cold War world would play a role similar to those of security organizations in the era following World War II.[1] Bank President James Wolfensohn cited the 2001 terrorist attacks as the event that demonstrated there were no walls between rich and poor.[2]

By then, David Wheeler and I had spent two years building a communication system designed to bring both ends of the spectrum into a virtual room. In the days that followed 9/11, the two of us came to the realization that the importance of B-SPAN's mission was greater than ever. It had to succeed in building bridges rather than in reinforcing the walls. We believed people would increasingly rely on the Bank in the years to come to accomplish its mission of creating a world free of poverty. But we wondered if the Bank was up to this enormous task.

It is worthwhile to consider the creation of B-SPAN holistically. Long before Islamic extremists arrived in vengeance, institutions such as the Bank were under siege. Fault lines decoupled by the Cold War's dissolution and the Internet's evolution unleashed a growing recognition of disparities between rich and poor. Discord focused on institutions serving as conduits between the two worlds.

The Bank along with a handful of other international organizations became Ground Zero for the storm. By the mid-1990s, an international coalition of NGOs called "50 Years is Enough" was chanting outside its front door. The movement grew increasingly radical, and by 1999 exploded into violence during the World Trade

Organization's meeting in Seattle. In a scene reminiscent of the Vietnam War era, protestors and police clashed in the streets. There was open speculation that violence would target the Bank and IMF during their spring meetings in 2000. In fact, there were several incidents of protestors endangering Bank staff that year.[3]

Wheeler and I saw B-SPAN as a vehicle to help alleviate tensions between the institution and its critics. At its heart, B-SPAN was a journalistic endeavor to provide access to the latest theories, research and activities on development. This would allow stakeholders and shareholders to understand issues or react to events shaping the world. It was not clear that the Bank wanted a transparent broadcasting system. We knew it would frighten many. Yet the need was obvious.

Marshall McLuhan coined the famous aphorism "the medium is the message." So it was with B-SPAN. Though its objective was seductively difficult, its concept was simple: Get honest information into the hands of people who wanted and needed it, and let them exchange ideas with one another and take action. It was about creating opportunities for people, so they could create their own opportunities.

During the three years its adversaries sought to reconfigure the transparency initiative to fit their personal ambitions, the model remained uncommonly pliant. That was because it was succinct, clear and precise. B-SPAN personified and implemented two important lessons learned from the Wheeler team's research on industrial pollution regulation and abatement. First, information that was public, accurate and transparently obtained could change people's behavior. Second, because information could be shared via the Internet, it provided extraordinary opportunities to people who did not have access to it previously. Subsequently, it could help them think anew about the challenges they faced.

That B-SPAN failed to fully reach its potential was both a surprise and predictable. A surprise because in some circles the model had enormous appeal, and paralleled the stated aim of the institution. Predictable because it was an entrepreneurial venture in an environment anesthetized against innovation. Organizations, after all, are human inventions, and as such are imperfect. For every person who acts to extend the boundaries of the status quo, a thousand will blindly reinforce it. It is a paradox of life that, given free will, most people conform.

In a sense, B-SPAN was appealing and distasteful to many within the institution for the same reason. It empowered event organizers with an exciting new way to communicate and build relationships with stakeholders. It connected staff in countries around the world with events and exchanges of information in Washington. It gave stakeholders a seat at the table. Before the inauguration of B-SPAN, all these groups had felt less connected with each other. Suddenly, a tool existed that could immediately and intimately link them together. B-SPAN escaped traditional rules of communication. It released control of information to the public. It empowered content providers and stakeholders rather than the Bank's management, because all had equal access to the new medium. B-SPAN built a bridge between the Bank and the rest of the world.

Its supporters inside the Bank saw additional and fundamental benefits to the transparency model as well. B-SPAN served as a counterpoint to the monolithic society that had engendered the public's wrath. Our model humanized the Bank with *imperfect* and uncensored information. It showed the organization debating key questions and struggling to find solutions just as its stakeholders did. Moreover, for most content providers, perfect information took too long to create, was often out of date by the time it could be made available, and would not stay current long.

The same qualities that appealed to some threatened others. Information is power, and the Bank is an organization very much guided by the principles of power. B-SPAN was giving information away; and to some, that meant it was diluting their authority.

There is also a strong sense within the Bank that its best face must be all the public should see. Anything less might suggest the Bank was not knowledgeable, capable or in control of everything within its domain. Therefore, only perfect information should be disseminated, and anything that does not make this grade is viewed as unsatisfactory. A medium that communicates transparently, and by caveat may provide unflattering information to the public, would be viewed with extreme suspicion. More likely, it would be an anathema.

Then, of course, the Bank is an institution filled with elites. Many have advanced degrees from the most prestigious universities in the world. Many have been cocooned in academia for years. A percentage act as if chosen to administer the world; so there is a natural intellectual disconnect about having a dialogue with those they have been groomed to govern. To have information that was not perfect, that was being released everywhere, and that was moving in reverberating directions—was a startling and unsettling experience.

At its most fundamental level, the transparency initiative was an experiment designed by Bank researchers. The subject was our own organization. In building a webcasting station, we wanted to see whether the culture of a bureaucracy—instinctively conservative, elitist and resistant to change—could be compelled to adopt a communication medium that was open, honest and transparent. We wanted to learn whether such a model would be accepted, rejected or homogenized as a propaganda tool. We wanted to identify the point at which the organization was willing to give up control over the flow of information.

In the end, B-SPAN was a voyage to find where those borders at the Bank intersected.

2

Long before the apocalyptic events of 2001, Wheeler and I believed that for the Bank to reach its potential, it was necessary to change the culture. We were not reactionaries, however. We were already immersed in compelling research, and what we learned saved lives. We could have been satisfied with that alone. Yet we continued to witness endemic structural defects in the bureaucracy's culture that prevented the Bank from reaching its potential.

Through a disparate set of unlikely circumstances, we came to realize it would be possible to create a new paradigm. By changing how people communicated, we believed we could change how they did business. B-SPAN became the vehicle.

But what is the culture of the Bank? It is not like Fortune 500 companies, small businesses or government agencies that are often highly homogenous. Rather, it is multi-cultural with employees from almost every country on the globe. Moreover, some from the same country have grown up in sub-cultures entirely different from each other. In such an environment, different people will look at the same thing and come to opposite conclusions. Our challenge was not to change one culture, but to change hundreds of cultures that had morphed into one uniquely its own.

After several years of watching our struggle to increase institutional transparency, Wheeler suggested this: The key cultural clash centered upon different perceptions North Americans and Europeans had toward public information and knowledge sharing.

The Americans—Wheeler, Shaman, de Nevers, Witzel, Means, Bowden, Johnson, Lawrence Macdonald and Ron Kim—saw public information via transparency as an opportunity to move the institution, and ultimately its stakeholders, toward accountability and enlightenment.

The Europeans—Tolstopiatenko, Laporte and Weber-Fahr—viewed information as a commodity to be managed and manipulated. By upbringing and instinct, they were leery about transparency as a methodology for transferring information. They believed information needed to be perfect, and therefore embraced the crafting of it. They also sensed messages generated by B-SPAN's model might compromise them within an organization highly conscious and concerned about image-making. So, while the Europeans smiled in public, they wielded knives behind closed doors.

In his study *Cultures and Organizations*, Geert Hofstede, a professor emeritus at Maastricht University, noted some cultures emphasize teamwork while others embrace individualism.[4] His research suggested Europeans were process-oriented while Americans were results-oriented.[5] He found Americans were employee-oriented while Europeans were job-oriented. Hofstede noted Europeans instinctively embraced closed systems with tight controls, while Americans gravitated toward open systems with loose controls.[6]

Within the fishbowl of the B-SPAN saga, one sees all these dynamics at play. Hofstede believed Germans valued standardization of skills, the French valued standardization of processes, and Americans valued standardization of outputs.[7] If one might think of a long factory line as an analogy for B-SPAN, different players valued different sections of the conveyer belt.

The multi-cultural Bank has a plethora of personalities, each with a different perception of the institution. Senior management has one view of what is important and how the organization should act. Economists, financiers, engineers, environmental auditors, transport specialists, urban planners, external affairs, unit managers, administrative staff and country-based staff have other opinions. Within the parameters of their distinct responsibilities, no group sees the same issue the same way. The result is an institution that often acts in conflicting ways, and thereby creates a hypocritical environment on a daily basis.

In 2005, the Bank's Staff Association (SA) addressed the issue of institutionalized hypocrisy.[8] It wrote, "One Bank-watcher, Robert Wade of the London School of Economics, points out that the necessity for a good image forces the Bank into what he calls 'the art of organized hypocrisy.' The hypocrisy comes about as the Bank tries to 'control its external environment and manage contradictory demands being made by states, NGOs and firms.' Wade defines the Bank as an 'action-cum-political organization' that produces both action/services and talk. Its customers and clients 'value primarily its goods and services' (in other words, its operations) while 'other entities—its spectators and watchdogs—value primarily its talk … the more disconnect between talk and actions, the more likely the organization's critics will, rightly, accuse it of hypocrisy. The disconnect is real … the organization must forcefully deny the charge and reassert that it does indeed have a rational alignment of mission, talk, decisions and action under the direction of senior management.'"[9]

The Staff Association continued by noting, "Wade goes on to say 'an action-cum-political organization faced with an external environment full of conflicting demands, many of them hostile, has an array of ways to maneuver. The organization can (1) increase the density of declarations and policies designed to satisfy and pacify spectators and watchdogs, and increase its promises to bring its actions into line with the policies, while not making the corresponding resource allocations; (2) reform its organizational structure to make it look more consistent with the model of a 'rational' organization, while de-coupling itself internally so as to lower the noticeability of its actions for customers in the eyes of the spectators and watchdogs; and (3) flatter the feedback on its actions so as to make the results of the actions—when the future becomes the present—look more consistent with its talk. These are some of the tactics of the statecraft of organized hypocrisy."

The Staff Association suggested there were a number of maneuvers by the Bank to institutionalize organized hypocrisy during the 1990s. It founded External Affairs and Internal Communications so as to increase the volume of declarations. It created an Inspection Panel to enhance the perception the Bank followed its own rules in operations. It created safeguard requirements for projects to mollify external critics concerned about the environment and population relocation (though it neglected to accompany it with adequate funding). And, it marketed the organization as a "knowledge bank" since knowledge was seen as being politically neutral.

During WBI's Knowledge Sharing Conference in June 2004, Bruno Laporte said, "Knowledge sharing is collecting and connecting. Collecting is about harvesting information and technology, and connecting is making sure people are talking to each other. And, the emphasis should be on connecting … increasingly, the Bank's role is to be a catalyst for development ideas, but not to be in the driver's seat. If we help bring knowledge to others, we will work together to find development solutions."[10] Yet the very next day, Laporte was able to formally divest himself of all responsibility for B-SPAN.

In the 2005 Global Communications Forum, EXT's Vice President Ian Goldin said, "Development is about the evolution of ideas. The greatest thing communicators can do is to find ways to make the ideas accessible. Our clients' ability to access and understand these ideas will do much to advance development."[11] A month later, EXT declined an opportunity to absorb B-SPAN into its work program.

"Rhetoric," as I told Wheeler during our odyssey, "is the reality."

3

B-SPAN was a virus that infected an organism called the World Bank. As the virus developed, like all organisms do, the institution began developing anti-bodies to preserve the status quo of its culture. WBI was the bureaucracy's antibiotic. While fate hung in the balance for five years, B-SPAN served as the fault line between two worlds within the organization and two histories that were yet to be written.

If the transparency model succeeded, it would become a unique global communications system allowing the Bank to promulgate uninhibited dialogues between thousands of economists, academics, policy makers, regulators, researchers and civil society stakeholders. The institution would potentially be transformed into a highly transparent and accountable partner with its stakeholders in an ongoing exchange of information, ideas and experiences.

On the other hand, if the bureaucracy remolded B-SPAN to fit a preordained concept of propaganda as communications, the existing relationships between the Bank and its stakeholders would be reinforced. The bureaucracy would have preserved the institution's autonomous practices of working behind closed doors. In life, most things are shades of gray. Indeed, a look at B-SPAN in 2007 revealed a mixture of objectives achieved by both sides. The outcome of this larger struggle, however, was black and white.

Our experiment demonstrated a key principle for getting things done in bureaucracies: It is better to ask for forgiveness than permission. For two years, out of view from the formal establishment, Wheeler and I remained under the radar screen, quietly analyzing scenarios, testing applications, and building institutional arrangements. The result was a remarkable system that worked.

A transparent webcasting station was, however, a double-edged sword. To reach its potential, it would inevitably have to appear on the radar screen. There was no other way. Once visible, it would be vulnerable to the bureaucracy's formal authority. As it became more prominent, the more likely it would attract attention from powerful players with vested interests in the status quo.

There seems to be an inverse curve inherent in bureaucracies: As fiefdoms grow, their owners' psyches become less tolerant of things that don't support the status quo. Here a powerful irony is revealed. To build a transparent medium of communications inside the Bank, it was necessary for us to operate in a clandestine manner.

Wheeler's model for research was a merger of theory and application. It synthesized hypotheses implemented on the ground with data gathered from results. The means for protecting B-SPAN resided in principles derived from our research on industrial pollution that analyzed environmental behavior of facilities from world-class to worst-case. The public information disclosure campaigns in Indonesia and the Philippines unveiled the impact of informal regulatory initiatives on firms concerned about their reputation. Formal authority relies on regulations and indicators. Informal authority relies on reputation and stakeholder influence.

B-SPAN had external and internal stakeholders. Support from external stakeholders could be measured anecdotally and by website traffic. Their understanding of the power struggle regarding the transparency initiative, however, was non-existent; so their influence was marginalized. For the experiment to succeed, we turned to the informal influence of internal stakeholders. During the difficult immersion into WBI, informal stakeholders were used to neutralize the formal authority of B-SPAN's antagonists. The behavior of WBI bureaucrats who supervised B-SPAN was mitigated by a concern for how informal stakeholders might compromise their reputations within the formal structure of WBI and the entire Bank.

Based on our experiences in East Asia and WBI, one might theorize informal mechanisms may be as powerful as formal tools of control. Formal tools, however, have certain advantages. They tend to be timeless. They form the infrastructure of an organization; so they will exist prior, during and after implementation of informal applications.

Additionally, informal mechanisms, by nature, will change over time. This was certainly true in our experiences. As key regulators in Indonesia and the Philippines left their agencies, public information activities stalled or disappeared.

In the case of B-SPAN, important stakeholders that protected the transparency model during its infancy were neutralized over time. Wheeler never had full control over appropriations, and ultimately had to cede authority to WBI bureaucrats. De Nevers changed positions within WBI, and as she focused on her new responsibilities, she became inversely less responsive to demands B-SPAN placed on her loyalty.

Leautier displayed characteristics of both an informal and formal stakeholder. She had formal authority for administering the program; but during B-SPAN's turbulent entrance into her department, she remained conspicuously removed from participation. Yet she often acted as a cheerleader from afar, providing Wheeler and me enough ammunition to keep opponents off balance. Ultimately, like de Nevers, other pressing matters captured her attention. As she became less cognizant of substantive issues surrounding B-SPAN's evolution, she became more reliant upon receiving information from vested sources: Her mid-level managers.

As the ability of informal stakeholders to protect B-SPAN waned, bureaucrats wedded to the hierarchical culture of the institution, and emboldened by their formal regulatory authority, were able to assert their influence.

To affect change in a bureaucracy, one must find a champion who is seen by others as powerful or as a rising star. A champion will protect a new initiative through the dangerous shoals and eddies of an organization. Unfortunately, Wheeler and I picked the wrong champions, but fate had been the deciding factor. We had sought a profound change in a conservative organization. Such changes take years and perhaps decades.

The Bank's culture is one that disdains selectivity and embraces the notion it must do many things well. As a result, staff is continually addressing new challenges, engineering temporary fixes, and moving on to the next problem. For Leautier and de Nevers, B-SPAN served as a passing interest. Their attention drifted far sooner than what was necessary for our purposes.

With Leautier as the key stakeholder, her public recognition of B-SPAN kept Laporte, Tolstopiatenko and even Weber-Fahr from moving more aggressively to eliminate the system or terminate its staff. Wheeler and I translated the vice president's lavish praise as support for how the system had been built and how it operated. She provided ample evidence to justify the perception.

In 2002, when two Bank economists asked us to edit video, the vice president codified her support of B-SPAN's policy to not edit.[12] At that point, the transparency principle that I was responsible for administering became her mandate. However, Leautier's unsolicited public compliments of B-SPAN became so common, colleagues joked I must have been sending her kickbacks. Her comments reinforced our perception she supported B-SPAN's objectives.

For three years I was in the uncomfortable position of protecting Leautier's principles against actions by her own managers—a case study of institutional hypocrisy. Leautier never indicated that her viewpoint of the transparency model had degenerated until after the ETC panel process. Had we sensed this earlier, Wheeler and I would have moved with alacrity to shore up support. Even during my pivotal meeting with her in February 2004, Leautier could have suggested she wanted to expand, change or modify the model. She only expressed her ongoing support.[13]

When the influence of B-SPAN's internal supporters dissolved, little foundation remained for the informal model to compete with the traditional mechanisms of formal authority. We never underestimated the intentions, determination or codified authority of WBI's bureaucrats to mitigate and undermine B-SPAN. It was clear from the outset these antagonists would either destroy the transparency model outright or redesign it to fit their parochial ambitions.

In hindsight, we did overestimate the loyalty of our benefactors. Until the very end, we acted with the understanding they valued in practice, not just principle, the vision we collectively shared. And, it wasn't until the end of the struggle that it became clear: The vision B-SPAN's opponents fought vigorously to achieve had become the vice president's vision as well.

B-SPAN's fate was decided by two watershed moments. The first came in 2002 when Wheeler could not convince the Research Department's management to finance the service. B-SPAN needed a new home. Ironically, the original model sought to outsource activities to other Bank departments, partly because we recognized we didn't have all the prerequisite skills to run the system alone, and partly because we did not have sufficient funding for a complete staff.

Paradoxically, as our volume and requirements increased, we found relevant service providers inefficient, and reluctant to expand their work programs. They treated us as a competitor. Therefore, as B-SPAN evolved, it became necessary to adjust the model to assume some activities internally. This resulted in a system that could provide content quickly, efficiently, and in some ways more cost-effectively. But it also inhibited our ability to increase volume, which was seen as the key strategy for making B-SPAN affordable.

GSD and ISG had the technological capacity and hardware to run the system, yet neither recognized its institutional value. Since both treated B-SPAN as outside their programmatic mandates, their services proved haphazard in the initial years. Their efficiency would improve; but during this crucial phase of the experiment, they were not safe havens for B-SPAN following the Research Department's abdication. We shied away from External Affairs because we realized the institution's public relations arm would view B-SPAN as a new propaganda tool. The only opportunity for funding resided within

WBI, a result of the personal relationship Wheeler had developed with Michele de Nevers.

WBI was not an unknown commodity to us, however, and we were keenly aware of how its officials viewed issues of collegiality. We had worked with the Economic Development Institute (EDI), its forerunner, on several occasions to prepare course materials based on our industrial pollution research.

One time, they had solicited our help in preparing a learning seminar on pollution management issues in Latin America.[14] Wheeler was asked to lead two panel seminars which focused almost exclusively on our research. In anticipation of the events, I featured an EDI component on NIPR's home page, and prepared a new section on Latin America's environmental issues. When we asked the manager of the event for a reciprocal link, he flatly refused.[15] "Thanks for the creative exercise in 'net diplomacy,'" Wheeler wrote me. "I'm not surprised at his first response—it's simply a Bank reflex borne of zero-sum thinking."[16] The seminar attendance was listless until we sent a newsletter to our email community. Then readership surged. A few months later, a team of our economists did a second event for EDI. We asked if we could include their environmental contacts in our NIPR database. They demurred, deferred and finally declined.[17] We had created content for them. We had driven stakeholders to their events. In fact, EDI's analysis determined marketing the events through NIPR was more effective than its paid advertising in *The Economist* magazine.[18] Yet suggestions EDI might reciprocate were rebuffed.

On the surface, there seemed a logical link between the transparency model and the branch of the institution charged with reconfiguring it into a "knowledge bank." It was, however, a philosophically insolvent partnership.

B-SPAN sought to communicate in a new way while WBI represented how the Bank had always communicated. Unknown to us, but understood elsewhere in the organization, WBI had evolved into a refuge for *über*-bureaucrats. Officials there invested themselves in building personal fiefdoms, wrestling away funds and programs from one another, and mitigating what they could not control.

A year after B-SPAN was absorbed into WBI, the department surveyed Bank staff to gain fuller understanding of how it was perceived. When the results were revealed, Leautier acknowledged WBI staffers "don't really share what they do," and many respondents found the department "mysterious" and difficult to navigate.[19] WBI's effectiveness was also marginalized by a quagmire of upheavals. The department was continually realigning objectives, units, managers, and staff. In less than three years, B-SPAN was housed in three different units and had six supervisors.

The second key moment occurred in early 2004. I asked Vice President Leautier to give B-SPAN autonomy from competing agendas within the department's bureaucracy. The forced migration of B-SPAN into GDLN had not yet synthesized. If some in the Bank viewed WBI as a refuge for those who had failed elsewhere in the institution, GDLN was seen as the department's final dumping ground.

President Wolfensohn created GDLN in the late 1990s to help foster the goal of re-engineering the institution into a knowledge bank. It quickly achieved a reputation as a poorly conceived boondoggle.[20] In 2004, at the cost of tens of millions of dollars, GDLN facilities entertained 36,000 visitors.[21] At the same time, at the cost of about $150,000, B-SPAN was closing in on 200,000 viewers.[22] As a didactic platform for training and learning courses, GDLN's programs were structured events with facilitators. The shotgun marriage with B-SPAN's collection of open, free-flowing forums of information exchanges offered a strange juxtaposition.

In the ongoing skirmishes between bureaucrats and reformers, B-SPAN had three consistent trip wires. The first fault line touched upon information quality. WBI was in the business of producing training and learning products that were highly choreographed and vetted. B-SPAN sought to demystify the monolithic nature of the organization by offering open-ended and ambiguous exchanges of dialogue. The wedding of perfect and imperfect information systems was an ideological mismatch. The transparency versus propaganda models created flashpoints over video quality, editing of content, the Chatham House rule (as a methodology to intimidate presenters and discussants) and blending of product lines. Sebastian Mallaby, author of *The World's Banker*, summarized the inevitable frictions succinctly. "The KS networks," he wrote, "fostered a perfectionist culture rather than a speedy one and it encouraged the powerful tendency in the Bank to focus on internal process rather than on outside clients."[23]

The second trip wire was budget. Budgets are practical matters. Individual departments and units operate on fixed budgets with competing demands. Managers spend money on their priorities. Upon B-SPAN's arrival in 2002, WBI's mid-level managers took a dim view of financing it. They would have terminated the system quickly had it not been for a tenacious effort by its inventors to save it.

When these managers realized their attempts to kill the transparency model had failed, they altered their strategy to treat it as an "unfunded mandate"—an activity a manager is forced to administer for a variety of reasons, but without appropriate funds from senior management. Or worse, an unfunded mandate may be seen as using funds a manager wishes to use elsewhere. In B-SPAN's case, its growing popularity among Bank staff and verbal support from Leautier kept it alive.

Managers, however, rarely divert resources from favored projects. Instead, they will surreptitiously siphon resources from unfunded mandates to drain them financially. This can be seen by the abandonment of the revenue generation proposal in favor of a cost recovery plan that recycled funds generated by B-SPAN into other GDLN activities.

Here also is an example of what Robert Wade suggested was organized hypocrisy: As the department increased promises to stakeholders about knowledge sharing, it did not make corresponding resource allocations.

The characterization of B-SPAN as an unfunded mandate by WBI's managers also provides an important clue about their motivation to undermine it. Why, in theory, would a manager not fund a project he or she is responsible for administrating? The answer might be found in who is getting credit.

B-SPAN was not a WBI invention. It was an established project with a considerable reputation by the time it formally arrived at WBI. Its new WBI managers realized the credit the system generated as a transparent medium was going to its original founders. They had been saddled with administering a program for which personal credit was going elsewhere. In the Bank's cauldron of power and ambition, B-SPAN warranted their retribution rather than their support. By re-engineering the service to fit WBI's pedagogical mandate, they could transfer credit back to themselves.

As a result, B-SPAN's supervisors ruthlessly engaged in acts to undermine the system. Instead, they could have easily benefited from its success by simply taking credit. In fact, if they had shown the slightest indication toward compromise, we certainly would have found ways to give them a sense of ownership of the service. That they showed no deviation from their instinctive antagonism toward B-SPAN posed a conundrum. Until I began a serious post-experience analysis to identify the underlying motivations of WBI's bureaucracy, I found the question perplexing.

The final trip wire was over control. B-SPAN was invented to serve the entire institution and its stakeholders. Its misfortune resulted from a quirk in its evolution: It was financed by a branch of the organization with a parochial mandate. WBI managers weren't inclined to propagate a system designed for the institution. Their mandate was pedagogical training for a subset of the organization's stakeholders. Since the incentives were not right, and B-SPAN could not be easily eliminated, logic dictated the model should change to meet their more narrowly defined objectives.

Unfortunately, for them, they met determined adversaries dedicated to preventing B-SPAN from becoming what it was not intended to be. It was the genesis of war. The B-SPAN experiment therefore goes beyond the assimilation of transparency within an institution that traditionally kept information hidden and managed. It is a case study of the accumulation of power by informal means, and the corruption of power through formal channels.

Fighting in bureaucracies is much different from fighting in politics where attacks are public, loud and flamboyant. In bureaucracies, criticisms are muted and attacks covert, because people join these organizations for long periods. They seek to protect their reputations among colleagues and supervisors; so warfare insists on a subdued decorum. The battle over the transparency model happened behind closed doors and out of view. Though the institution's identity was on trial, almost no one in the Bank knew what was taking place.

The Bank is an organization that, for the sake of appearances, likes to keep the lawn trimmed. Rare is the individual willing to become a blade of grass that has grown disproportionately. Nevertheless, as an agent of cultural change, I was, perhaps, suited for the endeavor. From my training in journalism, I was ingrained with a commitment to transparency. From my experiences in politics, I was endowed with a sense of urgency and distaste for bureaucracy. From my public relations background, I understood what would attract a market to Bank webcasts. From my work in the Research Department, I had learned about the power of formal and informal control of information. From Wheeler, I had learned how to manipulate the bureaucracy. I was also single. With no family to support, I could take stands on principles where others might have wavered. Like revolutionaries I had studied, I was passionate, committed, and would not be stopped on my own accord.

Tolstopiatenko, Laporte, Weber-Fahr and Sheram represented the bureaucracy's front line of defense. Each brought a different personality to the fray that in unison achieved a sum. Given the comparative norms of their environment, one might suggest their actions took a logical course. They themselves might proffer that they were involved in an ideological crusade to enhance the Bank's image, as well as mandated to implement policies within the framework of budget contractions. Still, on a substantive level, they represented a deeply entrenched mindset unnerved by transparency and resistant to change.

Tolstopiatenko was the first important antagonist. Raised in a Stalinist environment, he adopted an autocratic methodology of administration. Convinced of his infallibility, he sought to implement his ideas unilaterally. As a technician, he perceived B-SPAN as a technology to be manipulated in serving WBI's pedagogical mandate and keep his star rising. In arguing the merits of his agenda, he often used covert tactics to undermine the founding objectives of the service. The battles fought were largely on fields of his choosing; and yet he lost because sounder arguments and better tactics were deployed in B-SPAN's defense. Importantly, in this phase of the transparency experiment, informal stakeholders in the shadows kept the balance of power in check.

Weber-Fahr was the second key antagonist. Her instincts mirrored Tolstopiatenko's in many ways. Both were subservient to authority while also creatures of authority. Like Tolstopiatenko, she demanded control of every aspect of every initiative under her supervision. Deviation from total submission by subordinates was not tolerated. Alternative thinking by others was disdained. Each sought to establish a working environment that institutionalized chaos; this was not by chance, but rather as an orchestrated objective. Every issue or event was treated as a crisis. Every request was urgent and vital. Choreographed terror created a mechanism that allowed these managers to satisfy their most basic instincts: Control and domination. Symmetry and serenity made them feel dysfunctional.

In one way, they were quite different. Tolstopiatenko believed in the superiority of his ideas, argued their merits, and repositioned based on counterarguments. Weber-Fahr didn't tolerate ideas that were not her own. Since her instincts were so diametrically opposed to transparency, she refused to engage in any debate of ideas. Despite a reputation for brilliance, in some ways her mind was less facile. She made decisions quickly, and upon determining the objective would not allow new information to influence her. All that was left to resolve was how best to chart her course. Her tactics depended on manipulating the institution's codified rules. She used them as a vehicle to destroy anything she perceived as inhibiting her goals.

Weber-Fahr, however, enjoyed advantages not available to Tolstopiatenko (or Laporte). B-SPAN had been a full-time operation administered by short-term consultants for four years when the Human Resources Department created an ETC category. This handed Weber-Fahr a lever to orchestrate personnel changes. By converting the position of running B-SPAN from STC to ETC, a process was set in motion where the expiration of my existing contract would force a decision and create an opportunity.

Normally, Bank managers automate such conversions, but they do have the discretion of convening a panel selection process. Weber-Fahr made a callous but unerring calculation. As the only conduit of information, she could undermine my reputation with Leautier, thereby making a change palatable. By realigning the ETC requirements to include skill mixes she knew I did not possess, she could weaken my candidacy for the position. By using a panel process, she used the guise of transparency as a mechanism for identifying alternative candidates. By determining the composition of the panel, she could neutralize support previous accomplishments had engendered with the institution. She understood this: Large bureaucracies instinctively marginalize the value of any one individual; therefore all work in fear. If she removed me to mitigate the system, few would protest, and most would not even notice.

Another important issue moved in Weber-Fahr's favor. The influence of informal stakeholders had been mitigated over time. By mutual agreement, Wheeler was kept hidden from the stage. Though Tolstopiatenko and Laporte were highly aware of his influence, Wheeler was unknown to Weber-Fahr. However, the longer he was away from participation with B-SPAN, the less influence he had with Leautier. By the time B-SPAN fell, we both decided his interceding with the vice president no longer had value.

At the crucial moment of negotiating B-SPAN's future with Leautier in the spring of 2004, the intensity of battles waged with Tolstopiatenko and Laporte had also left me in a vulnerable position. To have an openly frictional relationship with Weber-Fahr would reinforce negative impressions created by her predecessors, and would undermine any ability I had to influence outcomes. It was a vulnerability Weber-Fahr could exploit, because she had regular access to Leautier and I did not. Since B-SPAN and its creators were synonymous, it was necessary for her to separate them in the vice president's mind by providing reports of an efficient service rapidly reducing backlog under her watch (which had been artificially exacerbated by her obfuscation during Johnson's administration), juxtaposed with unflattering personnel accounts. She influenced de Nevers in the same way. As we learned from our research on industrial pollution, reputations matter. By caveat, I concluded, reputation matters even for those who seek to use informal mechanisms to aid their cause.

As the tactics of our opponents changed, so did mine. I was a vocal defender of B-SPAN against Tolstopiatenko and Laporte, because they yielded to logical arguments documented by evidence and backed by informal stakeholders. None of this mattered to Weber-Fahr. Since informal stakeholder influence external to GDLN no longer existed, Weber-Fahr's actions needed no further adjustments other than to address a subordinate. After a period of observation, it became clear to me there was little logic in offering alternative opinions or arguments, even if based on fact or supported by evidence. Since logic was meaningless, negotiating over it was not meaningful. I adopted quieter and more nuanced tactics by design. At some point during the fall, I simply absorbed information offered by Weber-Fahr or Sheram, but offered no response, and worked in silence on strategies to protect B-SPAN.

Long before B-SPAN's official merger into GDLN, clues to Weber-Fahr's perception of the transparency model were available. For nearly two years, Claude Salem and I actively encouraged her to disseminate our content through the Distance Learning Centers that GDLN ran throughout the world.[24] The DLCs were desperate for content, and Salem was convinced our system of free off-the-shelf materials offered an excellent complement to their activities. Weber-Fahr, however, never responded or acknowledged us in any way. Moreover, she repeatedly rejected efforts by Johnson in the spring of 2004 to build a revenue generation system, and was silent when he pleaded for her counsel on resources for staffing.[25]

Her rejection of Johnson's overtures was designed to accomplish three things. First, though Johnson remained formally in charge of B-SPAN until the close of the fiscal year, she was signaling she no longer considered him relevant. Leautier's decision to move the system into GDLN had made Johnson a lame duck, and Weber-Fahr's disdain of him followed her own natural inclinations. As cognizance of his reduced status grew, Johnson became instinctively reluctant to move forward on his ideas to broaden B-SPAN. This became evident when he tried to broker a deal with GSD on sharing encoders. He immediately agreed to Weber-Fahr's demand to meet about the proposal, and quickly surrendered when she nixed the arrangement. He knew to do otherwise would come perilously close to treason.

Weber-Fahr's instincts were also at play with her second objective, not to let B-SPAN prosper. Since she was intellectually opposed to the transparency model, she was content to let the trend lines of high demand and inadequate resources continue until she took over. By introducing cost recovery with an increase in charges, she could reduce volume. By introducing a production log, she could focus available resources on the existing backlog. This would enable her to claim to senior management she had restored an ailing service.

Finally, there was the issue of our revenue generation proposal. If successfully deployed, the concept would have infused B-SPAN with a steady and dedicated source of revenue and content. In essence, it would have institutionalized the transparency initiative in perpetuity. By not announcing her position on our revenue generation model during the spring, Weber-Fahr believed she could effectively keep me in the dark about her intentions. This might have worked had the issue of purchasing encoders and lending them to GSD not arisen. When she destroyed the partnership Johnson and I arranged with GSD so GDLN "would be able to charge clients more," Weber-Fahr's intentions were revealed on cost recovery and other substantive issues.[26]

It wasn't until July, when B-SPAN was formally placed under GDLN that Weber-Fahr unveiled her true opinion of the transparency model, and her plans to implement changes. This was done under the guise that it was the official dictum of WBI's EILT, its senior management body.[27] But Weber-Fahr's vision was so far-reaching as to suggest the department rejected the model in totality.

Weber-Fahr's alternative model embraced editing B-SPAN's videos, merging its product line with training materials, offering content to selected internal audiences, deleting archives, and terminating most marketing activities.[28] Moreover, growing the system with a permanent professional staff was rejected.[29] B-SPAN, she announced, would be run as a "low-cost initiative" using consultants and college students to fill gaps. On the pivotal issue of revenue generation, she waited until I was on holiday before implementing a decision kept hidden until then. Although she suggested this was done in accordance with the wishes of the EILT, I learned subsequently she made the decision unilaterally.[30] And, then she decided revenues B-SPAN generated would be used to subsidize other activities within the new Multi-Media Unit. Weber-Fahr, thereafter, initiated a long list of activities reflecting personal antagonism.

The financing issue warrants a bit of further observation. Weber-Fahr understood that structural points in the model needed maintenance if the system was to continue its meteoric evolution. The principal input was content. Without regular infusions, B-SPAN's value would begin to decline.

One tactic for weakening the volume of content was to remain non-committal toward the revenue generation model designed by Johnson and me. Previously, content had been generated by aggressive marketing, quality results and growing audience share. A revenue generation model would institutionalize inputs of content by creating partnerships. If a partnership concept was eliminated and replaced by a pay-as-you-go model, clients would value the system less. It would create more logistical hurdles. It would require closer scrutiny by clients of their budget parameters. It would create more uncertainties. By keeping the revenue generation model at bay, an environment of disincentives could be created for clients wishing to use B-SPAN.

Separate, but closely related to how clients would pay, was the cost of the service. When Bruno Laporte unilaterally imposed a cost recovery policy to cover GSD's filming charges, an important threshold had been crossed. B-SPAN had begun a transition from a public service to a private one. I knew clients would be highly sensitive to pricing, and hoped the decision would not be fatal. Initially, about half our clientele abandoned the service; but perhaps in a testament to what B-SPAN provided them, many returned.[31] Active marketing and new ways of presenting content allowed us to resume robust growth in content and traffic during Johnson's management. Still, this was only possible because customers suffered no further pricing shocks.

When Weber-Fahr then imposed even greater costs to use B-SPAN, the decision consciously destabilized an already fragile client base. In a way similar to how revenue was raised, pricing disincentives could build a momentum of their own. As fees escalated and volume declined, the value clients associated with the system would also decline. This would begin a cyclical effect of further and further disuse. Over time, it would become a self-fulfilling prophesy. Patrons would be less likely to feel the sting of losing B-SPAN as a dissemination opportunity: Since it had become too expensive to use, they wouldn't use it, thereby making it less important to them.

It seems relevant to note at this point that the Bank was becoming acclimated to B-SPAN to some degree. By the fall of 2004, the transparency model had a large and supportive following. Thousands of Bank staff had watched B-SPAN; and hundreds had contracted with the system for their knowledge sharing needs. Accolades and compliments received from staff during its initial four years could have filled a novella.[32] And, substantively, EXT had made featuring our content a permanent part of its Internet communications strategy. This included disseminating, via the Bank's home page, controversial events such as Sachs and de Soto, as well as news-making interviews with key development practitioners.

Moreover, EXT was actively soliciting our services to conduct live webcasting of events. This reveals a subtle but important shift in its thinking. Perhaps without conscious realization, EXT had come to acknowledge the validity of B-SPAN's journalistic tendencies and proactive nature. In addition, our content was featured in numerous Bank newsletters and on dozens of its Internet sub-sites.

For these reasons, B-SPAN could not be terminated outright nor have its archives arbitrarily deleted in their entirety. Nevertheless, in large organizations with thousands of activities, people invariably focus on what directly concerns them. The nuances of any particular project will escape them; and ultimately, if the system fell into disrepair, they would not value it significantly anyway.

To carry this one step further, it's also useful to acknowledge that NGOs, as a collective group, never truly discovered B-SPAN. At an individual level, civil society activists responded with intense and enthusiastic support; but officially no NGOs mentioned B-SPAN as instrumental in their efforts to increase transparency and accountability at the Bank. Perhaps it suggests a lack of awareness or apathy over internal transparency initiatives within the Bretton Woods institutions, or a level of inoculation from stimuli originating outside their agendas. Perhaps it simply suggests something about our own inability to scale up quickly enough to make their awareness inevitable.

If B-SPAN only provided technical inputs, then it would have proven far less troubling for WBI's managers to dominate. But it had a human component, and here they sought a strategy of disengagement. Weber-Fahr enjoyed the most success with this tactic. Her objective was to minimize, and to the extent possible, eliminate my involvement with B-SPAN's clientele. To achieve this, she implemented a variety of tactics such as terminating my direct correspondence with clients, extinguishing almost all marketing activities, implementing a production log to emphasize the process of creating content rather than simply creating it, and immersing me in extraneous administrative activities. The logic behind reducing my contact with clients worked on several levels. I would be less able to promote B-SPAN. Moreover, if clients saw less of me, then they would find my value to them would also decline. Should I depart, they might find it unfortunate but not necessarily consequential.

On this front, I engaged a counter strategy. WBI's managers viewed me as a self-indulgent promoter. I was the one announcing new and exciting events and developments regarding B-SPAN. I wrote the newsletters, communicated with clients and answered viewer questions. When people spoke about B-SPAN, they routinely interchanged its name with mine. From their parochial perspective, WBI's managers instinctively viewed the issue as one of who was receiving credit.

As noted before, I did not view the matter as a luxury. I would have gladly traded this strategy for a healthy environment. Moreover, I recognized it would have been an appropriate tactic in moving my agenda forward, but only if the terrain was not hostile. B-SPAN, however, had been under attack the moment it entered WBI. I viewed public relations activities as a mechanism to insulate B-SPAN from attacks, and from attempts to remove me. And, by and large, the strategy proved successful. Every time Tolstopiatenko and Laporte wanted to remove me, they could not because of my popularity with clients and B-SPAN's reputation as a successful system. The tactic was used extensively during the ETC process, but here it was not successful because Weber-Fahr was able to use the panel as a shield to insulate her from bureaucratic recrimination.

Arguably the most effective tactic Weber-Fahr employed also offered a curious paradox. Almost universally among her staff, she was known as a blunt and plain-spoken individual. However, her most skilful trait was perhaps a talent for using ambiguity and half-truths to hide intentions. Her silence about staffing solutions prior to formally assuming control, resulting in an operation starved of resources, offers one example. Another example: Her vocal support of B-SPAN's transparency principles, and its strategy for multi-directional knowledge sharing, cloaked a determination to eliminate the principles and emasculate the system. Her obfuscation regarding the adoption of a revenue generation model reveals a third example. Her vacillation over B-SPAN's pricing unmasks another. The suggestion that pricing was decided by the EILT when in fact it was a decision she implemented unilaterally, is a fifth example. Her insinuation the panel process was merely a formality rather than a hanging jury offers more evidence. Additional examples abound, but no longer seem necessary to list.

Leautier was also skilled at couching intentions with misleading statements. In the spring of 2004, with the dissolution of the Global Knowledge Pillar underway, B-SPAN had become a free agent. Leautier, unsure of where to align the service, decided to fold it into GDLN, and Weber-Fahr, ever conscious of accruing power, was an active supporter of that idea. Knowing the ideological clash this would present, they embarked on a strategy of public praise and private reassurance to get me to accept the realignment. This began in earnest immediately when the vice president suggested that shifting B-SPAN would provide its staff with employment security, and would not mean it would become submerged in GDLN's agenda. Throughout the spring of 2004, Leautier complimented B-SPAN on numerous occasions before various audiences. It could be seen again in public comments of support for a revenue generation model with the Bank's board at a time when the question was open as to whether Weber-Fahr would adopt a cost recovery model. Concurrently, there were plans to re-engineer the transparency model.

The issue of B-SPAN's "massification" also poses an interesting hypothetical conundrum. While Leautier was applauding our prowess for attracting large audiences although we had limited resources, it might have proven vexing because of what we were broadcasting. During this same period, we webcast highly visible events with Sachs, Botchwey and Ebadi; and each offered tough critiques of the Bank. The divergent messages emanating from Leautier, and the evolving scenarios regarding B-SPAN's organizational alignment and its resource allocations, may directly relate to the nexus between rhetoric and action. Could the lack of attention by WBI's senior management to resource needs, and abandonment of revenue generation and multi-directional knowledge sharing plans, be attributable to B-SPAN's "massification" of messages by critics who questioned the institution's effectiveness?

Despite accolades and assurances that B-SPAN would be

adequately funded, resources never came. By late June, the system broke down when it finally became impractical to cover a Presidential Lecture with Juan Somavia of the International Labour Organization.

Leautier's reaction even then was couched. More reassurances were offered that resources would be committed, but the only infusion was to insure the Shanghai Conference tapes were processed. Philosophically and intellectually, Leautier might have supported the concept of transparency, but only to the extent it served her pedagogical needs, lightly impacted her budget, and provided valuable opportunities to market her to the development community. Her focus was elsewhere, and B-SPAN was tangential to her core work program. Weber-Fahr, on the other hand, was openly hostile toward B-SPAN, but for political reasons could not be seen as being overtly responsible for destroying it.

Two theories arise over the fading of Leautier as a supporter. Laporte and Weber-Fahr had regular access to the vice president, something not enjoyed by Wheeler or me. Over time, they had the opportunity to change her mind about B-SPAN's value to the department and its assimilation into WBI. Yet if B-SPAN was important enough for the vice president to praise in public, logic would dictate it would have been prudent to acquire full information if what she heard from her mid-level managers was unfavorable.

This leads to the second theory. Leautier was kept unaware of the turmoil surrounding the administration of B-SPAN. If true, then WBI was a bureaucracy out of her control. Moreover, at some point in the process, Laporte and Weber-Fahr understood that beyond Leautier's rhetoric, she found B-SPAN of limited value since she would not fund the system. It was the signal they needed to move ahead with their plans.

Nevertheless, despite all attempts to chart a methodical and error-free course for B-SPAN, hindsight suggests I made important tactical mistakes. Much of this I might attribute to a lack of full information that compelled me to move slowly when alacrity was called for. Some may be the result of my own shortcomings.

For example, Weber-Fahr was allowed to decide my ETC status when Leautier should have been pressured into a commitment. Twice Leautier suggested she would address the matter personally. Had I been able to make the vice president accountable on this point, admittedly an unusual scenario, the evolution of B-SPAN within GDLN would certainly have been different. After GDLN's formal takeover, Weber-Fahr announced her challenge was to mold B-SPAN into an agenda that no longer valued the transparency model. Logic would again dictate that I seek restitution with Leautier at this juncture. Yet by then, the environment had evolved enough to convince me Weber-Fahr had been fully empowered by the vice president to act as she pleased on a range of issues including the ETC status. It had become both too late to make a credible plea to the vice president on this point, and too early to consider the matter at endgame.

A second tactical mistake occurred when Weber-Fahr first announced she would force B-SPAN into blending product lines with learning content. Instead of hoping to keep B-SPAN unblemished, I might have been better served to move quickly as Johnson advised to create a WBI Presents. If Weber-Fahr had balked at a window on B-SPAN's home page that separated product lines, I would have been able to seek guidance from Leautier with a sound argument: Both product lines were sharing technological resources behind the scenes, but the separate skins protected B-SPAN's transparency. It was still soon enough into our immersion within GDLN for me to reach out to the vice president on this type of issue. Likely she would have agreed with my position, and Weber-Fahr would have been denied a key part of her agenda to change the model.

A third tactical error was not to have organized Wheeler, de Nevers and Johnson into a unified front to pressure Leautier quickly in the immediate aftermath of the ETC panel session. In the month that followed, I embarked on an aggressive campaign of public relations coups and solicitations of stakeholder support, because I believed Leautier would find it compelling while Weber-Fahr would feel it intimidating. Here I was obviously far from the truth. Wheeler also counseled patience in letting the process unfold without bias.

Leautier's ongoing verbal support for both me and the system supported this logic. Holding back seemed sensible if the vice president's words were to be taken at face value. By the time I learned otherwise, it was already too late to implement a new strategy.

In the aftermath of the ETC decision, I wondered if reconvening the Advisory Committee first orchestrated during the Tolstopiatenko's reign might have derailed Weber-Fahr's aggression. I concluded that perhaps it might have caused a temporary adjustment in her tactics, but that was all. B-SPAN's key protagonists had already been neutralized. De Nevers had disengaged. Millet had left the Bank. And Wheeler's influence as an informal stakeholder had waned.

Finally, the effort to save B-SPAN by moving it became the victim of unfortunate timing. In late 2004, most other Bank units including WBI were beginning annual 2.5% budget reductions that were to continue for the next three years. Also during this period, Wolfensohn convened a task force to look at the organizational effectiveness of the Bank. Rumors swirled that the task force would not treat WBI kindly. This viewpoint was reinforced with the highly critical Quality Assurance Group report. Concurrently, Wolfensohn's term as Bank president was expiring; and though he was pushing hard for reappointment from the Bush Administration, it was far from assured.

With the announced departure of Wolfensohn, a series of events fell into place. He was the driving force behind the task force, and its momentum was curtailed when he was ousted. With the advent of a new Bank president, all significant organizational changes froze. Key institutional players such as Van Pulley of GSD, Muhsin of ISG and Rice of EXT refrained from new initiatives. They were further inhibited by new budget limitations.

Had the reorganization process moved forward, WBI would likely have suffered real pain and no longer have been capable of administering B-SPAN. (In March 2007, following Leautier's resignation from the Bank, delays finding a successor launched new rumors about WBI's fate, including the possibility it would be downsized and its remnants folded into the Research Department). WBI's difficulties would have convinced GSD to act. That these events did not evolve does not change one strongly held belief: Had GSD launched a competitive service WBI would have been forced to fold B-SPAN or hand it to them.

Other Bank departments had a chance to champion B-SPAN. All failed to seize the opportunity. Moreover, it appears none understood what they were being offered. As previously noted, the Research Department was late to embrace the Internet as a marketing strategy, and predictably never realized the potential impact B-SPAN could have disseminating its research. Had they, the transparency model may well have proven to be a remarkable leap in the history of the department's influence. In 2005, GSD, ISG and EXT were afforded opportunities to make B-SPAN part of their strategic work programs. Each was given a detailed paper documenting how it was aligned with their objectives, and how it could generate revenue for their departments. All three decided not to act. Why? Because the Bank's culture is so overwhelmingly risk averse that staff is often frozen by fear, cynicism and indifference.

Wheeler wondered about the feasibility of launching a service external to the Bank. We could not identify a practical way to achieve it without a sizeable budget for start-up costs. B-SPAN's affordability was possible because the Bank's infrastructure allowed us to achieve economies of scale.

When I left WBI at the start of 2005, I explored pricing issues in the private sector and found the results unsatisfactory. Private sector sources wanted evidence of a model that could generate immediate profits. I was soliciting a model that reduced operating costs per unit by building volume. Finally, the Bank and external organizations I encountered understood traditional communications tools, and were comfortable with expected returns. Webcasting was still too cutting-edge.

But, there was another issue of critical importance. The Bank generated enormous amounts of content that allowed B-SPAN to thrive despite chronic financing problems and internal bureaucratic warfare. External content could enrich a healthy system that was functioning internally. It would not, however, replace internal content that was no longer available, at least not in the beginning. Barring a grant or infusion of funds from a benefactor, only the Bank or a similar international organization was positioned to house a B-SPAN. There had been no choice. We had had to fight.

4

B-SPAN continues today, but its decline has been dramatic. On the surface, a viewer might surmise little about the system has changed. The transparency principle of not editing content survives. There does not appear to be an overt evolution of the system into a warehouse of training and learning content. Hundreds of videos are available online. Dissemination of video content to selected audiences does not appear to have happened (but, then again, how would one know).

Nevertheless, upon closer inspection, the changes have been profound. "Three reviews of B-SPAN's evolution were conducted. The first occurred in March 2007, the second was conducted in December 2008, and the final review was done in June 2009. Upon my departure from B-SPAN, I had produced more than 700 events. In the two-and-three-quarter-year period that followed, 219 events were added.[33] In fact, volume declined from 363 events in Fiscal Year 2004 to 113 in FY 2005 and then further to only 83 in FY 2006.[34] In the first half of FY 2007, only 23 events were made available.[35] This represents a 69% decline in volume by GDLN during its first year of management and a 77% decline in its second. Trends during its third year suggested the decline would be even more precipitous. Moreover, the volume of webcasts during GDLN's supervision from July 2004 through March 2007 did not even match what B-SPAN produced in Fiscal Year 2004, when under Erik Johnson's supervision it was starved of resources by WBI senior officials. It amounts to 60% of the total of Johnson's one year.

Volume, however, is only one barometer that one can use to

measure B-SPAN's decline. Equally important is the quality of the content. Here the system's decline is quite evident. Of the 78 events during calendar year 2006, 18 events, or about 23%, were WBI's own events or ones where the department's input was substantial.[36] Nineteen events, or 24%, were launches of books or reports, almost all of which were written by Bank units or staff. Another 14 events or 18% were conferences, workshops or other Bank sponsored video conferences. Only 27 events for an entire year, about 35% of the total, could be considered seminar events of the kind B-SPAN was created to disseminate.

Moreover, though not yet substantial in number, training products are officially welcomed as part of B-SPAN's offerings. One therefore might conclude there is no need to enforce an agenda of editing content where the character of events is tightly controlled.

As of 2007, the official policy of B-SPAN was to guarantee events would be archived for as long as two years.[37] Though there was no fee in 2007 for storage beyond two years, the guarantee of permanent archiving on B-SPAN by GDLN was by caveat void. Unspoken was a rationale that GDLN wished to reserve the right to use this server space as it defined its priorities. In reality, server costs have declined over time. Moreover, the marginal cost of storing a file is nil once the initial server investment has been made (which neither GDLN nor WBI had ever subsidized).

The price of this policy has been that the concept of a virtual library of development dialogues for the benefit of practitioners, scholars and historians was terminated. GDLN might argue this poses nothing more than a theoretical exercise, yet a thorough count of the existing archives found about 600 video events were available.[38] Since 219 were produced (as of March 2007) after the system was merged into GDLN, about 380 remained from the period before.

Given that the overall volume B-SPAN produced since its inception would total more than 900 events, one-third of its archives were lost; and all these losses have come from the pre-GDLN era. The rest might go at any time. GDLN's counter-argument might be these events have been lost due to database migrations. But the enormous loss of content suggests they didn't seriously value the resource to begin with, and perhaps saw it as an opportunity to clear server space for content it could use to disseminate WBI learning events via VoD (the database system developed by Andrei Tolstopiatenko and the I Team for streaming edited content to Bank staff). In any event, the result is that the B-SPAN events available to the public stem largely from GDLN's vision.

The evolution of event pricing is also an interesting tale. In June 2004, Weber-Fahr suggested GDLN's charges for B-SPAN did not have to reach the full costs it incurred for producing an event.[39] Subsequently, I delivered an analysis that determined per-event costs were approximately $289.[40] Thereafter, Weber-Fahr decided to implement a policy that profited from Bank colleagues by charging them $350 for B-SPAN's services.[41] As of 2007, GDLN charged $500 to use B-SPAN.[42] This represented a 43% increase in two years, and a 73% increase from the estimate Weber-Fahr was provided as to actual costs. These charges did not include GSD's filming costs of $400, which made the cost of getting a video on B-SPAN $900. Clients wishing to webcast a conference would incur a price spike double what I recommended to Weber-Fahr in late 2004 and almost 50% higher than what was determined at that time. Conferences cost $2,000.[43] Including GSD's fee, a one-day conference charge approached $3,000. Not many Bank units could afford to make their events available on such an expensive outlet. Not surprisingly, volume plummeted.

B-SPAN also began offering podcasts in 2006. Podcasts are audio broadcasts created by individuals offering perspectives on an area of expertise. This concept diametrically counters the notion under which the transparency model was created, because the format promotes a form of communication in which Bank specialists offer sermons. Moreover, these selections are edited snippets of larger discussions. There is no opportunity for interaction, debate or questioning from those with alternative perspectives. It is another method of controlling information and ensuring it flows in one direction only.

It's also important to note how information is disseminated. The operating norm for B-SPAN until 2005 was to send out one newsletter each month to inform stakeholders of new offerings. Often, newsletters were sent more frequently. In the two-and-three-quarter-years that followed, little more than a half dozen had been sent out.[44] The result was marketing to external stakeholders virtually disappeared. Moreover, the newsletters I composed tried to convey critical information to readers. Those from GDLN's administration between 2005 and 2007 offered text so mundane that they commonly did not even mention involvement of influential personalities. Summaries placed online offered limited substance. And, as noted earlier, events were largely vetted to reduce opportunities for controversial dialogue. Nothing questioning Bank policies or actions was encouraged.

The final variable for analysis is a review of website traffic. In the spring of 2004, visitors coming to B-SPAN averaged between 20,000 and 25,000 each month.[45] Page views fluctuated between 350,000 and 400,000. Both trend lines at the time were marching rapidly upward. Even if no further growth was achieved, over a calendar year B-SPAN would have attracted between 240,000 and 300,000 visitors and provided between 4.2 million and 4.8 million page views. ISG did not monitor B-SPAN's traffic during 2005 but started again in mid-2006.[46] The reason is undetermined, but may have been because ISG installed a new traffic-monitoring system during this period, and it took time to gain access to B-SPAN's data. Perhaps it may have been because B-SPAN is housed on the VoD system which created additional hurdles for ISG, or that the Bank moved all its websites to a new publishing platform in 2004 and 2005, and this prevented traffic monitoring.

In any event, the ISG data from August 2006 to February 2007 revealed a shocking reduction for B-SPAN. In the Weber-Fahr era, the monthly average for visitors was 12, 643 and for page views it was 91,540.[47] If extrapolated over one full year, B-SPAN was hosting just over 150,000 visitors and providing less than 1.1 million page views. This represented reductions of as much as 50% in visitors and 77% in page views from levels we reached during the Johnson period.

Interestingly, for all the adamancy by Tolstopiatenko that WBI statistics were superior to ISG's, the department switched over to ISG's system in July 2006. Data from January 2005 to June 2006 for B-SPAN was not recoverable, but given the precipitous decline in late 2004 and to even lower levels in mid-2006, there is nothing to suggest what transpired in between would be complimentary to GDLN.

Within a few months of its absorption into GDLN, B-SPAN had morphed from a free-flowing and vibrant youth into an ossified and decrepit ancient. Volume of output declined to less than one-third and continued to drop. Reductions in traffic were also steep. Marketing to internal and external stakeholders ceased. The eclectic diversity of the system's content had dissolved into numbing familiarity.

That was the good news.

The second review of B-SPAN in December 2008 revealed a system that had essentially collapsed. When half of Fiscal Year 2008 concluded, B-SPAN had covered six events. The trends lines to its disintegration remained steady from the initial March 2007 review. When Fiscal Year 2006 concluded, B-SPAN had covered 55 events. In Fiscal Year 2007, it covered just 64 events. This represents an 85% drop in FY06 and 82% drop in FY07 from FY04 levels.

The cover story on B-SPAN's home page in December 2008 was an event from March 2008, nine months earlier. A section at the bottom of the home page was for the "10 Most Watched Presentations Last Month." Nothing was listed. A review of the site revealed it was littered with links that no longer worked, which suggests even routine website maintenance had been abandoned.

The last known newsletter on record was sent in August 2007. The history section on B-SPAN notes that it is distributed to 18,000 subscribers. This means the list had not grown at all since it was last administered by me in 2004. Reality suggests the subscriber list is smaller than that—and substantially so—because a certain percentage of email subscriptions routinely go out-of-date. Inputs to the system via content and newsletter distributions are essential if the distribution list size is to remain steady or grow.

To even find what is left of B-SPAN on the Bank's Internet infrastructure was extremely difficult. There is no longer a B-SPAN link on the Bank's home page. A "Video" link exists, but it is not really a video link at all. It goes to a general landing page with a multitude of "news" offerings including press releases, speeches, press reviews, issue briefs, photography galleries, podcasts and a guide to find a World Bank expert on a topic of interest. B-SPAN does not appear on this page either. One must search on "Broadcast and Media" on the side bar to find its link—two layers removed from where it had once been years before.

By 2007, a system that once had been uniformly used throughout the Bank by many dozens of units subsisted as a medium to release Bank publications, a few major conferences and as a showcase for WBI forums and video conferences. The "have" and "have not" society created by WBI's bureaucrats reflected an instinctive distaste for transparency, a belief that propaganda equals communications, and a desire to use the residual dissemination power generated by B-SPAN as a tool for parochial use. By the end of 2008, it didn't even do that much. June 2009's review showed no deviation.

What is inherently wrong with a transparency system evolving into a venue for major conferences, GDLN video conferences and launches of Bank publications? Such a development posed a deep concern for Wheeler and me. Most discussions, debates and cutting-edge research occur at the micro-level before becoming anointed as policy. It was with these events that the full value of the transparency model could bloom. Directly related was our ongoing concern that B-SPAN might become a platform for senior officials of the Bank. Whenever there were policy battles with WBI officials regarding B-SPAN's content, volume and pricing, these issues of perception weighed heavily.

Why was it critical for B-SPAN to continue its natural progression into a multi-directional hub of knowledge sharing and information exchanges? The perception of borrowers is when the Bank engages them in dialogues, it does less listening than prescribing, and its policy prescriptions reflect donor concerns rather than their concerns. Having information systems moving in one direction reinforces this viewpoint. Moreover, not providing opportunities for external content to flow back into the Bank robs the institution of valuable opportunities to learn about local developments. Finally, creating a venue where stakeholders and shareholders can engage, inform and learn reinforces the supposition that the Bank's expertise and role is central to development.

In response to how B-SPAN has evolved, WBI officials might suggest the system has remained an unedited medium. Such a defense, however, seems frail since few sources participate, and the primary disseminator of content via B-SPAN is WBI itself. The department facilitates pedagogical activities, so WBI might counter that as B-SPAN's financial backer its prerogative to mold the system into a platform for its products is sound and just, and the rest of the Bank should be considered secondary providers. However, such an argument carries less weight when WBI's cost recovery policy places much of the burden of financing the system upon its client base.

In addition, B-SPAN was invented as an institution-wide system and not one to implement a parochial mandate. By such a definition, it should not reside within WBI at all. That WBI has not yet followed through on moving B-SPAN suggests it recognizes the marketing advantages it provides the department within the Bank.

WBI might also argue budget contractions since FY04 made it impossible to expand something that was not a core service. Nevertheless, department officials imposed a cost recovery policy that provided disincentives for B-SPAN's clients. Despite numerous chances, they have never experimented with a revenue generation approach that would create a reliable revenue stream and growth opportunities. Nor would it be credible for them to claim that budget limitations make it impossible for a partnership approach to work, for they have no data to support such a position. And, finally, they channeled revenues raised by B-SPAN into GDLN's Multi-Media Unit to finance other activities, which suggests they never harbored serious support for the system in the first place.

Perhaps GDLN's rhetoric about editing content, blending product lines and limiting web streams to selected audiences was simply a tactic designed to inflame tensions. However, one has the sense GDLN views this as an unfinished agenda because it has been a lack of resources that have precluded their intentions to move forward. Video editing, blending product lines and creating password-protected sites to give some audiences access to content and prohibit others, is expensive.

In the environment in which B-SPAN was inherited, WBI and GDLN were facing serious budget cuts starting in 2004. This strict budget environment remained in place in the years that followed. Moreover, given that the department decided to implement a cost recovery policy, it in effect took steps to prevent itself from financing its own agenda. In other words, WBI wanted to move B-SPAN aggressively in a certain direction and then created roadblocks before it could get there. As a result, it has settled into a middling course in which B-SPAN remains largely unused outside WBI, little valued by internal clients and external stakeholders, and only disseminating messages the department is comfortable communicating, making the service largely benign by previous standards.

B-SPAN exists only because Wheeler and I had developed it to the point where it was not politically expedient for the bureaucrats to end it. By the time WBI's managers saw B-SPAN on their radar screen, it was too late to stop it. Denied the opportunity to terminate it outright, they sought to make it homogenous with the department's internal image-making instincts.

Is intellectual dishonesty and moral corruption the yardstick by which opposition or support for the transparency model is measured? I would not suggest this, but would note arguments advocating another philosophy, based on evidence that it rather than B-SPAN was more closely aligned with the Bank's mission, have never been raised.

5

Questions still remained for me. Why had WBI dismantled a system experiencing such astounding success? I wondered if my experience with WBI was an anomaly or endemic of the organization. To learn why institutional hypocrisy was ingrained upon the Bank, it would be necessary to slice deeply until the core issues driving behavior were revealed. But I could not view the issue as an academic who studied organizational behavior and culture. I could not study it as an external critic confounded by its actions. Nor could I pretend to be a passive observer. Rather I could view it from a unique vantage point. I was intimately involved with the institution. My understanding was as a participant active in its rhythms. I would begin from there.

Bruno Laporte once characterized B-SPAN as a sunrise activity, yet there is a sunrise industry at the Bank. It has been a growth business there since the 1980s. It's called organizational reform.

For two decades, reacting like a thermometer to external criticism and changing business theories, the Bank's management has switched directions and tactics for how it administers lending, budget and personnel.[48] New management paradigms go into effect, and when deficiencies are detected, they are jettisoned for the next cutting-edge application. The result is an organization that is constantly moving in new and often conflicting directions, creating the institutional hypocrisies suggested by Robert Wade.

In 1987, the Bank implemented a reorganization that has been considered a watershed in management-employee relations. It was launched in response to client concerns that lending was not closely enough aligned to what they wanted or needed. Following the reforms, the Bank established an Organization and Business Practices Unit to administer further reorganizations.[49] Several years thereafter, the Bank began reacting again as management theorists hailed the fall of the Soviet Union as proof centrally planned, command-and-control regimes would inevitably fail.[50] By the middle of the 1990s, even the Organization and Business Practices Unit had reorganized into the Change Management Unit.[51]

There is a palpable sense within the Bank that each new management team arrives looking to make their mark by instituting wide-ranging structural reforms. Reforms are partly driven by the difficulties of poverty reduction, but also partly by developments in the business world. When private sector companies successfully reengineer their business models, pressure grows on public institutions to adopt similar tactics to improve efficiency and growth.

The Bank, however, operates in an unusual prism: The world stage. The result is an impatient culture. Management looks for quick results that contradict the application of its lending programs which are implemented over decades. According to the Staff Association, a 2002 survey revealed even 21% of senior management did not have a clear sense of the Bank's strategic direction.[52]

Bank reorganizations have sought to improve efficiency, mollify critics and, to the extent possible, modify the institution's culture. Over two decades, reforms have followed a recurring theme: Bring resources closer to clients thereby reducing costs, while concurrently allowing staff to do more with less. The frequent shuffling, however, has led to staff downsizing through redundancies and realignments of "skill mixes" but without corresponding decreases in work programs. Reviews on whether these reorganizations have brought the Bank closer to its clients have been mixed. The Strategic Compact, a massive reorganization implemented from 1997 to 2001, provides a useful example.

James Wolfensohn took over as the Bank's president in 1995, promising to reform an institution facing severe criticism and an evaporating lending portfolio. By 1997, he had brokered a mammoth deal with the Bank's board to implement a series of far-reaching proposals. The Compact's agenda was to reposition the institution from building infrastructure and promoting macroeconomic reforms to promoting poverty reduction through social and environmentally sustainable development. In addition, Wolfensohn wanted to use new technologies such as the Internet to help the Bank create a repository of technical expertise so as to reinvent itself as a "knowledge bank." The Board agreed to an infusion of $100 million at the beginning of the Compact with a promise from senior management the budget would be reduced to 1997 levels by 2001.

Academics and organizational theorists have studied the

Compact to understand whether its objectives were successful, and if inroads were made to alter the Bank's culture. The findings have been startling.

Two years after the Compact concluded, Daniel Nielson of Brigham Young University, Michael Tierney of William and Mary College and Catherine Weaver of the University of Kansas wrote a paper entitled, *The Argument is the Incentive: Agency, Organizational Culture and the World Bank's Strategic Compact.*[53] They sought to measure changes in staff behavior from two baseline years, 1996, the year before the Compact's implementation, and 2001, the year of its conclusion. Since the Compact sought to achieve specific outcomes, the authors began with a hypothesis that the more they could measure actions taken by staff to achieve a management goal, the more likely the objective was met.

Formal institutions and personnel can be changed, the professors believed, but organizational culture, once entrenched, proves resistant to change. Cultural change in organizations is typically glacial. They noted Harvard Business School training sessions of Bank personnel suggested the institution had one of the strongest internal cultures the educators had ever seen. If organizational cultures in general are difficult to change, it appeared the Bank was a bellwether for resistance.

The authors' research revealed change, or the concept of change, was met with hostility. Partially, this can be attributed to human nature. As Woodrow Wilson once said, "If you want to make an enemy, try to change something." But in addition, there are also those who benefited from the status quo. Nielson et al suggest organizational culture will change slowly only when the objectives of reform find convergence with existing norms.

The researchers addressed similar themes to those Wheeler and I experimented on with B-SPAN during the same period. We intuitively understood the range of potential responses to the change we were fermenting. In the early years, we quietly developed the system, but eventually it was necessary to shock the culture into changing. To be successful, we knew B-SPAN needed champions who were not married to the status quo of the existing culture.

The issue of Bank culture poses an interesting conundrum because there are two aspects to it. To refer once again to Geert Hofstede's work, *Cultures and Organizations*, he suggests strong cultures are homogenous and weak cultures are heterogeneous.[54] Homogenous cultures are most capable of setting targets and achieving objectives. The Bank's workforce is comprised of a myriad of nationalities and cultures each with various viewpoints and objectives on development. From this perspective, the Bank's culture is highly heterogeneous and, using Hofstede's standard, likely ineffective. On the other hand, it has an unusually homogenous culture of internal norms that dictate how processes, activities and relationships are conducted. They bind together to form the Bank's unique environment: A homogenous and strong culture that is more accomplished at setting targets than achieving objectives.

Nielson and his colleagues assessed the impact of each objective and found the results dubious. For example, spending on environmental and social development increased, but the impact was mitigated by two other concurrent policies. As part of a decentralization effort, budget authority moved away from the Environment Department and toward individual country directors. Additionally, a new Country Assistance Management (CAM) system, designed to reduce supply-driven lending by creating internal markets for technical services, was introduced. The CAM system forced environmental specialists to sell their time to line managers, who in turn viewed environmental assessments as an albatross that would increase costs and extend project timelines. Demand for lenient auditors grew. Now that they had to compete to sell their services, incentives for auditors to become lenient increased. The quality of environmental audits declined.

Matrix management was introduced during the Compact as a system to create cross-fertilization between technical and country-based teams. According to the academics, it instead created ambiguities that resulted in a reduction in morale and a decrease in cooperation among staff. Low marks were also given to an effort to increase NGO participation during the project appraisal and implementation process. This goal came into conflict with the institution's cultural norm of moving projects quickly through its pipeline for board approval.

The authors cited a survey from 2001, the year the Compact concluded, that recorded the perception of representatives of borrowing countries. Only 14% thought the Bank had strengthened civic participation in national development efforts. On the other hand, 82% found the Bank remained effective in maintaining macroeconomic and trade policies to attract investments, the philosophy it had in place prior to the launch of the Compact. Finally, chronic weaknesses in the Bank's monitoring and evaluation process undermined another objective to show improved results for project sustainability and impact.

The authors gave higher marks to the Compact's decentralization process. As hundreds of staff moved to field offices over three years, they measured an increase in the amount of operational decisions made at the country-level. The length of projects cycles, which had been a key client concern, also declined. Still, their assessment was mixed. The researchers believed reduction of project cycles was due in large part to its convergence with the existing "approval culture." They found field staff felt disconnected from cutting-edge research taking place at headquarters (a key objective for the implementation of B-SPAN in 2000). Field staff felt disenfranchised as assignments and promotions were decided in Washington. They also felt pressured from headquarters to encourage clients to conform to Bank guidelines and policies. Clients concurred with this assessment and believed key decisions still remained within the purview of Washington.

Ralf Leiteritz, in his paper '*Our Poverty is a World Full of Dreams*': *Organizational Culture and Change at the World Bank*, explored how the embedded culture resisted Compact actions to change existing norms.[55] Leiteritz, a political science professor at the Universidad de los Andes in Colombia and former Bank consultant, calls culture the intervening variable between the external environment and organizational outcomes. His theoretical model suggests that inputs from change agents, whether external or internal, will compel the organization to choose one of three outcomes: Keeping the status quo by rejecting reforms; adapting to reforms to produce interpretations consistent with existing norms; or learning from and embracing reforms. He notes behavioral changes are directly tied to incentives that serve as the foundation for the organization's culture: If the Compact failed to change incentives, then it would fail to change the culture.

The Compact, Leiteritz suggests, sought to move the Bank away from the neoclassical economic heterodoxy of the "Washington Consensus" epitomized by the structural adjustment lending it embraced throughout the 1980s and early 1990s. He asserts the growing chorus of external discontent for Bank environmental policies and indigenous documents such as the Wapenhans Report unleashed newly emboldened internal catalysts for reform.

In 1996, sensing a mandate in the making, President Wolfensohn threw down the gauntlet. He castigated the institution for its lack of transparency and pointed to internal surveys that found half the staff said they did not trust management. The Compact created four new networks: Environmentally and Socially Sustainable Development; Human Development; Finance and Private Sector Infrastructure; and Poverty Reduction and Economic Management. It moved personnel increasingly into the field and brought more budgetary authority into the hands of country directors. It sought to build a new identity for the institution as a "knowledge bank." And, it implemented architectural reforms with matrix management and increased monitoring and evaluation.

Leiteritz believes, however, the ingrained culture proved more resilient than reformers expected. He observed a persistent pattern of objectives that were in conflict with one another and thus mitigated intended impacts. For instance, the attempt to cater to clients' desires for streamlined project cycles conflicted with efforts to provide greater participation to civil society stakeholders who were simultaneously pushing for increased safeguards. Bank public relations spokespersons cited increased NGO participation in project appraisals, but civil society actors complained they were often brought into the process so late that their influence was minimal. In the aftermath of the Compact, the Bank was quick to note a decrease in overall project cycles; but since this dovetailed with the existing norm of its approval culture, observers were not surprised.

Safeguards proved vexing in another way. In the aftermath of the Wapenhans Commission's report on the high failure rate of Bank projects, some blamed new environmental and social development safeguards as a chief cause.[56] Safeguards were first implemented during the 1980s in response to pressure from NGOs in the aftermath of environmental problems created by the Bank's lending activities. Critics of the Wapenhans Commission said safeguards created financial disincentives for lenders and borrowers.[57] The Bank estimated they added $300 million in direct and indirect costs to each project.[58] Safeguards compelled managers to seek projects that could meet these new requirements and still move quickly through the pipeline. This resulted in projects considered safe but marginally effective, thus reinforcing the institution's risk-averse culture. At a time when the stakes for the poor were growing more desperate, the Bank was moving in the opposite direction by taking fewer risks in its developmental lending.[59]

Other conflicts appeared. Matrix management was intended to reduce a supply driven culture by introducing an internal market for services. This reform, however, was inversely related to efforts to create a knowledge bank: If staff were directly in competition with colleagues to sell their services, what motivation would they have to engage in knowledge sharing?[60] As new networks such as Poverty Reduction and Environmentally and Socially Sustainable Development were being created, budget authority was concurrently moving into the hands of country directors. Dichotomous but unequal schools of thought on how funds should be spent were fostered.[61] Finally, at a time when the Compact sought greater emphasis on project evaluation, funding for supervision was often an early target when budgets began contracting toward the latter stages of the

Compact's implementation.

Leiteritz noted the Compact had minimal input and support from staff. It moved in different directions simultaneously. It emphasized reform through structures and systems, but failed to address the underlying incentives that sustained the Bank's culture. Leiteritz concluded the institution assimilated the Compact's goals by adapting to them. The final result of the three possibilities he defined more closely resembled retrenchment of the status quo rather than learning from the reforms.

A closer look at two pivotal reforms seems in order to illustrate the resiliency of the Bank's culture. A critical issue the Compact sought to address was the quality of the Bank's project evaluation. Throughout the 1980s, external observers—representing both NGOs and donor participants—became increasingly concerned about the Bank's lending effectiveness. Senior officials were diffident, but as the decibel level rose they commissioned an internal investigation.

The result was the 1991 Wapenhans Commission Report.[62] As noted in Part I, it was a watershed document that left the institution struggling to find stable ground. The report revealed more than 37% of the Bank's projects had failed. Ten years earlier, the failure rate had been 15%. This meant the Bank's measure of its own effectiveness found success rates had declined by 150% during the 1980s. The reviewers also said an additional 30% were seriously troubled by the fifth year of implementation. And, there was more. The report noted more than 60% of the audits either had insufficient information or had been done so soon after the final disbursement of lending that it was impossible to accurately gauge effectiveness. In other words, the Bank could tell when a project failed but it couldn't tell when a project succeeded.

The report sounded like a catalogue of charges leveled by critics. It noted Bank personnel ignored local input and bullied borrowing governments to adopt the prevailing mantra from headquarters. It said the approval culture was on full display. Project appraisals were slanted in such a way as to secure loan approvals that were pushed through quickly. Minimal project supervision was conducted to analyze and monitor impacts. Moreover, the Bank's Operations Evaluation Department (OED) was woefully under-funded and under-utilized. Since there was an absence of information, managerial accountability was also lacking. Furthermore, there was no means in place to capitalize on whatever lessons had been learned. The report could have been written by any one of a dozen American or European NGOs raging against the Bank at the time. But the investigation had been led by Willi Wapenhans, a former Bank vice president.

To be sure, the Commission had its critics. In the comprehensive compendium *The World Bank: In Its First Half Century,* authors Devesh Kapur, John Lewis and Richard Webb said it had not fully accounted for exacerbating factors such as the debt crises among client countries during the 1970s that compelled the Bank to expand portfolios and increase investment risks.[63] They suggest the report placed undue emphasis on the approval culture by highlighting weaknesses at the project supervision stage rather than the project appraisal phase.[64] Kapur et al also noted the implementation of safeguard requirements due to NGO pressure created further difficulties.[65]

Finally, the researchers suggested another factor for the decline: Unrealistic predictions about economic rates of return that had been caused by overly ambitious output goals or limited borrower capacity.[66] Whatever view about causes an observer might support, Wapenhans's or Kapur's, there is little debate about the outcome: Over the time period studied by the commission, Bank projects failed at a higher rate than they had previously; and its lending imposed further debt upon borrowing governments of poor countries.

The importance of the Wapenhans Commission findings cannot be underestimated. They questioned core reasons for the Bank's existence.[67] If the Bank's lending effectiveness was declining and its ability to evaluate success was in doubt, then the legitimacy of the institution would also be called into question. As the Compact went into effect, more funds were funneled into the Operations Evaluation Department's work. But the Compact also mandated the Bank return to 1997 budget levels when the reform package concluded in 2001. Increasing project supervision and evaluation were not tied to incentives as defined by the approval culture. As budgets declined, funds for project evaluation were among the first to contract. Bank personnel recognized the Compact's conflicting objectives, and Leiteritz suggested they simply adapted and internalized the reforms to fit existing cultural norms.[68]

Bank critics went one step further by questioning the objectivity of in-house evaluations. These observers have suggested biases can be expected from a system where evaluators were judging their own management. Consequently, they have advocated for the establishment of an independent auditing process.

Following the Compact, the Bank asserted successful lending had improved to nearly 80% by 2000. Adam Lerrick, a Carnegie Mellon University economist, questioned the declaration.[69] In a highly publicized rebuttal, he noted the same concerns raised by the Wapenhans Commission prior to implementation of Compact reforms still continued. The institution's approval culture, he said, continued to emphasize moving projects and then moving on.

Lerrick suggested personnel were conditioned to focus more on the interests of superiors than of clients, because that was how careers were made in the Bank. Since the study's evaluations took years to complete, accountability for mistakes during project design, preparation and implementation were minimized. "When the auditors are captive, when the timing of judgment is premature, when the criteria are faulty and when the numbers are selectively chosen, then conclusions are worthless," he concluded.[70]

A second part of the Strategic Compact's agenda was to address staff inequities. It provides another example of institutional hypocrisy and the difficulty of cultural reform. The Compact called for a phased elimination of Bank consultants who were classified as Non-Regular Staff (NRS). As part of the 1987 reorganization, the institution began a policy of "dollar budgeting" that allocated staff salaries directly to projects. Since higher grade-level personnel were more costly, managers began hiring consultants to keep within their budget parameters. Consultants who were continually rehired over long periods became known as NRS.[71] NRS earned half the salaries of staff, had fewer benefits and no pensions. The reorganization had reduced costs through downsizing, yet within a year many former staff had returned as NRS. By the early 1990s, the NRS ranks were growing dramatically.

Hiring NRS provided line managers with a number of incentives. Since managers were judged on how well they operated within their budget, reducing salary expenditures made sense. Contracts were generally six to twelve months and could be renewed just before expiration. NRS were not allowed access to the Administrative Tribunal, which made their situation difficult if they worked for an autocratic superior. They had no family leave, and though they received some abbreviated benefits, these costs were not charged to unit budgets.

Those NRS who were U.S. nationals faced additional financial burdens. They paid all their own Social Security. Moreover, the U.S. Internal Revenue Service classified NRS as common-law employees of the Bank. As such, they were ineligible to make contributions to retirement plans for the self-employed. Concurrently, the Bank refused to allow them to participate in its retirement plan. As the category swelled, the Staff Association and individual NRS began suggesting they had become second-class citizens.[72] As early as 1988, senior management said they were fully cognizant of the problem, and promised to seek a solution.[73] For almost a decade nothing changed. By the late 1990s, more than 4,000 employees, or one-fourth of all Bank workers, were NRS.[74] Some had been consultants for two decades. The Staff Association characterized it as an "apartheid-like system."[75]

Rising NRS tensions, increasing concern on the part of Bank watchdogs, and two external events finally prompted a management reaction. In 1997, a U.S. Circuit Court of Appeals ruled contractors and temporary agency workers at Microsoft who had been laboring full-time were in fact "common-law" employees of the company.[76] Microsoft's position that the workers were independent contractors was invalidated. The court ruled they should receive the same salaries and benefits Microsoft's full-time employees enjoyed. Microsoft appealed, but the U.S. Supreme Court reaffirmed the lower court's ruling.

Then in 1998, an NRS employee working for the Asian Development Bank (ADB) sought past pension credit for his services.[77] The ADB's Tribunal ruled in his favor. The decisions regarding equal pay for equal work and the right of NRS to have a retirement plan meant the Bank could no longer sidestep these issues.

A major overhaul of the status of personnel began to evolve. As part of the Compact, the NRS category would be eliminated. Workers could be converted to full-time staff or designated Short-Term Consultants (STCs), and allowed to work a maximum of 180 days or be terminated at the conclusion of their contracts. Managers would be forced to make a choice. The plan provided a two-year window for phasing out NRS. When the window finally closed, less than half had been converted to full-time staff.[78]

From a personal perspective, my not achieving a regular staff position was a mixed blessing. On the one hand, I never enjoyed the stability, wages or benefits afforded some colleagues. My contracts were always short-term and tenuous. On the other hand, had I been locked into a staff position, there would have been little opportunity to launch B-SPAN. Put more succinctly, a crusade to bring transparency to the Bank could never have been launched.

The reform, however, did not change the incentive structure for managers. STCs provided them the opportunity to continue the practice of hiring personnel on short-term contracts. Predictably the percentage of STCs grew. By 2001, the Human Resources Department recognized it had manufactured a situation similar to the one it had tried to solve.[79] In response, HR expanded the use of Junior Professional Associates (JPA), fixed-term positions for young professionals for up to two years.[80] But the incentives for managers to hire STCs had not changed, and their ranks continued to swell.

In 2004, HR launched a new strategy with the creation of an Extended Term Consultant (ETC) category. It allowed managers to hire someone full-time for two years with benefits. ETCs, however, could not continue beyond two years. When their time expired, managers would be forced to hire them as full-time staff, return them to STCs, or terminate them. Conversion was at the discretion of individual managers. Concurrently, HR reduced the amount of days STCs would be eligible to work to 150. The rationale, senior management said, was to make STCs truly part-time, and give them opportunities to find employment outside the Bank.[81] With few opportunities to find suitable work elsewhere for their specialized skill sets, most STCs continued to work full-time schedules with part-time salaries. Today, through the toil of hundreds of STCs, the Bank continues to operate normally. They represent the reincarnation of the old NRS.

Nor did the conversion of some NRS into regular staff end a key disagreement with management. Following the Supreme Court decision, HR set up a pension plan for newly converted employees, but past pension credit for former NRS was not provided. Despite vehement protests, management said consultants were fully cognizant their employment agreements did not include pension rights. They added that U.S. labor laws—which prohibited denial of pensions--were irrelevant, since the Bank was not beholden to U.S. law.[82]

The groundswell of anger from the original treatment of NRS gained new momentum. Management changed tactics. Past pension credit was unaffordable, they said, and would cost the institution more than $1 billion. The Staff Association then hired an actuarial firm to generate precise figures. That figure came to $125 million.[83] It represented one percent of total pension assets. In fact the fund was so flush with cash that the Bank had not even made a contribution during the four years leading up to the audit.[84] The Staff Association subsequently funded a test case of a former NRS employee before the Administrative Tribunal. When the employee received a favorable verdict, management was forced to capitulate entirely. In the end, thousands of NRS employees, I included, received pension money.

The Staff Association estimated continual reorganizations—those that readjusted skill mixes from 1987 to 2000—cost 3,000 individuals their jobs.[85] Many people who dedicated their lives to helping the world's poor have left the Bank. It is also a heavy price to pay in lost institutional expertise. The Staff Association has characterized HR as "incremental thinkers who have been brought up in a culture of small, rational, efficient changes that eventually drift into an uneconomical whole; that although they have determined to pull things apart, they may not have the skills in systems-thinking to implement an imaginative, holistic strategy any better than they've implemented all the other state-of-the-art strategies put down on paper since 1987."[86]

Following the Compact, there have been a series of smaller departmental reorganizations which included that of the World Bank Institute in 2002. When B-SPAN moved from the Research Department, it was positioned inside a new unit headed by Karen Millet called Knowledge Learning. Millet resigned two years later, and WBI's management chose to dissolve the unit instead of seeking continuity with a replacement. The Knowledge Learning teams were absorbed into remaining units and in B-SPAN's case by GDLN. This repositioning of activities was seen at the time as temporary while the department changed its strategic focus by placing greater emphasis on capacity building tasks and closer integration with country-level operations. The absorption of various teams from the dissolved Knowledge Learning pillar did not end GDLN's reorganization. The unit continued a rapid evolution which included decentralization of its business units into the regions, and creation of a multi-media services operation.

While WBI and GDLN were changing, an even greater undertow was taking shape. In early 2004, Managing Director Shengman Zhang announced the Bank's leadership was pleased with the institution's accomplishments. Therefore it had decided to convene a Task Force on Organizational Effectiveness (OETF) to "proactively reposition the organization."[87]

Legions of Bank employees shuddered. Management said there were several reasons for convening the task force, including a decline of lending to middle-income countries, a need to simplify an arcane budget process, a desire to increase selectivity of a pipeline that had expanded to 4,000 projects, and an interest in consolidating technical specialists with regional operations. Zhang said the results of two surveys had provided the impetus for the task force.[88]

The first survey had asked officials from client countries about their perception of the institution. One-third railed against the Bank's culture. They called it arrogant and bureaucratic. A second survey queried Bank staff. More than half responded that work was done on behalf of managers rather than in the interest of stakeholders.

Throughout the year, the task force sifted through proposals behind closed doors. By the time it submitted recommendations, word had leaked that Wolfensohn would be replaced as Bank president by Paul Wolfowitz. The proposals were dead on arrival, yet within a few months new rumors began about reforms the Wolfowitz team was planning. The game of musical chairs never stopped.

The Bank believes the Strategic Compact was a success, and management says it has the data to prove it.[89] Nevertheless, a question remains. The Compact's core goal was to stop an eroding lending portfolio by bringing the institution closer to its clients. If so, why did the Bank cite the same problems when launching the OETF just three years after the Compact concluded?[90] One Bank insider suggested the Compact was "trying to bring an organization from The Middle Ages, strategically. You cannot have dukedoms and have a strategy."[91] The reality is that the Bank's senior management is wedded to a middle management with a competing objective. High-level officials addressing large issues under the glare of global scrutiny frequently change strategic direction. The middle management bureaucracy, however, draws power from retention of the status quo. Caught in the middle is staff.

The habitual reorganizations, large and small, have engendered cynicism among staff, and created anxiety over a stable work environment. Cynicism has increased because lofty reforms have been muted by a powerful culture resistant to change. Anxiety has increased because positions have been right-sized, downsized, outsourced, and realigned to meet changing objectives.

Senior management's traditional reticence for sharing information or consulting with the Bank's workforce regarding reorganizations has fostered this tension. Moreover, management's lack of transparency on the necessity and depth of change is exacerbated by a tendency to enact the reorganizations quickly within a culture where all else evolves slowly. The lack of communication also creates an important structural problem. Staff is well positioned to offer insights on strengths and weaknesses of proposals because they work in the trenches. Yet senior management usually does not seek their input until the planning process is largely completed.

The workforce worries as it watches decisions being made behind closed doors: It was a Kafkaesque moment when senior officials expressed befuddlement about persistent rumors swirling among employees regarding the OETF. External stakeholders have long criticized the institution for not providing enough seats at the table. Internal stakeholders, the Bank's staff, have shared the same concern.

Some suggest the impetus for these continual reinventions is that, despite decades of research and application, the causes of development and poverty remain uncertain. Others believe senior management has traditionally been top-heavy, and bureaucrats will inevitably engineer reorganizations as a way to justify their existence.

Robert Wade suggests the impetus occurs whenever the disconnection between the bureaucracy's rhetoric and the reality becomes too noticeable.[92] What is clear: Constant reorganizations have fostered an environment of waste and fear. Some observers have noted that eventually productivity reaches a point of diminishing returns, and the institution becomes less effective in its mission.

By 2005, the Staff Association had essentially thrown in the towel. It suggested staff "accept that reorganizations and other painful changes made for public consumption are always going to occur: It is safer not to get too locked in to the organization."[93]

6

On one end of the spectrum are Bank consultants who are virtually powerless with regard to workplace protections. On the other end is the institutionalized power of the Bank's managerial corps. In 2004, the Staff Association began an assessment of what it believed had plagued the institution for decades: A management culture that controlled staff through fear and intimidation.[94]

The Staff Association said the breeding ground for managerial abuses were institutions that were disorganized and chaotic. But managerial harassment was not about demanding styles, personality clashes or poor communications. Rather, the Staff Association believed it was a pervasive, persistent and deliberate strategy for interpersonal destruction of Bank staff.[95] It cited research suggesting the more hierarchical an organization was the more staff were at risk for abuses.

What were the characteristics of abusive managers? The research noted punitive behavior was related to an insatiable desire to control or dominate others. Often these managers were insecure and viewed staff as a threat rather than a resource. Manipulation and intimidation were found to be long-existing traits, generally exhibited as early as childhood. Abusive managers also shared another common characteristic: They sought to keep their tactics of intimidation and retribution hidden from others, especially superiors.[96]

The Staff Association investigation studied both sides of the equation. They found submissive employees were not targeted. "Researchers have found that bullying bosses tend to target those who are strong, competent workers and show a personal sense of ethics. The workers share another essential: They have some psychological or economic vulnerability that traps them in the job."[97]

The research also suggested employees with certain characteristics were especially targeted by managers who ruled by fear and intimidation. These characteristics included integrity, idealism, humor, trustworthiness and the ability to see the big picture.[98]

If the parallels to B-SPAN were uncanny, then perhaps WBI was not particularly unique. Over the years, the Staff Association documented numerous employee experiences. Staff spoke about managers who appeared gracious in public and before superiors, only to unleash tirades and humiliate underlings behind closed doors. There were managers who: Declared positions redundant or changed position descriptions to dominate their staff; promised staff positions to consultants only to renege without explanation; conducted character assassinations of personnel they had dismissed so as to insulate themselves from accountability; used their office to advance their careers at the expense of work programs; used staff to camouflage their lack of knowledge before superiors; and used staff as personal valets.

Managers like these could live without fear of accountability, the Staff Association suggested, for in the culture of the Bank they were sacrosanct. If things did not work out, they were simply moved to a different part of the organization. The pattern of behavior had been consistent year in and year out. This was possible, the Staff Association said, because there was no transparency inside the institution to provide accountability.[99]

Internal theatrics are meaningful because of the Bank's mission to help people survive poverty; and not just a few people, but literally hundreds of millions. Institutions with an uncomfortable percentage of managers intent on self-promotion are ultimately not effective organizations. When staff has performed poorly, they have been fired. Yet when Bank managers have performed poorly, historically they have re-emerged elsewhere in the organization. There is, however, an internal mechanism for accountability that the Bank has established. It is called the Conflict Resolution System (CRS).

During the late 1970s, a series of wage and hiring decisions by the Bank engendered hostility among its staff. The growing chasm between management and staff led to the formation of the Staff Association, which began immediately to work on establishing a formal grievance process.[100] By 1980, it was able to negotiate the creation of an Administrative Tribunal.

From the start, however, the tribunal process was inordinately weighted in management's favor. Management had final authority to appoint members, and it chose judges and attorneys exclusively.

Mediation and labor experts were excluded and Staff Association input on appointments was advisory. Terms ran three years, and since management determined appointments, the Staff Association believed judicial independence was effectively eliminated.

According to Tribunal rules, class action suits were prohibited, which meant a favorable judgment for one plaintiff's filed grievance was inadmissible for others, no matter how representative. Additionally, a staff person had a 120-day limit to file an appeal from the date of their dismissal; yet the Tribunal was afforded as much time as it wanted to issue a ruling. Some decisions took as long as two years to be rendered. Staff in the Bank's country offices had no practical means of accessing the Tribunal in Washington.

Moreover the Tribunal defined its jurisdiction narrowly. It ruled only on what was appropriate for the staff member filing the grievance, but abstained from disciplining managers. If a plaintiff received a favorable judgment regarding a flagrant managerial abuse, the Tribunal could recommend the Bank take one of two actions: Reinstatement or monetary compensation. Historically, senior management always chose compensation, which meant the staff person's career at the Bank was over immediately. Unlike other international civil service organizations such as the International Labour Organization or the Pan-American Health Organization, monetary awards were capped at three times a worker's annual net salary.[101]

Unabated staff anger over an environment that continued to foster labor abuses finally led to a 1999 investigation by the U.S. Congress. Under the glare of its most important donor, the Bank moved preemptively to increase mediation opportunities. The CRS, instituted in the late 1990s, included several components in addition to the Tribunal. It created an Ethics Office, the Department of Institutional Integrity (INT), an Ombudsman's Office, a Mediation Office, and the Appeals Committee.

Limits, however, were placed on the authority and jurisdiction of each new office.[102] The Ethics Office addresses issues of corporate ethics rather than workplace abuses. The Department of Institutional Integrity handles issues of financial fraud and embezzlement. The

Ombudsman's Office plays an advisory role to staff, but has no formal authority to take action or render a decision. The Mediation Office seeks to use informal mechanisms to bring parties into agreement. The Appeals Committee is not empowered to render binding decisions, and does not handle cases involving harassment, retaliation, or hostile work situations.

The Bank created a Review Committee to oversee the implementation of the revised system, and the Staff Association subsequently complained the CRS had not gone far enough in addressing inequities. The Review Committee agreed but shied away from changing the new system, and subsequently rejected a proposal to add an external arbitration option. The Review Committee concluded more informal approaches such as mediation should be the emphasis of the CRS.

In reviewing the system, the U.S. General Accounting Office (GAO) found the measures did "not fundamentally alter the Bank's system."[103] With regards to Congress, however, some critics were mollified. The Bank had dodged a bullet.

The CRS system has remained untouched since these events took place at the end of the 1990s. Bank employees believe the system is flawed and ineffective.[104] Though some grievances are settled informally, a significant percentage of abuse is silently accepted. The numbers of staff seeking restitution via the CRS have paled in comparison to the anecdotal evidence about managerial abuses. Many believe pursuing a grievance, successfully or unsuccessfully, also leaves them vulnerable to retaliation. The situation is especially precarious for STCs and staff dependent upon their G-4 visas, which allows them and their families to remain in the U.S. Without monetary damages that have the capacity to cause the Bank real pain, the institution remains without a pivotal incentive to proactively root out or reactively punish abusive managers. Predictably, staff is reluctant to pursue grievances.

The Staff Association has emphasized that without independent oversight, the CRS remains "vulnerable to manipulation and improper influence. A privacy-seeking organization will always want to settle employee-employer conflicts as quickly and quietly as possible, especially whistleblower episodes.

"World Bank management set up the organization's conflict resolution and investigatory mechanisms at least partly with institutional privacy in mind, and in the early days of political meddling in the young Bank, self-protection in general was probably a good idea," the Staff Association goes on to say. "The concern with privacy now has become a barrier to fairness, though. For example, in some multi-national development banks staff is barred from speaking to the press about anything that would harm the institution's *mission*. At the World Bank, staff can't say anything that might harm the *institution*—in other words, management. Management of any organization in reality can't be neutral in staff grievance cases. The Bank cannot be police, prosecutor, and judge without many forms of conflict of interest arising. For due process, the institution needs broadly based independent oversight of its behavior toward staff."[105]

It seems relevant to note the following: Even an effective CRS system would not have been a venue I would have pursued regarding B-SPAN. The nature of my work was bringing about institutional change through a cultural revolution. It would have been difficult to argue I was trying to launch a revolution and WBI hard-headedly was refusing to cooperate.

Monika Weber-Fahr was also a consummate tactician. Her approach to wresting control of B-SPAN was couched in such a way as to insulate her from organizational scrutiny. Launching a panel process to evaluate candidates was orchestrated to cover her tracks within acceptable institutional practices. Even if those around her understood she was engineering a sham, creating a panel was akin to establishing an alibi. The charade was confirmed again when Sona Panajyan resigned a few months later to take a job elsewhere in the Bank. Weber-Fahr quickly replaced her with a GDLN consultant from overseas.

The Bank Ombudsman's 2005 annual report cited managerial abuse and the need to improve management skills as its top concerns.[106] The report recommended job evaluations become less weighted on program and budget administration and more on how staff is managed. "Technical competence is still perceived to be more important in management selections than managerial skills," the report noted.[107] The Ombudsman report also suggested there was a propensity for hiring managerial candidates with poor interpersonal skills.

These findings by the Staff Association and Ombudsman's Office have only codified an understanding held by Bank staff. For the last two decades, the Bank has surveyed staff to gauge perceptions about management, supervisors, work environments and organizational reforms. The results have proved remarkably consistent, indicating a malaise has descended upon the Bank's workforce.[108] Fear over job loss, downsizing, right-sizing, redundancy, decentralization, deportation following job loss, the inability to seek restitution for inequities, and the lack of a mentoring environment, were key factors.

Most staff lacked confidence in the institution's senior officials. Most distrusted their immediate supervisors. Many believed managers routinely put their personal agendas ahead of team objectives. Fear over job security was an underlying refrain, but other factors contributed to low morale. Those subjected to abusive work situations were incensed by double standards for managers. Staff understood the limitations of the CRS and feared retaliation. Some perceived racial or gender-based discrimination. Additionally, many found job mobility within the institution restrictive, the bureaucracy stifling and keeping an appropriate work-life balance, difficult.

Analysis the Bank has conducted parallels these findings. Myers-Briggs found Bank managers had extremely low levels of "emotional intelligence."[109] There was a disproportionate amount of "rational thinkers" who looked at a situation's logic but failed to take into account other viewpoints or the impact of their decisions on others. Managers were quick to criticize and slow to commend. Their perfectionism interfered with competent work.

In 2000, the Bank invited the British Institute of Development Studies (IDS) to conduct another analysis. IDS found Bank managers highly educated, verbally dexterous and forceful. They often went into poor countries and overpowered clients with their opinions. They were intimidating, arrogant and seemed to revel in their elitism. IDS noted Bank managers seemed little concerned about their behavior, as there was no competition for services they provided to developing country clients. Managers who weren't listening to staff weren't listening to clients either.

The Bank attracts ambitious people who understand success can lead to accruing vast power: The power to control billions of dollars; the power to manage thousands of staff; the power to dictate to governments and even continents what to do and how to do it. To accrue this power, they plot. They calculate. They ingratiate themselves with those above them. They believe they must subordinate those below them. Appearance takes precedence, and practice often mitigates policy. In such a culture, the rhetoric for change is treated as rhetoric. While the Bank has changed over the past two decades, it has done so at the margins. Below the surface, its DNA remains in many ways unchanged.

Nor is the Bank a normal business. It seeks to make a profit, but success is not measured by profits. Managers may be considered successful if their projects receive board approval. Managers are rewarded for administering units and tasks within annual budget allocations rather than for the texture of their administration. In an environment of strict funding allocations, short-term considerations take precedence over long-term interests.

The Bank's culture does not easily reward leadership skills; but it does require adherence to the dictums of superiors. Successful technical service and subservience lead to promotions. In an environment where loyalty is prized above competence, and where an internal Conflict Resolution System is deemed dubious, accountability for inappropriate management becomes problematic. As a result, a system of perverse incentives has been institutionalized at the Bank.

Layering these perverse incentives is a rigid hierarchy. The separation between senior officials and staff is stark and ingrained. Mid-level management, cognizant of and empowered by the separation, is diligent in enforcing it. Barriers are considered turf. Personnel who seek direct contact with officials above their immediate superiors are dealt with punitively.

Such an environment creates warped perceptions and information vacuums. Mid-level officials only want to present successes as a strategy for promotion. Senior officials, focused on the big picture, are often given a skewed view of how things actually operate at the staff level. Problems and potential problems become hidden as accurate information often fails to move up the chain of command. This is reinforced by what the Staff Association suggests is senior management's intense desire to not receive unpleasant information. The result is an institution-wide fear of candor, and it provides further incentives for mid-level officials to avoid transparency.

Management experts who study what makes organizations effective suggest that as hierarchies are reduced, staff become more empowered.[110] Empowered staff tend to be more independent, a concern for autocrats; but they are also more committed, innovative and responsive to challenges. The issue is not about eliminating hierarchy or creating situations where everyone answers to no one. Rather it is about finding a balance within an organization's layers, so an open flow of communication between levels allows everyone to operate with the best possible information.

The Bank's sheer size provides occasional gaps in the bureaucracy's instincts to stifle entrepreneurial activity. Innovators, when they are able to operate, must do so at the margins; and they must keep their activities carefully hidden until fruition. Based on personal experience, it is a difficult endeavor. Habitual reorganizations, periodic redundancies, continuous budget calamities, and the institutionalized culture of managerial abuse empower bureaucrats at the expense of entrepreneurs.

Internal surveys sought to identify the degree to which staff felt they had the freedom to be creative and innovative. All responded negatively with the exception of the most senior managerial cadre.[111] The nature of all bureaucracies is to favor risk aversion. As bureaucracy in an organization increases, innovation declines. Those who fear risk mitigate it by increasing their paper trails and other activities that have no relationship to producing results or products for their customers. The problem for an organization that doesn't value a degree of entrepreneurship: At some point its bureaucracy will reduce efficiency, increase costs, and produce fewer results. Since the Bank deliberately seeks managers with risk-adverse portfolios, this tendency is continually reinforced. Innovators fall by the wayside. As a result, an unbreakable loop is formed.

The risk-adverse nature of Bank managers exists in tandem with another ingrained characteristic known in the institution as its "approval culture." A key variable by which the Bank measures success is by the volume of outputs: The amount of projects approved and lending dispersed. Personnel who are successful in getting projects accepted by the board climb through the hierarchy.

Banks like to make money. So, lending projects that are approved are ones considered safe or of less risk. Careers are built on not taking risks, and those who take risks become risks. Ambitious managers have incentives to move many projects safely through the pipeline. This is good for volume and other indices that the Bank uses to demonstrate its effectiveness to donors and external watchdogs. But does it translate into insightful lending or successful projects? There is significant evidence to suggest it does not.

There is also significant anecdotal evidence suggesting the approval culture has another important manifestation: Its perverse incentives supported corruption in client countries in the past. Since staff promotions were tied to moving projects forward, ignoring corruption was good for business and careers. Ignoring client corruption, in turn, fostered an environment for ignoring internal corruption. The Department of Institutional Integrity audits weed out illegalities for personal gain, but internal corruption has usually revealed itself in abuses of authority.

This culture, institutionalized over six decades, is one where managers have little latitude to fail. Since failure is to be feared, there is little flexibility to innovate. Staff becomes fodder that cannot be trusted, and must be tightly controlled. They survive by facilitating what is in the best interest of their supervisors. In such an environment, one theory merits consideration. At some point close enough to the pinnacle of the pyramid of power, the ruler of a fief must become a chameleon. Now, in the public eye, he or she is will be seen as responsible for creating or perpetuating institutional inefficiencies. As such, they often seek to redefine their role into one of an agent of change. By instinct or training, however, they rarely possess the ability to play this role. Strategies are misguided. Reforms hollow. The institution lurches into new difficulties because its change agents are products of a reward system of the bureaucracy's status quo.

The Bank's Young Professionals (YP) Program also contributes heavily to its managerial cadre. Each year, from thousands of applicants, the few YPs chosen have come to represent an "anointed" class within the internal culture of the Bank. Over time this elite class, however, has also come to epitomize the arrogance of the institution.

"The Bank's culture is over bred, inbred and totally tied to process," said I.J. Singh, a former Research Department economist during a 1996 forum with Wolfensohn that discussed the institution's bureaucracy.[112] Years later, with little changed, the stifling bureaucracy had caused an institutionalized disillusionment among staff who believe the culture is largely unchangeable. Jim Adams, a former Bank vice president of operations policy, acknowledged the deep-seated nature of the issue after staff was surveyed in 2002.[113] Among the reasons cited for the institution's lethargy: Its managerial aversion to risk and striving for perfectionism.

Like a baseball scout trying to assess whether a youngster will develop into a major league performer, it is difficult for the Bank to identify whether a new manager will become an effective leader. Significant academic accomplishments and superior technical skills in one's field are valuable, but they don't necessarily make a candidate suited to lead others. For example, few Bank managers have started or run a business. Most are without practical experience in leading teams or motivating individuals. And, academics who are comfortable in theoretical environments often stumble in the highly politicized settings within which the Bank operates.

Perhaps their proficiency is only a matter of perception. Former Staff Association Chair John Alvey recalled an incident when a senior official told him of two managers the HR Department believed were examples of managerial excellence. Alvey had compiled a list of the worst managers in the Bank from the Staff Association's perspective. Both managers cited by HR as outstanding were rated as the two worst performers on his list.[114]

By 2003, the Staff Association had lost all patience. "Managers are incompetent at management," it said. "All too often managers have been promoted because they were highly skilled in their technical field and for that reason alone. A conscious effort was made a few years ago to make people-management skills an integral part of the management hiring process. The results, frankly, have been mixed, particularly with the host of new managers appointed in the past two-to-three years. Some might argue that there is now extensive management training to help managers become better managers. Again, however worthwhile the training—and there are questions there—it cannot (and does not) turn poor managers into good managers. The Harvard Executive Development Program (EDP) course, which may have made Bank managers better at managing processes and projects, did not make them better at managing people."[115]

Managers with strong technical skills and academic training are valuable. But it can be argued creating a culture of leadership is more valuable. Business environments are not static, and the field of international development is especially volatile. Organizations that encourage personnel to innovate and grow within their responsibilities are best able to adapt to evolving business climates.

That does not mean there are no good managers at the Bank. There are. In 1996, the Staff Association established an annual Good Manager Award for the best managers as voted by staff. Each year, staff described the winners with the same adjectives. These managers were supportive and accessible. They showed interest in staff professionally and personally. They listened. They used "we" instead of "I" to describe accomplishments. They treated staff as partners rather than as parts of an assembly line. There was open communication between both sides, and staff input was actively solicited. These managers encouraged innovation and problem solving. They openly praised accomplishments and allowed staff to share credit. They sought mentoring and training opportunities for staff. And critically, when given new information or logical advice, these managers had the capacity to admit mistakes or change direction. They were successful because they understood the most important thing about being managers: They understood people; they empathized with them; and they empowered them.[116]

Frannie Leautier received a Good Manager Award in 1999 as the sector manager in the South Asia region's Infrastructure unit.[117] Her technical competence was noted, but it was her people skills that had been appreciated the most. Her staff said she excelled at instilling confidence and trust.

How then did she so badly miscalculate when it came to B-SPAN and its strategic vision? One theory might suggest running a small unit in the Bank is vastly different from running a large department. Between the vice president and me was a layer of substantial insulation from a cadre of mid-level managers, each with fiefdoms and vested interests. The powerful monopolizing more power can prevent important information from rising through the ranks. She placed her trust in such managers. Or had she really miscalculated? Perhaps the root causes of the Bank's culture could reveal answers. To find out, I needed to dig even deeper.

7

The journey ends where it began with a crusade by "revolutionaries" to make the World Bank transparent. If B-SPAN was a crusade to increase transparency at the Bank, then what does transparency actually mean? Webster's Dictionary states, "Capable of transmitting light so that objects or images beyond can be clearly perceived; or easily detected; or readily understandable; or without guile, candid." In the policy arena, transparency means openness and accountability, but it also suggests something else: Inclusion. Without it, the rest of what transparency's proponents seek to achieve is hollow.

Increasing stakeholder empowerment and participation has been difficult, because the Bank is bureaucratic and operates with competing mandates. An examination about inclusion therefore should begin at the top of the structure.

The Bank's board of directors is a largely hidden world, even to staff. It is comprised of 24 executive directors (EDs) representing donor and recipient-member countries. Donor and recipient countries have different objectives driven by their own internal issues. Domestic politics often compel donors to reduce foreign aid. Simultaneously, recipient countries, though leery of adding debt, want to expand development opportunities. Into this mix, individual executive directors maneuver to secure opportunities for their domestic corporations to participate in Bank projects.[118] Board politics therefore becomes a game of three-level chess as directives mandating new projects with expansive tasks conflict with directives demanding costs be reduced. In examining the violent vibrations of how the Bank is administered, the initial ripples can be found here.

Management tailors lending, operational and administrative policies based principally on what it thinks it can sell to the board. In most organizations that is logical; but there is an issue particular to the Bank that in this case causes concern.

The board is perceived by many as being dominated by rich countries. The Bank's membership consists of 185 countries. Each owns shares of the institution and has voting rights. Voting rights are weighted by a country's relative economic strength, thereby making some nations more influential than others.

The U.S., which finances about 16% of the Bank's annual budget, has the most voting leverage of any member country. The weighted voting shares roughly reflect the standing of its members at the time the Bank was formed during the 1940s. Changes have occurred during capital replenishments, but have not been systematically adjusted to account for the changing economic and financial weights of the membership.[119] The U.S., the United Kingdom, France, Germany and Japan each have their own executive director. The 19 other EDs represent the rest of the world. One African director represents 24 nations. As noted in Part I, the Sub-Saharan Africa region accounts for 27% of the Bank's membership but only 8% of its voting shares.[120]

Some, however, have long suggested a strong case can be made for re-evaluating board representation at the Bank. Oxfam, a leading development NGO watchdog of the Bank, wrote in 2003, "Rich countries have failed to address the democratic deficits at the World Bank and IMF. African countries are chronically under-represented on the boards."[121] If the Bank's management is designing projects to be sanctioned by a governing body dominated by donor nations, it suggests recipient nations have less say in their own future. Oxfam and other organizations have continued to call for increasing the number of voting shares held by developing countries.

In 2006, Ngaire Woods, an Oxford University professor and author of *The Globalizers: The IMF, the World Bank, and their Borrowers*, said her research revealed a strategic shift in emphasis for the Bank's financing during the 1980s and 1990s. "By charging the borrower countries more for loans, [the Bank] built up reserves and investment income—relieving wealthy countries of responsibility," Woods wrote.[122] She goes on to note that "in the 1980s, the U.S. insisted (successfully) that borrowing countries in [the Bank] should shoulder the costs of bad loans." From Woods' perspective, the onus of financing the institution had increasingly moved from donors to borrowers.

Among reforms Woods recommends: Board votes should change from securing a simple majority of executive directors to securing a majority of countries represented by them as well.

Others are on record urging changes. The Center for Global Development, a think tank focused on World Bank governance and international development issues, issued a report in 2005 entitled "*The Hardest Job in the World: Five Crucial Tasks for the New President of the World Bank*." Written in advance of Paul Wolfowitz's term as Bank president, the report suggested reducing board representation in Europe, merging Saudi Arabia's seat with those of other Arab nations, and expanding representation in Africa by two seats.[123] Sebastian Mallaby, in *The World's Banker*, suggested extending the length of International Development Association replenishments beyond three years. He believes this would help de-politicize the atmosphere somewhat and reduce donor influence.[124] And, finally, borrowing countries have also spoken out on this matter. Over the last two decades, with less say in how the Bank is managed, they have turned increasingly to private sector sources for capital.

In 2006, the first signs that the Bretton Woods institutions would be forced to change appeared. Rodrigo de Rato, the IMF's managing director, announced the Fund would give four key developing countries greater say in how it was run. It represented a step, but Nancy Birdsall, president of the Center for Global Development (CGD), suggested it was a small one. Birdsall noted the Fund's impetus for increasing the shares of China, South Korea, Mexico and Turkey had been less about increasing their legitimacy and more about increasing the IMF's own relevance.

"China and its neighbors don't need the Fund (China's enormous reserves provide self-insurance against a financial crisis) but the Fund and G-7 increasingly need China's engagement," Birdsall said.[125]

In their assessment of the move, the Brookings Institute's Johannes Linn, a former Bank vice president for Europe and Central Asia, and Colin Bradford, a former Bank economist, also criticized the Fund. They complained it had not increased voting allocations or seating on its board for more developing countries and particularly not for those in Sub-Saharan Africa.[126]

Would the Bank join the Fund in this initial act? Not likely, according to Birdsall. "The World Bank does not yet face the same crisis of relevance as the IMF—since minimizing global systemic risks is not part of its mandate. And it is the Fund's relevance not 'legitimacy' that is motivating the G-7 to finally agree on quota changes. So we cannot expect that changes in quotas (and thus voting structure) at the Fund will translate soon into changes at the Bank."[127]

That remained true until November 2008, when a different crisis of relevance emerged on the world scene. In the midst of the 2008 global economic downturn, the G-20—the 20 largest industrialized and emerging economies—convened in Washington to address instability threatening international markets. Dubbed "Bretton Woods II", the meeting was hastily arranged, but among the measures adopted was a pledge to reform the Bank (and IMF) to increase the representation of developing countries that "more adequately reflect changing economic weights in the world economy."[128]

Sensing the wave that was about to overwhelm it, the Bank took a preemptive measure. In the days leading up to the G-20 meeting, the Bank announced it would form a commission to study the modernization of its governance structure. Among the reforms it would study was adjusting the composition of its board, increasing voting representation for developing countries and making the selection of future presidents merit-based rather than the prerogative of the U.S. government.[129] The commission was given a year to offer a report.

Without oversight over six decades, the board has developed a culture of secrecy. Here, admittedly, is an unorthodox proposal: Bank member countries also might be encouraged to consider creating a board seat for a civil society representative. Such a proposal does have carrots for the Bank. Most NGOs believe that donor nations, and particularly the U.S., hold too much sway over the Bank. In the past, civil society actors have been in the enviable position of criticizing Bank policies without being responsible for accountability. Giving an NGO coalition formal input in how the institution is run also makes them accountable for shortcomings. Bringing NGOs into the wheel-building business might mute their public criticisms.

NGO inclusion, however, does not suggest it is a panacea. Borrowers have expressed concern that their agendas might be co-opted by large NGOs reflecting Western values and traditions rather than their own. Lawrence Summers has said he did not believe NGOs had special claim to speak on behalf of the poor, nor did they know more about development than Bank staff.[130] Yet lack of stakeholder participation has been cited as a key reason why project failure rates hovered near 40% during the 1980s and are still believed by many to be significantly high.[131]

In *The World's Banker*, Mallaby said structural adjustment lending neglected social development, empowerment and participation issues, all of which impacted a client country's political stability. When the political stability of a government was at risk, then the Bank's financial packages were as well.[132] Moreover, civil society participation in other areas of the Bank's policy making has also moved against the grain of the institution's approval culture, and raised concern with its managerial corps and clients. Therefore, careful scrutiny is warranted in the composition of a group choosing an NGO representative who would reflect both industrialized and developing country values.

Inclusion dovetails into accountability, as they are of the same coin. In the private sector, company executives are accountable to their boards and shareholders. In the public sector, office holders are accountable to their constituents. Accountability for the Bank's board, senior management and mid-level bureaucracy, however, appears less clear. In theory, senior management answers to the board, but executive directors continually tack between the needs of the institution and the wishes of their home governments. Senior management, the sculptor of visionary reforms, is beholden to mid-level management for implementation, while this hardened bureaucracy is wedded to the culture of fiefdoms as its power base.

Accountability in such an environment does not seem obvious to many staff and the public. In 2002, former Staff Association Chair John Alvey called management accountability the biggest problem at the Bank.[133]

The Bank's mechanism for accountability inside the organization is the Conflict Resolution System. Its external mechanism is an Inspection Panel which was implemented by the Bank to chasten civil society actors. Several Bank debacles during the 1980s and early 1990s that caused environmental havoc and massive resettlement prompted NGOs in the U.S. to seek increased accountability in the Bank's lending process. In response to this pressure, then Bank President Lewis Preston ordered an internal review of Bank activities.

A commission led by Brad Morse, a former UN Development Programme administrator, found important failings by the Bank in complying with its own policies. The results had been catastrophic for the environment and indigenous populations. Concurrently, the Wapenhans Report suggested the failure rate of Bank lending had increased to unacceptable levels. These findings, along with NGO pressure on the U.S. Congress during the critical International Development Association replenishment negotiations, forced senior management to capitulate. The Inspection Panel was established in 1993.

The panel was not well received in Bank circles. Management which had previously convened its own inspections resented the intrusion into its affairs. In an overview of the panel entitled, *The Impact of Civil Society on the World Bank*, Dr. Sabine Schlemmer-Schulte, a Bank counsel, discussed calls by NGOs to increase the "democratization" of the Bank.

The analysis offers an institutional argument on why the Bank should retain legal immunity as an international organization. It also provides a perspective on the organization's sensibilities towards the panel.

Schlemmer-Schulte wrote, "Democratization, however, is not only the wrong term but should never conceptually be asked for because, unlike states, international organizations are not organisms that could within themselves establish a self-standing democratic structure. They do neither possess a territory nor a population to be looked after fairly, but have a much narrower purpose to fulfill ... thus, any calls for direct involvement of the people in the political decision-making process or their representation for that process as well as separation of powers, e.g., direct participation by people in Bank decisions or representation by them in the Board as well as establishment of an independent court judging in cases between Bank Management and affected people, or participation of NGOs in decision-making by the Bank's Board as part of involvement of people in the legislative process of the Bank, have their conceptual shortcomings."[134]

Some borrowing clients were not pleased with the creation of the Inspection Panel either. They sensed it made the Bank's decision-making process less efficient. They also sensed the development reflected the sensibilities of Western NGOs rather than the views of developing countries.

In the late 1990s, major borrowers, Brazil and India, led a counter-offensive to reduce the scope and autonomy of the panel. In 1999, their pressure induced the board to create a working group of several executive directors to review and recommend changes. The working group recommended reducing the panel's scope by limiting opportunities to gather information and increasing avenues for dissenting board members to block investigations. When an internal memo about the recommendations was leaked, the outcry from civil society stakeholders forced the board to incorporate public commentary. The impact of the working group's recommendations was mitigated, but only to an extent.[135]

Since then there have been other attempts to limit the Inspection Panel's scope. In 2000, a coalition of Western NGOs charged the Bank with violating its guidelines during a dam-building project in Qinghai, China that would displace thousands of rural farmers. In the furor, senior officials sought to diffuse the issue by invoking the panel's involvement. But the investigation turned against the Bank, and Chinese officials openly questioned the tenets of their borrowing program with the institution.[136] By incensing perhaps the most important client in its portfolio, the Bank was suddenly caught in an uncomfortable position.

At the height of the controversy, the board voted to keep the panel from commenting on a government's responsibility regarding a project under review. Instead, the board restricted inspections specifically to Bank actions.[137]

In 2004, a controversy over a pilot project in Mexico to test a new approach to environmental and social protection led the Bank Information Center (BIC), a Washington-based NGO that monitors the Bank and other international financial institutions, to suggest it was another attempt to rein in the scope of the panel. BIC said the

Bank's management was seeking "to limit the panel's review authority to the application of the Bank's supervision policy and procedures." Project implementation conducted by local authorities would be "beyond panel review."[138]

A number of academics have looked at the panel's effectiveness during its evolution. Jonathan Fox, a professor at the University of California at Santa Cruz, suggested in his *The World Bank Inspection Panel: Lessons from the First Five Years*, that there was significant ambiguity over whether the existence of the panel resulted in greater compliance.[139] He believed safeguards had not been uniformly met in lending activities, and leaked memos revealed Bank managers adhered only to the extent necessary for public relations reasons.

The process offered an important empirical test of the NGOs influence as well as the Bank's aptitude for accountability. It also revealed serious difficulties the Bank faced when balancing the interests of sovereign nations, accepted international standards of practice, and its own waning relevance as the lender of choice versus private sector capital.

Fox noted Bank safeguards were more rigorous than borrower practices. This revealed gaps in implementation. The Bank's inattention to borrower compliance was a key driver of complaints coming to the panel. This was also related to the issue of managerial accountability within the Bank's approval culture.

Managers are rewarded for moving projects through the pipeline rather than meeting safeguards. They feel secure in doing so. The Bank's evaluation process does not determine accountability until long after project approval, lending disbursement, and project implementation. By then, most players have moved up or moved on. Moreover, the Bank's inability to implement safeguards contrasted with its public discourse. Here, we may find another example of institutional hypocrisy.

Paul Nelson, an associate professor of international development at the University of Pittsburgh, examined the Inspection Panel in his essay *Whose Civil Society? Whose Governance? Decision Making and Practice in the New Agenda at the Inter-American Development Bank and the World Bank*. Nelson suggested the institution sought to limit the panel's influence by treating it as an advisory body.[140] To mitigate the impact of the panel, the board ruled it could make findings but not recommend actions the board or management should take. The board limited the range of policies the panel could investigate. It also sought to increase those limitations by reducing the list of operational directives subject to panel review, resulting in a shorter list of best-practice guidance for staff.

Bank legal representatives have also acknowledged that, should the panel find violations, management or the board may take remedial action but injured parties do not have the right to be provided remedial relief. Additionally, since the Bank has certain immunities as an international organization, injured parties cannot seek recourse in domestic courts. The result, Nelson believes, are policies on information disclosure and independent inspections that are strong on paper, but less effective in practice.[141]

Many critics have suggested more opportunities are needed for civil society stakeholders to provide input after filing the original complaint. They've also noted remedial actions taken by management have not addressed all inequities. Moreover, as the Bank acknowledged in its 2003 report, *Accountability at the World Bank: The Inspection Panel 10 Years On*, "Not all harm can be the subject of a Request for Inspection."[142]

Still, on balance, most observers believe the Bank's accountability has fared better via the panel process than through board representation, or through an independent project evaluation process, or under the Conflict Resolution System. The Inspection Panel is independent of management. Its members cannot have worked for the Bank within two years of their appointment; and following the expiration of a single five-year term, they are not eligible to be employed by the Bank again. Management's remedial action plans have addressed some, if not all, claimant grievances. The process has kept staff more cognizant of environmental and social concerns during the conduct of their lending activities. The existence of the panel has also served to mitigate the funding of questionable projects. And, this example of an accountability mechanism has spread to other lending institutions such as the IMF and the Inter-American Development Bank.

Fox believes the most practical method for ensuring safeguard compliance is for reform-minded Bank personnel to partner with civil society actors in borrower countries; together, they can pressure key policy makers in those governments. His supposition is that by definition, reformers rarely are dominant within their policy environments and their influence rests on forming broader alliances. Fox concludes the Inspection Panel is "a paradigm case both of the influence of transnational advocacy networks over international norms and policies and of their limited leverage over institutional behavior in practice. Because of the constraints on its mandate and its practice, at most the panel can deliver some degree of transparency, contributing only indirectly to accountability. More generally, the experience reminds us that transparency is necessary but not sufficient for accountability."[143] It is a hypothesis B-SPAN's founders understood well.

Bank observers believe a second critical way to improve institutional accountability is through the project evaluation process. Some critics wonder about evaluations where drafts have been vetted by the individuals being reviewed. They question a system without baseline indicators.

In 2004, a group of economists with MIT's Poverty Action Lab analyzed whether Bank aid had actually improved people's lives. The group concluded evidence of successful lending remained absent.[144] Then, two leading Bank economists offered a startling response to the Lab's findings: Contrition.

Lant Pritchett, a lead economist with the Research Department, and co-author of *Assessing Aid*, suggested rigorous impact evaluations were a rarity because the institution's highly educated staff believed they were infallible.[145] The Bank's Chief Economist Francois Bourguignon followed Pritchett's comments by acknowledging a strong evaluation process was not ingrained in the institution's culture.[146]

Opinions may differ as to whether funding levels for evaluations are sufficient or if evaluation methodologies are astute or whether Bank projects are having their intended impact. But funding and evaluation criteria sidestep an even more fundamental issue which is how Bank projects are assessed: Namely the impartiality of the process.

Critics openly question the legitimacy of an internal unit passing judgment on its own management. Their concern would abate if the unit was independent of the Bank, or if independent auditors conducted evaluations. And concern would abate further if there was ample funding for project maintenance rather than the current emphasis on project implementation. Such steps would increase the Bank's accountability and also mitigate the cultural norm of the approval process. If managers were being judged on project sustainability as well as their ability to get board approval, it would change the way projects were designed and implemented.

Many believe these developments would help the Bank make the case for increasing aid levels. When, in the final years of his tenure, James Wolfensohn implored donor countries to spend more on development assistance, the Bank's checkered record of lending results and its evaluation process impeded his case.

Increasing the scope and independence of the Inspection Panel and implementing independent audits of project evaluations are two important ways to increase the Bank's accountability to shareholders and stakeholders. Two other crucial reforms should be directed inward. Staff surveys in the last decade reveal a cynicism of management so deep President Wolfensohn was compelled to acknowledge: "We have failed in terms of staff … there is something in the place that is missing, and it is cohesion, it is trust, it is the enthusiasm to be together, mutual dependency."[147]

There is a catalyst for this behavior. Personnel abuses are not punished because there is no legal mechanism for punishment. Bank workers are especially vulnerable because, not only are many beholden to retaining their G-4 status as foreign nationals, most have specialties not marketable outside the development field. International organizations are exempt from fair labor practices in the U.S. So while the Bank is housed in the U.S. capital, American labor law is not applicable. The institution is immune from U.S. law governing lawsuits arising from labor disputes. U.S. Congressional oversight is conducted on how the Bank manages its personnel, but there is no binding authority. With some legitimacy, the Bank can claim it should not be beholden to labor laws of the U.S. or any other country, since its membership includes 185 countries.

That does not suggest *no* standard should apply. The Staff Association believes a reasonable approach would be for the Bank to adhere to a compilation of labor laws of democratic nations protecting worker rights.[148] Moreover, the introduction of the Bank's Inspection Panel represents an advance in international law, because for the first time the institution made itself accountable to citizens adversely affected by its actions.[149] Perhaps there is applicability in the case of Bank employees as well.

The Staff Association has noted accountability under the Conflict Resolution System can be achieved by introducing independent arbitrators with binding authority. This would eliminate the Bank's role in acting as judge and jury on allegations of managerial impropriety. With monetary rewards for successful plaintiffs currently capped at three times their annual salary, arbitrators might also be empowered to impose significant monetary awards that would cause the institution to feel the sting. Reforming the Conflict Resolution System would weaken fiefdoms. It would force the Bank to reevaluate how it recruits and trains managers. It would also reinvigorate a workforce that, though dedicated to poverty reduction, is itself mired in cynicism.

Related to the Conflict Resolution System is the issue of managerial selections. Monika Weber-Fahr freely acknowledged her belief that acting as an autocrat gave her an advantage in managing GDLN's staff. External analysis by Myers-Briggs and the Institute of Development Studies, and internal assessments by the Ombudsman's Office and the Staff Association confirmed this was true with managers in general. They revealed Bank managers were highly educated and technologically astute, but often arrogant with clients and autocratic with staff. Despite ongoing tension with staff, there has not been an evolution in senior management's thinking about the issue.

"Wolfensohns's meritocracy personnel system may have weakened clans a bit, but could not blow them clean away," Mallaby said in *The World's Banker*.[150] "A survey of the Bank in 2003 found that only 51% of the staff believed that promotions were made on an objective basis."

Technocrats remain in vogue. Managerial recruits are risk averse, and are judged by loyalty to superiors and adherence to budget parameters for the implementation of program or lending objectives.

When it comes to hiring, another issue generally escapes the scrutiny of employment experts, personnel strategists and employees as well. The hiring standards at the Bank are extraordinarily high. A small circle of elite institutions such as Harvard, the London School of Economics, and John Hopkins' Center for International Studies serve as a pipeline to the Bank. Most professional positions require a Master's Degree. It has been said more PhDs work at the Bank than at any organization in the world. Perhaps, it is too many.

While in theory, having access to so much intellectual capital seems sound, it does not necessarily mean having the most effective workers. The institution's bias in hiring candidates with post-secondary training means its emphasis is on securing academic excellence. Candidates with significant human development and practical, real-world experience tend to be overlooked. The Bank is also vulnerable to biases that may occur when a disparate percentage of personnel are chosen from a select group of elite universities in the U.S. and Europe.

The Bank might benefit from a more holistic approach. Noted management expert Tom Peters believes managers who need to be overly in control are weak at both leading and managing.[151] The Bank might be better served to recruit people recognized for their leadership skills and managerial successes outside the institution, and perhaps even outside the development field. It might seek out entrepreneurs who have launched their own businesses. It might seek out people who have grown up with and outgrown poverty. And, if they don't have a Master's degree or a PhD, the Bank should recognize that these people bring to the institution important qualities beyond academia.

One of the most interesting suggestions about managerial reform has been proposed over the years by a variety of sources. To the extent their health allows, make managers live one week each year or two in a poor village in exactly the same manner as the villagers do. It would humble many to discard the contrivances they garden in the name of development. Management guru Tom Peters believes great leaders are ones who develop opportunities for others to use their talents.[152] Leaders, he suggests, don't necessarily transform people. Rather, they give people a chance to transform themselves.

In the last few years, many development think tanks and NGOs, and now the G-20, have focused their attention on three possible reforms for the Bank: Changing the board's representation, giving emerging and developing country members greater voice and vote power in Bank operational decisions and changing the process for selecting its president. All have merit. These reforms will make the Bank's decision-making more representative of its membership. Nevertheless, my personal sense is other reforms noted above have greater potential for improving the institution's effectiveness and accountability because they will directly impact its internal functionality. Creating an evaluation process that is independent of the Bank and more focused on project sustainability will dilute the approval culture and increase managerial accountability. Reforming the Conflict Resolution System will improve staff morale and also increase managerial accountability. Revising the institution's process for selecting managers will improve its effectiveness and reduce its culture of fiefdoms. Implementation of these reforms will have a profound impact on the Bank's ability to reduce poverty.

Transparency is the final part of the paradigm. It means something different inside the institution than it does outside it. For the bureaucrats who sought to stifle B-SPAN, transparency meant a production process that identified all actions. It meant a hiring process that was officially vetted even if unofficially suspect. For WBI, which housed the Knowledge Management initiatives for the Bank, transparency was the fashion of the day that could be ignored in the appropriate climate. For the institution, the lack of transparency to the outside world represented a crisis to be skirted long enough so attention could be diverted to other issues. Following the environmental damages created by the ill-fated Narmada dam project in India, NGOs' alleged problems were traceable to the lack of transparency in the Bank's decision-making process. Reluctantly, the institution adopted a Disclosure of Information policy two years later in 1989. It would be five more years before the first Public Information Center (PIC) opened at Bank headquarters, and ten years before PICs operated throughout the Bank's global offices.

Throughout the 1990s, the Bank faced intense pressure from NGOs and the U.S. Congress regarding the confidentiality it maintained over documents. On the eve of a gargantuan demonstration in September 2001, the Board capitulated. It adopted a new disclosure policy, but critics were unimpressed. Key documents remained confidential. "This is a perfect example of the Bank's inability to transform its laudable rhetoric into concrete policy commitments," Graham Saul, the Transparency Program Manager of the Bank Information Center, a watchdog group, said then.[153] "The Bank says it wants communities to participate in decisions that affect their lives, but the Board refuses to release information until after most of the decisions are already made."

Over the years, the Board has loosened its grip on information as it has acclimated to an environment that has permanently changed. More lending and project evaluation documents are available, as are summaries of board discussions. In 2005, the board took another step by making public the minutes of its meetings, but these documents are largely superficial, recording final decisions without the nuances of debate. Meetings remain closed, and documents submitted to the board remain confidential until meetings and votes are concluded. The board maintains that releasing documents prior to their deliberations would politicize the process by allowing interest groups to pressure them unduly. But civil society stakeholders continue to believe they are excluded.

The Bretton Woods Project, a European NGO, has urged the Bank to publish the transcript of board meetings, adopt formal voting at board meetings and publish the board's voting records.[154] "Want to know the positions your government is taking at the World Bank?" asked Bruce Jenkins of the Global Transparency Initiative (GTI), another coalition of NGOs seeking greater public information disclosure of Bank documents. "That's off-limits as well. Aside from annual shareholder speeches, citizens are unable to monitor their government's actions at the Bank. The Bank's Board of Directors has thrown a virtual veil of secrecy over their proceedings."[155] In anticipation of a Bank review of its information disclosure policies in 2009, GTI has also put together a series of insightful proposals designed to increase public access to Bank project documents.

We wanted B-SPAN to webcast board meetings and felt that could be achieved without compromising the confidentiality of sensitive information. Wheeler and I discussed this frequently throughout 2000, because much of what the board discussed was suited for public consumption, even if some of it was off-limits.

Our motivation was partly generated by the burgeoning protest movement of the 1990s that criticized the monolithic nature of the institution. No entity within the Bank epitomized the closed-door decision-making process more than the board. Nor were we alone in that sentiment.

In the winter of 2000, U.S. Senators Daniel Patrick Moynihan and Ron Wyden called for board proceedings to be opened to the public via a "global C-SPAN." "If you look at the protests about globalization, the single most cited factor is that they do business behind closed doors," Wyden said.[156]

The Bank's response was to note it was starting to hold press conferences during its annual meetings.[157] If B-SPAN had been able to penetrate its inner sanctum, it may have served as a middle ground for both sides to find consensus on concerns about the Bank's transparency.

In 1994, when the chorus of critics was gaining volume, the Bank took the only action its culture understood. It expanded

External Affairs, its public relations arm, into a full-time operation. Wolfensohn even made it clear: Staff engaging in public criticism of the institution would be dismissed.

Though the Bank sits only about a mile away from where the U.S. Constitution is housed in the National Archives, freedom of speech is not part of its culture. Those who engage in criticism or offer contrary views, even if meant to improve the institution, do so at their peril. They are considered insurgents, and as such, become cultural security risks. In 2003, the Staff Association said there is "the lack of transparency in the organization. We are a secretive organization. Our critics accuse us of that and staff strongly feels it. There seems to be a reluctance to share information. When it is shared, there is often an element or, at the very least, a perception of spin. We often feel that we are not getting the whole truth."[158]

In 2004, an NGO called the Government Accountability Project (GAP) (www.whistleblower.org) issued a report titled "*Challenging the Culture of Secrecy: A Status Report on Freedom of Speech at the World Bank*." The report said, "The Bank is an extremely powerful institution with the ability to influence millions of people's lives ... It is unsurprising that a closed and insular culture has evolved within an institution having such power. It is also no surprise that the secrecy bias that exists within the Bank's culture has hurt its mission and standing in the international community." Among GAP's findings was that whistleblowers had been prohibited from disclosing information regarding fraud or corruption to the public; and without an external review party, the Conflict Resolution System had an institutionalized conflict of interest.[159]

The Bank was not amused by the report. It was even less amused when GAP made subsequent allegations in 2005 that senior management was using the Department of Institutional Integrity (INT) to deliberately harass and retaliate against staff that had become whistleblowers or activated the Conflict Resolution System process due to workplace grievances. "INT has developed a reputation as a legalized special operations unit for hidden management agendas: A unit that investigates whistleblowers far more actively than their charges of corruption," GAP said.[160]

It was an opinion also suggested by former Staff Association Chair John Alvey.[161] The allegations, the NGO said, were based on information from Bank staff who had sought their help. In writing the Bank's president to get his side of the story, GAP praised Wolfensohn for making anti-corruption a central plank in his development agenda. They implored him to make it a consistent principle within the Bank's internal operations as well. "Taking these steps now will lay the foundation for an enduring set of structural reforms that will substitute a transparency mandate for the legacy of secrecy enforced by repression," GAP urged.

The Bank's response would have sounded familiar to staff filing grievances: The messenger, not the message, was the problem. "GAP is not an impartial party, but a legal practice in active search of clients to represent in whistleblower litigation," wrote the Bank's deputy general counsel in a terse response.[162]

With this answer in hand, GAP turned its attention to strengthening reform legislation for the multilateral development banks that was then being debated in the U.S. Congress. In testimony before the Senate Foreign Relations Committee during the summer of 2005, Tom Devine, director of GAP's legal program, noted the ironies surrounding the Bank regarding freedom of speech. It included the Bank's refusal to make public a report it had commissioned on how to reform its whistleblower policies. Devine characterized the escapade as "secret transparency reform."

Though it sounded comical, GAP's counsel was making a serious point. He put it bluntly. "It is imperative that the policies and practices of the banks themselves reflect the values of transparency and respect for human rights that they expect by the rest of the world. That is because these practices can have life and death consequences."[163]

Former Bank Chief Economist Joseph Stiglitz is perhaps the institution's most famous dissenter. He condemned the Bank's adherence to the Washington Consensus, and railed against IMF policies during the East Asian financial crisis of the late 1990s. He was "retired" from the Bank.[164] Two years later, Stiglitz received the

Nobel Prize for economics.

To the chagrin of the Bank and IMF, he then published *Globalization and Its Discontents* which discussed his views in depth. On reflecting about transparency within these lending institutions during the East Asia financial crises of the late 1990s, Stiglitz noted, "It was maddening … because with everything going on behind closed doors it was impossible to know who was the real obstacle to change … but bad economics was only a symptom of the real problem: Secrecy. Smart people are more likely to do stupid things when they close themselves off from outside criticism and advice. If there's one thing I've learned in government, it's that openness is most essential in those realms where expertise seems to matter most …"[165]

Ravi Kanbur was another notable dissenter. Kanbur was the lead author of the *World Development Report*. In the Millennium edition of this prestigious Bank publication, he sought to emphasize the importance of empowerment in poverty reduction. He quit rather than be party to senior management's decision to keep this content suppressed.[166] Stiglitz and Kanbur are well-known dissenters but they have not been alone.

The case of one-time Research Department economist Bill Easterly also illustrates the issue.[167] In 2001, Easterly, with management's knowledge, wrote a book called *The Elusive Quest for Growth*. It encapsulated two decades of research on cross-country growth comparisons. Easterly looked at different methodologies for fostering development, such as foreign aid and investments in education and population reduction. He concluded the inability to achieve sustainable development was a systematic failure by the donor community to apply economic principles to practical policy work.

Moreover, he criticized structural adjustment lending by the Bank because it emphasized tightening monetary supplies as a methodology for stabilizing local currencies, and promoted fiscal austerity and privatization. Easterly's research suggested structural adjustment lending fostered consumption over investment that led to stagnant growth, and increased debt and more adjustment lending.

MIT Press published Easterly's book. Initially, all seemed well, but then Easterly published a subsequent article in *The Financial Times*, a key news source for the international community. That proved too public a forum to air a difference of opinion with the company elders.

The Bank's Ethics Office was prompted to launch an investigation. It charged Easterly with violating the institution's Administrative Manual by publicly suggesting the Bank change its policies. External Affairs said Easterly violated its Media Guidelines though no one could identify a previous infraction.

Easterly was then fired from the Bank. The incident sent ripples through the institution. The Staff Association noted the "Bank publicly commits itself to finding the best way to fight poverty and pays researchers to do so. How can the institution share 'best practice' that inspires any public confidence, if research staff cannot discuss 'poor practice' based on high quality research?"[168] This observation mirrored remarks made by Hernando de Soto three years later when he discussed his efforts to access the Bank's archives.

In the aftermath of the Easterly affair, Anita Baker, who managed the Ethics Office, offered a candid concession. She acknowledged rules were unclear, and Easterly's case may have been one of selective enforcement. "If the Bank were an American organization," she said, "we would have problems because we are not consistent in enforcement regarding publications … the Bank doesn't have a good self-governing structure."[169] She also suggested that without external checks, the Bank's self-policing capacity allowed management to abuse rules and censor staff that had legitimate issues to make public. Baker left her position the same year.

In 2000, an *internal* Bank report acknowledged structural adjustment lending had not been a boon to the poor.[170] For Easterly, the issue of telling the public what he had learned, however, was never in doubt. "I had an obligation to speak out," he said.[171]

Another example of the Bank's intolerance for research findings that differed from the institution's official viewpoints was Branko Milanovic, an economist researching poverty and inequality in transition economies, who investigated income disparities between rich and poor. Inequality, Milanovic believed, had increased between rich and poor nations during the Bank's existence. In addition, he wrote, income inequality within poor countries increased at the fastest rate during the previous two decades. At the start of the millennium the richest five percent of the world's population owned as much as the poorest 80 percent. Milanovic's research was based on household survey data rather than aggregated information normally used by researchers. Many scholars were impressed. But it was not in sync with the official views espoused by senior officials who had highlighted aggregate levels of poverty as dropping by 200 million people during the previous two decades.

Milanovic soon thereafter became a visiting professor at Johns Hopkins University's School for Advanced International Studies. Princeton University Press and not the Bank ultimately published the research under the title *Worlds Apart: Measuring International and Global Inequality*. Milanovic characterized the episode diplomatically. "The World Bank is indeed the only place in the world where this kind of information could be accessed, assembled, processed and even possibly written about," he wrote in the book's acknowledgements.[172] "Despite the sometime lack of enthusiasm in this line of research by some of my colleagues at the World Bank, I dare to believe that this may be one of the instances where the World Bank indeed played the role to which it aspires, that of a 'knowledge bank.' The views expressed in the book, however, are my own and should not be attributed to the World Bank or its affiliated organizations."

The high-profile cases of Stiglitz, Kanbur and Easterly, and to a lesser extent that of Milanovic, paralleled the nearly invisible case of B-SPAN. Each time there had been a break from adherence to the company line, the Bank's bureaucracy took action to silence dissent. B-SPAN, however, offered a variation, for it did not dissent from a particular cause. Rather it served as a platform to make diverging viewpoints public. Perhaps it was enough reason for the Research Department's management to refuse funding it during the incubation period under Wheeler. It was an obvious motivation for WBI's bureaucrats to kill it upon entry into their department. Dissent frightened them. The time had come to find out why.

The inherent muting of views by an institution dedicated to knowledge sharing, learning and world-class research has been noted by others. David Ellerman, another Research Department economist, examined the relationship between knowledge, truth and power in bureaucracies in a 2001 Bank paper entitled *Helping People Help Themselves: Toward a Theory of Autonomy-Compatible Help.*[173] Ellerman noted when truth and power are at odds within totalitarian regimes that it was truth that lost out.

"Power," he wrote, "corrupts the ecology of knowledge—the conditions under which knowledge grows and flourishes. Those in power in an organization tend to enshrine their views as the Official Views ... Experimentation, debate and the exercise of critical reasons are curtailed to stay within the safe boundaries of Official Wisdom. To those in power, others who argue within the organization against Official Views only reveal their unreliability and lack of fitness for positions of authority. Those who argue against Official Views *outside* the organization - particularly with any public notice—are seen as traitors being disloyal to the organization itself."

The Stiglitz, Kanbur and Easterly cases seems to be Ellerman's focus. His theorizing could just have well applied to actions by WBI regarding B-SPAN. By fostering a medium for debate and dissent to exist, WBI officials feared they too would be accused of not adhering to the company line.

Ellerman questioned whether a knowledge institution should even have Official Views when the issues, causes and questions surrounding development and poverty reduction are vast, complex and changing. He brooded over the ominous expansion of External Affairs: "When an organization adopts Official Views, then the public relations function seems to morph into the function of propagating the Official Messages and acting as the thought police to the black sheep in the organization who—within public view—are not 'on message' with the rest of the flock."

The concern regarding dissent from a public relations standpoint,

Ellerman surmised, is an irrational fear the organization will, using East Asian parlance, lose face. In the West, it is euphemistically known as "bad press." Rather, he suggested, by allowing debate to foster, the newsworthiness of debate itself will subside. It was a cognitive understanding Wheeler and I had from the very inception of B-SPAN.

Ellerman believes pedagogy by a development agency poses an interesting conundrum. "How can an outside party assist those undertaking autonomous activities without overriding or undercutting their autonomy?" he asks. His question begins to unravel the mystery of why WBI, the branch of the institution charged with facilitating knowledge sharing, treated B-SPAN—perhaps the most progressive information sharing tool in its domain—as a hostile and dangerous entity.

Under the current standard, Ellerman suggests, the Bank through the auspices of WBI, views its clients as passive recipients for the knowledge it shares. The knowledge sharing instrument, in this case WBI, measures its success in how many clients are trained, how well it can scale up training off-site, and how well its training has been assimilated by recipients. Seen within this modality, delivering knowledge nuggets is akin to delivering infrastructure projects. Rather than dollars moved or liters of concrete poured, results are quantified by variables such as head counts.

All of this amounts to tutelage and not active learning, Ellerman asserts. The model fosters dependency rather than helping clients to develop into autonomous stakeholders capable of building their own future. Ellerman quotes Immanuel Kant from *What is Enlightenment* to illustrate his point. "Tutelage," Kant said, "is man's inability to make use of his understanding without direction from another." Kant also states, "Enlightenment is man's release from self-incurred tutelage."

If Ellerman's supposition has truth, one may begin to identify crucial characteristics of WBI's personality. Knowledge via this format, according to his theory, moves in one direction. If information were no longer moving from the institution out to the field, then the need for WBI would become less obvious. Ultimately, based on the existing model, WBI would lose its identity and mission. Creating client dependency in turn means insuring WBI's survival within the Bank.

But that's not all. In recent years, WBI has sought to be at the forefront of the Bank's work on capacity building for clients. Within the prism of Ellerman's hypothesis, WBI would in fact be actively undermining capacity building. By force-feeding vetted messages to clients in need of aid, WBI is creating an environment of dependency rather than helping the poor build their own capacity to improve their condition.

"Prudent counsel is to scan globally for best practices but to test them locally since local adaptation often amounts to reinventing the 'best practice' in the new context," Ellerman notes. "It is the local component of knowledge that requires adaptation, which in turn requires the active participation of those who know and understand the local environment. Local adaptation cannot be done by the passive cognitively dependent recipients of 'development knowledge': It must be done by the 'doers of development' in the course of their self activity."

According to the former Bank economist, there is something else of significance. The knowledge delivered is coordinated by management and must be "on message." Ellerman suggests the prevailing wisdom is it would weaken the faith of recipients should the knowledge providers be seen as disagreeing amongst themselves. If WBI is the harbinger of "best practice" knowledge, it also fosters a tendency toward preaching "one size fits all."

Obviously, one size does not fit all, because the complexities of local conditions are affected by history, culture, capacity and circumstance. In recent years, Bank rhetoric has increasingly acknowledged revisionist thinking along these lines, but that is not how it often acts. "One size fits all" parallels some of the institution's strongest existing cultural norms, such as being risk averse, non-transparent, on message, and applying conditionality to its lending.

Ellerman asserts the concept of fostered learning is misguided. His supposition is the "poor already have a history of ineffectual action to better their condition, so any kind of assistance that reinforces that perceived inability to help themselves is simply the wrong kind of assistance, no matter how well intended." He suggests the current model be eliminated in favor of a model where the Bank adopts an approach similar to the one used by universities.

Universities do not pose as arbiters of truth, but serve as arenas for open and ongoing debate. In such an open-learning model, there is not only toleration but fostering of contradictory views. Moreover, he suggests knowledge sharing and learning activities, currently done by WBI, are best left to locally-based research institutions and think tanks. Ellerman believes these entities are better positioned to adapt development knowledge to local conditions.

He further suggests development agencies must choose between serving as library storehouses dispensing knowledge nuggets, or as knowledge brokers offering a variety of experiences, and allowing recipients to decide on their own which nuggets of information fit. The danger for the agency: It may seek to implement both models and do so poorly. And, in the current information revolution, he believes it is the library-storehouse model, the one on which WBI is based, that will lose influence over time.

Ellerman's analysis takes an obvious, but still startling, step. He writes, "The new rhetoric of 'learning' is applied as a veneer onto a Church-like or Party-like organization proselytizing its own messages."

The hypothesis manufactures an interesting image: WBI espousing dogma in a way one might find within the auspices of an authoritarian regime. WBI, empowered to disseminate "Official Views," was also empowered to attack agents who would question those views or seek alternatives.

"Members must adhere to the Party Line," Ellerman states. "The Church or Party model fits perfectly with the standard 'dissemination' or transmission belt methodology of knowledge-based development assistance. The agency has the best 'knowledge for development' and it is to be transmitted through various forms of aid-baited proselytizing to the authorities in the developing world."

The image of WBI taking on the characteristics of authoritarian regimes that it seeks to reform is unnerving.

Ellerman reinforces this notion further. He states, "One must marvel at the tendency of the major development agencies to rush forward with a universal 'best practice,'—a tendency based not on any methods resembling social science but on a bureaucratic need to maintain elite prestige by 'having an answer' for the client." The Party Line does not have room for alternative views; and Ellerman notes the discipline is vigorously enforced by instruments such as External Affairs. He believes a key motivation is fear that the news media might publicize conflicting views or uncoordinated messages. If allowing voice to be given to disparate views and theories were the norm, however, the relative news value of organizational disagreements would quickly dissipate. Instead, officials would be able to promote the organization as one of intellectual honesty and integrity, since it fosters debate to enhance development progress. Ellerman suggests just such an environment would foster active learning among clients, since they would then be forced to contemplate various ideas and findings rather than embrace a single message. What views the Bank believed were most sound would be validated by where it spent its money.

The instinct to conform messages is not simply a function of organizational culture, but also one of human nature. Ellerman quotes John Dewey's research on *Freedom and Culture*. Dewey said, "To hold theories and principles in solution, awaiting confirmation, goes contrary to the grain."

The Bank has invested six decades and many billions of dollars in espousing various development doctrines. During this period it has often found itself in the position of admitting its policies and practices have proven incorrect. The institution has even gone so far as to acknowledge the reasons behind development are not fully understood. Much of the Bank's self-imposed bloodletting might have substantially been avoided if it had forsaken dogma, or as Ellerman called it, "centrally planned and socially engineered reforms," in favor of an open forum of debate and discussion among staff and clients.

In quoting Richard Elmore's research in *Education for Judgment*, Ellerman searches for the core parameter. "The aim of teaching," Elmore states, "is not only to transmit information, but also to transform students from passive recipients of other people's knowledge into active constructors of their own and others' knowledge. The teacher cannot transform without the student's active participation, of course. Teaching is fundamentally about creating the pedagogical, social, and ethical conditions under which students agree to take charge of their own learning, individually and collectively."

Ellerman's persuasive thesis argues that transforming knowledge must be the fruit of one's own active learning. "On the direct or social engineering path," he writes, "the 'helper' helps the doer by supplying distorted motivation (conditional aid) and 'managed' knowledge (*ex cathedra* answers buttressed by biased information and one-sided arguments) to deliver (what the helper takes as) the right results ... direct methods can help others, but they cannot help others to help themselves."

WBI's approach mirrors the methodologies of imposed conditionality and absence of stakeholder participation—Bank practices that have been severely criticized since the 1980s. Moreover, others have informed WBI about the weakness of its mantra to implement uni-directional information flows.

In 2004, WBI hosted a knowledge sharing workshop with development practitioners from 24 countries. As reported afterwards by the Bank's Internal Communications, "One of the key messages which emerged from the event was that capacity is best built through a dynamic exchange of knowledge, not through teaching or passive documentation. Geoff Parcell (on [a temporary assignment] from British Petroleum to UNAIDS) captured this sentiment well in saying, 'I don't believe there is such a thing as best practice. We all have different backgrounds and sets of experiences and we can talk together and gain insights. But a real exchange of knowledge only occurs when we take action.' "[174]

In their 2004 analysis, *Knowledge for Development*, Kenneth King and Simon McGrath of the University of Edinburgh argued the

Bank had placed too much emphasis on knowledge-based aid for capacity development within agencies, rather than addressing the expressed needs of its clients.[175] More specifically, the authors argued the Bank implemented an agenda it had envisioned for itself. They openly wondered whether the capacity development the Bank was conducting was actually effective.[176]

In a review of *Knowledge for Development*, Simon Maxwell, former director of the Overseas Development Institute, said, "Knowledge management is popular. Aid agencies talk easily of sharing stories, communities of practice and double-loop learning. But are they ready to sacrifice a preoccupation with results and a concern to disseminate 'best practice' in favor of real partnership and mutual learning across divergent networks?"[177]

One of the objectives of the 1997 Strategic Compact was to transform the Bank into a knowledge sharing organization. The Economic Development Institute (EDI), WBI's forerunner, became designated as the lead agent for implementation, and quickly began incorporating video conferencing and web-based training technologies as tools for distance learning activities. Muthukumara Mani, an environmental economist on Wheeler's team, analyzed EDI's activities and discussed his findings with the NIPR team.[178] Based on Mani's research, Dave Witzel suggested EDI needed to jettison its existing culture of lecturing, and adopt a new methodology to fit changing times.[179]

"EDI needs to move beyond 'training' in a college classroom sense and think more in terms of collaborative, directed learning," he wrote. "Or maybe it could be called 'facilitated problem solving'—basically working with clients to write the case studies as they work out real problems."

Using the public information disclosure work as an example, Witzel suggested interested regulators and economists could "form a 'classroom of practice' where they can work together as they each develop a program for their country, supply 'instructors' to help guide development, provide materials from theory and past experience, and an infrastructure so that everyone can communicate (the web component), and then let the various countries help each other. The results will be better policy within the countries and great teaching materials." Witzel's reflections mirrored those codified by Ellerman four years later.

"Learning" and "knowledge sharing" are not the same. In some respect, the terms are at odds with one another. Culturally, the Bank is inclined to hoard information rather than share it. Moreover, EDI was launched during the 1950s to move information in one direction. Knowledge sharing, however, is meant to allow information to move in many directions simultaneously. Therefore, when EDI was designated as the branch of the organization charged with changing this part of the Bank's culture, it was in fact philosophically incapable of being such an agent.[180]

It is possible WBI officials might not agree with suggestions there are structural deficiencies in its knowledge sharing strategy. They might note the Bank has been recognized by the KNOW Network for the Most Admired Knowledge Enterprise (MAKE) award. The MAKE award acknowledges organizations for creating knowledge cultures and learning organizations, and for delivering knowledge-based products, as well as for several other categories.

The Bank's emphasis, however, has been on delivery of information to staff rather than informal, multi-directional dissemination. "In time, this translates into greater effectiveness, greater speed in the delivery of products and services, better quality work, and greater innovation and speed in disseminating that innovation within the organization," Bruno Laporte said in 2003.[181] Yet the reality was that by the time Laporte spoke, WBI was about to move on. The next year, with the departure of Karen Millet, the Knowledge Pillar was dissolved. Within a few months, Laporte and a couple of aides were all that remained of the Bank's knowledge sharing administrators. Careful observation might suggest that WBI's tacit admission was that knowledge sharing had been a fad from a former era.

B-SPAN fits seamlessly within *all* the parameters raised by Ellerman, King and McGrath. B-SPAN sought to make the Bank a forum for debate about development theories. A complete platform would have included development discussions from research sources outside the Bank. B-SPAN's impending evolution into a mechanism for two-way knowledge sharing, however, posed a significant threat to WBI's status quo.

What I hadn't realized when I broached the concept of B-SPAN as a multi-directional hub for information sharing and exchanges to WBI's leadership, was that this challenged their bureaucratic instincts and imperiled a deeply ingrained and valued cultural mantra. It would dilute WBI's ability to be on message, control the message, control the context for learning, create dependency among clients, use its facilities to mitigate potentially hostile stakeholders, and dilute its value as the institution's messenger. WBI's senior officials realized when the ultimate vision of B-SPAN was revealed to them that it was evolving from a malady to a lethal virus. For political reasons, it could not be killed, but to the extent possible, it had to be corralled. The options available were to slash funding and eliminate its driving force.

8

"To remain secure and prosperous themselves, wealthy nations must extend the kind of cooperation to the less fortunate members that will inspire hope, confidence, and progress," said President Eisenhower in his final State of the Union message in 1960. "A rich nation can for a time, without noticeable damage to itself, pursue a course of self-indulgence, making its single goal the material ease and comfort of its own citizens—thus repudiating its own spiritual and material stake in a peaceful and prosperous society of nations. But the enmities it will incur, the isolation into which it will descend, and the internal, moral, spiritual, economic and political softness that will be engendered will, in the long run, bring it to disaster."[182]

In accepting the 2006 Nobel Peace Prize, Muhammad Yunus, founder of the Grameen Bank in Bangladesh which pioneered micro-credit lending to the poor, said, "We must address the root causes of terrorism to end it for all time. I believe putting resources into improving the lives of poor people is better strategy than spending it on guns."[183]

From starkly different perspectives, these two views span the Bank's modern lifetime and arrive at the same place.

Some might ask why the Bank's leadership is important if it no longer holds a dominant position as an international lender. The Bank currently lends about $20 billion annually to the developing world, compared to private capital flows of $170 billion, and an overall private-investment level of about $1.5 trillion.[184] In terms relative to private lending, the Bank's financial impact is limited, but its influence on international development overall is still vast. Donor and borrower countries, other development and international organizations and civil society stakeholders, look to the Bank to set the standards and take the risks others cannot.[185]

The investment decisions the Bank makes affect the hundreds of millions of people in a world where tens of thousands die every day from poverty and preventable diseases. So, increasing the effectiveness of the institution becomes vitally important as the global population expands past six billion in the opening decades of the 21st century.

The Bank must remain relevant to make the case that the pendulum has swung too far, and donors must recommit themselves to the fight against poverty. To do so, the Bank will have to address its structural inefficiencies.

"Change is the law of life," President Kennedy once said. "And those who look only to the past or present are certain to miss the future." The mission is noble. The cause is just. Yet shortcomings prevent the Bank from reaching its potential. It needs to be more responsive, flexible, innovative, nimble and accepting of alternative viewpoints.

Nevertheless, reforming a bureaucracy means walking a fine line. If the pendulum swings too far, new problems may arise. Excessive re-engineering may actually lead to increased bureaucracy, making the environment more stifling rather than less so. Reforms that overreach might result in the greatest irony of all.

Therefore, changing the Bank's culture is a difficult challenge. Operating from within the organization provided us opportunities not available outside it. It also imposed limitations. There were times I came to believe that true change must be generated by external forces. At other times, I was less sure. As it turned out, the most effective lever for instigating reform may not be internal change agents or external critics but some sort of global crisis such as the financial downturn that forced the Bank to enact a study of its internal governance in late 2008.

There were also many lessons drawn from my experience. Among them: Individuals without authority still have the power to influence if they are careful and wise. Informal alliances can move ideas forward, sometimes more effectively than formal alliances. Rhetorical support is of value, but policy within bureaucracies is made by how funds are spent. And, as the 19th Century British philosopher Herbert Spencer once said, "The great aim of education is not knowledge but action." Sharing knowledge is only a means to an end. The value is in knowing what to do next.

It is useful to recall one of the truths we learned from our research on industrial pollution. We tend to think of knowledge as something that is gained; but we fail to remember knowledge can also be lost. At the Bank-sponsored Web for Development conference in 2005, one speaker noted, during the previous year the entertainer, Britney Spears, recorded 3.6 million search returns on Google, while the Bank and its sister organizations in international development recorded 500,000.[186]

Increasingly, geopolitical issues, international financial markets, terrorism, and private sector competitors are marginalizing the Bank. To remain viable and to move forward, it must embrace a different concept of communications. The international community looks to the Bank as perhaps the most important venue of development knowledge. The developing world cannot afford to have the Bank's flow of information slanted to provide particular viewpoints. The full potential of the institution can only be unleashed if it provides policy analysis in conjunction with a role as medium for multi-directional knowledge sharing and exchanges. Therefore, of all the reforms the Bank should enact, perhaps the most important would be to rejuvenate an uncensored webcasting system that provided all a voice.

The transparency model Wheeler and I invented was aligned with the institution's mission of providing stakeholders with insights on the range and depth of the Bank's lending and technical expertise. Such a system would not have weakened the Bank by giving information away. It would have strengthened it by reinforcing the Bank's role as the focal point on development. A multi-directional webcasting hub would have been a vehicle for driving the institution's market share.

On a concurrent theme, does openness reduce the opportunities for an organization to make mistakes? We thought so, but that would not have told our whole story. We wanted to make the institution a more humane entity and one stakeholders, shareholders, critics and supporters could embrace.

As my perception of modalities changed, the objective remained constant. Thousands of people at the Bank work tirelessly to improve the fate of the less fortunate. It was on their behalf that the transparency model was created as well.

The Bank is also an institution that suffers from various maladies not uncommon in other bureaucracies. Poverty remains an abstraction to some. Personal ambition often comes at the expense of the mission and mitigates the Bank's potential to help stakeholders. Some use obfuscation, censorship, reprisals, panels and reviews to cloak themselves in anonymity as their fiefdoms grow. Yet one solution would be to embrace the tenets of the transparency model by opening up the doors and windows of the World Bank and letting the sun shine in.

AFTERWORD

transparency, reform and development in the obama era

What is development? To be sure, it means different things to different groups, but by all accounts the answers and the ways they are measured are complex. Still, we know that increasing income levels for the poor, improving access to safe water and basic education, and effectively treating people with diseases that barely exist in richer societies are some of the ways to measure development. For the more than one and a half billion people who live in abject poverty today, the stakes are high. Events in 2008 only exacerbated their miseries. It was a year that began with escalating food prices that led to riots in some countries and ended with the sharpest global economic downturn since the Great Depression.

There can be no doubt that in 2009 we stand on a vastly changed landscape. Like the armies of the Great War who in 1915 looked at a no man's land of shattered tree trunks and earth torn asunder, the view from just a year ago is remarkably different. Yet for many millions the trench lines of the war on poverty have not moved noticeably. In fact, in some ways they have deepened. In advance of the 2002 International Conference on Financing for Development in Monterrey, Mexico, the World Bank proclaimed 200 million people have been lifted out of poverty during the previous two decades. But now in the grip of the worldwide economic contraction, the UN Educational, Scientific and Cultural Organization (UNESCO) projected a 20% decline in per capita income for 400 million Africans already living in poverty. Even the Bank predicts poverty will affect an additional 46 million people in 2009.

The question becomes: What happens as the world marches forward? Recent history offers a mixed record. A Bank report, "African Development Indicators 2007," suggested growth rates in Sub-Saharan Africa economies were five percent higher than those of the previous decade.[1] The United Nation's Millennium Development Goals (MDGs) report for 2008 also indicated success in some important areas. Halving absolute global poverty by 2015 remained possible, the report said. Primary school enrollment had improved. Fatalities from measles and AIDS had declined, and HIV infection rates were also down. Malaria prevention had increased. More people had access to safe drinking water. Furthermore, the share of developing countries' export earnings devoted to servicing their external debt had declined, allowing them to use more resources for reducing poverty.

These positive developments were saddled with less hopeful signs. While the Bank report on Africa was good news, given the starting position of countries enjoying this growth, by any measure this progress was modest. By February 2009, the Bank estimated the financial downturn will halve this growth rate for the region this year.[2] The 2008 UN report on the MDGs was finalized just prior to the collapse of the U.S. financial markets that precipitated the global downturn. The report itself was not optimistic Africa would reach the MDG targets.[3] It also noted progress remained elusive in other key areas. Almost one and a half billion people continue to live in extreme poverty. Half the world's population does not have adequate sanitation and access to safe drinking water. A quarter of all children living in the developing world were malnourished and underweight. Their mortality rate is 14 times that of children in the developed world, and higher food prices are exacerbating these trends.[4] A half million women die each year from their pregnancies. Few economic opportunities cause millions to migrate from rural areas to cities, while more than one-third of the developing world's urban dwellers live in slum conditions. Stalled trade negotiations strangle the exports of developing countries. Environmental degradation has increased morbidity and mortality rates. Climate change is already impacting populations living on lands vulnerable to natural disasters. And development aid expenditures have fallen short of promised commitments from wealthy nations.[5]

Development assistance remains a key issue for impoverished nations. Two important aspects emerge. One is the volatility of aid flows. Homi Kharas, a senior fellow at the Brookings Institution in Washington, points out aid volatility is typically five times that of a recipient country's Gross Domestic Product, and three times that of its exports.[6] Volatility retards opportunities for poor countries to achieve economic growth, Kharas suggests. For example, he points out, "Aid volatility results in distortions in the choice of investment projects. High return, but long gestation, projects are put off for fear that future funding might be hard to come by." One solution he offers: Multi-year financial programs should become standardized among donor countries. Long-term strategic planning and development depends upon long-term and consistent aid flows, he argues. Kharas ruefully notes, however, "Most aid depends on annual budget appropriations."

A second key issue is aid levels. As has been noted before, development aid from the U.S. and other wealthy nations has fallen woefully below the 0.7% of Gross National Income levels they promised at the Monterrey conference in 2002. In 2005, further assurances were voiced in Gleneagles, Scotland where the G-8 nations agreed to raise their aid levels to $130 billion by 2010. By 2008, the collective percentage of aid from the participants at Monterrey amounted to only 0.28%. Even this level of underperformance far exceeded U.S. assistance, which was only 0.16%. In fact, G-8 aid levels fell by 13% during the two years following Gleneagles.[7]

In critiquing the Global Poverty Act of 2007, the Heritage Foundation noted, "The Bush Administration has been very careful to express its support for the objectives of the Millennium Declaration without specifically endorsing many of the specific indicators or documents that the Declaration has spawned. For instance, the U.S. has consistently couched its commitment to increase aid as part of a pact with developing countries to adopt policies that would create an economic environment more conducive to growth."[8] The Foundation noted that, while the Bush Administration agreed to the MDGs, the declaration was never formally submitted to it for approval. This allowed the U.S. to sidestep specific indicators, including calls for it to provide development aid at 0.7% of its GNP. According to the Foundation, this made sense since "there is scant evidence that such a sum [$100 billion] is necessary or, if provided, would actually promote development."

In fact, the Foundation believed the 0.7% indicator cited by the MDGs had no legitimacy to begin with. It cited research from the Center for Global Development (CGD), a Washington think tank, that said, "Originally intended as a political tool to goad rich countries to modestly increase their aid budget, the specific figure of 0.7% was a compromise between educated guesses based on economic conditions in the early 1960s and on a crude and deeply flawed model of growth. Despite these origins, '0.7%' has taken on a life of its own and become a powerful rallying cry for aid proponents. Indeed, in 2005, advocates are demanding that rich countries reach this specific target (and with some success). But there has been little reflection on whether 0.7% is the right figure."[9] Moreover, the Foundation suggested MDG targets focus on the symptoms of poverty rather than the causes. The onus, it said, should be upon developing countries to implement policies that promoted good governance, the rule of law and economic liberalization.

In fact, some aspects of the Bush Administration's record on development have been viewed positively. For example, the administration has been praised for significantly increasing aid to Africa, which quadrupled according to former Secretary of State Condoleezza Rice.[10] Aid to other global regions also increased. The President's Emergency Plan for AIDS Relief (PEPFAR) has provided treatment to 1.7 million people in Sub-Saharan Africa.[11] Additional monies have been provided to reduce malaria by increasing distribution of bed nets and medicines. The Bush response to the MDGs was the Millennium Challenge Corporation (MCC). It has received recognition for increasing the accountability of development spending by linking aid to measurable results. This dovetailed with the administration's existing philosophy that increases in aid did not necessarily lead to development, and that aid must be tied to results. The MCC has received praise from observers for innovation in the application of lessons learned from past development practices toward an incentive-based selection process.

In other ways, the Bush Administration's performance has disappointed the development community. While aid levels rose in real terms, CGD's 2008 Commitment to Development Index (CDI) ranked the U.S. 17th out of 22 rich nations in helping poor countries increase prosperity, good governance and security.[12] While U.S. development assistance has grown in real terms, at 0.16% of GDP it is still far short of the commitments made in 2002. In addition, PEPFAR, which formed the bulk of U.S. spending, was focused only on a single disease. As for the MCC, actual funding never reached targets announced by the administration. Its eligibility criteria limited disbursements to a small group of recipient countries, and it has focused on preparing countries to become eligible for funds as opposed to implementing successful projects.

In addition, many in the development community suggest the decentralized nature of how the U.S. government implements aid programs is problematic. "President Bush leaves a mixed legacy on foreign assistance," said Carol Lancaster, author of *George Bush's Foreign Aid: Transformation or Chaos?*[13] "Development issues have received more attention and money under this administration than at any time since President Kennedy. But the lack of a clear strategic direction and jumble of agencies and missions undermines effectiveness and fails to serve U.S. interests."

Others have questioned whether the Bush Administration's increases of aid to Africa have actually promoted sustainable development. "Much of the aid is emergency food or medical aid, rather than true development assistance," said Nii Akuetteh, a former executive director of Africa Action, a Washington-based advocacy group.[14] "Then there are conditions that are attached where the emphasis is more on countries that open up their markets so American companies can go in and privatize things like water and electrical service or have access to certain resources." Africa, indeed, is rich in resources such as oil that are important to American national security. In fact, even former administration officials have suggested increased attention on Africa in part stems from concerns over terrorism.[15]

"The U.S. has been blind to the Millennium Development Goals on fighting poverty, hunger and disease," said macroeconomist Jeffrey Sachs in an opinion piece that appeared in *The Guardian* (United Kingdom) newspaper on October 21, 2008. "When George Bush addressed the UN in September—supposedly the mid-point in achieving the goals—he mentioned 'terror' 31 times while failing to mention the goals even once. All the big donors except Britain—including the U.S., Japan, France, Germany, Italy and Canada—are failing to live up to long-standing aid commitments."[16]

It can be argued then that the war on terrorism was the overarching framework of the Bush presidency's legacy, not just as it applied to foreign aid but also to development assistance as well. The Bush Administration often treated the Bretton Woods institutions as instruments of its foreign policy. Prior to the terrorist attacks of 2001, key officials including former Treasury Secretary Paul O'Neill vilified the World Bank as inefficient, incompetent and in need of restructuring. It sought to reinvent the Bank as a grant-making institution. Following the attacks, the pendulum swung markedly in a different direction. Both the Bank and IMF were used to channel funds to "friends" in the war on terrorism. For reasons noted throughout this text, the Bank was incapable of curbing this momentous shift.

Pakistan offers a useful example of this conflict between using multilateral lending institutions as tools of foreign policy and having a strategic agenda on development. As noted at the beginning of this book, the Bush Administration enacted a series of steps to increase aid to Pakistan following the 2001 terrorist attacks. This did not necessarily go hand in hand with a clear plan of how more aid to Islamabad would promote development. In 2005, the *Wall Street Journal* reported that Pakistan remained at the bottom of the world's rankings for investing in its public education system. Aid flows were also highly uneven. Development assistance from the U.S. to Pakistan rose from $100 million in the late 1990s to $880 million in 2001, then dropped to $113 million in 2003, and rose again to $480 million in 2006.[17] As of 2009, Pakistan remains deeply troubled. There is significant poverty, growing violence and terrorists seeking the government's nuclear arsenal. It is also the one country many knowledgeable observers believe is central to how the war on terrorism will end.

Now we have entered new terrain, far different than the one we traversed before. The 2001 terrorist attacks created a fissure in a landscape still vibrating with anxiety over globalization and the currency destabilization in East Asia in the late 1990s. The 2008 global financial downturn has shifted everything again. In November 2008, heads of state and finance ministers from the G-20 (the wealthy countries of the G-7 plus the largest emerging economies) met in Washington to discuss how to stabilize international markets in order to stave off financial collapses throughout the world.

The G-20 meeting emphasized the immediate need for regulatory reform of financial markets. It also focused its attention on the role of the IMF, which traditionally micro-manages the macroeconomic policies of emerging economies with financial problems. Participants stated that the IMF should play the lead role in stabilizing tottering economies through its short-term liquidity resources, and it should serve as a forum for the oversight of macroeconomic policies of countries during the downturn. As for the Bank, the G-20 was prepared to "ensure that the World Bank and other MDBs (multilateral development banks) have sufficient resources to continue playing their role in overcoming the crisis."[18]

The G-20 reconvened in April 2009 to assess the changing dynamics of the global economy and formally adopt and fund measures to stem its deterioration. A key schism that emerged between the U.S. and Britain, which sought additional national fiscal stimulus, and France and Germany, which sought cross-border regulation of financial markets, went unresolved. The G-20, however, did agree to provide $1.1 trillion in "new" funds to the IMF, Bank and other regional multilateral development banks to stabilize emerging and developing economies whose vulnerability had increased since the G-20 meeting the previous fall.

Critics, however, questioned how much of the $1.1 trillion pledge was new monies or announcements of existing but undistributed funds or redirected resources.[19] Given the urgency of the situation, concern was also raised about the speed in which funds would be dispersed. Without quick infusions, devoid of the conditions that made borrowers hesitate, developing countries would be without the resources necessary to undertake fiscal stimulus measures. Some observers thought this point was critical. "There is ample research that shows that the frequency and depth of downturns is more important for long-run average growth in poor countries than growth accelerations," said Kharas of the Brookings Institute. On this front there is good news. Kharas stated as much as $70 billion of monies approved by the boards of the various multilateral development banks had not yet been dispersed and could be used immediately.[20]

The G-20 also declared that "We reaffirm our historic commitment to meeting the Millennium Development Goals and to achieving our respective ODA (overseas development assistance) pledges, including commitments on Aid for Trade, debt relief, and the Gleneagles commitments, especially to Sub-Saharan Africa."[21] But given the failure to live up to promises made by rich countries at Monterrey and Scotland, these assurances were received by observers with lukewarm enthusiasm.

And, aside from the above statement, little discussion was devoted to debt relief. "Debt relief is a proven, effective and fast way to reduce poverty," said Sarah Anderson, director of the Global Economy Project of the Institute of Policy Studies in Washington.[22] In suggesting the G-20 invest in fiscal stimulus for poor countries in the days before the London conference, Homi Kharas offered this perspective. "Thanks to debt relief programs like the Heavily Indebted Poor Country Initiative, half of all low-income countries have debt below 36% of GDP," he said. "Half also have fiscal deficits (after grants) below 1.8% of GDP. While it is true that these hard-won gains should not be casually reversed, the creation of fiscal space through debt relief was done precisely to provide room for necessary spending. If this is not the appropriate time to use the space, then when is?"[23]

Another area of concern heading into London was a growing thread of protectionism precipitated by the global crisis. Protectionism, cited as a key factor for lengthening the Great Depression of the 1930s, was on the rise. In advance of the London meeting, the Bank issued a report that since the start of the downturn it found 47 trade measures had been implemented with various types of restrictions. Seventeen had been done by G-20 countries.[24] Developing countries are highly dependent on exports—a key vulnerability that the economic contraction has impacted—while trade credit shrunk by 40% during the last quarter of 2008.[25] The G-20 did direct that $250 billion of the $1.1 trillion would go to trade finance. They also said they would refrain from protectionism, minimize trade-distorting fiscal stimulus measures, and "name and shame" countries that erected trade barriers. The G-20 did not, however, commit to a deadline for the current Doha round of trade negotiations. On the eve of the London meeting, *The Economist* suggested that "a failure to agree on coordinating fiscal plans opens the door to forms of protectionism in stimulus packages motivated by worries about stimulus benefits 'leaking' abroad."[26]

It seems curious that the popular question we grow up asking in the West is: Why is there war? Perhaps we should instead be asking this question: Why is there peace? Most analysts acknowledge the underlying cause of terrorism is poverty. Poverty with its lack of food, medicines, sanitation, education and rule of law is a breeding ground for discontent and anarchy. The donor community and institutions such as the World Bank have no choice but to more effectively address global poverty, even in this perilous time. The pendulum of attention and action must swing toward sustainable poverty reduction and development, and decisively, and soon. Population trends over the coming decade will exacerbate existing conditions and create new ones over resource scarcities.

The changing landscape caused by the financial downturn has

nevertheless brought with it a new current in the wind. For the first time in nearly a decade there is optimism about the role the United States will play on the world's stage. The unilateralist philosophy of the previous administration has ended. In its place has come rhetoric of a distinctly different kind: Engagement.

Still, the challenges faced by President Barack Obama at the start of his term are enormous: A banking sector riddled with so-called toxic assets and a reluctance to engage in new lending; unemployment rates hovering at 30-year highs, and stock market indexes dramatically reduced; consumer spending, the centerpiece of the American economy in recent years, collapsing while manufacturing surpluses are growing; a housing market crippled by faulty loans and defaults; an automobile industry in need of restructuring and needing increasing bailout funds; the deficit at record levels; millions of families without access to affordable health care; entitlement programs such as Social Security, Medicare and Medicaid overwhelming the federal budget; an energy sector that will need to develop alternative sources; and two expensive wars draining the nation's coffers.

With all these costly problems confronting the new government, where will it find time and funds for international development? What we might expect to hear is promising rhetoric. But President Obama has suggested the domestic economic crisis he has inherited will not derail his global development agenda. Perhaps the reasons can be found in speeches he made in 2007 during the campaign. He stated, in part, "And since extremely poor societies and weak states provide optimal breeding grounds for disease, terrorism and conflict, the United States has a direct national security interest in dramatically reducing global poverty and joining with our allies in sharing more of our riches to help those most in need." He added, "In today's globalized world, the security of the American people is inextricably linked to the security of all people. When narco-trafficking and corruption threaten democracy in Latin America, it's America's problem, too. When poor villagers in Indonesia have no choice but to send chickens to market infected with avian flu, it cannot be seen as a distant concern. When religious schools in Pakistan teach hatred to young children, our children are threatened as well."[27] The linkages he made between poverty and terrorism with the need for the United States to commit more resources to development are clear and succinct.

The Obama agenda moves beyond where the Bush Administration and the Heritage Foundation attempted to go, most notably with a pledge to double aid to the developing world to $50 billion by 2012.[28] While $50 billion would not move the U.S. to the 0.7% target of the MDGs, here Obama is positioned with the majority of the development community, acknowledging that larger aid levels are not in themselves a panacea for global poverty, but nevertheless a critical component. On the campaign trail, Obama said, "The United Nations has embraced the Millennium Development Goals, which aim to cut extreme poverty in half by 2015. When I'm president, they will be America's goals."

In late 2007, he laid out a lengthy agenda. In addition to doubling aid, his initiatives included: Providing $2 billion for a new Global Education Fund that would increase primary education rates; committing $50 billion over five years to combat HIV/AIDS through an expansion of PEPFAR, as well as targeting malaria and tuberculosis; seeking 100% debt relief for the most heavily-indebted countries by ensuring they receive grants through the World Bank rather than loans, so as to not fall back into debt; launching an agricultural initiative to reduce the vulnerability of commodity exports to global shocks and improve access to markets for poor farmers; introducing a Rapid Response Fund to provide aid, debt relief and technical assistance to fledgling democracies and post-conflict societies; pursuing a climate change and alternative energy development agenda domestically while establishing an Emerging Market Energy Fund to expand the developing world's renewable energy portfolio; and consolidating the administration of U.S. foreign aid that is currently spread across more than 20 federal agencies.

The development community has also called for a series of new initiatives and reforms, many of which mirror Obama's campaign platform. The Overseas Development Institute is pushing for diversification of development assistance promoted under Bush. It noted that, of the $22 billion spent by the U.S. in 2007, almost $19 billion went into PEPFAR.[29] Numerous sources are calling for a consolidation of the extraordinarily decentralized administration of development aid.[30] CGD analysts have noted that despite the economic climate that will tighten budgets further, the MCC now must show that its best practice standards "actually translate into better results on the ground, and whether the incentive-based eligibility structure truly inspires and sustains policy reform in recipient countries."[31] CGD believes support in Congress for the MCC may wither if it cannot show concrete results. Among the reforms CGD suggests is the MCC should focus exclusively on low-income countries. Currently, only eight of the 26 eligible nations are classified as low-income.

During the 2008 campaign, CGD issued a report, *The White House and the World: A Global Development Agenda for the Next U.S. President*. The agenda is comprehensive, and seeks a parallel track of improving the quality of life for the world's poor with initiatives that will also enhance American economic and national security.[32] Its recommendations include: Revamping the U.S. trade agenda to reduce subsidies in key commodities, and removing other import barriers while providing duty-free and quota-free access to the poorest countries; launching a strategic framework on global health that moves beyond PEPFAR by leveraging the resources of multilateral partners and U.S. pharmaceutical companies to address other key health concerns; setting emission limits, establishing effective market mechanisms, and promoting clean technology to curb global climate change; promoting public and private research and development to increase agricultural production; and reorganizing the government's foreign assistance under a single cabinet-level agency. CGD also reiterated its long-held position that World Bank reforms include a more open selection process for its president, and more power sharing for developing countries on its board.

CGD estimates that "aside from the $50 billion that we recommend spending inside the United States to finance agriculture, clean energy and health research, the total cost of our recommendations for 'foreign aid' would amount to an increase in our development assistance of just $7 billion a year. That is less than the cost of one month of 'Iraq time' (in 2007), and only 1 percent of the $700 billion that Congress authorized to be spent for coping with the financial crisis."[33]

A comparison of spending on the war on terrorism and relief for the global financial sector with expenditures for development aid is dramatic. "Europe and the U.S. have mobilized around $3 trillion in the past month in guarantees and bailout funds for the banks but failed to mobilize even one ten-thousandth of that this year to help the world's poorest grow more food in the midst of a massive food price increase and hunger crisis," said Jeffrey Sachs in late 2008.[34]

Given the rapidly changing environment of U.S. domestic interests, the global economy and pressures from the G-20, reality suggests the Obama Administration will continually adjust its goals, strategies and tactics toward international development. To date, however, President Obama's rhetoric has moved in lockstep with this understanding: It is not sound policy to spend trillions stabilizing financial markets and bailing out banks, and not increase spending on development by a few billion more.

At his inauguration, President Obama's speech mirrored a State of the Union speech made in 1960, just months before he was born, by President Dwight D. Eisenhower.[35] "To the people of poor nations, we pledge to work alongside you," Obama said. "And to those nations like ours that enjoy relatively plenty, we say we can no longer afford indifference to the suffering outside our borders, nor can we consume the world's resources without regard to effect … a nation cannot prosper long when it favors only the prosperous. The success of our economy has always depended not just on the size of our Gross Domestic Product, but the reach of our prosperity, on our ability to extend the opportunity to every willing heart, not out of charity but because it is the surest route to our common good."[36]

Naturally, the development community appealed for quick action to reverse growing poverty rates, frozen investment capital and slumping exports in the developing world. Just two days after Obama's inauguration, World Bank president Robert Zoellick pressed the U.S. to pledge 0.7% of its economic stimulus package be directed to a vulnerability fund for assisting developing countries.[37] Such a fund, Zoellick suggested, could be used to increase investments in health, education and nutrition programs, foster more infrastructure expenditures, and support small and medium-size enterprise and micro-financing institutions.

The G-20 agreed to such a vulnerability fund during its London meeting in April 2009. The global crisis, which is replacing the post-9/11 period as the centerpiece of the development paradigm, has returned the Bank (and the IMF) to the forefront of importance. The G-20 pledge to infuse the Bank with new capital, however, did not exorcise the underlying issues plaguing the institution with its various constituencies. Despite British Prime Minister Gordon Brown's insistence the meeting marked the beginning of a "new world order" and summit language that stated the IMF would do "concessional and flexible finance for the poorest countries," Congressional Quarterly suggested "it is far from the end of the dominance of the Washington Consensus."[38] Borrowers remain hesitant to do business with the Bretton Woods institutions because of their appetite to impose conditions with their loans. Donors remain unclear whether the Bank's lending assistance is effective. Both groups plus civil society observers continue to be concerned about the Bank's transparency. The G-20 formally called upon the Bank (and the IMF) to implement reforms. Development think tanks and NGOs have also been forceful advocates for improving the governance of the international financial institutions. In the wake of the global financial crisis, the Bank acknowledged it could no longer avoid calls to "modernize" its governance and subsequently launched a commission to study the issue. But its reluctant to proactively implement reforms is undeniable. With all these problems working in tandem, it is unclear whether the Bank will be any more effective using the vulnerability funds and future aid to help the developing world than it had been before the global economic downturn.

Given all that has been discussed, it would be easy to be cynical about the Bank. But in the final analysis, the mission is to reduce global poverty. To reach that goal, it is necessary for society to reexamine the instruments used to foster those ends. If they are not up to the task, and if we do not make them so, then our best intentions will not be fulfilled. And, if in the past, these instruments have not been fully effective, it is beholden upon us not to ridicule them, but to make them better.

It is therefore reassuring to note what a then-candidate Obama said in 2007: "Today it's become fashionable to disparage the United Nations, the World Bank and other international organizations. In fact, reform of these bodies is urgently needed if they are to keep pace with fast-moving threats we face. Such real reform will not come, however, by dismissing the value of these institutions, or by bullying other countries to ratify changes we have drafted in isolation. Real reform will come because we convince others that they too have a stake in change—that such reforms will make their world, and not just ours, more secure."[39]

The new president has made transparency and accountability the pillars by which his administration will govern. During his campaign he promised to "end the practice of writing legislation behind closed doors" and said he would seek reform of Congressional rules to require all legislative sessions, including committee markups and conference committee sessions, be conducted in public. He pledged to have legislation online for public review five days before its enactment. He called for the establishment of Internet databases that would allow the public to read reports on federal contractors, lobbying, ethics records, and campaign finance filings.[40] His platform sought the establishment of an independent watchdog agency to oversee the investigation of congressional ethics violations. He stated that to reduce corruption abroad, America should lead by example by making its contracting decisions merit-based and transparent.

"Transparency and the rule of law will be the touchstones of this presidency," he declared.[41] Action began immediately. The first blogpost of his administration said, "President Obama has committed to making his administration the most open and transparent in history."[42] Then, on his first full day in office, he signed an executive order on new ethics guidelines for White House staff related to lobbying, and issued a memorandum ordering federal agencies to "harness new technologies to put information about their operations and decisions online and readily available to the public."[43]

Logic dictates the new administration may also look for opportunities beyond the scope of the federal government by pushing international financial institutions to embrace these tenets more aggressively. On the eve of his departure as president of the World Bank in 2005, James Wolfensohn noted that transparency reduced corruption. Less corruption led to better governance and better governance increased development. Transparency, Wolfensohn believed, was the key. This is the trail the Obama Administration has begun to blaze. If the Bank and other development institutions move with it in unison, then truly the landscape of 2009 and beyond, while fragile and full of fissures, offers all of us the audacity of hope.

footnotes

(Note: WBM = Official World Bank Memorandum)

PART I — A PATH TO PEACE

1 *Wikipedia*, "The Bank of the South"
2 *ZNet*, "The Bank of the South: An Alternative to IMF and World Bank Dominance," Stephen Lendman, October 30, 2007; *Alternet*, "Adios World Bank: The World Bank Continues its Downward Crisis of Legitimacy, at Least in Latin America," Nadia Martinez, May 9, 2007. http://alternet.org/blogs/peek/51662
3 Bloomberg.com, Jeb Blount, "South American Countries Agree to Found Banco del Sur," January 29, 2008.
4 NowPublic.com, "Banco del Sur: Breaking Washington's Grip," January 23, 2008.
5 Ibid.
6 MSNBC.com, *Associated Press*, "Chavez and Allies Challenge IMF, World Bank," December 9, 2007, www.msnbc.com/id/22171566/; NowPublic.com, "Banco del Sur: Breaking Washington's Grip," January 23, 2008.
7 World Bank Internal Communications, "World Bank Increases Support to Developing Countries," September 17, 2004; World Bank Publication, *Knowledge for Resources and Development*, January 2001, Stock # 31720; ZNet, "The Bank of the South: An Alternative to IMF and World Bank Dominance," Stephen Lendman, October 30, 2007; *MarketPlace*, "South America Set to Launch 'Banco del Sur,'" http://marketplace.publicradio.org, December 6, 2007.
8 *MarketPlace*, "South America Set to Launch 'Banco del Sur,'" http://marketplace.publicradio.org, December 6, 2007; *Christian Science Monitor*, Sara Miller Llana, Mathew Clark, "Latin America's Answer to the World Bank and IMF," July 12, 2007.
9 *MarketPlace*, "South America Set to Launch 'Banco del Sur,'" http://marketplace.publicradio.org, December 6, 2007.
10 Rudi Dornbusch, "Do We Really Need the World Bank Anymore?" *Business Week*, February 24, 1997
11 Adam Lerrick, "Has the World Bank Lost Its Way?" *Euromoney*, December 1999.
12 Adam Lerrick, "Why is the World Bank Still Lending?" *Wall Street Journal*, October 28, 2005.
13 *The Globalizers: The IMF, The World Bank and Their Borrowers*, Ngaire Woods, Cornell Press, 2006; Center for Global Development Brief, "The Globalizers in Search of a Future: Four Reasons Why the IMF and World Bank Must Change and Four Ways They Can," Ngaire Woods, April 2006.
14 Adam Lerrick, "Has the World Bank Lost Its Way?" *Euromoney*, December 1999; Adam Lerrick, "Why is the World Bank Still Lending?" *Wall Street Journal*, October 28, 2005.
15 World Bank Report of Task Force on Portfolio Management (*Wapenhans Report*), 1991.
16 World Bank Report, "The Role and Effectiveness of Development Assistance, 2002"; *World Bank Today*, "Development Effectiveness," March 12, 2002; *Washington Post*,

Paul Blustein, "World Bank Answers Skeptics on Aid; Report Says Assistance is More Effective Today than It Has Ever Been," March 12, 2002.

17 Paul Blustein, "World Bank Answers Skeptics on Aid; Report Says Assistance is More Effective Today than It Has Ever Been," *Washington Post*, March 12, 2002; Ken Ringle, "Bank Shot," *Washington Post*, March 20, 2002.

18 Paul Nelson, "Whose Civil Society? Whose Governance? Decision-making and Practice in the New Agenda at the Inter-American Development Bank and the World Bank," *Global Governance: A Review of Multilateralism and International Organizations*, October 1, 2000; *Foreign Policy*, Spring 2000, The FP Interview: "Lori's War."

19 *Washington Post*, Peter Goodman, "Bush to Pick Zoellick for World Bank," May 30, 2007; CNN Money.com, "Deal Said to be Offered for Wolfowitz Exit: European Countries Will Drop Demand that They Pick Next World Bank President if Wolfowitz Agrees to Leave Soon, Newspaper Says," May 8, 2007.

20 Center for Global Development, "The Hardest Job in the World: Five Crucial Tasks for the New President of the World Bank," June 1, 2005, Page 24.

21 *Washington Post*, Paul Blustein, "O'Neill Targets World Bank's Poverty-Fighting Strategy," May 16, 2001.

22 WBM, Sunetra Puri to WBI Staff, "MORE ON ANNUAL MEETINGS," August 20, 2001.

23 *Washington Post*, Paul Blustein, "A Tighter Hand in Doling Out Global Aid? IMF, World Bank Principles Face a New Policy Threat," September 30, 2001.

24 WBMs, Wheeler to Kristalina Georgieva, Michele de Nevers, "DECRG-IE, More Fallout ... Amazing ...," September 25, 2001; Shaman to Wheeler, "Gaining Speed," September 14, 2001.

25 World Bank Group Staff Association Newsletter, October 2001, "The Bank Group is Always Navigating Political Waters."

26 *Washington Post*, Paul Blustein, "A Tighter Hand in Doling Out Global Aid? IMF, World Bank Principles Face a New Policy Threat," September 30, 2001.

27 ZNet, "The Bank of the South: An Alternative to IMF and World Bank Dominance," Stephen Lendman, October 30, 2007.

28 *Wall Street Journal*, Steve LeVine Zahid Hussain, "Pakistan's Broad Education Ills: Public Schools May Stir Up More Extremism than Madrassas," August 19, 2005.

29 *Newsweek*, "The Most Dangerous Nation in the World Isn't Iraq. It's Pakistan," October 29, 2007.

30 *The New York Times*, Elizabeth Becker, "A World Bank Mission to Bring Help to the Poor," April 22, 2004; *World Bank Development News*, "Wolfensohn Sees Need for New Balance Between Rich and Poor Nations," September 23, 2003; WBMs, Shaman to Bowden, "Summary for Interfaith Conference: Celebrating 25 Years of Building Community," April 1, 2004; Shaman to B-SPAN List, *B-SPAN Newsletter*, April 2004, April 7, 2004.

31 World Bank Internal Communications, "WDI 2004: Global Poverty Cut by Half in 20 Years," April 23, 2004.

32 *The New York Times* Editorial, "Failing the World's Poor," September 24, 2008; *New York Times*, Elizabeth Becker, "A World Bank Mission to Bring Help to the Poor," April 22, 2004; FT.com, "Interest in Poverty Near a Low Point," Richard McGregor, May 25, 2004.

33 Council on Hemispheric Affairs, *Bush's Millennium Challenge Corporation: A New Approach to Overseas Development, or the Same Old Strategy?*, www.coha.org.

34 U.S. State Department, America.gov, "U.S. Millennium Challenge Corporation Overview: MCA Helps Countries Obtain Sustainable Economic Growth, Reduce Poverty," May 31, 2007; Millennium Challenge Corporation Press Release, "Leading

International NGOs, Think Tanks and Senators Join President Bush in Support of Full Funding for MCC," June 13, 2008.
35 Wikipedia, Millennium Challenge Account: *El Pais*, "Transcription of Talk Between George Bush and Jose Maria Aznar, Crawford, Texas," February 22, 2003; MSNBC, Andrew War, "New Light Cast on Bush's Plans for Iraq War," September 27, 2007.
36 *The New York Times*, David Leonhardt, "What $1.2 Trillion Can Buy," January 17, 2007; *The Guardian*, Jamie Wilson, "Iraq War Could Cost US Over $2 Trillion Says Nobel Prize Winning Economist," January 7, 2006; About.com, Deborah White, "Iraq War Results and Statistics at August 13, 2008."
37 *The New York Times* Editorial, "Failing the World's Poor," September 24, 2008.
38 *The Millennium Development Goals Report 2005*, United Nations.
39 *The Millennium Development Goals Report 2005*, United Nations.
40 CNN, "Advocacy Group Says G8 Nations Far Behind in African Aid Promises," June 7, 2007; *Washington Post*, Editorial Page, "Anticlimax," July 9, 2005; *Washington Post*, Jin VendeHei and Paul Blustein, "African Aid is Doubled by G-8," July 8, 2005.
41 CNN, "WTO Global Trade Talks Collapse," July 24, 2006.
42 World Bank Group Staff Association Newsletter, June 2004, "FY05 Budget Will Bring Yet Another Squeeze on Staff."
43 *The New York Times*, Steven Weisman, "World Bank Faces Doubts From Donors," September 25, 2007.
44 *Washington Post*, Peter Goodman and Krissah Williams, "Scandal May Jeopardize World Bank Funds," May 8, 2007.
45 Sebastian Mallaby, *The World's Banker: The Story of Failed States, Financial Crises, and the Wealth and Poverty of Nations*, Penguin Books, 2004, Page 143; *The New York Times*, Richard Stevenson, "World Bank Gets Bosnia Aid Role," April 17, 1996.
46 *Associated Press*, "Chavez: Venezuela to Ext IMF, World Bank," May 1, 2007.

PART 2 — THREADS

1 *The New York Times*, July 1, 1944 through July 30, 1944.
2 Shelby Stanton, *World War II Order of Battle, U.S. Army*, Presidio Publishers, 1984.
3 Sebastian Mallaby, *The World's Banker: The Story of Failed States, Financial Crises, and the Wealth and Poverty of Nations*, Penguin Books, 2004, Pages 14, 15.
4 Devesh Kapur, John Lewis, Richard Webb, *The World Bank: Its First Half Century, Volume 1*, The Brookings Institute, 1997, Page 57; Sebastian Mallaby, *The World's Banker: The Story of Failed States, Financial Crises, and the Wealth and Poverty of Nations*, Penguin Books, 2004, Page 15.
5 Devesh Kapur, John Lewis, Richard Webb, *The World Bank: Its First Half Century, Volume 1*, The Brookings Institute, 1997, Pages 9, 58.
6 Ibid., Pages 61, 62.
7 Ibid., Pages, 61, 62, 68.
8 Ibid., Pages 62, 66.
9 Devesh Kapur, John Lewis, Richard Webb, *The World Bank: Its First Half Century, Volume 1*, The Brookings Institute, 1997, Pages 3, 4; Sebastian Mallaby, *The World's Banker: The Story of Failed States, Financial Crises, and the Wealth and Poverty of Nations*, Penguin Books, 2004, Page 21.
10 Devesh Kapur, John Lewis, Richard Webb, *The World Bank: Its First Half Century, Volume 1*, The Brookings Institute, 1997, Volume 1, Pages 3, 4; Volume 2, Page 198 ; World Bank Group Staff Association Newsletter, "The Bank Group is Always Navigating Political Waters," October 2001.
11 Devesh Kapur, John Lewis, Richard Webb, *The World Bank: Its First Half Century, Volume 1*, The Brookings Institute, 1997, Pages 3, 3n.
12 Ibid., Page 63.
13 Ibid., Pages 64, 65.

14 Ibid., Pages 64, 65.
15 Ibid., Pages 16, 52, 207, 208.
16 Sebastian Mallaby, *The World's Banker: The Story of Failed States, Financial Crises, and the Wealth and Poverty of Nations*, Penguin Books, 2004, Pages 26-28.
17 Devesh Kapur, John Lewis, Richard Webb, *The World Bank: Its First Half Century, Volume 1*, The Brookings Institute, 1997, Pages 426-428.
18 Sebastian Mallaby, *The World's Banker: The Story of Failed States, Financial Crises, and the Wealth and Poverty of Nations*, Penguin Books, 2004, Pages 90-92, 379-385; World Bank Report, "The Effect of IMF and World Bank Programmes on Poverty, 2000"; Anup Shah, *Global Issues*, 'Structural Adjustment A Major Cause of Poverty," July 2, 2007, http://www.globalissues.org/article/3/structural-adjustment-a-major-cause-of-poverty.
19 Devesh Kapur, John Lewis, Richard Webb, *The World Bank: Its First Half Century, Volume 1*, The Brookings Institute, 1997, Volume 1, Page 34; Volume 2, Pages 698-701.
20 Raymond Kopp, "The Power of Ideas and the Public Policy Process, Resources for the Future," *Resources*, Winter 2003.
21 *The Environment and the Appropriate Development: The Parable of Four Paths?*, David Wheeler, 1991
22 *Outreach* #12, "Policy Views from the Policy Research Department, Promoting Cleaner Industrial Development," Shakeb Afsah, Paul Martin, David Wheeler, August 1993.
23 "The Economics of Industrial Pollution in Developing Countries: A Research Proposal," David Wheeler, Raymond Hartman, April 1994; *Determinants of Pollution Abatement in Developing Countries,* Hemala Hettige, Mainual Huq, Sheoli Pargal, David Wheeler, 1995.
24 "The Economics of Industrial Pollution in Developing Countries: A Research Proposal," David Wheeler, Raymond Hartman, April 1994; *Determinants of Pollution Abatement in Developing Countries*, Hemala Hettige, Mainual Huq, Sheoli Pargal, David Wheeler, 1995.
25 "The Economics of Industrial Pollution in Developing Countries: A Research Proposal," David Wheeler, Raymond Hartman, April 1994; *Economic Development, Environmental Regulation, and the International Migration of Toxic Pollution: 1960-88*, Robert Lucas, David Wheeler, Hemala Hettige, 1992; *The Economist*, "Economics Man, Cleaner Planet," September 27, 2001; *Trade Policy and Industrial Pollution in Latin America: Where are the Pollution Havens?*, Nancy Birdsall, David Wheeler, 1992; *Moving to Greener Pastures? Multinationals and the Pollution Haven Hypothesis*, Gunnar Eskeland, Ann Harrison, 1994.
26 *The Industrial Pollution Projection System*, Hemala Hettige, Paul Martin, Manjula Singh, David Wheeler, 1994
27 *The New York Times*, "Across Asia, A Pollution Disaster Hovers," November 28, 1997.
28 WBM, Wheeler to Maritta Koch-Weser, "Current Research and Papers in Preparation," April 29, 1991.
29 WBM, Wheeler to Maritta Koch-Weser, "Current Research and Papers in Preparation," April 29, 1991.
30 *The Industrial Pollution Projection System*, Hemala Hettige, Paul Martin, Manjula Singh, David Wheeler, 1994.
31 *The Industrial Pollution Projection System*, Hemala Hettige, Paul Martin, Manjula Singh, David Wheeler, 1994.
32 *The Cost of Air Pollution Abatement*, Raymond Hartman, Manjula Singh, David Wheeler, 1994.
33 World Bank Policy Research Report, *Greening Industry: New Roles for Communities, Markets, and Governments*, 1999, Page 23.

34 World Development Report 1992, *Development and the Environment*, Chapter 6, "Energy and Industry," Box 6.3, *Benign Technological Change: The Manufacture of Wood Pulp*, Page 129; *Economic Development, Environmental Regulation, and the International Migration of Toxic Pollution: 1960-88*, Robert Lucas, David Wheeler, Hemala Hettige, 1992; WBM, Wheeler to Extended List, "Neiman Marcus Information at K Mart Prices: A Plea for Support," October 29, 1992.

35 WBMs, Wheeler to Richard Ackerman, Nancy Birdsall, Carter Brandon, Carl Dahlman, Gloria Davis, Gunnar Eskeland, Gregory Ingram, Maritta Koch-Weser, Mark Kosmo, Dennis Mahar, Ijaz Nabi, Lant Pritchett, Sudhir Shetty, Andrew Steer, Lawrence Summers, Hemala Hettige, Lili Liu, "Nieman Marcus Information at K Mart Prices: A Plea for Support," October 29, 1992; Wheeler to Elizabeth Wyname-Green, "Wheeling and Dealing …," November 8, 1992.

36 WBMs, Wheeler to Elizabeth Wyname-Green, "Wheeling and Dealing …," November 8, 1992; Wheeler to Hemala Hettige, "Good News," November 10, 1992.

37 David Wheeler, Research Proposal, "Econometric Analysis of Pollution Abatement Costs, 1992."

38 WBM, Wheeler to Richard Ackermann, Robert Anderson, Roger Batstone, Carter Brandon, Arthur Bruestle, Antonio Estache, Mark Kosmo, Robert Mertz, Ijaz Nabi, "Next Steps," August 6, 1993.

39 WBMs, Shaman to Wheeler, Shakeb Afsah, "Progress Report," August 23, 1993; Shaman to Wheeler, Afsah, "IPPS Update," September 20, 1993.

40 WBMs, Cecilia Guido Spano to Lilibeth Hocson, "Salary Increase David Shaman (Staff #26335)," November 30, 1994; Shaman to Wheeler, "Bi-Annual Update," December 21, 1994; "World Bank Group Performance Record, David Shaman," January 1, 1995 to December 31, 1995.

41 WBM, Shaman to Sherif Arif, Wheeler, Hemala Hettige, "Comparison of IPPS and DSS," November 14, 1996.

42 WBM, Wheeler to Emmanuel Jimenez, Susmita Dasgupta, Benoit Laplante, Ken Chomitz, Craig Meisner, Hua Wang, Kiran Panday, Paul Martin, Shaman, Maria Teresa Serra, Zmarak Shalizi, "Manny's Maxim: The Continuing Adventures of IPPS," June 23, 2003.

43 Islam Faisal to Shaman, "Application of IPPS in Bangladesh," March 1, 2002; WBM, Craig Meisner to Anna Kukla, University of Warsaw, "Applying IPPS Project," July 25, 2002; WBM, Shaman to NIPR List, "NIPR Newsletter, February 2002," February 26, 2002.

44 *The Economics of Industrial Pollution in Developing Countries: The Role of Formal and Informal Regulation*, Wheeler et. al, 1994.

45 *Why Paper Mills Clean Up; Determinants of Pollution Abatement in Four Asian Countries*, Raymond Hartman, Mainul Huq, David Wheeler, 1997.

46 WBM, Shaman to Tanaporn Poshyandada, Wheeler, Hemala Hettige, Shakeb Afsah, Sudhir Shetty, "Thai Census Data," August 16, 1994; Timothy Whitington, Seatec International, to Wheeler, "Plant Level Statistics for Industrial Pollution Intensities," March 11, 1994.

47 WBM, Shakeb Afsah, Benoit Laplante, Sheoli Pargal to Wheeler, "Back-to-Office Report
Indonesia Mission, December 7-16, 1994," January 8, 1995

48 *The Economist*, "Economics Man, Cleaner Planet," September 27, 2001; The Right-to-Know Network, www.rtk.net.

49 WBM, Carter Brandon to Wheeler, Maritta Koch-Weser, Jean Aden, Nobuko Ichikawa, Esme Abedim, "Draft Proposal for a Study on Public Disclosure and Participation in Industrial Pollution," June 8, 1993; "Japan's Experience in Urban Environmental Management," Paper Presented to the Third Intercountry Workshop,

World Bank Metropolitan Environmental Improvement Program, Colombo, Sri Lanka, December 1992.

50 *Community Right-to-Know: The Impact of Toxic Release Inventory Reporting in the USA*, Paul Martin, 1992.

51 Shelly Hearne, "Tracking Toxics: Chemical Use and the Publics 'Right-to-Know,'" *Environment*, July-August 1996.

52 Shelly Hearne, "Tracking Toxics: Chemical Use and the Publics 'Right-to-Know,'" *Environment*, July-August 1996.

53 *The Atlantic Monthly*, "Regulation by Shaming," Mary Graham, April 2000; Shelly Hearne, "Tracking Toxics: Chemical Use and the Publics 'Right-to-Know,'" *Environment*, July-August 1996.

54 *The New York Times*, Keith Schneider, "For Communities, Knowledge of Polluters is Power," March 24, 1991; Shelly Hearne, "Tracking Toxics: Chemical Use and the Publics 'Right-to-Know,'" *Environment*, July-August 1996.

55 DEC Notes #31, "Creating Incentives to Control Pollution," Shakeb Afsah, Benoit Laplante, David Shaman, David Wheeler, July 1997.

56 WBMs, Wheeler to Nabile Makarim, Indonesia Ministry of Environment, Lyn Squire, Richard Calkins, no subject, December 19, 1994; Shakeb Afsah to Calkins, Wheeler, "BTO: Indonesia Mission for BPR Support to Bapedal," July 21, 1994; Afsah to Calkins, Zmarak Shalizi, Wheeler, "BTO
Six Month Advisory Mission to Bapedal, Indonesia," September 26, 1995.

57 World Bank Press Release, "Public Opinion, Markets Are New Weapons in Pollution Fight," August 20, 1996; *Persuasion and Incentives: New Ways to Achieve a Cleaner World*, World Bank Group Publication, *Environment Matters*, Winter/Spring 1997.

58 World Bank Press Release, "Public Opinion, Markets Are New Weapons in Pollution Fight," August 20, 1996; *Persuasion and Incentives: New Ways to Achieve a Cleaner World*, World Bank Group Publication, *Environment Matters*, Winter/Spring 1997.

59 World Bank Press Release, "Public Opinion, Markets Are New Weapons in Pollution Fight," August 20, 1996; *Persuasion and Incentives: New Ways to Achieve a Cleaner World*, World Bank Group Publication, *Environment Matters*, Winter/Spring 1997.

60 DEC Notes #31, "Creating Incentives to Control Pollution," Shakeb Afsah, Benoit Laplante, David Shaman, David Wheeler, July 1997; *Persuasion and Incentives: New Ways to Achieve a Cleaner World*, World Bank Group Publication, *Environment Matters*, Winter/Spring 1997.

61 WBM, Shakeb Afsah to Zmarak Shalizi, Wheeler, "BTO-Jakarta Mission: Update on Indonesia's PROPER Program," August 29, 1997.

62 World Bank Policy Research Report, *Greening Industry: New Roles for Communities, Markets, and Governments*, 1999, Page 71.

63 Bebet Gozun, *The Industrial Ecowatch Project, Business and Environment*, Vol. III, No. 4, March-April 1997.

64 Statement by Philippines Department of Environment and Natural Resources Undersecretary Elmer Mercado on Industrial Ecowatch Program, November 17, 1998; *Manila Times*, "DENR Blacklists 19 Firms for Polluting Environment," Novmeber 18, 1998; *Manila Standard*, "19 Firms Named Heavy Polluters," November 18, 1998; Bebet Gozun to Konrad von Ritter, Wheeler, "Update – Industrial Ecowatch," November 19, 1998; WBM, Shaman to Wheeler, "Dissemination Note for Environment Matters," September 19, 2000.

65 DEC Notes #31, "Creating Incentives to Control Pollution," Shakeb Afsah, Benoit Laplante, David Shaman, David Wheeler, July 1997; WBMs, Wheeler to Shaman, PRTR Section, October 28, 1997; Shaman to NIPR List, NIPR Newsletter, August 1999, August 30, 1999.

66 WBM, Shaman to NIPR List, NIPR Newsletter, August 1999, August 30, 1999.

67 WBMs, Susmita Dasgupta to Shaman, Pradeep Kumar, Uttar Pradesh State Pollution Control Board, Wheeler, Hua Wang, Benoit Laplante, Craig Meisner, "For the Next Round of Posting on NIPR," May 6, 2002; Kumar to Dasgupta, "Hello!," April 28, 2002; Dasgupta to Kumar, Wheeler, Wang, Meisner, Shaman, Laplante, "Hello!," April 24, 2002; Smita Misra to Michael Carter, Jeffrey Racki, SASE ENV, Stephen Howes, Rachid Benmessoud, Sonia Hammam, Vincent Gouarne, John Roome, Sumir Lal, Geetanjali Chopra, Karina Manasseh, Wheeler, Junaid Ahmad, Shantayanan Devarajan, Shekhar Shah, Monica Fernandes, Carter Brandon, Dasgupta, "UP Pilot Industrial Rating Program: Public Disclosure," January 29, 2004.

68 WBMs, Wheeler to Ian Johnson, Kristalina Georgieva, Michele de Nevers, "Important News from Europe and the U.S.," November 3, 2000; Wheeler to Zmarak Shalizi, Ken Chomitz, Maureen Cropper, Benoit Laplante, Susmita Dasgupta, Hua Wang, Shaman, David Witzel, "Forum One, Craig Meisner, Very Interesting News," November 3, 2000; *Business and The Environment*, "EU Emissions Register to Name Top Polluters," November 1998.

69 WBMs, Shaman to Wheeler, "Colombia Meets Indonesia and PROPER Wins," March 5, 1998; Thomas Black Arbelez, Colombia Ministry of Environment, to Wheeler, Shakeb Afsah, Susmita Dasgupta, "Visit to Colombia," March 4, 1998; DEC Notes #31, "Creating Incentives to Control Pollution," Shakeb Afsah, Benoit Laplante, David Shaman, David Wheeler, July 1997; Wheeler to Ian Johnson, Kristalina Georgieva, Michele de Nevers, "Important News from Europe and the U.S.," November 3, 2000; Shaman to Wheeler, David Witzel, "Forum One, Follow Up Questions on China Datasets," February 19, 1998.

70 WBM, Shaman to Shakeb Afsah, "International Resources Group, Transparency International," February 5, 1998.

71 WBM, Wheeler to Robert Crooks, Hua Wang, Craig Meisner, Susmita Dasgupat, Shaman, "Proposal for the Municipal Environmental Ratings Work," December 9, 1999.

72 *The New York Times*, Elisabeth Rosenthal, "China Officially Lifts Filter on Staggering Pollution Data," June 14, 1998.

73 WBM, Wheeler to Hua Wang, Shaman, Susmita Dasgupta, Benoit Laplante, "China GreenWatch Website," April 13, 2001; Wang to Dasgupta, Laplante, Craig Meisner, Shaman, Wheeler, Pradeep Kumar, Jun Bi, Lu Genfa, China State Environmental Protection Administration, Guomei Zhu, MIT, "Disclosure in Jiangsu," May 6, 2002; Wang to Wheeler, Zmarak Shalizi, Dasgupta, Laplante, Ken Chomitz, Maureen Cropper, Mead Over, Shaman, Jun, "China Work," July 8, 2000; Wang to Wheeler, "China Environmental Performance Disclosure and Community Dialogue Programs A BTO Report," June 13, 2002; Wang to Shalizi, Wheeler, "China Environmental Policy Research and Development Program BTO Report," January 16, 2001.

74 WBMs, Lawrence Macdonald to DEC Management, Extended List, "Excellent News from Vietnam (Example of Impact of Translated PRR)," June 21, 2002; Phuong Thi Thanh Tran to Andrew Steer, Christopher Gibbs, Giang Thanh Huong Le, Hoa Phuong Kieu, Kazi Mahbub-Al Matin, Patchamuthu Illangovan, Zafer Ecevit, "IDF Grant: Environmental Public Disclosure Announced Jun 21," June 21, 2002; Phuong Thi Thanh Tran to Shaman, Benoit Laplante, Wheeler, Illangovan, Susmita Dasgupta, "Vietnam and Public Information Disclosure Program," August 13, 2002; Laplante to Dasgupta, Wheeler, Shaman, Hua Wang, no subject, February 5, 2002.

75 WBM, Wheeler to Susmita Dasgupta, Hua Wang, Benoit Laplante, Craig Meisner, Shaman, Ken Chomitz, Zmarak Shalizi, Swati Ghosh, "You'll Like This One!," February 11, 2002.

76 *Measures on Open Environmental Information (for Trial Implementation)* (Adopted by the State Environmental Protection Administration of China on February 8, 2007; Effective May 1, 2008) http://www.epa.gov/ogc/china/open_environmental.pdf.

77 WBM, Wheeler to Carter Brandon, "On a More Substantive Note ...," October 2, 2000.
78 World Bank Policy Research Report, *Greening Industry: New Roles for Communities, Markets, and Governments, 1999*, Pages 2, 98-100.
79 World Bank Press Release, "Public Opinion, Markets Are New Weapons in Pollution Fight," August 20, 1996.
80 *Manila Times*, Howard Severino, "Info Age Can Let the Sun Shine In," April 29, 1997.
81 "Partnerships for Environmental Policy Reform: Working with Environmental Agencies in Developing Countries, A Proposal" by David Wheeler and the PRDEI Industry Team, June 1996.
82 Letter from Susmita Dasgupta, David Gray, Charles Griffiths, Cecilia Guido-Spano, Mala Hettige, Mainul Huq, Frannie Humplick, Benoit Laplante, Nlandu Mamingi, Muthukumara Mani, Ana Marie Maranon, Elizabeth Schaper, David Shaman, Nathalie Simon and David Witzel to Lyn Squire, Director, World Bank Policy Research Department, February 22, 1995.
83 WBMs, Shakeb Afsah to Wheeler, Benoit Laplante, Susmita Dasgupta, Zmarak Shalizi, Shaman, David Witzel, "Forum One, PROPER: Some Results on Impact," August 20, 1997; Shaman to Afsah, Wheeler, Laplante, "New PROPER Results," August 20, 1997; Wheeler to Dasgupta, Laplante, Shaman, Hua Wang, "Becoming the Conventional Wisdom," December 19, 2000.
84 WBMs, Lyn Squire to Michael Bruno, Alan Gelb, Gregory Ingram, Vinod Thomas, Shantayanan Deverajan, David Dollar, William Easterly, Emmanual Jimenez, Zmarka Shalizi, Mary Shirley, Wheeler, Lant Pritchett, no subject, August 22, 1995; Wheeler to Squire, "Outline for Possible Policy Research Report," August 22, 1995.
85 Presentation to the President of The World Bank Group by the Policy Research Department, December 18, 1996; *Controlling Industrial Pollution: A New Paradigm*, David Wheeler, Benoit Laplante, Shakeb Afsah, 1996; *Information in Pollution Management: The New Model*, David Wheeler, 1996; David Witzel, Forum One, to Shaman, Wheeler, "Wolfensohn Presentation on NIPR," January 24, 1997.
86 *Information in Pollution Management: The New Model*, David Wheeler, 1996.
87 "Environmental News in Argentina, Chile, Mexico and the Philippines," Susmita Dasgupta, Benoit Laplante, Craig Meisner, *Local Environment*, Vol. 5, No. 3, 351-359, 2000.
88 "Controlling Industrial Pollution in the Developing World," David Shaman, David Wheeler, *Environmental Quality Management*, Autumn 1998.
89 "Controlling Industrial Pollution in the Developing World," David Shaman, David Wheeler, *Environmental Quality Management*, Autumn 1998.
90 WBM, Wheeler to Lyn Squire, "PRDEI's Impact Strategy," October 28, 1994.
91 *Reuters News Service*, Michael Miller, "Rocky Road to Information Superhighway," September 2, 1999.
92 WBM, Shaman to Wheeler, "Deliverable Variables for FY'95," January 25, 1995.
93 WBM, Wheeler to Emmanuel Jimenez, Zmarak Shalizi, "Publications Cost-Effectiveness," July 29, 1997.
94 WWW Access Statistics for Research Department, "Totals for Summary Period: 95/04/07 to 95/04/30"; Memorandum, Shaman to PRDEI, "Report on the Policy Research Department's Environment, Infrastructure and Agriculture Division (PRDEI) Research on the Economics of Industrial Pollution for FY1993 through FY1996," July 1996.
95 WWW Access Statistics for Research Department, "Totals for Summary Period: 95/04/07 to 95/04/30."
96 WWW Access Statistics for Selected Special Research Documents, "Totals for Summary Period: 95/05/01 to 95/05/31."

97 WBM, Shaman to Cecilia Guido Spano, Anna Maranon, Elizabeth Schaper, Celia Tucker, Angela Williams, Wheeler, Hemala Hettige, David Witzel, Sheoli Pargal, Benoit Laplante, "IPPS and Internet," June 21, 1995.
98 David Witzel, Forum One, to Zmarak Shalizi, Wheeler, Shaman, "Internet Links to IPPS Working Paper," February 15, 1996.
99 WWW Access Statistics for Selected Special Research Documents, "Totals for Summary Period: 95/12/01 to 95/12/31."
100 WBM, David Witzel to Wheeler, Hemala Hettige, Shaman, Zmarak Shalizi, "FYI: IPPS Internet Page," September 29, 1995.
101 WBM, David Witzel to Wheeler, Hemala Hettige, Shaman, Zmarak Shalizi, "FYI: IPPS Internet Page," September 29, 1995.
102 WBMs, Shaman to Extended List, "PRDEI Research," January 31, 1996; Shaman to Extended List, "Your Thoughts – Comments on PRDEI Research," February 22, 1996.
103 WBM, Shaman to Wheeler, "Dissemination Note for Environment Matters," September 19, 2000.
104 WBM, David Witzel to Wheeler, Hemala Hettige, Shaman, Zmarak Shalizi, "FYI: IPPS Internet Page," September 29, 1995.
105 WBM, David Witzel to Wheeler, Hemala Hettige, Shaman, Zmarak Shalizi, "FYI: IPPS Internet Page," September 29, 1995.
106 WBM, Shaman to Wheeler, "Short List," September 11, 1995.
107 WWW Access Statistics for Research Department, "Totals for Summary Period: 95/04/07 to 95/04/30."
108 WWW Access Statistics for PRD Environment, Infrastructure and Agriculture Division Documents, "Totals for Summary Period: 96/01/01 to 96/01/31."
109 WBM, Shaman to Wheeler, "Marketing IPPS and Other PRDEI Work," January 17, 1996.
110 WBM, Gregory Ingram to Wheeler, Research Dissemination Grant Proposal, "IPPS Dissemination: Promoting Research with Impact," June 12, 1996.
111 WBM, Wheeler to Gregory Ingram, Zmarak Shalizi, "Interim Report on NIPR, Our RAD-Funded Website," March 5, 1997.
112 WBM, Gregory Ingram to Wheeler, Research Dissemination Grant Proposal, "IPPS Dissemination: Promoting Research with Impact," June 12, 1996.
113 WBMs, Shaman to Wheeler, "Traffic Building," April 15, 2002; Wheeler to Shaman, "Traffic Building," April 15, 2002.
114 Jim Cashel, Forum One, David Witzel, Forum One, to Michael Potashnik, "Benefits and Costs of Bank Websites," July 16, 1999.
115 David Witzel, Prosody Communications, to Shaman, "Industrial Pollution Site," September 25, 1996; WBM, Shaman to Witzel, "IPPS," September 25, 1996.
116 WBM, Wheeler to Gregory Ingram, Zmarak Shalizi, David Witzel, Forum One, Shaman, Shanz Khan, Evelyn de Castro, "Interim Report on NIPR, Our RAD-Funded Website," March 5, 1997.
117 WBM, Michael Bruno to All DEC Staff, "Research and Press Leaks," October 30, 1996.
118 WBM, Wheeler to Shaman, David Witzel, Forum One, "NIPR," November 20, 1996.
119 WBM, Wheeler to Shaman, David Witzel, Forum One, "NIPR," November 20, 1996.
120 David Witzel, Forum One, to Wheeler, Shaman, "NIPR," November 20, 1996.
121 WBM, Shaman to NIPR List, "New Ideas in Pollution Regulation," August 27, 1997.
122 WBMs, Shaman to Wheeler, "Dissemination Note for Environment Matters," September 19, 2000; Shaman to NIPR List, "New Ideas in Pollution Regulation," January 22, 1997; David Witzel, Forum One, to Shaman, Wheeler, "Introduction to NIPR," December 19, 1996.

123 WBM, Shaman to Wheeler, Shakeb Afsah, Susmita Dasgupta, David Gray, Charles Griffiths, Hemala Hettige, Benoit Laplante, Muthukumara Mani, Hua Wang, David Witzel, Forum One, "Your 15 Minutes," August 28, 1997.

124 WBMs, Shaman to David Witzel, Prosody Communications, Wheeler, "Reworking the On The Net Page," September 16, 1998; Shaman to NIPR List, NIPR Newsletter, October-November 1998, November 4, 1998; *The Scout Report for Business and Economics*, November 4, 1999.

125 David Witzel, Forum One, to Wheeler, Shaman, Chris Wolz, Forum One, Jim Cashel, Forum One, "Search Engine," October 27, 1998.

126 WBM, Shaman to NIPR List, NIPR Newsletter, April 1999, April 4, 1999.

127 WBMs, Wheeler to David Witzel, Forum One, Shaman, "P.P. S.," March 30, 1998; Shaman to NIPR List, NIPR Newsletter for February, 1998, February 27, 1998.

128 WBM, Shaman to Wheeler, David Witzel, Prosody Communications, Evelyn De Castro, "IPPS Completion Report Stats from NIPR Site," March 18, 1998; Witzel, Forum One, to Shaman, Wheeler, "NIPR Impact Summary: Forum One, NIPR Mid-Term Evaluation," March 3, 1997.

129 WBM, Shaman to Wheeler, David Witzel, Prosody Communications, Evelyn De Castro, "IPPS Completion Report Stats from NIPR Site," March 18, 1998; Witzel, Forum One, to Shaman, Wheeler, "NIPR Impact Summary: Forum One, NIPR Mid-Term Evaluation," March 3, 1997.

130 WBM, Shaman to Wheeler, David Witzel, Prosody Communications, Evelyn De Castro, "IPPS Completion Report Stats from NIPR Site," March 18, 1998; Witzel, Forum One, to Shaman, Wheeler, "NIPR Impact Summary: Forum One, NIPR Mid-Term Evaluation," March 3, 1997.

131 WBM, Wheeler to Sarwar Lateef, "Downloads from Our Website," July 30, 1997.

132 David Witzel, Forum One, to Wheeler, "Traffic Statistics for NIPR," January 31, 1998.

133 Nathan Bedford Forrest is best known for his military acumen. However, history also records this successful Confederate leader as the initial leader of the Ku Klux Klan when it came into existence after the Civil War.

134 WBMs, Wheeler to Shaman, David Witzel, Forum One, "More and More Good Stuff," October 16, 1997; Wheeler to Shaman, Witzel, "More and More Good Stuff," October 17, 1997.

135 "Partnerships for Environmental Policy Reform: Working with Environmental Agencies in Developing Countries, A Proposal" by David Wheeler and the PRDEI Industry Team, June 1996.

136 WBMs, Wheeler to Gregory Ingram, Zmarak Shalizi, "Interim Report on NIPR, Our RAD-Funded Website," March 5, 1997; Wheeler to Clara Else, Ingram, Anupa Bhaumik, Shaman, Evelyn De Castro, "Our New Proposals," March 5, 1998.

137 WBM, Trinidad Angeles to Zmarak Shalizi, Wheeler, Dave Shaman, April 9, 1997.

138 WBM, Wheeler to Shaman, "Well, We've Got Good News …," April 15, 1997.

139 WBMs, Shaman to Wheeler, Benoit Laplante, David Witzel, Forum One, "DEC Note and NIPR," April 17, 1997; Laplante to Shaman, Wheeler, Witzel, "DEC Note and NIPR," April 17, 1997; Wheeler to Laplante, Shaman, Witzel, "DEC Note and NIPR," April 17, 1997; Witzel to Laplante, Shaman, Wheeler, "DEC Note and NIPR," April 17, 1997; Shaman to Laplante, Wheeler, Witzel, "DEC Note and NIPR," April 17, 1997.

140 David Witzel, Forum One, to Benoit Laplante, Wheeler, Shaman, "DEC Note and NIPR," April 18, 1997; Witzel to Laplante, Wheeler, Shaman, "DEC Note and NIPR Take II," April 18, 1997.

141 WBM, Wheeler to David Witzel, Forum One, Benoit Laplante, Shaman, "DEC Note and NIPR Take II," April 18, 1997.

142 WBMs, Scott Johnson to Shaman, David Witzel, Forum One, Wheeler, Michael Lennon, "NIPR Site Now Under DEC," February 10, 1998; Wheeler to Gregory

Ingram, "Moving the NIPR Website Into the Bank," July 30, 1997; Witzel to Shaman, "NIPR's Up," August 13, 1997.
143 WBM, Wheeler to David Witzel, Forum One, Shaman, "The Golden Rule," July 9, 1997.
144 WBM, Shaman to Wheeler, David Witzel, Forum One, "The Golden Rule (aka) Throwing Darts at Shaman's Mug," July 9, 1997.
145 WBM, Shaman to Wheeler, David Witzel, Prosody Communications, "NIPRisms, Chatting with Macdonald, and the Upcoming Knowledge Fair, Feedback Needed Before Colombia Trip," March 5, 1998; Lawrence Macdonald to David Dollar, Emmanuel Jimenez, Margaret Grosh, Jeffrey Hammer, Paul Glewwe, Elizabeth Crayford, "Building a DRG Internet Site," January 9, 1998; Shaman to Wheeler, David Witzel, Forum One, "DRG Internet Site," January 15, 1998.
146 Forum One, "Overview of DEC Site Usage," January 1999.
147 WBMs, Shaman to NIPR List, NIPR Newsletter, September 1997, September 30, 1997; Shaman to David Witzel, Forum One, "Review of Makarim Tapes," February 26, 1997; Witzel to Shaman, "Review of Makarim Tapes," February 26, 1997; Wheeler to Soon Haut Ang, Shaman, Witzel, "Streaming Video," September 5, 1997; Shaman to Ang, Witzel, "Video Technology," September 5, 1997.
148 WBMs, Wheeler to Soon Haut Ang, Shaman, David Witzel, Forum One, "Streaming Video," September 5, 1997; Shaman to Ang, Witzel, "Video Technology," September 5, 1997; Wheeler to Shaman, Witzel, "It's A Hit," September 19, 1997; Wheeler to Shaman, Witzel, "New Web Page," September 23, 1997.
149 WBMs, Wheeler to Geoffrey Read, Shaman, David Witzel, Forum One, "The New Age," September 25, 1997; Shaman to Read, Lee Travers, Todd Johnson, Wheeler, Witzel, "China Department Video on NIPR," September 29, 1997.
150 WBMs, Wheeler to Extended List, "Latin America Month on Our NIPR Website," October 3, 1997; Wheeler to Joan Martin-Brown, Shaman, David Witzel, Forum One, "Linking Our Websites," October 3, 1997.
151 WBM, Joan Martin-Brown to Wheeler, "Linking Our Websites," October 3, 1997.
152 WBM, Wheeler to Shaman, David Witzel, Forum One, "More and More Good Stuff," October 16, 1997.
153 Forum One, "Example Web Traffic and Country Breakdown," May 1998.
154 David Witzel, Forum One, to Wheeler, Shaman, "Stats and Stats," November 25, 1997.
155 David Witzel, Forum One, to Wheeler, Shaman, "Stats and Stats," November 25, 1997.
156 Jim Cashel, Forum One, David Witzel, Forum One, to Michael Potashnik, "Benefits and Costs of Bank Web Sites," July 16, 1999; WBM, Shaman to David Witzel, Forum One, Wheeler, "NIPR Traffic," February 20, 1998.
157 Forum One, "Example Web Traffic and Country Breakdown," May 1998; David Witzel, Forum One, to Wheeler, Shaman, "Stats and Stats," November 25, 1997.
158 Suzan Hazen, Director, Environmental Assistance Division, U.S. Environmental Protection Agency, to Hemala Hettige, March 25, 1997.
159 WBM, Lawrence Macdonald to DEC Roster, "NIPR Named National Academy Press 'Cool' Website," December 2, 1998.
160 David Witzel, Forum One, to Shaman, Wheeler, "Yahoo," October 1, 1998; WBMs, Shaman to Wheeler, "FYI," January 22, 1999; Wheeler to Susmita Dasgupta, Hua Wang, Craig Meisner, David Witzel, Forum One, Shaman, Yasmin D'Souza, Benoit Laplante, "Pretty Neat," August 19, 1999.
161 WBM, Wheeler to David Witzel, Forum One, Shaman, "Stats and Stats," December 1, 1997.
162 David Witzel, Forum One, to Wheeler, Shaman, Jim Cashel, Forum One, "Can't Be Done," May 16, 1997.
163 David Witzel, Forum One, to Shaman, "NIPR Link," October 12, 1997.
164 WBM, Wheeler to Shaman, "Internet Proposal," August 26, 1998.

165 WBM, Gunnar Eskeland to Moshe Syrquin, Shantayanan Devarajan, Shaman, Clara Else, Gregory Ingram, Zmarak Shalizi, Wheeler, David Witzel, Forum One, Paul Collier, "Release of World Bank Journal Articles for Web-Posting with Lag: Knowledge Bank," November 6, 1998.

166 WBM, Lawrence Macdonald to Jo Ritzen, Paul Collier, Francis Ng, Nicholas Sambanis, Michael Potashnik, Katie Bannon, Stephen Denning, Shaman, Wheeler, David Witzel, Forum One, Anthony Venebles, Andrew Mason, Elizabeth King, "NIPR Kudos
The Scout Report for Business and Economics
November 4, 1999," November 5, 1999.

167 WBMs, Wheeler to David Hanrahan, "Pollution Abatement and Prevention Handbook," November 21, 1997; Shaman to NIPR List, "NIPR Newsletter, August 1997," August 20, 1997.

168 David Witzel, Forum One, to Wheeler, Shaman, "NIPR Stats," November 3, 1999.

169 David Witzel, Forum One, to Wheeler, Shaman, "NIPR Stats," October 6, 1998.

170 WBM, Scott Johnson, ISGIS, to Shaman, ISP Deployment Team, Web Admin Group, "ListMember Totals," February 18, 2004; "Shaman Operational Evaluation Performance, April 1, 1999 to March 31, 2000."

171 David Witzel, Forum One, to Wheeler, Shaman, "NIPR Usage Report," August 15, 2000.

172 WBMs, Shaman to Lawrence Macdonald, "NIPR Subscriptions," June 12, 2002; Shaman to Wheeler, "Traffic Stats," January 24, 2002.

173 WBM, Scott Johnson to Shaman, "Newsletter Ranking," October 6, 2004.

174 WBMs – Karen Shaines to Nicole Frost, Jeff McCoy, David Gray, Joelle Dehase, Ricardo Castro, Michael Kane, Barbara Ann Gregory, Lawrence Macdonald, "Web Quality Assessment Review," March 9, 2000; Shaman to Wheeler, "Web Quality Assessment Review," March 9, 2000; Shaman to Shaines, David Witzel, Forum One, Wheeler, "Web Quality Assessment Review," March 9, 2000; Forum One, "Web Quality Assessment, Prepared for World Bank Group," February 28, 2000; Lawrence Macdonald to DEC VP Roster, Uri Dadush, Paul Collier, Shaida Badier, Lyn Squire, Extended List, "World Bank Website Quality Review
Implications for DEC," March 31, 2000; Wheeler to Jo Ritzen, Paul Collier, Zmarak Shalizi, Lawrence Macdonald, Michele de Nevers, Shaman, Witzel, Forum One, Susmita Dasgupta, Benoit Laplante, Hua Wang, Craig Meisner, Yasmin D'Souza, Gregory Ingram, Muthukumara Mani, "Website Quality Review," March 10, 2000.

175 WBMs – Wheeler to Jo Ritzen, Paul Collier, Zmarak Shalizi, Lawrence Macdonald, Michele de Nevers, Shaman, Witzel, Forum One, Susmita Dasgupta, Benoit Laplante, Hua Wang, Craig Meisner, Yasmin D'Souza, Gregory Ingram, Muthukumara Mani, "Website Quality Review," March 10, 2000; Karen Shaines to Nicole Frost, Jeff McCoy, David Gray, Joelle Dehase, Ricardo Castro, Michael Kane, Barbara Ann Gregory, Lawrence Macdonald, "Web Quality Assessment Review," March 9, 2000; Shaman to Wheeler, "Web Quality Assessment Review," March 9, 2000; Shaman to Shaines, David Witzel, Forum One, Wheeler, "Web Quality Assessment Review," March 9, 2000.

176 *The New York Times*, Gladwin Hill, November 30, 1969.

177 Angela Conway, "Winds of Change: Eco-Glastnost in Eastern Europe," *The Kansas Journal of Law Public Policy*, Volume 1, Number 1, Summer 1991.

178 –Marina Ottaway, "Corporatism Goes Global: International Organizations, NGO Networks and Transnational Business," *Global Governance*, September 2001.

179 Sources: Numerous including Wikipedia http://en.wikipedia.org/wiki/Summers_memo

180 Susan Reed, "Enemies of the Earth," *PEOPLE* magazine, April 27, 1992.

181 "The FP Interview: Lori's War," *Foreign Policy*, Spring 2000.

182 Susan Aaronson, *Taking Trade to the Street: The Lost History of Public Efforts to Shape Globalization*, University of Michigan Press, 2001.
183 James Wolfensohn, "The Challenges of Globalization: The Role of the World Bank," Address to the Bundestag, Berlin, Germany, April 2, 2001.
184 Paul Nelson, "Whose Civil Society? Whose Governance? Decision-making and Practice in the New Agenda at the Inter-American Development Bank and the World Bank," *Global Governance: A Review of Multilateralism and International Organizations*, October 1, 2000.
185 Paul Nelson, "Whose Civil Society? Whose Governance? Decision-making and Practice in the New Agenda at the Inter-American Development Bank and the World Bank," *Global Governance: A Review of Multilateralism and International Organizations*," October 1, 2000.
186 Paul Nelson, "Whose Civil Society? Whose Governance? Decision-making and Practice in the New Agenda at the Inter-American Development Bank and the World Bank," *Global Governance: A Review of Multilateralism and International Organizations*, October 1, 2000.
187 "The FP Interview: Lori's War," *Foreign Policy*, Spring 2000.
188 "Opponents to Gather in Washington to Protest IMF Policies," *Agence France-Presse*, October 4, 1998.
189 "The FP Interview: Lori's War," *Foreign Policy*, Spring 2000.
190 "The FP Interview: Lori's War," *Foreign Policy*, Spring 2000; Dr. Sabine Schlemmer-Schulte, "The Impact of Civil Society on the World Bank, the IMF and the WTO: The Case of the World Bank," *ILSA Journal of International and Comparable Law*, Spring 2001; Marina Ottaway, "Corporatism Goes Global: International Organizations, NGO Networks and Transnational Business," *Global Governance*, September 2001.
191 Marina Ottaway, "Corporatism Goes Global: International Organizations, NGO Networks and Transnational Business," *Global Governance*, September 2001.
192 David Wheeler, Raymond Hartman, "The Economics of Industrial Pollution in Developing Countries: A Research Proposal," April 1994; Robert Lucas, David Wheeler, Hemala Hettige, *Economic Development, Environmental Regulation, and the International Migration of Toxic Pollution: 1960-88*, 1992; , Economics Man, Cleaner Planet, September 27, 2001; Nancy Birdsall, David Wheeler, "Trade Policy and Industrial Pollution in Latin America: Where are the Pollution Havens?" *The Economist*, 1992; Gunnar Eskeland, Ann Harrison, *Moving to Greener Pastures? Multinationals and the Pollution Haven Hypothesis*, 1994.
193 The Economics of Industrial Pollution in Developing Countries: A Research Proposal, David Wheeler, Raymond Hartman, April 1994; Economic Development, Environmental Regulation, and the International Migration of Toxic Pollution: 1960-88, Robert Lucas, David Wheeler, Hemala Hettige, 1992; The Economist, Economics Man, Cleaner Planet, September 27, 2001; Trade Policy and Industrial Pollution in Latin America: Where are the Pollution Havens?, Nancy Birdsall, David Wheeler, 1992; Moving to Greener Pastures? Multinationals and the Pollution Haven Hypothesis, Gunnar Eskeland, Ann Harrison, 1994.
194 David Wheeler, Raymond Hartman "The Economics of Industrial Pollution in Developing Countries: A Research Proposal," April 1994; Robert Lucas, David Wheeler, Hemala Hettige, *Economic Development, Environmental Regulation, and the International Migration of Toxic Pollution: 1960-88*, 1992;, Economics Man, Cleaner Planet, September 27, 2001; Nancy Birdsall, David Wheeler, "Trade Policy and Industrial Pollution in Latin America: Where are the Pollution Havens?" The Economist, 1992; Gunnar Eskeland, Ann Harrison, *Moving to Greener Pastures? Multinationals and the Pollution Haven Hypothesis*, 1994.

195 Thomas Black Arbelez, Colombia Ministry of Environment, to Vinod Thomas, "Post-Seminar in DC," November 3, 1998.
196 Nabiel Makarim, Indonesia Ministry of Environment, to Wheeler, "More Anak-anak PROPER," June 23, 2002.
197 Shakeb Afsah, "Impact of Financial Crisis on Industrial Growth and Environmental Performance in Indonesia," U.S.-Asia Environmental Partnership (US-AEPA), 1998.
198 "Retooling the Bank's Knowledge Base," ITS, World Bank, February 24, 1997.
199 "Retooling the Bank's Knowledge Base," ITS, World Bank, February 24, 1997.
200 "Retooling the Bank's Knowledge Base," ITS, World Bank, February 24, 1997.
201 WBM, Nathalie Simon, Shaman to Extended List, "Knowledge Management System," March 11, 1997.
202 WBMs, Shaman to NIPR List, "NIPR Newsletter, January 2001," January 10, 2001; Wheeler to Lawrence Macdonald, Shaman, David Witzel, Forum One, "Greening HTML Online, PDF for Free VH Paper for Payment Assessing the Trade Offs," January 11, 2001.
203 WBMs, Lawrence Macdonald to Shaman, Wheeler, "Greening HTML Online, PDF for Free VH Paper for Payment Assessing the Trade Offs," January 10, 2001; Wheeler to Macdonald, Shaman, David Witzel, Forum One, "Greening HTML Online, PDF for Free VH Paper for Payment Assessing the Trade Offs," January 11, 2001.
204 World Bank Policy Research Report, *Greening Industry: New Roles for Communities, Markets, and Governments*, 1999.
205 WBMs, Wheeler to Kristalina Georgieva, "Small Money, Big Opportunity," May 8, 2000; Georgieva to Wheeler, "Small Money, Big Opportunity," May 8, 2000; Wheeler to Shaman, "Small Money, Big Opportunity," May 10, 2000; Shaman to Mark Davis, "Vietnam," May 5, 2000; Wheeler to Shaman, "Greening Industry Vietnamese," November 22, 2000; Ha Thanh Hoang to Carlos Rossel, Phuong Thi Thanh Tran, Shaman, Anna Marie Rebueno, "Translation of the Book *Greening Industry* into Vietnamese," May 17, 2000.
206 WBM, Craig Meisner to Shaman, "New Addition to NIPR," October 15, 2001.
207 WBMs, Shaman to Miriam Razaq, Abdel Shabana, Wheeler, Phillip Hay, Carlos Rossel, Lawrence Macdonald, "*Greening Industry* Translation," December 7, 1999; Annice Brown to Shaman, Wheeler, Macdonald, Jean-Roger Mercier, Tiekoura Kome, Yves Andre Prevost, Jean-Michel Pavy, Akintola Fatoyinbo, Cythina Cook, Asha Ayoung, Mohammed Bekhechi, "New Publication: *Greening Industry: New Roles for Communities, Markets, and Governments*," October 6, 1999; Shaman to NIPR List, "NIPR Newsletter, May 2000," May 9, 2000; Valentina Kalk to Shaman, Carlos Rossel, "*Greening Industry* - Chinese Edition," January 9, 2001; Shaman to Kalk, Rossel, Wheeler, Hua Wang, "Four-color Production of *Greening Industry* in Chinese," March 29, 2001; Wheeler to Trinidad Angeles, Paul Collier, Shaman, "Spanish-Language *Greening Industry*," February 1, 2002; Maria Teresa Serra to Davinder Sakhuja, John Redwood, Mark Cackler, Shelton Davis, "Budget for Publications," January 30, 2002.
208 WBM, Lawrence Macdonald to DEC Management, Wheeler, Ha Thanh Hoang, Andrew Steer, Valentina Kalk, Hans Koehler, Julie Knowles, Shaman, Kristalina Georgieva, Sergio Jellinek, Caroline Anstey, Amanda Humm, Clara Else, "Excellent News from Vietnam (Example of Impact of Translated PRR)," June 21, 2002.
209 WBM, Wheeler to Anna Maranon, Benoit Laplante, Cecilia Guido Spano, Charles Griffiths, David Witzel, Forum One, Shaman, Debu Talukdar, Elizabeth Schaper, Evelyn De Castro, Hua Wang, I.J. Singh, Ken Chomitz, Koshy Mathai, "Nice Retreat!" January 17, 1997.
210 WBM, Wheeler to Ian Johnson, Kristalina Georgieva, Michele de Nevers, "Important News from Europe and the U.S." November 3, 2000.
211 WBMs, Kseniya Lvovsky to Carter Brandon, Sameer Akbar, Smita Misra, Bilal Rahill, Susmita Dasgupta, Richard Ackermann, "Letter for GoK and DEA, Karnataka

Mission," September 29, 2000; Brandon to Lvovsky, Akbar, Misra, Rahill, Dasgupta, Ackermann, "Letter for GoK and DEA, Karnataka Mission," October 1, 2000.

212 WBM, Wheeler to Carter Brandon, "Just Between You and Me ...," October 2, 2000.

213 WBM, Wheeler to David Witzel, Forum One, Shaman, "NIPRisms," May 10, 2000.

214 WBM, Shaman to NIPR List, "NIPR Newsletter, September 1998," October 2, 1998.

215 Susmita Dasgupta, Mainul Huq, David Wheeler, "*Village Development in the Digital Age: The Impact of the Internet on Rural Bangladesh*, Research Proposal," DECRGIE, November 2000.

216 Susmita Dasgupta, Mainul Huq, David Wheeler, *Village Development in the Digital Age: The Impact of the Internet on Rural Bangladesh*, Research Proposal, Development Economics Research Group Infrastructure/Environment Team, November 2000; Alvin Toffler, *The Third Wave*, Bantam Books, 1991; John Naisbitt, *Global Paradox*, Avon Books, 1995.

217 Sam Pitroda, "Development, Democracy, and the Village Telephone," *Harvard Business Review*, November-December 1993.

218 Susmita Dasgupta, Mainul Huq, David Wheeler, *Village Development in the Digital Age: The Impact of the Internet on Rural Bangladesh*, Research Proposal, DECRGIE, November 2000.

219 WBMs, Wheeler to Susmita Dasgupat, Shaman, Mainul Huq, David Witzel, Forum One, "MP Draft Aide Memoire," August 19, 1999; Wheeler to Luis Constantino, Ruth Alsop, Geeta Sethi, "India Internet Project," October 20, 1999; Constantino to Wheeler, Alsop, Sethi, "India Internet Project," October 19, 1999; Wheeler to Susmita Dasgupta, Mainul Huq, Hua Wang, David Witzel, Forum One, Shaman, "Things are Cookin'!" August 12, 1999.

220 "Global Development Gateway, Harnessing Knowledge and Technology for Sustainable Development and Poverty Reduction, Preliminary Business Plan," April 26, 2000.

221 Center for Balanced Development Press Release, "Open Joint Letter of Concern About the Global Development Gateway," October 2, 2000.

222 Thomas Lippman, "An Unlikely Alliance: Cisco, UN Plan Site to Fight Third World Poverty," *Washington Post*, August 12, 1999; Cisco Press Release, "Akami, KRMG Join Cisco, UNDP in Building NetAid Technology, NetAid Network Will be Unprecedented in Scale and Integration, 125,000 Simultaneous Live Streams, 1,500 Servers in Over 90 Data Centers Worldwide," August 13, 1999.

223 Thomas Lippman, "An Unlikely Alliance: Cisco, U.N. Plan to Fight Third World Poverty," *Washington Post*, August 12, 1999.

224 David Witzel, Forum One, to Shaman, Missy McCool, Forum One, Christopher Wolz, Forum One, Jason Lefkowitz, Forum One, "Colombia Draft Prez," January 25, 1999; WBMs, Shaman to NIPR List, "NIPR Newsletter, April 1999," April 28, 1999; Shaman to Witzel, "Just Lucky I Guess," February 19, 1999; *The Scout Report for Business and Economics*, May 6, 1999; Shaman to Thomas Black Arbelez, Susmita Dasgupta, Wheeler, "Mission Focus," June 8, 1998.

225 David J. Rothkopf, "Globalization at Work: The Disinformtion Age," *Foreign Policy*, Spring 1999.

226 B-SPAN Production, "How Does Culture Matter? with Amartya Sen," July 25, 2001.

227 Peter Cook, Jonathan Stevens, "Metropolitan Manila Public Performance Assessment Project, PPA Process and Initial Results," World Bank Forum, February 22, 2001; WBM, Wheeler to Susmita Dasgupta, Benoit Laplante, Shaman, Hua Wang, "Becoming the Conventional Wisdom," December 19, 2000.

228 Sebastian Mallaby, *The World's Banker: The Story of Failed States, Financial Crises, and the Wealth and Poverty of Nations*, Penguin Books, 2004, Pages 225, 226.

229 Sebastian Mallaby, *The World's Banker: The Story of Failed States, Financial Crises, and the Wealth and Poverty of Nations*, Penguin Books, 2004, Pages 202-206.

230 WBM, Shaman to Shakeb Afsah, International Resources Group, "Transparency International," February 5, 1998.

PART 3 — BUILD IT AND THEY WILL COME

1 WBM, Wheeler to Lawrence Macdonald, David Witzel, Forum One, Shaman, "B-SPAN Time?" November 5, 1999.
2 Blair Fuller, Netcast Incorporated, to David Witzel, Forum One, "Service Request Form," November 12, 1999.
3 WBM, Shaman to World Bank TV Distribution Network, David Witzel, Forum One, "Service Request Form," November 11, 1999.
4 WBM, Wheeler to Michele de Nevers, David Witzel, Forum One, Shaman, "The Road From Here," February 5, 2000.
5 WBM, Michele de Nevers to Anthony Bigio, Gayatri Acharya, Vincent Ferrer-Andrew, Sunetra Puri, Francois-Marie Patorni, Javier Jarquin, Shaman, Maria Rosa Schwartz, "Possible Person to Help Us on Website Management Communications," March 7, 2000.
6 WBMs, Jo Ritzen to DEC Roster, no subject (announcement of DEC Team Based Performance Awards to the NIPR/Greening Industry PRR Team), March 27, 2000; Karen Shaines to Nicole Frost, Jeff McCoy, David Gray, Joelle Dehase, Ricardo Castro, Michael Kane, Barbara Ann Gregory, Lawrence Macdonald, "Web Quality Assessment Review," March 9, 2000; Shaman to Wheeler, "Web Quality Assessment Review," March 9, 2000; Shaman to Shaines, David Witzel, Forum One, Wheeler, "Web Quality Assessment Review," March 9, 2000.
7 WBMs, Wheeler to Jo Ritzen, Paul Collier, Zmarak Shalizi, Lawrence Macdonald, Shaman, "Interesting Days Ahead," March 17, 2000; Wheeler to Shaman, David Strelneck, Forum One, Missy McCool, Forum One, Aldo Bello, "Mind and Media," April 17, 2000.
8 WBM, Wheeler to Jo Ritzen, Paul Collier, Zmarak Shalizi, Lawrence Macdonald, Shaman, "Interesting Days Ahead," March 17, 2000.
9 WBM, Wheeler to Jo Ritzen, Paul Collier, Zmarak Shalizi, Lawrence Macdonald, Shaman, "Interesting Days Ahead," March 17, 2000.
10 WBM, Shaman to Corrie Lam, Loews Hotel, "Webcasting Needs," March 15, 2000.
11 WBM, Shaman to TV Distribution Network/Services, "Service Request Form," November 10, 1999.
12 WBM, Wheeler to Nick Van Praag, Wilfredo Cruz, Michele de Nevers, Kristyn Ebro, "Let's Meet to Plan ENV Forum Reporting and Information Dissemination Plan," March 8, 2000.
13 WBM, Wheeler to Wilfredo Cruz, Shaman, Michele de Nevers, "Contracts with Forum One, etc.," March 15, 2000.
14 WBM, Wheeler to Ian Johnson, Kristalina Georgieva, Michele de Nevers, Shaman, Wilfredo Cruz, David Strelneck, Forum One, David Witzel, Forum One, Aldo Bello, Mind and Media, Nick Van Praag, Kristyn Ebro, "The Environment Forum on the Internet," April 17, 2000.
15 WBMs, Wheeler to Ian Johnson, Kristalina Georgieva, Michele de Nevers, Shaman, Wilfredo Cruz, David Strelneck, Forum One, David Witzel, Forum One, Aldo Bello, Mind and Media, Nick Van Praag, Kristyn Ebro, "The Environment Forum on the Internet," April 17, 2000; Shaman to de Nevers, Wheeler, "Post-Webcast Analysis," March 31, 2000.
16 Aldo Bello, Mind and Media, to Wheeler, David Strelneck, Forum One, Shaman, "WB Script 1," April 11, 2000; Vinod Thomas to WBI Staff, "WBI Weekly, Bi-Weekly," March 27, 2000.
17 WBM, Vinod Thomas to WBI Staff, "WBI Weekly, Bi-Weekly," March 27, 2000.

18 Aldo Bello, Mind and Media, to Wheeler, David Strelneck, Forum One, Shaman, "WB Script 1," April 11, 2000.
19 Aldo Bello, Mind and Media, to Wheeler, David Strelneck, Forum One, Shaman, "WB Script 1," April 11, 2000.
20 Aldo Bello, Mind and Media, to Wheeler, David Strelneck, Forum One, Shaman, "WB Script 1," April 11, 2000.
21 Aldo Bello, Mind and Media, to Wheeler, David Strelneck, Forum One, Shaman, "WB Script 1," April 11, 2000.
22 Aldo Bello, Mind and Media, to Wheeler, David Strelneck, Forum One, Shaman, "WB Script 1," April 11, 2000.
23 WBM, Shaman to Michele de Nevers, Wheeler, "Post-Webcast Analysis," March 31, 2000; David Strelneck, Forum One, to de Nevers, Judith Moore, Wheeler, Shaman, "Quick ENV Forum Website Statistics," March 23, 2000; Ramachandra Jammi to Shaman, Wilfredo Cruz, "Memo on Conference Discussion," March 27, 2000; Vinod Thomas to WBI Staff, "WBI Weekly, Bi-Weekly," March 27, 2000.
24 WBMs, Shaman to Michele de Nevers, Wheeler, "Post-Webcast Analysis," March 31, 2000; Shaman to NIPR List, "NIPR Newsletter, March 2000," March 16, 2000.
25 David Strelneck, Forum One, to Shaman, "Addition ENV Forum Site Hits," March 30, 2000; Shaman to Michele de Nevers, Wheeler, "Post-Webcast Analysis," March 31, 2000.
26 WBMs, Wheeler to Kristalina Georgieva, Michele de Nevers, Phillip Hay, Nick Van Praag, Shaman, Wilfredo Cruz, David Strelneck, Forum One, "An Excellent Opportunity to Demonstrate the New Bank," April 14, 2000; Wheeler to Shaman, Strelneck, David Witzel, Forum One, Missy McCool, Forum One, Aldo Bello, Mind and Media, "Thanks a Million," April 17, 2000.
27 WBM, Wheeler to David Strelneck, Forum One, Shaman, David Witzel, Forum One, Aldo Bello, Mind and Media, "ENV Forum Script," April 12, 2000.
28 WBMs, Wheeler to Shaman, "E-Conference Announcement," April 26, 2000; Shaman to Wheeler, "E-Conference Announcement," April 26, 2000.
29 WBMs, Michele de Nevers to Shaman, Wheeler, "Post-Webcast Analysis," April 5, 2000; Wheeler to Jo Ritzen, Paul Collier, Zmarak Shalizi, Lawrence Macdonald, "Keeping a Great Team Member," March 29, 2000, Wheeler to Shaman, "Keeping a Great Team Member," March 29, 2000; de Nevers to Wheeler, "Updates," May 24, 2000.
30 WBMs, Shantayanan Devarajan to Wheeler, "DECRG DMT, David Shaman," April 25, 2000; Wheeler to Shaman, "Hey Whatever …," April 26, 2000; Paul Collier to Wheeler, "David Shaman," April 20, 2000; Wheeler to Shaman, "Note from Paul Collier," April 26, 2000; Wheeler to Jo Ritzen, Paul Collier, Zmarak Shalizi, Lawrence Macdonald, "Keeping a Great Team Member," March 29, 2000, Wheeler to Shaman, "Keeping a Great Team Member," March 29, 2000.
31 WBMs, Michele de Nevers to Wheeler, "B-SPAN," September 21, 2000; Wheeler to Shaman, "The TOR," September 26, 2000; de Nevers to Wheeler, "Dave Shaman and the WBIEN Job," November 22, 2000; Wheeler to Shaman, "WBI and Me," December 16, 2000.
32 WBM, Wheeler to Shaman, "WBI and Me," December 16, 2000.
33 WBMs, Michele de Nevers to Wheeler, "Updates," May 24, 2000; Wheeler to Jo Ritzen, Paul Collier, Zmarak Shalizi, "Announcement of B-SPAN – Webcasting ESSD Events," July 12, 2000; Wheeler to de Nevers, "Your Call," October 16, 2000; Wheeler to Shaman, "Decisions, Decisions," October 16, 2000.
34 WBM, Wheeler to Michele de Nevers, David Witzel, Forum One, Shaman, "The Road From Here," February 5, 2000.

35 WBM, Shaman to Wheeler, "FYI – URGENT – Do Environmental Initiatives also Promote Poverty Alleviation? Using Video Clips from the Environment Forum to Promote Dialogue on Controversial Issues," March 24, 2000.

36 WBM, Shaman to Graeme Donovan, "Your Seminar Now Online at B-SPAN," June 4, 2002.

37 WBMs, Shaman to Wheeler, "B-SPAN – The Concept, May 15, 2000;" Shaman to Wheeler, "B-SPAN – The Concept and Related Questions," May 16, 2000.

38 WBMs, Wheeler to David Witzel, Forum One, Shaman, "Streaming Video Hosting," August 16, 2000; Witzel, to Wheeler, Shaman, "Streaming Video Hosting," August 16, 2000; Larissa Fastovsky to Witzel, "Streaming Video Hosting," August 15, 2000; Wheeler to Shaman, "Streaming Video Hosting," August 16, 2000; Wheeler to Shaman, "This Just In," August 10, 2000.

39 WBMs, Shaman to Wheeler, "B-SPAN – The Concept," May 15, 2000; Shaman to Wheeler, "B-SPAN – The Concept and Related Questions," May 16, 2000.

40 WBMs, Shaman to Wheeler, "B-SPAN
The Concept," May 15, 2000; Shaman to Wheeler, "B-SPAN – The Concept and Related Questions," May 16, 2000.

41 WBMs, Shaman to Wheeler, "B-SPAN – The Concept," May 15, 2000; Shaman to Wheeler, "B-SPAN – The Concept and Related Questions," May 16, 2000.

42 WBMs, Shaman to Wheeler, "B-SPAN – The Concept," May 15, 2000; Shaman to Wheeler, "B-SPAN – The Concept and Related Questions," May 16, 2000.

43 WBMs, Shaman to Clovis Fantinelli, "Camera Crew Request," September 28, 2000; Fantinelli to Shaman, "Camera Crew Request," September 27, 2000.

44 WBM, Shaman to Wheeler, "B-SPAN – A Little More," May 16, 2000.

45 WBM, Shaman to Wheeler, "B-SPAN – A Little More," May 16, 2000.

46 WBM, Michele de Nevers to Shaman, "Questions Re: B-SPAN," July 25, 2000.

47 WBMs, Michele de Nevers to Shaman, "Questions Re: B-SPAN," July 25, 2000; Shaman to de Nevers, Wheeler, "Questions Re: B-SPAN," July 27, 2000.

48 WBM, Shaman to Wheeler, "B-SPAN Cost Analysis," August 4, 2000.

49 WBMs, Charles Mann to Shaman, Sefik Cardak, Clovis Fantinelli, Paulette Wilmot, "Rates for DEC/Research Group," November 28, 2000; Edna Fogerty to Rachel Reyes Luz, "Conference/AV Support," March 16, 2001.

50 WBMs, Shaman to Witzel, Forum One, Wheeler, "B-SPAN Webdesign," August 17, 2000; Shaman to Wheeler, "B-SPAN Follow up to MdN," July 18, 2000; WBM, Shaman to David Witzel, Forum One, Wheeler, "B-SPAN Start Up," August 9, 2000; Wheeler to Shaman, "Could Be Really Good …," November 20, 2001; Geoffrey Read to John Middleton, Keshav Varna, Katrinka Ebbe, Michael Potashnik, "China: Urban Cultural Heritage Conference: Beijing July 5 to 7, 2000," June 29, 2000.

51 WBM, Wheeler to Shaman, "Update," November 30, 2000.

52 WBM, Shaman to Wheeler, "B-SPAN – A Little More," May 16, 2000.

53 WBMs, Shaman to Wei Zhang, Polly Means, "E-Finance Module 2," December 5, 2001; Shaman to Vesselina Hekimova, Bonnie Bradford, Julie Babinard, Cary Ann Cadman, Michele de Nevers, "Global Dialogues on Sustainable Development B-SPAN Coverage," October 31, 2001; Hekimova to Shaman, Bradford, Babinard, Cadman, de Nevers, "Global Dialogues on Sustainable Development B-SPAN Coverage," October 31, 2001; de Nevers to Wheeler, Shaman, "Internal Dialogue on Structural Adjustment Seminar Series," November 21, 2001.

54 WBMs, Shaman to Michele de Nevers, Wheeler, "Post-Webcast Analysis," March 31, 2000; Shaman to Thomas Scott Yarn, Drew Stewart, Donald Macdonald, "Post Production Capacity of WBI for Webcasts," May 22, 2000; Shaman to Wheeler, "FYI – URGENT – Do Environmental Initiatives also Promote Poverty Alleviation? Using Video Clips from the ENV Forum to Promote Dialogue on Controversial Issues," March 24, 2000.

55 WBMs, Michele de Nevers to Shaman, Wheeler, John Middleton, "Spanable Events," June 26, 2000; Shaman to de Nevers, Wheeler, Middleton, "Spanable Events," June 26, 2000; de Nevers to Philip Karp, Shaman, Wheeler, Judith Moore, Joshua Okoth Ogada, Alyson Kleine, Francois-Marie Patorni, Anthony Bigio, "WBIEN WEBSITE J4 101," June 28, 2000.
56 WBM, Kerry Mcnamara to Wheeler, Michele de Nevers, John Middleton, Philip Karp, Ron Kim, Shaman, "B-SPAN," September 20, 2000.
57 WBMs, Shaman to Wheeler, "B-SPAN – Some More," May 25, 2000; Shaman to Wheeler, "B-SPAN – The Costs," May 25, 2000; Shaman to Wheeler, "Final Update on B-SPAN Costs," May 26, 2000; Wheeler to Shaman, "El Spreadsheet Cosmico," May 16, 2000.
58 WBM, Shaman to Wheeler, "B-SPAN – Some More," May 25, 2000.
59 WBM, Wheeler to Shaman, "Pretty Cool," February 14, 2001.
60 WBM, Wheeler to Shaman, David Witzel, Forum One, "Now DAT's Hits," February 28, 2000.
61 WBM, Wheeler to David Witzel, Forum One, David Strelneck, Forum One, Shaman, "Killer App?" September 11, 2000.
62 WBM, Shaman to David Witzel, Forum One, Wheeler, "B-SPAN Start Up," August 9, 2000.
63 WBMs, Shaman to Witzel, Forum One, Wheeler, "B-SPAN Webdesign," August 17, 2000; Wheeler to Michele de Nevers, Shaman, Witzel, "B-SPAN – We're in Good Company," February 29, 2000.
64 WBM, Shaman to Edit Pena, Polly Means, Jennifer Prochnow, Wheeler, "Web Maintenance for B-SPAN," October 2, 2000.
65 WBMs, Wheeler to Shaman, Yasmin D'Souza, "B-SPAN: First Adventures," June 7, 2000; Wheeler to David Witzel, Forum One, "NIPR Usage Report," August 16, 2000; Shaman to WEB ADMIN, "Starting a New Bank Site," June 21, 2000.
66 WBM, Wheeler to David Witzel, Forum One, "NIPR Usage Report," August 16, 2000; David Strelneck, Forum One, to Shaman, Witzel, "B-SPAN TOR," August 3, 2000.
67 WBM, Shaman to David Witzel, Forum One, Wheeler, "B-SPAN Webdesign," August 17, 2000.
68 WBMs, Wheeler to Shaman, "Further Ruminations About Live Chat for B-SPAN," August 7, 2000; Shaman to Wheeler, "Further Ruminations About Online Chat for B-SPAN," August 3, 2000; Wheeler to Shaman, "Further Ruminations About Online Chat for B-SPAN," August 7, 2000.
69 WBMs, Shaman to Wheeler, "Further Ruminations About Online Chat for B-SPAN," August 3, 2000; Wheeler to Shaman, "Further Ruminations About Online Chat for B-SPAN," August 7, 2000.
70 WBM, Michele de Nevers to Wheeler, "WB-IMF Forum on Supporting Comprehensive and Country-led Poverty Reduction Strategies, April 24-25, 2000," April 24, 2000.
71 WBM, Shaman to Alyson Kleine, "US National Park Service Discovery 2000 Conference," July 13, 2000.
72 WBM, Shaman to Scott Johnson, "B-SPAN Subscribe Request," October 2, 2001.
73 David Strelneck, Forum One, to David Witzel, Forum One, Shaman, Michele de Nevers, "Mailing List," November 8, 2000.
74 WBM, Shaman to Wheeler, "One for Da Money, Two for Da Span …?," March 27, 2001.
75 WBM, Shaman to Wheeler, "B-SPAN Tidbits," March 28, 2001.
76 WBMs, Shaman to Michele de Nevers, Wheeler, "Brown Bags," September 12, 2000; Shaman to de Nevers, Joshua Okoth Ogada, Wheeler, "Reminder: BBL on Full Cost Accounting of Alternative Land Development Scenarios," July 12, 2000.

77 WBMs, Wheeler to Shaman, "B-SPAN Schedule," May 9, 2001; Shaman to Wheeler, "B-SPAN Schedule," May 9, 2001, Shaman to Polly Means, Wheeler, "B-SPAN Schedule," May 7, 2001.
78 WBM, Wheeler to Shaman, "Yo, Yo ...!" September 8, 2001.
79 WBM, Wheeler to Shaman, "Brown Bag on EA Capacity Building in Africa, Thursday September 14 at 12:30 in J8-044," September 6, 2000.
80 WBM, Wheeler to Shaman, "Today's Catch," September 15, 2000.
81 WBM, Shaman to Wheeler, "Spanning the Globe," June 8, 2000.
82 WBMs, Shaman to Wheeler, "Spanning the Globe," June 8, 2000; Shaman to Michele de Nevers, Wheeler, "Spanable Events," June 26, 2000; Shaman to Joshua Okoth Ogada, "Spanable Events," June 28, 2000.
83 WBMs, Michele de Nevers to Shaman, "Questions Re: B-SPAN," July 25, 2000; Shaman to de Nevers, Wheeler, "Questions Re: B-SPAN," July 27, 2000.
84 WBMs, Shaman to Kerry Mcnamara, "B-SPAN and DLC Studios," October 2, 2000; Michele de Nevers to Mcnamara, Shaman, John Middleton, Philip Karp, Ron Kim, Shaman, Alyson Kleine, "B-SPAN," September 20, 2000; de Nevers to Pietronella Van Den Oever, ENCORR, Alice Mary Faria, Maria Rosa Schwartz, Alyson Kleine, Rita Klees, Shaman, "Task Assignment Re: US National Park Service Discovery 2000 Conference – Due on: 7/19/2000," July 18, 2000; Shaman to Wheeler, "B-SPAN A Bit More," July 18, 2000.
85 WBMs, Kerry Mcnamara to Wheeler, Michele de Nevers, John Middleton, Philip Karp, Ron Kim, Shaman, "B-SPAN," September 20, 2000; de Nevers to Wheeler, "Good News for B-SPAN," June 12, 2000.
86 WBMs, Wheeler to Shaman, "Course Announcement: "Understanding Rural Institutions", December 12-13. 2000, MC C2-129," November 16, 2000; to Shaman, "Course Announcement: "Understanding Rural Institutions", December 12-13. 2000, MC C2-129," November 16, 2000.
87 WBM, Michele de Nevers to Wheeler, "New Customer for B-SPAN," February 7, 2001.
88 WBMs, Michele de Nevers to Ian Johnson, Vinodhini David, Kristalina Georgieva, Wheeler, Shaman, Christiane Kraus, Alyson Kleine, Joshua Okoth Ogada, "Announcement of B-SPAN
Webcasting ESSD Events," July 5, 2000; Johnson to ESSD Network, "Announcement of B-SPAN – Webcasting ESSD Events," July 12, 2000.
89 WBM, Shaman to Michele de Nevers, Wheeler, "Sample Note to Ian Johnson," June 30, 2000.
90 WBM, Wheeler to Michele de Nevers, "Progress on the B-SPAN Front," November 14, 2001.
91 WBMs, Wheeler to Jos Ritzen, Paul Collier, Zmarak Shalizi, "Announcement of B-SPAN – Webcasting ESSD Events," July 12, 2000; Lawrence Macdonald to Andrew Mason, Elizabeth King, Shaman, Wheeler, "DEC Gender Policy Seminar and Streaming Video (B-SPAN)," February 16, 2001; Wheeler to Michele de Nevers, "B-SPAN and Dave Shaman," January 22, 2001; Macdonald to Wheeler, "DEC and B-SPAN," February 1, 2001; Wheeler to Shaman, Polly Means, "DEC and B-SPAN," February 2, 2001.
92 WBM, Alex Norsworthy to Shaman, Nick Van Praag, "B-SPAN and ECA Strategies," July 28, 2000.
93 WBMs, Shaman to Wheeler, "B-SPAN Follow up to MdN," July 18, 2000; Shaman to David Witzel, Forum One, Wheeler, "B-SPAN Start Up," August 9, 2000; David Strelneck, Forum One, to Shaman, Witzel, "B-SPAN TOR," August 3, 2000.
94 David Strelneck, Forum One, to Shaman, Witzel, "B-SPAN TOR," August 3, 2000.
95 WBMs, Shaman to David Witzel, Forum One, Wheeler, "B-SPAN Start Up," August 9, 2000; Witzel to Wheeler, Shaman, David Stelneck, Forum One, "B-SPAN Start Up,"

August 9, 2000; Witzel to Wheeler, Shaman, "B-SPAN Web Design," August 28, 2000; Strelneck to Shaman, Witzel, "B-SPAN TOR," August 3, 2000.

96 WBM, Wheeler to Shaman, David Witzel, Forum One, "B-SPAN Web Design," August 18, 2000.

97 WBM, Shaman to David Witzel, Forum One, Wheeler, "B-SPAN Start Up," August 9, 2000.

98 WBMs, Shaman to David Witzel, Forum One, Wheeler, "B-SPAN Start Up," August 9, 2000; Shaman to NIPR List, "Introducing B-SPAN, the World Bank's New Broadcasting Station," January 25, 2001.

99 WBMs, Wheeler to Shaman, "B-SPAN: Working Da $$$," August 7, 2000; Shaman to Wheeler, "B-SPAN Cost Analysis," August 4, 2000.

100 WBM, Shaman to Wheeler, "B-SPAN Cost Analysis," August 4, 2000.

101 Dianelva Montas to Walter Vergara, Shaman, "Webcasting Monday's BBL," October 12, 2000.

102 WBM, Shaman to Wheeler, "B-SPAN Cost Analysis," August 4, 2000.

103 WBM, Wheeler to Michele de Nevers, "B-SPAN Updates," October 16, 2000.

104 David Strelneck, Forum One, to Shaman, "Response to Your Phone Call TOR," July 27, 2000; David Witzel, Forum One, to Wheeler, Shaman, "Streaming Video Hosting," August 16, 2000.

105 WBMs, Wheeler to Michele de Nevers, "B-SPAN," September 21, 2000; Wheeler to David Witzel, Forum One, "NIPR Usage Report," August 16, 2000; Wheeler to Steve Peace, Escene, David Witzel, Forum One, Shaman, "Thinking About Next Moves," September 15, 2000; Shaman to Wheeler, "B-SPAN Disses and Dats," March 7, 2001.

106 WBMs, Shaman to David Witzel, Forum One, Wheeler, "B-SPAN Web Design," August 17, 2000; Wheeler to Shaman, Missy McCool, Forum One, "B-SPAN Mockups," October 3, 2000; Shaman to Wheeler, McCool, "B-SPAN Mockups," October 3, 2000; Witzel to Shaman, Wheeler, "B-SPAN Layouts," September 5, 2000; Shaman, to Witzel, Wheeler, "B-SPAN Layouts," September 11, 2000; Witzel to Wheeler, Shaman, "B-SPAN Layouts," September 5, 2000; Wheeler to Shaman, McCool, "B-SPAN Mockups," October 19, 2000; Shaman to Witzel, McCool, Wheeler, "B-SPAN Mockups," October 18, 2000.

107 WBMs, Shaman to Guenter Riethmacher, "Your Discussion Now on B-SPAN," February 5, 2001; Shaman to Polly Means, "RealPlayer Downloading Instructions and Relevant Screens," February 27, 2001.

108 WBMs, Wheeler to Shaman, "B-SPAN: Workin' da $$$," August 7, 2000; Wheeler to Shaman, "B-SPAN $$," November 22, 2000; Wheeler to Shaman, "The Bottom Line(s)," February 28, 2001.

109 David Witzel, Forum One, to Wheeler, Shaman, "Streaming Video Hosting," August 15, 2000.

110 WBM, Shaman to Michele de Nevers, Wheeler, "Talk on Adapting Climate Change," September 5, 2000.

111 WBMs, Shaman to Wheeler, "B-SPAN Developments," November 2, 2000; Shaman to Wheeler, "B-SPAN – A Little More," May 16, 2000.

112 WBM, Shaman to Kerry McNamara, "B-SPAN and DLC Studios," October 2, 2000.

113 WBMs, Wheeler to Michele de Nevers, "B-SPAN Updates," October 16, 2000; Shaman to Larissa Fastovsky, Chongman Kim, Wheeler, "Tapes," September 25, 2000; Fastovsky to Shaman, Kim, "Tapes," September 22, 2000.

114 WBMs, Wheeler to Shaman, "You De Man," September 19, 2000; Shaman to Polly Means, "B-SPAN Video Summaries II," November 20, 2000; Michele de Nevers to Richard Klein, Potsdam Institute, Shaman, "Visit to Washington, DC," August 31, 2000.

115 WBM, Shaman to Michele de Nevers, Wheeler, "Talk on Adapting Climate Change," September 5, 2000.

116 WBM, Shaman to Alexandre Marc, "Your Interview on B-SPAN," February 5, 2001.
117 WBMs, Wheeler to David Witzel, David Strelneck, Forum One, "B-SPAN Idea," September 11, 2000; Shaman to Kayoko Shibati Medlin, Bowden, "MORE Feedback," February 3, 2003; Polly Means to Shaman, Bowden, "MORE Feedback," February 3, 2003; Wheeler to Shaman, Polly Means, "Details, Details," May 31, 2002; Shaman to Wheeler, Means, "Details, Details," May 31, 2002; Wheeler to Shaman, "Details, Details," May 31, 2002; Shaman to Wheeler, "Details, Details," May 31, 2002.
118 WBMs, Polly Means to Shaman, "Your Discussion, Now on B-SPAN," February 6, 2001; Jaime Yepez to Shaman, Gerd Fleischer, "Your Discussion, Now on B-SPAN," February 6, 2001; Means to Shaman, "Your Discussion, Now on B-SPAN," February 6, 2001.
119 WBMs, Nathaniel Dickinson to Shaman, "Pesticide Presentation on B-SPAN Webpage," February 8, 2001; Kim to Shaman, Wheeler, Means, "Your Discussion, Now on B-SPAN," February 7, 2001.
120 WBM, Shaman to Polly Means, "RealPlayer Downloading Instructions and Relevant Screens," February 27, 2001.
121 WBM, Shaman to B-SPAN List, "B-SPAN Newsletter," March 2001, March 1, 2001; Shaman to Michael Kane, Edit Pena, Barbara Murek, Bryan Waller, Cary Ann Cadman, Cenk Ozmen, John Didier, Latifah Alsegaf, Philip Karp, Vandana Sarna, "Response to External Web Feedback: Query on RealPlayer 8 Presentations," May 31, 2001; Shaman to Larissa Fastovsky, Chongman Kim, Wheeler, "B-SPAN Files," September 20, 2000; Kim to Shaman, Fastovsky, Wheeler, "B-SPAN Files," September 20, 2000; Shaman to Alex Norsworthy, Wheeler, Fastovsky, "How the Digitizing is Going," September 21, 2000.
122 WBMs, Wheeler to Shaman, Missy McCool, Forum One, "B-SPAN Mockups," October 3, 2000; Shaman to Wheeler, McCool, "B-SPAN Mockups," October 3, 2000; Wheeler to Shaman, "The Competition," September 21, 2000; Shaman to Wheeler, "Day Two," September 22, 2000.
123 WBM, Wheeler to Shaman, "Further B-SPAN Ruminations," October 13, 2000.
124 WBMs, Polly Means to Shaman, Thamnu Sihsobhon, "Problems with the Software/Hardware," December 13, 2000; Wheeler to Shaman, "Dat Gold's Been Spiked!," December 21, 2000; Means to Chongman Kim, Odis Hamilton, Shaman, "Advice If You Can Spare a Minute," January 19, 2001.
125 WBM, Wheeler to Shaman, "Life on the New Frontier," September 18, 2000.
126 WBMs, Odin Knudsen to Nalin Kishor, "Brown Bag This Thursday, 12:30," October 3, 2000; Kishor to Knudsen, Kerstin Canby, James Douglas, William Magrath, Shaman, Adriana Bianchi, "Webecast: Brown Bag This Thursday, 12:30," October 3, 2000.
127 WBMs, Wheeler to Michele de Nevers, "B-SPAN," September 21, 2000; Shaman to David Witzel, Forum One, "Digitizing," November 3, 2000.
128 WBMs, Wheeler to Shaman, "PRSP Training Announcement," June 4, 2001; Wheeler to Shaman, "B-SPAN Update," October 27, 2000; Shaman to Chongman Kim, Wheeler, "B-SPAN Not Connecting, Help," September 18, 2000.
129 WBM, Steve Peace, Escene, "Checking In," May 9, 2001.
130 WBMs, Wheeler to Michele de Nevers, "B-SPAN," September 21, 2000; Shaman to Wheeler, "Think About Next Moves," September 19, 2000; Wheeler to Steve Peace, Escene, David Witzel, Forum One, Shaman, "Think About Next Moves," September 15, 2000; Peace to Wheeler, Witzel, Shaman, "Think About Next Moves," September 18, 2000.
131 WBMs, Shaman to Michele de Nevers, Wheeler, "Workshop: Country Assistance Strategies and Drylands Issues," September 20, 2000; de Nevers to Guenter Riethmacher, Shaman, "Workshop: Country Assistance Strategies and Drylands Issues," September 20, 2000.

132 WBMs, Shaman to Wheeler, "B-SPAN – Some More," May 25, 2000; Shaman to Wheeler, "To Go Live or Not To Go Live, That is the Question on Global Dialogue on Sustainable Development Request for B-SPAN," October 16, 2001.
133 WBM, Michele de Nevers to Shaman, "Continuous Slow Sand Filtration," September 22, 2000.
134 WBM, Shaman to Polly Means, "Summary of Continuous Slow Sand Filtration," November 19, 2001.
135 WBM, Alyson Kleine to Shaman, Wheeler, Michele de Nevers, "RDV Series for B-SPAN," October 2, 2000.
136 WBM, Lynn Brown to Shaman, Cristin Cogley, "Rural Seminar Series," October 4, 2000.
137 WBMs, Shaman to Alejandro Deeb, "Your Discussion, Now on B-SPAN," February 5, 2001; Shaman to Michele de Nevers, Wheeler, "B-SPAN and IFC," October 18, 2000.
138 WBM, Wheeler to Polly Means, Shaman, "Today's Nitpicking," March 28, 2001.
139 WBMs, Shaman to Wheeler, "Latest B-SPAN Ruminations," October 12, 2000; Shaman to Wheeler, "Further B-SPAN Ruminations," October 12, 2000; Shaman to David Witzel, Forum One, "Digitizing," November 3, 2000.
140 WBMs, Shaman to Wheeler, "Latest B-SPAN Ruminations," October 12, 2000; Shaman to Wheeler, "Further B-SPAN Ruminations," October 12, 2000.
141 WBMs, Wheeler to Polly Means, Shaman, Thamnu Sihsobhon, "A Setback for B-SPAN," November 20, 2000; Wheeler to Shaman, "On The Side Panel," November 20, 2000.
142 WBM, Wheeler to Michele de Nevers, "B-SPAN Updates," October 16, 2000.
143 WBM, Shaman to Wheeler, Polly Means, Bowden, "Second System," May 15, 2002.
144 WBMs, Wheeler to Michele de Nevers, "B-SPAN Updates," October 16, 2000; Shaman to Wheeler, "Da Latest," October 17, 2000.
145 WBMs, Wheeler to Chongman Kim, Shaman, "High Capacity Drives for B-SPAN," November 3, 2000; Shaman to Wheeler, "High Capacity Drives for B-SPAN," November 21, 2000.
146 WBM, Shaman to Wheeler, "Some Missing Links," March 28, 2001.
147 WBMs, Shaman to Polly Means, "New Headline Section for B-SPAN," March 7, 2001; Wheeler to Shaman, "Grist for Da Span," January 22, 2001; Shaman to Means, "B-SPAN Edits," January 23, 2001.
148 WBM, Shaman to Wheeler, "Memo for WBI Meeting," January 17, 2001.
149 WBM, Wheeler to Polly Means, Shaman, "Thanks a Million," January 19, 2001; Michele de Nevers to Extended List, "Introducing B-SPAN, the World Bank's New Broadcasting Station," January 29, 2001; Wheeler to Shaman, "Beautiful," February 2, 2001.
150 WBMs, Lawrence Macdonald to Wheeler, Shaman, "B-SPAN and DEC Policy Seminars, Research Site," January 29, 2001; Macdonald to Wheeler, "DEC and B-SPAN," February 1, 2001, Wheeler to Polly Means, Shaman, "DEC and B-SPAN," February 2, 2001; Wheeler to Martin Rama, Shaman, "Webcasting the Poverty and Applied Micro Series," September 4, 2001.
151 WBMs, Wheeler to William Easterly, Shaman, Bowden, Polly Means, "Building the Web Audience for the Macro Seminars," September 6, 2001; Easterly to Wheeler, Karie Labrie, "Webcasting the Macro Brown Bag Series," April 2, 2001.
152 WBMs, Martin Rama to Wheeler, Vijayendra Rao, Patricia Sader, Ana Maria Maranon, Shaman, "Webcasting the Poverty and Applied Micro Series," September 6, 2001; Wheeler to Rama, Rao, Sader, Maranon, Shaman, "Webcasting the Poverty and Applied Micro Series," September 6, 2001; Rama to Shaman, "Webcasting," February 5, 2001; Shaman to Rama, "Webcasting," February 5, 2001.
153 WBM, Wheeler to Shaman, "Yo, Yo …!" September 10, 2001.

154 WBMs, Shaman to Wheeler, "Chongman's In," March 7, 2001; Wheeler to Michele de Nevers, Shaman, Michael Doyle, "Budget for B-SPAN," Novmeber 13, 2000; Shaman to Wheeler, "Nudder 'Cept," October 3, 2001.
155 WBMs, Polly Means to Chongman Kim, Shaman, "New Upgraded Card," April 2, 2001; Wheeler to Michele de Nevers, "Today's Items," April 16, 2001; Means to Shaman, Thamnu Sihsobhon, "Problems with the Software/Hardware," December 13, 2000; Shaman to Wheeler, "Size of RealPlayer Screen," February 5, 2001; Means to Shaman, Wheeler, Sihsobhon, "A Setback for B-SPAN," November 20, 2000; Shaman to Means, Wheeler, Sihsobhon, "A Setback for B-SPAN," November 20, 2000; Means to Wheeler, "A Setback for B-SPAN," November 20, 2000; Wheeler to Means, Shaman, Sihsobhon, "A Setback for B-SPAN," November 20, 2000.
156 WBMs, Wheeler to Shaman, "A Setback for B-SPAN," November 20, 2000; Wheeler to Means, Shaman, Sihsobhon, "A Setback for B-SPAN," November 20, 2000; Means to Wheeler, Sihsobhon, Shaman, "Price for Server for B-SPAN," May 10, 2001; Wheeler to Means, Sihsobhon, Shaman, "Price for Server for B-SPAN," May 11, 2001.
157 WBMs, Polly Means to Chongman Kim, Shaman, Jennifer Prochnow, "Digitizing Videos onto the External Bank Server," December 22, 2000; Shaman to Means, Wheeler, "Access to ISG Server," December 22, 2000; Shaman to Wheeler, "Access to ISG Server," December 22, 2000.
158 WBMs, Wheeler to Shaman, "Da Latest," October 18, 2000; Wheeler to Michele de Nevers, Shaman, Michael Doyle, "Budget for B-SPAN," November 13, 2000.
159 WBM, Wheeler to Michele de Nevers, "B-SPAN and Dave Shaman," January 19, 2001.
160 WBM, Roula Yazigi to Shaman, Raquel Reyes Luz, "# of Days," January 23, 2001.
161 WBMs, Shaman to Wheeler, "Draft Note to Michael Doyle," January 23, 2001; Wheeler to Michele de Nevers, "B-SPAN and Dave Shaman," January 19, 2001; Wheeler to Michael Doyle, de Nevers, Shaman, Roula Yazigi, "Contract Extension for Dave Shaman," January 23, 2001.
162 WBMs, Lawrence Macdonald to Shaman, Gunnar Eskeland, "Gunnar's B-SPAN Talk Proposed as Feature in Next World Bank Research E-News," March 16, 2001; Shaman to Macdonald, Eskeland, Wheeler, "Gunnar's B-SPAN Talk Proposed as Feature in Next World Bank Research E-News," March 16, 2001; Wheeler to Shaman, "One for Da Money, Two for Da Span ...?" March 26, 2001.
163 WBM, Shaman to NIPR List, "Introducing B-SPAN, the World Bank's New Broadcasting Station," January 24, 2001.
164 WBM, Shaman to Scott Johnson, "B-SPAN and NIPR Mailing List," September 24, 2001.
165 David Witzel, Forum One, to Wheeler, Shaman, "The Scout Report January 26, 2000 – HTML Version," January 29, 2001.
166 Marilynn Larkin, The Lancet, to Shaman, "LANCET Review of B-SPAN," February 3, 2001.
167 WBMs, Shaman to Tewodros Yilma, "Introducing B-SPAN, the World Bank's New Broadcasting Station," January 29, 2001; Lawrence Macdonald to Chongman Kim, Coralie Gevers, Dora Tzochevska, Francis Dobbs, Larissa Fastovsky, Polly Means, Wheeler, Shaman, "URGENT – Problems with Streaming Video (Nick Stern Video BTO on Indonesia)," February 1, 2001; Shaman to Macdonald, "URGENT – Problems with Streaming Video (Nick Stern Video BTO on Indonesia)," February 1, 2001; Means to Kim, Shaman, Macdonald, "URGENT – Problems with Streaming Video (Nick Stern Video BTO on Indonesia)," February 1, 2001.
168 WBMs, Michele de Nevers to WBIEN Staff, Cary Ann Cadman, Iliriana Mushkolaj, Sunetra Puri, Wheeler, Shaman, "WBIEN – Weekly Division Meeting – Thursday, February 1, 2001 – 4:00 pm in J4-044," January 31, 2001; de Nevers to Shaman, "Presentation on B-SPAN to WBI Management Team," April 9, 2001; Wheeler to de

Nevers, Maria Rosa Schwartz, Shaman, "Division Meeting This Week," January 17, 2001.

169 WBMs, Wheeler to Polly Means, Shaman, "PC Buy for B-SPAN," April 13, 2001; Shaman to Wheeler, "Memo for WBI Meeting," January 17, 2001.

170 WBM, Shaman to Polly Means, Wheeler, "B-SPAN Host Page," February 21, 2001.

171 WBMs, Wheeler to Gerard Caprio, Shaman, "B-SPAN Costs," July 11, 2001; Wheeler to Shaman, "Budget for B-SPAN," February 7, 2001; Wheeler to Daniel Kaufmann, Michele de Nevers, Shaman, Polly Means, "Streaming the Governance Series," April 2, 2001.

172 WBM, Shaman to Wheeler, "David Gray," February 2, 2001.

173 WBMs, Shaman to Wheeler, "David Gray," February 2, 2001; Shaman to Wheeler, "The Package," January 30, 2002.

174 WBM, Sarah Lipscomb to Shaman, Sara Guerschanik Calvo, "Posting of Exchange Rates Brainstorming Workshop on Website," March 20, 2001.

175 WBM, Michael Doyle to Lili-Ann Tabada, Shaman, Michele de Nevers, "Intellectual Property Rights Workshop and B-SPAN – March 14," April 23, 2001.

176 WBM, Wheeler to Nicholas Stern, Joseph Michael Finger, Paul Collier, Zmarak Shalizi, Lawrence Macdonald, Michele de Neverss, Shaman, Polly Means, "Webcast of the Conference on Intellectual Property Rights in Developing Countries," March 20, 2001.

177 WBM, Lawrence Macdonald to Shaman, "IDG??" April 19, 2001.

178 WBM, Margaret Miller to Shaman, Shahrokh Fardoust, Eric Swanson, Shantayanan Devarajan, Bilkiss Dhomun, "B-SPAN Filming of Seminar on International Development Goals," March 9, 2001.

179 WBMs, Wheeler to Shaman, "Budget for B-SPAN," February 7, 2001; Wheeler to Michele de Nevers, "New Customer for B-SPAN," February 7, 2001; de Nevers to Wheeler, "New Customer for B-SPAN," February 7, 2001; Shaman to Daniel Kaufmann, de Nevers, Wheeler, "Governance and B-SPAN," March 7, 2001.

180 WBMs, Christopher Walsh to Shaman, "B-SPAN," February 9, 2001; Shaman to Wheeler, "A B-SPAN Feeler – BUT Careful," February 8, 2001; Wheeler to Shaman, "A B-SPAN Feeler – BUT Careful," February 8, 2001.

181 WBM, Wheeler to Michele de Nevers, Shaman, "The Road from Here," February 5, 2000.

182 WBMs, Shaman to Wheeler, "Span Thoughts," September 27, 2001; Wheeler to Shaman, "Span Thoughts," October 1, 2001.

183 WBMs, Wheeler to Shaman, Missy McCool, Forum One, "B-SPAN Mockups," October 19, 2000; Wheeler to Michele de Nevers, Shaman, "Amazing Day – Sorry About This!" October 16, 2000; Wheeler to de Nevers, "MORE ON ANNUAL MEETINGS," August 27, 2001.

184 WBMs, Polly Means to Shaman, Bowden, Chongman Kim, "URGENT MATTER ABOUT B-SPAN, and Carbon and the Policy Nexus," December 10, 2001; Means to Kim, Shaman, "Cut-overs to the Streaming Server Needed," April 5, 2001; Means to Shaman, "B-SPAN Fiddles and Diddles," December 17, 2001; Shaman to Wheeler, "Chongman," December 14, 2001.

185 WBMs, Chongman Kim to Polly Means, Shaman, Bowden, "URGENT MATTER ABOUT B-SPAN, and Carbon and the Policy Nexus," December 10, 2001; Means to Kim, Larissa Fastovsky, Shaman, "In Need of Additional Space for Problem with Server," February 20, 2001; Kim to Means, Shaman, Fastovsky, "In Need of Additional Space for B-SPAN Video Files, February 26, 2001; Kim to Means, Shaman, In Need of Additional Space for B-SPAN Video Files," February 26, 2001; Means to Shaman, "Broken Links," February 21, 2001; Means to Fastovsky, Kim, Shaman, "Problem with Server, Still!" February 16, 2001.

186 WBMs, Shaman to Wheeler, "B-SPAN Follow up with MdN," July 18, 2000; Shaman to Wheeler, "In Need of Additional Space for B-SPAN Video Files," March 1, 2001; Chongman Kim to Polly Means, Shaman, "In Need of Additional Space for B-SPAN Video Files," February 26, 2001; WBMs, Wheeler to Chongman Kim, Shaman, "High Capacity Drives for B-SPAN," November 3, 2000; Shaman to Wheeler, "High Capacity Drives for B-SPAN," November 21, 2000; Shaman to Wheeler, "Thinking About Next Moves," September 19, 2000.

187 WBM, Wheeler to Shaman, "Maybe Time to Pop the Question," February 23, 2001.

188 WBMs, Wheeler to Shaman, "Vodium, etc.," February 3, 2001; Steve Peace, Escene Networks, "Checking In," May 7, 2001; Brandon Wick, Inktomi Corp, to Shaman, "Inktomi Solutions," July 30, 2001; Tim McMillan, Streampipe, "Streampipe, Sect 508 Compliance, Live Captioning," June 18, 2001; McMillan to Shaman, "Annual Hosting Proposal," March 27, 2001; Nate Pagel, SiteBurst, to Shaman, "Inquiry: B-SPAN," March 6, 2001; Aldo Bello, Mind and Media, to Shaman, "Webcasting Capabilities and Pricing," March 16, 2001; Mark Maxey, Digital Island, to Shaman, "Digital Island Streaming POPs and Sample URLs," March 20, 2001; Susan Kular, Virage, to Shaman, "Virage Video Solution," March 13, 2001.

189 WBMs, Lawrence Macdonald to Wheeler, Shaman, "B-SPAN and DEC Policy Seminars, Research Site," January 29, 2001; Macdonald to Wheeler, "DEC and B-SPAN," February 1, 2001; Wheeler to Polly Means, Shaman, "DEC and B-SPAN," February 2, 2001.

190 WBMs, Shaman to Wheeler, "Microphone Issues for B-SPAN Sessions," March 8, 2001; Wheeler to Shaman, "Microphone Issues for B-SPAN Sessions," March 9, 2001; Vijayendra Rao to Shaman, Dominique Van De Walle, "DECRG Micro Seminar," December 13, 2002.

191 WBMs, Shaman to Charles Mann, Clovis Fantinelli, Sefik Cardak, Wheeler, Bowden, "Taping Problem," August 24, 2001; Shaman to Cardak, "Today's Event," April 19, 2001.

192 WBM, David Witzel, Forum One, to Wheeler, Shaman, David Strelneck, Forum One, "B-SPAN in Ban's Swirled," April 4, 2001; Bank Swirled, B-SPAN is Proud to Present Survivor 3: The Challenge of Leadership, April 4, 2001

193 WBMs, Shaman to Lawrence Macdonald, Wheeler, "IDG and ABCDE," May 7, 2001; Shaman to Polly Means, Wheeler, "ABCDE Conference," June 15, 2001; Wheeler to Shaman, "A Must for De Span," March 22, 2001; Wheeler to Zeny Kranzer, Boris Pleskovic, Gerard Caprio, Shaman, "Video Taping Arrangements for ABCDE," April 10, 2001; Wheeler to Zeny Kranzer, Boris Pleskovic, Gerard Caprio, Shaman, "Video Taping Arrangements for ABCDE," April 13, 2001.

194 WBM, Shaman to B-SPAN List, "B-SPAN Newsletter, September 2001," September 10, 2001.

195 WBM, Ana Marie Maranon to DECRG, "Amartya Sen Lecture on 'Culture and Development' – July 25, 2001 at 9:00 am," J 1-050; Vijayendra Rao to DECRG, Prena Clark, Nadia Islam, Sabina Alkire, Michael Walton, "Amartya Sen's Paper," July 25, 2001; Wheeler to Kreszentia Duer, Bowden, Polly Means, Michele de Nevers, Shaman, "Record Time!" July 27, 2001.

196 WBM, Wheeler to William Easterly, Shaman, "Webcasting the Macro Seminar," April 27, 2001; Shaman to Wheeler, "Ooooppps," April 27, 2001.

197 WBMs, William Easterly to Wheeler, Shaman, "Webcasting the Macro Seminar," April 27, 2001; Shaman to Wheeler, "DEC Brown Bags," August 17, 2001; Wheeler to Shaman, "DEC Brown Bags," August 17, 2001.

198 WBMs, Shaman to Wheeler, "The Ultimate Spannable," December 4, 2001; Wheeler to Shaman, "The Ultimate Spannable," December 4, 2001.

199 WBM, Wheeler to Shaman, "Re-SPAN?" May 14, 2001.

200 WBMs, Shaman to Michele de Nevers, Wheeler, "B-SPAN Volume," June 4, 2001; de Nevers to Shaman, Wheeler, May 26, 2001; Shaman to de Nevers, Wheeler, "B-SPAN Volume," May 30, 2001.

201 WBMs, Shaman to Bonnie Bradford, Wheeler, Michele de Nevers, Anita Gordon, Polly Means, Natalie Magradze, "B-SPAN Schedule for Environment Month," June 4, 2001; Kristalina Georgieva to ENV HQ1, ENV HQ2, ESSD Management Team, "June is Environment Month in the World Bank …" April 13, 2001; Shaman to Sefik Cardak, Conference Services, "B-SPAN and Environment Month," May 18, 2001.

202 WBMs, Nicole Frost to Shaman, "B-SPAN Newsletter, March 2001," March 1, 2001; Frost to Shaman, "EXT Web, B-SPAN Promoting," June 4, 2001; Frost to Shaman, Wheeler, Jeff McCoy, "Pages for B-SPAN Links," September 19, 2001; Shaman to Frost, Wheeler, "Pages for B-SPAN Links," September 19, 2001; Shaman to Coralie Gevers, "Globalization PRR Seminar," December 11, 2001.

203 WBMs, Wheeler to Shaman, "B-SPAN Newsletter, March 2001," March 5, 2001; Shaman to Wheeler, "B-SPAN Newsletter, March 2001," March 5, 2001.

204 WBMs, Nicole Frost to Shaman, "EXT Web, B-SPAN Promoting," June 4, 2001; Bonnie Bradford to Shaman, Michele de Nevers, "Help with B-SPAN This Week?" June 6, 2001; Shaman to de Nevers, Wheeler, "Help with B-SPAN This Week?" June 6, 2001.

205 WBM, Wheeler to Bonnie Bradford, Shaman, Michele de Nevers, "Congrats on B-SPAN Coverage!!!!" June 6, 2001.

206 David Witzel, Forum One, to Wheeler, Shaman, "B-SPAN," June 8, 2001; Wheeler to Michele de Nevers, "First B-SPAN Stats," June 8, 2001; Witzel to Wheeler, Shaman, "NIPR, B-SPAN Usage Data," August 14, 2001.

207 WBMs, Anupa Bhaumik to Susmita Dasgupta, "Dissemination Grant Proposal: 'Greening Industry: New Roles for Communities, Markets, and Governments,' " June 21, 2000; Clara Else to Dasgupta, "Revised Dissemination Grant Request: Policy Research Report, 'Greening Industry: New Roles for Communities, Markets, and Governments,' " March 29, 2001.

208 WBMs, Anupa Bhaumik to Susmita Dasgupta, "Dissemination Grant Proposal: 'Greening Industry: New Roles for Communities, Markets, and Governments,' " June 21, 2000; Clara Else to Dasgupta, "Revised Dissemination Grant Request: Policy Research Report, 'Greening Industry: New Roles for Communities, Markets, and Goverments,' " March 29, 2001.

209 WBMs, Nathaniel Dickinson to Shaman, "Pesticide Presentation on B-SPAN Webpage," February 8, 2001; Shaman to Michele de Nevers, Bonnie Bradford, Chongman Kim, Polly Means, "B-SPAN Archive of Wednesday's Live Webcast and ED3 Deployment," June 8, 2001; Wheeler to de Nevers, "ISG," June 7, 2001; Shaman to Bradford, de Nevers, Wheeler, "Accessing B-SPAN's Archives," June 7, 2001; Dickinson to IWG Community, Michael Kingsberry, Teresa Tidwell, Chongman Kim, Brian Iori, ED3 Coordinators, "IWG Testing of RealPlayer 8 Upgrade: 5/3 – 5/9," May 1, 2001; Shaman to Michael Kane, Edit Pena, Barbara Murek, Bryan Waller, Cary Ann Cadman, Cenk Ozmen, John Didier, Latifah Alsegaf, Philip Karp, Vandana Sarna, "Response to External Web Feedback: Query on RealPlayer 8 Presentations," May 31, 2001; Means to Shaman, "Your Discussion, Now on B-SPAN," February 6, 2001; Kim to Shaman, Wheeler, Means, "Your Discussion, Now on B-SPAN," February 7, 2001.

210 WBMs, Bonnie Bradford to Cary Ann Cadman, Veit Burger, Cenk Ozmen, Shaman, Michele de Nevers, "Vinod's B-SPAN Access," June 13, 2001; Bradford to Edit Pena, Shaman, Natalie Magradze, "Changes to the B-SPAN Website Urgently Needed," June 7, 2001.

211 WBM, Philip Karp to Michele de Nevers, Vinod Thomas, "Environment Strategy Archives of Webcast," June 15, 2001.

212 WBM, Shaman to Wheeler, "Environment Strategy Archives of Webcast," June 18, 2001.

213 WBMs, Kurt Nemes to Philip Karp, "Response to External Web Feedback: Query on RealPlayer 8 Presentations," June 2, 2001; Karp to Michele de Nevers, John Middleton, Vinod Thomas, "Environment Strategy Archives of Webcast," June 15, 2001; Nemes to Karp, Peter Coppleston, "Response to External Web Feedback: Query on RealPlayer 8 Presentations," June 1, 2001.

214 WBM, Michele de Nevers to Shaman, "Environment Strategy Archives of Webcast," June 15, 2001.

215 WBM, Wheeler to Michele de Nevers, Hua Wang, Susmita Dasgupta, Benoit Laplante, Shaman, "Greening Industry Conference in Nanjing," April 19, 2001.

216 WBM, Wheeler to Shaman, Hua Wang, "Geoff Read's Interest," February 9, 2001.

217 WBMs, Wheeler to Martin Rama, Shaman, "Webcasting the Poverty and Applied Micro Series," September 4, 2001; Wheeler to DECRG DMT, Bowden, Shaman, Polly Means, "Webcasting of Your Brown Bags, Seminars and Conferences," July 17, 2001; Wheeler to Gershon Feder, Shaman, "Challenging the Rush for Community-Driven Development," May 11, 2001.

218 WBMs, Wheeler to William Easterly, Shaman, Bowden, Polly Means, "Building the Web Audience for the Macro Seminars," September 6, 2001; Martin Rama to Wheeler, Vijayendra Rao, Patricia Sader, Ana Maria Maranon, Shaman, "Webcasting the Poverty and Applied Micro Series," September 6, 2001; Wheeler to Rama, Rao, Sader, Maranon, Shaman, "Webcasting the Poverty and Applied Micro Series," September 6, 2001; Rama to Shaman, Rao, Wheeler, Sader, Maranon, "Seminar Webcast," October 26, 2001.

219 WBM, Beata Smarzynska to Wheeler, Paulina Flewitt, David Tarr, "Webcasting the Trade Seminars," December 11, 2001; Wheeler to Tarr, John Wilson, William Martin Tracy, Shaman, "Webcasting the Trade Seminars," December 11, 2001.

220 WBMs, Wheeler to Wei Zhang, Shaman, Michael Pomerleano, Demmet Cabbar, Cintya Vega, Colleen Mascenik, "B-SPAN and Financial Sector," August 10, 2001; Shaman to Zhang, Cabbar, Michael Doyle, "B-SPAN and Financial Sector," September 6, 2001; Zhang to Wheeler, Pomerleano, Daniel Kaufmann, Alexandra Russo Rancal, Shaman, Bowden, "B-SPAN," July 18, 2001.

221 WBM, Wheeler to Shaman, "Cookin' with $$," July 23, 2001.

222 David Witzel, Forum One, to Wheeler, Shaman, "NIPR, B-SPAN Usage Data," August 14, 2001.

223 WBM, Wheeler to Michele de Nevers, Shaman, Polly Means, Bowden, Lawrence Macdonald, "Is B-SPAN Leading Edge?" August 16, 2001; David Witzel, Forum One, to Wheeler, Shaman, "NIPR, B-SPAN Usage Data," August 14, 2001.

224 WBM, Wheeler to Shaman, Bowden, Polly Means, Michele de Nevers, Paul Collier, Lawrence Macdonald, Kristalina Georgieva, Trinidad Angeles, "Interest in Our B-SPAN Webcasting Service," August 31, 2001.

225 WBM, Philip Karp to Shaman, Wheeler, Michele de Nevers, "Brief Write-up Re B-SPAN," August 22, 2001.

226 WBM, Shaman to Philip Karp, Michele de Nevers, Wheeler, "Brief Write-up Re B-SPAN," August 23, 2001.

227 WBM, Sunetra Puri to WBI Staff, "MORE ON ANNUAL MEETINGS," August 20, 2001.

228 WBMs, Michele de Nevers to Mats Karlsson, Wheeler, Shaman, "B-SPAN and Annual Meetings Dialogue with Civil Society," September 6, 2001; Wheeler to de Nevers, Karlsson, Shaman, "B-SPAN and Annual Meetings Dialogue with Civil Society," September 7, 2001; de Nevers to Wheeler, "MORE ON ANNUAL MEETINGS," August 21, 2001.

229 WBMs, Wheeler to Michele de Nevers, Shaman, "Help on the Home Front?" September 4, 2001; Wheeler to Shaman, "Hey, Hey …" August 27, 2001.
230 WBM, Rafik Fatehali Hirji to Prabir Joardar, Walter Garvey, Ajit Pattnaik, David Grey, Lawrence Mbuya, Shaman, "B-SPAN," May 3, 2002.
231 WBMs, Polly Means to Wheeler, Shaman, Thamnu Sihsobhon, "Backup/Distribution of Tapes for B-SPAN," December 20, 2001; Wheeler to Means, Shaman, Sihsobhon, "Backup/Distribution of Tapes for B-SPAN," December 21, 2001.
232 WBM, Shaman to Don Beck, "Reminder that Your Video is Online at B-SPAN," February 19, 2002; Beck to Shaman, "Reminder that Your Video is Online at B-SPAN," February 16, 2002.
233 WBMs, Shaman to Wheeler, "Gaining Speed," September 14, 2001; Shaman to B-SPAN List, "B-SPAN Newsletter September 2001," September 10, 2001.
234 World Bank Information Service Group, "General Statistics for B-SPAN, 7-1-01 to 7-31-01," August 8, 2001.
235 World Bank Information Service Group, "General Statistics for B-SPAN, 8-1-01 to 8-31-01," September 11, 2001.
236 WBM, Shaman to Wheeler, "Traffic, and We Ain't Talking No Movie," December 14, 2001.
237 WBM, Bonnie Bradford to Shaman, Michele de Nevers, "B-SPAN Links from Bank's External Site," November 6, 2001.
238 WBMs, Wheeler to Gobind Nankani, "Webcasting PREM Events," October 10, 2001; Maria Ionata to Wheeler, "Meeting with PREM Managers," November 1, 2001; Shaman to Wheeler, Michele de Nevers, Bowden, Polly Means, "Can B-SPAN Do? You Bet It Can," June 13, 2002; Shaman to de Nevers, Wheeler, "B-SPAN Coverage for This Week," June 17, 2002.
239 WBM, Wheeler to Jo Ritzen, "Could You Spare Me 15 Minutes?" October 24, 2001.
240 WBMs, Wheeler to Jo Ritzen, Phillip Hay, "AIDS/PRSP: Very Good Seminar for B-SPAN," December 7, 2001; WBM, Wheeler to Michele de Nevers, "Progress on the B-SPAN Front," November 14, 2001; Hay to Ritzen, Wheeler, "AIDS/PRSP: Very Good Seminar for B-SPAN," December 18, 2001; Wheeler to Hay, Shaman, Ritzen, "AIDS/PRSP: Very Good Seminar for B-SPAN," December 10, 2001; Wheeler to Ritzen, Hay, Shaman, "AIDS/PRSP Seminar on B-SPAN," December 17, 2001.
241 WBMs, Steve Dingledine to Shaman, "B-SPAN and Macroeconomics," October 15, 2001; Wheeler to Shaman, "B-SPAN and Macroeconomics," October 16, 2001.
242 WBM, Shaman to Wheeler, "Today's Spannables," October 2, 2001; Chris Allen, US-Asia Environmental Partnership, to Shaman, Extended List, "Last Policy Forum of the Season!" December 13, 2001.
243 WBMs, Shaman to Wheeler, "Password Protected?" November 7, 2001; Wheeler to Shaman, "Bing!" November 8, 2001; Shaman to Wheeler, "Bing!" November 8, 2001.
244 WBMs, Wheeler to Michele de Nevers, "Progress on the B-SPAN Front," November 14, 2001; Polly Means to Shaman, "Edit," November 8, 2001; Shaman to Wheeler, "Edit," November 8, 2001; Wheeler to Shaman, Means, Bowden, "Peek-a-Boo," November 13, 2001; Shaman to Wheeler, Means, Bowden, "Peek-a-Boo," November 13, 2001; Means to Wheeler, Shaman, Bowden, "Peek-a-Boo," November 13, 2001; Means to Shaman, "About the World Bank Webcasting Email Account," November 19, 2001; Shaman to Wheeler, "Da Daze Spannables," November 12, 2001.
245 WBM, Jill Armstrong to John Middleton, "Did You Know," September 20, 2001.
246 WBMs, Michele de Nevers to Jill Armstrong, "B-SPAN," September 21, 2001; Armstrong to de Nevers, "B-SPAN," September 21, 2001.
247 WBMs, Shaman to McCoy, Wheeler, Polly Means, "Mary Robinson's Speech," December 5, 2001; Shaman to Nicole Frost, Jeff McCoy, Wheeler, "Mary Robinson Visit Dec. 3," November 29, 2001; Chris Allen, US-Asia Environmental Partnership, to Shaman, "Policy Forum and B-SPAN," October 24, 2001; Wheeler to Kristalina

Georgieva, Michele de Nevers, Zmarak Shalizi, Rusdian Lubis, "Excellent Opportunity to Dialogue with Indonesia's Environment Minister," November 29, 2001; Wheeler to de Nevers, "Progress on B-SPAN Front," November 14, 2001; Shaman to Jennifer Vito, "Summary of Environment, Strategy, Politics and Governance in Developing Countries, A Discussion with Nabiel Makarim, Minister of Environment, Indonesia," December 14, 2001; Wheeler to Shaman, "Date on the Braverman Talk," November 14, 2001; Jerri Dell to Extended List, "Learning from Afghanistan on the Cultural Dynamics that Spark Violence and Shape Globalization," December 2, 2001; Eileen Heffern to Shaman, "Don Beck BBL," December 5, 2001; Shaman to de Nevers, Philip Karp, Wheeler, "Reminder: 'The Cultural Dynamics of Nation Building in Afghanistan,' Monday, December 17, 12:30 – 2 pm, room JB 1-080," December 13, 2001; Shaman to Wheeler, "Spanning the Globe," October 24, 2001; Shaman to Polly Means, "New B-SPAN Cover Page," January 8, 2002; Shaman to B-SPAN List, "The UN High Commission on Human Rights, the Indonesian Minister of Environment, Middle East Peace and More on B-SPAN's January 2002 Newsletter," January 9, 2002.

248 WBMs, Shaman to Polly Means, "New Additions to B-SPAN Personalities and Link Pages," April 30, 2002; Shaman to Means, "New B-SPAN Links/Personalities," May 29, 2002; Shaman to Means, Bowden, Wheeler, "A Fiddle and Diddle," May 31, 2002; Shaman to Means, "New B-SPAN Personalities and Links," June 10, 2002; Shaman to Means, "Great Job," January 28, 2002; Wheeler to Shaman, "Spannin,'" January 18, 2002; Shaman to Wheeler, "Spannin,'" January 22, 2002; Shaman to Wheeler, Bowden, "Check Out the Latest, It's the Greatest," February 1, 2002; Wheeler to Shaman, Bowden, "Check Out the Latest, It's the Greatest," February 1, 2002; Wheeler to Shaman, David Witzel, Forum One, " 'Cept," September 19, 2000; Shaman to Polly Means, "B-SPAN History," June 4, 2002; Shaman to Means, "Great Job," January 28, 2002; Wheeler to Shaman, "Spannin,'" January 18, 2002; Shaman to Wheeler, "Spannin,'" January 22, 2002.

249 WBMs, Bowden to Shaman, Wheeler, Polly Means, "B-SPAN Shorts," January 9, 2002; Means to Bowden, Shaman, Wheeler, "B-SPAN Shorts," January 9, 2002; Shaman to Means, Bowden, Wheeler, "A Fiddle and Diddle," May 31, 2002; Shaman to Means, "New B-SPAN Personalities and Links," June 10, 2002.

250 WBMs, Shaman to Polly Means, "New Additions to B-SPAN Personalities and Link Pages," April 30, 2002; Shaman to Means, "New B-SPAN Links/Personalities," May 29, 2002; Shaman to Means, Wheeler, Bowden, "B-SPAN Links Section," March 28, 2002.

251 WBMs, Chongman Kim to Polly Means, Shaman, Bowden, "URGENT MATTER ABOUT B-SPAN, and Carbon and Policy Nexus," December 10, 2001; Wheeler to Michele de Nevers, "B-SPAN: News from the Front Lines," January 11, 2002; Means to Maria Lourdes Kasilag, Thamnu Sihsobhon, Shaman, "GEP Seminar Tape," January 4, 2002.

252 WBMs, Shaman to Wheeler, "Meeting with Chongman," December 18, 2001; Wheeler to Shaman, "Fuzzy Numbers from Chongman," December 21, 2001; Wheeler to Michele de Nevers, "B-SPAN: News from the Front Lines," January 11, 2002.

253 WBMs, David Gray to Shaman, "Video Hosting," January 4, 2002; Shaman to Gray, "Video Hosting," January 4, 2002; Shaman to Wheeler, "Video Hosting," January 4, 2002; Shaman to Wheeler, "Well?" January 10, 2002; Wheeler to Michele de Nevers, "B-SPAN: News from the Front Lines," January 11, 2002; Katie Bannon to Regional Webmasters, Charles Schueller, "Video Hosting – Request for IO," January 4, 2002; Shaman to Wheeler, "More on B-SPAN," January 11, 2002; Shaman to Gray, Means, "Server Access," January 15, 2002.

254 WBM, Wheeler to Michele de Nevers, "B-SPAN: News from the Front Lines," January 11, 2002.

255 WBMs, Wheeler to Michele de Nevers, "B-SPAN: News from the Front Lines," January 11, 2002; Wheeler to Shaman, Bowden, Polly Means, "Excellente!" October 1, 2001.

256 WBMs, Shaman to Alejandro Fernandez, "Catepillar Pitch on B-SPAN," January 10, 2002; Fernandez to Shaman, "Catepillar Pitch on B-SPAN," January 9, 2002; Wheeler to Shaman, Bowden, "Catepillar Pitch on B-SPAN," January 10, 2002; Shaman to Wheeler, Bowden, "Catepillar Pitch on B-SPAN," January 10, 2002; Wheeler to Michele de Nevers, "B-SPAN: News from the Front Lines," January 11, 2002; Shaman to Polly Means, "Summary of Continuous Slow Sand Filtration," November 19, 2001.

257 WBMs, Shaman to Wheeler, "DEC Gender Policy Seminar – and Streaming Video (B-SPAN)," February 21, 2001; Wheeler to Shaman, "DEC Gender Policy Seminar – and Streaming Video (B-SPAN)," February 21, 2001.

258 WBMs, Wheeler to Michele de Nevers, "B-SPAN: News from the Front Lines," January 11, 2002; de Nevers to Shaman, Wheeler, "INVITATION: Environment Strategy Implementation Roundtable on 'Country Environment Analysis,' " January 11, 2002; Shaman to Michele de Nevers, Wheeler, "INVITATION: Environment Strategy Implementation Roundtable on 'Country Environment Analysis,' " December 7, 2001.

259 WBM, Shaman to Sereen Juma, "B-SPAN," May 31, 2002.

260 WBMs, Sereen Juma to Shaman, Shaha Riza, Genalinda Gorospe, "B-SPAN," June 4, 2002; Shaman to Juma, Riza, Gorospe, "B-SPAN," June 5, 2002.

261 Paul Jepson, Oxford University, to Shaman, "Seminars on the Web," January 14, 2002; WBMs – Shaman to Jepson, "Seminars on the Web," January 14, 2002; Wheeler to Michele de Nevers, Shaman, "Flash: World Bank's Progressive Impact on Oxford," January 15, 2002.

262 Anne Marie DiNardo, C-SPAN, to Shaman, "Working at B-SPAN," January 7, 2002.

263 WBM, Wheeler to Shaman, "Glitch Patrol: ONE URGENT ITEM," January 16, 2002.

264 WBMs, Michele de Nevers to Wheeler, "More Thoughts on Today," January 16, 2002; Wheeler to Shaman, Bowden, Polly Means, "Note from Michele," January 17, 2002; Wheeler to Trinidad Angeles, Paul Collier, Lilliana Longo, David Dollar, Shaman, "Good News on B-SPAN," January 30, 2002.

265 WBMs, Wheeler to Shaman, "Yowzah!" January 28, 2002; Wheeler to Trinidad Angeles, Paul Collier, Lilliana Longo, David Dollar, Shaman, "Good News on B-SPAN," January 30, 2002.

266 WBM, Wheeler to Shaman, "Spinnin'," January 18, 2002.

267 WBM, Shaman to Wheeler, "A Thought," January 17, 2002.

268 WBMs, Shaman to Wheeler, "Streaming Streamline Update," February 1, 2002; Polly Means to Shaman, "Incompatibility of Real Producer with My Capture Card [#37209781]," February 12, 2002; Shaman to Means, Wheeler, "Incompatibility of Real Producer with My Capture Card [#37209781]," February 12, 2002.

269 WBM, Shaman to Wheeler, "Yowzah!," March 13, 2002.

270 WBMs, Shaman to Wheeler, "Streaming Streamline Update," February 1, 2002; Polly Means to Shaman, "Incompatibility of Real Producer with My Capture Card [#37209781]," February 12, 2002; Shaman to Means, Wheeler, "Incompatibility of Real Producer with My Capture Card [#37209781]," February 12, 2002.

271 WBMs, Shaman to Wheeler, Polly Means, Bowden, "Second System," May 15, 2002; Means to Shaman, "Good News," February 12, 2002; Means to Shaman, "Incompatibility of Real Producer with My Capture Card [#37209781]," February 12, 2002; Shaman to Means, Wheeler, "Incompatibility of Real Producer with My Capture Card [#37209781]," February 12, 2002.

272 WBM, Shaman to Wheeler, "Streaming Streamline Update," February 1, 2002.

273 WBMs, Shaman to Wheeler, Polly Means, Bowden, "Second System," May 15, 2002; Shaman to Wheeler, "Streaming Streamline Update," February 1, 2002; Shaman to

Wheeler, "Digital VCRs," February 7, 2002; Wheeler to Shaman, "Digital VCRs," February 7, 2002.

274 David Hobbs, Forum One, to Shaman, David Witzel, Forum One, "Wireframes and MOU," May 1, 2002; WBM, Shaman to Hobbs, Witzel, "Wireframes and MOU," May 1, 2002; Witzel to Shaman, Wheeler, Hobbs, "Project Planning Meeting," February 13, 2002; Witzel to Wheeler, Shaman, Hobbs, "B-SPAN-aganza," January 20, 2002; WBMs, Shaman to Wheeler, "The Search Thing," January 23, 2002; Wheeler to Shaman, "Friends," January 25, 2002; Shaman to Wheeler, Witzel, no subject (confirms a deal with Forum One to build a knowledge content database for $40K), January 28, 2002.

275 WBMs, Wheeler to Shaman, "Tidbits," May 3, 2001; Lawrence Macdonald to Wheeler, Shaman, "B-SPAN and DEC Policy Seminars, Research Site," January 29, 2001; Macdonald to Wheeler, "DEC and B-SPAN," February 1, 2001, Wheeler to Polly Means, Shaman, "DEC and B-SPAN," February 2, 2001; Shaman to Wheeler, "Spannin'," January 22, 2002; Shaman to Wheeler, "Spinnin'," January 18, 2002; David Witzel, Forum One, to Wheeler, Shaman, David Hobbs, Forum One, "B-SPAN-aganza," January 20, 2002; WBMs, Shaman to Wheeler, "The Search Thing," January 23, 2002; Wheeler to Shaman, "Friends," January 25, 2002; Shaman to Wheeler, Witzel, no subject (confirms a deal with Forum One to build a knowledge content database for $40K), January 28, 2002.

276 WBM, Shaman to Sunetra Puri, "Knowledge Content Management System for B-SPAN," January 31, 2002; David Witzel, Forum One, to Shaman, Wheeler, David Hobbs, Forum One, "TOR for B-SPAN 2002 Efforts," February 8, 2002; David Hobbs, Forum One, to Shaman, Wheeler, "B-SPAN Requirements Spreadsheet," March 5, 2002; Hobbs to Shaman, Wheeler, "Touch Base," February 27, 2002; WBMs, Wheeler to Hobbs, Shaman, "B-SPAN Website," April 22, 2002; Michael Doyle to Shaman, Michele de Nevers, "Request for Information on B-SPAN," April 9, 2002; Daily Luisa Martinez to Shaman, Doyle, "PAYMENT to 'Forum One Communications,' " June 11, 2002.

277 WBMs, Michele de Nevers to Philip Karp, Paul Procee, Wheeler, Shaman, "Converting WBI Teaching Tapes for B-SPAN," November 21, 2001; Wheeler to Shaman, "Converting WBI Teaching Tapes for B-SPAN," November 21, 2001.

278 WBMs, Michele de Nevers to Philip Karp, Wheeler, Shaman, "Trade Seminar on Tuesday, 29th: 'Trade and the Environment: Unmasking the Pollution Haven Effect,' " January 25, 2002; Shaman to de Nevers, Karp, Wheeler, "Trade Seminar on Tuesday, 29th: 'Trade and the Environment: Unmasking the Pollution Haven Effect,' " January 25, 2002; Wheeler to Shaman, "Good Test Case," January 25, 2002; Shaman to Wheeler, "Good Test Case," January 25, 2002.

279 WBMs, Philip Karp to Michele de Nevers, Shaman, "Trade Seminar on Tuesday, 29th: 'Trade and the Environment: Unmasking the Pollution Haven Effect,' " February 27, 2002; Shaman to Wheeler, "Trade Seminar on Tuesday, 29th: 'Trade and the Environment: Unmasking the Pollution Haven Effect,' " February 27, 2002.

280 WBMs, Shaman to Laura de Brular, Robert Chavez, Fallert Kessides, "Video Taping of Urban BBL's," March 1, 2002; Shaman to Lisa Abrams, Gerda Merwald, Jean-March Baissus, Elizabeth Lin, "B-SPAN Availability for International Advisory Council Meeting, March 25-26," March 4, 2002; Shaman to Zenaida Kranzer, Ritva Reinikka, Wheeler, "B-SPAN," February 11, 2002.

281 WBMs, Wheeler to Shaman, "B-SPAN," February 11, 2002; Shaman to Wheeler, "B-SPAN," February 6, 2002.

282 WBM, Shaman to Wheeler, "Yowzah!" March 13, 2002.

283 WBM, Wheeler to Shaman, "Access to New Server," February 27, 2002.

284 WBM, Shaman to Wheeler, "Server Update," February 27, 2002.

285 WBMs, Shaman to Polly Means, David Gray, Chongman Kim, "Access to New Server," February 27, 2002; Kim to Shaman, Gray, Means, "Access to New Server," February 28, 2002; Gray to Kim, Shaman, Means, Charles Schueller, Eric Englemann, Deborah Knight, Nicole Frost, Katie Bannon, "External Video – Server Now Available for Your Use, PLEASE READ," February 28, 2002.

286 WBMs, Shaman to Polly Means, Bowden, "Seven More Tapes: Coming Fast and Furious!" March 11, 2002; Means to Shaman, Bowden, "Six More Tapes," March 12, 2002; Shaman to Wheeler, "Yowzah!" March 13, 2002; Shaman to B-SPAN List, "B-SPAN Newsletter April 2002," April 10, 2002; Shaman to B-SPAN List, "B-SPAN Newsletter (2) April 2002," April 16, 2002; Shaman to B-SPAN List, "Drs. Jeffrey Sachs and Jane Goodall Featured on B-SPAN," April 17, 2002; Shaman to B-SPAN List, "The World Bank's Sustainable Development Month on B-SPAN," April 29, 2002; Shaman to B-SPAN List, "B-SPAN Newsletter, May 2002," May 13, 2002; Shaman to B-SPAN List, "B-SPAN Newsletter, May (2) 2002," May 20, 2002; Shaman to B-SPAN List, "B-SPAN Newsletter, May (3) 2002," May 28, 2002; Shaman to B-SPAN List, "B-SPAN Newsletter, June 2002," June 10, 2002; Means to Shaman, Bowden, "All Tapes Now Awaiting Action/Classification (Five New Today ...)," March 13, 2002; Shaman to Means, "More Tapes Done! I Have Given Them to Nick – Can You Classify Them Please?" March 26, 2002; Shaman to Bowden, "Catching Up," February 28, 2002.

287 WBM, Shaman to Wheeler, "Comments from the Field," May 9, 2002.

288 WBM, Shaman to Wheeler, "Dreamin'," January 31, 2002.

289 WBMs, Wheeler to Shaman, "Hmmm..." December 10, 2001; Shaman to Norman Loayza, "B-SPAN Description," December 10, 2001.

290 WBM, Vesselina Hekimova to Shaman, "Request Re: B-SPAN Link to Biotechnology VC on Jan 24, 2002," March 7, 2002.

291 WBMs, Shaman to Wheeler, "Circlin' in High Society," March 14, 2002; Wheeler to Michele de Nevers, "B-SPAN Gossip," March 14, 2002.

292 WBMs, Wheeler to Shaman, "Whaddya Think?" January 3, 2002; Shaman to Wheeler, "Whaddya Think?" January 3, 2002; Wheeler to Shaman, "2001 (+2?): And Beyond ...the Infinite?" January 25, 2002; Shaman to Wheeler, "2001 (+2?): And Beyond ... the Infinite?" January 25, 2002.

293 WBM, Shaman to Wheeler, "Streaming Streamline Update," February 1, 2002.

294 WBMs, Shaman to Wheeler, Polly Means, "New B-SPAN Acquisitions," April 2, 2002; Shaman to Wheeler, "On The Road," March 6, 2002; Means to Shaman, "Sony DSR 11 DVcam Stuff," March 7, 2002.

295 WBMs, Shaman to B-SPAN List, "B-SPAN Newsletter April 2002," April 10, 2002; Shaman to B-SPAN List, "B-SPAN Newsletter (2) April 2002," April 16, 2002; Shaman to B-SPAN List, "Drs. Jeffrey Sachs and Jane Goodall Featured on B-SPAN," April 17, 2002; Shaman to B-SPAN List, "The World Bank's Sustainable Development Month on B-SPAN," April 29, 2002; Shaman to B-SPAN List, "B-SPAN Newsletter May 2002," May 13, 2002; Shaman to B-SPAN List, "B-SPAN Newsletter May (2) 2002," May 20, 2002; Shaman to B-SPAN List, "B-SPAN Newsletter May (3) 2002," May 28, 2002.

296 Jay Henderson, U.S. Voice of America, to Shaman, "B-SPAN Newsletter April 2002," April 11, 2002; WBM, Shaman to Henderson, "B-SPAN Newsletter April 2002," April 11, 2002.

297 WBMs, Valentina Kalk to Shaman, "B-SPAN," April 22, 2002; Shaman to Kalk, Wheeler, "B-SPAN," April 22, 2002.

298 WBM, Wheeler to Shaman, "De Span," June 6, 2002.

299 WBM, Wheeler to Michele de Nevers, "B-SPAN Traffic Stats," May 10, 2002.

300 Neena Jacob, Indev, The British Council, "B-SPAN Newsletter, January 2001," February 7, 2001; WBM, Shaman to Wheeler, "Comments from the Field," May 9, 2002.

301 Vikas Nath, KnowNet Initiative, London School of Economics, "B-SPAN Newsletter, March 2001," March 2, 2001; WBM, Shaman to Wheeler, "Comments from the Field," May 9, 2002.
302 Lisa Bore, LakeNet/Monitor International, "B-SPAN Newsletter, November 2001," November 26, 2001; WBM, Shaman to Wheeler, "Comments from the Field," May 9, 2002.
303 Shola Aboderin, Africa Virtual Library, to Shaman, "B-SPAN Newsletter, February 2002," February 7, 2002; WBM, Shaman to Wheeler, "Comments from the Field," May 9, 2002.
304 Shaba Tabazoli to Shaman, "B-SPAN Newsletter, April 2002," April 18, 2002; WBM, Shaman to Wheeler, "Comments from the Field," May 9, 2002.
305 WBMs, Shaman to Wheeler, "B-SPAN Traffic Stats," May 20, 2002; Shaman to Wheeler, "B-SPAN Traffic by Country/Region," May 22, 2002.
306 WBMs, Wheeler to Shaman, "B-SPAN TOR," May 8, 2002; Michele de Nevers to Shaman, Wheeler, "Re: [tech.cid] Seminar: Novel Experiments in Global Governance for Sustainable Development," May 7, 2002; Shaman to Wheeler, "B-SPAN TOR," April 15, 2002; Shaman to Wheeler, "ID Update," June 13, 2002; Wheeler to Shaman, "ID Update," June 13, 2002; Wheeler to de Nevers, "TOR for B-SPAN Fixed-Term," April 18, 2002; Wheeler to Shaman, "TOR for B-SPAN Fixed-Term," April 18, 2002; Wheeler to Frannie Leautier, "Thanks," April 18, 2002; Wheeler to Shaman, "Stayin' on the Case," April 18, 2002; de Nevers to Wheeler, Shaman, "TOR for B-SPAN Fixed-Term," April 25, 2002; Wheeler to Shaman, "Way Cool," April 12, 2002.
307 WBM, Dina Abu-Ghaida to Shaman, "Maddrassas BBL," April 25, 2002.
308 WBM, Shaman to Dina Abu-Ghaida, "Maddrassas BBL," April 25, 2002.
309 WBMs, Dina Abu-Ghaida to Shaman, "Maddrassas BBL," April 25, 2002; Shaman to B-SPAN List, "B-SAN Newsletter May (3) 2002," May 28, 2002; Shaman to Polly Means, "New Homepage for B-SPAN," May 29, 2002.
310 WBM, Shaman to B-SPAN List, "The World Bank's Sustainable Development Month on B-SPAN," April 29, 2002.
311 WBM, Shaman to B-SPAN List, "The World Bank's Sustainable Development Month on B-SPAN," April 29, 2002.
312 WBM, Shaman to B-SPAN List, "The World Bank's Sustainable Development Month on B-SPAN," April 29, 2002.
313 WBMs, Shaman to B-SPAN List, "The World Bank's Sustainable Development Month on B-SPAN," April 29, 2002; Shaman to B-SPAN List, "Drs. Jeffrey Sachs and Jane Goodall Featured on B-SPAN," April 17, 2002; Timoteo Dar Juan to Shaman, "Jane Goodall Video," May 21, 2002.
314 WBMs, Shaman to B-SPAN List, "The World Bank's Sustainable Development Month on B-SPAN," April 29, 2002; Shaman to Polly Means, "Summary of a Presentation by Maurice Strong," April 29, 2002.
315 WBM, Shaman to B-SPAN List, "B-SPAN Newsletter May (3), 2002," May 28, 2002.
316 WBMs, Bowden to Shaman, "Quote from Oden Knudson's Interview in Internal Communication's Yesterday," April 26, 2002; Shaman to B-SPAN List, "The World Bank's Sustainable Development Month on B-SPAN," April 29, 2002; Shaman to B-SPAN List, "Drs. Jeffrey Sachs and Jane Goodall Featured on B-SPAN," April 17, 2002; Shaman to Polly Means, "Summary for the Economics of Sustainability: An Address by Dr. Jeffrey Sachs," April 17, 2002; Shaman to Means, "New B-SPAN Front Page," April 17, 2002.
317 WBM, Wheeler to Shaman, "Sachs n de Span," April 18, 2002.
318 WBM, Wheeler to Frannie Leautier, "Thanks," April 18, 2002.
319 WBM, Frannie Leautier to Wheeler, "Thanks," April 18, 2002.
320 WBM, Wheeler to Shaman, Bowden, Polly Means, "The Greatest," April 18, 2002.

321 WBMs, Chongman Kim to Shaman, "Video Server Cost," April 18, 2002; Shaman to Kim, Wheeler, "Video Server Cost," May 3, 2002.
322 WBM, Shaman to Wheeler, "Server Issues and Options," May 31, 2002.
323 WBMs, Shaman to Chongman Kim, Wheeler, "Dedicated Server for B-SPAN," June 6, 2002; Shaman to Wheeler, "Da Chong Man!" June 24, 2002.
324 WBMs, Shaman to Chongman Kim, Wheeler, "Dedicated Server for B-SPAN," June 6, 2002; Shaman to Wheeler, "Da Chong Man!" June 24, 2002.
325 David Hobbs, Forum One, to Shaman, Wheeler, "Touch Base," February 27, 2002; Hobbs to Shaman, Wheeler, "B-SPAN Invoice," March 4, 2002; WBMs, Wheeler to Shaman, "Sony DSR 11 DVcam Stuff," March 7, 2002; Shaman to Wheeler, "Sony DSR 11 DVcam Stuff," March 7, 2002.
326 David Witzel, Forum One, to Wheeler, David Hobbs, Forum One, Shaman, "B-SPAN Next Steps," March 18, 2002; WBM, Wheeler to Witzel, Hobbs, Shaman, "B-SPAN Next Steps," March 18, 2002; Hobbs to Shaman, Wheeler, "B-SPAN Website," April 19, 2002.
327 David Hobbs, Forum One, to Shaman, "B-SPAN Site Walk Through," May 23, 2002; WBM, Shaman to Hobbs, "B-SPAN Site Walk Through," May 20, 2002; Hobbs to Shaman, "B-SPAN Next Steps," June 10, 2002; Shaman to Hobbs, Bowden, Polly Means, Wheeler, "B-SPAN Next Steps," June 11, 2002.
328 Tim Shaw, Forum One, to Shaman, David Hobbs, Forum One, "Survey Questions," June 11, 2002.
329 WBM, Shaman to Wheeler, "Survey Questions," June 12, 2002.
330 WBM, Lawrence Macdonald to Shaman, "NIPR Subscription Number?" June 12, 2002.
331 WBMs, Shaman to Lawrence Macdonald, "NIPR Subscription Number?" June 12, 2002; WBM, Shaman to Wheeler, "NIPR Subscription Number?" June 12, 2002; Wheeler to Michele de Nevers, "Shaman's on the Case," June 12, 2002.
332 Samuel Paul, Public Affairs Centre, Bangalore, to Shekhar Shah, "Brown Bag Invitation, Do Public Services Get to the Public? India's Public Services at the Start of the Millennium," April 30, 2002; WBM, Shah to Shaman, "Video Interview with Sam Paul on the Millennium Strategy," May 1, 2002.
333 WBM, Shaman to Shekhar Shah, Salma Sulemanji, "B-SPAN and Dr. Paul," June 11, 2002.
334 WBMs, Veit Burger to Michele de Nevers, Philip Karp, Claude Salem, "Re: [tech.cid] Seminar: Novel Experiments in Global Governance for Sustainable Development," May 7, 2002; Burger to Shaman, "B-SPAN Newsletter, April 2002," April 11, 2002; Burger to Shaman, Chantal Dejou, Shawki Barghouti, Claude Salem, "Taping of Braverman," November 13, 2001.
335 WBM, Veit Burger to David Mikosz, Devrin David Weiss, Elena Karaban, Aslan Sarinzhipov, Vera Wilhelm, Gulmira Mchale, Gary Fine, Michele de Nevers, Claude Salem, Monika Weber-Fahr, Shaman, "Basic Question on B-SPAN," February 4, 2003; Claude Salem to Extended Distance Learning Center List, Philip Karp, Monika Weber-Fahr, John Middleton, Shaman, Maria Jesus Calvo Romerales, Veit Burger, Laurent Porte, Prita Chatroth, Mwangi Wachira, Kofi Anani, Marilyne Yaguibou, Bari Rabin, "Cooperation Between GDLN and the B-SPAN Resource Base," May 28, 2002; Salem to Karp, Weber-Fahr, Middleton, Shaman, Romerales, Burger, Porte, Chatroth, Wachira, Anani, Yaguibou, Rabin, "GDLN and B-SPAN: Some Preliminary Thoughts for Discussion," May 23, 2002; Salem to Burger, Shaman, de Nevers, Weber-Fahr, Karp, Middleton, Romerales, Burger, Porte, Chatroth, Wachira, Anani, Yaguibou, Rabin, "Uses of B-SPAN in Developing DLC 'Attentive Publics,' " June 11, 2002; Shaman to Wheeler, "Uses of B-SPAN in Developing DLC 'Attentive Publics,' " June 11, 2002.

336 WBMs, Lawrence Macdonald to Julius Warmey, "Note to Internal Communications on June 28 Stiglitz Book Launch," June 21, 2002; Macdonald to Guy Brussat, Shaman, "Re; Stiglitz Book Launch – Draft Kiosk Announcement," June 19, 2002.
337 WBMs, Lawrence Macdonald to Shaman, "Re; Stiglitz Book Launch Draft Kiosk Announcement," June 19, 2002; Macdonald to Guy Brussat, Shaman, William Murray, International Monetary Fund, "IMF Contact for Stiglitz Video Feed," June 20, 2002.
338 WBM, Shaman to B-SPAN List, "B-SPAN Newsletter, July 2002," July 11, 2002.
339 "Introductory Remarks to Discussion with Joseph Stiglitz on Globalization and Its Discontents" by Kenneth Rogoff, Economic Counselor and Director of Research, Internet Monetary Fund, June 28, 2002, As Prepared for Delivery; WBM, Ralf Juan Leiteritz to Zlatina Loudjeva, Jonathan Maack, Annika Silva-Leander, Clara Brillembourg, "Rogoff on Stiglitz," July 3, 2002.
340 Memorandum, Shaman to Wheeler, "Issues Surrounding B-SPAN's Webcast of the Stiglitz-Rogoff Debate," July 1, 2002.
341 Memorandum, Shaman to Wheeler, "Issues Surrounding B-SPAN's Webcast of the Stiglitz-Rogoff Debate," July 1, 2002; William Murray, International Monetary Fund, Lawrence Macdonald to Guy Brussat, Shaman, "IMF Contact for Stiglitz Video Feed," June 21, 2002.
342 WBMs, Lawrence Macdonald to Shaman, Polly Means, "Siglitz-Rogoff ETA?" July 1, 2002; Shaman to Macdonald, Means, Wheeler, "Siglitz-Rogoff ETA?" July 1, 2002; Macdonald to Extended List, "Stiglitz-Rogoff Discussion Now On-line for Bank Staff," July 1, 2002.
343 "Joseph Stiglitz and Kenneth Rogoff Discuss 'Globalization and Its Discontents,'" *Bank's World Today*, July 1, 2002.
344 –"IMF Economist Assails Author of Critical Book," *Washington Post*, July 2, 2002.
345 WBMs, Jeff McCoy to Shaman, Melissa Knutson, "Link to Stiglitz Discussion," July 2, 2002; Wheeler to DECRG-IE, "Interesting Stuff …" July 2, 2002; Wheeler to Shaman, Polly Means, Bowden, "Right On!" July 2, 2002.
346 "Top Economists Engage in Bickering," *Financial Times*, July 3, 2002.
347 WBM, Wheeler to Shaman, Lawrence Macdonald, Bowden, Polly Means, "*The Financial Times* Didn't Waste Any Time," July 2, 2002.
348 WBM, Shaman to Diana Shaman, "Another Win," July 2, 2002.
349 WBM, Michael Walton to CULTURE, CDD Group Extended 1, CDD Group Extended 2, Urban Staff, Carol Archambault, Brown University, Vijayendra Rao, "Invitation to Conference on Culture and Public Action," June 5, 2002.
350 WBMs, Vijayendra Rao to Wheeler, Michael Walton, Carol Archambault, Brown University, "B-SPAN," May 29, 2002; Wheeler to Rao, Walton, Archambault, Shaman, "B-SPAN," May 29, 2002.
351 WBM, Martin Ravallion to Wheeler, Vijayendra Rao, Jeffrey Hammer, "Edit of Jeff Hammer's Remark About George Bush," July 8, 2002.
352 WBM, Martin Ravallion to Wheeler, Vijayendra Rao, Jeffrey Hammer, "Edit of Jeff Hammer's Remark About George Bush," July 8, 2002.
353 WBM, Shaman to Vijayendra Rao, Wheeler, "B-SPAN Operating Principles," July 8, 2002.
354 WBM, Martin Ravallion to Wheeler, Vijayendra Rao, Jeffrey Hammer, "Edit of Jeff Hammer's Remark About George Bush," July 8, 2002.
355 WBM, Wheeler to Martin Ravallion, Vijayendra Rao, Jeffrey Hammer, Blind Copy to Shaman, "Edit of Jeff Hammer's Remark About George Bush," July 8, 2002.
356 WBM, Martin Ravallion to Wheeler, "Edit of Jeff Hammer's Remark About George Bush," July 8, 2002.
357 WBMs, Wheeler to Frannie Leautier, "Urgent B-SPAN Policy Issue," July 9, 2002; Wheeler to Shaman, "I Pre-empted," July 9, 2002.

358 WBM, Frannie Leautier to Wheeler, "Urgent B-SPAN Policy Issue," July 9, 2002.
359 Wheeler to Shaman, "The Word from Frannie Leautier," July 9, 2002.
360 WBMs, Wheeler to Martin Ravallion, "Culture Conference," July 18, 2002; Wheeler to Shaman, "Too Sweet," July 18, 2002; Shaman to Wheeler, "Too Sweet," July 18, 2002.
361 WBM, Vijayendra Rao to Shaman, Wheeler, Michael Walton, Carol Archambault, Brown University, "Culture Conference," July 15, 2002.
362 WBMs, Vijayendra Rao to Shaman, Carol Archambault, Brown University, Wheeler, Michael Walton, Polly Means, Jeffrey Hammer, "Culture Conference," July 17, 2002; Shaman to Rao, Archambault, Wheeler, Walton, Means, Hammer, "Culture Conference," July 17, 2002.
363 WBM, Bruno Laporte to Shaman, Wheeler, "Quick Question," May 29, 2002.
364 WBM, Wheeler to Shaman, Bowden, Polly Means, "Key B-SPAN Meeting with WBI Folks," June 28, 2002.

PART 4 — RED SKY IN MORNING, SAILOR'S WARNING

1 WBM, Wheeler to Bruno Laporte, Andrei Tolstopiatenko, Carol Evangelista, Shaman, Polly Means, Bowden, "Confirmation Re: B-SPAN Budget and Meeting – July 3, 10:00 am, J 2-131," July 2, 2002.
2 WBM, Shaman to Wheeler, "JVC Streamcorder," July 18, 2002.
3 WBM, Wheeler to Shaman, "JVC Streamcorder," July 19, 2002.
4 WMB, Wheeler to Michele de Nevers, "B-SPAN Payments," July 19, 2002.
5 WBM, Andrei Tolstopiatenko to Shaman, "Webstats and Meeting," July 15, 2002.
6 "Meet Andrei V. Tolstopiatenko," "People," *World Bank Group Directory,* World Bank Intranet.
7 WBMs, Shaman to Wheeler, "Tuesday Meeting with WBI Folks," July 30, 2002; Andrei Tolstopiatenko to Hector Montenegro, Patrick Tse, Dickson Tang, Arseny Malov, Sheila Jagannathan, Shaman, Bowden, Maureen Miller, "B-SPAN Draft WP," July 18, 2002.
8 WBM, Shaman to Hector Montenegro, Dickson Tang, Patrick Tse, Polly Means, Andrei Tolstopiatenko, "Digitizing for B-SPAN," July 18, 2002.
9 WBMs, Shaman to Wheeler, "For Everything Else, There's MasterCard ...," July 24, 2002; Shaman to Bruno Laporte, Andrei Tolstopiatenko, "BCC – Wheeler, More Comments on B-SPAN," July 26, 2002.
10 WBM, Shaman to Andrei Tolstopiatenko, "Meeting," July 17, 2002.
11 WBM, Sabina Alkire to Shaman, "De Soto," March 27, 2002.
12 WBMs, Lawrence Macdonald to Shaman, Wheeler, "Hernando de Soto – and B-SPAN Home Page – Congrats," July 15, 2002; Wheeler to Shaman, "de Soto on B-SPAN," July 17, 2002; Shaman to Wheeler, "de Soto on B-SPAN," July 17, 2002.
13 WBMs, Shaman to Lee Morrison, "Hernando de Soto Video on B-SPAN Now," July 18, 2002; Shaman to Polly Means, "Summary of 'The Mystery of Capital: Why Capitalism Triumphs in the West and Fails Everywhere Else, A Discussion with Hernando de Soto,'" July 19, 2002; World Bank Internal Communications, "Staff Discuss 'Mystery of Capital' with Hernando de Soto," July 24, 2002.
14 WBM, Shaman to Andrei Tolstopiatenko, Bowden, Hector Montenegro, Dickson Tang, Patrick Tse, "Video Server," July 18, 2002.
15 WBM, Andrei Tolstopiatenko to Shaman, Bowden, Hector Montenegro, Dickson Tang, Patrick Tse, "Video Server," July 18, 2002.
16 WBM, Andrei Tolstopiatenko to Shaman, Patrick Tse, Hector Montenegro, Dickson Tang, Bowden, "B-SPAN Meeting on Thursday at 11 am," July 17, 2002.
17 David Hobbs, Forum One, to Andrei Tolstopiatenko, Shaman, J. Roberts, Forum One, David Witzel, Forum One, "[Fwd: More B-SPAN Site Info]," November 1, 2002; Hobbs to Tolstopiatenko, Shaman, Roberts, Witzel, "B-SPAN Handoff," October 28, 2002; WBM, Tolstopiatenko to Hobbs, Shaman, Roberts, Witzel, "B-SPAN Handoff,"

October 28, 2002; Patrick Tse to Bowden, "FYI," September 3, 2002; Bowden to Shaman, Wheeler, "FYI," September 3, 2002.

18 WBM, Andrei Tolstopiatenko to Hector Montenegro, Patrick Tse, Dickson Tang, Arseny Malov, Sheila Jagannathan, Shaman, Bowden, Maureen Miller, "B-SPAN Draft WP," July 18, 2002.

19 WBM, Shaman to Wheeler, "B-SPAN Draft WP," July 19, 2002.

20 WBM, Shaman to Bruno Laporte, Andrei Tolstopiatenko, Bowden, "Comments on B-SPAN," July 19, 2002.

21 WBMs, Jonathan Maack to Shaman, "Thanks for Posting the Stiglitz-Rogoff Discussion," July 22, 2002; Shaman to Maack, "Thanks for Posting the Stiglitz-Rogoff Discussion," July 22, 2002.

22 WBM, Shaman to Andrei Tolstopiatenko, Bruno Laporte, "Thanks for Posting the Stiglitz-Rogoff Discussion," July 22, 2002.

23 WBM, Andrei Tolstopiatenko to Shaman, Bruno Laporte, Bowden, "de Soto on B-SPAN," July 22, 2002.

24 WBMs, Wheeler to Michele de Nevers, "BCC – Shaman, For Everything Else, There's Mastercard, "July 22, 2002; Wheeler to Shaman, "It's All Good ..." July 23, 2002.

25 WBM, Bruno Laporte to Extended List, "Knowledge and Learning Services Retreat," July 1, 2002.

26 WBMs, Bruno Laporte to Extended List, "Knowledge and Learning Services Retreat," July 1, 2002; Laporte to Extended List, "July 23 WBIKL Retreat," July 9, 2002.

27 WBMs, Bruno Laporte to Extended List, "July 23 WBIKL Retreat," July 9, 2002; Shaman to Bowden, "July 23 WBIKL Retreat," July 9, 2002.

28 "Shaman Remarks at WBIKL Retreat," July 23, 2002; WBM, Shaman to Wheeler, "It's All Good ..." July 24, 2002.

29 WBMs, Shaman to Evija Vestergaard, Bowden, "B-SPAN Note," July 26, 2002; Shaman to Beatrice Warmey, Bowden, "B-SPAN Note," July 26, 2002; Shaman to Maureen Miller, Bowden, "B-SPAN Note," July 26, 2002.

30 WBM, Shaman to Wheeler, "It's All Good ..." July 24, 2002.

31 WBM, Bruno Laporte to Carol Evangelista, Karin Millet, Michele de Nevers, Wheeler, "Meeting on B-SPAN," July 24, 2002.

32 WBMs, Karin Millet to Michele de Nevers, Bruno Laporte, "B-SPAN," July 24, 2002; Laporte to Millet, de Nevers, "Andrei Tolstopiatenko," July 24, 2002.

33 WBM, Shaman to Wheeler, "B-SPAN," July 25, 2002.

34 WBM, Bruno Laporte to Carole Evangelista, Karin Millet, Michele de Nevers, Wheeler, "Meeting on B-SPAN," July 24, 2002; Wheeler to Shaman, Bowden, Polly Means, "First Meeting on B-SPAN Advisory Committee," August 28, 2002.

35 WBMs, Andrei Tolstopiatenko to Bruno Laporte, Michele de Nevers, Karin Millet, "B-SPAN," July 24, 2002; Shaman to Wheeler, "B-SPAN," July 24, 2002.

36 WBMs, Shaman to Wheeler, "Tuesday Meeting with WBI Folks," July 30, 2002; Andrei Tolstopiatenko to Bowden, Sheila Jagannathan, Maureen Miller, Hector Montenegro, Shaman, Dickson Tang, Patrick Tse, Bruno Laporte, "B-SPAN: July 31 Meeting Notes," August 5, 2002; Tolstopiatenko to I Team, "Current Draft of PDS for Comments and Suggestions," July 31, 2002; WBM, Tolstopiatenko to Shaman, Laporte, Bowden, "B-SPAN Draft Work Program," August 5, 2002; Bowden to Shaman, "On Short Notice," September 17, 2002.

37 WBMs, Shaman to Wheeler, "Tuesday Meeting with WBI Folks," July 30, 2002; Shaman to Wheeler, "Critical Juncture," August 2, 2002; Andrei Tolstopiatenko to Bowden, Sheila Jagannathan, Maureen Miller, Hector Montenegro, Shaman, Dickson Tang, Patrick Tse, Bruno Laporte, "B-SPAN: July 31 Meeting Notes," August 5, 2002; WBM, Tolstopiatenko to Shaman, aporte, Bowden, "B-SPAN Draft Work Program," August 5, 2002.

38 WBM, Shaman to Wheeler, "Tuesday Meeting with WBI Folks," July 30, 2002.

39 WBM, Shaman to Wheeler, "Tuesday Meeting with WBI Folks," July 30, 2002.
40 WBM, Shaman to Wheeler, "Tuesday Meeting with WBI Folks," July 30, 2002.
41 WBMs, Shaman to Wheeler, "Critical Juncture," August 2, 2002; Andrei Tolstopiatenko to Bowden, Sheila Jagannathan, Maureen Miller, Hector Montenegro, Shaman, Dickson Tang, Patrick Tse, Bruno Laporte, "B-SPAN: July 31 Meeting Notes," August 5, 2002.
42 WBMs, Shaman to Wheeler, "Critical Juncture," August 2, 2002; Andrei Tolstopiatenko to Bowden, Sheila Jagannathan, Maureen Miller, Hector Montenegro, Shaman, Dickson Tang, Patrick Tse, Bruno Laporte, "B-SPAN: July 31 Meeting Notes," August 5, 2002.
43 WBM, Shaman to Andrei Tolstopiatenko, Bruno Laporte, Bowden, "B-SPAN Draft Work Program," August 5, 2002.
44 WBMs, Wheeler to Shaman, Bowden, "Powerpoints on B-SPAN," November 22, 2001; Shaman to Wheeler, Bowden, "Powerpoints on B-SPAN," November 22, 2001; Polly Means to Shaman, "NBFI Pages," September 6, 2001; Shaman to Wei Zhang, Michael Pomerleano, Demet Cabbar, Wheeler, Means, Ken Kenworthy, Knowledge Realm, "NBFI Conference," September 6, 2001; Wheeler to Daniel Kaufmann, Michele de Nevers, Shaman, "Streaming the Governance Series," March 29, 2001; Means to Wheeler, "Governance and B-SPAN," March 14, 2001; Wheeler to Kaufmann, Shaman, de Nevers, Martin Getzendanner, Means, "Governance and B-SPAN," March 14, 2001.
45 WBM, Shaman to Polly Means, Bowden, BCC – Wheeler, "Indexing of Home Page Tapes," November 27, 2002.
46 WBM, Shaman to Bruno Laporte, "Upcoming Issues for B-SPAN," September 20, 2002.
47 WBM, Shaman to Wheeler, "Re: FEEDBACK FROM K4D FORUM FOR MENA, MARSEILLES, SEPT," October 10, 2002.
48 WBM, Andrei Tolstopiatenko to Shaman, Bruno Laporte, Bowden, "B-SPAN Draft Work Program," August 5, 2002.
49 Shaman Memorandum, "Yes and No," August 9, 2002.
50 WBM, Shaman to Andrei Tolstopiatenko, Bruno Laporte, Bowden, Dickson Tang, Patrick Tse, Hector Montenegro, BCC – Wheeler, "B-SPAN Draft Work Program," August 13, 2002.
51 WBMs, Bowden to Wheeler, Shaman, "A Ray of Hope," August 13, 2002; Shaman to Wheeler, Bowden, "A Ray of Hope," August 13, 2002.
52 WBMs, Bowden to Wheeler, "How Convenient Postscript," August 14, 2002; Andrei Tolstopiatenko to I Team, "Weekly I Team Meeting – Tuesday, August 30, – 10:00 a.m. – J-2-160," August 19, 2002; Bowden to Wheeler, Shaman, "Meeting with Karin Millet," August 20, 2002.
53 WBMs, Bowden to Wheeler, Shaman, "Updated WBI Web Statistics Site with Reports for July!" August 19, 2002.
54 WBM, Wheeler to Shaman, Bowden, Polly Means, "First Meeting with B-SPAN Advisory Committee," August 28, 2002.
55 WBM, Wheeler to Michele de Nevers, "Welcome Back!" August 29, 2002.
56 WBM, Bruno Laporte to Shaman, Carol Evangelista, "Coffee," September 6, 2002.
57 WBMs, Andrei Tolstopiatenko to Shaman, "Reminder: Results Agreement," November 4, 2002; Shaman to Tolstopiatenko, "Reminder: Results Agreement," April 22, 2003; Shaman to Andrei Tolstopiatenko, "Reminder: Results Agreement," October 21, 2002; Tolstopiatenko to I Team, "Results Agreement," August 14, 2002; Shaman to Tolstopiatenko, "Results Agreement," September 10, 2002.
58 WBMs, Bowden to Wheeler, Shaman, "Performance Assessment," September 2, 2002; Bowden to Shaman, "Justify Your Existence: Performance Assessment," September

4, 2002; Shaman to Andrei Tolstopiatenko, "Performance Assessment," September 6, 2002.

59 WBM, Shaman to Andrei Tolstopiatenko, Bruno Laporte, BCC – Bowden, Wheeler, "B-SPAN Follow Up," September, 17, 2002.

60 WBM, Shaman to I Team, "B-SPAN Draft Work Program," September 9, 2002.

61 WBM, Patrick Tse to I Team, "Video on Demand (VoD) is Ready for Testing," January 27, 2003.

62 WBM, Shaman to Andrei Tolstopiatenko, Bruno Laporte, BCC – Bowden, Wheeler, "B-SPAN Follow Up," September, 17, 2002.

63 WBM – Shaman to Bowden, Jennifer Vito, Viktor Soukhanov, Wheeler, Polly Means, "B-SPAN Training," September 17, 2001.

64 WBM, Shaman to Andrei Tolstopiatenko, Bruno Laporte, BCC – Bowden, Wheeler, "B-SPAN Follow Up," September, 17, 2002.

65 "Meet Bruno Andre Laporte!" "People," *World Bank Group Directory*, World Bank Intranet.

66 WBMs, Shaman to I Team, Bruno Laporte, "B-SPAN Traffic Update," September 11, 2002; Wheeler to Michele de Nevers, "Up, Up and Away …" September 12, 2002; Bowden to Shaman, Wheeler, Opps, "These Are the Numbers for July: Food for Thought," September 18, 2002.

67 WBMs, Shaman to I Team, Bruno Laporte, "B-SPAN Traffic Update," September 11, 2002; Wheeler to Michele de Nevers, "Up, Up and Away …" September 12, 2002; Bowden to Shaman, Wheeler, Opps, "These Are the Numbers for July: Food for Thought," September 18, 2002.

68 WBM, Bruno Laporte to Shaman, I Team, "B-SPAN Traffic Update," September 11, 2002.

69 WBM, Shaman to Bruno Laporte, "Upcoming Issues for B-SPAN," September 20, 2002.

70 WBM, Andrei Tolstopiatenko to Shaman, Bowden, Patrick Tse, Hector Montenegro, Sheila Jagannathan, Maureen Miller, Dickson Tang, "Meeting on Monday," September 18, 2002.

71 WBMs, Hector Montenegro to Shaman, Bowden, Dickson Tang, Maureen Miller, Patrick Tse, Sheila Jagannathan, Andrei Tolstopiatenko, Bruno Laporte, "B-SPAN Statistics," September 23, 2002; Veaceslav Revutchi to Tolstopiatenko, Montenegro, Tse, Larissa Fastovsky, "Standard FTP Available on WBWebcast Machines," September 29, 2002.

72 WBM, Andrei Tolstopiatenko to Veaceslav Revutchi, ISGGC, Hector Montenegro, Patrick Tse, "Standard FTP Available on WBWebcast Machines," September 29, 2002.

73 WBM, Shaman to B-SPAN List, "B-SPAN Newsletter, September 2002," September 16, 2002.

74 WBM, Edith Wilson to Richard Uku, Bruno Laporte, Caroline Anstey, Cecilia Verzosa, Sunetra Puri, Maya Brahmam, Angelica Silvero, "World Bank Symposium on 'Commanding Heights' w/ D Yergin," July 5, 2002.

75 WBMs, Bruno Laporte to Edith Wilson, Richard Uku, Caroline Anstey, Cecilia Verzosa, Sunetra Puri, Maya Brahmam, Angelica Silvero, Shaman, "World Bank Symposium on 'Commanding Heights' w/ D Yergin," July 5, 2002; Shaman to Laporte, Wilson, Uku, Anstey, Verzosa, Puri, Brahmam, Silvero, BCC – Wheeler, "World Bank Symposium on 'Commanding Heights' w/ D Yergin," July 5, 2002; Patricia Overend to Wilson, Brahmam, Silvero, "Videotaping, Streaming, B-SPAN, etc., for 'Commanding Heights,' " September 16, 2002; Shaman to Laporte, Tolstopiatenko, Bowden, BCC – Wheeler, " 'Commanding Heights,' " September 19, 2002.

76 WBM, Sefik Cardak to Shaman, Clovis Fantinelli, "no subject (Cardak apologies for technical difficulties that made Commanding Heights video of poor quality)," September 18, 2002; Shaman to Bruno Laporte, Andrei Tolstopiatenko, Bowden, BCC – Wheeler, " 'Commanding Heights,' " September 19, 2002.
77 WBMs, Bruno Laporte to WBIKL Staff, " 'Commanding Heights: The Battle for the World Economy,' Wednesday, September 18, H Auditorium from 1:00 – 3:00 p.m.," September 17, 2002; Shaman to Daniel Yergin, CERA, Nicholas Stern, Nemat Shafik, Mats Karlsson, Edith Wilson, Frannie Leautier, B. Genier, CERA, K. Graves, CERA, Laporte, Maya Brahmam, Patricia Overend, Angelica Silvero, Cecilia Verzosa, Richar Uku, Lawrence Macdonald, Caroline Anstey, Damien Milverton, Ana Luna Barros, Ron Kim, Andrei Tolstopiatenko, Nick Van Praag, Sunetra Puri, Guy Brussat, Claude Salem, Veit Burger, Bonnie Bradford, Paul Mitchell, Bowden, Polly Means, Jennifer Vito, Sefik Cardak, Clovis Fantinelli, Ira Chalphin, Kathy Sheram, " 'Commanding Heights' Now Online at B-SPAN," September 19, 2002.
78 WBM, Bruno Laporte to Shaman, Andrei Tolstopiatenko, "URGENT: 'Commanding Heights,' " September 19, 2002.
79 WBM, Andrei Tolstopiatenko to Shaman, Bruno Laporte, Bowden, " 'Commanding Heights' Now Online at B-SPAN," September 19, 2002.
80 WBMs, Edith Wilson to Shaman, Ira Chalphin, Daniel Yergin, "!!!! Re: 'Commanding Heights' Now Online at B-SPAN," September 19, 2002; Shaman to Wilson, Chalphin, Yergin, Bruno Laporte, Bowden, Polly Means, BCC – Wheeler, "!!!! Re: 'Commanding Heights' Now Online at B-SPAN," September 19, 2002; Shaman to Andrei Tolstopiatenko, "Lunch," September 19, 2002.
81 WBMs, Shaman to Bruno Laporte, Andrei Tolstopiatenko, Bowden, BCC – Wheeler, " 'Commanding Heights,' " September 19, 2002; Shaman to Peter Midgley, Dany Jones, Katherine Fishburne, "Camera Guidelines," September 19, 2002.
82 WBMs, Shaman to Bruno Laporte, "On Short Notice," September 17, 2002; Laporte to Andrei Tolstopiatenko, Shaman, Ron Kim, "On Short Notice," September 17, 2002.
83 WBM, Peter Midgley to Shaman, Dany Jones, Katherine Fishburne, "Camera Guidelines," September 20, 2002.
84 WBMs, Shaman to Bruno Laporte, Andrei Tolstopiatenko, Bowden, " 'Commanding Heights' Update (Two)," September 20, 2002; Tolstopiatenko to Shaman, Laporte, Tolstopiatenko, Bowden, " 'Commanding Heights' Update (Two)," September 20, 2002; Shaman to Laporte, Tolstopiatenko, Bowden, " 'Commanding Heights' Update," September 20, 2002.
85 WBM, Sefik Cardak to Shaman, Clovis Fantinelli, "Video Recording," September 20, 2002.
86 WBM, Bruno Laporte to Shaman, Andrei Tolstopiatenko, Bowden, " 'Commanding Heights' Update (Two)," September 20, 2002.
87 WBM, Bruno Laporte to Shaman, Andrei Tolstopiatenko, Bowden, " 'Commanding Heights' Update (Two)," September 20, 2002.
88 WBM, Hector Montenegro to Shaman, Bowden, Dickson Tang, Maureen Miller, Patrick Tse, Sheila Jagannathan, Andrei Tolstopiatenko, Bruno Laporte, "B-SPAN Statistics," September 23, 2002.
89 WBM, Shaman to Andrei Tolstopiatenko, Hector Montenegro, "Draft Survey Questions," September 24, 2002.
90 WBM, Shaman to Andrei Tolstopiatenko, Hector Montenegro, "Draft Camera Guidelines," September 25, 2002.
91 WBM, Polly Means to Shaman, Bowden, "Our Video Output," September 24, 2002.
92 WBM, Polly Means to Shaman, Bowden, "Sigh ..." September 25, 2002.
93 WBM, Shaman to Andrei Tolstopiatenko, Bruno Laporte, Hector Montenegro, Dickson Tang, Maureen Miller, Sheila Jagannathan, Bowden, Patrick Tse, "Our Video Output," September 24, 2002.

94 WBM, Andrei Tolstopiatenko to Shaman, Bruno Laporte, Hector Montenegro, Dickson Tang, Maureen Miller, Sheila Jagannathan, Bowden, Patrick Tse, "Our Video Output," September 24, 2002.

95 WBMs, Polly Means to Shaman, "Our Video Output," September 25, 2002; Andrei Tolstopiatenko to Shaman, Bruno Laporte, Hector Montenegro, Dickson Tang, Maureen Miller, Sheila Jagannathan, Bowden, Patrick Tse, "Our Video Output," September 24, 2002.

96 WBM, Andrei Tolstopiatenko to Shaman, Bowden, "Power Points," October 7, 2002.

97 WBM, Polly Means to Shaman, Bowden, "Over Hearing Hector with Bowden," October 8, 2002.

98 WBMs, Shaman to B-SPAN List, "B-SPAN Newsletter," October 29, 2002; Shaman to Polly Means, "Summary of What Will Make Countries Rich or Poor? A Discussion with Jared Diamond, Author of 'Guns, Germs and Steel: The Fate of Human Societies,'" December 5, 2002; Shaman to Means, "New Cover Page," October 24, 2002; Shaman to Extended List, "Your Conference on Poverty Day 2002 is Now Online at B-SPAN," November 25, 2002; Anna Corsi to Shaman, Kristyn Ebro, "Jared Diamond Talk," September 19, 2002; World Bank Internal Communications, "Six Billion and Growing," October 22, 2002.

99 WBM, Andrei Tolstopiatenko to Shaman, "Results Agreement," September 11, 2002.

100 WBMs, Shaman to Bruno Laporte, Andrei Tolstopiatenko, Bowden, BCC – Wheeler, "Last Year's Output on B-SPAN," October 1, 2002; Shaman to Polly Means, Bowden, "Number of B-SPAN Events," April 25, 2003; Polly Means to Shaman, "Edited List," September 26, 2002; Tolstopiatenko to Shaman, "Means," September 25, 2002.

101 WBM, Andrei Tolstopiatenko to Bruno Laporte, Bowden, Last Year's Output on B-SPAN, October 1, 2002

102 WBM, Bruno Laporte to Andrei Tolstopiatenko, Shaman, Bowden, Carol Evangelista, "Last Year's Output on B-SPAN," October 1, 2002.

103 WBM, Lawrence Macdonald to Shaman, "B-SPAN Newsletter, September 2002," September 25, 2002

104 WBMs, Shaman to I Team, "B-SPAN Newsletter, September 2002," September 25, 2002; Wheeler to Michele de Nevers, "B-SPAN Newsletter, September 2002," September 25, 2002.

105 WBMs, Bruno Laporte to Andrei Tolstopiatenko, Shaman, Bowden, Carol Evangelista, "Last Year's Output on B-SPAN," October 1, 2002; Tolstopiatenko to Laporte, Shaman, Bowden, Hector Montenegro, Patrick Tse, "B-SPAN Meeting on Oct 7, 12 pm," October 3, 2002.

106 WBM, Shaman to Bruno Laporte, "Lighting and Event Issues," November 27, 2002.

107 WBM, Bruno Laporte to WBIKL Staff, "WBIKL in the First Quarter," October 9, 2002.

108 WBMs, Jeanette Murry to Shaman, Donald Macdonald, Dominick Egan, "Webcasting," September 24, 2002; Shaman to Murry, Macdonald, Egan, "Webcasting," September 25, 2002; Murry to Peter Midgley, Macdonald, Barbara Lee, Egan, George Tharakan, Shaman, Katherine Fishburne, Kyung Min In, Dany Jones, Samule Taylor, Steve Wattenmaker, Simulconference, Julia Morelli, Capitol Connection, "Invitation," October 17, 2002.

109 WBMs, Jeanette Murry to Extended List, "Web Streaming BBL – Summary Presentations and Contacts," October 25, 2002; Murry to Phyllis Pomerantz, Bruno Laporte, Andrei Tolstopiatenko, Kathy Sheram, "Invitation," October 17, 2002.

110 WBM, Shaman to Wheeler, "Not Bad, Perhaps Pretty Good," January 30, 2003.

111 WBMs, Barbara Burns to Shaman, DECWD Roster, EDU Fam, Extended List, "Your Seminar on Eight Years of System-wide Education Reform in Brazil with Minister Paulo Renato Souza is Now Online at B-SPAN," November 25, 2002; Bruno Laporte to Shaman, "Your Seminar on Eight Years of System-wide Education Reform in Brazil

with Minister Paulo Renato Souza is Now Online at B-SPAN," November 25, 2002; Shaman to Laporte, "Your Seminar on Eight Years of System-wide Education Reform in Brazil with Minister Paulo Renato Souza is Now Online at B-SPAN," November 25, 2002; Shaman to Bruno Laporte, I Team, BCC – Wheeler, "Your Conference on Poverty Day 2002 is Now Online at B-SPAN," November 25, 2002.

112 WBM, Shaman to Wheeler, Bowden, "B-SPAN Issues," October 31, 2002.

113 WBM, Nicholas Stern to DEC Roster, EAP Roster, Frannie Leautier, " 'China: One Year into the WTO Process' – Speech by Jin Linqun, Vice Minister of Finance, PRC, Now Online," October 25, 2002.

114 "Web Trends Report, Default Report," WBI Intranet, October 21, 2002; "Web Trends Report, Default Report," B-SPAN Logs, November 1, 2002; "Web Trends Report, Default Report," B-SPAN Logs, December 2, 2002; WBMs, Andrei Tolstopiatenko to Danial Pincock, Bruno Laporte, Shaman, Hector Montenegro, Maureen Miller, Sheila Jagannathan, Bowden, "B-SPAN Team Meeting," December 4, 2002; Tolstopiatenko to Laporte, Pincock, Shaman, Montenegro, Miller, Jagannathan, Bowden, Patrick Tse, "For B-SPAN Team Meeting," December 5, 2002; Tolstopiatenko to I Team, "B-SPAN Webtrends Stats," October 23, 2002.

115 David Witzel, Forum One, to Shaman, "B-SPAN Web Trends stats," November 5, 2002.

116 WBMs, Shaman to Polly Means, Bowden, "B-SPAN Charts," November 5, 2002; Means to Shaman, Bowden, "B-SPAN Charts," November 5, 2002; Means to Shaman, Bowden, "Web Stats Graph Again," November 6, 2002; Means to Shaman, "Graphs Contained in Word Document," November 6, 2002; Shaman to Wheeler, "B-SPAN Traffic Statistics," November 6, 2002; David Witzel, Forum One, to Shaman, Wheeler, "B-SPAN Stats," November 18, 2002.

117 WBM, Shaman to Wheeler, "B-SPAN Traffic Statistics," November 6, 2002.

118 WBM, Andrei Tolstopiatenko to I Team, "B-SPAN Web Trends Stats," October 23, 2002; WBI Intranet Reports, "Web Trends, June 20, 2002 through November 30, 2002."

119 WBM, Wheeler to Michele de Nevers, "I Don't See Why They're Worried Anyway," November 22, 2002.

120 WBMs, Wheeler to Shaman, "Under the Hat: The Continuing Series," November 22, 2002; Shaman to Polly Means, "B-SPAN Charts," November 5, 2002.

121 WBMs, Shaman to I Team, Bruno Laporte, "B-SPAN Implementation of Recent Requests," November 7, 2002; Shaman to Polly Means, Bowden, BCC – Wheeler, "Seminar Tips," October 29, 2002; Shaman to Means, Bowden, "Sample of Four Encoding Styles," October 31, 2002; Means to Shaman, Bowden, "FAQs," November 5, 2002; Andrei Tolstopiatenko to Shaman, Bowden, "Power Points," October 7, 2002; Shaman to Tolstopiatenko, Bowden, "Power Points," October 7, 2002; Shaman to Sefik Cardak, Clovis Fantinelli, BCC – Wheeler, Bowden, "B-SPAN Camera Guidelines," October 8, 2002; Shaman to Laporte, "Lighting and Event Issues," November 27, 2002.

122 WBM, Andrei Tolstopiatenko to Shaman, "ID Input for B-SPAN," October 25, 2002; Shaman to Bowden, "ID Input for B-SPAN," October 25, 2002; Shaman to Wheeler, "ID Input for B-SPAN," October 25, 2002.

123 WBMs, Shaman to I Team, Bruno Laporte, "B-SPAN Team Meeting;" Andrei Tolstopiatenko to Shaman, I Team, Bruno Laporte, "B-SPAN Team Meeting."

124 WBM, Shaman to Polly Means, "Add Link," November 13, 2002.

125 WBM, Bruno Laporte to WBI Staff, KL Coordinators, "Knowledge Learning News, November 2002/Issue No. 1," November 11, 2002.

126 WBMs, Andrei Tolstopiatenko to WBI Staff, "WBI Web Statistics in October," November 12, 2002; Tolstopiatenko to WBI Staff, "WBI Web Statistics in November: We Moved," December 11, 2002.

127 WBM, Andrei Tolstopiatenko to Pierre Giardier, Jean-Christophe Bas, I Team, Bruno Laporte, Karin Millet, "Netd@ys and Films on Development Issues," November 13, 2002.
128 WBM, Shaman to Wheeler, "Netd@ys and Films on Development Issues," November 13, 2002.
129 WBMs, Shaman to Bruno Laporte, "Lighting and Event Issues," November 27, 2002; Sefik Cardak to Shaman, Paulette Wilmot, Clovis Fantinelli, "Video Recording," November 22, 2002.
130 WBMs, Andrei Tolstopiatenko to Shaman, Bruno Laporte, "Lightening for B-SPAN Events," November 25, 2002; Shaman to Tolstopiatenko, Laporte, I Team, BCC – Wheeler, "Video recording," November 25, 2002.
131 WBM, Andrei Tolstopiatenko to Shaman, Bruno Laporte, I Team, "Video Recording," November 25, 2002.
132 WBM, Shaman to Bruno Laporte, "Lighting and Event Issues," November 27, 2002.
133 WBM, Jeff McCoy to Shaman, "EXT Web, Highlighting B-SPAN Events on the Home Page," November 13, 2002.
134 David Witzel, Forum One, to Shaman, Wheeler, "B-SPAN Stats," November 18, 2002; WBMs, Wheeler to Michele de Nevers, "I Don't See Why They're Worried Anyway," November 22, 2002; Wheeler to de Nevers, "What's the Problem (II)," November 22, 2002.
135 WBM, Michele de Nevers to Bruno Laporte, Karin Millet, "Sowing and Reapin," November 21, 2002.
136 WBM, Wheeler to Michele de Nevers, "Sowing and Reapin," November 22, 2002.
137 WBM, Andrei Tolstopiatenko to Bruno Laporte, Ron Kim, Erik Johnson, Martha Pattilo Siv, Yahaka Doha, Donald Macdonald, Kathy Sheram, I Team, "I Team Slide for KL Presentation," December 3, 2002.
138 WBM, Andrei Tolstopiatenko to Bruno Laporte, Dan Pincock, Shaman, Hector Montenegro, Maureen Miller, Sheila Jagannathan, Bowden, "B-SPAN Team Meeting," December 5, 2002.
139 "Disability in Developing Countries: World Bank Conference Marks the International Day of the Disabled," *World Bank Today*, December 5, 2002; WBM, Andrei Tolstopiatenko to Shaman, Bruno Laporte, I Team, "Disability Conference on B-SPAN," December 4, 2002.
140 WBM, Shaman to Polly Means, Bowden, "Disability Conference," December 4, 2002.
141 WBM, Bowden to Shaman, "Disability Conference," December 4, 2002.
142 WBM, Shaman to Wheeler, Bowden, "Bruno Meeting," December 3, 2002.
143 WBM, Shaman to Wheeler, Bowden, "B-SPAN Good Vibes Continue," December 2, 2002.
144 WBM, Bowden to Wheeler, Polly Means, Shaman, "Latest B-SPAN Stats," January 3, 2003; Memorandum, Shaman, Bowden to Bruno Laporte, I Team, "B-SPAN Traffic Update, January 2003."
145 WBM, Bowden to Wheeler, Polly Means, Shaman, "Latest B-SPAN Stats," January 3, 2003; Memorandum, Shaman, Bowden to Bruno Laporte, I Team, "B-SPAN Traffic Update, January 2003."
146 WBM, Bowden to Wheeler, Polly Means, Shaman, "Latest B-SPAN Stats," January 3, 2003; Memorandum, Shaman, Bowden to Bruno Laporte, I Team, "B-SPAN Traffic Update, January 2003."
147 Shaman Memorandum to Bruno Laporte, I Team, "B-SPAN Issues," December 3, 2002; Shaman Memorandum to Laporte, I Team, "B-SPAN Traffic," December 3, 2002.
148 WBM, Andrei Tolstopiatenko to Shaman, Bruno Laporte, "Meeting with Bruno This Morning," December 5, 2002.

149 WBM, Shaman to Bruno Laporte, Andrei Tolstopiatenko, Bowden, BCC – Wheeler, "Contract Renewal," December 6, 2002.

150 WBM, Shaman to Bruno Laporte, I Team, "B-SPAN's Traffic Momentum," December 17, 2002.

151 WBM, Bowden to Wheeler, Shaman, Polly Means, "Latest B-SPAN Stats," January 3, 2003; Bruno Laporte to Shaman, I Team, "B-SPAN's Traffic Momentum," December 17, 2002; Shaman to Laporte, I Team, BCC – Wheeler, "B-SPAN's Traffic Momentum," December 17, 2002; Andrei Tolstopiatenko to Shaman, Laporte, I Team, "B-SPAN's Traffic Momentum," December 17, 2002; Shaman to Tolstopiatenko, Laporte, I Team, BCC – Wheeler, "B-SPAN's Traffic Momentum," December 17, 2002.

152 WBM, Shaman to Bruno Laporte, Andrei Tolstopiatenko, Bowden, "Contract Renewal," December 19, 2002.

153 WBMs, Wheeler to Shaman, "Old Times, New Times," January 15, 2003; Shaman to Wheeler, Bowden, "Contracts," December 19, 2002.

154 WBM, Mark Davis to Shaman, "The Seminar on Jared Diamond, 'What Will Make Countries Rich or Poor?' is Now Online at B-SPAN," January 10, 2003.

155 WBMs, Vijayendra Rao to Shaman, Dominique Van De Walle, "DECRG Micro Seminar," December 5, 2002; Rao to Shaman, Van De Walle, "DECRG Micro Seminar," December 13, 2002.

156 WBM, Shaman to Vijayendra Rao, Dominique Van De Walle, Wheeler, Bowden, "DECRG Micro Seminar," January 16, 2003.

157 WBMs, Andrei Tolstopiatenko to WBI Staff, "Webstats in December, Trends in 2002, and WBI Web Audience," January 16, 2003; Andrei Tolstopiatenko to WBI Staff, "Web Statistics and Audience Analysis for January," February 24, 2003.

158 WBMs, Wheeler to Bowden, Shaman, Polly Means, "Webstats in December, Trends in 2002, and WBI Web Audience," January 16, 2003; Shaman to Wheeler, Bowden, Polly Means, "Web Stats in December, Trends in 2002, and WBI Web Audience," January 16, 2003.

159 WBMs, Martha Pattilo Siv to Shaman, "1/30/03 David Shaman/Questions about WB Newsletters Available to Staff," January 30, 2003; Ijeoma Akunyili to Shaman, Lawrence Macdonald, "B-SPAN Article for Up Coming Newsletter," February 3, 2003; Shaman to Evija Vestergaard, Bowden, "B-SPAN Material for Your Newsletter," February 6, 2003; Karolina Ordon to Shaman, "Community Radio Video on B-SPAN," May 5, 2003; Shaman to Giovanna Prennushi, "B-SPAN and Poverty Net Newsletter," February 20, 2003; Shaman to Mirian Van Dyck, "Past B-SPAN Events on ECA," February 19, 2003; Samantha Constant to Shaman, Bonnie Bradford, "Past B-SPAN Events Related to Your Clean Air Newsletter," February 19, 2003; Hywon Cha Kim to Shaman, "Past B-SPAN Events on Water and Sanitation Issues," February 20, 2003; Shaman to Karolina Ordon, "Past B-SPAN Events Related to Civil Society," February 19, 2003; Shaman to Claudia Gabarain, "Past B-SPAN Events on Latin America and Caribbean," February 19, 2003; Shaman to Shahidur Khandker, "Past B-SPAN Events on Poverty," February 19, 2003; Katrina Sharkey to Shaman, "Past B-SPAN Events on PRSP Issues," February 19, 2003; Francis Ng to Shaman, "Past B-SPAN Events on Trade," February 19, 2003; Karina Manasseh to Shaman, "Past B-SPAN Events on South Asia," February 19, 2003; Shaman to Wheeler, "Check It Out," March 7, 2003.

160 WBMs, Nick Harrison to Shaman, "Item for the WB Newsletter," February 12, 2003; Harrison to Shaman, "New B-SPAN Events," April 23, 2003.

161 WBMs, Nick Harrison to Shaman, "New B-SPAN Events Which May be of Interest to You," September 9, 2003; Harrison to Shaman, "Item for the WB Newsletter," February 12, 2003; Harrison to Shaman, Nick, "New B-SPAN Events Which May be of Interest to You," July 21, 2004.

162 WBM, Shaman to Bank Staff Various, "B-SPAN Video on Marine Pollution and Oil Spill Contingency in the Indian Ocean Now Online," March 3, 2003.
163 WBM, Miriam Van Dyck to Shaman, Merrell Tuck-Primahl, "Material for B-SPAN," December 20, 2002.
164 WBM, Shaman to Miriam Van Dyck, "Material for B-SPAN," December 20, 2002.
165 WBMs, Veaceslav Ravutchi to Donald Andrew Brasek, "Video Files Servers," December 13, 2002; Veaceslav Revutchi to Andrei Tolstopiatenko, Shaman, Chongman Kim, Larissa Fastovsky, "B-SPAN on New Hardware," July 22, 2003; Tolstopiatenko to Revutchi, Shaman, Kim, Fastovsky, Patrick Tse, Hector Montenegro, Bruno Laporte, "B-SPAN on New Hardware," July 22, 2003.
166 WBMs, Patrick Tse to I Team, "Video on Demand (VoD) is Ready for Testing," January 27, 2003; Bowden to Polly Means, Wheeler, Shaman, "The Future Look of B-SPAN," May 20, 2003; Andrei Tolstopiatenko to WBI Staff, "Introducing WBI Video on Demand Service," July 8, 2003; 164A – WBM, Patrick Tse to Bowden, "FYI," September 3, 2002; Bowden to Shaman, Wheeler, "FYI," September 3, 2002.
167 WBM, Bruno Laporte to Shaman, Andrei Tolstopiatenko, "Your Bank Seminar Linking Policy Actions to Results in Education: New Tools for Shaping Our Thinking is Now Online at B-SPAN," January 28, 2003.
168 WBMs, Ludmilla Melnikova to WBIGK, "Forthcoming Move: Important Issues," January 6, 2003; Shaman to Wheeler, "Not Bad, Perhaps Pretty Good," January 30, 2003; Bowden to Vandana Sarna, Shaman, Hector Montenegro, Marthe Motley, Andrei Tolstopiatenko, Dan Pincock, Carole Evangilista, "Moving and Resetting Up of B-SPAN Equipment," February 25, 2003.
169 WBMs, Wheeler to Shaman, "Old Times, New Times," January 15, 2003; Shaman to Wheeler, Susmita Dasgupta, Hua Wang, Benoit Laplante, Ken Chomitz, Uwe Deichmann, Craign Meisner, Yasmin D'Souza, Bowden, "Moving? Oh, Please," January 9, 2003.
170 WBM, Shaman to Wheeler, "Not Bad, Perhaps Pretty Good," January 30, 2003.
171 WBMs, Shaman to Bowden, "FYI," January 30, 2003; Shaman to Wheeler, "Not Bad, Perhaps Pretty Good," January 30, 2003; Memorandum, Shaman to Bruno Laporte, "B-SPAN Update," January 30, 2003; Andrei Tolstopiatenko to Kabir Ahmed, Bruno Laporte, Caroline Adams-Brezina, Dan Pincock, Joanna Yue Sun, Karin Millet, Karlene Phillips, I Team, "Preliminary WBI Web Statistics for December," January 6, 2003; Tolstopiatenko to WBI Staff, "Web Stats in December, Trends in 2002 and WBI Web Audience," January 16, 2003; Shaman to Bowden, Polly Mean, Wheeler, "Da Stats," February 3, 2003.
172 WBMs, Andrei Tolstopiatenko to Veaceslav Revutchi, Larissa Fastovsky, Shaman, "December Log," January 7, 2003; Shaman to Asel Mukeyeva, "Your Global Dialogues on Microfinance is Now Online at B-SPAN," January 7, 2003; Shaman to Bowden, Polly Mean, Wheeler, "Da Stats," February 3, 2003.
173 WBMs, Elizabeth Campbell-Page to Kayoko Shibata Medlin, Cindy Alexis, "Dec 2nd Workshop on 'Empowering the Poor Through Rural Information Centers: What Works and What is Sustainable,' " January 30, 2003; Kayoko Shibata Medlin to Bowden, Shaman, "Feedback," January 30, 2003; Gordon Johnson to Shaman, Kelly Vielmo, Lisa Abrams, Mia Oh, Scott White, "Your Bank Event, The Global forum on Insolvency and Risk Management, A Discussion with Harvey Miller is Now Online at B-SPAN," February 4, 2003; Michael Carnahan, World Affairs Council of Oregon, "B-SPAN – New Additions," April 10, 2003; Marianne Stigset to Shaman, Jeff McCoy, Melissa Knutson, Bowden, Andrew Kircher, Nazanine Atabaki, Richard Romm, "Harvey Miller on B-SPAN," February 4, 2003; Edwin Maclellan, University of Cape Bretton, to Shaman, "Jared Diamond Lecture," December 14, 2002; Katya Gutierrez to Shaman, Jeff McCoy, Judith Heumann, Karen Peffley, Melissa Knutson, "Your Conference on Disability and Development is Now Online at B-SPAN,"

December 5, 2002; Thomas Sterner, University of Gothenburg, to Shaman, "Your Bank Seminar Policy Instruments for Environmental and Natural Resources is Now Online at B-SPAN," January 28, 2003; Shrikant Jagtup, University of Florida, "B-SPAN Newsletter, June 2002," February 8, 2003.

174 WBMs, Dany Jones to Shaman, "From Dany; Terms of Reference from Transport," February 26, 2003; Shaman to Bruno Laporte, Andrei Tolstopiatenko, "Short Term Consultant for B-SPAN," March 13, 2003; Shaman to Dany Jones, Bowden, "Assignment," March 13, 2003.

175 WBM, Shaman to Wheeler, "Not Bad, Perhaps Pretty Good," January 30, 2003.

176 WBMs, Claude Salem to Veit Burger, Shaman, "B-SPAN Pilot Events in the Regions ..." February 10, 2003; Mwangi Wachira to Shaman, Claude Salem, Marilyne Yaguibou, "Visiting DLC Tanzanian Team B-SPAN," January 29, 2003.

177 WBM, Shaman to Mwangi Wachira, "B-SPAN and Tanzania's DLC," June 25, 2003.

178 WBM, Shaman to Charles Senkondo, Tanzania GDLN, Claude Salem, Mwangi Wachira, Veit Burger, Bowden, "Disseminating B-SPAN Events to the Tanzanian DLC and Related Issues," February 14, 2003.

179 WBMs, Shaman to Bruno Laporte, I Team, "Disseminating B-SPAN to the Tanzanian DLC and Related Issues," February 21, 2003; Mwangi Wachira to Charles Senkondo, Tanzania DLC, Claude Salem, Shaman, Monika Weber-Fahr, "Disseminating B-SPAN to the Tanzanian DLC and Related Issues," February 22, 2003.

180 WBMs, Claude Salem to Shaman, Mwangi Wachira, Bruno Laporte, Monika Weber-Fahr, Robert Hawkins, "Disseminating B-SPAN to the Tanzanian DLC and Related Issues," February 14, 2003; Wachira to Abdul Mdimu, Salem, Shaman, Weber-Fahr, "Disseminating B-SPAN to the Tanzanian DLC and Related Issues," February 22, 2003; Gary Fine to Shaman, Aslan Sarinzhipov, Laporte, Salem, David Mikosz, Devrin Weiss, Elena Karaban, Gulmira Mchale, I Team, Michele de Nevers, Weber-Fahr, Veit Burger, Vera Wilhelm, "B-SPAN," February 23, 2003; Claude Salem to Anthony Bloome, Weber-Fahr, "Tape for GDLN?: HIV/AIDS and ICT Brown Bag, Thursday, February 6th, 12-1:30 p.m. – 'Using Print, Radio, Television and Internet to Combat HIV/AIDS,' " February 4, 2003; Veit Burger to David Mikosz, Devrin David Weiss, Elena Karaban, Aslan Sarinzhipov, Vera Wilhelm, Gulmira Mchale, Gary Fine, Michele de Nevers, Salem, Weber-Fahr, Shaman, "Basic Question on B-SPAN," February 4, 2003; Salem to Enrique Calgano, Drew Stewart, Peter Copplestone, Weber-Fahr, Prita Chathoth, Sharon Cheevers Newell, Burger, Shaman, "Videotaping and Dissemination of Regional Consultation Sessions," May 12, 2003; Salem to Stewart, Shaman, Bruno Laporte, Weber-Fahr, "School-Based Telecenters Videoconference – Uganda, Ethiopia, Ghana, Nigeria, Monday, 5/19, 8:00-9:00AM, MC-C2 131," May 12, 2003; Shaman to Mikosz, Bruno Laporte, Weiss, Karaban, Sarinzhipov, Wilhelm, Mchale, Fine, de Nevers, Salem, Weber-Fahr, I Team, "B-SPAN and Kazakhstan PIC," February 21, 2003; Salem to Burger, Wachira, Prita Chathoth, Ronny Adhikarya, Bari Rabin, Laurent Porte, Peter Auer, Aref Adamali, Coura Badiane, Nicholas Meyer, Shaman, Weber-Fahr, "Meeting with David Shaman on B-SPAN – 11/26 @ 2pm in J2-127," November 19, 2002; Salem to Weber-Fahr, Burger, Laporte, "Uses of B-SPAN in Developing DLC 'Attentive Publics,' " July 16, 2002.

181 WBMs, Claude Salem to Shaman, "C-SPAN and GDLN," March 4, 2003; Salem to Shaman, "ABCD-SPAN and GDLN," March 5, 2003; Shaman to Salem, "B-SPAN-GDLN Trust Fund Proposal Draft," March 6, 2003.

182 Abdulrahman Mdimu, Tanzania DLC, to Shaman, Charles Sekondo, Tanzania DLC, "B-SPAN Newsletter, May (II) 2003," May 23, 2003; Sekondo to Shaman, M. Salika, Tanzania DLC, Bowden, Veit Burger, Claude Salem, Mwangi Wachira, "Disseminating B-SPAN to the Tanzanian DLC and Related Issues," February 23, 2003; Mdimu to Shaman, "Two New B-SPAN Events for Your DLC," March 16, 2003;

Mdimu to Shaman, Senkondo, "Disseminating B-SPAN to the Tanzanian DLC and Related Issues," February 17, 2003; Mdimu to Shaman, "B-SPAN Newsletter, June 2003," June 24,2003; Mdimu to Shaman, Sekondo, M. Salika, Tanzania DLC, "B-SPAN Newsletter July 2003," July 24, 2003; Sekondo to Shaman, Wachira, Salem, Burger, "B-SPAN Events for Your DLC Dissemination," May 8, 2003.

183 WBMs, Veit Burger to Claude Salem, Shaman, "B-SPAN Pilot Events in the Regions..." February 10, 2003; Burger to David Mikosz, Devrin David Weiss, Shaman, "Basic Question," February 3, 2003; Veit Burger to David Mikosz, Devrin David Weiss, Elena Karaban, Aslan Sarinzhipov, Vera Wilhelm, Gulmira Mchale, Gary Fine, Michele de Nevers, Claude Salem, Monika Weber-Fahr, Shaman, "Basic Question on B-SPAN," February 4, 2003.

184 WBMs, David Mikosz to Shaman, Veit Burger, Erik Johnson, "How Does B-SPAN Work," February 26, 2003; Shaman to Mikosz, Bruno Laporte, Devrin Weiss, Elena Karaban, Aslan Sarinzhipov, Vera Wilhelm, Gulmira McHale, Gary Fine, Michele de Nevers, Claude Salem, Monika Weber-Fahr, "B-SPAN and Kazakhstan PIC," February 21, 2003; Mikosz to Burger, Weiss, Karaban, Sarinzhipov, Wilhelm, McHale, Fine, de Nevers, "Basic Question," February 4, 2003.

185 WBM, Shaman to David Mikosz, Veit Burger, Erik Johnson, "How Does B-SPAN Work," March 4, 2003.

186 WBMs, Shaman to Wheeler, "This Just In," February 13, 2003; Wheeler to Shaman, "This Just In," February 14, 2003; Shaman to Wheeler, "This Just In," February 14, 2003; Andrei Tolstopiatenko to WBI Staff, "Introducing WBI Video on Demand Service," July 8, 2003.

187 WBM, Shaman to Wheeler, "The Latest Insult," July 9, 2003.

188 WBMs, Wheeler to Shaman, "This Just In," February 14, 2003; Shaman to Wheeler, "This Just In," February 13, 2004

189 WBM, Trinidad Angels to Shaman, Wheeler, "Polly's Work on B-SPAN," January 21, 2003.

190 Jackie Sims, World Health Organization to Navin Rai, Miscellaneous UN Staff, Shaman, "For Your Consent: World Bank's Webcasting Station Wants to Film Your Tuesday Morning Presentation," February 14, 2003; WBMs, Shaman to Sims, Rai, Miscellaneous UN Staff, "For Your Consent: World Bank's Webcasting Station Wants to Film Your Tuesday Morning Presentation," February 14, 2003; Shaman to Alejandro Pero, UN Development Programme, Rai, Sims, Miscellaneous UN Staff, "Requesting Jackie to Reconsider Filming Tuesday Morning Presentation," February 14, 2003; Shaman to Rae, "B-SPAN," February 14, 2003.

191 WBM, Polly Means to Shaman, Bowden, "Number of Events We Have Covered," March 10, 2003.

192 WBM, Shaman to Polly Means, Bowden, "Summary of Irish Prime Minister Bertie Ahern's Address on Globalization, Partnership and Investment in People: Ireland's Experience for the World Bank's Presidential Lecture Series," March 13, 2003; World Bank Internal Communications, "Lessons from a Celtic Tiger," March 17, 2003.

193 WBMs, Maya Brahmam to Shaman, Jeff McCoy, Melissa Knutson, "Thursday's Presidential Lecture – Webstreaming?" March 13, 2003; Shaman to Brahmam, McCoy, Knutson, "Thursday's Presidential Lecture – Webstreaming?" March 13, 2003; Shaman to Polly Means, Bowden, "Summary of Irish Prime Minister Bertie Ahern's Address on Globalization, Partnership and Investment in People: Ireland's Experience for the World Bank's Presidential Lecture Series," March 13, 2003.

194 WBM, Shaman to Polly Means, Bowden, "Schedule," March 14, 2003.

195 WBM, Daniel Pincock to Bruno Laporte, Shaman, Bowden, Hector Montenegro, Patrick Tse, Dickson Tang, Sheila Jagannathan, Andrei Tolstopiatenko, "B-SPAN Meeting," March 6, 2003.

196 WBM, Shaman to I Team, Bruno Laporte, "B-SPAN Meeting," March 6, 2003.

197 WBM, Andrei Tolstopiatenko to Shaman, Bruno Laporte, I Team, Carole Evangelista, "B-SPAN Meeting Cancelled," March 6, 2003.
198 WBM, Andrei Tolstopiatenko to Vandana Sarna, Hector Montenegro, Jeeyeon Seo, Dickson Tang, Bruno Laporte, Karin Millet, Kabir Ahmed, Frannie Leautier, "Congratulations," March 6, 2003.
199 WBM, Bruno Laporte to Andrei Tolstopiatenko, Dickson Tang, Frannie Leautier, Hector Montenegro, Jeeyeon Seo, Kabir Ahmed, Karin Millet, Vandana Sarma, WBIKL Staff, "Congratulations," March 7, 2003.
200 WBM, Shaman to Bruno Laporte, Andrei Tolstopiatenko, "Short-Term Consultant for B-SPAN," March 13, 2003.
201 WBM, Shaman to Bowden, "Dany," March 14, 2003.
202 WBMs, Andrei Tolstopiatenko to Bowden, "Inquiry," March 18, 2003; Bowden to Tolstopiatenko, "Inquiry," March 18, 2003.
203 WBM, Bowden to Bruno Laporte, Andrei Tolstopiatenko, Martha Pattilo Siv, Shaman, Jeeyeon Seo, "Draft Version of B-SPAN Brochure," March 24, 2003.
204 WBM, Andrei Tolstopiatenko to Bowden, Bruno Laporte, Shaman, Jeeyeon Seo, Martha Pattillo Siv, Daniel Pincock, "Draft Version of B-SPAN Brochure," March 25, 2003.
205 WBM, Shaman to Andrei Tolstopiatenko, Bowden, Bruno Laporte, Jeeyeon Seo, Martha Pattillo Siv, Daniel Pincock, "Draft Version of B-SPAN Brochure," March 25, 2003.
206 WBMs, Shaman to Wheeler, "B-SPAN Traffic," April 2, 2003; Andrei Tolstopiatenko to Kabir Ahmed, Bruno Laporte, Caroline Adams-Brezina, Dan Pincock, Joanna Yue Sun, Karin Millet, Karlene Phillips, I Team, "Preliminary Web Statistics for March," April 3, 2003; Tolstopiatenko to WBI Staff, "WBI Web Stats in March," April 16, 2003; ISG Executive Summary Report, "B-SPAN General Statistics, March 1 to March 31, 2003," April 1, 2003.
207 WBM, Shaman to Wheeler, "Choppy Seas Again," April 7, 2003.
208 WBMs, Bruno Laporte to Andrei Tolstopiatenko, Shaman, "Short-Term Consultant for B-SPAN," April 3, 2003; Tolstopiatenko to Laporte, Shaman, "Short-Term Consultant for B-SPAN," April 3, 2003.
209 WBM, Shaman to Wheeler, "Choppy Seas Again," April 7, 2003.
210 WBM, Shaman to Wheeler, "Choppy Seas Again," April 7, 2003.
211 WBM, Shaman to Wheeler, "Choppy Seas Again," April 7, 2003.
212 WBM, Shaman to Wheeler, "Choppy Seas Again," April 7, 2003.
213 WBMs, Andrei Tolstopiatenko to Shaman, "Our Meeting," April 4, 2003; Shaman to Tolstopiatenko, "Our Meeting," April 4, 2003.
214 WBM, Carter Brandon to Michele de Nevers, Laura Tlaiye, Shaman, Bowden, "April 2 Videoconference with Jeff Sachs," March 26, 2003.
215 WBM, Shaman to Polly Means, Bowden, "Summary of Global Change and Sustainable Development with Jeff Sachs, Earth Institute," April 7, 2003.
216 WBM, Shaman to Jeff Sachs, Earth Institute, "B-SPAN – New Additions," April 11, 2003; Ravi Rajakumar, Earth Institute, to Shaman, "B-SPAN and the Earth Institute Website," June 19, 2003; WBM, Shaman to Rajakumar, "B-SPAN and the Earth Institute Website," June 19, 2003; Shaman to Rajakumar, "B-SPAN and the Earth Institute Website," June 23, 2003; Rajakumar to Shaman, "B-SPAN and the Earth Institute Website," June 23, 2003.
217 Michael Carnahan, World Affairs Council of Oregon to Shaman, "B-SPAN New Additions," April 10, 2003.
218 WBM, Mariam Britel-Swift to Shaman, Jocelyn Albert, Angie Wahl, Galina Arkusinski, Faduma Farah Hayir, Reza Firuzabadi, Karim M'chich, "B-SPAN Request for ESSD Week – Updated Version," March 4, 2003.

219 WBM, Mariam Britel-Swift to Shaman, Jocelyne Albert, Angie Wahi, Galina Arkusinski, Faduma Farah Hayir, Reza Firuzabadi, Karim M'chich, "B-SPAN Request for ESSD Week," March 4, 2003.
220 WBM, Galina Arkusinski to Mariam Britel-Swift, Shaman, "Is It Appropriate to Have The State of the Environment Broadcast Externally on B-SPAN," April 11, 2003.
221 WBMs, Shaman to Reza Firuzabadi, Galina Arkusinski, Mariam Britel-Swift, ESSD Week, April 14, 2003; Shaman to Wheeler, Bowden, http://www.worldbank.org/wbi/B-SPAN/essdweek2003/sub_essdweek2003_9_index.htm, April 21, 2003.
222 WBM, Jocelyn Albert to Shaman, Reza Firuzabadi, Galina Arkusinski, Mariam Britel-Swift, "B-Spanning ESSD Week," April 14, 2003.
223 WBM, Shaman to B-SPAN Distribution List, "B-SPAN Newsletter, April 2003," April 10, 2003; World Bank Weekly Web Update - April 21, 2003, April 21, 2003.
224 WBM, Andrei Tolstopiatenko to Shaman, "Policy, Guidelines (Draft)," April 11, 2003.
225 Memorandums, Shaman to I Team, "Potential B-SPAN Funding Options," April 15, 2003; Shaman, Bowden to I Team, "B-SPAN Update," April 15, 2003.
226 WBMs, Shaman to Andrei Tolstopiatenko, Bowden, Marthe Motley, Hector Montenegro, "RealPresenter License," April 15, 2003; Tolstopiatenko to Shaman, Bowden, Marthe Motley, Hector Montenegro, "RealPresenter License," April 15, 2003.
227 "Rebuilding the Trust," *World Bank Today*, February 4, 2003; "A Civil Discourse," *World Bank Today*, February 11, 2003; WBM, Shaman to Polly Means, Bowden, "Summary of Dr. Kumi Naidoo Discussing Civil Society, Governance and Globalization at the World Bank's Presidential Fellows Lecture," February 10, 2003.
228 WBM, Andrei Tolstopiatenko to I Team, "Video Stats," April 7, 2003.
229 WBM, Andrei Tolstopiatenko to Bruno Laporte, Shaman, Bowden, Hector Montenegro, Patrick Tse, Sheila Jagannathan, Arseny Malov, "B-SPAN Meeting – April 15, 2003 – 4:00p.m. – 5:00 p.m. – Conference Room J-2 -131," April 15, 2003.
230 WBM, Shaman to I Team, Bruno Laporte, "Possible B-SPAN Survey Questions," April 16, 2003.
231 WBMs, Shaman to I Team, Bruno Laporte, "B-SPAN Meeting Minutes," April 18, 2003; Tolstopiatenko to Shaman, Laporte, "B-SPAN Meeting Minutes," April 18, 2003; Shaman to Tolstopiatenko, Laporte, "B-SPAN Meeting Minutes," April 21, 2003.
232 WBM, Jocelyn Albert to Shaman, Galina Arkusinski, Mariam Britel-Swift, "ESSD Week on B-SPAN," April 18, 2003.
233 WBMs, Jocelyn Albert to Kristalina Georgieva, Lars Vidaeus, Kevin Cleaver, Galina Arkusinski, Shaman, "ESSD Week on B-SPAN," April 22, 2003; Shaman to Jocelyn Albert, Galina Arkusinski, Mariam Britel-Swift, "ESSD Week on B-SPAN," April 18, 2003.
234 WBM, Kevin Cleaver to Jocelyn Albert, "ESSD Week on B-SPAN," April 22, 2003.
235 WBM, Wheeler to Kristalina Georgieva, "ESSD Week on B-SPAN," May 2, 2003.
236 WBMs, Galina Arkusinski to Wheeler, Jeannine Djaky, "ESSD Week on B-SPAN, Requesting External Clearance on Session," May 6, 2003; Wheeler to Arkusinski, Djaky, "ESSD Week on B-SPAN, Requesting External Clearance on Session," May 6, 2003; Arkusinski to Shaman, Wheeler, Jocelyn Albert, Lars Vidaeus, "ESSD Week on B-SPAN, Requesting External Clearance on Session," May 6, 2003.
237 WBMs, Shaman to Wheeler, "Your Bank Seminar on AIDSWEB: HIV/AIDS and ICT Project Update is Now Online at B-SPAN," April 29, 2003; Shaman to Wheeler, "April Set Records across the Board," May 2, 2003; Andrei Tolstopiatenko to WBI Staff, "WBI Webstats in April," June 9, 2003; Memorandum, Shaman, Bowden, to I Team, "Recent B-SPAN Traffic Stats," June 4, 2003.
238 WBM, Shaman to Wheeler, "Some Traffic Information to Pass Along to Michele," May 5, 2003.
239 WBM, Nicole Frost to Shaman, "Your Bank Seminar on AIDSWEB: HIV/AIDS and ICT Project Update is Now Online at B-SPAN," April 29, 2003.

240 WBMs, Craig Mauro to Shaman, "CD," May 1, 2003; Shaman to Polly Means, Bowden, "Summary of Community Radio, Voice and Empowerment," May 1, 2003; *World Bank Today*, "Tapping the Power of Grassroots Radio," May 5, 2003.

241 WBMs, Shaman to Extended List, "B-SPAN Survey," May 8, 2003; Shaman to Bowden, I Team, "Possible B-SPAN Survey Questions," April 16, 2003.

242 WBMs, Shaman to Andrew Tolstopiatenko, Bowden, "B-SPAN Expenditures," May 20, 2003; Shaman to Bank Staff various, "B-SPAN Survey," May 8, 2003.

243 –WBM, Andrei Tolstopiatenko to Shaman, Bowden, Bruno Laporte, "B-SPAN Expenditures," May 21, 2003.

244 WBM, Shaman to Andrei Tolstopiatenko, Bowden, "B-SPAN and Charging for Brown Bags," May 22, 2003.

245 Shaman to Andrei Tolstopiatenko, Bowden, "B-SPAN Costs," May 22, 2003.

246 WBM, Shaman to Polly Means, Bowden, "Summary for Steering by the Stars, Being Young in South Africa," May 21, 2003.

247 John Clark, United Nations, to Veit Burger, Judy Henderson, Australian Ethical, "Your New Posting at UN and the FMG," June 10, 2003; WBM, Burger to Clark, Henderson, Shaman, Anna Amato, Katherine Marshall, June 10, 2003; Shaman to Polly Means, "Summary of Worlds Apart with John Clark," May 16, 2003.

248 WBMs, Roberto Zagha to Shaman, Sunetra Puri, Frannie Leautier, Michele de Nevers, Roumeen Islam, Ruben Lamdany, "Hello and a Request," May 13, 2004; Leautier to Zagha, Shaman, de Nevers, Islam, Lamdany, Sunetra Puri, Karin Millet, Bruno Laporte, Monika Weber-Fahr, "Hello and a Request," May 13, 2003; Shaman to Zagha, Puri, Leautier, de Nevers, Islam, Lamdany, "Hello and a Request," May 14, 2004.

249 WBM, Shaman to Polly Means, Bowden, "Summary of The Washington Consensus and Beyond with John Williamson," May 13, 2003.

250 WBMs, Sunetra Puri to Elizabeth Campbell-Page, Ana Maria Chasseloup, Shaman, Iskander Sulaiman, Nathalie Tavernier, Roberto Zagha, "Logistics for Foxley Lecture …" May 29, 2003; Campbell-Page to Zagha, Indermit Gill, Darlington, Tavernier, Abhijit Kulkarni, Madjiguene Seck, Puri, Shaman, Lawrence Macdonald, Michele de Nevers, Amy Lynn Stilwell, Gobind Nankani, Cindy Alexis, "Thank You for Successfully Launching Practitioners in Development Series," June 2, 2003; Shaman to B-SPAN Distribution List, "B-SPAN Newsletter June 2003," June 23, 2003.

251 WBM, Wheeler to Shaman, Bowden, "Good Meeting with Michele (and Karin)," May 27, 2003.

252 WBMs, Shaman to Wheeler, "B-SPAN Meeting Minutes," June 4, 2003; Shaman to Bruno Laporte, I Team, "B-SPAN Minutes and Tasks," June 4, 2003; Memorandum, Shaman and Bowden to I Team, "Recent B-SPAN Traffic Stats," June 4, 2003; Memorandum, Shaman and Bowden to I Team, "B-SPAN Meeting," June 4, 2003.

253 WBMs, Shaman to I Team, Bruno Laporte, "B-SPAN Minutes and Tasks," June 4, 2003; Shaman to Wheeler, "B-SPAN Meeting Minutes," June 4, 2003; Shaman to Wheeler, "Some Back and Forth with Michele," June 20, 2003.

254 WBMs, Shaman to Wheeler, "B-SPAN Meeting Minutes," June 4, 2003; Shaman to Bruno Laporte, I Team, "B-SPAN Minutes and Tasks," June 4, 2003.

255 WBM, Shaman to Wheeler, "Additional B-SPAN Information," June 4, 2003.

256 WBMs, Shaman to Bruno Laporte, Andrei Tolstopiatenko, I Team, "B-SPAN Updates," June 12, 2003; Bowden to Barbara Bitondo, Shaman, "B-SPAN Focus Group – Please ID Location and Confirm," June 19, 2003; Laporte to Bank Staff Various, "B-SPAN: Consultation on How We Can Meet Your Needs," June 20, 2003.

257 WBM, Bruno Laporte to Shaman, Andrei Tolstopiatenko, I Team, Karin Millet, "B-SPAN Updates," June 24, 2003; Shaman to Laporte, Tolstopiatenko, I Team, "B-SPAN Update," June 12, 2003.

258 WBM, Shaman to Bruno Laporte, Andrei Tolstopiatenko, I Team, "B-SPAN Updates," June 12, 2003.
259 WBM, Shaman to Bruno Laporte, "Request," July 24, 2003.
260 WBMs, Wheeler to Michele de Nevers, "They Never Quit ..." June 11, 2003; Wheeler to de Nevers, "B-SPAN: Consultation on How We Can Meet Your Needs," June 20, 2003.
261 WBMs, Shaman to Wheeler, "Sermon from the Mount? Perhaps Seminar from the Mount," June 17, 2003; Wheeler to Shaman, "Sermon from the Mount? Perhaps Seminar from the Mount," June 17, 2003; Shaman to Wheeler, "Sermon from the Mount? Perhaps Seminar from the Mount," June 17, 2003.
262 WBMs, Galina Arkusinski to Shaman, Jocelyn Albert, Mariam Britel-Swift, "Removing the Making an Impact Session from ESSD Week B-SPAN Feature," June 18, 2003; Arkusinski to Shaman, "Removing the Making an Impact Session from ESSD Week B-SPAN Feature," June 23, 2003; Albert to Arkusinski, Shaman, "Removing the Making an Impact Session from ESSD Week B-SPAN Feature," June 25, 2003.
263 WBMs, Shaman to Jocelyn Albert, "Removing the Making an Impact Session from ESSD
Week B-SPAN Feature," June 25, 2003; Shaman to Wheeler, "Help as Soon as Time Allows," June 25, 2003.
264 WBM, Michele de Nevers to Shaman, "Got Your Message – I Can't Come Tomorrow – I Have a VC w. EAP," June 25, 2003.
265 WBM, Carole Evangelista to Shaman, Bowden, "Response," June 25, 2003.
266 WBMs, Shaman to Bruno Laporte, I Team, "Focus Group Minutes," June 27, 2003; Shaman to Laporte, I Team, Kathy Sheram, Erik Johnson, Yahaya Doka, Lesley-Ann Schneier, Martha Patillo Siv, Ron Kim, "B-SPAN Focus Group Results," June 27, 2003.
267 WBM, Bowden to Lesley-Ann Schneier, Shaman, "Bullets from B-SPAN Focus Group," June 26, 2003; Shaman to Bruno Laporte, I Team, Kathy Sheram, Eric Johnson, Yahaya Doka, Lesley-Ann Shneier, Martha Pattilo Siv, Ron Kim, "B-SPAN Focus Group Results," June 27, 2003.
268 WBMs, Bruno Laporte to Shaman, "Out of Office," June 27, 2003; Laporte to Karin Millet, Phyllis Pomerantz, WBIKL Staff, WBI EILT, WBI EAMT, "Delegation of Authority – WBIKL," June 27, 2003; Laporte to WBI EILT, "eBusiness Transformation for World Bank," June 27, 2003; Andrei Tolstopiatenko to I Team, "eBusiness Transformation for World Bank," July 9, 2003.
269 WBM, Shaman to Bruno Laporte, "Request," July 24, 2003.
270 WBM, Shaman to Bruno Laporte, Andrei Tolstopiatenko, I Team, Karin Millet, "B-SPAN Updates," July 7, 2003.
271 WBM, Shaman to Bruno Laporte, Karin Millet, I Team, "Productive Summer," August 18, 2003.
272 WBMs, Bruno Laporte to Andrei Tolstopiatenko, WBIKL Staff, Karin Millet, "Introducing WBI Video on Demand Service," July 8, 2003; Tolstopiatenko to WBI Staff, "Introducing WBI Video on Demand Service," July 8, 2003.
273 "Turkey's Return from the Brink," *World Bank Today*, July 8, 2003; WBM, World Bank Weekly Web Update, July 21, 2003; Shaman to B-SPAN Distribution List, "B-SPAN Newsletter, July 2003," July 23, 2003.
274 WBMs, Shaman to WBI Staff, "Stern-Goldin Article on Today Featured by B-SPAN," June 17, 2003; Shaman to WBI Staff, "Stern-Goldin Article on Today Featured by B-SPAN," June 18, 2003; Shaman to B-SPAN List, "B-SPAN Newsletter June 2003," June 23, 2003.
275 WBMs, Shaman to Polly Means, Jennifer Vito, "Summary for Water Sanitation and Supply Lecture Series: Millennium Development Goals – Desirable, but are They Deliverable?," June 9, 2003; Shaman to Means, Bowden, Vito, "Summary of Town

Hall Meeting on Ideas, Operations and Communications with Nicholas Stern and Ian Goldin," June 12, 2003; Shaman to Means, Vito, Bowden, "New Home Page for B-SPAN," June 13, 2003; Shaman to Means, "Summary for Accelerating the Response to HIV/AIDS in the Caribbean," June 16, 2003; "How Chile Cut Its Poverty Rate in Half," World Bank Internal Communications, June 9, 2003; "Sachs, Others Discuss MDGs and Water," World Bank Internal Communications, June 3, 2003; "AIDS in the Caribbean: 'We Must Win This War,'" World Bank Internal Communications, June 17, 2003.

276 WBM, Bruno Laporte to Shaman, Andrei Tolstopiatenko, "Your Bank Lecture Practitioners in Development is Now Online at B-SPAN," July 8, 2003.

277 WBM, Wheeler to Shaman, "The Latest Insult," July 14, 2003.

278 WBM, Karin Millet to WBIGK Staff, "WBIGK Staff Meeting," July 16, 2003; Millet to WBIGK Pillar, "Some Organizational Announcements," June 27, 2003; Barbara Bitondo to Shaman, "WBIGK Staff Meeting," July 16, 2003.

279 WBMs, Bruno Laporte to Tara Sharafudeen, Andrei Tolstopiatenko, Shaman, Bowden, "B-SPAN: Consultation on How We Can Meet Your Needs," June 20, 2003; Carole Evangilista to Bowden, Shaman, "Invitees to B-SPAN Meeting Who are Out of the Office," June 25, 2003.

280 WBM, Shaman to Wheeler, "Epiphany," September 10, 2003.

281 WBM, Shaman to Frannie Leautier, Anna Lawton, "Your Global Dialogue on Trade for Development is now Online at B-SPAN," August 6, 2003.

282 WBM, Frannie Leautier to Shaman, "Your Global Dialogue on Trade for Development is now Online at B-SPAN," August 6, 2003; "Africans Want Trade as an Engine of Growth," *World Bank Today*, August 4, 2003.

283 WBMs, Shaman to B-SPAN List, "B-SPAN Newsletter, September 2004," September 8, 2003; Shaman to Maria Dawn Dolores Arribas Banos, "B-SPAN Link on Intranet Page," September 2, 2003.

284 WBM, Shaman to Wheeler, "Odds and Oddities," August 6, 2003.

285 WBM, Shaman to Wheeler, "Odds and Oddities," August 6, 2003.

286 WBM, Shaman to Bruno Laporte, Karin Millet, I Team, "Productive Summer," August 18, 2003.

287 WBM, Shaman to Wheeler, "Odds and Oddities," August 6, 2003.

288 WBMs, Sona Panajyan to Shaman, Bowden, Erich Vogt, "B-SPAN and DG: Further Cross-Linking Efforts," August 8, 2003; Development Gateway to B-SPAN Team, Account Information, August 12, 2003; Michael Pereira to Shaman, "B-SPAN Resources," September 2, 2003; Panajyan to Shaman, Michael Peiera, "Your Development Gateway Content (3)," September 25, 2003; Panajyan to Bowden, Shaman, Bjorn-Soren Gigler, Erich Vogt, "Example of Content Exchange Between Development Gateway and B-SPAN," July 22, 2003; Bowden to Polly Means, "Content Exchange Between Development Gateway and B-SPAN," July 29, 2003; Panajyan to Michael Pereira, Vogt, Shaman, Gigler, "Rescheduled: Development Gateway and B-SPAN: Opportunities for Collaboration (Jul 17 11:00 AM EDT in I4-060)," July 15, 2003; Bowden to Vogt, Gigler, Panajyan, Shaman, "B-SPAN Links to Community Radio Events," July 17, 2003; Panajyan to Bowden, Vogt, Gigler, Shaman, "B-SPAN Links to Community Radio Events," July 17, 2003.

289 WBM, Shaman to Bruno Laporte, Karin Millet, I Team, "Productive Summer," August 18, 2003.

290 WBM, Shaman to Mary Caperton Means, Bowden, "Last Batch," August 19, 2003.

291 WBMs, Shaman to Wheeler, "Seminar on ICT in Schools is Now on B-SPAN," August 20, 2003; Shaman to Wheeler, Bowden, "Today Article and B-SPAN Link to Presentation of 2002 HDR," January 23, 2003.

292 WBM, Andrei Tolstopiatenko to WBI Staff, "WBI Statistics for July," August 27, 2003.

PART 5 — BY DAWN'S EARLY LIGHT

1 WBM, Ron Kim to KS Group, "Another Last Minute Request," August 28, 2003.
2 WBM, Erik Johnson to Shaman, Bowden, "Meeting on Thursday," September 2, 2003.
3 WBMs, Erik Johnson to Elisabeth Goller, Shaman, Juan Blazquez Ancin, "08/18/03 Elisabeth Goller/KS Services," August 29, 2003; Shaman to Elisabeth Goller, "08/18/03 Elisabeth Goller/KS Services," August 29, 2003.
4 Unsent Draft WBM, Shaman, "Revenue Generation by Subscription for B-SPAN," August 18, 2003.
5 WBM, Shaman to Wheeler, "Ephiphany," September 10, 2003.
6 WBM, Wheeler to Shaman, "Ephiphany," September 10, 2003.
7 WBM, Shaman to Wheeler, "Ephiphany," September 10, 2003.
8 WBMs, Bruno Laporte to Shaman, Ron Kim, "Cost Recovery for B-SPAN," September 11, 2003; Kim to Laporte, Shaman, "Cost Recovery for B-SPAN," September 11, 2003.
9 WBM, Bruno Laporte to Shaman, Erik Johnson, Ron Kim, Bowden, Marshall Schreier, "B-SPAN GSD Charges," September 10, 2003.
10 WBMs, Bruno Laporte to Shaman, Ron Kim, "Cost Recovery for B-SPAN," September 11, 2003; Kim to Laporte, Shaman, "Cost Recovery for B-SPAN," September 11, 2003.
11 WBM, Shaman to Wheeler, "Odds and Oddities," August 6, 2003.
12 WBM, Shaman to Wheeler, "Why Not Get Up and Go?" September 12, 2003.
13 WBM, Shaman to Wheeler, "Why Not Get Up and Go?" September 12, 2003.
14 WBM, Paulina Maribel Flewitt to Shaman, Beata Smarzynska, "B-SPAN," September 17, 2003.
15 WBMs, Paulina Flewitt to Shaman, Beat Smarzynska, "B-SPAN," September 17, 2003; Shaman to Wheeler, "B-SPAN," September 17, 2003.
16 WBM, Wheeler to Frannie Leautier, "B-SPAN," September 18, 2003.
17 WBMs, Frannie Leautier to Wheeler, "B-SPAN," September 18, 2003; Wheeler to Shaman, Bowden, "The Word from Frannie," September 18, 2003.
18 WBMs, Shaman to Erik Johnson, "Paying GSD," October 3, 2003; Johnson to Bruno Laporte, Ron Kim, Shaman, "New GSD Arrangements for B-SPAN," October 3, 2003; Shaman to Wheeler, "B-SPAN," September 22, 2003.
19 WBMs, Shaman to Polly Means, "Summary for Women in Post-Conflict Iraq," September 17, 2003; Shaman to Audrey Liounis, Nicole Frost, Jeff McCoy, Bowden, "B-SPAN Link to Chairman Oxley Discussion Yesterday," September 17, 2003; "World Bank Weekly Update - October 13, 2003," October 14, 2003.
20 WBMs, Shaman to Wheeler, "This Just In," October 2, 2003; Andrei Tolstopiatenko to WBI Staff, "Web Statistics - September 2003," October 10, 2003.
21 WBM, Shaman to Wheeler, "This Just In," October 2, 2003.
22 WBM, Andrei Tolstopiatenko to WBI Staff, "Web Statistics - September 2003," October 10, 2003.
23 WBM, Shaman to Wheeler, "Ephiphany," September 10, 2003.
24 WBMs, Jeeyeon Seo to Dickson Tang, Patrick Tse, Hector Montenegro, Shaman, Bowden, Andrei Tolstopiatenko, Erik Johnson, "Invitation: B-SPAN Migration/ Maintenance Issues," September 9, 2003; Shaman to Wheeler, "New Format for B-SPAN," October 7, 2003.
25 WBM, Shaman to Polly Means, "Maybe the Last Time?" October 17, 2003.
26 WBMs, Erik Johnson to Patrick Tse, Andrei Tolstopiatenko, Shaman, Bowden, "New B-SPAN Web Site," October 8, 2003; Johnson to Bowden, Tolstopiatenko, Shaman, Tse, "New B-SPAN Web Site," October 8, 2003; Jeeyeo Seo to Tse, Tolstopiatenko, Johnson, Bowden, Shaman, "B-SPAN Changes," October 8, 2003.

27 WBM, Shaman to Mary Caperton Means, Patrick Tse, Erik Johnson, Bowden, Laure Charvin, "New Site/Old Site Issues," January 12, 2004; Bowden to Shaman, Tse, "New Site/Old Site Issues," December 16, 2003; Shaman to Nicole Frost, McCoy, "Please Remove Old B-SPAN Website," January 16, 2004; Frost to Shaman, McCoy, "Please Remove Old B-SPAN Website," January 15, 2004.

28 WBM, Jeeyeon Seo to Patrick Tse, Erik Johnson, Andrei Tolstopiatenko, Bowden, Shaman, "B-SPAN Changes," October 8, 2003.

29 WBM, Shaman to Erik Johnson, Patrick Tse, Bowden, "Special Focus Section," October 21, 2003.

30 WBMs, Shaman to Erik Johnson, Patrick Tse, Bowden, "Special Focus Section," October 21, 2003; Johnson to Shaman, Tse, Bowden, "Special Focus Section," October 21, 2003; Bowden to Shaman, Johnson, Tse, "Special Focus Section," October 22, 2003; Shaman to Johnson, Tse, Bowden, "Special Focus Section," October 22, 2003.

31 WBMs, Shaman to Patrick Tse, Erik Johnson, Bowden, "The About B-SPAN Page," October 16, 2003; Johnson to Shaman, Tse, "New What People are Saying and Host Sections for B-SPAN," October 20, 2003.

32 WBM, Shaman to Erik Johnson, Patrick Tse, "New What People are Saying and Hosts Section for B-SPAN," October 21, 2003.

33 WBMs, Shaman to Han Fraeters, Blanco Moreno-Dodson, John Didier, Erik Johnson, Bowden, Ron Kim, "B-SPAN and Shanghai," September 23, 2003; Shaman to Johnson, "B-SPAN and Shanghai," September 30, 2003; Johnson to Shaman, October 3, 2003; Shaman to Fraeters, Dodson, Didier, Johnson, Bowden, "B-SPAN and Shanghai," October 3, 2003.

34 WBMs, Shaman to Erik Johnson, "B-SPAN and Shanghai," October 2, 2003; Shaman to Han Fraeters, Blanca Moreno-Dodson, John Didier, Bowden, Johnson, October 3, 2003.

35 WBM, Shaman to Wheeler, "This Just In," October 3, 2003.

36 WBM, Shaman to Wheeler, "This Just In," October 3, 2003.

37 WBMs, Marshall Schreier to Shaman, Kathy Sheram, Bruno Laporte, "Poverty Day," October 7, 2003; Sheram to Shaman, Laporte, Schreier, "Poverty Day," October 7, 2003; Schreier to Shaman, Andrei Tolstopiatenko, I Team, Laporte, "B-SPAN Budget Issues," April 18, 2003.

38 WBMs, Marshall Schreier, WBICA, to Shaman, Bruno Laporte, Kathy Sheram, Maria Lourdes Abundo, "Poverty Day," October 9, 2003; Schreier to Shaman, Laporte, Sheram, "Poverty Day," October 7, 2003.

39 WBMs, Marshall Schreier to Shaman, Andrei Tolstopiatenko, "B-SPAN," May 29, 2003; Tolstopiatenko to Schreier, Shaman, "B-SPAN," May 29, 2003.

40 WBM, Shaman to Wheeler, "This Just In," October 2, 2003.

41 WBM, Erik Johnson to Bruno Laporte, Ron Kim, Shaman, "New GSD Arrangements for B-SPAN," October 3, 2003.

42 WBM, Bowden to Shaman, Latifah Alsegaf, Daria Laventieva, Erik Johnson, Patrick Tse, "As Promised, Fun for All B-SPAN Quality Control Checks," October 24, 2003.

43 WBM, Craig Mauro to Shaman, "Today Story," October 14, 2003.

44 WBM, Craig Mauro, EXTCC, to Shaman, "Today Story," October 14, 2003.

45 WBM, Shaman to Sunetra Puri, Erik Johnson, "B-SPAN and *World Bank Today*," October 17, 2003.

46 WBMs, Erik Johnson to Bruno Laporte, Karin Millet, WBIKL, "New and Improved B-SPAN Website," October 27, 2003; Bruno Laporte to WBI Staff, "This Month in WBIKL," October 31, 2003.

47 WBM, Craig Mauro to Shaman, "Draft Today Story," October 29, 2003.

48 WBM, Shaman to Erik Johnson, WBIKL, Sunetra Puri, WBIVP, "Subject: B-SPAN draft article for WB Today," October 28, 2003; WBM, Johnson to Shaman, Puri, October 28, 2003.

49 WBMs, Sunetra Puri, to Shaman, Erik Johnson, "B-SPAN Draft Article for WB Today," October 28, 2003; Johnson to Shaman, Puri, "B-SPAN Draft Article for WB Today," October 28, 2003.

50 WBM, Andrei Tolstopiatenko to Erik Johnson, Bruno Laporte, Shaman, Patrick Tse, Ron Kim, "Frannie's Video Feedback from Dubai, Istanbul, Rome and Marseille Mission, September 21 – October 2, 2003," October 27, 2003; Tolstopiatenko to Adarsh Desai, I Team, "Introducing WBI Video on Demand Service," July 8, 2003.

51 WBM, Erik Johnson to Andrei Tolstopiatenko, Patrick Tse, Shaman, Bruno Laporte, Ron Kim, "Frannie's Video Feedback from Dubai, Istanbul, Rome and Marseille Mission, September 21 – October 2, 2003," October 27, 2003.

52 WBM, Erik Johnson to Andrei Tolstopiatenko, Patrick Tse, Shaman, Bruno Laporte, Ron Kim, "Frannie's Video Feedback from Dubai, Istanbul, Rome and Marseille Mission, September 21 – October 2, 2003," October 27, 2003.

53 WBM, ISG Executive Summary Report, "B-SPAN General Statistics, October 1 through October 31, 2003."

54 WBM, Shaman to Erik Johnson, Karin Millet, Bruno Laporte, "B-SPAN Skyrocketing," November 3, 2003.

55 WBM, Erik Johnson to Shaman, Karin Millet, Bruno Laporte, "B-SPAN Skyrocketing," November 3, 2003.

56 WBM, Karin Millet to WBI EILT, "B-SPAN Skyrocketing," November 3, 2003.

57 WBM, Bruno Laporte, to Shaman, Erik Johnson, Karin Millet, "B-SPAN Skyrocketing," November 3, 2003.

58 WBM, Shaman to B-SPAN Distribution List, "B-SPAN Newsletter," November 3, 2003.

59 "B-SPAN: The Bank's Backdoor Window," *World Bank Today*, November 4, 2003.

60 WBM, Shaman to WBI Staff, "B-SPAN on *World Bank Today*," November 4, 2003.

61 WBM, Frannie Leautier to Shaman, Sunetra Puri, Bruno Laporte, Karin Millet, Ziad Alahdad, "B-SPAN on *World Bank Today*," November 5, 2003.

62 WBMs, Karin Millet to Shaman, "B-SPAN on *World Bank Today*," November 4, 2003; Sunetra Puri to Shaman, "B-SPAN on *World Bank Today*," November 4, 2003; Millet to Erik Johnson, Andrei Tolstopiatenko, Bruno Laporte, WBI Roster, Patrick Tse, Shaman, "Take a Closer Look," November 5, 2003.

63 WBMs, Erik Johnson to Andrei Tolstopiatenko, Karin Millet, Bruno Laporte, "Take a Closer Look," November 5, 2003; Millet to Johnson, "Take a Closer Look," November 5, 2003; Shaman to Audrey Liounis, Craig Mauro, EXTCC, "Request for Addition to B-SPAN Article," November 5, 2003.

64 WBMs, Shaman to Nicole Frost, EXT, "B-SPAN Web Casting," November 5, 2003; Shaman to Wheeler, "B-SPAN on *World Bank Today*," November 5, 2003.

65 WBMs, Carole Evangelista to Kathy Sheram, Erik Johnson, Ron Kim, Andrei Tolstopiatenko, Don McDonald, Y. Doka, Dan Pincock, Barbara Bitondo, Latifah Alsegaf, L. Shawbarry, Bruno Laporte, "New Employment Categories," November 5, 2003; Carol Evangelista to WBIKL, "Q&A – Extended Term Consultants (ETC) and Extended Term Temporaries (ETT)," November 14, 2003.

66 WBM, Shaman to Wheeler, "B-SPAN on *World Bank Today*," November 10, 2003.

67 WBM, Shaman to Wheeler, "B-SPAN on *World Bank Today*," November 11, 2003.

68 WBM, Wheeler to Shaman, "B-SPAN on *World Bank Today*," November 11, 2003.

69 WBMs, Shaman to Millet, "B-SPAN Alert for Joe Stiglitz," November 12, 2003; "Former Chief Economist Stiglitz Dissects the '90's Boom," *World Bank Today*, November 12, 2003; Shaman to B-SPAN List, "B-SPAN Newsletter, November (II) 2003," November 17, 2003.

70 WBMs, Shaman to Bowden, "Summary for WTO, LDC's and Cancun: A Practitioner's Perspective," November 11, 2003; Shaman to B-SPAN Distribution List, "B-SPAN Newsletter, November 2003," November 17, 2003.

71 WBMs, Shaman to Bowden, "Summary for Practitioners in Development for Development: Mario Blejer, Former Governor of the Central Bank of Argentina on Argentina, Managing the Financial Crisis," October 27, 2003; Shaman to B-SPAN List, "B-SPAN Newsletter, November 2003," November 3, 2003; Blejer, World Bank Internal Communications, "Confronting Argentina's Crisis," October 28, 2003.

72 WBM, Erik Johnson to Shaman, "Your Bank Seminar on Does CDD Work in ECA? Is Now Online at B-SPAN," November 17, 2003.

73 WBMs, Shaman to Karin Millet, WBIKL, "B-SPAN's Coverage of Eduardo Aninat on WB Today This Morning," November 11, 2003; Shaman to Millet, Erik Johnson, Jeeyeon Seo, "B-SPAN Alert for Eduardo Aninat," November 11, 2003; World Bank Internal Communications, "Eduardo Aninat on Education Reform in Chile," November 11, 2003.

74 WBI Town Hall Meeting, November 24, 2003.

75 WBI Town Hall Meeting, November 24, 2003.

76 Conversation between Erik Johnson and Shaman, December 3, 2003; Memorandum, Shaman to Wheeler, December 16, 2003.

77 WBMs, Bowden to Erik Johnson, "B-SPAN Event Analysis," January 30, 2004; Johnson to Bowden, Shaman, "B-SPAN Event Analysis," February 2, 2004.

78 WBM, Bowden to Erik Johnson, "B-SPAN Event Analysis," January 30, 2004.

79 "AIDS is a Major but One with a Possible Solution: UNAIDS Chief Talks About How the Epidemic has Changed the Development Business," Development Media Center and *World Bank Today*, November 21, 2003; WBM, Shaman to Karin Millet, "B-SPAN Alert for Dr. Piot's Presidential Lecture Yesterday," November 21, 2003.

80 WBMs, Shaman to Bowden, "Summary for Practitioners in Development with Leszek Balcerowicz, President of the National Bank of Poland on the Post-Communist Transition in Comparative Perspective," November 18, 2003; Shaman to Karin Millet, no subject, November 25, 2003; "Assessing ECA's Transition," *World Bank Today*, November 25, 2003.

81 WBM, Shaman to Wheeler, "Joe Stiglitz's Presentation on The Roaring Nineties Now on B-SPAN," November 13, 2003.

82 Shaman Diary, December 4, 2003.

83 Shaman Diary, December 9, 2003.

84 WBMs, Bowden to Shaman, "ImageBank Taxonomy," November 25, 2003; Shaman to Martha Patillo Siv, WBIKL, "ImageBank Taxonomy," November 25; Patillo Siv to Denise Ann Dowding Bedford, Michael Kingsberry, Luis Angel Rivas, ISG, Shaman, Bowden, Patrick Tse, Daria Lavrentieva, "B-SPAN, World Bank Taxonomy and the ImageBank," December 4, 2003.

85 Shaman Diary, December 17, 2003.

86 Shaman Diary, December 4, 2003.

87 WBMs, Shaman to Erik Johnson, "WBI Presents," December 11, 2003; Johnson to Shaman, "WBI Presents," December 11, 2003.

88 Shaman Diary, December 12, 2003.

89 WBMs, Bowden to Sefik Cardak, GSD, Shaman, "Meeting to Address Videoconferencing Issues," December 31, 2003; Bowden to Shaman, "Serious Quality Control Issues," November 26, 2003; Bowden to Shaman, "Next Week," December 12, 2003.

90 Shaman Diary, December 4, 2003; December 5, 2003; January 5, 2004.

91 WBM, Claude Salem to Extended List, "Moving From GDLN to the Office of WBI's Vice President," July 10, 2003.

92 WBMs, Claude Salem to Ruben Lamdany, "GDLN: An Efficacious and Efficient Delivery Tool?" August 28, 2003; Salem to Lamdany, Frannie Leautier, Ziad Alahdad, "Country Development Kit for B-SPAN Materials," September 9, 2003; Salem to Karen Millet, "Off the Shelf Offerings and Nurturing Our 'Country Audiences,' "

September 11, 2003; Salem to Nicole Frost, Shaman, Ron Kim, Erik Johnson, Veit Burger, Mwangi Wachira, "B-SPAN/GDLN and Project 60," September 24, 2003; Shaman to Salem, "Country Development Kits," August 8, 2003.

93 WBMs, Nicole Frost, EXT, to N.Ahmed, "Giving Works, Margaret Bergen, Country Dialogues and P60," September 23, 2003; Claude Salem, GDLN, to Frost, Shaman, Ron Kim, Erik Johnson, Veit Burger, Mwangi Wachira, "B-SPAN/GDLN and Project 60," September 25, 2003.

94 WBM, Nicole Frost to Claude Salem, Shaman, Erik Johnson, Ron Kim, Veit Burger, Mwangi Wachira, "B-SPAN/GDLN and Project 60," September 25, 2003.

95 WBM, Frannie Leautier to Ruben Lamdany, WBIVP, Michele de Nevers, Phil Karp, Karin Millet, "Subject: Support to the Philippines," September 25, 2003.

96 WBMs, Michele de Nevers to Robert Van Pulley, Alice Mary Faria, Lystra Antoine, Karin Millet, Monika Weber-Fahr, Phillip Karp, Ruben Lamdany, Frannie Leautier, Shaman, Maria Gonzalez De Asis, Anders Zeijlon, Claude Salem, Joel Turkewitz, Jeffrey Gutman, "Support to the Philippines," November 3, 2003; Shaman to de Nevers, Bruno Laporte, Erik Johnson, Claude Salem, "Support to Philippines," October 29, 2003; Shaman to Claude Salem, "Country Development Kit," August 8, 2003.

97 WBMs, Shaman to Bowden, "Summary of B-SPAN Interviews President Fernando Henrique Cardoso," December 11, 2003; Shaman to Roberto Zagha, Indermit Gill, PREM, Wheeler, "Cardoso Interview and Lecture," December 12, 2003.

98 WBMs, Shaman to Bowden, "Summary for Practitioners in Development Lecture with President Fernando Henrique Cardoso Discussing Reflections and Lessons from a Decade of Social Reform," December 10, 2003; "Former President Cardoso on Brazil's Social Sector Advances," *World Bank Today*, December 16, 2003; WBM, Karin Millet to WBI Staff, "New B-SPAN Featuring Former Brazilian President Cardoso," December 16, 2003; Shaman to B-SPAN List, "B-SPAN Newsletter, January 2004," January 7, 2004.

99 WBM, Shaman to Bowden, "Summary for Practitioners in Development Lecture with President Fernando Henrique Cardoso Discussing Reflections and Lessons from a Decade of Social Reform," December 10, 2003.

100 WBMs, IMF Memorandums, Shaman to John Starrels, IMF, "B-SPAN Coverage of Economic Forum," December 4, 2003; Starrels to Shaman, "B-SPAN Coverage of Economic Forum," December 8, 2003; Shaman to Starrels, "B-SPAN Coverage of Economic Forum," December 8, 2003; Pradeep Mitra, ECAVP, to ECA Staff, "Presentation of EBRD 2003 Transition Report," November 19, 2003; EBRD Memorandum, Georgina Savic, EBRD, to Shaman, "EBRD Transition Report 2003," November 25, 2003; Mandakini Sud, ECAVP, to Shaman, "Presentation of EBRD's 2003 Transition Report," November 20, 2003; Shaman to Bowden, "Summary of EBRD Transition Report 2003," November 25, 2003.

101 WBM, IMF Memorandums, John Starrels, IMF, to Shaman, "B-SPAN Coverage on the Economic Forum," December 4, 2003; Shaman to Starrels, "Next Week," December 11, 2003; Shaman to Bowden, "Next Week," December 12, 2003; Shaman Diary, December 11, 2003.

102 WBM, Nicole Frost to Alex McKenzie, Ana Elisa Luna Barros, Andrew Kirchner, Carolyn Reynolds, Christopher Neal, Claudia Gabarain, Craig Mauro, Damian Middleton, Jeff McCoy, Joaquin Lopez, Jr., Julius Gwyer, Katie Bannon, Lawrence Macdonald, Lee Morrison, Margaret Bergen, Maria Velez, Maria Dolores Arribas-Banos, Nick Harrison, Nina Vucenik, Phillip Hay, Rebecca Post, Ricardo Castro, Richard Fix, Richard Newfarmer, Roger Morier, Ron Kim, Rosemary O'neill, Sidney Maher, Steven Jackson, Sunetra Puri, "External Home Page: Please Comment!" November 19, 2003.

103 WBM, Shaman to Nicole Frost, "External Home Page: Please Comment!" November 20, 2003.

104 WBMs, Ron Kim, to Nicole Frost, Jeff McCoy, "External Home Page: Please Comment!" November 21, 2003; Erik Johnson to Frost, Alex McKenzie, Ana Elisa Luna Barros, Andrew Kirchner, Carolyn Reynolds, Christopher Neal, Claudia Gabarain, Craig Mauro, Damian Middleton, Jeff McCoy, Joaquin Lopez, Jr., Julius Gwyer, Katie Bannon, Lawrence Macdonald, Lee Morrison, Margaret Bergen, Maria Velez, Maria Dolores Arribas-Banos, Nick Harrison, Nina Vucenik, Phillip Hay, Rebecca Post, Ricardo Castro, Richard Fix, Richard Newfarmer, Roger Morier, Ron Kim, Rosemary O'neill, Sidney Maher, Steven Jackson, Sunetra Puri, "External Home Page: Please Comment!" November 20, 2003; Johnson to Frost, McCoy, Bannon, ISG, "A Couple More Suggestions for New Lovely Home Page," November 26, 2003.

105 WBM, Nicole Frost to Erik Johnson, Jeff McCoy, Katie Bannon, Ron Kim, Shaman, "A Couple More Suggestions for New Lovely Home Page," November 30, 2003.

106 WBM, Erik Johnson to Nicole Frost, Jeff McCoy, Katie Bannon, Ron Kim, Shaman, "A Couple More Suggestions for New Lovely Home Page," November 26, 2003.

107 WBM, Nicole Frost to Erik Johnson, Jeff McCoy, Katie Bannon, Ron Kim, Shaman, "A Couple More Suggestions for New Lovely Home Page," November 30, 2003; Bannon to Frost, Shaman, Johnson, McCoy, Kim, "A Couple More Suggestions for New Lovely Home Page," December 2, 2003; Frost to Shaman, Katie Bannon, Jeff McCoy, Erik Johnson, "A Couple More Suggestions for New Lovely Home Page," December 4, 2003.

108 WBMs, Shaman to Nicole Frost, Katie Bannon, Jeff McCoy, Erik Johnson, "A Couple More Suggestions for New Lovely Home Page," December 3, 2003; Shaman to Frost, Bannon, McCoy, Johnson, "A Couple More Suggestions for New Lovely Home Page," December 5, 2003.

109 WBMs, Erik Johnson to Nicole Frost, Shaman, "A Couple of Things on B-SPAN," December 16, 2003; Shaman to Frost, Jeff McCoy, Johnson, "B-SPAN Follow Up Requests," December 17, 2003.

110 WBM, Erik Johnson to Nicole Frost, Shaman, "A Couple More Things on B-SPAN," December 16, 2003; Shaman Diary, December 16, 2003.

111 WBM, Shaman to Erik Johnson, "B-SPAN Conference Events," December 9, 2003.

112 WBMs, Bruno Laporte to Frannie Leautier, Karen Millet, Erik Johnson, Shaman, Ron Kim, Bowden, "Cost Recovery for B-SPAN," December 17, 2003; Frannie Leautier to Bruno Laporte, Karen Millet, Shaman, Erik Johnson, Ron Kim, Bowden, "Cost Recovery for B-SPAN," December 18, 2003.

113 WBMs, Bowden to Shaman, "Hot Topics," January 8, 2004; Shaman to Bowden, "Hot Topics," January 8, 2004; Shaman to Wheeler, "Hot Topics," January 8, 2004; Bowden to Erik Johnson, "More Information on B-SPAN Material Used for Transforming Institutions for a Sustainable Future Event in South Asia," January 6, 2004; Bowden to Erik Johnson, "More Information on B-SPAN Material Used for Transforming Institutions for a Sustainable Future Event in South Asia," January 7, 2004; Bowden to Shaman, Sefik Cardak, "Meeting to Address Videoconferencing Issues," December 31, 2003.

114 WBM, Shaman to Bowden, Patrick Tse, Erik Johnson, "New Site/Old Site Issues," December 16, 2003.

115 WBM, Shaman to Wheeler, "Itinerary Jan. 6-12, 2004," January 7, 2004.

116 Shaman Diary, January 8, 2004.

117 Memorandum, Shaman to Wheeler, December 16, 2003; Shaman Diary, January 8, 2004.

118 Shaman Diary, January 9, 2004.

119 WBM, Nicole Frost, EXT, to Shaman, "B-SPAN and JDW," January 12, 2004.

120 WBM, Wheeler to Shaman, "B-SPAN and JDW," January 12, 2004.

121 WBMs, Shaman to Bowden, "Summary of The Washington Consensus as a Policy Prescription for Development: A Practitioners in Development Lecture with John Williamson," January 15, 2004; "Evaluating the Washington Consensus," *World Bank Today*, January 21, 2004; Shaman to B-SPAN List, "B-SPAN Newsletter, February 2004," February 2, 2004.

122 WBM, Andrei Tolstopiatenko to Bruno Laporte, Erik Johnson, Ron Kim, "For VoD – B-SPAN Meeting, January 21, 2004."

123 WBM, Shaman to Erik Johnson, "WBI Presents," December 11, 2003.

124 WBM, Erik Johnson, to Andrei Tolstopiatenko, Bruno Laporte, Shaman, Dickson Tang, Hector Montenegro, Patrick Tse, Ron Kim, Nick Bowden, Jeeyeon Seo, "WBIKL Webcasting and Video Library for Knowledge and Learning Services," January 30, 2004.

125 WBM, Andrei Tolstopiatenko to Bruno Laporte, Erik Johnson, Ron Kim, "For VoD – B-SPAN Meeting," January 21, 2004.

126 WBM, Andrei Tolstopiatenko to Erik Johnson, Bruno Laporte, Shaman, Dickson Tang, Hector Montenegro, Patrick Tse, Ron Kim, Nick Bowden, Jeeyeon Seo, "WBIKL Webcasting and Video Library for Knowledge and Learning Services," February 3, 2004.

127 WBM, Shaman to Wheeler, "Larry Summers," January 28, 2004.

128 Shaman Diary, January 22, 2004; January 23, 2004.

129 WBMs, Andrei Tolstopiatenko to Erik Johnson, Bruno Laporte, Shaman, Dickson Tang, Hector Montenegro, Ron Kim, Bowden, Patrick Tse, "WBIKL Webcasting and Video Library for Knowledge and Learning Services," January 27, 2004; Johnson to Tolstopiatenko, Laporte, Shaman, Tang, Montenegro, Kim, Bowden, Tse, "WBIKL Webcasting and Video Library for Knowledge and Learning Services," January 30, 2004; Tolstopiatenko to Johnson, Laporte, Shaman, Tang, Montenegro, Kim, Bowden, Tse, "WBIKL Webcasting and Video Library for Knowledge and Learning Services," February 3, 2004.

130 WBM, Shaman to Wheeler, "New Format for B-SPAN," October 7, 2003.

131 WBMs, David Hobbs to Shaman, "B-SPAN Comparison," January 23, 2004; Shaman to Hobbs, "B-SPAN Newsletter, November 2003," November 17, 2003; David Hobbs, Forum One, to Shaman, David Witzel, Forum One, "B-SPAN Key Points for ISG Discussion," January 27, 2003.

132 WBMs, Shaman to KS Team, Karen Millet, Bruno Laporte, "B-SPAN Dominating the Bank's Home Page," January 20, 2004; Frannie Leautier to Shaman, "B-SPAN Dominating the Bank's Home Page," January 20, 2004; Millet to Shaman, Laporte, KS Team, "B-SPAN Dominating the Bank's Home Page," January 20, 2004.

133 WBM, "World Bank Weekly Web Update," January 19, 2004, January 20, 2004.

134 WBM, Tolstopiatenko to WBI Staff, "December – Web Statistics Report for WBI," January 16, 2004.

135 WBM, Erik Johnson, to Shaman, Bowden, "December – Web Statistics Report for WBI," January 16, 2004.

136 WBMs, Shaman to Bowden, "Summary of Dr. Yegor Gaidar, former Acting Prime Minister of Russia, Discusses Post-Socialist Recession: Some Lessons Learned for the Practitioners in Development Lecture Series," January 27, 2004; Shaman to Bowden, "Summary of B-SPAN Interviews Dr. Yegor Gaidar on the Post-Socialist Russian Economy," January 27, 2004; Shaman to B-SPAN List, "B-SPAN Newsletter February 2004," February 2, 2004.

137 "Understanding Post-Socialist Russia," *World Bank Today*, January 28, 2004.

138 WBM, Shaman to Wheeler, "B-SPAN Dominating the Bank's Home Page," January 21, 2004.

139 Shaman Diary, January 16, 2004.

140 WBM, Erik Johnson to Bowden, Shaman, "B-SPAN Event Analysis," February 2, 2004.

141 Shaman Diary, January 16, 2004; January 28, 2004.

142 Bank-Wide Tools for Knowledge Sharing: B-SPAN and DevForum, WBIKL Staff Meeting, February 2, 2004.

143 Shaman Diary, February 2, 2004.

144 WBM, Kathy Sheram to Erik Johnson, Shaman, Bowden, "Meeting on B-SPAN," February 2, 2004.

145 WBMs, Jane Madden to Shaman, Sheila Jagannathan, "Copyright Resources," February 6, 2004; Debra Beattie to Learning Program, Erik Johnson, Shaman, Bowden, "Minutes of LDT Meeting, February 10th, 2004," February 12, 2004.

146 WBM, Jennifer Whitfield to Liball HQ, Jerry Floyd, "Invitation: Copyright: FAQ, Facts and Fiction," January 26, 2004.

147 Shaman Diary, February 10, 2004.

148 WBM, Shaman to Bowden, "Summary of Lawrence Summers on Speaking from Experience," February 3, 2004; "Speaking from Experience," *World Bank Today*, February 5, 2004.

149 WBMs, Claude Salem to Drew Stewart, Shaman, Bruno Laporte, Monika Weber-Fahr, "School-Based Telecenters Videoconference – Uganda, Ethiopia, Ghana, Nigeria, Monday, 5/19, 8:00-9:00AM, MC-C2 131," May 12, 2003; Shaman to David Mikosz, Laporte, David Devrin Weiss, Elena Karaban, Aslan Sarinzhipov, Vera Wilhelm, Gulmira Mchale, Gary Fine, Michele de Nevers, Salem, Weber-Fahr, I Team, "B-SPAN and Kazakhstan PIC," February 21, 2003; Shaman to de Nevers, Laporte, Erik Johnson, Salem, Karin Millet, "Support to the Philippines," October 29, 2004; Salem keeping MWF informed about B-SPAN long term, WBM, Claude Salem to Veit Burger, Mwangi Wachira, Prita Chathoth, Ronny Adhikarya, Bari Rabin, Laurent Porte, Peter Auer, Aref Adamali, Coura Badiane, Nicholas Meyer, Shaman, Weber-Fahr, "Meeting with David Shaman on B-SPAN – 11/26 @ 2pm in J2-127," November 19, 2002; Salem to Weber-Fahr, Veit Burger, Laporte, "Uses of B-SPAN in Developing DLC 'Attentive Publics,' " July 16, 2002; Laporte to Andrei Tolstopiatenko, Shaman, "Uses of B-SPAN in Developing DLC 'Attentive Publics,' " July 16, 2002.

150 WBM, Shaman to Bowden, "Summary of IMF Economic Forum on Russia Rebounds," February 4, 2004.

151 WBM, Christopher Neal to Shaman, Jean Gray, Coralie Gevers, DECRG, "B-SPAN Interview with Francois Bourguignon?" February 4, 2004.

152 WBMs, Shaman to Wheeler, "B-SPAN Interview with Francois Bourguignon?" February 5, 2004; Wheeler to Shaman, "B-SPAN Interview with Francois Bourguignon?" February 5, 2004.

153 WBM, Shaman to Bowden, "Summary for B-SPAN Interview with Bank Chief Economist Francois Bourguignon," February 10, 2004; World Bank Internal Communications, "Bank's Chief Economist Visits India," February 18, 2004.

154 Shaman Diary, February 18, 2004.

155 WBMs, Shaman to Jocelyn Albert, "ESSD and Environment Week: March 1-5, 2004 – PLEASE REGISTER," February 11, 2004; Shaman to Albert, Rebecca Ellison, "ESSD and Environment Week, March 1-5, 2004 – PLEASE REGISTER," January 23, 2004; Shaman to Albert, "ESSD and Environment Week, March 1-5, 2004 – PLEASE REGISTER," February 11, 2004.

156 WBMs, Galina Arkusinski, ENV, to Shaman, Payton Deeks, Anita Gordon, Kristyn Ebro, Jocelyn Albert, Kulsum Ahmed, "Request for B-SPAN Services," February 12, 2004; Shaman to Wheeler, "Request for B-SPAN Services – ESSD Week," February 23, 2004.

157 Shaman Diary, February 12, 2004.

158 WBMs, Nicole Frost to Shaman, Jeff McCoy, "This Will be of Huge Interest – and Possible External Too," January 9, 2004; Frost to Shaman, "No Live Webcasting on Monday – Will You Put It Up on B-SPAN (Archives?)," January 29, 2004.
159 WBM, Shaman to Erik Johnson, "Live Webcasting," January 30, 2004.
160 WBM, Bruno Laporte to Erik Johnson, Ron Kim, "Live Webcasting on B-SPAN," February 1, 2004.
161 WBMs, Wheeler to Kristalina Georgieva, "Debate with Herman Daly and Paul Portney During Environment Day – Tuesday, March 12, 11:30 am, Preston Auditorium," February 24, 2004; Wheeler to Shaman, "Progress, Or at Least No Regress?" February 24, 2004.
162 WBM, Shaman to Wheeler, "Request for B-SPAN Services – ESSD," February 23, 2004
163 Shaman Diary, February 24, 2004.
164 WBMs, Roger Morier, EXTCC, to Shaman, "McNamara Talk," February 24, 2004; Morier to Shaman, "McNamara on B-SPAN," February 23, 2004.
165 Shaman Diary, April 23, 2004.
166 WBMs, Karla McEvoy to Bank Staff various, "Invitation to a Presentation by Dr. Carmelo Mesa-Lago on Cuba's Social Services," April 21, 2004; Shaman to Laura Rawling, "B-SPAN's Current Coverage of Cuba's Social Services," April 23, 2004; World Bank Weekly Update, May 10, 2004.
167 WBM, Shaman to Shantayanan Devarajan, Raghuram Rajan, IMF, "Sixty Years Later: Why the IMF is Still Embraced Yet Misunderstood," May 27, 2004.
168 WBM, Shantayanan Devarajan to Shaman, "Second Thoughts on 'Sixty Years Later: Why the IMF is Still Embraced Yet Misunderstood,' " May 27, 2004
169 WBM, Shaman to Shantayanan Devarajan, "Second Thoughts on 'Sixty Years Later: Why the IMF is Still Embraced Yet Misunderstood,' " May 28, 2004.
170 WBM, Vijayendra Rao, DECRG, to Shaman, "McNamara Talk," February 24, 2004.
171 Shaman Diary, February 12, 2004.
172 WBM, Bruno Laporte to WBIKL Staff, "WBI's Management Alignment," February 17, 2004.
174 Shaman Diary, February 12, 2004.
175 Shaman Diary, February 19, 2004.
176 Shaman Diary, February 24, 2004.
177 Shaman Diary, February 18, 2004.
178 WBMs, Shaman to Wheeler, "Conversations with Michele, Others about the Future," February 19, 2004; Wheeler to Shaman, "Conversations with Michele, Others about the Future," February 20, 2004.
179 WBM, Frannie Leautier to WBI Staff, "Town Hall Meeting on Thursday, February 19, 2004," February 10, 2004; World Bank Institute Town Hall Meeting, February 19, 2004.
180 Shaman Diary, March 20, 2004.
181 WBM, Shaman to Wheeler, "Conversations with Michele, Others about the Future," February 19, 2004.
182 Shaman Diary, February 20, 2004.
183 Memorandum, Shaman to Frannie Leautier, "B-SPAN's Development, FY'05-FY'07."
184 WBM, Erik Johnson to Bowden, Shaman, "B-SPAN Event Analysis," February 2, 2004.
185 WBM, Shaman to Wheeler, "Meeting with Frannie," February 27, 2004.
186 WBM, Shaman to Frannie Leautier, "B-SPAN Meeting," February 26, 2004.
187 WBM, Frannie Leautier to Shaman, "B-SPAN Meeting," February 26, 2004.
188 WBM, Shaman to Wheeler, "Meeting with Frannie," February 27, 2004.

PART 6 — THE CRUCIBLE

1 WBM, Andrei Tolstopiatenko to WBI Staff, "February – Web Statistics Report for WBI," March 15, 2004.
2 WBMs, Claudia Gabarain to Shaman, "Logo for B-SPAN?" April 15, 2004; Gabarain to Shaman, "New B-SPAN EventsWhich May Be of Interest to You," August 6, 2003.
3 WBM, Shaman to Kristyn Ebro, Galina Arkusinski, "Request for B-SPAN Services ESSD Week," February 23, 2004.
4 WBMs, Shaman to Bowden, "Summary for Jeff Sachs on ESSD and MDGs," March 4, 2004; Shaman to B-SPAN List, "B-SPAN Newsletter for March (II) 2004," March 12, 2004.
5 Ravi Rajakumar, Earth Institute, to Shaman, "B-SPAN Newsletter March (II) 2004," March 15, 2004.
6 WBM, Shaman to Gordon McCord, Rajan Rajakumar, Earth Institute, Columbia University, "B-SPAN Coverage of Sachs Address," April 23, 2004; Rajakumar to Shaman, "World Bank Video," May 5, 2004.
7 Shaman Diary, March 12, 2004.
8 WBMs, Shaman to Bowden, "ESSD Week Text for Front Page," March 12, 2004; Shaman to B-SPAN Distribution List, "B-SPAN Newsletter, March (II) 2004," March 12, 2004.
9 Shaman Diary, March 5, 2004.
10 Shaman Diary, March 12, 2004.
11 "How the Bank is Helping Achieve the MDGs," *World Bank Today*, March 23, 2004.
12 World Bank Weekly Web Update, March 22, 2004.
13 WBMs, Shaman to Erik Johnson, Bowden, Jeff Sachs, "B-SPAN and the World Bank," March.
14 WBM, Shaman to Wheeler, Jeff Sachs, "B-SPAN and the World Bank aka The Rumble in the Jungle," March 25, 2004.
15 WBM, Shaman to Bowden, "Summary for Kwesi Botchwey on Theory and Practice of African Development in the New Millennium," March 9, 2004; World Bank Internal Communications, "Africa Requires Higher Growth Rates to Meet MDGs," March 18, 2004.
16 WBMs, Shaman to Bowden, Ann Vroom, "Summary for African Development Indicators 2004," April 28, 2004; Shaman to B-SPAN List, "B-SPAN Newsletter for May 2004," May 5, 2004; World Bank's *African Development Indicators 2004.*
17 WBMs, Shaman to Bowden, Ann Vroom, "Summary for African Development Indicators 2004," April 28, 2004; Shaman to B-SPAN List, "B-SPAN Newsletter for May 2004," May 5, 2004; World Bank's *African Development Indicators 2004.*
18 WBM, Shaman to Bowden, "Summary for B-SPAN Interview Kwesi Botchwey on African Development Issues," March 10, 2004; World Bank Internal Communications, "Africa Requires Higher Growth Rates to Meet MDGs," March 18, 2004.
19 WBM, Shaman to Bowden, Ann Vroom, "Summary for Practitioners in Development Lecture Series with Zhou Xiaochuan, Governor, People's Bank of China on Experience and Lessons from China's Gradual Reforms."
20 WBM, Shaman to Bowden, "Summary for IMF Economic Forum: In Defense of Globalization with Jagdish Bhagwati," March 3, 2004.
21 WBM, Shaman to Frannie Leautier, "Transparency Takes Hold," March 29, 2004.
22 WBM, Frannie Leautier to Shaman, "Transparency Takes Hold," March 29, 2004.
23 Shaman Diary, March 5, 2004.
24 WBM, Shaman to Wheeler, Jeff Sachs, "B-SPAN and the World Bank aka The Rumble in the Jungle," March 25, 2004.
25 Shaman Diary, February 26, 2004.

26 WBM, Shaman to Monika Weber-Fahr, "B-SPAN's FY'05 Work Program," March 29, 2004.
27 WBM, Shaman to Monika Weber-Fahr, "B-SPAN's FY'05 Work Program," March 29, 2004.
28 WBMs, Shaman to Erik Johnson, "B-SPAN Draft Work Program in Preparation for Meeting with Monika," March 25, 2004, ; Shaman to Wheeler, "B-SPAN Draft Work Program in Preparation for Meeting with Monika," March 25, 2004.
29 WBMs, Wheeler to Shaman, "B-SPAN Draft Work Program in Preparation for Meeting with Monika," March 26, 2004; Johnson to Shaman, "B-SPAN Draft Work Program in Preparation for Meeting with Monika," March 26, 2004.
30 Memorandum, Shaman to Himself, "B-SPAN Chronology/Options, March 10 – Monika Weber-Fahr tells Jee Seo that she views B-SPAN as a digitization service;" Shaman Diary, March 10, 2004.
31 WBMs, Kathy Sheram to B-SPAN Team, Monika Weber-Fahr, "B-SPAN Status Meeting #1 – Notes and Next Steps," September 9, 2004; Weber-Fahr to Sheram, Shaman, "B-SPAN Marketing Initiatives – Follow Up from This Morning's Meeting," October 20, 2004; Sheram to Weber-Fahr, Shaman, "B-SPAN Marketing Initiatives – Follow Up from This Morning's Meeting," October 14, 2004; Sheram to Bruno Laporte, Donald Macdonald, Shaman, Ann Spencer, Weber-Fahr, "B-SPAN Presentation to the Learning Board," October 14, 2004; Sheram to Kwaljit Bhutan, Shaman, "Scorecard Indicators for FY05," July 12, 2004; Sheram to Shaman, "IMPT: Your Results Agreement and Scorecard," July 2, 2004; Shaman to Wheeler, "Welcome to My World," July 22, 2004; Memorandum, Shaman to Himself, "B-SPAN Chronology/Options, March 22 – Monika Weber-Fahr tells Nick Bowden that B-SPAN will feature WBI learning and course materials and will increase coverage of GDLN VC's."
32 WBMs, Shaman to Wheeler, "Flown the Coop," March 29, 2004; Wheeler to Shaman, "Flown the Coop," March 29, 2004.
33 WBM, Shaman to Wheeler, "Flown the Coop," March 29, 2004.
34 WBMs, Shaman to Wheeler, "Flown the Coop," March 29, 2004; Wheeler to Shaman, "Flown the Coop," March 29, 2004.
35 Memorandum, Shaman to Himself, "B-SPAN Chronology/Options, March 10 – Frannie Leautier acknowledges her support of B-SPAN's branding in a WBIGK Pillar."
36 Monika Weber-Fahr's biography as catalogued on the World Bank's Intranet website
37 Memorandum, Shaman to Himself, March 24, "Monika Weber-Fahr tells Shaman she supports B-SPAN strategy note, supports a cost recovery plan that seeks unit support rather than task manager level support, and supports seeking out external content providers."
38 Shaman Diary, March 31, 2004.
39 Shaman Diary, April 1, 2004.
40 Shaman Diary, April 1, 2004.
41 WBMs, Wheeler to Shaman, "Draft Note to Frannie," April 2, 2004; Shaman to Wheeler, "Draft Note to Frannie," April 2, 2004.
42 WBMs, Shaman to Frannie Leautier, "My Meeting with Monika," April 2, 2004; Leautier to Shaman, "My Meeting with Monika," April 4, 2004; Shaman to Erik Johnson, "My Meeting with Monika," April 2, 2004; Johnson to Shaman, "My Meeting with Monika," April 5, 2004.
43 WBM, Leautier to Shaman, "My Meeting with Monika," April 4, 2004.
44 WBMs, Monika Weber-Fahr to Kathy Sheram, Andrei Tolstopiatenko, Shaman, Marilyn Yaguibou, "Short Presentation at the Next WBIGD Division Meeting on Your Teams?" March 29, 2004; Weber-Fahr to WBIGD, "Next GDLN Division Meeting –

April 6, Short Presentations – 'What Do They Do – The Internet Strategy Team, The B-SPAN Team, Development Forum, The Instructional Design Team,' " April 1, 2004.

45 WBM, Shaman to Monika Weber-Fahr, "B-SPAN Text from Today," April 6, 2004; Memorandum, Shaman to GDLN Staff, "B-SPAN Meeting with GDLN," April 6, 2004.

46 *Bank Swirled*, Volume 20/Number 1, April 1, 2004.

47 WBMs, Shaman to B-SPAN List, "B-SPAN Newsletter, April 2004," April 7, 2004; Shaman to Bowden, "Summary for Interfaith Conference: Celebrating 25 Years of Building Community," April 1, 2004.

48 WBM, Scott Johnson, ISGIS, to Shaman, "ISP Deployment Team, Web Admin Group, ListMember Totals," February 18, 2004.

49 WBM, Shaman to B-SPAN List, "B-SPAN Newsletter, April 2004," April 7, 2004.

50 WBM, Karin Millet to WBIGK, "Pillar Wide Staff Meeting on March 10 from 9:30 am to 11:00 am in JB 1-075 – Note Expanded Time for Meeting!" March 4, 2004; Shaman Diary, March 10, 2004.

51 WBMs, Monika Weber-Fahr to Shaman, Erik Johnson, "David – Your Help in Planning Ahead for B-SPAN?" April 8, 2004; Shaman to Weber-Fahr, Johnson, "Potential Cost Recovery Options and Usage Analysis," April 20, 2004.

52 WBMs, Shaman to Erik Johnson, "B-SPAN Cost Recovery Scenarios," April 13, 2004; Shaman to Johnson, "Second Cost Recovery Draft," April 16, 2004, Shaman to Johnson, "Third Cost Recovery Draft," April 20, 2004.

53 Shaman Diary, March 31, 2004.

54 WBMs, Shaman to Erik Johnson, "B-SPAN Cost Recovery Scenarios," April 13, 2004; Shaman to Johnson, "Third Cost Recovery Draft," April 20, 2004; Johnson to Shaman, "Third Cost Recovery Draft," April 20, 2004; Shaman to Kathy Sheram, Monika Weber-Fahr, "Another B-SPAN Cost Question in VPU Letter," July 13, 2004.

55 WBM, Shaman to John Starrels, IMF, "Your IMF Economic Forum on In Defense of Globalization is Now Online at B-SPAN," March 16, 2004.

56 IMF Memorandum, John Starrels, IMF, to Martha Pattilo Siv, KS Team, "Knowledge Sharing: IMF Interest in Advisory Services," March 22, 2004.

57 Shaman Diary, April 2, 2004.

58 WBM, Shaman to John Starrels, IMF, "May 11th IMF Book Event with Gerry Cohen," April 20, 2004; Shaman Diary May 5, 2004.

59 WBMs, Shaman to Najat Yamouri, Omer Karasapan, Erik Johnson, "B-SPAN in Arabic," May 13, 2004; Karasapan to Yamouri, Bachir Abdaym, Ferid Belhaj, Sridhar Srinivasam Iyer, Hasan Tuluy, Shaman, Johnson, Lara Saade, "B-SPAN in Arabic," April 8, 2004; Shaman to Karasapan, Yamouri, Abdaym, Belhaj, Srinivasam Iyer, Tuluy, Johnson, Saade, "B-SPAN in Arabic," April 16, 2004.

60 WBM, Shaman to Erik Johnson, "B-SPAN Acquisitions," April 8, 2004; Johnson to Shaman, "Budget," April 21, 2004.

61 Shaman Diary, April 16, 2004.

62 Memorandum, Shaman to Himself, "April – 2004, Erik Johnson repeatedly seeks a meeting with Monika Weber-Fahr to discuss staffing shortfalls, the impact on production, and cost recovery options. Weber-Fahr does not respond to any requests."

63 WBM, Shaman to Erik Johnson, "My Time – Re: Decentralization Conference, Tapes 1-5," April 29, 2004.

64 WBMs, Bowden to Shaman, "Looking Ahead," April 8, 2004; Shaman to Bowden, Erik Johnson, Ann Vroom, "B-SPAN Request InfoShop, OED and UD Unit Invite You to Launch 'Improving Lives of the Poor Through Investment in Cities,' May 10 at 3:30 pm," May 5, 2004.

65 WBM, Bowden to Shaman, Erik Johnson, Ann Vroom, "B-SPAN Request InfoShop, OED and UD Unit Invite You to Launch 'Improving Lives of the Poor Through Investment in Cities,' May 10 at 3:30 pm," May 4, 2004.
66 WBMs, Shaman to Erik Johnson, Bowden, Ann Vroom, "Temp or 2nd Machine? – 2nd Machine First!" May 6, 2004; Shaman to Bowden, Johnson, Vroom, "B-SPAN Request InfoShop, OED and UD Unit Invite You to Launch 'Improving Lives of the Poor Through Investment in Cities,' May 10 at 3:30 pm," May 4, 2004; Shaman Diary, May 5, 2004.
67 WBM, Latifa Alsegaf to Shaman, Erik Johnson, Bowden, "Meeting with Ann Vroom, Manpower, Wed. April 14 at 9:30 AM," April 14, 2004.
68 WBM, Andrei Tolstopiatenko to WBI Staff, "March – Web Statistics Report for WBI with Top 10 e-Learning Courses," April 19, 2004.
69 GDLN statistics based on WBI traffic data for FY'04; WBM, Deborah Touboul-Compagnon to WBI Staff, "June – Web Statistics Report for WBI," August 4, 2004.
70 WBM, Monika Weber-Fahr to Misc. Bank Staff, "INVITATION: Brainstorming on "Business Model for GDLN's ++ Division," April 9, 2004.
71 GDLN ++ Meeting, April 20, 2004; WBM, Monika Weber-Fahr to GDLN Staff, "Slides and Other Resources: Next Steps Towards Forming the New GDLN ++ Division," April 20, 2004; Memorandum, Shaman to Himself, "Weber-Fahr in a GDLN staff meeting says Leautier wants to reach 'mass audiences'and the unit would need to scale up with resource constraints."
72 Shaman Diary, April 20, 2004.
73 WBM, Monika Weber-Fahr to GDLN Staff, "Brainstorming on Business Model for GDLN++ Division, April 22nd," April 20, 2004.
74 WBM, Shaman to Wheeler, "Practitioners in Development Lecture Series presents Mr. Zhou Xiaochuan, Governor People's Bank of China: Experience and Lessons from China's Gradual Reforms," April 21, 2004.
75 Shaman Diary, April 23, 2004; Memorandum, Shaman to Himself, April 21, "Frannie Leautier says in GDLN retreat that B-SPAN is a shining example of 'massification.' "
76 Shaman Diary, March 31, 2004; May 7, 2004.
77 Shaman Diary, March 31, 2004.
78 WBM, Monika Weber-Fahr to GDLN Staff, "Outcome/Notes from April 22 Brainstorming on 'The New Unit' – What do Our Clients and Partners Expect, and How Can We Help Them Reach More Clients with More Impact?" April 23, 2004.
79 WBMs, Shaman to Monika Weber-Fahr, "Work Program Choices for B-SPAN," April 27, 2004; Shaman to Weber-Fahr, "B-SPAN Client Use Synopsis," April 30, 2004.
80 Meeting for Brainstorming the New Unit – Organizational Options, April 29, 2004.
81 WBM, Monika Weber-Fahr to GDLN Staff, "Outcome/Notes from April 29 Brainstorming on 'The New Unit' – What do Our Clients and Partners Expect, and How Can We Help Them Reach More Clients with More Impact? Everyone Invited for BRIEFING on Tuesday May 4 at 11:30 (Studio)," May 2, 2004
82 WBM, Shaman to Maya Brahmam, Erik Johnson, Bowden, "Live Webcasting of Next Presidential Lecture in May," March 2, 2004.
83 WBMs, Maya Brahmam to Shaman, Erik Johnson, Bowden, "Live Webcasting of Next Presidential Lecture in May," March 3, 2004; Shaman to Laure Charvin, Brahmam, Angelica Silvero, Sefik Cardak, Johnson, "Live Webcast Meeting Request," April 22, 2004.
84 WBM, Shaman to Laure Charvin, Hector Montenegro, Maya Brahmam, Sefik Cardak, "Live Webcast – Shirin Ebadi's Lecture on May 3rd," April 27, 2004.
85 WBM, Shaman to Laure Charvin, Hector Montenegro, Maya Brahmam, Sefik Cardak, "Live Webcast – Shirin Ebadi's Lecture on May 3rd," April 27, 2004.
86 WBM, Laure Charvin to Shaman, Larissa Fastovsky, "Tentative URL's for Shirin Ebadi's Lecture Broadcast," April 30, 2004.

87 WBM, Erik Johnson to Bruno Laporte, Karin Millet, Frannie Leautier, Monika Weber-Fahr, WBIKL, Ann Vroom, "B-SPAN's First Live Broadcast!!" May 5, 2004.
88 WBMs, Shaman to B-SPAN List, "B-SPAN Newsletter, May 2004," May 5, 2004; "Nobel Winner Rates Freedom as Most Precious Possession," *World Bank Today*, May 4, 2004; Shaman to Bowden, Ann Vroom, Patrick Tse, "Summary for Presidential Lecture with Shirin Ebadi, 2003 Nobel Peace Prize Winner on Human Rights and Development," May 4, 2004.
89 WBM, Shaman to Christopher Neal, "Annual Bank Conference on Development Economics Link," April 12, 2004.
90 WBM, Christopher Neal to Shaman, "ABCDE Link," May 2, 2004.
91 WBM, Bowden to Erik Johnson, Shaman, Ann Vroom, "MY TIME – Re: Decentralization – Conference Tapes 1-5," April 29, 2004.
92 Erik Johnson to Bowden, Shaman, Ann Vroom, "COB, Wed 5-5-04 Update," May 6, 2004.
93 WBM, Ann Vroom to Erik Johnson, Shaman, Bowden, "Temp or 2nd Machine? – Second Machine First!" May 6, 2004.
94 WBM, Erik Johnson to Ann Vroom, Shaman, Bowden, "Temp or 2nd Machine? – Second Machine First!" May 6, 2004.
95 WBMs, Monika Weber-Fahr to GDLN Core Team, I Team, Shaman, Bowden, Kathy Sheram, Barbara Bitondo, Debra Beattie, Han Fraeters, Jane Madden, Jiping Zhang, Sheila Jagannathan, Shobha Kumar, "EVERYONE Invited – Discussion on Organizational Options for the New Unit – Thursday, April 19 – 12:30-2:00 – But You Must Register with Sharon by Tuesday, COB and Be on Time at the Meeting and Stay the Whole Time," April 26, 2004; Weber-Fahr to Shaman, "Rescheduled: Meeting with David Shaman (Jun 29 09:00 am EDT)," June 28, 2004.
96 Memorandum, Shaman to Monika Weber-Fahr, "GDLN Model Options," May 7, 2004.
97 WBM, Monika Weber-Fahr to Shaman, "Our Meeting Today … Dave Shaman," May 7, 2004; Shaman Diary May 5, 2004.
98 Memorandum, Shaman to Himself, "Weber-Fahr tells Shaman B-SPAN needs to do smaller projects that are different to its strategic vision but does not elaborate."
99 WBM, Monika Weber-Fahr to Shaman, Kathy Sheram, Sharon Cheevers Newell, "B-SPAN: Next Step and First Six Months of FY05," June 29, 2004; Memorandum, Shaman to Himself, May-2004, "Weber-Fahr says she will staff B-SPAN with short-term consultants from local schools."
100 WBMs, Kathy Sheram to B-SPAN Team, Monika Weber-Fahr, "B-SPAN Status Meeting #1 – Notes and Next Steps," September 9, 2004; Weber-Fahr to Sheram, Shaman, "B-SPAN Marketing Initiatives – Follow Up from This Morning's Meeting," October 20, 2004; Sheram to Weber-Fahr, Shaman, "B-SPAN Marketing Initiatives – Follow Up from This Morning's Meeting," October 14, 2004; Sheram to Bruno Laporte, Donald Macdonald, Shaman, Ann Spencer, Weber-Fahr, "B-SPAN Presentation to the Learning Board," October 14, 2004; Sheram to Kwaljit Bhutan, Shaman, "Scorecard Indicators for FY05," July 12, 2004; Sheram to Shaman, "IMPT: Your Results Agreement and Scorecard," July 2, 2004; Shaman to Wheeler, "Welcome to My World," July 22, 2004.
101 WBM, Erik Johnson to Shaman, "CV Followup," January 31, 2005.
102 WBM, Andrei Tolstopiatenko to WBI Staff, "April – Web Statistics Report for WBI," May 13, 2004.
103 Memorandum, Shaman to himself, "Based on Web Statistic Reports for WBI, January through April, 2004," May 13, 2004.
104 WBMs, Bowden to Erik Johnson, Shaman, Ann Vroom, "MY TIME: Decentralization Conference Tapes 1-5," April 29, 2004; Shaman to Johnson, "MY TIME: Decentralization Conference Tapes 1-5," April 29, 2004; Shaman to Bowden, Johnson,

Vroom, "B-SPAN Request InfoShop, OED and UD Unit Invite You to Launch of 'Improving the Lives of the Poor Through Investments in Cities,' May 10 at 3:30 pm," May 4, 2004; Johnson to Shaman, Bowden, Vroom, "B-SPAN Request InfoShop, OED and UD Unit Invite You to Launch of 'Improving the Lives of the Poor Through Investments in Cities,' May 10 at 3:30 pm," May 4, 2004.

105 WBMs, Marshall Schreier, WBICA, to Shaman, Latifah Alsegaf, Erik Johnson, "B-SPAN Charges for PREM Conference," May 6, 2004; Schreier to Shaman, Caldwell, Alsegaf, "Updated Agenda for Course: Impact of International Trade in Goods and Services on Public Health," May 6, 2004; Shaman to Johnson, Alsegaf, "B-SPAN Charges," May 7, 2004; Alsegaf to Shaman, "Social Sector Decentralization," May 12, 2004; Muriel Darlington to Ana Maria Chasseloup, Shaman, Alsegaf, "B-SPAN Charges for PREM Conference," May 12, 2004.

106 WBMs, Bryan Waller to Shaman, Bowden, Erik Johnson, "2nd Encoder Machine," April 30, 2004; Waller to Johnson, Shaman, Bowden, "Where We Stand," April 30, 2004; Waller to Johnson, Shaman, "PO for Camera," May 6, 2004; Johnson to Waller, Shaman, Vandana Sarna, Bowden, "Update," May 11, 2004; Waller to Johnson, Shaman, Sarna, Bowden, "Update," May 11, 2004; Shaman to Laure Charvin, Waller, Hector Montenegro, Johnson, Sarna, "Encoder," May 18, 2004; Waller to Johnson, Shaman, Bowden, "Where We Stand," April 26, 2004.

107 WBMs, Shaman to Najat Yamouri, Omer Karasapan, Erik Johnson, "B-SPAN in Arabic," May 13, 2004; Karasapan to Ferid Belhaj, Yamouri, Bachir Abdaym, Johnson, Shaman, Yarissa Lyngdoh, Sridhar Srinivasan Iyer, Roby Charles Fields, "Talking Points or Mouhammed II PIC Opening," April 27, 2004; Shaman to Yamouri, Abdaym, Belhaj, Iyer, Hasan Tuluy, Johnson, Lara Saade, "B-SPAN in Arabic," April 16, 2004.

108 WBM, Monika Weber-Fahr to WBI Staff, GDLN Management Team, Karin Millet, Bruno Laporte, "WBIGD (GDLN) on Retreat Together with I-Team, LDesign Team and B-SPAN – May 14, 8:30 – 5:30," May 13, 2004.

109 Shaman Diary, July 29, 2004; Shaman Diary, September 28, 2004; This footnote is based on conversations with WBI's Instructional Design Team staff which was managed by Sheram prior to her joining GDLN in the July, 2004 departmental reorganization.

110 GDLN Memorandum, "Shaping Our Work Program Retreat for New GDLN++ Unit, Instructions to the Integrators and Special Purpose Teams for the First Work Session," May 13, 2004.

111 WBM, Shaman to Mark Davis, "Still Wresting with Monsters," October 29, 2004; Memorandum, Shaman to Himself, May 14, "Weber-Fahr designates Sheram as her B-SPAN liaison. Sheram immediately states B-SPAN should provide private access events."

112 WBMs, Bryan Waller to Erik Johnson, Shaman, Bowden, "Where We Stand," April 28, 2004; Bryan Waller to Erik Johnson, Shaman, Bowden, "Where We Stand Update," April 30, 2004.

113 WBM, Erik Johnson to Bryan Waller, Shaman, "Hold Off on Purchase," May 14, 2004.

114 WBM, Erik Johnson to Bryan Waller, Shaman, "Hold Off on Purchase," May 14, 2004.

115 WBM, Erik Johnson to Bryan Waller, Shaman, "Hold Off on Purchase," May 14, 2004.

116 Shaman Dairy, May 12, 2004.

117 WBMs, Erik Johnson to Hector Montenegro, Shaman, "Mobile Encoder," May 14, 2004; Shaman to Laure Charvin, Bryan Waller, Erik Johnson, Hector Montenegro, Vandana Sarna, "Encoder," May 18, 2004; Charvin to Shaman, "Encoder," May 18, 2004.

118 WBMs, Shaman to Bryan Waller, Vandana Sarna, Hector Montenegro, Erik Johnson, "Encoding Meeting with Monika Weber-Fahr," May 19, 2004; Weber-Fahr to Andrei Tolstopiatenko, Johnson, Kathy Sheram, Shaman, Sharon Cheevers Newell, "Meeting

on B-SPAN – Tomorrow, Thursday, May 19, 2004;" Memorandum, Shaman to Himself, May 20, "Shaman, Erik Johnson meet with Weber-Fahr on encoder purchase option with remaining Knowledge Learning funds. Weber-Fahr says she wants the encoder to be used by GDLN."

119 WBMs, Shaman to Monika Weber-Fahr, Erik Johnson, "Potential B-SPAN Cost Recovery Options and Usage Analysis," April 20, 2004; Weber-Fahr to Shaman, Johnson, "David – Your Help in Planning Ahead for B-SPAN?" April 8, 2004.

120 WBMs, Bryan Waller to Monika Weber-Fahr, Erik Johnson, Shaman, Hector Montenegro, "Waiver for Video Encoder," May 21, 2004; Johnson to Weber-Fahr, Kathy Sheram, Waller, Shaman, "NiagraMax," June 10, 2004.

121 WBMs, Erik Johnson to Monika Weber-Fahr, Kathy Sheram, Bryan Waller, Shaman, "NiagraMAX," June 10, 2004; Waller to Weber-Fahr, Johnson, Shaman, Hector Montenegro, "Waiver for Video Encoder," May 21, 2004.

122 WBM, Bryan Waller to Erik Johnson, Shaman, Kathy Sheram, Monika Weber-Fahr, "NiagraMAX," June 10, 2004.

123 WBM, Erik Johnson to Bryan Waller, Shaman, Kathy Sheram, Monika Weber-Fahr, "NiagraMAX," June 10, 2004.

124 WBMs, Shaman to Omer Karasapan, Najat Yamouri, Bachir Abdaym, Ferid Belhaj, Sridhar Srinvasam Iyer, Hasan Tuluy, Erik Johnson, Lara Saade, "B-SPAN in Arabic," April 8, 2004; Karasapan to Shaman, Najat Yamouri, Bachir Abdaym, Ferid Belhaj, Sridhar Srinvasam Iyer, Hasan Tuluy, Erik Johnson, Lara Saade, "Talking Points on Mohammed II PIC Opening," April 27, 2004.

125 WBM, Moira Enerva to Shaman, "I'm In DC," May 19, 2004.

126 WBMs, Shaman to Moira Enerva, "B-SPAN and Philippines PICs," May 26, 2004; Shaman to Enerva, Erik Johnson, Ron Kim, "B-SPAN and Philippines PICs," June 3, 2004; Johnson to Shaman, "B-SPAN and Philippines PICs," June 3, 2004.

127 Shaman Diary, May 21, 2004.

128 WBM, Bruno Laporte to KS Group, "Any Suggestions?" May 5, 2004.

129 WBMs, Laure Charvin to Shaman, Chongman Kim, Han Fraeters, Hector Montenegro, John Didier, Kathy Sheram, Le Anh Vu, Nansia Constantinou, "Urgent Shanghai Questions," May 20, 2004; Shaman to Fraeters, "Requirements for Shanghai," March 17, 2004; Vu to Sunetra Puri, Shaman, Didier, "More on Webcasting from Shanghai," May 12, 2004.

130 WBM, Shaman to Chongman Kim, Le Anh Vu, "Draft Questions for China – Chongman, if you have additional questions, please list, many thanks," March 15, 2004.

131 WBMs, Shaman to Han Fraeters, "Requirements for Shanghai," March 17, 2004; Shaman to Michele de Nevers, Fraeters, Erik Johnson, "Live Webcasting Shanghai," March 18, 2004; Shaman to Le Anh Vu, Chongman Kim, Fraeters, de Nevers, Yan Wang, "B-SPAN Requirements for Live Webcasting of Shanghai;" March 25, 2004.

132 WBMs, Shaman to Han Fraeters, "Requirements for Shanghai," March 17, 2004; Shaman to Jiping Zhang, Han Fraeters, Blanca Moreno-Dodson, "Technical Requirements," November 18, 2003; Shaman to Fraeters, "B-SPAN and Shanghai," October 3, 2003.

133 WBMs, Han Fraeters to Shaman, Erik Johnson, "B-SPAN and Shanghai," March 18, 2004; Shaman to Han Fraeters, "Requirements for Shanghai," March 17, 2004; Yan Wang to Michele de Nevers, Shaman, Le Anh Vu, Sunetra Puri, Chongman Kim, Fraeters, "Webcasting Shanghai and a Question," April 5, 2004; Sunetra Puri to Austin Hu, Annie Seys, Shaman, David Leonard, Galina Voytsekhovska, Vu, Patricia Davies, Sheng Li, Wei Wang, Yukon Huang, Yan Wang, de Nevers, "Proposed Agenda Items for Shanghai Next Week," April 7, 2004; De Nevers to Puri, Hu, Seys, Shaman, Leonard, Voytsekhovska, Vu, Davies, Li, Wei Wang, Huang, Yan Wang, "Proposed Agenda Items for Shanghai Next Week," April 7, 2004.

134 WBM, Shaman to Michele de Nevers, Han Fraeters, Erik Johnson, "Live Webcasting Shanghai," March 18, 2004.
135 WBM, Erik Johnson to Shaman, "NYTimes.com Article: 'Chinese Gave Cheney Speech Their Own Form of Openness' (Joseph Kahn, April 19, 2004)," April 19, 2004.
136 WBMs, Erik Johnson to Shaman, "NY Times.com Article: 'Chinese Gave Cheney Speech Their Own Form of Openness,' " April 19, 2004; Shaman to Johnson, "NY Times.com Article: 'Chinese Gave Cheney Speech Their Own Form of Openness,' " April 19, 2004.
137 WBM, Shaman to Le Anh Vu, Chongman Kim, Han Fraeters, Michele de Nevers, Yan Wang, "B-SPAN Requirements for Live Webcasting of Shanghai," March 25, 2004; Vu to Shaman, Kim, Fraeters, de Nevers, Wang, "B-SPAN Requirements for Live Webcasting of Shanghai," March 26, 2004; Shaman to Wang, Kim, Fraeters, "Shanghai and B-SPAN," March 8, 2004.
138 Shaman Diary, March 10, 2004.
139 WBMs, Shaman to Michele de Nevers, Le Anh Vu, Austin Hu, Sheng Li, David Leonard, Sunetra Puri, Carl Nai-Kang Fu, Chongman Kim, "Technical Requirements for TV Broadcast and Internet Webcast," April 26, 2004; Shaman to Han Fraeters, "Requirements for Shanghai," March 17, 2004; Vu to de Nevers, Alice Faria, Hu, Nai-Kang Fu, Kim, Shaman, Leonard, Frannie Leautier, Lystra Antoine, Sheng Li, Puri, "Technical Requirements for TV Broadcast and Internet Webcast," April 19, 2004; Shaman to Vu, de Nevers, Faria, Hu, Nai-Kang Fu, Kim, Leonard, Leautier, Antoine, Li, Puri, "Technical Requirements for TV Broadcast and Internet Webcast," April 19, 2004; Shaman to Vu, de Nevers, Faria, Hu, Nai-Kang Fu, Kim, Leonard, Leautier, Antoine, Li, Puri, "Technical Requirements for TV Broadcast and Internet Webcast," April 26, 2004; Shaman to Wheeler, "Practitioners in Development Lecture Series Presents: Mr. Zhou Xiaochuan, Governor, People's Bank of China: 'Experience and Lessons from China's Gradual Reform,' April 26, 2004 – J-1050," April 21, 2004.
140 WBM, Shaman to Michele de Nevers, Alice Faria, Austin Hu, Carl Nai-Kang Fu, Chongman Kim, David Leonard, Frannie Leautier, Han Fraeters, Li Li, Lystra Antoine, Sheng Li, Sunetra Puri, Le Anh Vu, Erik Johnson, "Technical Requirements for TV Broadcast and Internet Webcast," April 26, 2004.
141 WBM, Chongman Kim to Shaman, Han Fraeters, Hector Montenegro, John Didier, Kathy Sheram, Laure Charvin, Le Anh Vu, Nansia Constantinou, "Final Links List to the Live Section," May 25, 2004.
142 WBMs, Laure Charvin to Nansia Constantinou, Chongman Kim, Shaman, "Urgent – Shanghai Links to Live Webcast," May 25, 2004; Patrick Tse to Constantinou, Montenegro, Shaman, "Urgent – Shanghai Links to Live Webcast," May 25, 2004; Kim to Shaman, Tse, Constantinou, Montenegro, "Final Links," May 25, 2004.
143 WBMs, Patrick Tse to Nansia Constantinou, Hector Montenegro, Shaman, "Shanghai Links to Live Webcast," May 25, 2004; Tse to Shaman, Constantinou, Montenegro, "Shanghai Links to Live Webcast," March 25, 2004; Shaman to Chongman Kim, Han Fraeters, Montenegro, John Didier, Kathy Sheram, Laure Charvin, Le Anh Vu, Constantinou, "Final Links List to the Live Sessions," May 25, 2004; Kim to Shaman, "Final Links List to the Live Sessions," May 25, 2004.
144 WBMs, Shaman to Chongman Kim, Laure Charvin, Patrick Tse, Hector Montenegro, "Streaming Issues that Arose on Day One in Shanghai," May 26, 2004; Kim to Shaman, Charvin, Tse, Montenegro, "Streaming Issues that Arose on Day One in Shanghai," May 26, 2004; Tse to Nansia Constantinou, Han Fraeters, John Didier, Oxana Minchenko, Montenegro, Shaman, "B-SPAN Live Webcast Update," May 26, 2004.
145 WBMs, Shaman to Chongman Kim, Laure Charvin, Patrick Tse, Hector Montenegro, "First Day of Shanghai Conference Sessions Archived on B-SPAN," May 26, 2004; Han Fraeters to John Didier, Shaman, Nansia Constantinou, Oxana Minchenko,

"First Day of Shanghai Conference Sessions Archived on B-SPAN," May 26, 2004; Shaman to Kim, Charvin, Tse, Montenegro, "Streaming Issues that Arose on Day One in Shanghai," May 26, 2004; Kim to Shaman, Charvin, Tse, Montenegro, "Streaming Issues that Arose on Day One in Shanghai," May 26, 2004.

146 WBM, Shaman to Chongman Kim, Laure Charvin, Patrick Tse, Hector Montenegro, John Didier, "Second Day Streaming Problems/Issues," May 27, 2004.

147 WBMs, Shaman to Han Fraeters, Hector Montenegro, Nansia Constantinou, John Didier, Oxana Michenko, "Conference Tape Problems," June 4, 2004; David Leonard to Constantinou, Shaman, Fraeters, Montenegro, Didier, Minchenko, Sefik Cardak, Carl Nai-Kang Fu, Chongman Kim, Le Anh Vu, "Shanghai Conference Tapes," June 7, 2004; Leonard to Maria Rosa Schwartz, "Question … re Shanghai of Course," June 16, 2004; Fraeters to Michele de Nevers, Didier, Montenegro, Erik Johnson, Kathy Sheram, Shaman, "The Shanghai Tapes: Update on Audio Problems," June 18, 2004; Leonard to Fraeters, Montenegro, Shaman, Cardak, "Shanghai: Tapes," June 22, 2004; Leonard to Michele de Nevers, Yan Wang, Le Anh Vu, Han Fraeters, Carl Nai-Kang Fu, Chongman Kim, Shaman, Gonzalo Perez Constanzo, "Shanghai Video Tapes," June 28, 2004; Leonard to Fraeters, Shaman, Montenegro, "Shanghai Tapes," June 28, 2004.

148 Shaman Diary, June 7, 2004.

149 Meg Keller, "Resources for the Future," to Shaman, RFF, May 27, 2004.

150 WBM, Shaman to Meg Keller, "Resources for the Future, RFF," May 28, 2004.

151 Meg Keller, "Resources for the Future," to Shaman, RFF, May 28, 2004; Keller, "Resources for the Future," to Shaman, RFF, June 4, 2004.

152 WBMs, Ann Vroom to Shaman, Erik Johnson, Bowden, "Summary for Visions for Development in the Arab World," June 7, 2004; Vroom to Manpower.com, Johnson, Maureen Blassou, "Problem w. My Timesheets – From 'Bad' to 'Worse,' " June 7, 2004; Vroom to Manpower.com, Johnson, Blassou, "Problem w. My Timesheets," June 7, 2004.

153 WBM, Erik Johnson to Monika Weber-Fahr, Kathy Sheram, Bruno Laporte, Ron Kim, Shaman, Bowden, "B-SPAN Temp – Ann Vroom," June 7, 2004.

154 Memorandum, Shaman to Himself, June 6, "Sheram calls B-SPAN an unfunded mandate and a project rather than a service; Shaman Diary, June 11, 2004.

155 WBM, Shaman to Michele de Nevers, "Next Pres. Lecture by Head of ILO," June 9, 2004.

156 WBMs, Maya Brahmam to Shaman, Nicole Frost, EXT Web, Julius Mberiley Warmey, Roger Morier, Angelica Silvero, "Next Pres. Lecture by Head of ILO," June 8, 2004; Frost to Shaman, Brahmam, EXT Web, Julius Mberiley Warmey, Roger Morier, Angelica Silvero, "Next Pres. Lecture by Head of ILO," June 8, 2004.

157 WBM, Shaman to Wheeler, "B-SPAN's Collapsing," June 9, 2004.

158 WBM, Shaman to Maya Brahmam, Erik Johnson, Ron Kim, Bruno Laporte, Monika Weber-Fahr, Kathy Sheram, Frannie Leautier, "Next Pres. Lecture by Head of ILO," June 9, 2004.

159 WBMs, Michele de Nevers to Shaman, "Next Pres. Lecture by Head of ILO," June 9, 2004; Kabir Ahmed to de Nevers, Frannie Leautier, Caroline Adams-Brezina, Irina Sergeeva, "Additional Budget for Shanghai Related Expenses," June 9, 2004.

160 WBMs, Kabir Ahmed to Michele de Nevers, Frannie Leautier, Caroline Adams-Brezina, Irina Sergeeva, "Additional Budget for Shanghai-Related Expenses," June 10, 2004; de Nevers to Han Fraeters, John Didier, Shaman, Ahmed, "Additional Budget for Shanghai-Related Expenses," June 10, 2004; de Nevers to Leautier, Yan Wang, Sheng Li, E. Cuenco, Bintao Wang, Fraeters, Didier, Sunetra Puri, Shaman, Adriana Costa, Djordjijna Petkoski, Katia Nemes, Riad Berdayi, B. Dodson, "Post-Shanghai Follow Up Actions," June 9, 2004; Fraeters to Shaman, Erik Johnson, Kathy Sheram, "B-SPAN Needs and Shanghai," June 9, 2004; Johnson to Fraeters, Shaman, Didier,

Sheram, "B-SPAN Needs and Shanghai," June 9, 2004; Ahmed to de Nevers, Leautier, Adam-Brezina, Sergeeva, "Additional Budget for Shanghai-Related Expenses," June 9, 2004.

161 WBMs, Erik Johnson to Monika Weber-Fahr, Bruno Laporte, Shaman, Kathy Sheram, Ron Kim, Bowden, Drew Stewart, "Interim Arrangements to Ensure B-SPAN's Staffing Through Early July," June 14, 2004; Johnson to Weber-Fahr, Sheram, Laporte, Shaman, Kim, Bowden, "B-SPAN Temp – Ann Vroom," June 7, 2004; Johnson to Han Fraeters, Shaman, John Didier, Sheram, "B-SPAN Needs and Shanghai," June 9, 2004.

162 WBM, Monika Weber-Fahr to Erik Johnson, Bruno Laporte, Shaman, Kathy Sheram, Ron Kim, Bowden, Drew Stewart, "Interim Arrangements to Ensure B-SPAN's Staffing Through Early July," June 14, 2004; Sheram to Johnson, Weber-Fahr, Laporte, Shaman, Kim, Bowden, "B-SPAN Temp – Ann Vroom," June 8, 2004; Sheram to Manpower.com, Vroom, Shaman, Newell Cheevers, Marilyne Yaguibou, "Ann Vroom for B-SPAN," July 2, 2004; Sheram to Marilyne Yaguibou, Manpower Temp Agency, Shaman, Maureen Blassou, Sharon Cheevers Newell, "FM Project Finished, COB Friday, July 9, 2004," July 12, 2004; Sheram to Shaman, Ann Vroom, "Ann Vroom," July 12, 2004.

163 WBM, Andrei Tolstopiatenko to WBI Staff, "May – Web Statistics Report for WBI," July 1, 2004.

164 Shaman Diary, July 2, 2004.

165 Felipe Manteiga to Shaman, "Would Like to Change My EM to This One, How?" June 28, 2004.

166 WBM, Monika Weber-Fahr to Shaman, Kathy Sheram, Sharon Cheevers Newell, "B-SPAN: Next Steps and the First Six Months of FY'05," June 29, 2004.

167 WBMs, Kathy Sheram to B-SPAN Team, Monika Weber-Fahr, "B-SPAN Status Meeting #1 – Notes and Next Steps," September 9, 2004; Sheram to B-SPAN Team, Drew Stewart, Weber-Fahr, "B-SPAN Status Meeting #2 – Notes and Next Steps," September 16, 2004; Weber-Fahr to Sheram, Shaman, "B-SPAN Marketing Initiatives – Follow Up from This Morning's Meeting," October 20, 2004; Sheram to Weber-Fahr, Shaman, "B-SPAN Marketing Initiatives – Follow Up from This Morning's Meeting," October 14, 2004; Sheram to Bruno Laporte, Donald Macdonald, Shaman, Ann Spencer, Weber-Fahr, "B-SPAN Presentation to the Learning Board," October 14, 2004; Weber-Fahr to Macdonald, Spencer, Laporte, Shaman, Sheram, "B-SPAN Presentation to the Learning Board," October 27, 2004; Weber-Fahr to Shaman, Sheram, Sharon Cheevers Newell, "B-SPAN: Next Step and First Six Months of FY05," June 29, 2004; HRLOA to Shaman, Sharon Cheevers Newell, Weber-Fahr, "Personnel Image Archiver, Letter of Appointment: SHAMAN, DAVID I. (UPI=86922) (Case=125679, 12 ….. (NOAFT=1)," July 13, 2004; Sheram to Kwaljit Bhutan, Shaman, "Scorecard Indicators for FY05," July 12, 2004; Sheram to Shaman, "IMPT: Your Results Agreement and Scorecard," July 2, 2004; Shaman to Wheeler, "Welcome to My World," July 22, 2004; Shaman to Mark Davis, "Still Wresting with Monsters," October 29, 2004; Memorandum, Shaman to Himself, July 2, "Weber-Fahr says EILT is debating whether to keep B-SPAN or give it to EXT. If WBI keeps B-SPAN, it should offer edited learning products. She said she will run B-SPAN on a low-cost strategy of short-term consultant temporaries."

168 WBMs, Kathy Sheram to Shaman, "IMPT: Your Results Agreement and Scorecard," July 2, 2004; Monika Weber-Fahr to Shaman, Kathy Sheram, "Draft Results Agreement," July 14, 2004; Weber-Fahr to GDMM All, Kiron Bhandari, "EVERYONE: Your Results Agreement for FY05 and Your Learning Program," July 15, 2004.

169 WBMs, Kathy Sheram to Shaman, "IMPT: Your Results Agreement and Scorecard," July 2, 2004; Sheram to B-SPAN Team, Monika Weber-Fahr, "B-SPAN Status Meeting #1 – Notes and Next Steps," September 9, 2004; Weber-Fahr to Sheram, Shaman,

"B-SPAN Marketing Initiatives – Follow Up from This Morning's Meeting," October 20, 2004; Sheram to Weber-Fahr, Shaman, "B-SPAN Marketing Initiatives – Follow Up from This Morning's Meeting," October 14, 2004; Sheram to Bruno Laporte, Donald Macdonald, Shaman, Ann Spencer, Weber-Fahr, "B-SPAN Presentation to the Learning Board," October 14, 2004; Sheram to Kwaljit Bhutan, Shaman, "Scorecard Indicators for FY05," July 12, 2004; Sheram to Shaman, "IMPT: Your Results Agreement and Scorecard," July 2, 2004; Shaman to Wheeler, "Welcome to My World," July 22, 2004.

170 WBM, Shaman to Monika Weber-Fahr, Kathy Sheram, "Draft Results Agreement," July 9, 2004.

171 WBM, Monika Weber-Fahr to Shaman, Kathy Sheram, "B-SPAN Partnership Letters for Bank VPs," July 13, 2004; Weber-Fahr to Shaman, Sheram, Sharon Cheevers Newell, "B-SPAN: Next Step and First Six Months of FY05," June 29, 2004.

172 WBM, Monika Weber-Fahr to Shaman, Kathy Sheram, Sharon Cheevers Newell, "B-SPAN: Next Step and First Six Months of FY05," June 29, 2004.

173 WBM, Shaman to Monika Weber-Fahr, Kathy Sheram, "B-SPAN Partnership Letters to VPs," July 6, 2004.

174 WBM, Shaman to Kathy Sheram, Monika Weber-Fahr, "Another B-SPAN Cost Question in VPU Letter," July 13, 2004.

175 WBM, Kathy Sheram to Shaman, "New On-Line Video Editing Tool From SiSTeR Technologies," July 1, 2004.

176 WBM, Monika Weber-Fahr to Shaman, Kathy Sheram, "B-SPAN Partnership Letters to VPs," July 13, 2004.

177 WBM, Shaman to Monika Weber-Fahr, Kathy Sheram, "B-SPAN Partnership Letters for Bank VPs," July 16, 2004.

178 WBMs, Shaman to Monika Weber-Fahr, Kathy Sheram, "B-SPAN Partnership Letters for Bank VPs," July 16, 2004; Shaman to Wheeler, "Here Tis," January 7, 2005.

179 WBM, Shaman to Monika Weber-Fahr, "B-SPAN Partnership Letters for Bank VPs," July 16, 2004.

180 WBM, Kathy Sheram to Monika Weber-Fahr, Shaman, "B-SPAN Partnership Letters to VPs," July 13, 2004.

181 Shaman Diary, July 2, 2004.

182 WBM, Shaman to Meg Keller, "Resources for the Future, RFF," June 30, 2004.

183 WBM, Shaman to Meg Keller, "Resources for the Future, RFF," July 13, 2004.

184 Meg Keller, "Resources for the Future," to Shaman, RFF, July 13, 2004.

185 Michael Hensler-Mcginnis, "Resources for the Future," to Shaman, World Bank/RFF Partnership, July 14, 2004.

186 Shaman Diary, July 2, 2004.

187 WBMs, Kathy Sheram to Shaman, Spencer, Stewart, "Our Weekly B-SPAN Meeting with Monika Tomorrow, Thursday," September 15, 2004; Sheram to Monika Weber-Fahr, Shaman, Ann Vroom, Michael Kurdyla, Georgetown University, Han Fraeters, Barbara Bitondo, "B-SPAN Production Process," July 21, 2004.

188 WBMs, Sharon Cheevers Newell to WBIGM, "GDMM AWS Schedule and Working Hours," September 3, 2004; Kathy Sheram to Monika Weber-Fahr, Shaman, Ann Vroom, Michael Kurdyla, Georgetown University, Han Fraeters, Barbara Bitondo, "B-SPAN Production Process," July 21, 2004.

189 WBMs, Kathy Sheram to Ann Vroom, Shaman Monika Weber-Fahr, Michael Kurdyla, Georgetown University, Sharon Cheevers Newell, "B-SPAN 'Whereabouts' Sheets on Office Door," August 3, 2004; Weber-Fahr to Shaman, Vroom, Kurdyla, Fraeters, Bitondo, "B-SPAN Production Process," July 23, 2004; Newell to GDMM All, "Small Reminder: If You Haven't Picked Up a Small White Board for Your Door, Please Do So Today. Also Those of You Who Do Not Have an Eraser, I Have Them

Now at My Desk. Please Stop by to Pick One Up. Cheers," October 26, 2004; Newell to GDMM All, "Small Door White Boards," October 20, 2004.

190 WBM, Kathy Sheram to Shaman, Ann Vroom, "B-SPAN Key," July 15, 2004.

191 WBMs, Monika Weber-Fahr to GDMM All, "Our Division Meeting Last Week – and Next Steps on a Number of Items We Discussed," November 22, 2004; Kathy Sheram to Shaman, Ann Vroom, Han Fraeters, Weber-Fahr, "B-SPAN Meeting with Han on the Production Process," July 16, 2004; Sheram to Shaman, Vroom, Fraeters, "Confirmation: Our Meeting with Han, Thursday," July 19, 2004.

192 Han Fraeters biography as catalogued on the World Bank's Intranet website; WBM, Kathy Sheram to WBI Staff, "Please Welcome Mr. Han Fraeters," March 14, 2003.

193 WBM, Shaman to Han Fraeters, "Tuesday Would be OK – 12pm?" July 16, 2004; Shaman Diary, July 23, 2004.

194 WBMs, Monika Weber-Fahr to Shaman, Ann Vroom, Kathy Sheram, Marilyne Yaguibou, "B-SPAN Work Program Meeting Tomorrow," Wednesday at 2pm, July 20, 2004; Weber-Fahr to GDMM All, "Handover Notes: Monika > Kathy, Michael, Veit," July 23, 2004; Shaman Diary, July 23, 2004.

195 WBMs, Kathy Sheram to Ann Vroom, Shaman, Michael Kurdyla, Georgetown University, Bowden, "Status of PREM Postings," July 13, 2004; Vroom to Weber-Fahr, Sheram, Yaguibou, "B-SPAN Work Program Meeting Tomorrow, Wednesday at 2pm – Vroom Slideshow," July 20, 2004; Sheram to Monika Weber-Fahr, Shaman, Vroom, Kurdyla, Han Fraeters, Barbara Bitondo, "B-SPAN Production Process," July 21, 2004.

196 WBM, Shaman to Mark Davis, "Still Wresting with Monsters," October 29, 2004.

197 Shaman Diary, September 9, 2004.

198 WBM, Monika Weber-Fahr to Shaman, Ann Vroom, Kathy Sheram, Bruno Donat, "B-SPAN Announcements – Our Discussion 2 Days Ago – How Best to Publish 'What's Going On,'" July 22, 2004.

199 WBM, Kathy Sheram to Ann Vroom, Shaman, Michael Kurdyla, Georgetown University, Bowden, "Status of PREM Postings," July 13, 2004.

200 WBM, Kathy Sheram to Shaman, Ann Spencer, Drew Stewart, "Our Weekly B-SPAN Meeting with Monika Tomorrow, Thursday," September 15, 2004.

201 WBM, Kathy Sheram to Monika Weber-Fahr, Shaman, Ann Vroom, Michael Kurdyla, Georgetown University, Han Fraeters, Barbara Bitondo, "B-SPAN Production Process," July 21, 2004.

202 WBM, Shaman to Mark Davis, "Still Wresting with Monsters," October 29, 2004.

203 WBM, Shaman to Wheeler, "Welcome to My World," July 22, 2004; Shaman Diary, July 23, 2004.

204 WBM, Wheeler to Shaman, "Welcome to My World," July 23, 2004.

205 WBM, Shaman to Wheeler, "Welcome to My World," July 22, 2004.

206 Shaman Diary, July 28, 2004.

207 WBM, Kathy Sheram to Andrei Tolstopiatenko, Shaman, Monika Weber-Fahr, "B-SPAN Question Please, David and Andrei," September 9, 2004.

208 WBMs, Shaman to Monika Weber-Fahr, "Camera Guidelines," July 22, 2004; Weber-Fahr to Kathy Sheram, Ann Vroom, Drew Stewart, "B-SPAN Camera Guidelines," July 23, 2004; Sheram to Stewart, Vroom, Shaman, "Feedback Please: Camera Guidelines," August 30, 2004.

209 WBMs, Kathy Sheram to Shaman, Drew Stewart, Ann Spencer, "B-SPAN 'Public Event' Notice," September 16, 2004; Sheram to B-SPAN Team, Stewart, "B-SPAN 'Public' Notice and 'Open House' Handout," September 16, 2004.

210 Shaman Diary, July 28, 2004; Shaman Diary, September 9, 2004.

211 WBM, Shaman to Monika Weber-Fahr, Kathy Sheram, "B-SPAN Letters to VPUs Version 3," August 2, 2004.

212 WBM, Shaman to Monika Weber-Fahr, Kathy Sheram, "B-SPAN Letters to VPUs Version 3," August 2, 2004.

213 WBM, Kathy Sheram to Shaman, Monika Weber-Fahr, "IMPT: David, Status Report Needed Before You Go on Leave," July 28, 2004.
214 WBM, Shaman to Monika Weber-Fahr, Kathy Sheram, "B-SPAN Letters to VPUs, Version 3," August 2, 2004.
215 WBM, Kathy Sheram to Shaman, Ann Vroom, Han Fraeters, Weber-Fahr, "B-SPAN Meeting with Han on the Production Process," July 16, 2004; Sheram to Shaman, Vroom, Fraeters, "Confirmation: Our Meeting with Han, Thursday," July 19, 2004.
216 WBMs, Kathy Sheram to B-SPAN Team, Monika Weber-Fahr, "B-SPAN Status Meeting #1 – Notes and Next Steps," September 9, 2004; Weber-Fahr to Sheram, Shaman, "B-SPAN Marketing Initiatives – Follow Up from This Morning's Meeting," October 20, 2004; Sheram to Weber-Fahr, Shaman, "B-SPAN Marketing Initiatives – Follow Up from This Morning's Meeting," October 14, 2004; Sheram to Bruno Laporte, Donald Macdonald, Shaman, Ann Spencer, Weber-Fahr, "B-SPAN Presentation to the Learning Board," October 14, 2004; Sheram to Kwaljit Bhutan, Shaman, "Scorecard Indicators for FY05," July 12, 2004; Sheram to Shaman, "IMPT: Your Results Agreement and Scorecard," July 2, 2004; Shaman to Wheeler, "Welcome to My World," July 22, 2004.
217 Shaman Diary, July 28, 2004.
218 Shaman Diary, July 28, 2004.
219 Memorandum, Shaman to Himself, July 24, "Shaman fallout with Voom prompts Weber-Fahr and Sheram to seek arbitration with Bank mediator though Vroom has had arguments with a number of other Bank staff. Erik Johnson calls the move a deliberate ploy by Weber-Fahr;" Shaman Diary, July 28, 2004.
220 WBMs, Kathy Sheram to Shaman, Monika Weber-Fahr, "ACTION PLEASE: Pending B-SPAN Events and Tapes," July 28, 2004; Shaman to Sheram, Weber-Fahr, "ACTION PLEASE: Pending B-SPAN Events and Tapes," July 28, 2004; Sheram to Shaman, Monika Weber-Fahr, "ACTION PLEASE: B-SPAN Event CD's," July 28, 2004; Sheram to Hector Montenegro, Ann Spencer, Drew Stewart, Shaman, Patrick Tse, Han Fraeters, "B-SPAN – IMPT – NEW PROCEDURES," October 4, 2004.
221 WBMs, Kathy Sheram to Shaman, Monika Weber-Fahr, "B-SPAN Closing Down for the Month of August?" July 2, 2004; Sheram to Shaman, Weber-Fahr, Michael Kurdyla, Georgetown University, Marilyne Yaguibou, Drew Stewart, Barbara Bitondo, Han Fraeters, "B-SPAN in August," July 26, 2004; Sheram to Weber-Fahr, Shaman, Stewart, Bitondo, "B-SPAN 'Absence' Email and Voice Mail," July 26, 2004; Sheram to Weber-Fahr, Shaman, Stewart, Bitondo, "B-SPAN 'Absence' Email and Voice Mail – Final Version," July 27, 2004.
222 WBM, Kathy Sheram to Shaman, Monika Weber-Fahr, "IMPT: David, Status Reports Needed Before You Go on Leave," July 28, 2004.
223 WBM, Shaman to Kathy Sheram, Monika Weber-Fahr, "IMPT: David, Status Reports Needed Before You Go on Leave," July 28, 2004.
224 WBMs, Kathy Sheram to B-SPAN Team, Drew Stewart, Monika Weber-Fahr, "B-SPAN Status Meeting #2 – Notes and Next Steps," September 16, 2004; Sheram to B-SPAN Team, Weber-Fahr, "B-SPAN Status Meeting #1 – Notes and Next Steps," September 9, 2004; Weber-Fahr to Donald Macdonald, Ann Spencer, Bruno Laporte, Shaman, Sheram, "B-SPAN Presentation to the Learning Board," October 27, 2004; Weber-Fahr to Shaman, Sheram, Sharon Cheevers Newell, "B-SPAN: Next Step and First Six Months of FY05," June 29, 2004; Sheram to Kwaljit Bhutan, Shaman, "Scorecard Indicators for FY05," July 12, 2004; Sheram to Shaman, "IMPT: Your Results Agreement and Scorecard," July 2, 2004; Shaman to Wheeler, "Welcome to My World," July 22, 2004.
225 WBMs, Monika Weber-Fahr to Donald MacDonald, Ann Spencer, Bruno Laporte, Shaman, Kathy Sheram, "B-SPAN Presentation to the Learning Board," October 27, 2004; Shaman to Mark Davis, "Still Wrestling with Monsters," October 28, 2004;

Davis to Shaman, "Still Wrestling with Monsters," October 29, 2004; Shaman to Davis, "Still Wrestling with Monsters," October 29, 2004.

226 WBMs, Kathy Sheram to Shaman, "Test Absence Message," August 3, 2004; Ann Vroom to Shaman, "Testing Out of Office Message," August 3, 2004; Bryan Waller to Sheram, Sharon Cheevers Newell, Monika Weber-Fahr, Drew Stewart, Shaman, "David I. Shaman/Person/World Bank is Out of the Office," August 4, 2004.

227 WBM, Wheeler to Shaman, "Coffee with Michele," August 19, 2004.

228 WBM, Claude Salem to Bank Staff Various, "Au Revoir … for Now!" September 9, 2004.

229 WBM, Bruno Donat to GDMM All, "FYI – Principles in Behavior," August 16, 2004.

230 WBMs, Monika Weber-Fahr to GDLN Management Team, GDMM All, WBI EILT, Nicholas Gorjestani, Gerard Byam, Marc Jean Yves Lixi, Bobak Rezaian, Micahel Broemmel, Mwangi Wachira, "Towards New Challenges in the Africa GDLN Team," October 8, 2004.

231 Shaman Diary, July 28, 2004.

232 WBMs, Kathy Sheram to Shaman, Drew Stewart, Monika Weber-Fahr, Ann Vroom, "B-SPAN Team Meeting," September 7, 2004; Sheram to Shaman, Stewart, Weber-Fahr, Vroom, "B-SPAN Meeting Please – 2pm Today," September 7, 2004; Sheram to Shaman, Stewart, "Hi Drew and David
This is to Confirm Our 2pm B-SPAN Meeting Today in My Office. Thanks Kathy," September 7, 2004.

233 WBMs, Kathy Sheram to Ann Vroom, Ann Spencer, Shaman, Drew Stewart, "3 New Events in the Log," September 7, 2004; Shaman to Sheram, Vroom, Spencer, Stewart, "3 New Events in the Log," September 7, 2004.

234 WBM, Kathy Sheram to Shaman, Drew Stewart, "David – Please Handle Today, Wednesday – Re: AUDIO PROBLEM – Enabling Environment for Civic Engagement Advisory Board Meeting – June 7th Tape," September 8, 2004.

235 WBM, Kathy Sheram to Shaman, "B-SPAN Routing Slip," September 8, 2004.

236 WBM, Kathy Sheram to Ann Vroom, Ann Spencer, Shaman, Drew Stewart, "3 New Events in the Log," September 7, 2004; Sheram to B-SPAN Team, "B-SPAN Client Information Checklist," September 7, 2004; Sheram to B-SPAN Team, Stewart, "B-SPAN – Client Checklist," September 16, 2004.

237 WBMs, Kathy Sheram to Shaman, "Please Note Format for BSPAN Summaries," September 10, 2004; Sheram to Ann Spencer, Shaman, Hector Montenegro, "BSPAN Summaries as Word Documents," October 6, 2004; Sheram to Spencer, Shaman, Montenegro, "B-SPAN – Template for Summaries," October 6, 2004; Sheram to B-SPAN Team, "Guidelines for Summaries – Host and Notification Information," August 16, 2004.

238 WBM, Kathy Sheram to Hector Montenegro, Shaman, Ann Spencer, Drew Stewart, "BSPAN Work Load," October 5, 2004.

239 WBMs, Kathy Sheram to Shaman, Andrei Tolstopiatenko, Monika Weber-Fahr, "B-SPAN – Questions Please, David and Andrei," September 9, 2004; Tolstopiatenko to Sheram, Shaman, Weber-Fahr, "B-SPAN Questions Please, David and Andrei," September 9, 2004; Memorandum, Shaman to Himself, September 7, "Sheram reiterates the goal of eliminating the archives. She notes Weber-Fahr has terminated the usage of 'webcasting station' and said we are a 'service.' This change is reflected in the What is B-SPAN web page the Host Section is deleted."

240 WBM, Kathy Sheram to Ann Vroom, Ann Spencer, Shaman, "Help Please: Your Bank IP," September 1, 2004; Shaman Diary, September 9, 2004.

241 Shaman Diary, September 16, 2004.

242 WBM, Kathy Sheram to B-SPAN Team, Drew Stewart, Han Fraeters, Kawaljit Bhutani, "Scorecard Data: July and August for B-SPAN," September 8, 2004.

243 WBM, Ann Vroom to Kathy Sheram, B-SPAN Team, Monika Weber-Fahr, Han Fraeters, "Scorecard?" September 8, 2004.

244 WBM, Ann Vroom to Veit Burger, Kathy Sheram, Hector Montenegro, Patrick Tse, Monika Weber-Fahr, "Your CD Request," September 8, 2004.

245 WBMs, Ann Vroom to Veit Burger, Kathy Sheram, Han Fraeters, Hector Montenegro, Patrick Tse, Monika Weber-Fahr, "Your CD Request," September 8, 2004; Sheram to B-SPAN Team, "Welcome to Anne Spencer," July 26, 2004; Weber-Fahr to WBI Staff, GDLN Management Team, "Welcome to Annie Spencer!" August 10, 2004.

246 WBM, Ann Vroom to Kathy Sheram, Manpower Temporaries, Sharon Cheevers Newell, Sarika Jain, Roula Yazigi, Monika Weber-Fahr, Ann Spencer, Hector Montenegro, Patrick Tse, "Won't Be In – Please Fax My Timesheet for this Last Week w. B-SPAN (Ending 9/12/04 – Job # 20588)," September 8, 2004; Vroom to Tse, B-SPAN Team, "Just for Training Events Shows Up on B-SPAN Even though Not Posted!" September 29, 2004.

247 WBMs, Kathy Sheram to B-SPAN Team, "IMPT: Today – 11am Meeting with Monika in J2-155," September 9, 2004; Sheram to B-SPAN Team, Monika Weber-Fahr, "B-SPAN Status Meeting #1 – Notes and Next Steps," September 9, 2004; Memorandum, Sheram to B-SPAN Team, Weber-Fahr, "B-SPAN Status Meeting," September 9, 2004; B-SPAN Team (via Kathy Sheram) to Ann Vroom, "Hi Ann – Just a Note to Say How Wonderful It Is to Have the B-SPAN Account Cleaned Up! THANK YOU!!! Kathy (eom)," September 2, 2004; Sheram to Kwaljit Bhutan, Shaman, "Scorecard Indicators for FY05," July 12, 2004; Sheram to Shaman, "IMPT: Your Results Agreement and Scorecard," July 2, 2004; Shaman to Wheeler, "Welcome to My World," July 22, 2004.

248 WBM, Monika Weber-Fahr to Shaman, Ann Vroom, Kathy Sheram, Bruno Donat, "B-SPAN Announcements – Our Discussion 2 Days Ago – How to Best Publish 'What's Going On,'" July 22, 2004.

249 WBMs, Kathy Sheram to Shaman, Drew Stewart, Ann Spencer, "B-SPAN 'Public Event' Notice," September 16, 2004; Sheram to B-SPAN Team, Stewart, "B-SPAN 'Public' Notice and 'Open House' Handout," September 16, 2004; Sheram to Shaman, Spencer, Stewart, Han Fraeters, "IMPT: DAVID – Open House for Multi Media Center and B-SPAN," September 15, 2004; Sheram to Fraeters, Bruno Donat, Shaman, Spencer, Stewart, "Help Please: Public Notice for B-SPAN Events," September 15, 2004; Sheram to Shaman, Spencer, "IMPT: David, Regarding New B-SPAN Events," September 10, 2004; Monika Weber-Fahr to Shaman, Ann Vroom, Sheram, Bruno Donat, "B-SPAN Announcements – Our Discussion 2 Days Ago – How Best to Publish 'What's Going On,'" July 22, 2004; Sheram to B-SPAN Team, Weber-Fahr, "B-SPAN Status Meeting #1 – Notes and Next Steps," September 9, 2004; Sheram to Kwaljit Bhutan, Shaman, "Scorecard Indicators for FY05," July 12, 2004; Sheram to Shaman, "IMPT: Your Results Agreement and Scorecard," July 2, 2004; Shaman to Wheeler, "Welcome to My World," July 22, 2004.

250 WBM, Kathy Sheram to Hector Montenegro, Drew Stewart, Ann Spencer, Shaman, Han Fraeters, Patrick Tse, "B-SPAN – Help Please, Hector," October 4, 2004.

251 WBM, Shaman to Roberto Zagha, Muriel Darlington, "Practitioners in Development Lecture Series: Rima KHALAF HUNAIDI, Tuesday September 14, 2004, 12:00-2: pm," September 9, 2004; Memorandum, Shaman to Himself, August 26, "Monika Weber-Fahr decides on cost recovery at task manager level without further discussion. It is $350, representing a $61 profit on every event. Under Bank rules described by WBI's senior budget analyst, Marshall Schreier, WBI staff is not allowed to knowingly profit on services provided to Bank staff."

252 WBMs, WBMs, Monika Weber-Fahr to Donald MacDonald, Ann Spencer, Bruno Laporte, Shaman, Kathy Sheram, "B-SPAN Presentation to the Learning Board," October 27, 2004; Shaman to Mark Davis, "Still Wrestling with Monsters," October

28, 2004; Davis to Shaman, "Still Wrestling with Monsters," October 29, 2004; Shaman to Davis, "Still Wrestling with Monsters," October 29, 2004; Kathy Sheram to B-SPAN Team, Drew Stewart, Monika Weber-Fahr, "B-SPAN Status Meeting #2 – Notes and Next Steps," September 16, 2004; Weber-Fahr to Shaman, Sheram, Sharon Cheevers Newell, "B-SPAN: Next Step and First Six Months of FY05," June 29, 2004; Memorandum, Shaman to Himself, September 8, "Monika Weber-Fahr says at B-SPAN staff meeting that she supports restricted access materials. Reiterates need to announce Chatham House Rules. She said without funding support from WBI, the cost recovery model will assess demand which will determine if the service is to be continued. Sheram reiterates her belief the charge should actually increase to include indirect costs. Sheram adds that edited materials on B-SPAN is consistent with the principles in the new model."

253 WBMs, Dhalia Khalifa to Shaman, Hafed Al Ghwell, Patricia Singer, "Event on September 23 from 1 to 3pm in J1-050 – Please Confirm," September 10, 2004; Louise Cord to Shaman, Esteban Hernandez, Ignacio Fiestas, "BBL on Pro-Poor Growth and Inequality – China's (Uneven) Progress Against Poverty – Wednesday, September 15th, 12:30 – 2:00 pm, Room MC6-W150," September 11, 2004; Asuka Sato to Shaman, Marco Nicoli, "Request for B-SPAN," September 24, 2004; Yvette Atkins to Shaman, B-SPAN Team, Drew Stewart, Olusoji Adeyi, Suprotik Basu, "B-SPAN Coverage of Improving Health Status and Promoting Equity – Cancellation," September 30, 2004; Francis Muraya to Sona Panajyan, "Seminar on 'City Strategic Planning and Local Economic Development' – on B-SPAN," February 25, 2005; Tara Sharafudeen to B-SPAN Team, Panajyan, Luis Constantino, Juanid Kamal Ahmad, "Your Event 'Challenge of Urban Finance and Governance in India,' " February 18, 2005; Shaman Diary, October 20, 2004.

254 WBM, Shaman to Wheeler, "Loose Ends," September 20, 2004.

255 WBM, Mojgan Sami to Shaman, Reidar Kvam, "B-SPAN Request: INVITATION SD ROUNDTABLE: 'From Empire to Community' Wednesday, September 22, 3-5PM, JB 1-075," September 13, 2004.

256 WBM, Mojgan Sami to Shaman, Reidar Kvam, Najma Siddiqi, "B-SPAN Price Increase from $350 – $750 (Concerns)," September 13, 2004.

257 WBM, Monika Weber-Fahr to Shaman, Kathy Sheram, "For Your Comment: B-SPAN Price Increase from $350 – $750 (Concerns)," September 15, 2004.

258 WBM, Mogjam Sami to Shaman, "B-SPAN REQUEST PLEASE – SD ROUNDTABLE: Empowered Participatory Governance: Enhancing Accountability and Capacity, Thursday December 16, 2004; 10:30am – 12:00pm (Room JB1-075)," December 13, 2004.

259 WBMs, Kathy Sheram to B-SPAN Team, Drew Stewart, Monika Weber-Fahr, "BSPAN Status Meeting #2 – Notes and Next Steps," September 16, 2004; Weber-Fahr to Donald Macdonald, Ann Spencer, Bruno Laporte, Shaman, Sheram, "B-SPAN Presentation to the Learning Board," October 27, 2004.

260 WBM, Mogjam Sami to Shaman, "B-SPAN and WDR Workshop," November 14, 2004.

261 WBM, Ann Spencer to Shaman, Kathy Sheram, "Encoding," September 15, 2004.

262 WBMs, Rachel Beth Kaufman to Shaman, Kimberly Switlick, Erika Yanick, Monika Weber-Fahr, "Water, Sanitation, Hygiene & Health BBL – B-SPAN Filming," September 24, 2004; Shaman to Kaufman, Switlick, Yanick, Weber-Fahr, "Water, Sanitation, Hygiene & Health BBL – B-SPAN Filming," September 24, 2004; Weber-Fahr to Shaman, Kathy Sheram, "Kathy/David – Could I Have Your Recommendations on What to Do With This – and With Background … Re: Water, Sanitation, Hygiene & Health BBL – B-SPAN Filming," September 27, 2004; Shaman to Weber-Fahr, Sheram, "Kathy/David – Could I Have Your Recommendations on

What to Do With This – and With Background … Re: Water, Sanitation, Hygiene & Health BBL – B-SPAN Filming," September 27, 2004.

263 WBMs, Kathy Sheram to Ann Spencer, Shaman, Drew Stewart, "B-SPAN Handover Meeting," September 16, 2004; Sheram to B-SPAN Team, Veit Burger, Drew Stewart, "My Annual Leave 18-25 August," August 17, 2004; Shaman to Wheeler, "Loose Ends," September 20, 2004.

264 Shaman Diary, September 16, 2004.

265 WBMs, Kathy Sheram to Drew Stewart, Shaman, Ann Spencer, "Rescheduled: BSPAN Handover Meeting (Sep 16 03:00PM EDT)," September 14, 2004; Sheram to Shaman, Spencer, Stewart, "B-SPAN Handover Meeting," September 16, 2004; Memorandum, Shaman to Himself, September 16, "In a follow up meeing, Sheram said cost recovery price for WB clients set by Monika Weber-Fahr alone, but she needed/received approval from EILT for extending the coverage to WBI clients;" Memorandum, Shaman to Himself, September 13, "Sheram states that Monika Weber-Fahr has decided not to send cost recovery letters to VPU's but rather clients instead."

266 WBMs, Wheeler to Shaman, "This Sucks," September 16, 2004; Shaman to Wheeler, "Brewin'," September 9, 2004.

267 Shaman Diary, September 17, 2004.

268 WBMs, Shaman to Wheeler, "Loose Ends," September 20, 2004; Wheeler to Shaman, "Loose Ends," September 22, 2004.

269 WBM, Lee Morrison to B-SPAN Team, "Concern about the B-SPAN Web Page …" September 16, 2004.

270 WBMs, Lee Morrison to B-SPAN Team, "Concern about the B-SPAN Web Page…" September 17, 2004; Shaman to Morrison, B-SPAN Team, "Concern about the B-SPAN Web Page…" September 17, 2004; Shaman to Morrison, B-SPAN Team, "Concern about the B-SPAN Web Page…" September 22, 2004; Hector Montenegro to Shaman, "Banner," September 27, 2004.

271 WBM, Kathy Sheram to B-SPAN Team, Drew Stewart, Monika Weber-Fahr, "B-SPAN Status Meeting #2 – Notes and Next Steps," September 16, 2004; Weber-Fahr to Donald Macdonald, Ann Spencer, Bruno Laporte, Shaman, Sheram, "B-SPAN Presentation to the Learning Board," October 27, 2004; Weber-Fahr to Shaman, Sheram, Sharon Cheevers Newell, "B-SPAN: Next Step and First Six Months of FY05," June 29, 2004; Shaman to Mark Davis, "Still Wresting with Monsters," October 29, 2004; Memorandum, Shaman to Himself, September 16, "At B-SPAN staff meeting, Monika Weber-Fahr and Kathy Sheram agree that edited materials will be accepted from internal clients by Shaman and according to Weber-Fahr 'for the moment' will be housed on B-SPAN with some accompanying identification noting that the event has been edited. Weber-Fahr said discussion would continue over the next few months on what business lines the new model will take including whether to host edited versus non-edited events, open versus restricted access events. Weber-Fahr wants her email response from the previous day on charges to be sent to anyone who complains."

272 WBM, Shaman to Michael Hensler-McGinnis, Resources for the Future, "Posting RFF Event on China on B-SPAN," November 2, 2004; Hensler-McGinnis, Resources for the Future, to Shaman, "Posting RFF Event on China on B-SPAN," November 1, 2004.

273 WBM, Kathy Sheram to Ann Spencer, Shaman, "B-SPAN Procedure – Event Cancellations," October 14, 2004; Shaman to Wheeler, "Loose Ends," September 20, 2004.

274 WBMs, Shaman to B-SPAN Distribution List, "B-SPAN Newsletter, September 2004," September 27, 2004; Shaman to Wheeler, "Loose Ends," September 20, 2004; Wheeler to Shaman, "Loose Ends," September 22, 2004.

275 WBM, Shaman to Wheeler, "Loose Ends," September 22, 2004; World Bank *Internal Communications*, "Immediate Dangers Versus Longer Term Actions," September 21, 2004; Shaman to Wheeler, "Loose Ends," September 20, 2004.

276 Shaman Diary, September 9, 2004.

277 Shaman Diary, September 15, 2004.

278 WBMs, Shaman to Wheeler, "Loose Ends," September 20, 2004; Jeeyeon Seo to Shaman, "Link to PPT," September 21, 2004.

279 WBM, Shaman to David Leonard, Sefik Cardak, "October 11, Tuesday, 11am in Dave Leonard's Office," September 23, 2004.

280 WBMs, Shaman to Jeff McCoy, Nicole Frost, "B-SPAN Link for the Practitioners in Development Lecture with Rima Khala Hunaidi," September 23, 2004; Shaman to Bart Stevens, Julius Wamey, "B-SPAN Link for the Practitioners in Development Lecture with Rima Khala Hunaidi," September 23, 2004; Frost to Shaman, McCoy, "B-SPAN Link for the Practitioners in Development Lecture with Rima Khala Hunaidi," September 24, 2004.

281 World Bank Weekly Update, September 20, 2004.

282 WBM, Hafed Al Ghwell to Shaman, "B-SPAN," September 29, 2004.

283 WBM, Shaman to Hafed Al Ghwell, B-SPAN Team, "B-SPAN," September 29, 2004.

284 WBMs, Hafed Al Ghwell to Frannie Leautier, Monika Weber-Fahr, "B-SPAN," September 29, 2004; Hafed Al-Ghwell to Shaman, "B-SPAN," September 22, 2004

285 WBM, Frannie Leautier to Hafed Al Ghwell, Monika Weber-Fahr, Kathy Sheram, Shaman, "B-SPAN," October 1, 2004.

286 WBMs, Kathy Sheram to Ann Vroom, J. Serrano, K Force, Monika Weber-Fahr, Sharon Cheevers Newell, Marilyne Yaguibou, Mirza Hamner, "WBI/B-SPAN Assignment," September 27, 2004; Vroom to Sheram, Serrano, Weber-Fahr, Newell, Yaguibou, Hamner, "WBI/B-SPAN Assignment," September 27, 2004; Sheram to Vroom, Shaman, Ann Spencer, "B-SPAN Assignment," September 27, 2004.

287 WBMs, Kathy Sheram to Ann Vroom, J. Serrano, K Force, Monika Weber-Fahr, Sharon Cheevers Newell, Marilyne Yaguibou, Mirza Hamner, "WBI/B-SPAN Assignment," September 27, 2004; Vroom to Sheram, Serrano, Weber-Fahr, Newell, Yaguibou, Hamner, "WBI/B-SPAN Assignment," September 27, 2004; Sheram to Vroom, Shaman, Ann Spencer, "B-SPAN Assignment," September 27, 2004.

288 WBMs, Ann Vroom to B-SPAN Team, Monika Weber-Fahr, "BSPAN Production Room Equip. – I'm Gonna Go Get a Cup of Coffee – Most of the Equip is "Down" – Didn't Anybody Check?" September 28, 2004; Vroom to B-SPAN Team, Weber-Fahr, "B-SPAN Prod. Room Equip.," September 28, 2004.

289 WBMs, Kathy Sheram to Ann Vroom, B-SPAN Team, Monika Weber-Fahr, "B-SPAN Prod. Room Equip. – I'm Going to Get a Cup of Coffee – Most of the Equip is "Down" – Didn't Anybody Check?" September 28, 2004; Vroom to Sheram, B-SPAN Team, Weber-Fahr, "B-SPAN Prod. Room Equip. – I'm Going to Get a Cup of Coffee – Most of the Equip is "Down" – Didn't Anybody Check?" September 28, 2004.

290 WBM, Kathy Sheram to Hector Montenegro, Drew Stewart, Ann Spencer, Shaman, Han Fraeters, Patrick Tse, "B-SPAN – Help Please, Hector," October 4, 2004.

291 WBMs, Erik Johnson to Kathy Sheram, "Restoring Global Balance Together – Re: Tapes 3 & 4," August 13, 2004; Johnson to Sheram, "Problem w. My Timesheets – From 'Bad' to 'Worse,'" August 18, 2004.

292 WBMs, Bryan Waller to B-SPAN Team, "B-SPAN Lotus Notes Cleanup," August 31, 2004; Waller to Shaman, "B-SPAN Lotus Notes Cleanup," October 19, 2004.

293 WBMs, Monika Weber-Fahr to Shaman, Kathy Sheram, "Circulating a CV for an ETC Position Among Communications Staff," September 28, 2004; Weber-Fahr to GDMM All, GDLN Management Team, K. Bhandara, "Towards More Continuity in the B-SPAN Team: Announcing a Job Opening (Either ETC or DA)," October 1, 2004; Weber-Fahr to Robert King, Kathy Sheram, "Circulating a CV for an

ETC Position among the Communication's Staff," September 28, 2004; WBI Job Description, "B-SPAN Coordinator, 92704," November 9, 2004.
294 WBI Job Description, "B-SPAN Coordinator, 92704," November 9, 2004.
295 Kathy Sheram to Shaman, Ann Spencer, Hector Montenegro, Patrick Tse, Sundeep Kalidindi, Drew Stewart, "B-SPAN Event Mystery: Practitioners w/ Rima Khalif Hunaidi - THANKS," October 21, 2004.
296 WBMs, Wheeler to Shaman, "B-SPAN Newsletter - Edits, Please," November 2, 2004; Shaman to Mark Davis, "B-SPAN Newsletter - Edits, Please," November 2, 2004; Davis to Shaman, "B-SPAN Newsletter - Edits, Please," November 2, 2004.
297 WBM, Shaman to Wheeler, "Fair and Balanced Coverage..." October 21, 2004.
298 WBM, Monika Weber-Fahr to Shaman, Kathy Sheram, Veit Burger, "David - Are They B-SPAN Clients? Veit - Are They GDLN Clients? (ESMAP in Principle has $$ - Though Not Necessarily for Bank Staff - to Cover Knowledge Type Work)," September 28, 2004; Marco Nicoli to Shaman, "Disability and Development Conference, B-SPAN Coverage," October 22, 2004; Judith Heumann to Shaman, "2004 International Day of Disabled Persons, Disability and Development Conference, B-SPAN Coverage," October 19, 2004; Kathy Sheram to Sona Panajyan, Ann Spencer, B-SPAN Team, Drew Stewart, Sundeep Kalidindi, "Pricing Question," February 3, 2005.
299 WBMs, Barbara Yale to B-SPAN Team, Shaman, Julius Gwyer, Osman Cuadros, "B-SPAN Coverage of OED Conference on Effectiveness of Policies and Reforms for October 4, 2004," September 29, 2004; Shaman to Yale, B-SPAN Team, Shaman, Gwyer, Cuadros, "B-SPAN Coverage of OED Conference on Effectiveness of Policies and Reforms for October 4, 2004," September 29, 2004; B-SPAN Team (via Sheram) to Yale, B-SPAN Team, Shaman, Gwyer, Cuadros, "B-SPAN Coverage of OED Conference on Effectiveness of Policies and Reforms for October 4, 2004," September 29, 2004; Shaman Diary, September 29, 2004.
300 WBMs, B-SPAN Team sent by Shaman to Barbara Yale, "B-SPAN Coverage of OED Conference on Effectiveness of Policies and Reforms for October 4, 2004," September 29, 2004; Wadee Deeprawat to Anis Dani, Mogjam Sami, Joyce Chinsen, "B-SPAN of WDR Workshop," November 10, 2004.
301 WBM, Ann Vroom to Patrick Tse, B-SPAN Team, "Just for Training Event Shows Up on BSPAN Even Tho NOT Posted!" September 29, 2004.
302 WBMs, Shaman to Wheeler, "Fair and Balanced Coverage..." October 21, 2004; Kathy Sheram to Drew Stewart, Hector Montenegro, Bryan Waller, Patrick Tse, Ann Spencer, Han Fraeters, "B-SPAN: Equipment Room Needs and Next Steps," October 6, 2004.
303 WBM, Andrei Tolstopiatenko to WBI Staff, "July - Web Statistics Report for WBI," September 13, 2004.
304 WBM, Andrei Tolstopiatenko to WBI Staff, "September - Web Statistics Report for WBI," October 13, 2004.
305 Shaman Diary, October 5, 2004.
306 Shaman Diary, October 5, 2004.
307 WBM, Shaman to Kathy Sheram, Monika Weber-Fahr, "B-SPAN CV," October 14, 2004.
308 WBM, Arseny Malov to Shaman, "B-SPAN Statistics with WB CO Added," June 26, 2003; Malov to Tolstopiatenko, "B-SPAN Statistics with WB CO Added," June 11, 2003.
309 WBMs, Shaman to Bruno Laporte, I Team, Karin Millet, "Productive Summer," August 18, 2003; Shaman to Lawrence Macdonald, Nick Harrison, (web4dev) "World Bank Offer to Swap Web Traffic Data," September 24, 2004.
310 WBI Web Statistics for FY04, July 2003 through June 2004.
311 WBM, Scott Johnson to Shaman, "Newsletter Ranking," October 6, 2004.

312 WBM, Shaman to Julius Warmey, Patricia Overend, "B-SPAN Links for Existing *World Bank Today* Articles," October 12, 2004.
313 Shaman Diary, October 7, 2004.
314 World Bank's Information Solution Newsletter, ISG, September 30, 2004.
315 Shaman Diary, October 12, 2004.
316 Shaman Diary, October 14, 2004.
317 WBM, Monika Weber-Fahr to WBI Staff, "Welcome Sundeep Kalindindi to WBI's GDLN and Multimedia Family," October 28, 2004; Kathy Sheram to Hector Montenegro, Ann Spencer, Shaman, Drew Stewart, Han Fraeters, Andrei Tolstopiatenko, Sharon Cheevers Newell, "B-SPAN Technical Assistant," October 15, 2004.
318 WBM, Kathy Sheram to Donald MacDonald, Ann Spencer, Bruno Laporte, Shaman, Monika Weber-Fahr, "B-SPAN Presentation to the Learning Board," October 14, 2004; Shaman Diary, October 14, 2004.
319 WBM, Jerry Floyd to Shaman, Andres Mcalister, Elisa Liberatori-Prati, "To: Dave Shaman Re: Would Like to meet with You on Friday 10/15 Re: B-SPAN Telecast of 10/25 Lecture by Hernando de Soto," October 14, 2004.
320 WBM, Andres Mcalister to Hajrudin Beca, Larissa Fastovsky, David Leonard, Shaman, Elisa Liberatori-Prati, Jerry Floyd, "Channel 13 and Video Streaming of October 25 Event at Preston 3-6," October 21, 2004; Shaman to Mark Davis, "Still Wresting with Monsters," October 29, 2004.
321 WBM, Shaman to Hernando de Soto, Institute for Liberty and Democracy, "B-SPAN Coverage of Your World Bank Speech on October 25th," October 15, 2004.
322 WBM, Shaman to Wheeler, "Fair and Balanced Coverage..." October 21, 2004.
323 WBM, Shaman to Mark Davis, "Still Wresting with Monsters," October 29, 2004.
324 WBMs, Kathy Sheram to Ann Spencer, Shaman, Sundeep Kalidindi, Sharon Cheevers Newell, Drew Stewart, "B-SPAN and My Schedule," October 19, 2004; Sheram to Spencer, Shaman, Kalidindi, "B-SPAN Production Meeting, 20 Oct: MINUTES," October 20, 2004.
325 WBM, Shaman to Wheeler, "Fair and Balanced Coverage..." October 21, 2004.
326 WBM, Shaman to Wheeler, "New Intelligence," November 17, 2004.
327 WBM, Shaman to Wheeler, "Fair and Balanced Coverage..." October 21, 2004.
328 WBM, Shaman to Wheeler, "Fair and Balanced Coverage..." October 21, 2004.
329 WBM, Shaman to Wheeler, Fair and Balanced Coverage..." October 21, 2004.
330 WBM, Shaman to Sundeep Kalindindi, Ann Spencer, Hector Montenegro, B-SPAN Team, "Summary of Knowledge, Archives and Development with Hernando de Soto," October 26, 2004; "De Soto Inaugurates New Archives," *World Bank Today*, October 28, 2004.
331 The Millennium Development Goals Report 2005, United Nations.
332 WBM, Shaman to Sundeep Kalindindi, "Home Page Update," October 27, 2004.
333 WBM, Deborah Campos to Jerry Floyd, Elisa Liberatori-Prati, Shaman, "Coverage of the President's 10/25 Reception on Mr. Wolfensohn's Website," October 27, 2004; "De Soto Inaugurates New Archives," *World Bank Today*, October 28, 2004.
334 WBM, Shaman to B-SPAN Distribution List, "B-SPAN Newsletter, October 2004," October 28, 2004.
335 Odelia Funke, U.S. Environmental Protection Agency, to Shaman, "B-SPAN Newsletter, October 2004," November 1, 2004; Dr. Donald Beck to Shaman, "B-SPAN Newsletter, October 2004," November 1, 2004; WBM, Elisa Liberatori-Prati to Shaman, "B-SPAN Newsletter, October 2004," October 28, 2004; Jim Kessler, Third Way, to Shaman, "B-SPAN Newsletter, October 2004," October 28, 2004.
336 WBM, Shaman to Hernando de Soto, "New Event on B-SPAN: Knowledge, Archives and Development with Hernando de Soto," October 26, 2004.

337 WBM, Sharon Cheevers Newell to Shaman, Drew Stewart, Han Fraeters, Stuart Machir, Andrei Tolstopiatenko, "Interview for the B-SPAN Coordinator Position – JPS #200409102," October 25, 2004.
338 WBMs, Monika Weber-Fahr to WBI EILT, Andrei Tolstopiatenko, GDMM All, Andrei – Tolstopiatenko: "SMO for October 29-November 17, 2004, TOT Trip to India, Philippines and Japan," October 26, 2004; Shaman to Wheeler, "Interview for the B-SPAN Coordinator Position – JPS #200409102," October 27, 2004.
339 WBM, Nicole Frost to Shaman, "Where Are U Going?" October 21, 2004.
340 Shaman Diary, September 9, 2004.
341 WBM, Kathy Sheram to Shaman, Ann Spencer, Sundeep Kalidindi, Monika Weber-Fahr, Han Fraeters, Drew Stewart, "B-SPAN Newsletter – Edits, Please," November 1, 2004.
342 Shaman Diary, September 28, 2004.
343 WBM, Mohamed Muhsin to Frannie Leautier, Ronald Maclean-Abaroa, Roumeen Islam, Shaman, Monika Weber-Fahr, Andres Mcalister, Elisa Liberatori-Prati, "Oct. 25 de Soto Lecture," November 3, 2004.
344 WBM, Monika Weber-Fahr to Shaman, Kathy Sheram, Annie Seys, Sundeep Kalidindi, Drew Stewart, "Compliments to the B-SPAN Team … Oct. 25, de Soto Lecture," November 3, 2004.
345 WBM, Frannie Leautier to Mohamed Muhsin, Andres Mcalister, Shaman, Elisa Liberatori-Prati, Monika Weber-Fahr, Ronald Maclean-Abaroa, Roumeen Islam, "de Soto Lecture," November 4, 2004.
346 WBM, Shaman to Frannie Leautier, "Oct. 25 de Soto Lecture," November 8, 2004.
347 Shaman Diary, November 13, 2004.
348 WBM, Shaman to David Leonard, Sefik Cardak, "B-SPAN Traffic Data," November 1, 2004.
349 WBM, Shaman to Maya Brahmam, Angelica Silvero, "B-SPAN – Presidential Lectures," November 2, 2004.
350 WBMs, Sharon Cheevers Newell to Shaman, Drew Stewart, Han Fraeters, Stuart Machir, Andrei Tolstopiatenko, "Interview for the B-SPAN Coordinator Position – JPS #200409102," October 25, 2004; Wheeler to Shaman, "Go For It!" November 11, 2004; World Bank Institute Annual Report, Fiscal Year 2004; World Bank Institute's Development Outreach, Special Report, October 2004.
351 WBM, Shaman to Wheeler, "US Elections 2000-2004: What Changed?" November 15, 2004; Monika Weber-Fahr, "Schedule for November 15-November 22, 2004."
352 WBM, Han Fraeters to MM All, "Please Mark Your Calendars – All MM Staff Expected to Contribute: MM Center, 2nd Open House, 11/18 12-2pm," October 22, 2004; Shaman Diary, November 19, 2004.
353 WBMs, Monika Weber-Fahr to GDMM All, "News Arrangements for the GDLN-AMS Team," December 6, 2004; Kathy Sheram to Sundeep Kalindindi, Drew Stewart, Han Fraeters, ann Spencer, Shaman, "Your Work Program," November 11, 2004.
354 WBM, Kathy Sheram to Ann Spencer, Shaman, Sundeep Kalidindi, Drew Stewart, Sharon Cheevers Newell, "B-SPAN Production Meeting and Handover Meeting," November 16, 2004.
355 WBM, Sona Panajyan to Shaman, "Brief Meeting?" November 5, 2004; Shaman Diary, November 19, 2004.
356 WBM, Sona Panajyan to Shaman, "Thanks," November 17, 2004.
357 WBMs, Sona Panajyan to Shaman, "Thanks," November 17, 2004: Shaman to Panajyan, "Thanks," November 17, 2004.
358 Shaman Diary, November 19, 2004.
359 WBMs, Shaman to Wheeler, "New Intelligence," November 17, 2004; Sunetra Puri to WBI Staff, Commnet Steering Group, "TODAY Story on BUILDING STATE CAPACITY IN AFRICA," November 22, 2004.

360 WBM, Shaman to Wheeler, "New Intelligence," November 17, 2004.
361 WBMs, Shaman to Wheeler, "Fair and Balanced Coverage..." October 21, 2004; Memorandum, Shaman to Wheeler, "Revenue Log," November 11, 2004; Shaman to Wheeler, "New Intelligence," November 17, 2004.
362 WBMs, Shaman to Frannie Leautier, Claire Marshall, Institute of Governance, Laura Edgar, Institute of Governance, Mary McNeil, Paula Duggan, Julie Bockarie, "New Event on B-SPAN: Partnerships and Communications: Linking Civil Society and Government," November 19, 2004; Shaman to Sundeep Kalidindi, B-SPAN Team, "Summary for Partnerships and Communications: Linking Civil Society and Government," November 18, 2004.
363 WBM, Shaman to Frannie Leautier, Hafed Al-Ghwell, "The Partnerships and Communications Event is Now Online and Some Further Thoughts on a B-SPAN Interview," November 18, 2004.
364 WBM, Shaman to Kathy Sheram, B-SPAN Team, "Partnerships and Communications Event Now Online," November 18, 2004.
365 WBM, Kathy Sheram to Ann Spencer, Shaman, Sundeep Kalidindi, Drew Stewart, Sharon Cheevers Newell, "BSPAN Production Meeting and Handover Meeting," November 16, 2004.
366 WBM, Shaman to Frannie Leautier, Hafed Al Ghwell, "The Partnerships and Communications Event is Now Online and Some Further Thoughts on a B-SPAN Interview," November 18, 2004.
367 WBM, Frannie Leautier to WBI Staff, "2004 Disability and Development Conference, November 30-December 1, 2004," November 17, 2004.
368 WBM, Shaman to Frannie Leautier, Monika Weber-Fahr, Drew Stewart, Kathy Sheram, "2004 Disability and Development Conference, November 30-December 1, 2004," November 23, 2004.
369 WBM, Marco Nicoli to Shaman, "Thanks," December 2, 2004.
370 WBMs, Shaman to Frannie Leautier, "2004 Disability and Development Conference, November 30-December 1, 2004," November 23, 2004; Judith Heumann to Shaman, "2004 International Day of Disabled Persons, Disability and Development Conference, B-SPAN Coverage," October 19, 2004.
371 WBMs, Roberto Zagha to Shaman, Muriel Darlington, Michele de Nevers, Frannie Leautier, "Practitioners in Development Lecture Series on B-SPAN," November 23, 2004; Shaman to Zagha, "Practitioners in Development Lecture Series on B-SPAN," November 22, 2004.
372 WBM, Shaman to Wheeler, "New Intelligence," November 17, 2004.
373 WBMs, Shaman to B-SPAN Distribution List, "B-SPAN to Live Webcast the Disability and Inclusive Development Conference on November 30th and December 1st," November 29, 2004; Mmenyane Seoposengwe to Ferial H., Mallory Saleson, Phillip Hay, Shaman, "Op-Ed Offer for Business Day," November 24, 2004; Shaman to Masami Morigami, Judith Heumann, Marco Nicoli, "Webcast of Disability Conference," December 1, 2004; EXT Internal Communications, December 7, 2004; Shaman to Sundeep Kalidindi, Ann Spencer, B-SPAN Team, "Summary for 2004 World Bank Conference on Disability and Development," January 7, 2005.
374 WBM, James Wolfensohn to World Bank Staff, "Invitation to 2004 Disability and Development Conference, November 30-December 1, 2004, Preston Auditorium," November 29, 2004.
375 WBMs, Marco Nicoli to Shaman, "Thanks," December 2, 2004; Shaman to Nicoli, "Thanks," December 2, 2004; Shaman Diary, December 4, 2004.
376 WBM, Shaman to Hafed Al Ghwell, "InfoShop Events on B-SPAN," December 1, 2004.
377 WBM, Shaman to Wheeler, "Speaker Invitation: Environment, Security and Development: Lessons from India," December 2, 2004.

378 WBM, Shaman to Wheeler, "One Thing Answered," December 3, 2004.
379 WBMs, Monika Weber-Fahr to Marthe Motley, Sharon Cheevers Newell, "Marthe Pls Make Sure This Does Not Happen," December 2, 2004; Motley to William Gillis, Weber-Fahr, bcc: Shaman, "Marthe – Pls Make Sure This Does Not Happen," December 2, 2004.
380 Shaman Diary, December 4, 2004.
381 WBM, Shaman to Wheeler, "One Thing Answered," December 3, 2004.
382 WBM, Shaman to Wheeler, "One Thing Answered," December 3, 2004.
383 WBM, Shaman to Roger Morier, Gerald Rice, "B-SPAN and Mr. Wolfensohn," December 7, 2004.
384 WBM, Monika Weber-Fahr to Shaman, Kiron Bhandari, "Your Contract with WBI – B-SPAN," December 7, 2004.
385 WBMs, Shaman to Monika Weber-Fahr, Kiron Bhandari, "Your Contract with WBI – B-SPAN," December 9, 2004; Shaman to Weber-Fahr, Bhandari, "Your Contract with WBI-B-SPAN," December 9, 2004.
386 Shaman Diary, December 8, 2004.
387 Shaman Diary, December 8, 2004.
388 WBMs, Nicole Frost to Bank Staff Miscellaneous, "IWG Community Event: Annual Web in Review Presentation, Wednesday, December 8th, 3-4pm," November 18, 2004; Lawrence Macdonald to Jeff McCoy, Katie Bannon, Sekkappa Nagappan, Nicole Frost, "VPU List for Web Traffic Analysis, Are Any Important Directories Missing? (Tell Us by Aug. 4, Please)," July 30, 2004.
389 WBM, B-SPAN Statistics based on WBI traffic data for FY'04.
390 WBMs, Larissa Fastovsky to Shaman, "B-SPAN Charges," November 24, 2004; Shaman to Fastovsky, "B-SPAN Charges," November 29, 2004; Fastovsky to Shaman, "B-SPAN Costs," December 13, 2004; Shaman to Fastovsky, "B-SPAN Costs," December 13, 2004.
391 WBM, Larissa Fastovsky to Andre Mcalister, "Streaming Video Request Procedures," October 21, 2004.
392 WBM, Larissa Fastovsky to Shaman, "B-SPAN Costs," December 13, 2004.
393 Memorandum, Shaman to David Leonard, "Webcasting Services," December 9, 2004.
394 Shaman Diary, December 9, 2004.
395 Shaman Diary, December 10, 2004.
396 Shaman Diary, December 18, 2004.
397 WBM, Shaman to Frannie Leautier, Request, December 15, 2004.
398 WBM, Frannie Leautier to Shaman, Request, December 15, 2004.
399 WBMs, Wheeler to Shaman, "Request," December 17, 2004; Shaman to Wheeler, "Request," December 17, 2004.
400 Shaman Diary, December 18, 2004.
401 Shaman Diary, December 18, 2004.
402 Shaman Diary, December 25, 2004.
403 Shaman Diary, December 25, 2004.
404 Memorandum, Shaman to Himself, September 7, 2004 – "Sheram reiterates the goal of eliminating the archives. She notes Weber-Fahr has terminated the usage of 'webcasting station' and said we are a 'service.' This change is reflected in the What is B-SPAN web page the Host Section is deleted."
405 Shaman Diary, December 25, 2004.
406 WBM, Frannie Leautier to WBI, Staff, Shengman Zhang, "Best Wishes for the Holidays and Happy New Year," December 22, 2004.
407 WBM, Andrei Tolstopiatenko to WBI Staff, "July – Web Statistics Report for WBI," September 13, 2004.

408 WBMs, Andrei Tolstopiatenko to WBI Staff, "November – Web Statistics Report for WBI," December 15, 2004; Tolstopiatenko to WBI Staff, "October – Web Statistics Report for WBI," November 6, 2004.
409 WBI Web Statistics for FY04 and FY05.

PART 7 – OUR DREAM

1 WBMs, Mojgan Sami to Shaman, "CV Follow Up," January 26, 2005; Anthony Bloome to Phillip Hay, Stevan Jackson, Shaman, "David Shaman's CV," January 25, 2005; Nicole Frost to Shaman, "CV Follow Up," January 25, 2005; Katie Bannon to Shaman, "CV," January 26, 2005; Najaragjo Rao Harshadeep to Shaman, "CV Follow Up," January 26, 2005; Elizabeth Campbell-Page to Shaman, "CV Follow Up," January 26, 2005.
2 WBM, Ron Kim to KS Group, "Sigh," February 23, 2004.
3 WBM, Kathy Sheram to Shaman, Drew Stewart, Monika Weber-Fahr, Sharon Cheevers Newell, "BSPAN – Your New Contract Offer," January 14, 2005.
4 WBM, Monika Weber-Fahr to GDMM All, "(for information and action) Minutes and Materials from Today's Division Meeting," January 4, 2005.
5 Shaman Diary, January 5, 2005.
6 WBMs, Mojgan Sami to Shaman, "CV Follow Up," January 26, 2005; Anthony Bloome to Phillip Hay, Stevan Jackson, Shaman, "David Shaman's CV," January 25, 2005; Nicole Frost to Shaman, "CV Follow Up," January 25, 2005; Katie Bannon to Shaman, "CV," January 26, 2005; Najaragjo Rao Harshadeep to Shaman, "CV Follow Up," January 26, 2005; Elizabeth Campbell-Page to Shaman, "CV Follow Up," January 26, 2005; Paul Martin to Shaman, "CV Followup," January 25, 2005; Nick Harrison to Web4Dev List, "Web Editor/Webcasting Producer Available," January 14, 2005.
7 WBMs, Wheeler to Shaman, "Your Request for a Meeting with Frannie Leautier," December 17, 2005; Alice Mary Faria to Shaman, "Your Request for a Meeting with Frannie Leautier," December 17, 2004.
8 Shaman Diary, January 5, 2005.
9 Shaman Diary, January 5, 2005.
10 WBMs, Shaman to Monika Weber-Fahr, Kathy Sheram, "B-SPAN Partnership Letters for Bank VPs," July 16, 2004; Shaman to Wheeler, "Here Tis," January 7, 2005.
11 Shaman Diary, January 8, 2005.
12 WBM, Shaman to Wheeler, "Here Tis," January 7, 2005.
13 WBM, Shaman to Frannie Leautier, "Project Proposal for Low Cost Webcasting Service," January 7, 2005.
14 WBM, Shaman to Wheeler, "Role Model," January 12, 2005.
15 WBMs, Laure Charvin to Jeffrey McCoy, Shaman, Veaceslav Revutchi, Bart Stevens, Nicole Frost, Cynthia Carol Case McMahon, Larissa Fastovsky, Merat Salassie, Le Ahn Vu, Diane Vincent, Chongman Kim, "Tomorrow's JDW Press Conference – Request for Live Internal and External Webcast," January 12, 2005; Shaman to Charvin, McCoy, Revutchi, Stevens, Frost, McMahon, Fastovsky, Salassie, Vu, Vincent, Kim, "Tomorrow's JDW Press Conference Request for Live Internal and External Webcast," January 12, 2005.
16 WBM, Kathy Sheram to Shaman, Drew Stewart, Monika Weber-Fahr, Sharon Cheevers Newell, "BSPAN – Your New Contract Offer," January 14, 2005.
17 Drew Stewart to Shaman, "Are You In on Tuesday? Would Like to Talk About B-SPAN Events for 2nd Half of January?" January 14, 2005; Shaman Diary, January 15, 2005.
18 Shaman Diary, January 15, 2005.
19 Shaman Diary, January 15, 2005.
20 WBM, Ann Spencer to Kathy Sheram, Drew Stewart, Shaman, Sundeep Kalidindi, "B-SPAN in the Classroom (My Classroom)," January 18, 2005.

21 WBM, Kathy Sheram to Ann Spencer, Drew Stewart, Shaman, Sundeep Kalidindi, "B-SPAN in the Classroom (My Classroom)," January 18, 2005.
22 EXT Internal Communications, Sachs Report on Millennium Development Goals, January 18, 2005.
23 World Bank Weekly Update, January 17, 2005.
24 WBMs, B-SPAN Team to Melanie Faltas, "New Event on B-SPAN: Training Course on Trade and Poverty," February 22, 2005; B-SPAN Team to Alexandra Sears, "New Event on B-SPAN: Training Course on Solid Waste Outsourcing," February 22, 2005; B-SPAN Team to Paul Procee, Sebastian Anapolsky, "Event 679: WBI Training Course on Solid Waste Outsourcing is Now on B-SPAN," February 23, 2005.
25 Shaman Diary, January 18, 2005.
26 WBM, Andrei Tolstopiatenko to WBI Staff, "December – Web Statistics Report for WBI," January 19, 2005.
27 WBM, Carl Hanlon to Shaman, "CV Followup," January 25, 2005.
28 Shaman Diary, January 15, 2005; Shaman Diary, January 20, 2005.
29 Shaman Diary, January 20, 2005.
30 WBM, Frannie Leautier to Extended List, "Best Wishes for the Holidays and Happy New Year," December 22, 2004.
31 WBM, Kathy Sheram to Shaman, Drew Stewart, Monika Weber-Fahr, Sharon Cheevers Newell, "BSPAN – Your New Contract Offer – FINAL NOTICE," January 24, 2005.
32 Shaman Diary, February 2, 2005.
33 Shaman Diary, February 2, 2005.
34 Shaman Diary, February 2, 2005.
35 WBM, Shaman to Wheeler, "All Good Wishes," January 31, 2005.
36 WBMs, Ken Chomitz to Shaman, Wheeler, Craig Meisner, Susmita Dasgupta, Uwe Deichmann, Somik Lall, Piet Buys, "Beer for Shaman on Tuesday?" January 31, 2005; Wheeler to Shaman, "All Good Wishes," February 1, 2005.
37 WBMs, Kathy Sheram to Sona Panajyan, Drew Stewart, "Pricing Question," February 3, 2005; Panajyan to Sheram, Stewart, Ann Spencer, Sundeep Kalidindi, February 2, 2005.
38 WBMs, Sona Panajyan to Library Marketing and Communications, "RSS Feeds: Come to a Demo and Lesson How to Use RSS to Track Frequently Changing Websites," February 15, 2005; Panajyan to Youth Community, B-SPAN Team, " 'Y2Y for You in a Dynamic Bank' with Mr. Shigeo Katsu, Regional Vice President ECA, on Thursday, Feb. 17, 2005 from 12:30-1:30," February 15, 2005.
39 WBMs, B-SPAN Team to Melanie Faltas, "New Event on B-SPAN: 'Training Course on Trade and Poverty,' " February 22, 2005; B-SPAN Team to Alexandra Sears, "New Event on B-SPAN: 'Training Course on Solid Waste Outsourcing,' " February 22, 2005; Sona Panajyan to Laura de Brular, B-SPAN Team, "Urban Learning Week; March 7-11 on B-SPAN," February 22, 2005; Fatu Kokul Ama Gbedema to Panajyan, "Event #693 'Communicating Effectively in Multicultural Environments' is now on B-SPAN," February 23, 2005; B-SPAN Production, Training Course on Local Knowledge and Health Practices for Multi-Country and Project Teams and National AIDS Commissions, September 8, 2005 to September 9, 2005; B-SPAN Production, Learning Dialogue: Equitable Development and the MDGs, June 2, 2005; WBMs, Thomas Wilburn to Craig Meisner, Maria-Martina Yalamova, "Some Further Questions About B-SPAN," March 28, 2007; Wilburn to Meisner, "Some Questions About B-SPAN," March 2, 2007.
40 WBMs, Francis Muraya to Sona Panajyan, "Seminar on 'City Strategic Planning and Local Economic Development' – on B-SPAN," February 25, 2005; Tara Sharafudeen to B-SPAN Team, Panajyan, Luis Constantino, Juanid Kamal Ahmad, "Your Event 'Challenge of Urban Finance and Governance in India,' " February 18, 2005.

41 WBMs, Andrei Tolstopiatenko to WBI Staff, "February – Web Statistics Report for WBI," March 23, 2005; Tolstopiatenko to WBI Staff, "January – Web Statistics Report for WBI," February 11, 2005.
42 WBM, Richard Fix to Shaman, "Further to Your Idea," January 14, 2005.
43 WBMs, Tara Sharafudeen to Sona Panajyan, "Your Event 'Challenge of Urban Finance and Governance in India,' " February 18, 2005; Oykiao Koo Tze Mew to Panajyan, "Seminar on 'OED Ghana Study: Promoting Improvements in Ghana's Basic Education' on B-SPAN?" February 23, 2005.
44 "How Well do You Know the World Bank Institute?" *World Bank Today*, March 9, 2005.
45 B-SPAN Coverage of The End of Poverty: Economic Possibilities for Our Time by Jeffery Sachs, March 22, 2005.
46 B-SPAN Team to B-SPAN List, "B-SPAN March Newsletter," March 31, 2005; B-SPAN Coverage of The End of Poverty: Economic Possibilities for Our Time by Jeffery Sachs, March 22, 2005.
47 "Jeffrey Sachs to Staff: 'MDGs are Attainable,' " *World Bank Today*, March 23, 2005.
48 "Transparency Key to Development in Resource-Rich Countries," *World Bank Today*, March 17, 2005.
49 B-SPAN Coverage of A Chance for the World Bank by Jo Ritzen, April 6, 2005; WBM, Events at InfoShop to Extended List, "Jozef Ritzen Talks About 'A Chance for the World Bank' at the InfoShop on Wednesday, April 6, 2005 at 4pm in J1-050," March 23, 2005.
50 WBM, B-SPAN Team, B-SPAN Distribution List, "B-SPAN April Newsletter," April 30, 2005.
51 B-SPAN Team to B-SPAN List, "B-SPAN February Newsletter," February 28, 2005.
52 WBM, Shaman to David Leonard, "Webcasting Follow Up," April 12, 2005; Memorandum, Shaman to Leonard, "New Low-Cost Webcasting Initiative," April 12, 2005.
53 WBMs, Shaman to Wheeler, "This Just In ..." April 14, 2005; Shaman to Wheeler, "Pulley Leads," April 25, 2005; Wheeler to Shaman, "Pulley Leads," April 25, 2005.
54 WBMs, Shaman to Wheeler, "Pulley Leads," April 25, 2005; Wheeler to Shaman, "Pulley Leads," April 25, 2005; Shaman to Wheeler, "B-SPAN Intelligence," May 18, 2005; Wheeler to Shaman, "B-SPAN Intelligence," May 19, 2005.
55 WBM, Shaman to Wheeler, "This Just In …" April 14, 2005.
56 "World Bank-IMF Protests Set This Week," *Washington Post*, April 13, 2005.
57 WBM, B-SPAN Team, B-SPAN Distribution List, "B-SPAN April Newsletter," April 30, 2005.
58 A second example can be seen with the B-SPAN Newsletter from February 2005 which gave similar passing reference to former U.S. President Jimmy Carter addressing the Organization of American States, and noted psychologist and best selling author Deborah Tannen discussing effective communications in multicultural environments.
59 World Bank Weekly Update, April 11, 2005; World Bank Weekly Update, April 18, 2005; World Bank Weekly Update, June 20, 2005.
60 "Stern to Staff: 'Celebrate the Nature of the Bank,' " *World Bank Today*, May 3, 2005.
61 WBM, Aye Mon Myo to WBI Staff, "May – Web Statistics Report for WBI," June 15, 2005.
62 WBMs, Andrei Tolstopiatenko to WBI Staff, "March – Web Statistics Report for WBI," April 11, 2005; Tolstopiatenko to WBI Staff, "April – Web Statistics Report for WBI," May 12, 2005.
63 World Bank Institute Web Statistics for FY04 and FY05.
64 "Wolfensohn on Bank Communications: No Cosmetics, No Spin," *World Bank Today*, May 11, 2005.

65 The Web for Development Conference, Telling the Development Story to the World, May 9-11, 2005, Washington, DC.
66 Nicole Frost presentation, Session I, Making Key Connections – A Content Odyssey, The Web for Development Conference, Telling the Development Story to the World, May 9, 2005, Washington, DC.
67 Christopher Strebel, UNESCO, presentation, Session I, Making Key Connections – A Content Odyssey, The Web for Development Conference, Telling the Development Story to the World, May 9, 2005, Washington, DC.
68 Earl Mardle, KeyNet presentation, Session I, Making Key Connections – A Content Odyssey, The Web for Development Conference, Telling the Development Story to the World, May 9, 2005, Washington, DC.
69 Gerry McGovern presentation, Session III and Session IV, Unlocking Successful Content, The Web for Development Conference, Telling the Development Story to the World, May 9-10, 2005, Washington, DC.
70 Gerry Rice presentation, Keynote Address, The Web for Development Conference, Telling the Development Story to the World, May 11, 2005, Washington, DC.
71 WBM, Shaman to Wheeler, "B-SPAN Intelligence," May 18, 2005.
72 WBM, Shaman to Wheeler, "B-SPAN Intelligence," May 18, 2005.
73 WBM, Shaman to Wheeler, "B-SPAN Intelligence," May 18, 2005.
74 WBM, Shaman to Wheeler, "B-SPAN Intelligence," May 18, 2005.
75 WBM, Shaman to Wheeler, "B-SPAN Intelligence," May 18, 2005.
76 WBM, Shaman to Wheeler, "B-SPAN Intelligence," May 18, 2005.
77 "The Charlie Rose Show," A Conversation with the President of the World Bank, James Wolfensohn, May 24, 2005.
78 WBMs, Shaman to Nicole Frost, "B-SPAN Proposal," May 27, 2005; Shaman to Michael Kingsberry, "B-SPAN Proposal," June 13, 2005.
79 WBM, Shaman to Nicole Frost, "B-SPAN Proposal," May 27, 2005.
80 WBM, Shaman to Wheeler, "B-SPAN Proposal," June 2, 2005.
81 WBM, Aye Mon Myo to WBI Staff, "May – Web Statistics Report for WBI," June 15, 2005.
82 Shaman to Wheeler, "ISG Proposal," June 24, 2005; Wheeler to Shaman, "ISG Proposal," June 24, 2005.
83 WBM, Shaman to Michael Kingsberry, "B-SPAN Proposal," June 13, 2005.
84 WBM, Shaman to Michael Kingsberry, "ISG Low Cost Webcasting Service," June 24, 2005.
85 WBM, Shaman to Wheeler, "Just a Final Check," July 1, 2005; B-SPAN Production, Second Annual OED Good Practice Award Ceremony, June 8, 2005.
86 WBI Web Statistics for June, 2005.

PART 8 – BECOME THE CHANGE YOU WISH TO SEEK

1 Sebastian Mallaby, *The World's Banker: The Story of Failed States, Financial Crises, and the Wealth and Poverty of Nations*, Penguin Books, 2004, Page 143; Richard Stevenson, "World Bank Gets Bosnia Aid Role," *The New York Times*, April 17, 1996.
2 James Wolfensohn, Commencement address at Massachusetts Institute of Technology, June 7, 2002; Interview with Margaret Warner, PBS "News Hour with Jim Lehrer," March 22, 2002; Interview with Jim Lehrer, PBS "News Hour with Jim Lehrer," May 30, 2005.
3 World Bank Group Staff Association Newsletter, January 2001.
4 Geert Hofstede, *Cultures and Organizations: Software of the Mind*, McGraw Hill, 1997; WBG Staff Association Newsletter, May 1998, Book Review.
5 Geert Hofstede, *Cultures and Organizations: Software of the Mind*, McGraw Hill, 1997; WBG Staff Association Newsletter, May 1998, Book Review.

6 Geert Hofstede, *Cultures and Organizations: Software of the Mind*, McGraw Hill, 1997; WBG Staff Association Newsletter, May 1998, Book Review.
7 Geert Hofstede, *Cultures and Organizations: Software of the Mind*, McGraw Hill, 1997; WBG Staff Association Newsletter, May 1998, Book Review.
8 World Bank Group Staff Association Newsletter, January-February 2005, "Political Pressures on the Bank - and Staff - in 2005."
9 World Bank Group Staff Association Newsletter, January-February 2005, "Political Pressures on the Bank - and Staff - in 2005."
10 WBM, Bruno Laporte to WBI Staff, "5th Staff Exchange and Knowledge Sharing Program," June 28, 2004; Restoring Global Balance Together, Fifth Annual Staff Exchange Program and Knowledge Sharing Conference and Expo, June 28-29, 2004.
11 World Bank Internal Communications, "Wolfensohn on Bank Communications: No Cosmetics, No Spin," May 12, 2005.
12 WBMs, Frannie Leautier to Wheeler, "Urgent B-SPAN Policy Issue," July 9, 2002; Wheeler to Leautier, "Urgent B-SPAN Policy Issue," July 9, 2002.
13 WBM, Frannie Leautier to Shaman, "B-SPAN Meeting," February 26, 2004.
14 WBMs, Shaman to Michael Doyle, "EDI Seminar and Environmental Network," September 14, 1998; Shaman to Wheeler, David Witzel, Forum One, "EDI Meeting," October 6, 1997; Wheeler to Shaman, Witzel, "EDI Meeting," October 6, 1997; Witzel to Shaman, Wheeler, "EDI Meeting," October 7, 1997; Wheeler to Shaman, "Score One for NIPR," October 20, 1997.
15 WBMs, Shaman to Michael Doyle, "EDI Seminar and Environmental Network," September 14, 1998; Shaman to Wheeler, David Witzel, Forum One, "EDI Meeting," October 6, 1997; Wheeler to Shaman, Witzel, "EDI Meeting," October 6, 1997; Witzel to Shaman, Wheeler, "EDI Meeting," October 7, 1997; Wheeler to Shaman, "Score One for NIPR," October 20, 1997.
16 WBMs, Shaman to Michael Doyle, "EDI Seminar and Environmental Network," September 14, 1998; Shaman to Wheeler, David Witzel, Forum One, "EDI Meeting," October 6, 1997; Wheeler to Shaman, Witzel, "EDI Meeting," October 6, 1997; Witzel to Shaman, Wheeler, "EDI Meeting," October 7, 1997; Wheeler to Shaman, "Score One for NIPR," October 20, 1997.
17 WBMs, Shaman to Michael Doyle, "EDI Seminar and Environmental Network," September 14, 1998; Shaman to Wheeler, David Witzel, Forum One, "EDI Meeting," October 6, 1997; Wheeler to Shaman, Witzel, "EDI Meeting," October 6, 1997; Witzel to Shaman, Wheeler, "EDI Meeting," October 7, 1997; Wheeler to Shaman, "Score One for NIPR," October 20, 1997.
18 WBMs, Shaman to Michael Doyle, "EDI Seminar and Environmental Network," September 14, 1998; Shaman to Wheeler, David Witzel, Forum One, "EDI Meeting," October 6, 1997; Wheeler to Shaman, Witzel, "EDI Meeting," October 6, 1997; Witzel to Shaman, Wheeler, "EDI Meeting," October 7, 1997; Wheeler to Shaman, "Score One for NIPR," October 20, 1997; Jim Cashel, Forum One, David Witzel, Forum One, to Michael Potashnik, "Benefits and Costs of Bank Web Sites," July 16, 1999.
19 World Bank Internal Communications, "How WBI is Responding to Perception Survey," May 28, 2003.
20 "Pushed to the Edge by Budget Cuts,"World Bank Group Staff Association Newsletter, December 2000-January 2001; "The Bank's Formal Strategy for FY01-03: Maintain Direction, Increase Momentum, on Much Less Money," World Bank Group Staff Association Newsletter, June 2000.
21 The Global Development Learning Network (GDLN): The Bank's Use of GDLN's Opportunities - and its Support to the Network, Update Note, October 2004, October 22, 2004.
22 World Bank Institute Web Statistics, FY04.

23 Sebastian Mallaby, *The World's Banker: The Story of Failed States, Financial Crises, and the Wealth and Poverty of Nations*, Penguin Books, 2004, Page 160.

24 WBMs, Claude Salem to Shaman, Mwangi Wachira, Bruno Laporte, Monika Weber-Fahr, Robert Hawkins, "Disseminating B-SPAN to the Tanzanian DLC and Related Issues," February 14, 2003; Wachira to Abdul Mdimu, Salem, Shaman, Weber-Fahr, "Disseminating B-SPAN to the Tanzanian DLC and Related Issues," February 22, 2003; Gary Fine to Shaman, Aslan Sarinzhipov, Laporte, Salem, David Mikosz, Devrin Weiss, Elena Karaban, Gulmira Mchale, I Team, Michele de Nevers, Weber-Fahr, Veit Burger, Vera Wilhelm, "B-SPAN," February 23, 2003; Claude Salem to Anthony Bloome, Monika Weber-Fahr, "Tape for GDLN?: HIV/AIDS and ICT Brown Bag, Thursday, February 6th, 12-1:30 p.m. – Using Print, Radio, Television and Internet to Combat HIV/AIDS," February 4, 2003; Veit Burger to David Mikosz, Devrin David Weiss, Elena Karaban, Aslan Sarinzhipov, Vera Wilhelm, Gulmira Mchale, Gary Fine, Michele de Nevers, Salem, Weber-Fahr, Shaman, "Basic Question on B-SPAN," February 4, 2003; Salem to Enrique Calgano, Drew Stewart, Peter Copplestone, Weber-Fahr, Prita Chathoth, Sharon Cheevers Newell, Burger, Shaman, "Videotaping and Dissemination of Regional Consultation Sessions," May 12, 2003; Salem to Stewart, Shaman, Bruno Laporte, Weber-Fahr, "School-Based Telecenters Videoconference – Uganda, Ethiopia, Ghana, Nigeria, Monday, 5/19, 8:00-9:00AM, MC-C2 131," May 12, 2003; Shaman to Mikosz, Bruno Laporte, Weiss, Karaban, Sarinzhipov, Wilhelm, Mchale, Fine, de Nevers, Salem, Weber-Fahr, I Team, "B-SPAN and Kazakhstan PIC," February 21, 2003.

25 Memorandum, Shaman to Himself, April – 2004, "Erik Johnson repeatedly seeks a meeting with Monika Weber-Fahr to discuss staffing shortfalls, the impact on production, and cost recovery options. Weber-Fahr does not respond to any requests."

26 WBMs, Bryan Waller to Monika Weber-Fahr, Erik Johnson, Shaman, Hector Montenegro, "Waiver for Video Encoder," May 21, 2004; Johnson to Monika Weber-Fahr, Kathy Sheram, Waller, Shaman, "NiagraMax," June 10, 2004; Waller to Erik Johnson, Shaman, Sheram, Weber-Fahr, "NiagraMAX," June 10, 2004; Johnson to Waller, Shaman, Sheram, Weber-Fahr, "NiagraMAX," June 10, 2004.

27 WBMs, Kathy Sheram to B-SPAN Team, Monika Weber-Fahr, "B-SPAN Status Meeting #1 – Notes and Next Steps," September 9, 2004; Sheram to B-SPAN Team, Drew Stewart, Weber-Fahr, "B-SPAN Status Meeting #2 – Notes and Next Steps," September 16, 2004; Weber-Fahr to Sheram, Shaman, "B-SPAN Marketing Initiatives – Follow Up from This Morning's Meeting," October 20, 2004; Sheram to Weber-Fahr, Shaman, "B-SPAN Marketing Initiatives – Follow Up from This Morning's Meeting," October 14, 2004; Sheram to Bruno Laporte, Donald Macdonald, Shaman, Ann Spencer, Weber-Fahr, "B-SPAN Presentation to the Learning Board," October 14, 2004; Weber-Fahr to Macdonald, Spencer, Laporte, Shaman, Sheram, "B-SPAN Presentation to the Learning Board," October 27, 2004; Weber-Fahr to Shaman, Sheram, Sharon Cheevers Newell, "B-SPAN: Next Step and First Six Months of FY05," June 29, 2004; HRLOA to Shaman, Sharon Cheevers Newell, Weber-Fahr, "Personnel Image Archiver, Letter of Appointment: SHAMAN, DAVID I. (UPI=86922) (Case=125679, 12 ….. (NOAFT=1)," July 13, 2004; Sheram to Kwaljit Bhutan, Shaman, "Scorecard Indicators for FY05," July 12, 2004; Sheram to Shaman, "IMPT: Your Results Agreement and Scorecard," July 2, 2004; Shaman to Wheeler, "Welcome to My World," July 22, 2004; Shaman to Mark Davis, "Still Wresting with Monsters," October 29, 2004; Memorandum, Shaman to Himself, July 2, "Weber-Fahr says EILT is debating whether to keep B-SPAN or give it to EXT. If WBI keeps B-SPAN, it should offer edited learning products. She said she will run B-SPAN on a low-cost strategy of short-term consultant temporaries."

28 WBMs, Kathy Sheram to B-SPAN Team, Monika Weber-Fahr, "B-SPAN Status Meeting #1 – Notes and Next Steps," September 9, 2004; Sheram to B-SPAN Team, Drew Stewart, Weber-Fahr, "B-SPAN Status Meeting #2 – Notes and Next Steps," September 16, 2004; Weber-Fahr to Sheram, Shaman, "B-SPAN Marketing Initiatives – Follow Up from This Morning's Meeting," October 20, 2004; Sheram to Weber-Fahr, Shaman, "B-SPAN Marketing Initiatives – Follow Up from This Morning's Meeting," October 14, 2004; Sheram to Bruno Laporte, Donald Macdonald, Shaman, Ann Spencer, Weber-Fahr, "B-SPAN Presentation to the Learning Board," October 14, 2004; Weber-Fahr to Macdonald, Spencer, Laporte, Shaman, Sheram, "B-SPAN Presentation to the Learning Board," October 27, 2004; Weber-Fahr to Shaman, Sheram, Sharon Cheevers Newell, "B-SPAN: Next Step and First Six Months of FY05," June 29, 2004; HRLOA to Shaman, Sharon Cheevers Newell, Weber-Fahr, "Personnel Image Archiver, Letter of Appointment: SHAMAN, DAVID I. (UPI=86922) (Case=125679, 12 ..... (NOAFT=1)," July 13, 2004; Sheram to Kwaljit Bhutan, Shaman, "Scorecard Indicators for FY05," July 12, 2004; Sheram to Shaman, "IMPT: Your Results Agreement and Scorecard," July 2, 2004; Shaman to Wheeler, "Welcome to My World," July 22, 2004; Shaman to Mark Davis, "Still Wresting with Monsters," October 29, 2004; Memorandum, Shaman to Himself, July 2, "Weber-Fahr says EILT is debating whether to keep B-SPAN or give it to EXT. If WBI keeps B-SPAN, it should offer edited learning products. She said she will run B-SPAN on a low-cost strategy of short-term consultant temporaries; Monika Weber-Fahr to Donald MacDonald, Ann Spencer, Bruno Laporte, Shaman, Kathy Sheram, "B-SPAN Presentation to the Learning Board," October 27, 2004; Shaman to Mark Davis, "Still Wrestling with Monsters," October 28, 2004; Davis to Shaman, "Still Wrestling with Monsters," October 29, 2004; Shaman to Davis, "Still Wrestling with Monsters," October 29, 2004; Kathy Sheram to B-SPAN Team, Drew Stewart, Monika Weber-Fahr, "B-SPAN Status Meeting #2 – Notes and Next Steps," September 16, 2004; Weber-Fahr to Shaman, Sheram, Sharon Cheevers Newell, "B-SPAN: Next Step and First Six Months of FY05," June 29, 2004; Memorandum, Shaman to Himself, September 8, "Monika Weber-Fahr says at B-SPAN staff meeting that she supports restricted access materials. Reiterates need to announce Chatham House Rules. She said without funding support from WBI, the cost recovery model will assess demand which will determine if the service is to be continued. Sheram reiterates her belief the charge should actually increase to include indirect costs. Sheram adds that edited materials on B-SPAN is consistent with the principles in the new model; Kathy Sheram to B-SPAN Team, Drew Stewart, Monika Weber-Fahr, "B-SPAN Status Meeting #2 – Notes and Next Steps," September 16, 2004; Weber-Fahr to Donald Macdonald, Ann Spencer, Bruno Laporte, Shaman, Sheram, "B-SPAN Presentation to the Learning Board," October 27, 2004; Weber-Fahr to Shaman, Sheram, Sharon Cheevers Newell, "B-SPAN: Next Step and First Six Months of FY05," June 29, 2004; Shaman to Mark Davis, "Still Wresting with Monsters," October 29, 2004; Memorandum, Shaman to Himself, September 16, "At B-SPAN staff meeting, Monika Weber-Fahr and Kathy Sheram agree that edited materials will be accepted from internal clients by Shaman and according to Weber-Fahr "for the moment" will be housed on B-SPAN with some accompanying identification noting that the event has been edited. Weber-Fahr said discussion would continue over the next few months on what business lines the new model will take including whether to host edited versus non-edited events, open versus restricted access events. Weber-Fahr wants her email response from the previous day on charges to be sent to anyone who complains; Kathy Sheram to Shaman, Ann Spencer, Sundeep Kalidindi, Monika Weber-Fahr, Han Fraeters, Drew Stewart, "B-SPAN Newsletter – Edits, Please," November 1, 2004; Kathy Sheram to Shaman, "IMPT: Your Results Agreement and Scorecard," July 2, 2004; Sheram to B-SPAN Team, Monika Weber-Fahr, "B-SPAN Status Meeting #1

– Notes and Next Steps," September 9, 2004; Weber-Fahr to Sheram, Shaman, "B-SPAN Marketing Initiatives – Follow Up from This Morning's Meeting," October 20, 2004; Sheram to Weber-Fahr, Shaman, "B-SPAN Marketing Initiatives – Follow Up from This Morning's Meeting," October 14, 2004; Sheram to Bruno Laporte, Donald Macdonald, Shaman, Ann Spencer, Weber-Fahr, "B-SPAN Presentation to the Learning Board," October 14, 2004; Sheram to Kwaljit Bhutan, Shaman, "Scorecard Indicators for FY05," July 12, 2004; Sheram to Shaman, "IMPT: Your Results Agreement and Scorecard," July 2, 2004; Shaman to Wheeler, "Welcome to My World," July 22, 2004; Kathy Sheram to B-SPAN Team, Monika Weber-Fahr, "B-SPAN Status Meeting #1 – Notes and Next Steps," September 9, 2004; Weber-Fahr to Sheram, Shaman, "B-SPAN Marketing Initiatives – Follow Up from This Morning's Meeting," October 20, 2004; Sheram to Weber-Fahr, Shaman, "B-SPAN Marketing Initiatives – Follow Up from This Morning's Meeting," October 14, 2004; Sheram to Bruno Laporte, Donald Macdonald, Shaman, Ann Spencer, Weber-Fahr, "B-SPAN Presentation to the Learning Board," October 14, 2004; Sheram to Kwaljit Bhutan, Shaman, "Scorecard Indicators for FY05," July 12, 2004; Sheram to Shaman, "IMPT: Your Results Agreement and Scorecard," July 2, 2004; Shaman to Wheeler, "Welcome to My World," July 22, 2004; Ann Vroom to Veit Burger, Kathy Sheram, Hector Montenegro, Patrick Tse, Monika Weber-Fahr, "Your CD Request, September 8, 2004; Ann Vroom to Kathy Sheram, Manpower Temporaries, Sharon Cheevers Newell, Sarika Jain, Roula Yazigi, Monika Weber-Fahr, Ann Spencer, Hector Montenegro, Patrick Tse, "Won't Be In – Please Fax My Timesheet for this Last Week w. B-SPAN (Ending 9/12/04 – Job # 20588)," September 8, 2004; Vroom to Tse, B-SPAN Team, "Just for Training Events Shows Up on B-SPAN Even though Not Posted!" September 29, 2004; Kathy Sheram to B-SPAN Team, Drew Stewart, Monika Weber-Fahr, "B-SPAN Status Meeting #2 – Notes and Next Steps," September 16, 2004; Sheram to B-SPAN Team, Weber-Fahr, "B-SPAN Status Meeting #1 – Notes and Next Steps," September 9, 2004; Weber-Fahr to Donald Macdonald, Ann Spencer, Bruno Laporte, Shaman, Sheram, "B-SPAN Presentation to the Learning Board," October 27, 2004; Weber-Fahr to Shaman, Sheram, Sharon Cheevers Newell, "B-SPAN: Next Step and First Six Months of FY05," June 29, 2004; Sheram to Kwaljit Bhutan, Shaman, "Scorecard Indicators for FY05," July 12, 2004; Sheram to Shaman, "IMPT: Your Results Agreement and Scorecard," July 2, 2004; Shaman to Wheeler, "Welcome to My World," July 22, 2004; Ann Vroom to Patrick Tse, B-SPAN Team, "Just for Training Event Shows Up on BSPAN Even Tho NOT Posted!" September 29, 2004; Shaman to Mark Davis, "Still Wresting with Monsters," October 29, 2004; Memorandum, Shaman to Himself, May 14, "Weber-Fahr designates Sheram as her B-SPAN liaison. Sheram immediately states B-SPAN should provide private access events;" Shaman Diary, September 9, 2004; Kathy Sheram to Andrei Tolstopiatenko, Shaman, Monika Weber-Fahr, "B-SPAN Questions Please, David and Andrei," September 9, 2004; Kathy Sheram to Shaman, Andrei Tolstopiatenko, Monika Weber-Fahr, "B-SPAN Questions Please, David and Andrei," September 9, 2004; Tolstopiatenko to Sheram, Shaman, Weber-Fahr, "B-SPAN Questions Please, David and Andrei," September 9, 2004; Memorandum, Shaman to Himself, September 7, "Sheram reiterates the goal of eliminating the archives. She notes Weber-Fahr has terminated the usage of 'webcasting station' and said we are a 'service.' This change is reflected in the What is B-SPAN web page the Host Section is deleted;" Kathy Sheram to Ann Vroom, Ann Spencer, Shaman, "Help Please: Your Bank IP," September 1, 2004; Shaman Diary, September 9, 2004; Shaman Diary, December 25, 2004; Monika Weber-Fahr to Shaman, Ann Vroom, Kathy Sheram, Bruno Donat, "B-SPAN Announcements – Our Discussion 2 Days Ago – How Best to Publish 'What's Going On,'" July 22, 2004.

29 WBM, Monika Weber-Fahr to Shaman, Kathy Sheram, Sharon Cheevers Newell, "B-SPAN: Next Step and First Six Months of FY05," June 29, 2004; Memorandum, Shaman to Himself, May-2004, "Weber-Fahr says she will staff B-SPAN with short-term consultants from local schools;" Memorandum, Shaman to Himself, July 2, "Weber-Fahr says EILT is debating whether to keep B-SPAN or give it to EXT. If WBI keeps B-SPAN, it should offer edited learning products. She said she will run B-SPAN on a low-cost strategy of short-term consultant temporaries."

30 WBMs, Kathy Sheram to Drew Stewart, Shaman, Ann Spencer, "Rescheduled: BSPAN Handover Meeting (Sep 16 03:00PM EDT)," September 14, 2004; Sheram to Shaman, Spencer, Stewart, "B-SPAN Handover Meeting," September 16, 2004; Memorandum, Shaman to Himself, September 16, "In a follow up meeing, Sheram said cost recovery price for WB clients set by Monika Weber-Fahr alone, but she needed/received approval from EILT for extending the cleage to WBI clients;" Memorandum, Shaman to Himself, September 13, "Sheram states that Monika Weber-Fahr has decided not to send cost recovery letters to VPU's but rather clients instead."

31 WBMs, Bowden to Erik Johnson, "B-SPAN Event Analysis," January 30, 2004; Johnson to Bowden, Shaman, "B-SPAN Event Analysis," February 2, 2004.

32 WBM, Shaman to Wheeler, Bowden, "B-SPAN Issues," October 31, 2002.

33 These statistics are based on a comprehensive count of B-SPAN's archives in March 2007.

34 These statistics are based on a comprehensive count of B-SPAN's archives in March 2007.

35 These statistics are based on a comprehensive count of B-SPAN's archives in March 2007.

36 This statistic is based on analysis of B-SPAN's event composition from its existing archives in March 2007.

37 WBM, Thomas Wilburn to Craig Meisner, Maria-Martina Yalamova, "Some Further Questions About B-SPAN," March 28, 2007; B-SPAN website, FAQ: General.

38 This statistic is based on a comprehensive count of B-SPAN's archives in March 2007. Emails from Thomas Wilburn to Craig Meisner confirm that some of B-SPAN's archives during my management no longer exist or are no longer available. WBMs, Thomas Wilburn to Craig Meisner, Maria-Martina Yalamova, "Some Further Questions About B-SPAN," March 28, 2007; Wilburn to Meisner, "Some Questions About B-SPAN," March 2, 2007.

39 WBM, Monika Weber-Fahr to Shaman, Kathy Sheram, "B-SPAN Partnership Letters to VPs," July 13, 2004.

40 WBM, Shaman to Monika Weber-Fahr, "B-SPAN Partnership Letters for Bank VPs," July 16, 2004.

41 WBMs, Monika Weber-Fahr to Shaman, Kathy Sheram, "For Your Comment: B-SPAN Price Increase from $350 – $750 (Concerns)," September 15, 2004; WBM, Shaman to Roberto Zagha, Muriel Darlington, "Practitioners in Development Lecture Series: Rima KHALAF HUNAIDI, Tuesday September 14, 2004, 12:00-2: pm," September 9, 2004; Memorandum, Shaman to Himself, August 26, "Monika Weber-Fahr decides on cost recovery at task manager level without further discussion. It is $350, representing a $61 profit on every event. Under Bank rules described by WBI's senior budget analyst, Marshall Schreier, WBI staff is not allowed to knowingly profit on services provided to Bank staff."

42 WBM, Thomas Wilburn to Craig Meisner, "Some Questions About B-SPAN," March 2, 2007.

43 WBM, Thomas Wilburn to Craig Meisner, "Some Questions About B-SPAN," March 2, 2007.

44 There were six newsletters and eight single event notices disseminated since the end of 2004. The last recorded B-SPAN dissemination was on February 5, 2007. This data is derived from newsletter e-mailings received by me and others subscribed to B-SPAN electronic newsletter distribution list.
45 WBMs, Andrei Tolstopiatenko to WBI Staff, "February – Web Statistics Report for WBI," March 15, 2004; Tolstopiatenko to WBI Staff, "March – Web Statistics Report for WBI with Top 10 e-Learning Courses," April 19, 2004; Deborah Touboul-Compagnon to WBI Staff, "June – Web Statistics Report for WBI," August 4, 2004.
46 WBMs, Arvind Bhand to Craig Meisner, "Case: HD0000001325445; Assigned: ARVIND G. BHAND; Requestor: UWE DEICHMANN; Priority: Medium; Summary: Client Wants to Monitor Web Traffic Statistics," April 2, 2007; Meisner to Bhand, "Case: HD0000001325445; Assigned: ARVIND G. BHAND; Requestor: UWE DEICHMANN; Priority: Medium; Summary: Client Wants to Monitor Web Traffic Statistics," March 28, 2007.
47 WBM, Erik Johnson to Shaman, no subject, March 20, 2007.
48 World Bank Group Staff Association Newsletter, June-July 2001, "The Fad of the Week: Management Theories Come, Management Theories Go."
49 World Bank Group Staff Association Newsletter, June-July 2001, "The Fad of the Week: Management Theories Come, Management Theories Go."
50 World Bank Group Staff Association Newsletter, June-July 2001, "The Fad of the Week: Management Theories Come, Management Theories Go."
51 World Bank Group Staff Association Newsletter, June-July 2001, "The Fad of the Week: Management Theories Come, Management Theories Go."
52 World Bank Group Staff Association Newsletter, Staff Association Editorial, July/August 2002, "Let's Reconsider Our Work/Life Balance."
53 "The Argument is the Incentive: Agency, Organizational Culture and the World Bank's Strategic Compact," Daniel Nielson, Brigham Young University, Michael Tierney, College of William and Mary, Catherine Weaver, University of Kansas, Paper prepared for the ISA International Annual Conference, Budapest, Hungary, June 27-28, 2003.
54 Geert Hofstede, *Cultures and Organizations: Software of the Mind*, McGraw Hill, 1997; WBG Staff Association Newsletter, May 1998, Book Review.
55 " 'Our Poverty is a World Full of Dreams': Organizational Culture and Change at the World Bank," Ralf Leiteritz, 2002.
56 Sebastian Mallaby, *The World's Banker: The Story of Failed States, Financial Crises, and the Wealth and Poverty of Nations*, Penguin Books, 2004, Pages 59, 149-150.
57 " 'Our Poverty is a World Full of Dreams': Organizational Culture and Change at the World Bank," Ralf Leiteritz, 2002; "The Argument is the Incentive: Agency, Organizational Culture and the World Bank's Strategic Compact," Daniel Nielson, Brigham Young University, Michael Tierney, College of William and Mary, Catherine Weaver, University of Kansas, Paper prepared for the ISA International Annual Conference, Budapest, Hungary, June 27-28, 2003; Sebastian Mallaby, *The World's Banker: The Story of Failed States, Financial Crises, and the Wealth and Poverty of Nations*, Penguin Books, 2004, Page 59.
58 Sebastian Mallaby, *World's Banker*, page 283; Sebastian Mallaby, "Saving the World Bank," Foreign Affairs, May-June 2005.
59 " 'Our Poverty is a World Full of Dreams': Organizational Culture and Change at the World Bank," Ralf Leiteritz, 2002.
60 " 'Our Poverty is a World Full of Dreams': Organizational Culture and Change at the World Bank," Ralf Leiteritz, 2002; "The Argument is the Incentive: Agency, Organizational Culture and the World Bank's Strategic Compact," Daniel Nielson, Brigham Young University, Michael Tierney, College of William and Mary, Catherine

Weaver, University of Kansas, Paper prepared for the ISA International Annual Conference, Budapest, Hungary, June 27-28, 2003.

61 " 'Our Poverty is a World Full of Dreams': Organizational Culture and Change at the World Bank, Ralf Leiteritz, 2002; "The Argument is the Incentive: Agency, Organizational Culture and the World Bank's Strategic Compact," Daniel Nielson, Brigham Young University, Michael Tierney, College of William and Mary, Catherine Weaver, University of Kansas, Paper prepared for the ISA International Annual Conference, Budapest, Hungary, June 27-28, 2003.

62 World Bank Report of Task Force on Portfolio Management (Wapenhans Report), 1991.

63 Devesh Kapur, John Lewis, Richard Webb, "The World Bank: Its First Half Century, Volume 1," The Brookings Institute, 1997, Pages 40-46.

64 Ibid.

65 Ibid.

66 Ibid.

67 "World Bank Job," *Wall Street Journal*, Editorial, March 19, 2002.

68 " 'Our Poverty is a World Full of Dreams': Organizational Culture and Change at the World Bank," Ralf Leiteritz, 2002.

69 Adam Lerrick, "Are the World Bank Claims of Success Credible? It Is Time for an External Performance Audit," Quarterly International Economics Report, March 2002, Gailliott Center for Public Policy, Carnegie Mellon University.

70 Adam Lerrick, "Are the World Bank Claims of Success Credible? It Is Time for an External Performance Audit," Quarterly International Economics Report, March 2002, Gailliott Center for Public Policy, Carnegie Mellon University.

71 "ETCs/ETTs – Another NRS?" World Bank Group Staff Association Newsletter, December 2003.

72 "Staff Association Concludes NRS Struggle After More Than Fifteen Years," World Bank Group Staff Association Newsletter, September 2002.

73 "Staff Association Concludes NRS Struggle After More Than Fifteen Years," World Bank Group Staff Association Newsletter, September 2002; "When it Comes to Pensions, We Are 'One Bank' in Rhetoric Only," World Bank Group Staff Association Newsletter, May 2000; "Bank Group Promises to Nonregular Staff: Do They Sound Familiar?" World Bank Group Staff Association Newsletter, May 1997.

74 "Staff Association Concludes NRS Struggle After More Than Fifteen Years," World Bank Group Staff Association Newsletter, September 2002.

75 "Staff Association Concludes NRS Struggle After More Than Fifteen Years," World Bank Group Staff Association Newsletter, September 2002.

76 "Staff Association Concludes NRS Struggle After More Than Fifteen Years," World Bank Group Staff Association Newsletter, September 2002; U.S. Supreme Court Lets Decision Stand on Microsoft NRS Pension," World Bank Group Staff Association Newsletter, March 1998; "Court Holds that Microsoft Owes Benefits to Agency Temps, Too," World Bank Group Staff Association Newsletter, July-August 1999.

77 "U.S. Supreme Court Lets Decision Stand on Microsoft NRS Pension," World Bank Group Staff Association Newsletter, March 1998; "Staff Association Concludes NRS Struggle After More Than Fifteen Years," World Bank Group Staff Association Newsletter, September 2002.

78 "Staff Association Concludes NRS Struggle After More Than Fifteen Years," World Bank Group Staff Association Newsletter, September 2002.

79 "ETCs/ETTs – Another NRS?" World Bank Group Staff Association Newsletter, December 2003.

80 "Are Junior Associates New Competition?" World Bank Group Staff Association Newsletter, August 2001.

81 "ETCs/ETTs – Another NRS?" World Bank Group Staff Association Newsletter, December 2003.
82 "Staff Association Concludes NRS Struggle After More Than Fifteen Years," World Bank Group Staff Association Newsletter, September 2002.
83 "Staff Association Concludes NRS Struggle After More Than Fifteen Years," World Bank Group Staff Association Newsletter, September 2002; "When it Comes to Pensions, We Are 'One Bank' in Rhetoric Only," World Bank Group Staff Association Newsletter, May 2000.
84 "Staff Association Concludes NRS Struggle After More Than Fifteen Years," World Bank Group Staff Association Newsletter, September 2002; "When it Comes to Pensions, We Are 'One Bank' in Rhetoric Only," World Bank Group Staff Association Newsletter, May 2000.
85 "The Fad of the Week: Management Theories Come, Management Theories Go," World Bank Group Staff Association Newsletter, June-July 2001.
86 "Needed: A New Way to Do HR Strategy," World Bank Group Staff Association Newsletter, July 1997.
87 "On the Table: Proposals for Major Changes in Bank; No Details Known Yet," World Bank Group Staff Association Newsletter, July 2004.
88 "On the Table: Proposals for Major Changes in Bank; No Details Known Yet." World Bank Group Staff Association Newsletter, July 2004.
89 Memorandum to the Executive Directors on the Assessment of the Strategic Compact from World Bank President James Wolfensohn, March 13, 2001; http://www.worldbank.org/html/extdr/strategypapers/assessment.pdf
90 World Bank Internal Communications, "Open Forum on Organizational Change, HR Issues and Budget," July 19, 2004.
91 "Where Are We Going and How Do We Get There?" World Bank Group Staff Association Newsletter, May 1999.
92 "Political Pressures on the Bank – and Staff – in 2005," World Bank Group Staff Association Newsletter, January-February 2005.
93 "Political Pressures on the Bank – and Staff – in 2005," World Bank Group Staff Association Newsletter, January-February 2005.
94 "Bullying Bosses Damage Staff and the Bank Group: Controlling Through Fear," World Bank Group Staff Association Newsletter, September 2004.
95 "Bullying Bosses Damage Staff and the Bank Group: Controlling Through Fear," World Bank Group Staff Association Newsletter, September 2004; WBM, Ralf Leiteritz to SDV KM Workers, SRMSG Staff, "MENA on Bank Culture," January 18, 2001.
96 "Bullying Bosses Damage Staff and the Bank Group: Controlling Through Fear," World Bank Group Staff Association Newsletter, September 2004.
97 Ibid.
98 Ibid.
99 Ibid.
100 "Twenty Five Years of Standing Up for Staff," World Bank Group Staff Association Newsletter, February 1997.
101 "Bank Makes Little Progress on Important Tribunal Reforms," World Bank Group Staff Association Newsletter, April 2001.
102 "Independent Justice System Needed: Staff Want Greivances Handled," World Bank Group Staff Association Newsletter, June 2005.
103 "World Bank Status of Grievance Process Reform," U.S. General Accounting Office Report to Congressional Committees, May 1999.
104 "Independent Justice System Needed: Staff Want Greivances Handled," World Bank Group Staff Association Newsletter, June 2005.
105 Ibid.

106 World Bank Conflict Resolution System, Office of the Ombudsman, Ombuds Services Annual Report for CY2004, May 9, 2005.
107 Ibid.
108 "1997 All-Staff Survey Coming: Be Sure to Fill It, SA Urges Staff to Respond," World Bank Group Staff Association Newsletter, September 1997.
109 "SA Good Managers Exemplify 'Emotional Intelligence,' " World Bank Group Staff Association, June 2000; "The Bank and Myers Briggs: Why We Are the Way We Are," World Bank Group Staff Association Newsletter, December 1996; "Does the Bank Suffer from Low 'Emotional Intelligence,' " World Bank Group Staff Association Newsletter, October 1999; On two occasions Monika Weber-Fahr acknowledged to me that she believed she had low emotional intelligence. Then, with unusual candor, she admitted that she considered this personality trait an asset in her ability to control staff.
110 "The Fad of the Week: Management Theories Come, Management Theories Go," World Bank Group Staff Association Newsletter, June-July 2001.
111 "Survey Demographics Reveal Bank Weaknesses and Strengths," World Bank Group Staff Association Newsletter, February 1998.
112 Sebastian Mallaby, *The World's Banker: The Story of Failed States, Financial Crises, and the Wealth and Poverty of Nations*, Penguin Books, 2004, Page 146.
113 World Bank Internal Communications, "Jim Adams on Beating Back Bureaucracy," November 21, 2002.
114 Editorial by John Alvey, SA Chair, "What is a Good Manager? Here's What Staff Say," WBG Staff Association Newsletter, July 2004.
115 "Are Managers Accountable?" World Bank Staff Association Newsletter, December 2003.
116 Editorial by John Alvey, SA Chair, "What is a Good Manager? Here's What Staff Say," WBG Staff Association Newsletter, July 2004.
117 "Good Managers: Brown, Humplick, Parra," WBG Staff Association, June 1999.
118 Devesh Kapur, John Lewis, Richard Webb, "The World Bank: Its First Half Century, Volume 1," The Brookings Institute, 1997, Page 37.
119 "The Hardest Job in the World: Five Crucial Tasks for the New President of the World Bank," Center for Global Development, June 1, 2005, Page 24.
120 Ibid.
121 "Political Pressures on the Bank – and Staff – in 2005," World Bank Group Staff Association Newsletter, January-February 2005.
122 Ngaire Woods, *The Globalizers: The IMF, the World Bank and Their Borrowers*, Cornell University Press, 2006; Woods, "The Globalizers in Search of a Future: Four Reasons Why the IMF and World Bank Must Change and Four Ways They Can," Center for Global Development Brief, April 2006.
123 "The Hardest Job in the World: Five Crucial Tasks for the New President of the World Bank," Center for Global Development, June 1, 2005, Page 27.
124 Sebastian Mallaby, *The World's Banker: The Story of Failed States, Financial Crises, and the Wealth and Poverty of Nations*, Penguin Books, 2004, Page 391.
125 Global Development: "Views from the Center, World Bank Unlikely to Quickly Follow Smart IMF Lead on Representation – Too Bad!" Nancy Birdsall, April 25, 2006.
126 Johannes Linn, Colin Bradford, "The Next Phase of IMF Reform," WashingtonPost.com, September 27, 2006.
127 Global Development: "Views from the Center, World Bank Unlikely to Quickly Follow Smart IMF Lead on Representation – Too Bad!" Nancy Birdsall, April 25, 2006.
128 G-20 Declaration on the Financial Crisis, November 15, 2008.

129 Sebastian Mallaby, *The World's Banker: The Story of Failed States, Financial Crises, and the Wealth and Poverty of Nations*, Penguin Books, 2004, Page 297

130 Ibid., Page 298.

131 Ibid., Pages 90-92, 379-385; Paul Blustein, "World Bank Answers Skeptics on Aid; Report Says Assistance is More Effective Today than It Has Ever Been," *Washington Post,* March 12, 2002.

132 "An Interview with Incoming Chair John Alvey," World Bank Group Staff Association Newsletter, December 2002.

133 Sabine Schlemmer-Schulte, "The Impact of Civil Society on the World Bank, The International Monetary Fund and the World Trade Organization: The Case of the World Bank," ILSA Journal of International and Comparative Law, Vol. 7, N. 2: 399-428, Spring 2001.

134 Daniel Bradlow, "Precedent-Setting NGO Campaign Saves the World Bank's Inspection Panel," Human Rights Brief, Volume 6, Number 3, 1999, http://www.wcl.american.edu

135 "A Misguided World Bank Project," *The New York Times*, July 5, 2000; "Bending Rules in China," *Washington Post*, July 5, 2000.

136 Stefanie Ricarda Roos, "The World Bank Inspection Panel in its Seventh Year: An Analysis of its Process, Mandate, and Desirability with special reference to the China (Tibet) case," Max Planer Yearbook of United Nations Law, Volume 5, 2001, 473-521.

137 "Outlines Concern That First Safeguard Pilot Project Will Weaken Role of Inspection Panel," Bank Information Center Letter to World Bank Executive Directors, June 7, 2004.

138 Jonathan Fox, "The World Bank Inspection Panel: Lessons from the First Five Years," *Global Governance* (6) 2000, 279-318.

139 Paul Nelson, "Whose Civil Society? Whose Governance? Decision-making and Practice in the New Agenda at the Inter-American Development Bank and the World Bank," *Global Governance: A Review of Multilateralism and International Organizations*, October 1, 2000.

140 Ibid.

141 "Accountability at the World Bank: The Inspection Panel Ten Years On," World Bank Publication, 2003, page 7.

142 Jonathan Fox, "The World Bank Inspection Panel: Lessons from the First Five Years," Global Governance (6) 2000, 279-318.

143 Ceclia Dugger, "World Bank Challenged: Are the Poor Really Helped?" *The New York Times*, July 28, 2004.

144 Ibid.

145 Ibid.

146 "Survey Demographics Reveal Bank Weaknesses and Strengths," World Bank Group Staff Association Newsletter, February 1998.

147 "Independent Justice System Needed: Staff Want Greivances Handled," WBG Staff Association Newsletter, June 2005.

148 David Hunter, "The World Bank's New Inspection Panel: Will It Increase the Bank's Accountability," Center for International Environmental Law, April 1994, http://www.ciel.org/Publications/issue1.html

149 Sebastian Mallaby, *The World's Banker: The Story of Failed States, Financial Crises, and the Wealth and Poverty of Nations, Penguin Books*, 2004, Page 378.

150 "Tom Peters Re-Imagines," MWorld, Winter 2004.

151 Ibid.

152 Paul Blustein, "Critics Get World Bank to Ease Disclosure Policy," *Washington Post*, September 6, 2001.

153 WBM – Wheeler to Michele de Nevers, Shaman, "Amazing Day – Sorry About This!" October 16, 2000; "Global Lenders Urged to Make Meetings Public," *World Bank Development News*, October 15, 2000; David Witzel, Forum One, to Wheeler, Shaman, "Global C-SPAN," October 15, 2000.
154 "Global Lenders Urged to Make Meetings Public," *World Bank Development News*, October 15, 2000; David Witzel, Forum One, to Wheeler, Shaman, "Global C-SPAN," October 15, 2000; WBM – Wheeler to Michele de Nevers, Shaman, "Amazing Day – Sorry About This!" October 16, 2000.
155 "Are Managers Accountable?" World Bank Staff Association Newsletter, December 2003.
156 "Challenging the Culture of Secrecy: A Status Report on the Freedom of Speech at the World Bank," Government Accountability Project, July 2004.
157 Thomas Devine, Director, Legal Program, Government Accountability Project, Memorandum to U.S. Congressional Oversight Committees, January 7, 2005.
158 "Interview with John Alvey, Outgoing SA Chair," World Bank Group Staff Association Newsletter, December 2004.
159 Scott White, World Bank Deputy General Counsel, to Thomas Devine, Director, Legal Program, Government Accountability Project, and Melanie Beth Oliviero, Director, International Program, Government Accountability Project, December 15, 2004.
160 Thomas Devine, Melanie Beth Oliviero, Sophia Sahaf, Government Accountability Project, Testimony before the U.S. Senate Foreign Relations Committee on Whistleblower Protection Policies of Regional Development Banks, April 21, 2005.
161 Greg Palast, "Joe Stiglitz: Today's Winner of the Nobel Prize in Economics," *London Observer*, October 10, 2001.
162 Joseph Stiglitz, "What I Learned at the World Economic Crisis," The Insider, *The New Republic*, April 17, 2000.
163 Sebastian Mallaby, *The World's Banker: The Story of Failed States, Financial Crises, and the Wealth and Poverty of Nations*, Penguin Books, 2004, Pages 268-269.
164 "Freedom of Speech, Freedom of Conscience and the World Bank," World Bank Group Staff Association Newsletter, November-December 2001; Ken Ringle, "Bank Shot," *Washington Post*, March 20, 2002.
165 "Freedom of Speech, Freedom of Conscience and the World Bank," World Bank Group Staff Association Newsletter, November-December 2001.
166 Ibid.
167 "The Effect of IMF and World Bank Programmes on Poverty, 2000," World Bank Report; Anup Shah, "Structural Adjustment – A Major Cause of Poverty," *Global Issues*, July 2, 2007. http://www.globalissues.org/article/3/structural-adjustment-a-major-cause-of-poverty
168 "Freedom of Speech, Freedom of Conscience and the World Bank," World Bank Group Staff Association Newsletter, November-December 2001.
169 Branko Milanovic, *World's Apart: Measuring International and Global Inequality*, Princeton University Press, 2005.
170 David Ellerman, "Helping People Help Themselves: Toward A Theory of Autonomy-Compatible Help," World Bank Research Paper 2693, 2001.
171 "WBI, External Partners Share Learning," World Bank Internal Communications, August 25, 2004.
172 Kenneth King, Simon McGrath, *Knowledge for Development: Comparing British, Japanese, Swedish and World Bank Aid*, Zed Books, April 2004.
173 Ibid.
174 Simon Maxwell, Review of *Knowledge for Development*. Source: Development Gateway Bookstore.

175 WBM, Muthukumar Mani to Wheeler, David Witzel, Forum One, Shaman, "Distance Learning and Us," September 11, 1997.
176 David Witzel, Forum One, to Muthukumara Mani, Wheeler, Shaman, "Distance Learning and Us," September 16, 1997.
177 "Retooling the Bank's Knowledge Base," ITS, World Bank, February 24, 1997; WBM, Nathalie Simon, Shaman to Extended List, "Knowledge Management System," March 11, 1997.
178 "Bank Recognized as Leading Knowledge Enterprise," *World Bank Today*, July 14, 2003; WBM, Sunetra Puri to WBI Staff, "Knowledge in the Bank Acclaimed," July 14, 2003.
179 President Dwight D. Eisenhower, State of the Union delivered to a Joint Session of Congress, January 7, 1960.
180 " 'Banker to the Poor' Receives Nobel Peace Prize," *The Associated Press,* December 10, 2006.
181 World Bank Internal Communications, Mamphele Ramphele: Knowledge at the Center of Development, July 30, 2002.
182 Sebastian Mallaby, *The World's Banker: The Story of Failed States, Financial Crises, and the Wealth and Poverty of Nations*, Penguin Books, 2004, Pages 111-112; In response to Adam Lerrick's article in the *Wall Street Journal*, ("Why is the World Bank Still Lending?" October 28, 2005) World Bank President James Wolfensohn said, "Many of these countries ... do not have continuous access to international capital in the amount they need or on terms that are manageable to them. Moreover, as our own research and experience shows, World Bank lending has a catalytic effect: it crowds in private capital. It doesn't crowd it out."
183 The Web for Development Conference, Telling the Development Story to the World, May 9-11, 2005, Washington, DC.

AFTERWORD

1 World Bank, African Development Indicators 2007; World Bank Communications, "Africa Achieving Healthy and Steady Growth Rate," November 14, 2007.
2 United Nations, Millennium Development Goals Report 2008.
3 Peter Heinlein, Addis Ababa , "World Bank Predicts Up to 50 Percent Decline in Africa's Economic Growth This Year," Voice of America News, February 2, 2009.
4 "Failing the World's Poor," Editorial, *The New York Times*, September 23, 2008.
5 United Nations, Millennium Development Goals Report 2008.
6 Homi Kharas, "Reform the Aid System to Fix the Slow-Burning Global Poverty Crisis," Brookings Global Economy and Development, November 2008.
7 "Failing the World's Poor," Editorial, *The New York Times*, September 23, 2008.
8 Ambassador Terry Miller, Brett D. Schaefer, "The Global Poverty Act: The Wrong Track for U.S. Aid Policy," The Heritage Foundation, April 1, 2008; David McKeeby, "Bush Showcases International Development Progress: U.S. Foreign Aid Strategy Empowering People, Delivering Results," America.gov, October 21, 2008.
9 Michael A. Clemens, Todd J. Moss, "Ghost of 0.7%: Origins and Relevance of the International Aid Target," Worlding Paper 68, Center for Global Development, September 6, 2005. www.cgdev.org/content/publications/detail/3822
10 David McKeeby, "Bush Showcases International Development Progress: U.S. Foreign Aid Strategy Empowering People, Delivering Results," America.gov, October 21, 2008.
11 Ibid.
12 Center for Global Development, Commitment to Development Index 2008. http://www.cgdev.org/section/initiatives/_active/cdi/

13 "George Bush's Foreign Aid: Transformation or Chaos?" Center for Global Development, May 20, 2008, http://cgdev.org/content/article/detail/16099/
14 Michael A. Fletcher, "Bush Has Quietly Tripled Aid to Africa," *Washington Post*, December 31, 2006.
15 Ibid.
16 Homi Kharas, "Reform the Aid System to Fix the Slow-Burning Global Poverty Crisis," Brookings Global Economy and Development, November 2008.
17 G-20 Declaration on Financial Crisis, November 15, 2008.
18 Homi Kharas, "Reform the Aid System to Fix the Slow-Burning Global Poverty Crisis," Brookings Global Economy and Development, November 2008
19 Obama '08, Remarks of Senator Barack Obama to the Chicago Council on Global Affairs, April 23, 2007. http://mybarackobama.com/page/content/fpccga/
20 Obama '08, "Strengthening Our Common Security by Investing in Our Common Humanity," November 2007.
21 Ajoy Datta, "Obama and USAID: The Need for Genuine Evaluation," Overseas Development Institute (ODI) Blog, January 19, 2009.
22 "Bush Hosting International Aid Summit, *The Associated Press*, October 21, 2008; Simon Maxwell, "Obama and the Global Development Agenda," Overseas Development Institute (ODI) Blog, June 20, 2009; "The White House and the World: A Global Development Agenda for the Next U.S. President," The Center for Global Development, 2008.
23 Inauguration of President Barack Hussein Obama, January 20, 2009.
24 Sheila Herrling, Molly Kinder, Steve Radelet, "From Innovation to Impact: Next Steps for the Millennium Challenge Corporation," Center for Global Development, January 16, 2009.
25 Nancy Birdsall, "Why Global Development Matters and What the Next U.S. President Should Do About It," Policy Brief, Center for Global Development, August 22, 2008.
26 To read the related quote from President Eisenhower's 1960 State of the Union, visit the last section of Part VIII, Overview and Analysis of the World Bank: Become the Change You Wish to Seek.
27 Nancy Birdsall, "Why Global Development Matters and What the Next U.S. President Should Do About It," Policy Brief, Center for Global Development, August 22, 2008.
28 Robert Zoellick, World Bank President, "A Stimulus Package for the World," Op-Ed, *The New York Times*, January 22, 2009.
29 Obama '08, Remarks of Senator Barack Obama to the Chicago Council on Global Affairs, April 23, 2007. http://mybarackobama.com/page/content/fpccga/
30 Eric Umansky, "Obama Details Promises for Transparency," ProPublica, November 7, 2008. www.propublica.org/article/obama-details-promises-for-transparency-1107
31 "Vowing Transparency, Obama OKs Ethics Guidelines," CNN Politics, January 21, 2009.
32 Chris Bowers, "BARF: Pushing President Obama on Transparency," Open Left, February 10, 2009. www.openleft.com/showDiary.do?diaryId=11509
33 The White House, Memorandum for the Heads of Executive Departments and Agencies, "Transparency and Open Government," January 21, 2009.

index